# COUNSELING DIVERSE POPULATIONS

## THIRD EDITION

### Donald R. Atkinson
University of California, Santa Barbara

### Gail Hackett
Arizona State University

Mc
Graw
Hill

Boston   Burr Ridge, IL   Dubuque, IA   Madison, WI   New York
San Francisco   St. Louis   Bangkok   Bogotá   Caracas   Kuala Lumpur
Lisbon   London   Madrid   Mexico City   Milan   Montreal   New Delhi
Santiago   Seoul   Singapore   Sydney   Taipei   Toronto

# Higher Education

COUNSELING DIVERSE POPULATIONS, THIRD EDITION

Published by McGraw-Hill, a business unit of The McGraw-Hill Companies, Inc., 1221 Avenue of the Americas, New York, NY 10020. Copyright © 2004 by The McGraw-Hill Companies, Inc. All rights reserved. Previous edition(s) 1998, 1995. All rights reserved. No part of this publication may be reproduced or distributed in any form or by any means, or stored in a database or retrieval system, without the prior written consent of The McGraw-Hill Companies, Inc., including, but not limited to, in any network or other electronic storage or transmission, or broadcast for distance learning.

Some ancillaries, including electronic and print components, may not be available to customers outside the United States.

Domestic      2 3 4 5 6 7 8 9 0 DOC/DOC 0 9 8 7 6 5 4

ISBN 0-697-36184-5

Vice president and editor-in-chief: *Thalia Dorwick*
Publisher: *Stephen D. Rutter*
Freelance developmental editor: *Rebecca Smith*
Marketing manager: *Melissa Caughlin*
Project manager: *Mary Lee Harms*
Manager, New book production: *Sandra Hahn*
Manager, Design: *Laurie Entringer*
Cover designer: *JoAnne Schopler*
Cover image: *Corbis*
Associate art editor: *Cristin Yancey*
Associate photo research coordinator: *Natalia Peschiera*
Senior supplement producer: *David A. Welsh*
Compositor: *ElectraGraphics, Inc.*
Typeface: 10/12 *Times Roman*
Printer: *R. R. Donnelley/Crawfordsville, IN*

The credits section for this book begins on page C-1 and is considered an extension of the copyright page.

### Library of Congress Cataloging-in-Publication Data

Counseling diverse populations / [edited by] Donald R. Atkinson, Gail Hackett.—3rd ed.
    p. cm.
  Includes bibliographical references and indexes.
  ISBN 0-697-36184-5 (alk. paper)
      1. Counseling. 2. Aged—Counseling of. 3. Women—Counseling of. 4. Handicapped—
  Counseling of. 5. Gays—Counseling of. I. Atkinson, Donald R. II. Hackett, Gail.

  BF637.C6C6372 2004
  158'.3'08—dc21                                                        2003047730

The Internet addresses listed in the text were accurate at the time of publication. The inclusion of a website does not indicate an endorsement by the authors or McGraw-Hill, and McGraw-Hill does not guarantee the accuracy of the information presented at these sites.

www.mhhe.com

# Contents in Brief

# Detailed Contents

## 8   Counseling and Psychotherapy with Clients with Disabilities

John F. Kosciulek, Michigan
State University                                           194

*Describes four "common factors" that contribute to positive therapeutic outcomes when counseling clients with disabilities, describes major counseling principles and intervention strategies that may be particularly effective, and explains counseling etiquette when working with people with disabilities*

Part III

**THE OLDER
CLIENT**

*Identifies principles critical to conducting culturally rele-
vant interventions with women of color and discusses the
implications of cultural processes that influence their psychological functioning—drawing on both feminist therapy
approaches and the emerging literature on multicultural
counseling competencies*

## 17 Affirmative Counseling with Gay Men
Eric C. Chen, Thomas I. Stracuzzi,
and Daniel E. Ruckdeschel,
Fordham University 388

*Highlights issues related to interpersonal relationships, work, and health that affect the well-being of gay male clients, describes the challenges and principles of counseling gay men, and discusses effective individual and group counseling strategies*

# Preface

This third edition of *Counseling Diverse Populations* has the same goals as the first two editions, to direct the attention of mental health practitioners to the unique experiences and needs of four groups within the American society that, along with ethnic and selected other groups, share the common experience of oppression. These four groups are people with disabilities, older people, women, and lesbian, gay, and bisexual (LGB) people. Each of these four groups has a common physical or behavioral characteristic that identifies individuals as members of the group and that has served to single them out for differential and inferior treatment. Each of these groups has in the past experienced (and continues to experience) discrimination as a result of their physical or behavioral uniqueness. Discrimination for all four groups has ranged from negative stereotypes to physical violence. Our thesis is that mental health practitioners need to be aware of the unique experiences of these groups in order to effectively intervene on their behalf.

This edition represents a complete revision of the second edition. Part I and VI, which are written by the coeditors of the book, have been rewritten and updated. The first chapter describes how traditional psychotherapeutic approaches have ignored the experiences of, and failed to meet the needs of, people with disabilities, older people, women, and LGB people. The first chapter also provides a rationale for identifying the four groups as minorities, as well as a brief profile of each group. In chapters 2 to 5, we review the past and present treatment of each group by society in general and mental health care providers in particular. The last chapter (chapter 18), which examines the implications of diversity issues for counseling practice, counselor training, and counseling research, also has been updated for the current edition.

We are praticularly excited about the changes to Parts II–IV. These parts cover the mental health needs of, respectively, clients with disabilities, older clients, female clients, and sexual minority clients. In the past, we have used reprinted journal articles for chapters in these sections. For this edition, we have commissioned original articles by experts who bring both their professional knowledge and their personal experience to bear in writing about each of these client populations. Furthermore, we developed outlines of what we wanted each chapter author to address. The result is more continuity and less redundancy between chapters than is possible with an edited volume composed of reprinted articles. We are especially pleased that the chapter authors have been very successful in integrating research and scholarship with useful guidelines for practice.

This book is intended as a textbook for undergraduate and graduate courses in counseling, counseling psychology, clinical psychology, social work, student personnel services, and other mental health professions where human rights issues are discussed. The book might be used as a primary text in courses where diversity or human rights issues are the primary focus or as a supplemental textbook in counseling theory and technique courses. When used in conjunction with another McGraw-Hill publication, *Counseling American Minorities,* the book provides an excellent introduction to a broad range of diversity issues.

We hope the book will help mental health professionals look beyond the current *Diagnostic and Statistical Manual of Mental Disorders* when diagnosing clients and beyond conventional psychotherapeutic strategies when treating clients. We believe that experiences, behaviors, attitudes, values, and needs based on membership in the groups discussed in this book must be taken into account as part of diagnosis and treatment. Furthermore, we hope that counselors and other mental health providers will reconceptualize their roles as facilitators of behavioral *and social* change when working with the diverse populations discussed in this book.

## ACKNOWLEDGMENTS

In addition to the chapter authors, there are a number of people who have contributed to this edition of *Counseling Diverse Populations* in one way or another. First, we are grateful for the feedback provided by the following professors, who scrutinized the second edition and suggested many of the changes that have guided this revision: Anthony Bandele, University of Denver; John M. Dillard, University of Louisville; Aneneosa A. Okocha, University of Wisconsin, Whitewater; Maxine Rawlins, Bridgewater State College; and Edil Torres-Rivera, University of Nevada, Reno. We would also like to thank Mary Lee Harms, Rebecca Smith, and other McGraw-Hill employees who contributed to the current edition through their careful editing and thoughtful suggestions.

D. R. A.
G. H.

# About the Contributors

**Donald R. Atkinson** is Professor Emeritus in the combined psychology program (Gevirtz Graduate School of Education) at the Unversity of California–Santa Barbara. He is a coauthor of three books, *Counseling American Minorities: A Cross-Cultural Perspective* (now in its sixth edition), *Counseling Non-Ethnic American Minorities, Counseling Diverse Populations* (now in its third edition), and *Counseling Across the Lifespan,* and author or coauthor of over 130 journal articles and book chapters, most of which report the results of research on diversity variables in counseling. Professor Atkinson is a Fellow in the American Psychological Society and Divisions 17 and 45 of the American Psychological Association and in 2001 he received the Lifetime Research Award from Division 45 (Society for the Psychological Study of Ethnic Minority Issues). Dr. Atkinson earned his Ph.D. at the University of Wisconsin-Madison in 1970.

**Angela Byars-Winston** received her doctorate in counseling psychology from Arizona State University in 1997. Her primary research interests include the examination of cultural influences on the career development of African American women, specifically the influence of race and gender on career-related self-efficacy. To date, Dr. Byars-Winston's publications have appeared in the *Journal of Applied and Preventive Psychology,* the *Career Development Quarterly,* and in the edited books *Career Counseling for African Americans, Handbook of Multicultural Counseling* (2nd ed.), and *Handbook on Racial-Cultural Psychology.* She has been involved in the American Psychological Association serving as the 1999 program Co-Chair for the Section for Ethnic and Racial Diversity within Division 17 and as the Town Hall Co-Chair for the 2001 National Counseling Psychology Conference. She is currently a member of Division 35's Task Force on Early Career Mentoring. Dr. Byars-Winston joined the faculty in the Department of Counseling Psychology at the University of Wisconsin–Madison in 1997.

**Eric C. Chen,** Ph.D., is an associate professor and Chair of the Division of Psychological and Educational Services in the Graduate School of Education at Fordham University. He was born and raised in Taiwan and received his doctorate in counseling psychology from Arizona State University in 1995. His research interests and publications have encompassed topics of clinical supervision, group counseling, multicultural issues and competencies, and career choice and development of immigrant youth. He received the 2003 Outstanding Research Award in Counseling from the American Educational Research Association for a group research journal he co-authored. He has served on the editorial board of the *Journal of Counseling and Development* and is a member of the editorial boards for the *Group Dynamic: Theory, Research, and Practice,* the *Journal of Counseling Psychology,* and the *Journal of Multicultural Counseling and Development.*

**Eve H. Davison,** Ph.D., is clinical director of the Women's Stress Disorder Treatment Team in the Women's Health Sciences Division of the National Center for Post-Traumatic Stress Disorder, Veterans Boston Healthcare System, and is an instructor of psychiatry in the Boston University School of Medicine. She earned her doctorate from the Counseling, Clinical, and School Psychology program at the University of California–Santa Barbara in 1999 and completed a clinical geropsychology postdoctoral fellowship at Hillside Hospital, Long Island Jewish Medical Center in 2000. Her interests lie primarily in the areas of geropsychology and the effects of trauma in late life. She provides treatment to female military veterans with sexual trauma histories, and she is currently conducting research examining late-onset stress symptomatology in aging male and female military veterans.

**Timothy R. Elliott** obtained his Ph.D. in counseling psychology from the University of Missouri–Columbia. He is an associate professor in the Department of Physical Medicine and Rehabilitation at the University of Alabama–Birmingham, where he also serves as a scientist in the Center for Nursing Research, and as an associate scientist in the Injury Research and Control Center. He was among the first diplomates in rehabilitation psychology awarded by the American Board of Professional Psychology, and he is a Fellow in three divisions of the American Psychological Association (including the divisions of Rehabilitation, Health, and Counseling Psychology). He is a past president of the Division of Rehabilitation Psychology within the APA, and his research has been funded by grants from the Centers for Disease Control, the National Institute of Disability Rehabilitation and Research, and the National Institute of Child and Human Development. The American Association of Spinal Cord Injury Psychologists and Social Workers recently presented him with the Essie Morgan Excellence Award for his research achievements in the area of spinal cord injury.

**Carolyn Zerbe Enns** is a professor of psychology and Co-Chair of the Women's Studies program at Cornell College in Mt. Vernon, Iowa. Carolyn completed her Ph.D. (1987) in counseling psychology at the University of California–Santa Barbara, and she is a licensed psychologist in the state of Iowa. She is the current Chair (2002–2004) of the American Psychological Association (APA) Division 17 (Counseling Psychology) Section for the Advancement of Women. Carolyn is also a Co-Chair of the APA interdivisional task force, which is sponsored by the APA Divisions of Counseling Psychology and Psychology of Women. This task force is charged with revising the 1979 Principles for Counseling and Psychotherapy with Women. Carolyn's primary areas of research and scholarship are feminist theory, feminist psychotherapy, and feminist pedagogy. She is the author of *Feminist Theores and Psychotherapies: Origins, Themes, and Variations* (published in 1997), which reflects her interdisciplinary interests and works toward integrating feminist perspectives within women's studies and psychology.

**Laura Urbanski Forrest** received her Ph.D. in counseling psychology from Arizona State University. She is currently an assistant professor in the MS in Counseling program at California State University–Long Beach. Her research interests center on feminist therapy, women's career issues, and self-efficacy.

**Gail Hackett** received her Ph.D. from Pennsylvania State University. She served on the faculty at the Ohio State University and the University of California–Santa Barbara and is now a professor of counseling psychology in the Division of Psychology in Education and vice provost at Arizona State University. Her research interests include: (a) career self-efficacy theory; (b) social cognitive applications to career counseling and development; (c) gender and ethnicity in career counseling and career development; and (d) feminist approaches to counseling and therapy. She has served as associate editor of the *Journal of Counseling Psychology*, vice president for Division E of the American Educational Research Association, and vice president for Scientific Affairs of Division 17 of the American Psychological Association. She is a Fellow of Divisions 17 and 35 of the American Psychological Association.

**Rosemany B. Hughes,** Ph.D., is the director of the Center for Research on Women with Disabilities, and an assistant professor in the Department of Physical Medicine and Rehabilitation, at Baylor College of Medicine in Houston, Texas. Dr. Hughes earned a Ph.D. in counseling psychology from the University of Houston. She holds an M.S. in education and a B.A. in sociology. She is a licensed psychologist in the state of Texas. She has clinical, teaching, and research expertise related to the health and mental health of women with disabilities. At the Center for Research on Women with Disabilities, Dr. Hughes serves as principal investigator on various federally funded research grants investigating health promotion, stress, depression, and self-esteem among women with disabilities.

**Tania Israel** is an assistant professor in the Counseling, Clinical, and School Psychology program at the University of California–Santa Barbara. She received her doctoral degree in counseling psychology from Arizona State University in 1998, and she has a background in women's studies and sexuality education. Her professional interests include gender issues, feminist psychology, sexuality education and counseling, and diversity training. Her current research focuses on the development and assessment of counselor competence with lesbian, gay, bisexual, and transgendered clients.

**Audrey Kim** is a licensed psychologist at the University of California–Santa Cruz's Counseling and Psychological Services. She received her Ph.D. in counseling, clinical, and school psychology from the University of California–Santa Barbara. Audrey is committed to research and practice that serves the needs of traditionally underserved and/or marginalized populations, including racial/ethnic minorities and older adults. She is a strong believer in the importance of incorporating research into practice and focusing research around clinical applications.

**John Kosciulek** is an associate professor in the Department of Counseling, Educational Psychology, and Special Education at Michigan State University. Dr. Kosciulek has over 15 years of experience as a practicing counselor, educator, and researcher. He has published over 30 articles and book chapters and has presented his research to a variety of state, national, and international professional counseling and rehabilitation groups. He also is a certified rehabilitation counselor (CRC). Dr. Kosciulek's clinical and research interests include consumer direction in disability policy development and rehabilitation service delivery, community rehabilitation organizations, family adaptation to brain injury, rehabilitation and disability theory and model development, and research methodology. Dr. Kosciulek is currently coeditor of the journal *Rehabilitation Education,* the flagship journal of the National Council on Rehabilitation Education (NCRE). He was awarded the 2001 American Rehabilitation Counseling Association (ARCA)

Research Award. Dr. Kosciulek is a past recipient of a Mary E. Switzer Rehabilitation Research Fellowship (1996–97) from the National Institute on Disability and Rehabilitation Research (NIDRR). In addition, he was selected as a Mary E. Switzer Scholar by the National Rehabilitation Association (NRA) and presented a key action paper at the 1999 Switzer Seminar on the topic of consumer direction in disability policy development.

**Susan L. Morrow** is an associate professor in the Educational Psychology Department at the University of Utah, where she directs the Counseling Psychology Program. She graduated from Arizona State University in 1992. She is a qualitative researcher and methodologist. Her research and counseling interests include women's issues, multicultural counseling and education, lesbian/gay/bisexual concerns, adult survivors of childhood trauma, and feminist therapy.

**Larry L. Mullins,** Ph.D., is a professor of clinical psychology at Oklahoma State University and a clinical professor of psychiatry at the University of Oklahoma Health Sciences Center. He also serves as associate director of clinical training. Dr. Mullins completed his internship in pediatric psychology at the OU Health Sciences Center and received his Ph.D. from the University of Missouri–Columbia in 1983. Dr. Mullins's research interests focus on the relationship of cognitive appraisal mechanisms and children's adjustment to various chronic illnesses.

**Margaret (Peg) A. Nosek** is professor and executive director of the Center for Research on Women with Disabilities in the Department of Physical Medicine and Rehabilitation at Baylor College of Medicine. She holds a Ph.D. in rehabilitation research and an MA in rehabilitation counseling from the University of Texas–Austin and is an internationally recognized authority on women with disabilities and independent living for persons with disabilities. She has done considerable research and writing on developments in public policy that affect the ability of people with disabilities to live independently in the community, and she has contributed significantly to the scientific literature on the health issues and violence issues of women with disabilities. Her recent studies examined the cost of depression and other secondary conditions, self-esteem enhancement, health promotion, and aging with a disability. Dr. Nosek's accomplishments are reflected in her many publications and presentations at national and international conferences. She is recipient of numerous awards for her research and advocacy by local, state, and national organizations. As a person with a severe physical disability, she has been both a pioneer and an activist in the disability rights movement, including vigorously supporting passage of the Americans with Disabilities Act. The President's Committee on Employment of People with Disabilities has honored her as a "Disability Patriot."

**Sara Honn Qualls,** Ph.D., is a professor in the Psychology Department at the University of Colorado at Colorado Springs where she also serves as the director of the Center on Aging. She has published two books *Pscyhology and the Aging Revolution* and *Aging and Mental Health.* Her research and writing focus on marital and family development in later life and clinical interventions for later life couples and families. She is also a practicing clinical psychologist who helped establish the CU Aging Center, a community-based geriatric mental health training clinic.

**Daniel E. Ruckdeschel,** M.S.Ed., is a Ph.D. student in counseling psychology at Fordham University. Born in Boston and raised in rural upstate New York, he has experience as a counselor in both college counseling center and hospital settings. His research interests include multicultural issues and topics related to social justice, as well as counseling outcomes.

**Thomas I. Stracuzzi,** M.S.Ed., is a Ph.D. candidate in the counseling psychology program at Fordham University. He has been working as a counselor at St. Vincent's Catholic Medical Centers of New York, Westchester Division in Harrison, New York, since 1997. His research focuses on the counseling relationship, particularly in relation to lesbian, gay, and bisexual clients.

# Part I    A CONTEXT
FOR COUNSELING
DIVERSE
POPULATIONS

# CHAPTER 1

An Introduction
to Nontraditional
Interventions
and Diverse
Populations

This book focuses on two groups who are perceived as different and treated in a negative fashion because of physical characteristics (women and elders), one group because of behavioral characteristics (lesbian, gay, and bisexual [LGB] people), and one group because of either physical or behavioral characteristics (people with disabilities). As we shall see in chapters 2 and 3, these four groups have experienced discrimination and victim-blaming much like ethnic minorities have.

Our readings relating to these four groups by necessity focus on the distinctiveness of each group and may serve to reinforce the view that they are mutually exclusive populations. Nothing could be further from the truth. For example, the greater survival rate of Americans with lifelong disabilities and the growing number of elders with later-life disabilities (Ansello, 1991) means that there is considerable overlap between these two groups. Further, the fact that there are only 67 elderly men for every 100 elderly women in the United States suggests that a large number of elderly women have disabilities. Since some of those elderly women with disabilities are also lesbians, the overlap of all four groups on which we have chosen to focus becomes obvious. That the four groups are not mutually exclusive is significant because it suggests that many individuals in our society are subject to multiple layers of discrimination.

## TRADITIONAL APPROACHES TO COUNSELING
## AND PSYCHOTHERAPY

Most, if not all, mental health professions that practice counseling and psychotherapy can trace their roots to Freud and psychoanalysis; Shilling (1984) refers to Freud as "grandfather to all of us . . . who are psychologists and/or counselors" (p. 17). According to Sharf (2000), "Sigmund Freud's contribution to the current practice of psychoanalysis, psychotherapy, and counseling is enormous. . . . Virtually every major theorist discussed in this book [*Theories of Psychotherapy and Counseling*] was originally trained in Freudian psychoanalysis" (p. 25). Many of the concepts and constructs Freud developed are still perceived as necessary and sufficient conditions for psychotherapy. In particular, many contemporary psychotherapists draw heavily upon Freud's assumption that feelings and unconscious drives must be brought into consciousness for behavior to change, and many still rely on techniques he developed to facilitate this process. Although many of Freud's contributions to the mental health professions have been widely applauded, some of his ideas have been criticized as erroneous or even deleterious.

Two of the unfortunate legacies that Freud left to mental health professionals are the overemphasis on intrapsychic etiologies for mental health problems and the exclusive reliance on one-to-one psychotherapy for the treatment of psychological disturbances. Freud believed an individual's behavior was the result of instinctual, biological drives, thus originating within the individual. Although neo-Freudians and subsequent theorists have moved away from the heavy stress Freud placed on sexual instinct and aggression as determinants of behavior, they continue to emphasize an internal model of psychopathology, one that views the etiology of the client's problem (and the resources to resolve it) as residing within the client. Thus, for example, advocates of person-centered therapy believe that psychological maladjustment occurs when "the *organism denies* to awareness, or *distorts* in awareness, significant experiences" (italics added; Meador & Rogers, 1984, p. 159). Gestalt therapists believe that "*people are responsible* for what they choose to do" (italics added; Simkin & Yontef, 1984, p. 291). And even behavior therapists, who eschew needs, drives, motives, traits, and conflicts as underlying causes of behavior, believe that "a crucial factor in therapy is the *client's motivation* and *willingness to cooperate* in the arduous and challenging task of making significant changes in real-life behavior" (italics added; Wilson, 1984, p. 253). The following quote from the *Diagnostic and Statistical Manual of Mental Disorders-Fourth Edition (DSM-IV)* demonstrates just how thoroughly this intrapsychic view of psychological problems has permeated the mental health establishment:

> In *DSM-IV,* each of the mental disorders is conceptualized as a clinically significant behavioral or psychological syndrome or pattern that occurs in an individual and that is associated with present distress (e.g., a painful symptom) or disability (i.e., impairment in one or more important areas of functioning) or with significantly increased risk of suffering death, pain, disability, or an important loss of freedom. In addition, this syndrome or pattern must not be merely an expectable and culturally sanctioned response to a particular event, for example, the death of a loved one. *Whatever its original cause, it must currently be considered a manifestation of a behavioral, psychological, or biological dysfunction in the individual. Neither deviant behavior (e.g., political, religious, or sexual) nor conflicts that are primarily between the individual and society are mental disorders unless the deviance or conflict is a symptom of a dysfunction in the individual.* (italics added; American Psychiatric Association, 2000, xxi–xxii)

If the primary mechanisms that shape and maintain affect, behavior, and cognition reside within the individual, then it follows that psychotherapy should focus attention on the individual. Freud's use of the psychoanalytic situation, a one-to-one therapeutic environment in which the analyst facilitates critical self-examination, had a significant and enduring impact on counseling and psychotherapy. This emphasis on intrapsychic pathology and psychotherapy is evident in the goals therapists have for counseling. Although the client may be encouraged to state therapeutic goals as part of the counseling process, therapists conventionally pursue metagoals of changing the client's affect, behavior, and/or cognitions. The therapist works on these metagoals by encouraging catharsis, interpreting feelings, challenging negative self-perceptions, assigning homework, and a myriad of other counseling strategies. Regardless of the counselor's material and the strategies employed to reach it, an underlying assumption of nearly all conventional counseling approaches is that some aspect of the client must change in order to resolve the problem. With the exception of embryonic group and family counseling efforts, counseling and psychotherapy prior to the 1950s involved the one therapist, one client model.

Family therapists were among the first to recognize the limitations of focusing therapy solely on the individual. According to Nichols (1984), Freud actively discouraged psychotherapists from involving other family members when they were treating a patient because it would undermine the transference process, considered essential for treatment success. As a result, early attempts at interviewing with families were little more than individual psychotherapy for each family member. It was not until the early 1950s that researchers examining communication patterns in the families of schizophrenics developed a systems theory approach to therapy and with it the concept that it is more effective to treat a family system conjointly than a single family member individually (Nichols, 1984).

## THE BEGINNINGS OF NONTRADITIONAL APPROACHES TO THERAPY

The social conditions of the 1960s set the stage for a second, more disparate, group of mental health professionals to criticize the shortcomings of conventional psychopathology and psychotherapy theory. Civil rights, antiwar, feminist, and other human rights movements directly and indirectly motivated many disfranchised groups to seek (and in some cases demand) mental health services. Counselors and other mental health professionals soon discovered that their training did not prepare them to work with such issues as discrimination, alienation, and basic survival (Aubrey & Lewis, 1983). The result of pressure by disfranchised groups for counseling services has been referred to as a "fundamental if not revolutionary change" (Larson, 1982, p. 843) in counseling.

By the late 1960s, radical psychiatrists, social change psychologists, feminist counselors, and others were suggesting that psychological problems experienced by many clients were the result of oppressive environments, not intrapsychic pathology. Concurrently, a number of authors began criticizing the mental health professions for their neutral stance with respect to social issues. Seymour Halleck (1971) indicted psychotherapists for helping to maintain the status quo in social institutions that are oppressive. According to Halleck, psychotherapists, whether they intend to or not, commit a political act every time they reinforce the positions of persons who hold power. Intrapsychic views of client problems were criticized for being shortsighted and for promoting institutional oppression through passive acceptance. Claude Steiner (1975) articulated this position in its extreme in his Manifesto for psychiatrists:

> Extended individual psychotherapy is an elitist, outmoded, as well as nonproductive, form of psychiatric help. It concentrates the talents of a few on a few. It silently colludes with the notion that people's difficulties have their source within them while implying that everything is well with the world. It promotes oppression by shrouding its consequences with shame and secrecy. . . . People's troubles have their source not within them but in their alienated relationships, in their exploitation in polluted environments, in war, and in the profit motive. (Steiner, 1975, pp. 3–4)

Sarason (1981) also chastised American psychology as "quintessentially a psychology of the individual organism, a characteristic that, however, it may have been and is productive has severely and adversely affected psychology's contribution to human welfare" (p. 827). In examining the social issues and counseling needs of the 1980s and 1990s, Aubrey and Lewis (1983) expressed concern that "counselors still tend to overlook the impact of environmental factors on individual functioning, to distrust the efficacy of preventative interventions, and to narrow the scope of their attention to the individual psyche" (p. 10). More recently, the steering committee for the National Institute of Mental Health (NIMH) Group on Culture, Diagnosis and Care (consisting of 50 cultural experts, both clinicians and scholars) criticized the *DSM-IV* and its predecessors for failing to recognize the role of the environment in development and maintenance of psychological problems:

> The *DSM* has traditionally concentrated on pathology conceptualized as rooted and fixed in the biological individual. This ignores the way in which many psychiatric problems are not only substantially more prevalent among individuals facing social disadvantage but, in important ways, constituted by those same economic, family, social, and cultural predicaments. (Mezzich et al., 1999, p. 461)

We share these concerns that counselors and psychologists ignore environmental sources of mental health problems and rely almost exclusively on an intrapsychic model of psychopathology. We believe that for some of the issues clients bring to counseling, particularly for clients from groups that are victims of oppression, counselors need to consider alternatives to the intrapsychic pathology and individual psychotherapy models. This book examines the experiences of four oppressed groups with the goal of sensitizing mental health practitioners to the external sources of the psychological problems and to the nontraditional interventions designed to assist them with these problems.

## DEFINING OPPRESSED GROUPS AS MINORITIES

The term *minority* has been widely used in the United States since the 1950s with reference to racial and ethnic groups and more recently with respect to nonethnic groups. Based on Wirth's (1945) definition that minorities are groups who "because of physical or cultural characteristics, are singled out from the others in the society in which they live for differential and unequal treatment" (p. 347), the term has been generalized to any group oppressed by those in power. The concept of minorities being groups that are singled out for differential and unequal treatment allows us to expand the list of minorities beyond ethnic groups who are a numerical minority in the society. As applied to Blacks in South Africa and women in the United States, the term applies to groups that are actually a numerical majority of the population. Religious groups, young children, and older people, to the extent they are oppressed by the social system in which they live, also can be identified as minorities.

A. G. Dworkin and R. J. Dworkin (1976) proposed that "a minority group is a group characterized by four qualities: identifiability, differential power, differential and pejorative treatment, and group awareness" (p. 17). Biological (skin color, eye shape and color, facial structure) and cultural (religion, dress, behavior) variables serve to identify a minority group as does the position of inferior power relative to a power group (a group that uses power to influence and control others). When such differential power exists between two groups, it is probably inevitable that the dominant group exercises its power, resulting in differential and discriminatory treatment of the minority group. One effect of experiencing differential and discriminatory treatment is to make minority group members more aware of their common bond.

A definition Kinloch (1979) offered also addresses the issue of power. Kinloch (1979) defined a minority as "any group that is defined by a power elite as different and/or inferior on the basis of certain perceived characteristics and is consequently treated in a negative fashion" (p. 7). Further, he identified four types of minorities, those who are identified as different or inferior based on physiological criteria (e.g., non-White racial minorities, women, elders), cultural criteria (non-Anglo-Saxon ethnic groups), economic criteria (the poor and/or lower class), and behavioral criteria (e.g., gay men and lesbians, persons with mental disabilities, persons with physical disabilities).

Similarly, Larson (1982) identified minorities as groups of people who are stigmatized by the majority group in some way. He referred to Goffman's (1963) classification system for identifying conditions subject to stigma. The system consists of three categories:

> (a) physical—for example, visible manifestations of disability; (b) blemishes of character—for example, conditions that are viewed as voluntary deviant choices such as political dissidents, alternate sexual orientations, criminals, some categories of mental illness, such as addictions; and (c) tribal—for example, racial, ethnic, linguistic, or religious groups. (Larson, 1982, p. 845)

These definitions by A. G. Dworkin and R. J. Dworkin (1976), Kinloch (1979), and Larson (1982) stipulate that oppressed individuals be recognized or perceived as a group sharing common characteristics in order to qualify as a minority. However, Pope (1995) made the interesting point that even those individuals who attempt to "pass" as members of the dominant society (e.g., gay men or lesbians who hide their sexual orientation, people of color who are not visibly identifiable and deny their ethnic heritage, older people who forswear their age) experience oppression in the form of lower self-esteem, feelings of inferiority, and internalization of negative self-concepts (p. 303). Thus, the recognition or perception of membership in a minority group need not be public for a member of that group to experience the effects of oppression.

Although counselors and mental health professionals have long recognized that people with disabilities, older people, women, and gay people qualify as minorities based on their experiences of discrimination and oppression, only recently have these populations been included under the banner of multiculturalism. Writing about the first National Multicultural Conference and Summit (NMCS) held in January 1999, Sue, Bingham, Porche-Burke, and Vasquez (1999) pointed out that "It has become apparent at the NMCS that the term multiculturalism must include the broad range of significant differences (race, gender, sexual orientation, ability and disability, religion, class, etc.) that so often hinder communication and understanding among people" (p. 1063). They argued that multiculturalism is about social justice, and oppression of any minority group involves denial of social justice. However, when the Council of Representatives of the American Psychological Association adopted as policy the *Guidelines on Multicultural Education, Training, Research, Practice, and Organizational Change for Psychologists* in August 2002, *multicultural* was specifically defined "to refer to interactions between individuals from ethnic and racial groups" (American Psychological Association, 2002, p. 3). Thus, readers will find that the term *multicultural* is sometimes used in the mental health literature to encompass the four groups covered in this book, and sometimes not. However, there does seem to be general agreement that these groups qualify as minorities according to definitions of minorities cited earlier.

## THE EFFECTS OF VICTIM-BLAMING

Not only are minority groups singled out for stigmatization and discrimination, they are placed in double jeopardy by a society that blames them for the social conditions they experience as a result of discrimination. This phenomenon, known as *victim-blaming,* "is the tendency when examining a social problem to attribute that problem to the characteristics of the people who are its victims" (Levin & Levin, 1980, p. 36). For example, early forms of victim-blaming of ethnic minorities were often racially based and usually cited assumed biological inferiority as a cause of the groups' social problems (e.g., the assumed intellectual inferiority of Mexican Americans cited as a reason for Mexican American underachievement in school). More recently, cultural deviance has been cited as a cause of social problems experienced by ethnic minorities (e.g., the breakdown of the traditional two-parent family cited as a reason for a myriad of problems experienced by African Americans). The argument that a child's seductive behavior is the cause of child sexual abuse (Muller, Caldwell, & Hunter, 1995) and rape (Bell, Kuriloff, & Lottes, 1994) is another example of blaming the victim. Thus, victim-blaming overlooks the societal and institutional causes of social problems experienced by minorities and instead blames the problem on assumed biological or cultural inferiority.

Victim-blaming is particularly insidious when the minority group toward which it is directed begins to accept the blame for problems caused by oppression.

> The ultimate personal consequence of victim-blaming occurs when victims come to see themselves as those who blame them do. Lower self-esteem, even self-hatred, are outcomes more likely to emerge for those who are already marginalized and devalued in society. One's adoption of negative images from others can be viewed as a form of auto-oppression which has within it the seeds of self-destruction. Tragically and ironically, self-destruction accomplishes for society what social isolation and genocide do, but without raising the spectre of rights violations. (Dressel, Carter, & Balachandran, 1995, p. 118)

A further negative effect of victim-blaming is to misdirect the resources expended to resolve the social problems faced by a minority. Once we identify a social problem, we study the group affected by it to determine how they are different from the rest of us. We next define those differences as the source of the problem and develop a bureaucratic program to correct the differences, not the social cause of the problem. Further, we often withhold resources from minorities needed to resolve the social sources of their problems because we assume they are incapable of resolving their own difficulties. Thus, huge resources are often directed toward solving a problem experienced by a minority population, but most of those resources end up supporting the bureaucracy that is created and very little trickles down to the individuals experiencing the problem.

## PROFILES OF SELECTED MINORITIES

Brief profiles of people with disabilities, older people, women, and LGB people are provided in the following sections.

### People with Disabilities

Any discussion of people with disabilities by necessity must begin with a discussion of the terms *handicap, handicapped, disability,* and *disabled.*

**Definitions**    Those who have followed the literature on people with disabilities have witnessed an evolution in terminology (not unlike the evolution in terminology used to designate members of racial/ethnic minority groups) applied to this population. Professional articles and federal laws in the 1970s followed the convention of referring to people with disabilities as *handicapped people* or *people with handicaps*. During the 1970s the terms *handicapped person* and *disabled person* were often used interchangeably. By the 1980s, however, advocates for people with disabilities began to make distinctions between handicap and disability. The term *disability* began to be used with reference to some physical or mental diagnosis, one that may or may not limit the individual's major life activities. The term *handicap* began to be used to indicate the restricting consequences of the diagnosed disability. Thus, a handicap was seen as more situationally defined than was a disability.

The disability may be considered as the person's observable, measurable characteristic that is judged to be deviant or discrepant from some acceptable norm. In contrast, the handicap may be considered as the barriers, demands, and general environmental press placed on the person by various aspects of his or her environment, including other persons. (Fagan & Wallace, 1979, p. 216)

*Disability* has been defined as "the functional limitation within the individual caused by physical, mental, or sensory impairments," while *handicapped* has been defined by as "the loss or limitation of opportunities to take part in the normal life of the community on an equal level with others due to physical and social barriers" (McNeil, 1993, p. 1). Thus, an individual may have a disability (e.g., hearing loss) but may not define it as a handicap if he or she is not restricted from taking part in normal activities of life. On the other hand, people in the environment may create a handicap for the disabled person if they restrict the person from living a normal life.

By the mid-1980s, most health professionals had dropped the term *handicapped person* in favor of *disabled person,* and by the early 1990s, *person with disabilities* became the more accepted terminology. According to Grealish and Salomone (1986), *disabled person* implies that the person is disabled in a total sense (physically, emotionally, intellectually). Although more cumbersome, *person with a disability* puts the emphasis on the whole person and recognizes that the disability is just one aspect of their personhood. In fact, some advocates for people with disabilities prefer to use the expression *differently able* since it more accurately reflects the fact that we all have varying levels of mental and physical ability given the environmental conditions in which we happen to be (in the case of a blind and a sighted person in an unlighted room, being sightless may actually be an asset). However, some people with disabilities object to this terminology since it tends to deny their impairment and their status as an oppressed person. At this point most professionals and advocates for people with disabilities have accepted the term *people with disabilities.*

The preceding definitions of disability notwithstanding, there is some ambiguity about what constitutes an impairment or functional limitation; according to Kuehn (1991), "disability resists precise definition and measurement" (p. 8). One approach has been to identify specific mental or physical conditions that are medically or educationally diagnosable. Thus, the Education for All Handicapped Act (Public Law [PL] 94-142) includes the following categories of disabilities for children: (a) hearing impaired, (b) deaf-blind, (c) visually impaired, (d) speech impaired, (e) mentally retarded, (f) learning disabled, (g) emotionally disturbed, (h) orthopedically impaired, (i) other health impaired, and (j) multihandicapped (Fagan & Wallace, 1979). Disabling conditions in the "other health impaired" category range from asthma to lead poisoning and include many chronic or acute health problems.

Another approach to defining disability is to identify the life activity affected. Thus, the Rehabilitation Act of 1973 defines an "individual with severe handicaps" as a person:

1. who has a severe physical or mental disability which seriously limits one or more functional capacities (such as mobility, communication, self care, self-

direction, interpersonal skills, work tolerance or work skills) in terms of employability;

2. whose vocational rehabilitation can be expected to require multiple vocational rehabilitation services over an extended period of time; and
3. who has one or more physical or mental disabilities resulting from a list of disorders/diseases or a combination of disabilities determined on the basis of an evaluation of rehabilitation potential to cause comparable substantial functional limitation (Perlman & Kirk, 1991, p. 21).

More recently, the Americans with Disabilities Act (ADA; PL. 101-336) of 1990 defined disability very broadly, encompassing such chronic diseases as AIDS and diabetes:

> Under the ADA, an individual is considered to have a disability if the person: (a) has a physical or mental impairment that substantially limits one or more of the major life activities; (b) has a record of such an impairment; or (c) is regarded as having such an impairment. (McNeil, 1993, p. 1)

Ability to perform an activity or role is often used to define disability. For the 1990 census, the U.S. Bureau of the Census based its definition of a person with a *work disability* on the concept that "a person has a disability if he or she has a limitation in the ability to perform one or more of the life activities expected of an individual within a social environment" (U.S. Bureau of the Census, 1989, p. 1). The bureau defined a person with a work disability as someone for whom one or more of the following conditions are met:

1. Identified by a question that asks "does anyone in this household have a health problem or disability which prevents them from working or which limits the kind or amount of work they can do?"
2. Identified by a question that asks "Is there anyone in this household who ever retired or left a job for health reasons?"
3. Did not work in the survey week because of a long term physical or mental illness or disability which prevents the performance of any kind of work (based on the "main activity last week" question on the basic CPS [Current Population Survey] questionnaire).
4. Did not work at all in previous year because ill or disabled (based on the "reason did not work last year" question on the March CPS supplement).
5. Under 65 years of age and covered by Medicare.
6. Under 65 years of age and a recipient of Supplemental Security Income (SSI). (U.S. Bureau of the Census, 1989, p. 1)

The person is considered to have a "severe" work disability if one or more of the final four conditions are met.

Lack of comparability of disability definitions used by the Census Bureau from one census to the next is part of the problem in both identifying the proportion of the population that has a disability and tracking that proportion over time. For the 2000 census, disability status was derived from two items:

> Item 16 was a two-part question that asked about the existence of the following long-lasting conditions: (a) blindness, deafness, or a severe vision or hearing impairment (sensory disability) and (b) a condition that substantially limits one or

more basic physical activities such as walking, climbing stairs, reaching, lifting, or carrying (physical disability). . . . Item 17 was a four-part question that asked if the individual had a physical, mental, or emotional condition lasting 6 months or more that made it difficult to perform certain activities. The four activity categories were: (a) learning, remembering, or concentrating (mental disability); (b) dressing, bathing, or getting around inside the home (self-care disability); (c) going outside the home alone to shop or visit a doctor's office (going outside the home disability); and (d) working at a job or business (employment disability). . . . Individuals were classified as having a disability if any of the following three conditions was true: (1) they were five years old and over and had a response of "yes" to a sensory, physical, mental or self-care disability; (2) they were 16 years old and over and had a response of "yes" to going outside the home disability; or (3) they were 16 to 64 years old and had a response of "yes" to employment disability. (U.S. Bureau of the Census, 2002, p. 1)

Using definitions of disability applied to the 1990 census, a recent census brief (U.S. Bureau of the Census, 1997b) reported that approximately 1 in 10 Americans have a disability of some kind, and 1 in 20 Americans have a severe disability. Using the disability definitions adopted in the 2000 census, however, nearly 1 in 5 (or 49,746,248) people ages 5 and over had a disability when the most recent census was conducted (U.S. Bureau of the Census, 2000).

**Criteria**   Even when agreement exists about the categories of disabilities, disagreement may arise about whether an individual satisfies the criteria for the category. According to Bowe (1985), two trained observers may differ as to whether a person has a disability or not. Questions used by the Census Bureau to identify persons with a work disability "may screen out some legitimately disabled persons; less often, they may screen in some individuals who may not be disabled" (Bowe, 1985, p. 2). Perhaps because there is not a clear consensus on what constitutes a disability, even among U.S. governmental agencies, there are no clear-cut national estimates of the number of people with disabilities.

The Survey of Income and Program Participation, conducted by the Census Bureau in 1994 and 1995 and summarized in McNeil (1997), is the most comprehensive study of people with disabilities to date. According to this survey, about 53 million people in the United States had some level of disability, 26 million of whom had a severe disability. Among 237 million people 6 years of age and older in 1994, the study found that 1.8 million used a wheelchair, 4.1 million needed assistance with one or more activities of daily living, 8.8 million had difficulty seeing, and 10.1 million had difficulty hearing. This study found a direct correlation between age and disability rate; as might be expected, the likelihood of having a disability or severe disability increases with age (see Figure 1.1). Within each age category beginning with 22 years of age, women are more likely to have a severe disability than are men (see Figure 1.2). Also, within each age category beginning with 22 years of age, Blacks and Hispanics are more likely to have a severe disability than are non-Hispanic Whites (see Figure 1.3).

Clinical identification of people with disabilities may be improved with the recent adoption by the World Health Organization (2001) of the International

**FIGURE 1.1**  Disability prevalence by age.

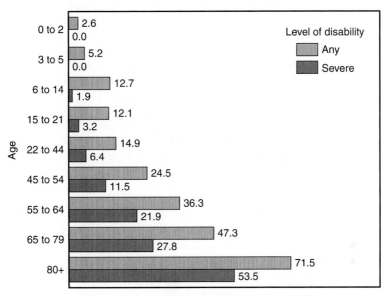

Percentage with specified level of disability

Figure 1 from McNeil, J. M. (1997). *American with disabilities: 1994–95* (U.S. Bureau of the Census Current Populations Reports, P70-61). Washington, DC: U.S. Government Printing Office, p. 2.

**FIGURE 1.2**  Percentage of men and women with a severe disability by age.

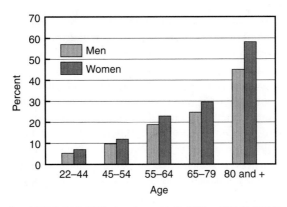

Based on data taken from McNeil, J. M. (1997). *Americans with disabilities: 1994–95* (U.S. Bureau of the Census Current Populations Reports, P70-61). Washington, DC: U.S. Government Printing Office, Table 1, p. 6.

Classification of Functioning, Disability and Health (ICF). The ICF, which culminates seven years of development involving 65 countries, replaced the International Classification of Impairments, Disabilities and Handicaps (ICIDH), which was first published by the World Health Organization in 1980 and revised in 1994.

**FIGURE 1.3**   Percentage of Whites, Hispanics, and Blacks with a severe disability by age.

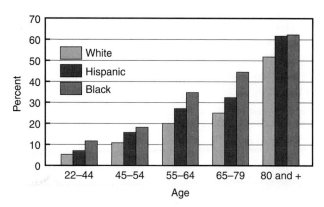

Based on data taken from McNeil, J. M. (1997). *American with disabilities: 1994–95* (U.S. Bureau of the Census Current Populations Reports, P70-61). Washington, DC: U.S. Government Printing Office, Table 1, p. 6.

In essence, the ICF provides a means of classifying human functioning and defines disabilities as impairments, activity limitations, or participation restrictions. The ICF classifies disabilities according to body functions and structures, activities, and participation, while taking the environment into account. The ICF can be contrasted with the International Classification of Diseases-Tenth Edition (ICD-10), the system for classifying health conditions (diseases, disorders, injuries, etc.). Thus, disability is viewed within the context of human functioning rather than disease.

There is every reason to believe that both the absolute number of people with disabilities and their proportion in the population will grow well into the 21st century. A sizable portion of the number of persons with disabilities are elderly, since the incidence of disability increases in old age; nearly half of the people who are 65 years old or older have a disability (U.S. Bureau of the Census, 1997b; U.S. Bureau of the Census, 2000). Thus, as the number and percentage of the U.S. population that are elderly increases (discussed in the next section), the number and percentage of people with disabilities will increase. It should be noted, however, that disabilities are a fact of life among a sizable number of young people as well; approximately 1 in 8 children ages 6 to 14 have some type of disability (U.S. Bureau of the Census, 1997b).

## Older People

The terms used to refer to older people, like those used with people with disabilities, have gone through a metamorphosis over the past three decades.

**Definitions**   In the past, *aged, old people, senior citizens,* and other more derogatory terms were used to refer to people 65 years of age and older. More recently, *elders* and *elderly* were commonly used in reference to this group. Most recently, the term *older people* has been used with increasing frequency and seems least objectionable to the people to whom it is applied. We follow this convention when we are referring to people aged 65 or older. Because the Census Bureau and most gerontological researchers still refer to people age 85 or older as the "oldest-old," we have adopted that convention as well.

The determination of who is an "older person" and who is not is arbitrary at best. Although chronological age is frequently used for this purpose (as it is in the current text), it is often not an accurate indicator of biological age (measured by skin texture, hair color and thickness, reflex speed, etc.), psychological age (feelings, attitudes, way of looking at things, etc.), or social age (social roles and activities) (Aiken, 1995). Defining the term *aging* is also problematic. According to Griffiths and Meechan (1990), the definition of aging most widely accepted by biologists is one offered by Vander, Sherman, and Luciano (1985); these authors defined aging as a "progressive failure of the body's various homeostatic adaptive responses" (Griffiths & Meechan, 1990, p. 45).

> This definition has the advantage that it allows us to distinguish the aging process from degenerative changes that result from diseases. Although diseases such as cancer and atherosclerosis can interact and compound the aging process, they do not always accompany aging and therefore must be thought of as distinct processes. (Griffiths & Meechan, 1990, p. 45)

As we shall see in chapter 2, however, the disease model of aging was in vogue for the major part of the 20th century, and only recently has functional capacity been used to assess the aging process.

**Aging Assessment Measures**   Biologists, physicians, and chemists who have studied the physiological aging process (senescence) have long recognized that it occurs at varying rates among individuals (Satlin, 1994; Strehler, 1962). Various measures of physical aging have been employed; for example, hair color and loss, skin tone and texture, and muscle tone and flexibility have been examined as evidence of senescence. But because individuals evidence changes in these physical attributes at widely varying chronological ages, physical standards of aging are averages for the population as a whole and are seldom useful in assessing a particular individual's status in the aging process. Increasingly, aging is being assessed in terms of functional capacity or the ability to engage in purposeful activity. Two types of activities, activities of daily living (ADLs) and instrumental activities of daily living (IADLs), are used to measure functional capacity. ADLs include getting in and out of a chair or a bed, bathing, and using the toilet; IADLs include preparing meals, doing light housework, and shopping. Quite clearly, some individuals who are in their 40s have greatly restricted ADLs and IADLs, while others in their 70s and even 80s may have retained full functional capacity (Aiken, 1995).

The Social Security Act of 1935 had a major impact on our current perceptions about who is an older person when it identified 65 as the magic age for determining who will receive full Social Security benefits. According to Achenbaum (1978), however, "at least six other birthdays (60, 62, 68, 70, 72, and 75) were used as an eligibility criterion in public and private schemes operating in the 1930s" (p. 149). Legislators selected age 65 for Social Security purposes in the final analysis on the basis of cost estimates, actuarial data, and the spirit of compromise rather than on scientific information about the aging process. These same considerations (costs and actuarial data in particular) came into play when the government raised the age at which older people can begin receiving full Social Security benefits. The full retirement age remains at 65 for persons born before 1938; however, the age gradually rises until it reaches 67 for persons born in 1960 or later. Although the original decision to make 65 the age at which full benefits begin has shaped our view of when "old age" sets in, it seems unlikely that the new age for full Social Security benefits will have a similar effect. The Bureau of the Census, other government agencies, and the general public all continue to use 65 as the magical cutoff between middle and old age.

The decision to raise the age of qualification for full Social Security benefits is the result of people living longer than ever before and a shrinking number of people paying into Social Security.

> For the first time in history, most people can expect to live into the "long late afternoon of life." Whereas American life expectancy in 1900 was about forty-nine, today's children will live an average of about seventy-five years (seventy-one for men, seventy-eight for women). This increase represents two-thirds of all the gains in life expectancy achieved since the emergence of the human species! (Cole, 1991, p. 25)

**The Impact of Increased Life Expectancy**　　Due to an increasing life expectancy, the number of older people living in the United States has been growing steadily since 1830, the first year for which census data are available. In 1830 there were less than one half million White persons (non-Whites were not counted in the early reports) over 60 years of age. In 1870 the Census Bureau reported over 1.1 million citizens were age 65 or older. By 1900 that figure had more than doubled to just over 3 million. The number of citizens 65 and older had increased to 9 million by 1940, 20 million by 1970, and 31.2 million by 1990. As of the 2000 census, there were 35 million people age 65 and over, a 12% increase over the 1990 figure (Hetzel & Smith, 2001). The number of persons 65 and over is projected to increase to 53.2 million by 2020 and almost 79 million by 2050 (U.S. Bureau of the Census, 1997a). The highest percentage increase is occurring among those people 85 years of age and older. Between 1990 and 2000, the 85-and-over population grew from 3.1 million to 4.2 million, a 38% increase (Hetzel & Smith, 2001). Furthermore, it is projected that those 85 and older will increase in number to 6.5 million by 2020 and 18.2 million by 2050. Most of this growth in the first half of the 21st century will be due to the aging of the baby boomers. A rapid acceleration in the projected growth of the older population will occur between 2010 and 2020 as the peak of the baby-boom generation turns 65 (U.S. Bureau of the Census, 1997a).

Until the 1990s, not only was the older population increasing in absolute numbers, but they were increasing in proportion to the rest of the population. At the same time that life expectancy has been increasing, the birthrate has been declining steadily since 1790 (with the exception of the post–World War II baby boom), causing the proportion of older people in the American population, as well as their absolute number, to increase dramatically. However, this pattern of older people representing an increasing percentage of the total population was temporarily halted in the 1990s; their proportion of the total population actually dropped slightly from 12.6% in 1990 to 12.4% in 2000 (Hetzel & Smith, 2001). This leveling off of the proportion of older people in the total population is the result of a lower birthrate during the depression years of the 1930s. However, as mentioned, the pattern of the older population growing proportionately faster than the total population is expected to resume at an accelerated pace by 2010 as the baby boomers begin reaching age 65. Between 2010 and 2030, the age-65 and older population is expected to grow by 57% while the under-age-65 population is expected to grow by only 6.5% (U.S. Bureau of the Census, 1997a). In 1990, 1 in 35 Americans were 80 or older. By 2050 as many as 1 in 13 will be 80 or older (U.S. Bureau of the Census, 1992).

As might be expected, the differing life expectancies for men and women noted earlier affect their representation in the older population. According to Hobbs and Damon (1996), the sex ratios of older men and women were approximately equal in 1930 but have changed dramatically since then. According to the most recent census data, there were 14.4 million men and 20.6 million women in 2000. By multiplying the number of men by 100 and dividing by the number of women, the Bureau of the Census calculates this to be a male-female ratio of 70. The male-female ratio decreases steadily with age group. For the 65–74 age group, the male-female ratio is 82; for the 75–84 age group, it is 65; and for the 85-and-older age group, it is 41. However, men are living longer than in the past and the male-female ratio for each of these age groups is on the rise (Hetzel & Smith, 2001).

**Diversity and Aging**   Although there is a great deal of diversity among older people in terms of demographics, needs, abilities, and resources, there is less ethnic diversity in the older population than in the younger population. Using a cut-off of age 55, the Bureau of the Census determined that in 1999 non-Hispanic Whites made up 68% of the population under age 55, and 82% of those 55 and older (Smith & Tillipman, 2000). In part this phenomenon is due to the youthfulness of immigrants from Central and South America, Asia, and Africa over the past two or three decades. However, it is also due in part to the shorter life expectancy among ethnic minorities than among Whites. For example, the life expectancy of a Black male born in 1991 was 64.6 years, whereas that of a White male was 72.9 years. Although Black females born that year could expect to live 73.8 years, they still had a shorter life expectancy than did White females (79.6 years; Hobbs & Damon, 1996). Nonetheless, because of the growing numbers of ethnic minorities in the younger population, the older population is expected to become increasingly ethnically diverse in the future. By 2050, the percentage of Whites in the age 65 or older population will drop to 67%. By the middle of the 21st century Hispanics will make up 16%, Blacks will make up 10%, and Asian and Pacific Islanders will make up 7% of those over age 65.

**Retirement**   Contrary to earlier generations, most of today's older men (comparable figures for women are not reported) retire before age 65. According to the U.S. Bureau of the Census (1992):

> In 1950, two-thirds (68.6%) of men 55 or older, and nearly half (45.8%) of men 65 and older were in the labor force. In 1990, about 2 in 5 (39.3%) men 55 and over, and about 1 in 6 (16.4%) elderly men were in the labor force. (p. 4-1).

This pattern is expected to reverse itself, however, due to increases in the qualifying age for Social Security benefits, less generous pension plans in the future, and the demand for older workers. Evidence also indicates that an increasing number of men who retire before age 65 are taking part-time and even full-time jobs in "retirement." A number of factors send retirees back into the labor force, including improved health, longer life expectancies, unplanned forced retirements, loss of health insurance coverage, and erosion of retirees' retirement income due to inflation.

**Health and Living Arrangements**   Convention has it that older people experience declining health, especially after age 85. Although this stereotype has some truth, most older people report that they are relatively healthy compared with others in their same age group. Surveys have consistently found that about 70% of older people report their health to be good, very good, or exceptional. A common misperception is that the majority (or at least a large percentage) of older people live in nursing homes; in reality, however, fewer than 1 in 20 do. In 2000, only 4.5% (down from 5.1% in 1990) were living in nursing homes, although the number does increase with advancing age. For people ages 65 to 74, only about 1.1% lived in a nursing home in 2000. The percentage increases to 4.7% for ages 75 to 84 and 18.2% for ages 85 and above (Hetzel & Smith, 2001). Because many older people are admitted to nursing homes for both recuperative and end-of-life care, approximately 35% of older people are admitted to a nursing home at some point after they turn 65 years of age (Hobbs & Damon, 1996).

Almost 91% of all older married couples (and 75% of all older people) own and live in their own home (Hobbs & Damon, 1996). For most elderly householders, their home is their major asset. However, the property values of the homes owned by older people are lower than those owned by younger homeowners. In many cases the homes owned by older people are at least 40 years old and in need of structural repairs (Hess, 1991). Older Whites (79%) are more likely to be homeowners than older Blacks (64%) or Hispanics (59%; Hobbs & Damon, 1996).

Contrary to still another common misperception, most noninstitutionalized older people do not live with a relative. The majority (63%) of persons ages 65 to 74 were married and living with their spouse in 1992, while 25% lived alone and 10% lived with relatives. However, the living arrangements of older people are, to some extent, a function of age, ethnicity, and sex. For persons 75 and over, the percentage living with their spouses decreases (41%), the percentage living alone increases (41%), and the percentage living with other relatives increases (16%).

Older Blacks are more likely to live alone (36% vs. 31%), less likely to live with a spouse (37% vs. 56%), and more likely to live with other relatives (25% vs. 11%) than their White counterparts (U.S. Bureau of the Census, 1993). When adult children do provide care for their aging parents, it often occurs when the children themselves are older. A survey of caregivers revealed that their mean age was 63.5 years, which means that many of their aging parents were in their 80s and 90s (Schwiebert & Myers, 1994).

With women outliving men, it is not surprising that older women are more likely than older men to be living alone. Of 9.4 million noninstitutionalized persons aged 65 and older living alone in 1993, over 79% were women and 70% were White women (Hobbs & Damon, 1996). By age 85, White women are twice as likely as White men to be living alone (59% and 28%, respectively). Black and White women are more likely to live alone than Hispanic women. Because women live longer than men and are often married to men 10 years their senior, older men are more likely than older women to be living with their spouse. The majority of men (76%) ages 65–84 were married and living with their spouse in 1999, while this was true for less than half (46%) of the women in this age group. Almost half (49%) of the men 85 years of age and older were married and living with their spouse that year, while this applied to only 12% of the women (Smith & Tillipman, 2000).

Another misperception is that most older people need assistance with living (bathing, dressing, moving out of beds and chairs, toileting, and eating). However, even among the oldest age group, less than half need this kind of assistance. Compared with the 2% of persons under age 65 who need assistance with living activities, "the proportion requiring assistance ranged from 9% for those aged 65 to 69 up to 45% for those aged 85 or older" (U.S. Bureau of the Census, 1992, p. 3-12). The need for assistance is also related to demographic variables. Older women are more likely to need assistance than are older men, and older Blacks are more likely to need assistance than are older Whites. "Those who needed assistance were more likely to live in households with lower income levels than persons who did not require assistance" (U.S. Bureau of the Census, 1992).

It is estimated that 5 million older people who are ill or have severe disabilities live in the community, a figure that is almost four times the number living in nursing homes. Most of these older people are women who are being cared for by a relative, usually a daughter; only 22% of the care providers are husbands or sons. As we point out in chapter 3, caring for an older person with a severe disability places incredible stress on the care provider and not infrequently leads to older adult abuse. The strain on care providers may become worse in the near future as the number of offspring available to provide the care decreases (due to smaller families) and the financial pressures on women in their middle years to work increases (Hess, 1991).

Several patterns should be clear from these voluminous data. One is that in terms of ability, needs, and resources, the effects of aging differ considerably by sex and ethnicity. Another pattern is that the most severe effects of aging occur after age 85. This has led many scholars of aging to refer to the two tiers of aging, the young-old and the old-old. The young-old are characterized by relatively good health and financial condition while the old-old experience declining financial, physical, social, and psychological resources. To some extent this division between the young-old and the old-old is an artifact due to the varying economic, medical, and social opportunities available to different age cohorts and to the fact that more and more older people are "aging successfully" (Satlin, 1994). Therefore, the reader is cautioned that the comprehensive data on age discrimination cited in chapter 3 will necessarily overstate the privations of the young-old while understating those of the old-old.

## Women

Although women are ostensibly the easiest of the four groups under discussion to define and identify, the issues related to women's status as an oppressed group are actually quite complex. Social scientists have had great difficulty clarifying the issues, much less reaching agreement; conflicting definitions of terms plague the field (Henley, 1985; Swann, Langlois, & Gilbert, 1999). We use descriptors in keeping with the consensus of opinion in the literature on the psychology of women, with the caveat that the usage of other writers may differ considerably.

**Definitions**   Ask anyone to describe the crucial differences between men and women and you will get a hodgepodge of physical, mental, behavioral, and characterological distinctions. Yet contained within commonplace descriptions of sex differences are innumerable unfounded assumptions. There are some very real physical and genetic differences (e.g., average height, weight, muscle mass) between the sexes, but there are not the widespread intellectual, personality, and behavioral differences assumed by so many. In fact, as first documented in the landmark study by Maccoby and Jacklin (1974), supported by subsequent investigations, and contrary to common stereotypes, *very few* consistent sex differences exist. The research literature on the psychology of sex differences supports the contention that there are many more similarities than differences between boys and girls, men and women, and the few consistent differences that have been identified are of negligible import (Gilbert & Sher, 1999). Why, then, are assumptions of significant sex differences so prevalent? The answer rests in society's gender-based attitudes, norms, and expectations (Gilbert, 1992; Swann et al., 1999).

   Fundamental to this discussion of women and women's status in society is the crucial distinction between *sex* and *gender* (Gilbert & Sher, 1999; Unger, 1979). *Sex* refers to the biological condition of maleness or femaleness, the possession of the XY chromosomal configuration for men and boys, and the XX pattern for women and girls, along with the corresponding anatomical, hormonal, reproductive, and physiological structures. In sociological parlance, sex is an *ascribed* status; we are assigned to a sex at birth (Richardson, 1981). Gender, on the other hand, is an *achieved* status, that is, one we learn. *Gender* refers to the psychological, social, and cultural aspects of being female or male within a particular social context (Gilbert & Sher, 1999; Richardson, 1981). Gender, therefore, is a social label describing the aspects of male and female behavior that are a result of socialization to the culturally prescribed norms for women and men. *Gender identity* is one's self-defined sex, male or female, which usually, but not always (e.g., in the case of transsexuals), corresponds with one's ascribed sex. Despite a voluminous literature on this topic, a great deal of confusion and misunderstanding remains over the differences between sex and gender (Swann et al., 1999).

Far from semantic nit-picking, these distinctions reflect a crucial point: Most differences assumed to exist between the sexes have been found to be socially based rather than innate. Our language affects how we see the world, and the continuing use of the term *sex* differences to characterize observed differences in personality, cognitive functioning, interpersonal behavior, and vocational behavior only serves to reinforce outdated notions of the biological source of such observed differences (Swann et al., 1999). As Fassinger (2000) noted:

> the primary barrier to appropriate language is rooted in Western culture's dichotomization of sex into two separate, distinct categories (male and female), and the linking—both conscious and nonconscious—of these biological categories with particular meanings, characteristics, and behaviors that are determined by sociocultural consensus to be associated with one sex or another. (p. 347)

Further, observed or assumed sex differences have often been overemphasized and employed to support arguments for the inferiority of women. Conversely, similarities between the sexes are just as often minimized or ignored. Employing the term *gender* emphasizes the social construction of behavior and the existence of environmental causes for behavioral differences between women and men. To briefly illustrate: There do not seem to be any overall differences between men and women in the capacity to act assertively, yet in certain situations women *do* act less assertively than men, because they have learned what is expected of them as women (Gilbert, 1992).

**Gender-Role Socialization**   Immediately upon sex assignment at birth, the process of differential socialization begins. Our society holds certain beliefs about personality differences between, and appropriate behavior for, boys and girls. These gender-role stereotypes (sometimes inaccurately referred to as sex-role stereotypes), or widely held but simplistic beliefs about the roles of women and men, influence how we act, what we see, how we interpret behavior, and how we respond to others. Studies have documented the content of the gender-role stereotypes commonly held within the mainstream American culture (Swann et al., 1999). Women are characteristically seen as expressive, that is, compassionate, tactful, emotional, nurturing, and dependent; men are seen as instrumental, for example, objective, aggressive, independent, dominant, and competitive (Bem, 1974; Spence & Helmreich, 1978; Swann et al., 1999). Parents, family, the educational system, the media—all significant sources of influence on a growing child—communicate these expectations. As a result of gender-role socialization we learn what behaviors and attitudes to exhibit according to our label, male or female. When men act in a culturally approved, gender-appropriate way they are viewed as *masculine;* women are viewed as *feminine* when they act in ways considered appropriate for women in their culture.

Gender beliefs operate to influence judgments, memories, and actions, even in areas seemingly totally unrelated to gender. "The term *gender,* as social scientists have come to realize, is a very large umbrella, encompassing a wide array of beliefs and actions" (Deaux, 1999, pp. 20–21); the "lenses of gender" are pervasive (Bem, 1994; Deaux, 1999). Current research in the social sciences has, in fact, moved beyond studying sex and gender, and gender stereotypes of masculinity and femininity, to explorations of the social construction and representations of gender in all aspects of our lives (Deaux, 1999).

The importance of understanding the social construction of gender lies not only in its pervasiveness in our lives, but also in the consequent exposure of the political ideology underlying gender roles, and the costs of adherence to this political ideology that result for both women and men. Margaret Mead's classic anthropological study (1935/1971) convincingly demonstrated the cultural relativity of gender roles and the place of social conditioning rather than biology in the development of gender differences in personality. She investigated three tribes in New Guinea, finding one in which both men and women displayed what our culture would consider "feminine" traits; another in which both sexes displayed the instrumental traits we usually describe as "masculine"; and a third in which adult males demonstrated expressive ("feminine") characteristics while normal adult females displayed the aggressive, instrumental behaviors we label as "masculine."

Despite Mead's research and other anthropological studies refuting the universality of the content of gender-role expectations, and thus their biological immutability, within a given culture people tend to assume that what they are used to is "normal" and therefore good, desirable, and natural. It has been argued that our culture (along with many others) is patriarchal, or male dominated. The ideology underlying patriarchy is sexism, a political ideology resting squarely on the assumed inequality of women and men. As a consequence, our assumption that this culture's gender-role expectations for women are "normal," and our failure to question these stereotypical expectations, produces a situation where society is training over half of its population to behave and think in ways detrimental to the achievement of gender equality. Further, many of the gender-appropriate feminine characteristics, traits, and behaviors adhered to in our society are devalued; and some are inherently harmful to the mental and physical health and well-being of women (Gilbert & Sher, 1999; Swann et al., 1999). Men, too, pay a price for strict adherence to the cultural masculine gender role (O'Neil, 1980).

**Women as a Minority**    Thus, gender stereotyping, the result of sexist ideology, functions to maintain the status quo. The dominant group, men, are socialized to behave in culturally defined masculine ways that serve to preserve the dominance of men as a group. It takes informed and concerted efforts on the part of men to circumvent their conditioning and societal pressures, even when they consciously ascribe to gender equality (O'Neil, 1980). Women, too, are socialized to think and behave in ways that serve to preserve their relatively inferior status (Gilbert & Sher, 1999).

Of course, the reality of gender stereotyping and sexism is far more complex than this simple description. For example, differential expectations of girls and boys are communicated to shape behavior in a number of ways; for example, adults apply greater pressure on boys to conform to gender-role expectations and the enhanced value attached to and communicated about being male in Western cultures (Enns, 2000). That parents are largely unaware of their differential attitudes, expectations, and treatment of their children does not mitigate the negative impact of traditional gender-role socialization on all children.

Another example of these complexities is reflected in recent work on types of sexist ideologies (Glick & Fiske 1996, 1999). Glick and Fiske (1996) identified different types of sexism reflecting the multifaceted reality of the relations between men and women in different circumstances. Glick and Fiske (1996) contended that hostile sexism exists in situations where men's status is high and women's status is low (where men dominate politically, economically, socially, and/or religiously); negative stereotypes of women serve to provide a rationale for men's advantaged status. However, women have some power in all situations, particularly in intimate relationships. Glick and Fiske (1999) have analyzed what they call "dyadic power" and its consequences, namely, benevolent sexism, or subjective positive feelings toward women, which are manifested in protectiveness and paternalism. Benevolent sexism is fostered when men are dependent on and value women in their lives; however, men's positive feelings toward women are nevertheless often very traditional and stereotypical, and are not the same as support for the best interests of those women, and thus are a more palatable but nevertheless problematic variation of sexist ideology (Glick & Fiske, 1999). The consequence of sexism in any of its forms is social and economic inequality, resulting in women's disadvantaged status in society. It is this inequitable situation, both a determinant and a result of long-standing and continuing sex discrimination, that defines women as a "minority" or oppressed group (Hacker, 1975).

The minority status of women, then, is due to their economic, legal, political, and social disadvantages rather than their numerical minority, as is the case with other minority groups. However, we must remember as we are discussing women's status throughout this book that gender combines with other minority statuses to produce multiple, nonadditive sources of oppression. For example, because of the gender differences in mortality rates, the ratio of women to men increases greatly with age (Costello & Stone, 2001); thus, most women experience at least a dual oppression as they grow older. Older women suffer differentially from problems of loneliness, isolation, and lack of potential partners (Worell & Remer, 2003). Different standards of physical attractiveness for the sexes produce a situation where women generally encounter a type of age discrimination that is much more profound than that encountered by men (Collier, 1982). Women of color experience multiple forms of oppression, extending well beyond the "double jeopardy" of sexism and racism as gender interacts complexly with ethnicity, race, and social class; lesbians encounter homophobia as well as sexism, and that homophobia takes on a different form than what is experienced by gay men; older lesbian women and lesbian women of color face multiple forms of discrimination layered over homophobia and nurtured by sexism; women with disabilities face similar multiple forms of discrimination. We could continue indefinitely with the possibilities for multiplication of sources of oppression, discrimination, and bias.

But how can such a situation exist in a country founded on the concepts of freedom and human equality? Are we exaggerating the scope of the problem? Once again the answer is complicated, but it is intimately tied to the ideology of sexism, the oppression that is common to all women. As Amundsen (1971) stated:

> Sexism, then, is an "ideology" in the sense that its beliefs and postulates are well-integrated, it functions to direct and guide social and political activity, and it rests on assumptions that are not reliably tested, but that to some degree are accepted on faith. (p. 108)

Because of the pervasiveness of sexism in our culture, many client problems and concerns are influenced by gender-role stereotyping and socialization. Feminism, defined simply as the advocacy of equality between men and women, can be a potent force in exposing unexamined and harmful sexist beliefs and behaviors. Despite the widespread pejorative associations with the term *feminist*, its essential meaning is simply one who advocates for equality between the sexes.

Conversely, popular wisdom has it that we have been in a postfeminist era for years, a time when women have finally achieved equality and where sexism no longer holds sway. However, compelling evidence to the contrary exists, despite the real gains made by women on a variety of fronts. Faludi (1991), in particular, argued persuasively that the 1980s were a period of profound backlash against women's quest for equality: "The antifeminist backlash has been set off not by women's achievement of full equality but by the increased possibility that they might win it. It is a preemptive strike that stops women long before they reach the finish line" (p. xx). The new century brings more evidence of the truth of this statement, as evidenced by continuing and vitriolic antifeminist volleys in the popular media (e.g., Sommers, 2000) and the ongoing existence of gender differences in the workforce, such as the difficulties and harsh choices faced by even women who have seemingly "achieved it all"; high-achieving women often pay a price not paid by men (e.g., Hewlett, 2002).

The history of sexism is long, and though its specific manifestations have changed over time, its potency as an ideology remains with us today. What is "normal" is seen as right and correct, and largely goes unquestioned. As John Stuart Mill, an early advocate of women's rights, so aptly stated, "So true is it that unnatural generally means only uncustomary and that everything which is usual appears natural. The subjection of women to men being a universal custom, any departure from it quite naturally appears unnatural" (1869/1970, p. 14). Women are in a much better position than they were when Mill wrote these words, but equality in education, the workforce, politics, and the family is still far from being achieved.

In chapter 4 we examine the status of women from a historical perspective, tracing the origin and development of sexism over time, and we also discuss the legacy of sexism and its current manifestations in society, psychology, and the practice of counseling. As we will see, women's equality with men has not been one of linear, forward-moving progress, but rather one of fits and starts, progression and regression.

## Lesbians, Gay Men, and Bisexuals

There are ongoing debates in the research and theoretical literature about the components of sexual identity, arguments about whether sexual orientation is fixed or fluid, and disagreements about whether lesbian, gay, and bisexual identities are socially constructed and how they develop (Broido, 2000; S. H. Dworkin, 2000). All of these discussions have implications for the terminology employed. We use fairly traditional terms and definitions, at the same time acknowledging that these are in the process of reappraisal and the literature is not uniform in their use.

**Descriptors**   As is the case with labels employed for and by racial/ethnic minority groups, the nomenclature used when referring to LGB people reveals strongly held assumptions about the group. *Homosexual* is the term often applied to individuals whose sexual preferences are predominantly for those of the same sex. Yet the term *homosexuality* places primary emphasis on sexual preference, which is but one aspect of the life experience of the people so labeled (Broido, 2000).

An alternative term, *gay,* as with the labels preferred by other minorities (e.g., African American, Chicano), emphasizes the positive and was developed within the homosexual community itself:

> Gay is a descriptive label we assign ourselves as a way of reminding ourselves and others that awareness of our sexuality facilitates a capacity rather than creating a restriction. It means that we are capable of fully loving a person of the same gender by involving ourselves emotionally, sexually, spiritually, and intellectually. (Clark, 1977, p. 73)

Thus, the term *gay* affirms all aspects of this orientation. Further, in Western culture the designation *homosexual* is a clinical term with many negative associations, a term often used to separate gay people from the rest of society (Broido, 2000). The label *gay,* on the other hand, goes beyond a rigid classification of people into one group or the other:

> It may even imply a frequent or nearly constant preference or attraction for people of the same gender, meaning I (as a Gay man) might notice more men than women on the street or might notice men before women. But the label does not limit us. We who are Gay can still love someone of the other gender. Homosexual and heterosexual when used as nouns are naive and destructive nonsense in the form of labels that limit. (Clark, 1977, p. 73)

In this book we generally use *gay,* although the term *homosexual* is employed when referring to sexual behavior or when it is most descriptive of the issue under discussion. We note, however, that in some circles the term *queer,* once offensive and derogatory, has been embraced and is used in preference to *gay* to refer to "a spectrum of variant sexualities—gay, lesbian, transgendered, transsexual, and bisexual" (Fone, 2000, p. 411). As much as possible we refer to gay women as lesbian women in order to make visible a group of people who are often relegated to invisibility (Faderman, 1991; Martin & Lyon, 1972; Rothblum, 2000). The designation *lesbian* has been embraced by gay women because of the tendency of society to assume that gay people are exclusively male (Moses & Hawkins, 1982).

Historically, rigid and dichotomous conceptions of sexual orientation have led to confusion and misperceptions of bisexuals, and only in the 1990s have self-identified bisexuals come to be embraced by the lesbian and gay community (Reynolds & Hanjorgiris, 2000). Bisexuals still often feel alienated from both the gay and heterosexual communities (S. H. Dworkin, 2000). Although, as we will see, "a substantial proportion of women and men have reported participation in some sort of same-sex sexual activity during their lives, only some self-identify as bisexual. . . . In other words, same-sex behavior does not always lead to self-labeling as gay, lesbian, or bisexual" (Reynolds & Hanjorgiris, 2000, p. 43). Finally, we avoid the use of the term *straight* to describe heterosexuals; if one is "straight," the implication is that the other is somehow crooked, deviant, or criminal (Woodman & Lenna, 1980). Gays often use the word *nongay* rather than either heterosexual or straight.

**Sexual Orientation**    Homosexuality has traditionally been viewed as a rare and deviant form of behavior, in contrast to the societal norm of heterosexuality; the two are often seen as mutually exclusive categories. Yet in the landmark Kinsey studies, researchers found that over 60% of male respondents had engaged in same-sex sexual behavior before the age of 16, and 30% had homosexual experiences in their early 20s (Kinsey, Pomeroy, & Martin, 1948). Findings for women were not as dramatic but were consistent with the data regarding men; homosexuality is far from rare, and homosexuality-heterosexuality is not, in the general population, a clear dichotomous classification (Kinsey et al., 1948; Kinsey, Pomeroy, Martin, & Gebhard, 1953).

The Kinsey reports (Kinsey et al., 1948; Kinsey et al., 1953) and subsequent research (Churchill, 1971; Kingdon, 1979) demonstrated that, conservatively, about 10% of the population are predominantly homosexual, and this figure appears to be fairly stable throughout history and across cultures. Thus, although gay people are clearly a minority due to their oppressed status (which is documented in chapter 5) and their numbers, they are a significant minority.

Kinsey and his associates (1948, 1953) argued that sexual preference should be viewed along a continuum. They developed a 7-point scale to measure the degree to which respondents in their studies were "homosexual" or "heterosexual" in their sexual behaviors. The 0 point on the Kinsey Scale means that a man or woman has never had *any* overt homosexual experience, while a 6 on the scale indicates no overt heterosexual experience. Moving up the scale from 0, a 1 means that an individual has some minimal amount of homosexual experience, but that this is overshadowed by heterosexual experiences; a person scoring 2 on the Kinsey Scale has had significantly more homosexual experience but is still predominantly heterosexual; a Kinsey 3 indicates a person with about equal experience of both a homosexual and heterosexual nature; a 4 describes a person who has had a great deal of heterosexual experience but is predominantly homosexual; 5 indicates some minimal heterosexual experience in a very dominantly homosexual individual; and as discussed before, a Kinsey 6 is an exclusive homosexual.

In the Kinsey research, surprisingly few people fell on either end of the continuum, that is, "exclusively" heterosexual or homosexual. About half of all

American men fell somewhere *between* the two end points. Women's responses were also distributed across the continuum, but, as mentioned previously, fewer women than men indicated that their behavior was exclusively homosexual. Individuals falling at the midpoint of the Kinsey Scale sometimes describe themselves as "bisexual," but they may have a preference for one sex or the other, in spite of their ability to relate to both, and may or may not be self-identified as bisexual (Broido, 2000; S. H. Dworkin, 2000; Moses & Hawkins, 1982).

Thus, we see one way in which the issue of sexual orientation is more complex than it appears at first glance (Broido, 2000; Fassinger, 2000). But Kinsey and his colleagues only addressed sexual *behavior.* Sexual preference is only one aspect of sexual orientation; affectional/emotional factors are, for many, far more important than the sexual attraction to a partner. Moses and Hawkins (1982) identified two of the major components of sexual orientation: "(1) the physical, which includes gender preference for sexual partners and sexual relationships, and (2) the affectional, which includes gender preference for primary emotional relationships" (p. 36). One's exploration of partners in fantasy and one's personal history must also be taken into account. A person may have had various types of sexual, affectional, or fantasy experiences in the past but have different types of experiences currently. If all components of an individual's sexual orientation are congruent, labeling is fairly easy. However, factors influencing sexual orientation may be inconsistent, defying simple categories (Fassinger, 2000). Some authors disentangle sexual identity, defined as "socially constructed experiences of identity and of membership in groups (gay men, lesbians, and bisexual people) that have developed their own cultures" (S. H. Dworkin, 2000, pp. 171–172), and sexual orientation, or "core knowledge from early childhood about the nature of their inclination and capacities—whether they are homoerotic or heteroerotic" (S. H. Dworkin, 2000, p. 172).

Due to their unique status, LGB individuals encounter barriers not experienced by other minority group members. First, LGB people represent a statistically significant minority group in this country (i.e., well over 20 million individuals) and suffer from various forms of intolerance and oppression, including lack of legal protection, harassment, loss of their jobs, and violence, all of which usually serve to identify a minority group (Fone, 2000). Yet many still deny that LGB people are a true minority (Fone, 2000; Woodman & Lenna, 1980). Some of the arguments against affording minority status to LGBs hinge on religious beliefs, others on the view that sexual orientation is a choice rather than a natural orientation, and some of the arguments are simply reflective of ignorance and/or bias (S. H. Dworkin & Gutierrez, 1992; Fassinger, 2000; Fone, 2000). Interestingly, virulently antigay statements routinely appear in the media, and these are accepted in due course in a way that would be considered unconscionable if such statements were directed at any other minority group. Bias and discrimination against LGB people is "the last acceptable prejudice" (Fone, 2000).

Second, lesbians, gay men, and bisexuals grow up learning the same negative attitudes and hostility toward homosexuality that nongays do. *Homophobia* is the term used to describe "the irrational fear of anyone gay or lesbian, or of anyone perceived to be gay or lesbian" (S. H. Dworkin & Gutierrez, 1992, p. xx). Coined in the 1960s, *homophobia* was originally defined as "the dread of being in close quarters with homosexuals" (Weinberg, 1972). Although variations of these definitions are commonly used, some believe that the emphasis on fear alone (*homophobia*) does not adequately impart the severity of responses, including violence, toward LGB people in U.S. society. A wide range of alternate terms have been proposed as more adequate descriptors of antigay prejudice, gay and lesbian hatred, and "fear and dislike of difference that homosexual individuals allegedly embody—stereotypically, effeminacy in homosexual men, mannishness in homosexual women" (Blumenfeld, 1992; Fone, 2000, p. 5).

*Heterosexism* refers not only to the belief that heterosexuality is the only acceptable sexual orientation, but also to the accompanying fear, disgust, and hatred of LGB people that results in discrimination (Blumenfeld, 1992). We retain the term *homophobia* but employ it in the expanded sense to indicate not only the fear of, but also the prejudice and hatred toward, gay men and lesbians. Further, some writers have developed and employed other terms to describe negative and biased reactions, including *biphobia,* referring to "fear or dislike of people who do not behave as either lesbian, gay, or heterosexual" (S. H. Dworkin, 2000, p. 158). Homophobia and its variants are likened to and connected with other *isms,* including sexism and racism (Fone, 2000).

Homophobic reactions are prevalent in society at large and also characterize the responses of friends and family of LGB people, as well as LGB individuals themselves (S. H. Dworkin & Gutierrez, 1992; Reynolds & Hanjorgiris, 2000; Weinberg, 1972). LGB people experience a unique situation among minority groups in that they are reared in heterosexual families that rarely provide the type of support needed in coping with a socially oppressed self-identity (Fassinger, 2000; Reynolds & Hanjorgiris, 2000). Families of LGB individuals are therefore often an additional source of oppression, and the task of developing a positive LGB identity is both complex and challenging (Beane, 1981; Reynolds & Hanjorgiris, 2000). *Internalized* homophobia is also a major obstacle for LGB people wrestling with their sexual orientation, further complicating an already complex process of self-definition. Heterosexuality is expected of everyone.

> Youth who eventually become lesbian, gay, or bisexual often report feeling different from others during childhood, although the nature of their difference may not become clear until adolescence, by which time they may have internalized a great deal of negativity regarding self-identity. . . . Thus, for LGB youth, socialization is even more complex than for their heterosexual counterparts, because all developmental tasks related to gender and sexuality must be negotiated within a context of stigma and shame. (Fassinger, 2000, p. 354)

When people begin to realize that they are not heterosexually oriented, they struggle with a highly charged and stigmatized self-label. "Coming out" or "coming out of the closet" is argot for acknowledging to oneself, being open about, or asserting one's gay identity. Being "in the closet" is to conceal that identity. Among gays, the idea of coming out is more than just asserting a gay identity; it is a process by which an individual moves from the realization of homoerotic feelings to the acceptance of the sexual-affectional preference for people of the same sex. The next crucial step is to integrate those feelings positively into one's total self so that they can be asserted and to find affirmation in interactions with others. To use clients' phraseology, the process involves a "coming out to self" and a "coming out to others" (Woodman & Lenna, 1980, p. 13).

More recently, the theory and research literature has moved beyond the common aspects of gay and lesbian identity development to explore the complexity of the identity development process for LGB people, differences across subgroups of LGB people, and the intersections of sexual identity development with gender, race, and class (Reynolds & Hanjorgiris, 2000). For example, the terms used to self-identify as LGB or transgendered are clearly situated in a sociohistorical and cultural context; meanings and self-identities differ across cultures and have changed over time (Fone, 2000). Although having some shared aspects, the process of identity development for lesbians, gay men, and bisexuals is undoubtedly different in key respects (Reynolds & Hanjorgiris, 2000), and the "multiple layers of identity" of people of color interact to profoundly affect the process of sexual identity development (Fukuyama & Ferguson, 2000). For example

> LGB people of color may be coping with feelings of visibility or invisibility in at least two communities in which they live and function: the mainstream LGB community and their respective ethnic communities. . . . They are often differentially treated in the White, heterosexual community as well as in their respective heterosexual ethnic communities. (Fukuyama & Ferguson, 2000, pp. 85–86)

Further, views about women's roles, expectations of appropriate gender-role behavior, and attitudes toward LGB people differ across cultures and subcultures and by class within and across groups to vastly confound any effort to make broad generalizations about LGB identity development and the coming-out process. Other identities, for example, disability status, likewise significantly affect LGB self-identification and behavior.

**Gender Identity Versus Sexual Orientation**   As discussed in the previous section, the term *gender identity* refers to one's self-identity as a male or female (Richardson, 1981; Swann et al., 1999). Sexual orientation (or sexual identity) should not be mistaken for gender identity. Gay men are men and lesbians are women. The stereotype in Western cultures of the gay man as feminine equates sexual orientation with *gender role,* not gender identity, and though the stereotypes do fit some gay men, they do not fit many others. Most gay men exhibit the same range of masculine gender-role behavior as heterosexual men. Likewise, lesbian women may act in feminine or masculine ways, just as nongay women do; their gender identity as women is not dependent on their sexual orientation (Rothblum, 2000). And, as emphasized previously, our very conceptions of what is male and female vary across cultures and time.

Neither should sexual orientation be confused with transsexuality or transvestism. *Transsexuals* are individuals whose gender identity is different from their sex assignment, for example, a man who feels he is a women "trapped" in a man's body (Richardson, 1981). Some individuals who encounter such gender incongruence seek sex-reassignment surgery to resolve their dilemma, but transsexuality is fundamentally different from sexual orientation. *Transvestites* are people who enjoy dressing in clothing considered socially inappropriate for their sex. Because of the more stringent sanctions for gender-inappropriate behavior for men in our society, cross-dressing appears to be much more of an issue for men than women; despite the stereotypes, cross-dressing is unusual among gay men (Fone, 2000; Moses & Hawkins, 1982). Many men whose sexual orientation is predominantly or exclusively heterosexual cross-dress; gender identity and sexual orientation are often not issues for transvestites (Moses & Hawkins, 1982). *Transgendered* individuals are only recently being more widely considered a part of the gay community. As Fone (2000) stated: "In the 1980s, the 'gay people' of the 1970s became 'lesbians' and 'gay men'. In the 1990s out 'queers' challenged society—and disturbed some now old-fashioned 'gays'—by including transgendered and bisexual people under the rubric of difference" (p. 409). As can be seen from this briefest of overviews, LGB people are a complex and diverse group, and the literature is changing far more dramatically than in most other areas.

In chapter 5 we briefly describe the history of oppression of LGB people and explore some of the current societal attitudes and the responses of the mental health establishment. Counseling issues related to the concepts introduced in this chapter are expanded upon in later chapters.

## REFERENCES

Achenbaum, W. A. (1978). *Old age in the new land: The American experience since 1790.* Baltimore: Johns Hopkins University Press.

Aiken, L. R. (1995). *Aging: An introduction to gerontology.* Thousand Oaks, CA: Sage.

American Psychiatric Association. (2000). *Diagnostic and statistical manual of mental disorders* (4th ed.). Washington, DC: Author.

American Psychological Association. (2002). *Guidelines on multicultural education, training, research, practice, and organizational change for psychologists* [Electronic version]. Washington, DC: Author.

Amundsen, K. (1971). *The silenced majority.* Englewood Cliffs, NJ: Prentice Hall.

Ansello, E. F. (1991). The intersecting of aging and disabilities. In B. B. Hess & E. W. Markson (Eds.), *Growing old in America* (4th ed., pp. 207–218). New Brunswick, NJ: Transaction Books.

Aubrey, R. F., & Lewis, J. (1983). Social issues and the counseling profession in the 1980s and 1990s. *Counseling and Human Development, 15*(10), 1–15.

Beane, J. (1981). "I'd rather be dead than gay": Counseling gay men who are coming out. *Personnel and Guidance Journal, 60,* 222–226.

Bell, S. T., Kuriloff, P. J., & Lottes, I. (1994). Understanding attributions of blame in stranger rape and date rape situations: An examination of gender, race, identification, and students' social perceptions of rape victims. *Journal of Applied Social Psychology, 24,* 1719–1734.

Bem, S. L., (1974). The measurement of psychological androgyny. *Journal of Consulting and Clinical Psychology, 42,* 155–162.

Bem, S. L. (1994). *The lenses of gender.* New Haven, CT: Yale University Press.

Blumenfeld, W. J. (Ed.). (1992). *Homophobia: How we all pay the price.* Boston: Beacon Press.

Bowe, F. (1985). *Disabled adults in American: A statistical report drawn from Census Bureau data.* Washington, DC: U.S. Government Printing Office.

Broido, E. (2000). Constructing identity: The nature and meaning of lesbian, gay, and bisexual identities. In R. M. Perez, K. A. DeBord, & K. J. Bieschke (Eds.), *Handbook of counseling and psychotherapy with lesbian, gay, and bisexual clients* (pp. 13–34). Washington, DC: American Psychological Association.

Churchill, W. (1971). *Homosexual behavior among males: A cross-cultural and cross-species investigation.* Englewood Cliffs, NJ: Prentice Hall.

Clark, D. (1977). *Loving someone gay.* Millbrae, CA: Celestial Arts.

Cole, T. (1991). The specter of old age: History, politics, and culture in an aging America. In B. B. Hess & E. W. Markson (Eds.), *Growing old in America* (4th ed., pp. 23–37). New Brunswick, NJ: Transaction Books.

Collier, H. V. (1982). *Counseling women.* New York: Free Press.

Costello, C. B., & Stone, A. J. (Eds.). (2001). *The American woman, 2001–2002: Getting to the top.* New York: W. W. Norton.

Deaux, K. (1999). An overview of research on gender: Four themes from three decades. In W. B. Swann, J. H. Langlois, & L. A. Gilbert (Eds.), *Sexism and stereotypes in modern society* (pp. 11–34). Washington, DC: American Psychological Association.

Dressel, P. L., Carter, V., & Balachandran, A. (1995). Second-order victim-blaming. *Journal of Sociology and Social Welfare, 22*(2), 107–122.

Dworkin, A. G., & Dworkin, R. J. (1976). *The minority report.* New York: Praeger.

Dworkin, S. H. (2000). Individual therapy with lesbian, gay, and bisexual clients. In R. M. Perez, K. A. DeBord, & K. J. Bieschke (Eds.), *Handbook of counseling and psychotherapy with lesbian, gay, and bisexual clients* (pp. 157–181). Washington, DC: American Psychological Association.

Dworkin, S. H., & Gutierrez, F. J. (1992). Introduction: Opening the closet door. In S. H. Dworkin & F. J. Gutierrez (Eds.), *Counseling gay men and lesbians: Journey to the end of the rainbow* (pp. xvii–xxvii). Alexandria, VA: American Association of Counseling and Development.

Enns, C. Z. (2000). Gender issues in counseling. In S. D. Brown & R. W. Lent (Eds.), *Handbook of counseling psychology* (3rd ed., pp. 601–638). New York: Wiley.

Faderman, L. (1991). *Odd girls and twilight lovers.* New York: Penguin.

Fagan, T., & Wallace, A. (1979). Who are the handicapped? *Personnel and Guidance Journal, 58,* 215–220.

Faludi, S. (1991). *Backlash: The undeclared war against American women.* New York: Crown.

Fassinger, R. E. (2000). Gender and sexuality in human development: Implications for prevention and advocacy in counseling psychology. In S. D. Brown & R. W. Lent (Eds.), *Handbook of counseling psychology* (3rd ed., pp. 346–378). New York: Wiley.

Fone, B. (2000). *Homophobia: A history.* New York: Picador.

Fukuyama, M. A., & Ferguson, A. D. (2000). Lesbian, gay, and bisexual people of color: Understanding cultural complexity and managing multiple oppressions. In R. M. Perez, K. A. DeBord, & K. J. Bieschke (Eds.), *Handbook of counseling and psychotherapy with lesbian, gay, and bisexual clients* (pp. 81–105). Washington, DC: American Psychological Association.

Gilbert, L. A. (1992). Gender and counseling psychology: Current knowledge and directions for research and social action. In S. D. Brown & R. W. Lent (Eds.), *Handbook of counseling psychology* (2nd ed., pp. 383–416). New York: Wiley.

Gilbert, L. A., & Sher, M. (1999). *Gender and sex in counseling and psychotherapy.* Boston: Allyn & Bacon.

Glick, P., & Fiske, S. T. (1996). The ambivalent sexism inventory: Differentiating hostile and benevolent sexism. *Journal of Personality and Social Psychology, 70,* 491–512.

Glick, P., & Fiske, S. T. (1999). Sexism and other "isms": Independence, status, and the ambivalent content of stereotypes. In W. B. Swann, J. H. Langlois, & L. A. Gilbert (Eds.), *Sexism and stereotypes in modern society* (pp. 193–222). Washington, DC: American Psychological Association.

Goffman, D. (1963). *Stigma: Notes on the management of spoiled identity.* Englewood Cliffs, NJ: Prentice Hall.

Grealish, C. A., & Salomone, P. R. (1986). Devaluing those with disability: Take responsibility, take action. *The Vocational Guidance Quarterly, 34,* 147–150.

Griffiths, T. D., & Meechan, P. J. (1990). Biology of aging. In Kenneth F. Ferraro (Ed.), *Gerontology: Perspectives and issues* (pp. 45–57). New York: Springer.

Hacker, H. M. (1975). Women as a minority group. In R. K. Unger & F. L. Denmark (Eds.), *Woman: Dependent or independent variable* (pp. 85–115). New York: Psychological Dimensions.

Halleck, S. L. (1971). Therapy is the handmaiden of the status quo. *Psychology Today, 4,* 30–34, 98–100.

Henley, N. M. (1985). Psychology and gender. *Signs, 11,* 101–119.

Hess, B. B. (1991). Growing old in the 1990s. In B. B. Hess & E. W. Markson (Eds.), *Growing old in America* (4th ed., pp. 5–22). New Brunswick, NJ: Transaction Books.

Hetzel, L., & Smith, A. (2001). *The 65 years and over population: 2000.* Retrieved November 6, 2002, from U.S. Census Bureau website: http://www.census.gov/prod/2001pubs/c2kbr01-10.pdf.

Hewlett, S. A. (2002). *Creating a life: Professional women and the quest for children.* New York: Talk Miramax Books.

Hobbs, F. B., & Damon, B. L. (1996). *65+ in the United States* [Electronic version] (U.S. Bureau of the Census Current Population Reports P23-190). Washington, DC: U.S. Government Printing Office.

Kingdon, M. A. (1979). Lesbians. *The Counseling Psychologist, 8,* 44–45.

Kinloch, G. C. (1979). *The sociology of minority group relations.* Englewood Cliffs, NJ: Prentice Hall.

Kinsey, A. C., Pomeroy, W. B., & Martin, C. E. (1948). *Sexual behavior in the human male.* Philadelphia: Saunders.

Kinsey, A. C., Pomeroy, W. B., Martin, C. E., & Gebhard, P. H. (1953). *Sexual behavior in the human female.* Philadelphia: Saunders.

Kuehn, M. D. (1991). Agenda for professional practice in the 1990s. *Journal of Applied Rehabilitation Counseling, 22,* 6–15.

Larson, P. C. (1982). Counseling special populations. *Professional Psychology, 13,* 843–858.

Levin, J., & Levin, W. C. (1980). *Ageism: Prejudice and discrimination against the elderly.* Belmont, CA: Wadsworth.

Maccoby, E. E., & Jacklin, C. N. (1974). *The psychology of sex differences.* Stanford, CA: Stanford University Press.

Martin, D., & Lyon, P. (1972). *Lesbian woman.* San Francisco: New Glide.

McNeil, J. M. (1993). *Americans with disabilities: 1991–92* (U.S. Bureau of the Census Current Populations Reports, P70-33). Washington, DC: U.S. Government Printing Office.

McNeil, J. M (1997). *American with disabilities: 1994–95* [Electronic version] (U.S. Bureau of the Census Current Populations Reports, P70-61). Washington, DC: U.S. Government Printing Office.

Mead, M. (1971). *Sex and temperament in three primitive societies.* New York: Dell. (Original work published 1935)

Meador, B. D., & Rogers, C. R. (1984). Person-centered therapy. In R. J. Corsini (Ed.), *Current psychotherapies* (pp. 142–195). Itasca, IL: F. E. Peacock.

Mezzich, J. E., Kirmayer, L. J., Kleinman, A., Fabrega, H., Parron, D. L., Good, B. J., et al. (1999). The place of culture in DSM-IV. *The Journal of Nervous and Mental Disease, 187,* 457–464.

Mill, J. S. (1970). *The subjection of women.* Cambridge, MA: MIT Press. (Original work published 1869)

Moses, A. E., & Hawkins. R. O. (1982). *Counseling lesbian women and gay men.* St. Louis: Mosby.

Muller, R. T., Caldwell, R. A., & Hunter, J. E. (1995). The construct dimensionality of victim blame: The situations of physical child abuse and rape. *Personality and Individual Differences, 19,* 21–31.

Nichols, M. P. (1984). *Family therapy: Concepts and methods.* New York: Gardner Press.

O'Neil, J. M. (1980). Male sex role conflicts, sexism, and masculinity: Psychological implications for men, women, and the counseling psychologist. *The Counseling Psychologist, 9,* 61–80.

Perlman, L. G., & Kirk, F. S. (1991). Key disability and rehabilitation legislation. *Journal of Applied Rehabilitation Counseling, 22,* 21–27.

Pope, M. (1995). The "salad bowl" is big enough for us all: An argument for the inclusion of lesbians and gay men in any definition of multiculturalism. *Journal of Counseling and Development, 73,* 301–304.

Reynolds, A. L., & Hanjorgiris, W. F. (2000). Coming out: Lesbian, gay, and bisexual identity development. In R. M. Perez, K. A. DeBord, & K. J. Bieschke (Eds.), *Handbook of counseling and psychotherapy with lesbian, gay, and bisexual clients* (pp. 35–55). Washington, DC: American Psychological Association.

Richardson, L. W. (1981). *The dynamics of sex and gender: A sociological perspective* (2nd ed.). Boston: Houghton Mifflin.

Rothblum, E. D. (2000). "Somewhere in Des Moines or San Antonio": Historical perspectives on lesbian, gay, and bisexual mental health. In R. M. Perez, K. A. DeBord, & K. J. Bieschke (Eds.), *Handbook of counseling and psychotherapy with lesbian, gay, and bisexual clients* (pp. 57–80). Washington, DC: American Psychological Association.

Sarason, S. B. (1981). An asocial psychology and a misdirected clinical psychology. *American Psychologist, 36,* 827–836.

Satlin, A. (1994). The psychology of successful aging. *Journal of Geriatric Psychiatry, 27,* 3–7.

Schwiebert, V. L., & Myers, J. E. (1994). Midlife care givers: Effectiveness of a psychoeducational intervention for midlife adults with parent-care responsibilities. *Journal of Counseling & Development, 72,* 627–632.

Sharf, R. S. (2000). *Theories of psychotherapy and counseling: Concepts and cases* (2nd ed.). Belmont, CA: Wadsworth Brooks/Cole.

Shilling, L. E. (1984). *Perspectives on counseling theories.* Englewood Cliffs, NJ: Prentice Hall.

Simkin, J. S., & Yontef, G. M. (1984). Gestalt therapy. In R. J. Corsini (Ed.), *Current psychotherapies* (pp. 279–319). Itasca, IL: F. E. Peacock.

Smith, D., & Tillipman, H. (2000). *The older population in the United States: Population characteristics* [Electronic version] (U.S. Bureau of the Census Current Population Reports, P20-532). Washington, DC: U.S. Government Printing Office.

Sommers, C. H. (2000). *The war against boys: How misguided feminism is harming our young men.* New York: Simon & Schuster.

Spence, J. T., & Helmreich, R. L. (1978). *Masculinity and femininity: Their psychological dimensions, correlates, and antecedents.* Austin: University of Texas Press.

Steiner, C. (1975). *Readings in radical psychiatry.* New York: Grove.

Strehler, B. L. (1962). *Time, cells and aging.* New York: Academic.

Sue, D. W., Bingham, R. P., Porche-Burke, L., & Vasquez, M. (1999). The diversification of psychology: A multicultural revolution. *American Psychologist, 54,* 1061–1069.

Swann, W. B., Langlois, J. H., & Gilbert, L. A. (Eds.). (1999). *Sexism and stereotypes in modern society.* Washington, DC: American Psychological Association.

Unger, R. K. (1979). Toward a redefinition of sex and gender. *American Psychologist, 34,* 1085–1094.

U.S. Bureau of the Census. (1989). *Labor force status and other characteristics of persons with a work disability: 1981 to 1988* (Current Population Reports, P23-160). Washington, DC: U.S. Government Printing Office.

U.S. Bureau of the Census. (1992). *Sixty-five plus in America* (Current Populations Reports, Special Studies, P23-178RV). Washington, DC: U.S. Government Printing Office.

U.S. Bureau of the Census. (1993). *Marital status and living arrangements: March, 1992* (Current Population Reports, P20-468). Washington, DC: U.S. Government Printing Office.

U.S. Bureau of the Census. (1997a). *Aging in the United States—Past, present, and future.* Retrieved November 6, 2002, from http://www.census.gov /ipc/prod/97agewc.pdf.

U.S. Bureau of the Census. (1997b). *Disabilities affect one-fifth of all Americans.* Retrieved November 6, 2002, from http://www.census.gov/prod/3/97 pubs/cenbr975.pdf.

U.S. Bureau of the Census. (2000). *Profile of selected social characteristics: 2000.* Retrieved November 6, 2002, from http://censtats.census.gov/data/US/ 01000.pdf.

U.S. Bureau of the Census. (2002). *Definition of disability items in Census 2000.* Retrieved November 6, 2002, from http://www.census.gov/hhes/www/ disable/disdef00.html.

Vander, A. J., Sherman, J., & Luciano, D. (1985). Homeostatic mechanisms. In *Human physiology: The mechanisms of body function* (pp. 147–171). New York: McGraw-Hill.

Weinberg, G. H. (1972). *Society and the healthy homosexual.* New York: St. Martin's.

Wilson, G. T. (1984). Behavior therapy. In R. J. Corsini (Ed.), *Current psychotherapies* (pp. 239–278). Itasca, IL: F. E. Peacock.

Wirth, L. (1945.) The problem of minority groups. In R. Linton (Ed.), *The science of man in the world crisis* (pp. 347–372). New York: Columbia University Press.

Woodman, N. J., & Lenna, H. R. (1980). *Counseling with gay men and women.* San Francisco: Jossey-Bass.

Worell, J., & Remer, P. (2003). *Feminist perspectives in therapy: Empowering diverse women* (2nd ed.). New York: Wiley.

World Health Organization. (2001). *International classification of functioning, disability and health.* Retrieved November 8, 2002, from http://www3.who. int/icf/onlinebrowser/icf.cfm.

# CHAPTER 2

# Oppression of People with Disabilities: Past and Present

This chapter examines the various forms of oppression experienced by people with disabilities. Basically, three ways of viewing people with disabilities have evolved over time; all three views are reflected in contemporary society. To understand current discrimination, it is helpful to first examine past discrimination

## PAST DISCRIMINATION

Across the millennia, people with disabilities have been discriminated against in a variety of ways by other members of the society in which they live. In addition to examining discrimination by society in general, this section discusses how mental health professionals have contributed to discrimination against people with disabilities over the past century.

### Society's Treatment of People With Disabilities

Hohenshil and Humes (1979) summarized the treatment of persons with disabilities since prehistoric times as follows:

> Throughout the course of recorded human history, those persons who were different have often been destroyed, tortured, exorcised, sterilized, ignored, exiled, exploited, and even considered divine. Their problems have been crudely explained in terms of superstition and varying levels of scientific understanding. In the earliest primitive societies, physical abnormalities were not common beyond infancy because many tribes permitted the killing of such newborn children. . . . In more recent societies the handicapped have been pitied and cared for, and finally, they have been gradually accepted, educated, and often employed, with the same rights as those who are not handicapped. (p. 221)

As Hohenshil and Humes suggest, three views of persons with disabilities have been widely held from prehistoric through contemporary times in Western culture. Each is still present to some extent in modern society in the United States.

**Burdensome View**    The first view, that persons with disabilities are a burden on the community, originated with our first human ancestors. Early humans were almost certainly nomads, foraging for fruit, nuts, and plants and following game for food. Communities of humans presumably formed to enhance self-protection and food-gathering efficiency. Under these conditions individuals who could not ambulate well enough to keep up with the group or who could not contribute to the food-gathering activities were rejected, destroyed, or left to survive on their own (Obermann, 1965). In addition to the ability to ambulate, visual acuity, hearing ability, and other physical capabilities were presumably needed to contribute to group welfare. Limited mental ability was probably not viewed by the group as a burden, but no doubt lessened the ability of individuals to survive in an environment in which humans were both predators and prey.

As agricultural societies developed, permanent villages began to appear. Although ambulation and other physical and mental abilities were still needed for farming activities, individuals no longer needed to keep up with the nomadic movements of the group. Persons with mild disabilities often were able to contribute to the welfare of the community and to maintain themselves to a degree not possible in earlier stages of human development. Some people with disabilities could plant fields, use hand tools, make pottery, and contribute to the commonweal in other ways. Severe physical disabilities were still viewed as "deformities," however, and the belief that disabilities were somehow supernaturally inspired, a belief dating back to prehistoric times, still persisted (Bowe, 1978):

> Lacking the technical means to find and demonstrate germs or histopathology, ancient doctors had to explain disease and physiological disorders in terms of evil spirits and cures had to be offered in terms of exorcism and magic. If the gods were smiling upon the well and the whole and the strong, the sick and the disabled and the weak must be the special property of demons. Thus the disadvantaged individual not only felt the frustrations resulting from lack of capability, he [*sic*] suffered social ostracism and personal feelings of unworthiness as well. (Obermann, 1965, p. 54)

Even in the golden era of Greek culture it was common practice in Sparta, for example, to destroy babies and children with disabilities because they were viewed as a burden on their families and because it was a means of "upgrading" the race (Obermann, 1965; Rubin & Roessler, 2001). Although Aristotle and other Greek philosophers began to question negative societal attitudes toward persons with disabilities, the view that people with disabilities are a burden on society persisted, even as it does today among some circles. Centuries later the Romans engaged in the same barbaric practice and were known to dispose of "some deformed and unwanted children . . . in sewers, located, ironically, outside the Temple of Mercy" (Garrett, 1969, p. 31).

Evidence that the burdensome view of persons with disabilities still exists in modern society is provided by studies of employment attitudes. In general, it can be concluded that negative attitudes toward persons with disabilities have severely limited their employment opportunities (Schall, 1998; Stefan, 2001). In essence, an attitude exists that employing people with disabilities would place a burden on most businesses. This is particularly true of human-services occupations, where employees have contact with consumers and the employees' "appearance" presumably enters into hiring decisions. Businesses engaged in sales or service are less likely to hire persons with disabilities than are manufacturing firms (Harris and Associates, 1986; Satcher & Hendren, 1991).

**Charitable View**   In Western society at least, a second attitude toward people with disabilities, that of charitable concern for their welfare, emerged as a forceful theme when Jesus Christ drew attention to this population through his teachings. As a result, Christian churches accepted the plight of persons with disabilities as one of their charitable causes. This view of persons with disabilities held that they were among the "deserving poor." Providing food, shelter, and other services for people with disabilities became an important activity of the developing church and other charitable organizations. Unfortunately, the provider-receiver relationship that was created too often serves as a model for modern efforts to assist individuals with disabilities. This second view of people with disabilities, although motivated by sincere concern for their welfare, frequently translates into sympathy, pity, and a paternalistic attitude toward persons with disabilities (Bowe, 1978).

The charitable treatment of persons with disabilities received a setback in the Middle Ages, due in part to the poor economic conditions and the strict religious attitudes of the times (Rubin & Roessler, 2001). According to Scotch (2001), during the Middle Ages persons with disabilities were often placed in institutions that offered little more than custodial care. The belief that disabilities were the result of supernaturalism returned in full force. "Disabled people were to be feared or ridiculed, objects of persecution on the one hand and court jesters on the other" (Bowe, 1978, pp. 7–8). Frequently they were placed in asylums with "other individuals who did not play a productive role in the social and economic life of the community" (Scotch, 2001, p. 15). By the 16th century, however, the theory that mentally ill people were sick began to compete with the view that they were possessed by demons (Rubin & Roessler, 2001).

One of the first institutions for people with disabilities in the United States was a school for blind persons established in Baltimore, Maryland, in 1812. A school for the deaf was founded in Hartford, Connecticut, by 1817, and in 1893 the first school for children with physical disabilities was founded in Boston, Massachusetts (Obermann, 1965). By the late 19th century a number of voluntary charitable organizations had been established in the United States that were concerned with the welfare of individuals with disabilities. The Salvation Army, which had been organized in England, established an office in the United States in 1879. This was followed by the American Red Cross in 1881 and Goodwill Industries in 1902 (Scotch, 2001).

Although they helped to establish special schools for the blind, deaf, and mentally ill in the 1800s, state and federal governments did not become significantly involved with the needs of people with disabilities until the 20th century (Hohenshil & Humes, 1979). "With the ushering in of the Progressive Era at the turn of the century, the time was ripe for the passage of worker's compensation legislation" (Rubin & Roessler, 2001, p. 24). State worker compensation laws providing medical treatment and financial compensation for injured workers were first passed in 1909 and by 1921, 45 states and territories had worker compensation laws. The first pillar of a federal vocational rehabilitation program was set in place when the Smith-Sears Veterans Rehabilitation Act was passed in 1918 mandating vocational training for veterans with disabilities. This was followed by the Smith-Fess Act of 1920, which provided limited services for people with physical disabilities (including vocational counseling). The Smith-Fess Act provided for federal funding to participating states on a 50-50 basis. By 1935 all the states had vocational rehabilitation programs in operation. Also in 1935, passage of the Social Security Act gave the vocational rehabilitation program permanent authorization. In 1940 the program was expanded to include previously unserved populations, and the federal government's share of the funding was increased to 75%. Further expansion and strengthening of the federal rehabilitation program occurred with the Barder-LaFollette Act of 1943 and with the Vocational Rehabilitation Acts of 1954, 1965, and 1968 (Scotch, 2001).

Funk (1987) described the 40-year period from 1920 to 1960 as follows:

> From a broad disability/human rights perspective, the era reflects an increasing humanization of certain classes of disabled people based on qualities of "deservedness" and "normalcy" and "employability," and a move from total societal indifference to a recognition that the remaining "unfortunates" must receive some level of minimum care. However, the handicapped still retained their caste status in the public mind as dependent, unhealthy deviants, who would, in the great majority, always require segregated care and protection. (pp. 13–14)

Currently, more than a third (37.1% in 1994–95) of all adults ages 22 to 64 with severe disabilities receive federal means-tested assistance from the federal or state governments (McNeil, 1997).

**Egalitarian View**    Although the concept of rehabilitation was an important step in the evolution of attitudes toward people with disabilities, it was still based on a medical or deficiency model and a view that society was performing a charitable act by providing assistance to qualifying individuals. The focus of efforts by charitable organizations and governmental programs until the late 1960s was on rehabilitation, that is, helping people with disabilities to adapt as much as possible to their impairment and to the environment in which they lived. Furthermore, some rehabilitation statutes actually operated to restrict the activities of people with disabilities. According to Laski (1978), these statutes

> reflected common stereotypes of disabled persons as dependent and inferior. Laws characteristically excluded handicapped persons from services, benefits and protections provided, as a matter-of-course, to all persons. Specialized legislation enacted to protect the disabled was premised on notions of charity rather than enlightenment and implemented so as to segregate the disabled and suffocate their ability to participate in society. (p. 1)

By the late 1960s a third view of persons with disabilities was emerging in the United States, a view that they are a disparate but identifiable group of individuals whose civil rights have been severely restricted, often through the efforts of well-meaning supporters. Central to this view was the philosophy that the civil rights of people with disabilities were being denied if government-supported institutions were not socially and architecturally designed to accommodate them.

> Advocates argued that disabled people should receive not special education at a special school, but supplemental services as part of a regular educational program in a regular classroom shared with able-bodied students; not sheltered workshops for the construction of handicrafts and the repair of discards, but participation in the mainstream labor market; not separate arrangements for transportation, recreation, and access to public facilities, but equal access to facilities and services used by the general public. By rejecting separate facilities, whether equal or unequal, disability rights advocates rejected the association of disabled persons with the "deserving poor" and launched a civil rights movement demanding full integration into the mainstream of American life, a movement parallel to those demanding equal rights without regard to race, gender, or age. (Scotch, 2001, pp. 10–11)

The resulting civil rights movement for people with disabilities is the most recent in a series of movements that have sought rights for laborers, people of color, women, and gay men and lesbians (Driedger, 1989). Rather than providing services to help people with disabilities adjust to their environment, the egalitarian movement pushed for environmental and social changes to adapt to the needs of people with disabilities.

According to Scotch (2001), the groundwork for this egalitarian view of people with disabilities was laid when the National Federation for the Blind and other groups lobbied state legislatures in the 1930s for guide dog and white cane laws. These laws were precedent setting because they nullified restrictions placed on people with disabilities by the larger society (e.g., allowing the use of guide dogs in public places where dogs are prohibited) and required able-bodied persons to adjust to their presence (e.g., drivers must take precautions upon seeing a white cane in use). The fact that young people who became disabled as the result of World War II were living longer and were more mobile than earlier generations of people with disabilities also contributed to a climate for recognizing disability rights (Driedger, 1989). Further groundwork was laid with the Architectural Barriers Act of 1968, the first federal civil-rights-oriented statute affecting people with disabilities. This act required that a barrier-free design be employed in all new federal building construction.

For many years the formation of a cohesive social or political group representing people with disabilities was impeded by their diverse experiences and communication differences. With the social movements of the 1960s, however, came a recognition that they shared a common experience of oppression and exclusion, and a disability civil rights movement began to take form. Initially, informal and formal interaction took place among individuals sharing similar disabilities, and later interaction and political activity took place across disability lines (Scotch, 2001). The decade from 1965 to 1975 has been referred to by Abeson (1976) as the "era in which the battle cry for public policy advances changed from charitable solicitations to declarations of rights" (p. 5) on behalf of people with disabilities.

In 1972 the most comprehensive piece of legislature affecting people with disabilities up to that date was signed into law by President Richard Nixon. It was entitled The Rehabilitation Act of 1973 and was intended to expand and improve the federal rehabilitation program. Section 504 of the Act, however, included language borrowed from Title VI of the Civil Rights Acts of 1964 and has been referred to by Scotch (2001) as a civil rights law for persons with disabilities. The single sentence that constitutes Section 504 reads: "No otherwise qualified handicapped individual in the United States . . . shall, solely by reason of his [sic] handicap, be excluded from the participation in, be denied the benefits of, or be subjected to discrimination under any program or activity receiving Federal financial assistance." Bowe (1978), a leading disability rights activist, referred to Section 504 as "the single most important civil rights provision ever enacted on behalf of disabled citizens in this country" (p. 205). Unfortunately, however, the disability rights provided by the Rehabilitation Act of 1973 were limited to programs receiving federal assistance and did not apply to the private sector (White & Fawcett, 2000).

The Education of Handicapped Children Act (PL 94-142), which President Gerald Ford signed into law in November 1975, also included important provisions for disability rights. This law (which is now referred to as the Individuals with Disabilities Education Act [IDEA]) stipulated that states must provide free and appropriate education to all children with disabilities and included federal funding toward this end. In addition to provisions calling for the involvement of parents in development of individual educational plans (IEPs) for children with disabilities, the law mandated the concept of mainstreaming. In essence, this requirement stipulates that, whenever possible, children with disabilities must receive their education in the least restrictive environment, including regular classrooms with nondisabled students.

The list of rights won by people with disabilities through disability rights legislation during the period from 1965 to 1975 is indeed impressive. In addition to the right to public-supported education, the list includes

> the right of institutionalized handicapped persons to be free from unusual and cruel treatment; the right of institutionalized handicapped persons to be freed from employment without reimbursement and without rehabilitative purpose; the right to avoid involuntary institutionalization on the part of persons who represent neither a danger to society nor to themselves; the right of the handicapped to exercise the power to vote; the right of the handicapped both to marry and to procreate; the right of the handicapped to travel on the nation's public conveyances; and the right of the handicapped to access America's buildings by means of removal of environmental barriers. (Abeson, 1976, p. 5)

For a period of time in the early 1980s, the disability rights movement in the United States appeared to have reached a plateau. According to Scotch (2001), the disability rights movement peaked in effectiveness in 1978, and he cited failure by Congress to pass an extension to the Civil Rights Act prohibiting discrimination on the basis of disability in all employment to support his position. He also suggested that many government officials sympathetic to disability rights had been removed from government agencies following the 1980 presidential election. By the mid-1980s, however, a number of federal and state laws had been enacted that were designed to promote and enhance the career development of students with disabilities. Brolin and Gysbers (1989) listed the Job Training Partnership Act of 1982, the 1983 Amendments to the Education of the Handicapped Act of 1975, the Carl D. Perkins Vocational Education Act of 1984, the Developmental Disabilities Act Amendments of 1984, and the Rehabilitation Act Amendments of 1986 as evidence of continuing concern for the employment and civil rights of persons with disabilities.

Disability rights groups continued to lobby Congress, and by the late 1980s, support for a comprehensive disabilities rights bill was gaining strength (White & Faucett, 2000). In 1990, the Congress passed the Americans with Disabilities Act (ADA, PL 101-336), "the most sweeping civil-rights bill in more than 25 years" (Karr, 1990, p. B1). The ADA was signed into law by President George Bush on July 26, 1990, and took effect 2 years later. The purposes of the ADA are

1.  to provide a clear and comprehensive national mandate for the elimination of discrimination against individuals with disabilities;
2.  to provide clear, strong, consistent, enforceable standards addressing discrimination against individuals with disabilities;
3.  to ensure that the Federal Government plays a central role in enforcing the standards established in this Act on behalf of individuals with disabilities; and
4.  to invoke the sweep of congressional authority, including the power to enforce the fourteenth amendment and to regulate commerce, in order to address the major areas of discrimination faced day-to-day by people with disabilities. (Karr, 1990, p. B1)

The ADA prohibits discrimination against persons with mental or physical disabilities in the private sector in four different areas: (1) employment, (2) telecommunications, (3) transportation, and (4) public services and accommodations. With respect to employment, the ADA specifies that employers with 15 or more employees must "make reasonable accommodation to the known limitations of qualified persons with disabilities and to ensure that their hiring practices are nondiscriminatory" (Satcher & Hendren, 1991, p. 15). According to Youngstrom (1992), reasonable accommodations could include "hiring a reader for a blind employee; adjusting schedules so an employee can see a therapist in the middle of the day; and writing instructions for people who become anxious at oral directions" (p. 26). The law also requires that persons with disabilities must be provided access to public buildings, telephone service, mass transportation, and government services.

Several other important disability laws were passed subsequent to passage of the ADA. The IDEA, amended and renamed several times since 1975, was amended most recently in 1997; the newly amended statute is usually referred to as IDEA 97. Despite the fact that mainstreaming children with disabilities and involvement of their parents in their educational planning was initially mandated over 20 years earlier, federal legislators found that some children with disabilities still faced unacceptable barriers to obtaining an education. IDEA 97 ostensibly was an attempt to address some of these barriers. Among other things, IDEA 97

- reemphasized that parents need to be involved in developing, reviewing, and revising their child's IEP;
- ensured that regular education teachers are involved in planning and assessing children's progress;
- included children with disabilities in assessments, performance goals, and reports to the public;
- reinforced the concept of mainstreaming and required that an explanation be provided in the IEP if a child with a disability is to be excluded from any regular class in the general curriculum;
- required that measurable, annual goals be developed for each child with a disability; and
- stipulated that quality professional development be provided for all personnel who are involved in educating children with disabilities (Department of Education, 2001; The Family Network on Disabilities of Florida, n.d.).

In 1998, President Bill Clinton signed into law the Crime Victims with Disabilities Awareness Act. This law is designed to address the current lack of information about victimization (including abuse) of people with disabilities, raise public awareness of victimization of people with disabilities, identify risk factors associated with victimization of people with disabilities, assess how the criminal justice system responds to crimes against people with disabilities, and develop a centralized computer database for tracking crimes against people with disabilities. The law authorizes the attorney general to conduct a study to address these various purposes (Mitchell & Buchele-Ash, 2000).

The No Child Left Behind (NCLB) Act of 2001 (Executive Summary, 2001) was signed into law by President George W. Bush on January 8, 2002. The NCLB is the reauthorization of the Elementary and Secondary Education Act that was originally enacted in 1965. Although it was not specifically aimed at children with disabilities, the NCLB contains several features that have implications for them. In addition to giving local educational agencies greater flexibility to shift funds from one federal program to another, the NCLB provides for increased accountability, expanded options for parents, and a stronger emphasis on empirically supported teaching methods. With regard to increased accountability, the NCLB requires states to set progress objectives and report assessment results by groups based on poverty, race, ethnicity, disability, and limited English proficiency. Theoretically, this should allow for better tracking of how children with disabilities are performing in school. With respect to expanded options for parents, local educational agencies are required to give students attending a school that has not met performance standards an opportunity to attend a better public school within the school district. For students attending a school that has failed to meet state standards for at least 3 of the 4 preceding years, the local educational agency must provide low-income students the opportunity to obtain supplemental educational services from public- or private-sector providers selected by the students and their parents. Assuming special education services within a school district failed to meet state standards, this provision could further strengthen IDEA regulations regarding education services for children with disabilities. With regard to the emphasis on

**TABLE 2.1**   Comparison of the Moral, Medical, and Social Models of Disability

| Measure | Moral | Medical | Social |
|---|---|---|---|
| Meaning of disability | Disability is a defect caused by moral lapse or sins, failure of faith, evil, test of faith. | A defect in or failure of a bodily system that is inherently abnormal and pathological. | Disability is a social construct. Problems reside in the environment that fails to accommodate people with disabilities. |
| Moral implications | The disability brings shame to the person with the disability and his or her family. | A medical abnormality due to genetics, bad health habits, person's behavior. | Society has failed a segment of its citizens and oppresses them. |
| Sample ideas | "God gives us only what we can bear" or "There's a reason I was chosen to have this disability." | Clinical descriptions of "patients" in medical terminology. Isolation of body parts. | "Nothing about us without us" or "Civil rights, not charity." |
| Origins | Oldest model and still most prevalent worldwide. | Mid-19th century. Most common model in the United States. Entrenched in most rehabilitation clinics and journals. | In 1975 with the demonstrations by people with disabilities in support of the yet-unsigned Rehabilitation Act. |
| Goals of intervention | Spiritual, or divine, acceptance. | "Cure" or amelioration of the disability to the greatest extent possible. | Political, economic, social, and policy systems changes, increased access and inclusion. |
| Benefits of model | An acceptance of being selected, a special relationship with God, a sense of greater purpose to the disability. | A lessened sense of shame and stigma. Faith in medical intervention. Spurs medical and technological advances. | Promotes integration of the disability into the self. A sense of community and pride. Depathologizing of disability. |
| Negative effects | Shame, ostracization, need to conceal the disability or person with the disability. | Paternalistic, promotes benevolence and charity. Services for but not by people with disabilities. | Powerlessness in the face of broad social and political changes needed. Challenges to prevailing ideas. |

Table 1 on page 133 from Olkin, R. (2002). Could you hold the door for me? Including disability in diversity. *Cultural Diversity and Ethnic Minority Psychology, 8,* 130–137. Reprinted with permission.

empirically supported teaching methods, promoting the acquisition of reading skills by the third grade is a primary focus. Theoretically, this could result in fewer children being identified for special education services simply on the basis of inadequate reading skills and, in turn, retain more resources for students with disabilities. State educational agencies were still developing guidelines for the implementation of the NCLB at the time this book went to press, so the actual impact on the lives of children with disabilities remains to be seen.

As this brief review of disability legislation suggests, a number of laws have been passed since 1970 that are intended to eliminate barriers confronted by children and adults with disabilities. Despite the best of intentions, each law has included loopholes that allow private businesses, local educational agencies, and local governments to continue to discriminate against this population. As a result, earlier laws have been modified and rewritten in an attempt to close these loopholes and provide more rights for people with disabilities.

Although considerable attention has been given to disability rights since 1970, it is important to recognize that all three views of persons with disabilities (burdensome, charitable, egalitarian) are represented in modern society. In fact, our "three views" of people with disabilities are closely related to the moral, medical, and social models of disability described by Olkin (2002) that are currently operational in the United States. The basic tenets of each model are listed in Table 2.1. According to Olkin, "some clients [with disabilities] may have beliefs mostly consistent with one model, but others may hold views that cross the three models, some of which may even be contradictory" (p. 133). Although Olkin believes that it is imperative that counselors subscribe to the social model, as we shall see in the next section, some mental health practitioners still work primarily from a medical-model perspective.

## Psychology's Treatment of People With Disabilities

The counseling profession's involvement with persons with disabilities can be traced to the vocational rehabilitation movement that emerged in the second decade of the 20th century. The National Civilian Rehabilitation Conference first convened in 1924 and was renamed the National Rehabilitation Association (NRA) in 1927. Vocational rehabilitation over the next three decades moved from an educational emphasis, to a social work approach, to a vocational guidance approach (Cull & Hardy, 1972). The National Rehabilitation Counseling Association was established as a division of the NRA to meet the specialized needs of rehabilitation counselors, a profession struggling to identify itself.

**History of Rehabilitation Psychology**   By the mid-1950s research psychologists began to take an interest in disabilities and their psychological impact, and rehabilitation psychology emerged as a specialization. Rehabilitation psychologists have focused their research on people with disabilities and their self-perceptions and on nondisabled individuals and their perceptions of individuals with disabilities. Considerable research has also focused on the clinical process—developing a helping relationship, predicting work adjustment, and promoting successful rehabilitation (Fenderson, 1984).

Rehabilitation psychology was not formally recognized as a division (Division 22) of the American Psychological Association (APA) until 1958. Although research psychologists had formed a division to promote the study of the psychological effects of disabilities, the APA itself still neglected to offer leadership in the area of disability rights. By the mid- to late 1970s, however, psychologists with disabilities within the APA began to lobby for greater access to APA conventions (i.e., to remove the architectural and communication barriers at convention centers). Their efforts resulted in the establishment of the Task Force on Psychology and the Handicapped by the APA Board of Social and Ethical Responsibility for Psychology in 1979. This task force attempted to draw the attention of psychologists to barriers faced by psychologists with disabilities. In its final report published in 1984 (Task Force on Psychology and the Handicapped, 1984), the task force recommended the establishment of a permanent Committee on Psychology and Handicaps. The committee was renamed the Committee on Disabilities and Handicaps in 1986 and was placed under the aegis of the APA Board of Social and Ethical Responsibility. In 1991 it was again renamed, this time as the Committee on Disability Issues in Psychology, with oversight by the Board for the Advancement of Psychology in the Public Interest. At that time its responsibilities were broadened to include sensitizing and educating the APA membership about the role psychology can play to assist all persons with disabilities, not just psychologists with disabilities, to realize their potential (Tomes, 1992).

**Controversy About Rehabilitation Psychologists' Roles**    Throughout the history of the rehabilitation counseling profession, there has been internal controversy regarding the appropriate role and function of the rehabilitation counselor. Within what we might call the traditional rehabilitation counseling movement, the controversy has centered on the roles of counselor and coordinator. In the *counselor role,* the focus is on helping clients resolve the personal adjustment problems associated with their impairment. In the *coordinator role,* the focus is on assessment, case management, and placement of people with disabilities (Rubin & Roessler, 2001).

Both of these roles fit within Olkin's medical model of disability, where the focus is on "rehabilitating" the client with a disability. Gilson and DePoy (2002) provided evidence that rehabilitation counselors are still being trained for this traditional rehabilitation model; they examined the content of courses in social work training programs and found that disability is still generally discussed and treated from a diagnostic, medical perspective. However, the goal of rehabilitating clients with disabilities has come under criticism in recent years for failing to adequately address the needs of people with disabilities. According to Roberts (1989), the medical rehabilitation model that emerged in the 1940s actually contributes to negative images of persons with disabilities, even among members of this population themselves. Roberts suggested that millions of persons with disabilities who could not be rehabilitated to "normal" functioning have come to perceive themselves as rehabilitative failures (p. 233).

More recently, some rehabilitation counselors and psychologists have adopted the consultant role. In the *consultant role,* the focus is on working with "the client's family, friends, and employers to redesign the environment in order to maximize access and opportunity for people with disabilities" (Rubin & Roessler, 2001, p. 253). Other rehabilitation counselors have adopted an *advocacy role,* one in which a primary goal is to push for independent living and total access for people with disabilities.

It can be argued that rehabilitation counselors can (and should) perform all these roles. However, the supported-living goals often come in conflict with the environmental-change and independent-living goals for people with disabilities. Szymanski, Johnston-Rodriguez, Millington, Rodriguez, and Lagergren (1995) pointed out that this is just one of many paradoxes within the rehabilitation counseling profession:

> Independence and community integration have been generally regarded as important rehabilitation goals. . . . However, it has been suggested that some disability services can isolate consumers from normal activities and supports . . . and that the financial policies related to disability can actually impede independence. (p. 17)

Further, some individuals within the rehabilitation counseling profession suggest that securing rights for persons with disabilities has actually worked to the detriment of people in this group. For example, Nelson (1989) stated that "the perspective of justice has distorted our moral responsibility toward the disabled" (p. 228). Batavia (2001) argued that portraying people with disabilities as an oppressed minority is in and of itself a new form of paternalism on the part of disability advocates. He suggested that the majority of people with disabilities in contemporary society are not oppressed, and that to characterize people with disabilities as oppressed contradicts the antipaternalistic roots of the disability rights and independent living movements.

This book is aimed at mental health practitioners who are not rehabilitation specialists but who, in the normal course of their professional practice, may come in contact with clients with disabilities. We believe this brief overview of the rehabilitation counseling movement can be useful to readers because it suggests the kinds of choices that mental health counselors may have to make when working with people with disabilities. When working with an unemployed client with a disability, do we focus on helping them gain job skills, or on pushing prospective employers to modify their work environment, or both? When working with a depressed client with a disability, do we engage in counseling with the client, consultation with the family, or both? Chapters 6, 7, and 8 will help the reader examine some of these issues in greater depth.

## CURRENT DISCRIMINATION

Despite the passage of ADA and other legislation, people with disabilities continue to report that they are being discriminated against in a number of ways (Balser, 2002; Perry, Hendricks, & Broadbent, 2000). Oppression of people with disabilities persists in the form of social, educational, economic, and environmental discrimination, and abuse.

## Social Discrimination

As with all minority groups, discrimination against people with disabilities has its roots in negative attitudes and stereotypes that develop at an early age. Harper (1999) reviewed a series of prospective longitudinal studies carried out in the 1980s and 1990s to explore nondisabled children's attitudes toward peers with visible physical disabilities. In general, the more functionally limiting and/or less common the disability, the more aversion nondisabled children have for the children with the disability. Harper discussed several theories about how and why children acquire stereotypes about peers with disabilities. One theory of *how* children develop these attitudes is based on cognitive categorization, "a social cognition process of viewing and labeling visible physical differences of others" (p. 132). Factors that affect the saliency of an impairment include the perceived concealability, course over time, disruptiveness, aesthetic quality, origin, and dangerousness of the physical disability. One theory of *why* nondisabled children develop stereotypes of peers with disabilities is that they are learned; as children mature, they develop an increasingly complex set of expectations about how people should appear, move, behave, and so on. Stereotypes of peers who "violate" these expectations are categorized and solidified over time. Another theory is that stereotypical and prejudicial attitudes are a function of cognitive immaturity. This theory draws heavily on moral development theory; negative attitudes about peers with disabilities presumably reflect lower levels of cognitive development.

Regardless how stereotypes develop, it is generally recognized that attitudes toward some people with disabilities are more negative than others, depending on the nature of the disability (Olkin, 1999; Thomas, 2000). Thomas found that university students ranked the acceptability of 16 physical disabilities almost identically to the rankings made by students 30 years earlier. In general, physical disabilities are more accepted and have less stigma associated with them than do sensory disabilities, and sensory disabilities were ranked more acceptable than social, psychological, or cognitive impairments.

Given the negative attitudes associated with cognitive disabilities, it should come as no surprise that one of the currently most discriminated against disabilities groups is people with mental disorders. According to Stefan (2001), people with mental disabilities are discriminated against in ways that would be unthinkable for other minority groups (or even people with physical disabilities). She listed the following examples of laws that discriminate against people with mental disabilities to make her point:

- Laws that prohibit marriage based on mental illness
- Laws that permit states to deny people professional licenses as dental hygienists, social workers, and veterinarians if they voluntarily admit themselves to mental institutions
- Laws that permit divorce based on mental illness
- Laws that permit the termination of parental rights based on a parent's mental illness
- Laws that give people with mental illness fewer rights in the execution and enforcement of advance directives

- Laws that give people with mental illness fewer rights in guardianship proceedings
- Laws that give people who have received mental health treatment fewer rights of access to their treatment records
- Worker's compensation laws that cover workers' physical injuries on the job but not emotional injuries, such as the reaction to a sexual assault on the job or witnessing the violent death of a coworker
- Laws that permit evidence of psychiatric treatment to be introduced in court to attach a witness's credibility
- Laws that permit the denial of the right to vote based on mental disability (p. xii)

Furthermore, recent decisions by the U.S. Supreme Court make it difficult for people with mental illnesses (and others) to qualify for protection under ADA. In 1999, the Court issued three decisions that, in essence, stipulate that if a disability is correctable, it must be assessed in its corrected state. This, in effect, places the burden of proof on the individual to prove he or she has a disability (Petrila & Brink, 2001).

Unfortunately, psychologists and mental health counselors may share this bias against people with mental limitations. Butz, Bowling, and Bliss (2000) pointed out that, with the exception of cognitive appraisals, psychologists historically have avoided addressing the mental health needs of people with mental limitations or developmental disabilities. Butz et al. identified several reasons why psychological researchers and practitioners may neglect the mental health needs of mentally limited people: (a) intellectual deficits are assumed to account for concurrent emotional symptomatology, (b) mental retardation is assumed to immunize individuals from mental illness, (c) limited verbal skills are assumed to exclude discussion of cognitive or psychodynamic concepts; and (d) dichotimization of mental retardation and mental health has inhibited professional interest in clients who manifest a combination of these problems.

Olkin (1999) identified a number of key factors that affect attitudes toward people with disabilities, one of the most important of which is information provided in the media. Unfortunately, portrayals of people with disabilities in the media help to perpetuate negative stereotypes of this group. Balter (1999) examined media portrayals of people with disabilities and concluded that the depictions have not changed since the passage of ADA in 1990; in general, the media either stigmatizes or patronizes people with disability. Haller (2000) reviewed research on how people with disabilities are represented in televised, photographic, and print news and found that these mass media continue to provide stigmatizing representations of disability. Furthermore, she concluded that these stigmatizing representations in the mass media promote stereotyping in the general population. Similarly, Wolfson and Norden (2000) examined over 300 films dating back to the 1890s and identified 10 movie disability stereotypes. These authors concluded that Hollywood's treatment of people with disabilities tends to isolate them from the mainstream, and that the stereotypes portrayed have little resemblance to what people with disabilities actually experience. Although they judged that there has been a general trend toward improvement of the images portrayed, they also observed that stereotypes of people with disabilities are still being promoted through films.

Scotch (2000) pointed out, "the stigma associated with disability is so embedded and reinforced within our culture and social structure that it will take tremendous effort to root out" (p. 281). For example, there is some evidence that nondisabled people use different, sometimes discriminatory, interaction styles with people who have disabilities; more specifically, people without disabilities use more redundant and concrete speech when approached by someone using a wheelchair than when approached by someone not using a wheelchair. Gouvier, Coon, Todd, and Fuller (1994) found that people in general (but particularly women) were more likely to use "motherese" speech (exaggerated prosodic inflections, diminutives in naming, and shortened phrase and sentence length) when addressing a person in a wheelchair than when speaking to a nondisabled person. They proposed that "prosodic variations constitute the key element that determines whether a speech pattern is perceived as discriminatory or not" (p. 267).

Antonak and Livneh (1995) found some evidence of a trend toward more positive attitudes toward people with disabilities in several reviews of research. This trend notwithstanding, these authors concluded that "the acceptance and integration of persons with disabilities continue to be limited by the negative attitudes, misconceptions, and prejudicial stereotypes of health professionals, employers, coworkers, educators, peers, and neighbors" (Antonak & Livneh, 1995, p. 3).

## Educational Discrimination

Despite the fact that the IDEA was originally passed back in 1975, children with disabilities are still being excluded from full participation in the educational opportunities afforded children without disabilities (Scotch, 2000). According to a recent Bureau of the Census report (McNeil, 2002), people with a severe disability are much less likely to climb up the educational ladder than are those people with no disabilities. In 1997, only 67.4% of people ages 25 to 64 with a severe disability had finished high school, compared with 89.3% of those with no disability. Similarly, among those people 25 to 64 years of age with a severe disability, only 9.4% had finished college; the comparable figure for people with no disability was 28.5%. The Overview of IDEA 97 web page for the U.S. Department of Education lists the following unfulfilled promises to children with disabilities:

- Twice as many children with disabilities drop out of school.
- Dropouts do not return to school, have difficulty finding jobs, and often end up in the criminal justice system.
- Girls who drop out often become young unwed mothers—at a much higher rate than their nondisabled peers.
- Many children with disabilities are excluded from the curriculum and assessments used with their nondisabled classmates, limiting their possibilities of performing to higher standards of performance. (Department of Education, 2001)

Despite language in IDEA 97 designed to increase the involvement of all children with disabilities in the general curriculum, key educators may not believe access is appropriate for children with severe disabilities. Agran, Alper, and Wehmeyer (2002) surveyed teachers certified in severe disabilities and found that the majority did not believe the general curriculum has much relevance for students with severe disabilities. Furthermore, many of the school districts from which the teachers surveyed came did not have a clear policy on access to the general curriculum for children with severe disabilities.

Educational discrimination against children with disabilities means they are less qualified for most jobs as adults, contributing to economic discrimination they are likely to experience for the rest of their lives.

## Economic Discrimination

To the extent that low employment, income, and poverty rates of any group reflect oppression of that group, there is considerable evidence of economic discrimination against people with disabilities. According to recent census data, employment and poverty rates vary according to severity and type of disability. With regard to employment, individuals with a severe disability had an employment rate of 31.4%, compared with 82.0% for those with a nonsevere disability and 84.4% for those with no disability (McNeil, 2002). An earlier census brief, the U.S. Bureau of the Census (1997) reported that people who have difficulty hearing are most likely to be employed (64.4%), followed by people who have difficulty seeing (43.7%), mental disability (41.3%), and difficulty walking (33.5%). Scheid (1999) conducted a random telephone survey of 117 businesses in a southern metropolitan area and found that 37.6% had hired individuals with mental disabilities, but only 33% had an ADA Title I implementation plan and only 15.4% had specific policies for hiring persons with mental disabilities.

For those individuals with disabilities who are fortunate enough to be employed, there is evidence that they are likely to earn less than those without disabilities. The average annual income for workers with no disabilities in 2000 was $40,713, compared with $22,973 for workers with a work disability. The disparity in mean income between the two types of workers is greater for men ($26,879 vs. $50,001) than it is for women ($18,839 vs. $30,293; U.S. Bureau of the Census, 2002b).

With so many people with disabilities unemployed or earning low incomes, it is not surprising that they are more likely to live in poverty than are people without disabilities. According to 2000 census data, 8.3% of people ages 25 to 64 years who have no disability live in poverty, compared with 10.4% of those with a nonsevere disability and 27.9% of those with a severe disability (McNeil, 2002). In addition to increasing the probability of being unemployed, having a low income, and living in poverty, having a disability is also associated with a low probability of having private health insurance and high probability of having a government health plan or no health plan at all. Among people with a severe disability ages 22 to 64, 43.7% are covered by a private health insurance plan, 39.6% have no private coverage but are covered by a government plan, and 16.7% have no health insurance at all. This compares with 79.9% private insurance coverage, 3.0% government health coverage, and 17.1% no health insurance coverage for people without a disability (McNeil, 1997).

Very clear evidence shows a relationship between disability, education, and employment. For example, a strong correlation exists between years of school completed and likelihood of having a severe work disability. Among persons 25 to 64 years old in year 2000, 26.3% of those with only a seventh- to eighth-grade education, 18.8% of those with some high school education but no diploma, 9.5% of those with a high school education, 6.5% of those with some college education, and 2.4% of those with at least a bachelor's degree had a severe work disability. Because the opportunity for education typically comes after people are identified as having a disability (except in cases of disability acquired in young adulthood or later), it seems safe to conclude that despite almost 30 years of IDEA, people with disabilities do not have the same opportunities to move up the educational ladder as do people with no disability (U.S. Bureau of the Census, 2002a).

Although the elimination of physical barriers in work settings is the focus of much of the legislation to create accommodation for people with disabilities, negative attitudes by employers may be the greater barrier to their employment (Colella, DeNisi, & Varma, 1998; Colella & Varma, 1999). For example, employers frequently believe that persons with disabilities are accident-prone and will increase worker's compensation costs, are frequently absent from work, have low rates of productivity, and will not relate well with coworkers (Conti, 1995). As might be expected, employers with the least exposure to people with disabilities have the most negative attitudes (McFarlin, Song, & Sonntag, 1991, cited in Berry & Meyer, 1995).

Colella and Varma (1999) provided direct evidence of how social stereotypes might influence employment and promotion decisions involving employees with disabilities. In a laboratory experiment, undergraduates evaluated past and future job performance of, and made training recommendations for, people with and without a disability. The results indicated that evaluators did have stereotypes of what types of disabilities will lead to poor job performance in the future, and that these stereotypes affected personnel decisions despite past performance that indicated they are invalid. This suggests that even when people with disabilities are able to demonstrate ability to perform a job, they may not be hired because employers will still hold negative stereotypes about future performance. Furthermore, these results suggest that even when people with disabilities are able to obtain a job, unjustified stereotypes about their limitations may create a glass ceiling with regard to advancement. Similarly, Hazer and Bedell (2000) had psychology students and human resources professionals review and evaluate applications materials from a hypothetical job candidate. In this analogue study, they varied the disability status of the job candidate (none, physical, psychiatric) and whether or not the applicant was seeking accommodation for the disability. They found that asking for reasonable accommodation and having a psychiatric disability lowered employment suitability ratings.

Although 26 states and the District of Columbia had laws barring discrimination against people with disabilities by employers prior to the enactment of the ADA of 1990 (as did the federal government for employers receiving federal funds), discrimination still occurred. Discrimination against persons with disability also occurred despite Section 503 of the Rehabilitation Act of 1973, which for the past 30 years has required that any employer doing business with the federal government take affirmative action to hire persons with disabilities. In fact, personnel managers for state government organizations covered by the Rehabilitation Act reported that the passage of ADA has had no significant effects on their departments (Kellough, 2000). It remains to be seen if the Americans with Disabilities Act of 1990, which extends nondiscrimination against persons with disabilities to employment in the private sector, can have a significant impact on employment statistics. However, to date the signs are not hopeful. Schall (1998) analyzed data from a number of sources and concluded that little has changed regarding the employment of people with disabilities. Basically, she found that the same patterns of employment discrimination against people with disabilities still prevail a number of years after the passage of ADA. As observed by Scotch (2001):

> In its first decade of implementation the ADA appears to have fallen short of its optimistic goal to change fundamentally the lives of most Americans with disabilities. In the aggregate, people with disabilities are still as disproportionately unemployed and underemployed as before the ADA's enactment, and their incomes still are significantly below those of people without disabilities. (p. 177)

Furthermore, court cases have made it more difficult for people with some disabilities to obtain protection under ADA. Although Title I of ADA prohibits employment discrimination against people with disabilities, recent rulings by the U.S. Supreme Court exclude people with psychiatric disabilities from enjoying those benefits (Dalgin, 2001).

## Access Discrimination

Although Section 504 of the Rehabilitation Act required the removal of architectural, communication, and transportation barriers that affect people with disabilities in federal agencies and agencies supported by federal money beginning back in 1973, public accommodations were not mandated in the private sector until after the passage of ADA in 1990. Public accommodation under Title III provides accessibility and nondiscrimination in public and private settings where people with disabilities might seek food, lodging, health care, and recreation. Ten years after ADA became law, employed college graduates with disabilities still reported access discrimination, and access discrimination was found to be related to current job satisfaction (Perry et al., 2000).

Although Title I of ADA (which has to do with nondiscrimination in employment) has received the most attention, Title III (having to do with nondiscrimination in public services and accommodations) is in many ways equally or more important because it applies to all people with disabilities, not just those seeking employment. In part, the greater attention to Title I may be due to the lack of success to date in overcoming discrimination in employment, whereas considerable success has been achieved in overcoming discrimination in public services and accommodations. In the decade of the 1990s, our public-supported environment became much more accessible to people with physical disabilities, particularly those with mobility impairments (Batavia, 2000).

However, although the local, state, and federal governments have been fairly good about reducing physical barriers at street corners, entrances to buildings, restrooms, and so on, the private sector has been less responsive to the access needs of people with disabilities. As suggested by Colker (2000), "voluntary compliance is difficult to measure, but any casual observation of the accessibility of places of public accommodation [by private businesses] reveals that there is much work to be done in order to attain compliance" (p. 310). In many cases, individuals with disabilities have to bring a lawsuit against a restaurant, hotel, bank, or other business establishment in order to bring about compliance with Title III.

Colker (2000) reviewed appellate decisions, verdict data, and settlements under Title III that have taken place up until 1998. A typical case involved a person with a disability as the plaintiff, and a business establishment as the defendant, although the Department of Justice sometimes prosecutes Title III cases. Colker found, among other things, that (a) plaintiffs seldom sue under ADA; (b) defendants usually prevail in lower courts; (c) defendants usually prevail in appellate decisions; (d) plaintiffs prevail about 50% of the time in state and federal courts; (e) plaintiffs have a lower chance of prevailing in a judge trial than a jury trial; (f) when compensatory and punitive damages were justified, juries did not make excessive awards; and (g) "there is little incentive for private individuals to seek settlements unless the Department of Justice initiates an enforcement proceeding" (p. 310). Furthermore, not all environmental barriers that confront people with disabilities are covered by the ADA.

According to Schriner and Scotch (2001), accessibility continues to be a problem because the ADA provides a legal definition for physical barriers and discrimination, and not all forms of oppression confronting people with disabilities fall under the legal definition of discrimination. Thus, communication barriers exist in the form of audio-only announcements (inaccessible to the deaf) and visual-only announcements (inaccessible to the blind) in stores, hotels, transportation centers, employment settings, and public buildings. Nor are personnel in these settings trained to assist deaf and blind people. Transportation barriers still exist in subway, train, and bus systems that are inaccessible to the orthopedically handicapped.

It is likely to be a long time before the accessibility mandates of the ADA will have an impact on some parts of the country, particularly on rural areas (Associated Press, 1992). Areas in which no public transportation is currently provided are not required to develop a new transportation service for people with disabilities.

## Abuse

Although the data are limited, it is evident that children and adults with disabilities are disproportionately represented among people who are abused. Relatively little is known about the maltreatment prevalence for children with disabilities nationally, despite the fact that the Child Abuse Prevention, Adoption and Family Services Act of 1988 and the Crime Victims with Disabilities Awareness Act of 1998 mandated the study of abuse among children with disabilities (Mitchell & Buchele-Ash, 2000). According to Bonner, Crow, and Hensley (1997), only seven states currently document the presence of disability for their abuse records. Based on small-scale local studies, investigators generally conclude that children with disabilities in North America are at 2 to 3 times the risk of being abused as are children without disabilities. Furthermore, almost 1 in 3 children who have a disability have been abused at least once during childhood (Sobsey, 2002; Vig & Kaminer, 2002). For children in particular, abuse and disability are interactive; that is, children who have a disability are at higher risk of being abused than are children without a disability, and many children acquire a disability as a result of maltreatment.

In a recent large-scale study involving the school, social services, and law enforcement records for 50,278 students from public and archdiocesan schools in Omaha, Nebraska, Sullivan and Knutson (2000) found that 31% of the children with disabilities had a record of abuse. This rate of abuse was 3.4 times higher than the 9% rate of abuse for children with no disability. The authors developed a relative risk matrix that compared risk for children with specific disabilities to risk for children with no disabilities across four types of maltreatment (neglect, physical abuse, emotional abuse, sexual abuse). The risk rates ranged from children with visual disabilities being 1.2 times more likely than children without a disability to have experienced sexual abuse, to children with a behavior disorder being 7.3 times more likely than children without disabilities to have experienced physical abuse. They also found a relationship between gender and disability status; for children with disabilities, boys were more likely than girls to be abused, whereas the reverse was true for children with no disabilities. Furthermore, the authors reported that first-time abuse was more likely to be experienced by children with disabilities (as well as those without disabilities) between the ages of 6 and 9 than those in preschool, middle school, or high school.

Although men with disabilities experience more abuse than men without disabilities, women with disabilities are more likely to experience maltreatment than any other gender-by-disability group (Curry, Hassouneh-Phillips, & Johnston-Silverberg, 2001). Disability specialists attribute higher rates of abuse among women with disabilities to their increased vulnerability; rather than being a protective factor, disability places a woman at greater risk. Unfortunately, like the research on children with disabilities, very few large-scale studies have focused on women with disabilities. Hassouneh-Phillips and Curry (2002) reviewed the quantitative and qualitative research to date on abuse of women with disabilities and, despite limitations and disparities in methodology, arrived at the following general conclusions:

- There is a high incidence of abuse of women with disabilities, as high or higher than among women without disabilities.
- Typically, women with disabilities are abused in their home or place of residence.

- Male partners are most often the assailants, but women with disabilities are also at risk of abuse from friends, family members, personal assistance providers, transportation employees, and health care workers.
- "In addition to emotional, physical, and sexual abuse, women with disabilities also experienced various forms of disability-specific abuse, for example, damage or removal of assistive devices, theft of valuables and/or medications, and unwanted sexual touch during dressing and bathing" (p. 102).

In a study not reported in the Hassouneh-Phillips and Curry review, Nosek, Foley, Hughes, and Howland (2001) shed additional light on disability-specific abuse. Nosek et al. examined the relationship between abuse and types of disability and found that women who needed personal assistance with daily living were most likely to experience abuse.

Curry et al. (2001) described an ecological model to help understand abuse among women with disabilities. The model, based on an earlier model by Sobsey (1994) addressing abuse of all persons with disability, includes environmental and cultural factors that contribute to the vulnerability of potential for abuse, characteristics of women with disabilities that increase their vulnerability to abuse, and the characteristics of potential offenders. Basically, environmental and cultural factors include stigmatization and marginalization of women with disabilities in the media, health care settings, and society at large, as well as poverty and dependence on caregivers for essential personal care services. Characteristics that increase vulnerability to abuse include dependence on others for basic needs (women with physical and cognitive disabilities), limited problem-solving skills (women with cognitive disabilities), and internalized devaluation. Characteristics of potential offenders include need for control, low self-esteem, exposure to abusive models, poor impulse control, anxiety, and antisocial behavior.

Although children and adults with disabilities may be more vulnerable to abuse than are their counterparts who have no disabilities, it is important to distinguish between vulnerability and responsibility. Calderbank (2000) suggested that abuse experienced by people with disabilities is the result of societal attitudes held regarding this group, rather than the result of individual vulnerability per se. By identifying people (especially children and women) with disabilities as vulnerable to abuse, there is a danger of promoting a victim-blaming attitude among social service professionals and the general public that people with disabilities somehow are responsible for their own mistreatment.

## The Future

Schriner and Scotch (2001) suggested that one reason the ADA has been so ineffective in bringing about changes in the lives of people with disabilities is that it is modeled after laws that prohibit discrimination based on demographic categories like race and gender. However, eliminating barriers that face people with disabilities, they pointed out, is much more difficult than preventing discrimination against ethnic minorities and women. For one thing, the category of people with disabilities contains within it many different subcategories (e.g., blindness, deafness, mobility, mental, emotional) that each require unique accommodations to eliminate discrimination. Furthermore, accommodations may vary within a subcategory of people with disabilities, and for any one individual accommodations may need to change to reflect changes in the individual's impairment over time. Schriner and Scotch (2001) suggested that to eliminate oppression of people with disabilities, it may be useful to look beyond antidiscrimination laws to human rights theories, "which seek to establish positive rights to economic, social, and political justice for all" (p. 103). By defining *disability* as a "mismatch between physical and mental attributes and the present (but not the potential) ability of social institutions to incorporate those attributes" (p. 104) and accepting human rights theory, accessibility becomes a universal entitlement rather than a right that individuals with disabilities must win on a case-by-case basis. The authors pointed out that policies based on human rights theories are even less popular with the public and its political and legal establishments than are antidiscrimination policies, but their thesis deserves thoughtful consideration as advocates consider future steps to promote equality of opportunity for people with disabilities.

## REFERENCES

Abeson, A. (1976). Overview. In F. J. Weintraub, A. Abeson, J. Ballard, & M. L. LaVor (Eds.), *Public policy and the education of exceptional children* (pp. 1–28). Reston, Virginia: The Council for Exceptional Children.

Agran, M., Alper, S., & Wehmeyer, M. (2002). Access to the general curriculum for students with significant disabilities: What it means to teachers. *Education and Training in Mental Retardation and Developmental Disabilities, 37,* 123–133.

Antonak, R. F., & Livneh, H. (1995). Direct and indirect methods to measure attitudes toward persons with disabilities, with an exegesis of the error-choice test method. *Rehabilitation Psychology, 40,* 3–24.

Associated Press. (1992, October 6). Rural disabled find barriers slow to fall. *Santa Barbara New Press,* p. B-1.

Balser, D. B. (2002). Agency in organizational inequality: Organizational behavior and individual perceptions of discrimination. *Work and Occupations, 29,* 137–165.

Balter, R. (1999). From stigmatization to patronization: The media's distorted portrayal of physical disability. In L. L. Schwartz (Ed.), *Psychology and the media: A second look* (pp. 147–171). Washington, DC: American Psychological Association.

Batavia, A. I. (2000). Ten years later: The ADA and the future of disability policy. In L. P. Francis & A. Silvers (Eds.), *Americans with disabilities: Exploring implications of the law for individuals and institutions* (pp. 283–292). New York: Routledge.

Batavia, A. I. (2001). The new paternalism: Portraying people with disabilities as an oppressed minority. *Journal of Disability Policy Studies, 12,* 107–113.

Berry, J. O., & Meyer, J. A. (1995). Employing people with disabilities: Impact of attitude and situation. *Rehabilitation Psychology, 40,* 211–222.

Bonner, B. L., Crow, S. M., & Hensley, L. D. (1997). State efforts to identify maltreated children with disabilities: A follow-up study. *Children Maltreatment, 2*, 56–60.

Bowe, F. G. (1978). *Handicapping America: Barriers to disabled people.* New York: Harper & Row.

Brolin, D. E., & Gysbers, N. C. (1989). Career education for students with disabilities. *Journal of Counseling and Development, 68*, 155–159.

Butz, M. R., Bowling, J. B., & Bliss, C. A. (2000). Psychotherapy with the mentally retarded: A review of the literature and the implications. *Professional Psychology: Research and Practice, 31*, 42–47.

Calderbank, R. (2000). Abuse and disabled people: Vulnerability or social indifference? *Disability and Society, 15*, 521–534.

Conti, J. V. (1995). Job discrimination against people with a cancer history. *Journal of Applied Rehabilitation Counseling, 26*(2), 12–16.

Colella, A., DeNisi, A. S., & Varma, A. (1998). The impact of ratee's disability on performance judgments and choice as partner: The role of disability-job fit stereotypes and interdependence of rewards. *Journal of Applied Psychology, 83*, 102–111.

Colella, A., & Varma, A. (1999). Disability-job fit stereotypes and the evaluation of persons with disabilities at work. *Journal of Occupational Rehabilitation, 9*, 79–95.

Cull, J. G., & Hardy, R. E. (1972). *Vocational rehabilitation: Profession and process.* Springfield, IL: Charles C Thomas.

Curry, M. A. A., Hassouneh-Phillips, D., & Johnston-Silverberg, A. (2001). Abuse of women with disabilities: An ecological model and review. *Violence against women, 7*, 60–79.

Dalgin, R. S. (2001). Impact of Title I of the Americans with Disabilities Act on people with psychiatric disabilities. *Journal of Applied Rehabilitation Counseling, 32*, 45–50.

Department of Education (2001). *IDEA overview.* Retrieved November 11, 2002, from http://www.ed.gov/offices/OSERS/Policy/IDEA/overview.html.

Driedger, D. (1989). *The last civil rights movement.* London: Hurst.

Executive Summary. (2001). *No Child Left Behind Act of 2001.* Retrieved November 11, 2002, from http://www.ed.gov/offices/OESE/esea/exec-summ.html.

The Family Network on Disabilities of Florida. (n.d.). *Questions and answers on IDEA 97.* Retrieved November 12, 2002, from http://www.fndfl.org/rinterp.html.

Fenderson, D. A. (1984). Opportunities for psychologists in disability research. *American Psychologist, 39*, 524–528.

Funk, R. (1987). Disability rights: From cast to class in the context of civil rights. In A. Gartner & T. Joe (Eds.), *Images of the disabled, disabling images* (pp. 7–30). New York: Praeger Publishers.

Garrett, J. F. (1969). Historical background. In D. Malikin & H. Rusalem (Eds.), *Vocational rehabilitation of the disabled* (pp. 29–38). New York: New York University Press.

Gilson, S. F., & DePoy, E. (2002). Theoretical approaches to disability content in social work education. *Journal of Social Work Education, 38*, 153–165.

Gouvier, W. D., Coon, R. C., Todd, M. E., & Fuller, K. H. (1994). Verbal interactions with individuals presenting with or without physical disability. *Rehabilitation Psychology, 39,* 263–268.

Haller, B. (2000). If they limp, they lead? News representations and the hierarchy of disability images. In D. O. Braithwaite & T. L. Thompson (Eds.), *Handbook of communication and people with disabilities: Research and application* (pp. 273–288). Mahwah, NJ: Erlbaum.

Harper, D. C. (1999). Social psychology of difference: Stigma, spread, and stereotypes in children. *Rehabilitation Psychology, 44,* 131–144.

Harris and Associates. (1986). *The ICD survey of disabled Americans: Bringing disabled Americans into the mainstream. A nationwide survey of 1,000 disabled people.* New York: Author.

Hassouneh-Phillips, D., & Curry, M. A. (2002). Abuse of women with disabilities. *Rehabilitation Counseling Bulletin, 45,* 96–104.

Hazer, J. T., & Bedell, K. V. (2000). Effects of seeking accommodation and disability on preemployment evaluations. *Journal of Applied Social Psychology, 30,* 1201–1223.

Hohenshil, T. H., & Humes, C. W. (1979). Roles of counseling in ensuring the rights of the handicapped. *Personnel and Guidance Journal, 58,* 221–227.

Karr, A. R. (1990, May 23). Disabled-rights bill inspires hopes, fears. *Wall Street Journal,* pp. B1, B2.

Kellough, J. E. (2000). The Americans with Disabilities Act: A note on personnel policy impacts in state government. *Public Personnel Management, 29,* 211–224.

Laski, F. (1978, May). *Legal strategies to secure entitlement to services for severely handicapped persons.* Paper presented at the Conference on Habilitation of Severely Handicapped Adults, Public Interest Law Center, Philadelphia, PA.

McNeil, J. (1997). *Americans with disabilities: 1994–95* (Current Population Reports, P70-61). Washington, DC: Bureau of the Census. Retrieved November 12, 2002, from http://www.census.gov/prod/3/97pubs/p70-61.pdf.

McNeil, J. (2002). *Americans with disabilities: 1997.* Washington, DC: Bureau of the Census. Retrieved November 12, 2002, from http://www.census.gov/hhes/www/disable/sipp/disab97/asc97.html.

Mitchell, L. M., & Buchele-Ash, A. (2000). Abuse and neglect of individuals with disabilities: Building protective supports through public policy. *Journal of Disability Policy Studies, 10,* 225–243.

Nelson, R. M. (1989). Ethics and the physically disabled. In B. W. Heller, L. M. Flohr, & L. S. Zegans (Eds.), *Psychosocial interventions with physically disabled persons* (pp. 222–230). New Brunswick, NJ: Rutgers University Press.

Nosek, M. A., Foley, C. C., Hughes, R. B., & Howland, C. A. (2001). Vulnerabilities for abuse among women with disabilities. *Sexuality and Disability, 19,* 177-189.

Obermann, C. E. (1965). *A history of vocational rehabilitation in America.* Minneapolis: Denison.

Olkin, R (1999). *What psychotherapists should know about disability.* New York: Guilford Press.

Olkin, R. (2002). Could you hold the door for me? Including disability in diversity. *Cultural Diversity and Ethnic Minority Psychology, 8,* 130–137.

Perry, E. L., Hendricks, W., & Broadbent, E. (2000). An exploration of access and treatment discrimination and job satisfaction among college graduates with and without physical disabilities. *Human Relations, 53,* 923–955.

Petrila, J., & Brink, T. (2001). Mental illness and changing definitions of disability under the Americans with Disabilities Act. *Psychiatric Services, 52,* 626–630.

Roberts, E. V. (1989). A history of the independent living movement: A founder's perspective. In B. W. Heller, L. M. Flohr, & L. S. Zegans (Eds.), *Psychosocial interventions with physically disabled persons* (pp. 231–244). New Brunswick, NJ: Rutgers University Press.

Rubin, S. E., & Roessler, R. T. (2001). *Foundations of the vocational rehabilitation process* (5th ed.). Austin, TX: PRO-ED.

Satcher, J., & Hendren, G. R. (1991). Acceptance of the Americans with Disabilities Act of 1990 by persons preparing to enter the business field. *Journal of Applied Rehabilitation Counseling, 22*(2), 15–18.

Scotch, R. K. (2000). Making change: The ADA as in instrument of social reform. In L. P. Francis & A. Silvers (Eds.), *Americans with disabilities: Exploring implications of the law for individuals and institutions* (pp. 275–282). New York: Routledge.

Scotch, R. K. (2001). *From good will to civil rights* (2nd ed.). Philadelphia: Temple University Press.

Schall, C. M. (1998). The Americans with Disabilities Act—are we keeping our promise? An analysis of the effect of the ADA on the employment of persons with disabilities. *Journal of Vocational Rehabilitation, 10,* 191–203.

Scheid, T. L. (1999). Employment of individuals with mental disabilities: Business response to the ADA's challenge. *Behavioral Sciences and the Law, 17,* 73–91.

Sobsey, D. (1994). *Violence and abuse in the lives of people with disabilities.* Baltimore: Paul H. Brookes.

Sobsey, D. (2002). Exceptionality, education, and maltreatment. *Exceptionality, 10,* 29–46.

Stefan, S. (2001). *Unequal rights: Discrimination against people with mental disabilities and the Americans with Disabilities Act.* Washington, DC: American Psychological Association.

Sullivan, P. M., & Knutson, J. F. (2000). Maltreatment and disabilities: A population-based epidemiological study. *Child Abuse and Neglect, 24,* 1257–1273.

Szymanski, E. M., Johnston-Rodriguez, S., Millington, M. J., Rodriguez, B. H., & Lagergren, J. (1995). The paradoxical nature of disability services: Illustrations from supported employment and implications for rehabilitation counseling. *Journal of Applied Rehabilitation Counseling, 26*(2), 17–21.

Task Force on Psychology and the Handicapped. (1984). Final report of the task force on psychology and the handicapped. *American Psychologist, 39,* 545–550.

Thomas, A. (2000). Stability of Tringo's hierarchy of preference toward disability groups: 30 years later. *Psychological Reports, 86,* 1155–1156.

Tomes, H. (1992). Disabilities are major public interest issue. *APA Monitor, 20*(3), 13.

U.S. Bureau of the Census. (1997). *Disabilities affect one-fifth of all Americans* (census brief). Retrieved November 12, 2002, from http://www.census.gov/prod/3/97pubs/cenbr975.pdf.

U.S. Bureau of the Census. (2002a). *Disability—Selected characteristics of persons 16 to 74: 2002.* Retrieved November 12, 2002, from http://www.census.gov/hhes/www/disable/cps/cps102.html.

U.S. Bureau of the Census. (2002b). *Disability—Work experience and mean earnings in 2000—Work disability status of civilians 16 to 74 years old, by educational attainment and sex: 2000.* Retrieved November 12, 2002, from http://www.census.gov/hhes/www/disable/cps/cps302.html.

Vig, S., & Kaminer, R. (2002). Maltreatment and developmental disabilities in children. *Journal of Developmental and Physical Disabilities, 14,* 371–386.

White, G. W., & Fawcett, S. B. (2000). Independent living and people with physical disabilities. In J. Rappaport & E. Seidman (Eds.). *Handbook of community psychology* (pp. 979–982). New York: Kluwer Academic/Plenum.

Wolfson, K., & Norden, M. F. (2000). Film images of people with disabilities. In D. O. Braithwaite & T. L. Thompson (Eds.), *Handbook of communication and people with disabilities: Research and application* (pp. 289–305). Mahwah, NJ: Erlbaum.

Youngstrom, N. (1992). ADA is super advocate for those with disabilities. *APA Monitor, 23*(7), 26.

# CHAPTER 3

Oppression of Older
People: Past
and Present

*We ought not to heap reproaches on old age, seeing that we all hope to reach it.*
—(BION, quoted in Diogenes Laertius's *Lives and Opinions
of Eminent Philosophers,* 3rd century A.D.)

*How good we all are, in theory, to the old; and how in fact we wish them to
wander off like old dogs, die without bothering us, and bury themselves.*
—(EDGAR WATSON HOWE, *Ventures in Common Sense,* 1919)

## PAST DISCRIMINATION

In general, society's treatment of older people is a function of their ability to control and contribute to the economy. In order to place society's current attitudes toward older people in a proper context, it is important to first understand how society has treated older people in the past.

### Society's Treatment of Older People

According to Hendricks and Hendricks (1981), attitudes toward, and treatment of, older people have varied across the three major types of human societies; namely, nomadic, agricultural, and industrial. In nomadic hunting and gathering societies, life was precarious and marginal. Under such circumstances older people were often left to die on their own when they could no longer contribute to the food supply or keep up with the movements of the group. However, some older people who were a source of valued knowledge related to the group's physical and cultural survival were no doubt supported by members of the group as long as possible.

In agricultural societies where property rights often became inherited and immutable, power and prestige were accorded older people (usually men) who held these rights. Thus, the status of older adults was generally better in agricultural societies than in nomadic tribes. However, sociologist Leo Simmons (1945), in his study of aging in 71 "primitive" nomadic and agricultural societies, found that although some degree of prestige for older people was prevalent in all societies, it applied to a "prime of life" old age and not to disability in old age. In all of the societies studied, he also found that older people obtained support from others by rendering, in turn, essential services to the young and strong. In many of the societies he studied, when older people could no longer contribute a valued service, they were left to fend for themselves. The need to contribute to society was not necessarily an obstacle for older people in Ancient Greek and Roman societies, however. Kebric (1988) cited overwhelming evidence that many people lived active, productive lives into their 70s and 80s during the Greek and Roman Empires. In Greek society, men were expected to serve in the military until age 60.

Although earlier societies may have accorded older adults a measure of prestige, recorded evidence also shows that negative stereotypes of older people have been with us since the pre-Christian era. According to Aiken (1995), ancient Romans considered old age a disease and expended considerable energy trying to find a "cure" for old age. Aristotle, in *Treatise on Rhetoric,* describes old age as a time of conservatism and small-mindedness. Authors during the Middle Ages and the Renaissance reflected a similar theme. Pope Innocent III, in the 13th century, referred to old men as stingy, avaricious, sullen, and quarrelsome. Shakespeare's depiction of older people in his second sonnet is anything but flattering, where he describes the end of a man's life as a second childishness marked by loss of teeth, hearing, and virility (Hendricks & Hendricks, 1981). The negative stereotypes of older people were not restricted to men. In a review of terminology used historically to refer to older people, Covey (1988) found that gender was a critical factor:

> The English language has a long history of separating old men from old women. Terms for old men tend to be focused on their being old-fashioned, uncouth, conservative, feeble, stingy, incompetent, narrow-minded, eccentric, or stupid. Terms for old women are focused on mysticism, bad temper, disagreeableness, spinsterhood, bossiness, unattractiveness, spitefulness, and repulsiveness. . . . Although women have longer lifespans than men, women are viewed as being old much earlier than men. Thus women have been subjected to old-age labels much earlier in life and for much longer periods during their lifespans. (pp. 291–292)

In the United States, older adults commanded power and respect during the colonial period, due in part to their role as property owners. Fischer (1977) suggested that respect for old age in colonial America also may have been due to the fact that it was comparatively rare (see data on changing American demographics in chapter 1). According to Fischer (1977), the undermining of the esteem with which older Americans were held began about the time of the American revolution. He identified 1770 to 1820 as a period of decline in hierarchically oriented institutions and a questioning of the hierarchies of sex, race, and age in particular. Furthermore, he cited the strong American cultural value of individualism as one of the forces that began to undermine the privileged status older people enjoyed in the 18th century.

Historian Andrew Achenbaum (1978) examined experiences of older adults from 1790 to 1970 and found marked differences between the way older people were perceived and treated in colonial and modern America. Prior to the Civil War, those older people who were physically able to work were expected to do so. They were also greatly valued for their moral wisdom and practical sagacity. After the Civil War, however, Americans

> began to challenge nearly every favorable belief about the usefulness and merits of age that had been set forth by republican and romantic writers and that still appeared in contemporary literature. . . . By the outbreak of World War I, if not before, most Americans were affirming the obsolescence of old age. (Achenbaum, 1978, p. 39)

Although disagreement exists about the factors that precipitated the decline in prestige accorded older people, most authors agree that the industrial revolution contributed significantly to the increasingly negative attitudes toward older adults in the United States. In its evolution from an agricultural to an industrial society, older people lost prestige as economic power moved from land to currency and greater emphasis was placed on change, mobility, and competition (Cowgill & Holmes, 1972; Hendricks & Hendricks, 1981). The shift from an economy based on agriculture to one based on production, service, and technology usurped the power that older family members held as property owners. The development of large-scale businesses and organizations had a profound effect on American values and lifestyles. Efficiency became the sine qua non of successful enterprise, and individuals within a corporate structure became dispensable (Achenbaum, 1978).

Perceptions of older people and their contribution to the labor force began to change. Businesses began discharging employees at a predetermined age rather than on the basis of their productivity. "Between 1861 and 1915, the federal government and especially private industry began to design and implement policies that discharged workers because they were considered too old to stay on the job" (Achenbaum, 1978, p. 48). The first federal retirement law was passed by Congress in 1861, when it mandated that naval officers must retire at age 62. The first private pension plan, motivated in part by a desire to remove older workers from the labor force, was implemented by the American Express Company in 1875. As a result of these and subsequent laws and policies mandating a retirement age, the proportion of the labor force composed of persons over age 65 declined steadily from 1900 to 1970 (Achenbaum, 1978).

The rapid changes that accompanied the industrial revolution helped to promote a valuing of youth. The young could better adapt to the many changes, it was assumed, and wisdom previously attributed to older people was supplanted in importance by intelligence attributed to the young. Advertisements that played upon a desire to appear young and behave youthfully began to make their appearance after the Civil War (Achenbaum, 1978).

As U.S. society moved away from an agrarian base and the value of older people began to decline, responsibility for caring for parents and older relatives began to shift from the extended family to the government. Recognizing the need to provide medical care for older adults, presidential candidate Teddy Roosevelt in 1912 endorsed the Progressive Party's call for federal medical insurance. The concept of national medical insurance was dropped, however, when Woodrow

Wilson won the election. The concept was reintroduced later in the decade by other Progressive reformers but was again opposed by medical societies and the American Federation of Labor (Fein, 1992). Thus, many older people who were forced to retire and whose families were no longer willing or capable of acting as a safety net faced extended and sometimes terminal illness without adequate medical care.

Between World War I and World War II, theories developed and were supported by preliminary research that physical decay, mental decline, deviant psychological functioning, and personal isolation accompanied old age.

> Americans between 1914 and 1940 described the status of the aged more pessimistically than did their predecessors. . . . Americans after World War I perceived and voiced concern that current demographic and socioeconomic conditions were making old age per se a national problem as well as a personal misfortune. (Achenbaum, 1978, p. 109)

Levin and Levin (1980) suggested this developing view of older people as a societal "problem" is another example of blaming the victim. Thus, older people who had mandatory retirement policies forced on them by the federal government and private industry became a societal problem because they were not able to support themselves. Numerous surveys between 1914 and 1940 by civic groups, the U.S. Bureau of Labor, and state legislatures revealed that urbanization, industrialization, and the shortened working period of life were the real culprits of financial hardship experienced by older people (Achenbaum, 1978).

Initial efforts after World War I to cope with economic insecurity of older people included the federal compulsory old age and disability insurance program for civil service employees enacted in 1920 and the expansion of retirement plans in the private sector at about the same time. Evidence that traditional solutions died hard can be found in the fact that five states enacted laws requiring children to support their indigent parents. Other states, however, began to pass old age assistance programs in the late 1920s, a trend that was accelerated by the depression (Achenbaum, 1978).

The Great Depression of the 1930s was hard on many people, but particularly on older people. Older people were the first to lose their jobs and the last to be hired. In addition, many lost lifelong savings when banks were unable to fulfill their obligations to depositors. Several bills were introduced in Congress during the early 1930s aimed at meeting the economic needs of older people, but they failed to become law, due in part to pressure from groups that perceived old-age pensions to be un-American. It is interesting to note, in fact, that the United States was one of the last Western industrialized nations to grant retirement pensions. The first was Germany in 1889. Most of the others passed such legislation in the next 25 years (Rich & Baum, 1984).

Finally, the Congress passed, and President Franklin Roosevelt signed into law (on August 14, 1935), the Social Security Act of 1935. Although Title I of the Act granted states considerable flexibility in determining the amounts of assistance older people would receive, it did include a provision with important ramifications for the self-esteem of individuals receiving funds: "By permitting applicants to appeal administrative decisions, the federal government made old-age assistance a right that could be legally enforced. Public relief in old age was no longer a gratuity" (Achenbaum, 1978, p. 135).

However, the Social Security Act did not include any provisions for medical benefits. Although Roosevelt originally envisioned national health insurance for older people as part of the Social Security bill, his cabinet-level Committee on Economic Security convinced him that to include it could jeopardize any form of social assistance for older people. Once again older people were left without a safety net for health problems. President Harry Truman took up the national health insurance banner when he proposed an economic bill of rights for all American citizens on September 6, 1945. However, the American Medical Association, invoking the fear of communism, successfully fought against the concept of national health insurance (Fein, 1992).

About the time the United States entered World War II, older people began to organize to fight discrimination against them. Older citizens began to form lobby groups to push for legislation to assist oppressed older adults. Groups like the National Association of Retired Federal Employees, the National Retired Teachers Association, and the Gray Panthers became active lobbyists and played a major role in the establishment of a number of programs for older people. "Originally formed to promote life insurance and other group benefits, AARP [American Association of Retired Persons] has slowly developed into a powerful political force" (Hess, 1991). The AARP currently has a membership of over 35 million persons age fifty and over (American Association of Retired Persons, 2002).

Since the passage of the Social Security Act the federal government has evolved into a major clearinghouse for ideas related to aging. The first National Conference on Aging was held in 1950 with subsequent White House conferences on aging in 1961, 1971, 1981, and 1995. These conferences set forth recommendations concerning housing, nutrition, transportation, and other areas. Medicare and Medicaid, hospital insurance programs for older people, were passed in 1965, and Congress insured all older adults of a minimal income by passing the Supplementary Security Income program in 1972 (Achenbaum, 1978).

Although Social Security and other programs have produced an overall improvement in the economic security of older citizens, the effects have not been evenly distributed across all groups of older people. For example, people who supplement benefits from income from savings or pensions plans are better off than those on Social Security alone. Also, people who minimally satisfy requirements for Social Security payments receive significantly lower retirement incomes than do those who made larger contributions to the system. As Margolis (1990) suggested:

> Social Security has never fulfilled its ample promise. From the working poor's perspective, the program's ideological reach has consistently exceeded its practical grasp. The reason is no secret: To the notion of equal entitlement, society has appended a typically American extenuation—the idea of just deserts, which tends to reward winners and penalize losers. (p. 23)

In linking benefits to a citizen's wage-based payments into the Social Security trust fund, the government has overlooked the contributions of the unpaid housewife and the volunteer worker. This policy also overlooks the widespread employment discrimination experienced by women, people with disabilities, African Americans, Hispanics, and others that depresses their wages and thus their Social Security benefits (Margolis, 1990). As a result, "old-age dependency remains a serious predicament, especially for minorities and women" (Achenbaum, 1978, p. 151).

While state and federal laws were being enacted, attitudes toward aging and older people changed considerably during the 20th century, not always in a positive direction. Hirshbein (2001) examined representations of old age in popular magazines published between 1900 and 1950 and found three phases. In the first phase (1900–1920), most articles on aging were written by older people themselves, and they tended to emphasize their strengths as older adults. In the second phase (1920–early 1930s), "there was a shift toward a more negative reporting of the effects of old age" (p. 1556). During the third phase (late 1930s–1950), older people were often portrayed as a burden on society, largely as a result of the prioritization of younger workers for employment during the depression. A Louis Harris poll in 1975 revealed that most people still held the images of older people that prevailed prior to World War II:

> Americans continue to disparage the elderly's usefulness even though recent research lends substantial support for a concept of old age that recognizes the diversity in older person's abilities and conditions and that emphasizes positive as well as negative aspects of senescence. (Achenbaum, 1978, p. 163)

In the 1990s, retired people were actually viewed as a resource that could be tapped to address labor shortages in a number of employment sectors. However, in the first decade of the 21st century, older people are again being perceived as a drag on an economy that is staggering under rising unemployment, growing budget deficits, and falling stock markets.

In summary, treatment of older people in Western society has been a function of their role in the economy. The most power and prestige were accorded older people in agricultural societies and the least in nomadic and industrial and technological societies. The United States has responded more slowly than other nations to security problems of older people arising out of the industrial revolution. However, since the passage of the Social Security Act in 1934, a number of programs have been established to address these problems.

## Psychology's Treatment of Older People

Although humans have probably been concerned about the aging process since prehistoric times, the formal study of aging by psychologists is relatively new. Aiken (1995) pointed out that Roger Bacon, Francis Bacon, Benjamin Franklin, and Francis Galton all wrote about aging during the 13th to 19th centuries, and that an 18th-century British astronomer, Sir Edmund Halley, conducted the first scientific analysis of life expectancy. However, according to Birren (1964), "an empirically based psychology of aging did not appear until about 1835 with the work of Quetelet, and it showed a very slow growth in factual information until after World War II" (p. 9).

In reviewing the history of the psychology of aging, Birren (1961) identified three phases: Early Period (1835–1918); Beginning Systematic Studies (1918–1940); and Period of Expansion (1946–1960). The Early Period is typified by descriptive studies of human aging; that is, descriptions of how human senses develop and change with advancing age. It was near the end of this period (1914) that an American, Ignaz Nascher, coined the term *geriatrics* to identify the branch of medicine that deals with the health problems of older people (Aiken, 1995). During the Beginning Systematic Studies, numerous studies were conducted relating age to physical ability, reaction time, drive, mental ability, and other measures. Much of the research and writing of this period, as exemplified by G. Stanley Hall's (1923) *Senescence,* focused on the psychological decline of the aging individual.

The Period of Expansion was just that; more psychology of aging research was published in the 1950–1959 decade than had been published in the preceding 115 years (Birren, 1961, p. 127). It was also during this period (1945 to be exact) that the Division on Maturity and Old Age of the American Psychological Association was organized. Other significant events during this time included the convening of the National Conference on the Psychological Aspects of Aging (1953) and the publishing of the *Handbook of Aging and the Individual* (Birren, 1959). The fields of gerontology and geriatrics grew rapidly during this time, but unfortunately, the declining ability of older people remained a central theme of the professional research and writing in these fields (Johnson, 1995). A review of research on the psychology of aging by Levin and Levin (1980) revealed a continuing theme of decline in sensory and perceptual processes, psychomotor performance, cognitive processes, drives, and personality research. Similarly, a review of research on the creativity of artists and scientists led to a rather pessimistic view of productivity in the later years:

> Beginning somewhere in the 20s, output first increases fairly rapidly until a peak is reached, usually sometime in the 30s or 40s, after which a gradual decline sets in. This age curve holds even after introducing all varieties of statistical controls for potential artifacts and spurious relationships. . . . Hence the age decrement in creativity after the midlife optimum seems very real. Indeed, evidence strongly suggests that the longitudinal changes in creative achievement are cross-culturally and transhistorically invariant. (Simonton, 1990, p. 627)

These negative views of aging are now being challenged, and the most studies in recent years have documented that older people are aging well rather than aging ill. For example, Simonton (1990) identified a number of reasons why creative individuals can anticipate continued productivity during the latter part of their life and led him to conclude that "aging need not silence outstanding creativity in the last years" (p. 630). According to Johnson (1995), the White House Conference on Aging held in May 1995 recognized the need to focus on positive aging rather than just looking for ways to respond to a dependent population. Although he applauded this shift from viewing aging as negative to viewing it as positive, Johnson added a cautionary caveat:

> If we push the perception pendulum in the opposite direction in an effort to overcome the inaccurate exaggerations about negative views of aging from the past,

we may produce an equally exaggerated image that older adults are all aging in health and wholeness. . . . Homogenizing older adults in this way could do as much harm as grouping them into the negative category. Both are unrepresentative. The reality is that older adults will not fit into a single profile. Some age in good health and some age ill, some are unremarkable either way, and some have varying experiences within their own particular life course. (pp. 124–125)

Although experimental psychologists have shown some interest in the effects of aging on mental capacities since the turn of the century, applied psychologists have only recently turned their attention to the psychological needs of older people. In a review of research on utilization of psychological services by older people, Gatz, Karel, and Wolkenstein (1991) found substantial evidence of underutilization even though mental health needs do not decrease with age and despite evidence that psychotherapy is effective with older people. Although some underutilization can be explained by the stigma older people attach to psychological services, another important factor is therapist resistance to working with older people (Kent, 1990). At an April 1992 conference cosponsored by the APA's Practice Directorate, the National Institute of Mental Health, and the Retirement Research Foundation, several myths emerged as the reasons why psychologists have resisted serving the needs of older people (Moses, 1992). The prevailing myths or stereotypes held by psychologists are that "mental health issues disappear after mid-life, or that depression, anxiety and other problems are to be expected in the elderly and aren't worth treating" (p. 34). Related to this is the view that the mental health needs of older people have been neglected because it was assumed that the older people are developmentally static and coping mechanisms learned in their youth should suffice in old age. Other reasons why psychologists have not addressed the needs of older people can be hypothesized. For example, applied psychologists traditionally have been more interested in the needs of children and young adults than in the needs of older adults. Also, in the absence of a national health insurance that guarantees remuneration for working with older people, many mental health practitioners have simply focused their services on more lucrative populations.

However, underutilization cannot be totally explained as ageism on the part of mental health workers. Robb, Chen, and Haley (2002) reviewed the research on age bias among health and mental health professionals and concluded: (a) older people do underutilize mental health care services; (b) there is substantial evidence of differential diagnosis and treatment in physical health care; (c) evidence of ageism bias among mental health workers is less clear cut; and (d) "systemic factors [in mental health delivery] . . . may be stronger determinants of underservice than attitudes" (p. 9). According to Raschko (cited in Cavaliere, 1995), "disjointed government programs, scarce funds, and the inherent difficulties in locating people who rarely seek help" (p. 11) contribute to underutilization of mental health services by older people.

Also, it is true that most older people are socialized to handle their own problems and to not be a burden on others; therefore, they are reluctant to request counseling and other mental health services. In a survey of 100 older people, Kunkel and Williams (1991) found that recourse to a counselor or psychologist was considered to be neither relevant nor worthwhile except in the most extreme circumstances. The independence and guardedness themes suggested by other researchers among elderly persons were strongly present in this sample. . . . Few elderly persons in this sample thought that counselors were appropriate sources of help for retirement difficulties, fear of death, or sexual problems. . . . Many elderly persons may be part of a cohort that tends to view counseling services as irrelevant and even contrary to life experience. (p. 319)

However, there is reason to believe that this reluctance to use psychological services is changing with each new group of retiring cohorts and that future generations of older people will seek services on their own, rather than be referred by doctors, courts, home-health agencies, and adult children (Kent, 1990).

Notwithstanding the "reduced need" explanation for underutilization, a widely held belief exists among many mental health experts that psychological impairment increases with old age. Feinson (1991, p. 125) cited a number of quotes from policy-making individuals and commissions that document this belief. For example, The President's Commission on Mental Health concluded that "depression escalates decade by decade;" the former director of the Center for the Study of Mental Health and Aging at the National Institute of Mental Health stated that "the prevalence of mental illness and emotional distress is higher among those over 65 than in the general population"; and an official at the National Center for Health Statistics testified that "I have been told that depression is very prevalent among the elderly." However, after reviewing epidemiological studies conducted in the United States since 1950, Feinson (1991) concluded the following:

The one consistent finding from all cross-sectional studies conducted during the past forty years is that, to the extent that a relationship exists between impairment and age, more disorders are found among younger, rather than older, age groups! (p. 133)

Due in part to the negative views about serving older people held by counselors and psychologists, training programs seldom provide course work on aging. With respect to courses on aging and sexuality, there is actually evidence that health professionals in general are learning less than they did in the past. Karlen and Moglia (1995) surveyed sex educators in a variety of health professional programs and found "an overwhelmingly negative picture of what health professionals know, want to learn, and are taught about sex and aging" (p. 196). With respect to declining trainee interest in the topic, Karlen and Moglia concluded that their respondents' comments "underline the enduring strength of our society's traditional taboo against sex as a normal part of later life, and younger adults' emotional discomfort with seeing their elders as sexual beings" (p. 197). The respondents cited two reasons why less time and attention is being given to sexuality and aging in professional training than in the 1970s and 1980s: (a) the current important focus on problem areas of sex (HIV/AIDS, STDs, rape, sexual harassment, sexual abuse, unwanted pregnancies) takes time away from instruction about sex in middle and later life; and (b) classes on sexuality have never been incorporated as part of the mainstream of health education and, as the generation of pioneering sexuality educators reach retirement, sexuality courses are being cut back or even dropped. Thus, although a substantial number of mental health practitioners have older clients among their caseload, few have had any training for working with this client population (Gatz et al., 1991).

Several conferences convened by the American Psychological Association have addressed the need for more training in this area. A conference held in 1981 in Boulder, Colorado, resulted in a number of recommendations but no action plans. According to Dr. John Santos, a trustee of the Retirement Research Foundation, "APA just fell asleep at the wheel. . . . APA failed to set up mechanisms for helping psychologists develop curricula and service in this field" (quoted in Moses, 1992). An APA conference convened in Washington, D.C., in April 1992 also resulted in a number of recommendations for training for gerontological practice, but most students in APA-accredited programs still do not receive training specific to working with older clients.

The American Counseling Association (ACA), on the other hand, has taken several steps to promote training of counselors who have at least a minimum competence in gerontological issues. According to Myers (1992), the ACA (or more accurately, its predecessor, the American Association for Counseling and Development) conducted five national projects on aging between 1977 and 1991 with total funding from the U.S. Administration on Aging for these projects exceeding $1 million. All five projects focused on developing models and resources for preparing counselors to work with older persons. The most recent of the five projects identified "both generic competencies designed for training all counselors in gerontological issues and specialty competencies for training of gerontological counselors" (Myers, 1992, p. 37) and resulted in a proposal for a specialty credential in gerontological counseling that was accepted by the National Board for Certified Counselors (NBCC) in 1989. Gerontological competencies identified in these projects also contributed to the standards for training in gerontological counseling adopted by the Council for Accreditation of Counseling and Related Educational Programs (CACREP) in March 1992. Further, the ACA submitted standards to CACREP that were designed to infuse gerontological counseling into the common core preparation areas required for accreditation of counselor training programs. "This model would make it possible for all counselors (in accredited programs, at least) to graduate with some knowledge of the needs of older people and of ways to work successfully with them" (Myers, 1992, pp. 35–36).

With the aging of a significant proportion of our society and the lengthening of the life span came a growing recognition by mental health workers in the 1980s and 1990s that they must begin serving the older population. By sheer numbers older people are making us increasingly aware of their special needs. Counselors and psychologists can make a significant contribution to their well-being through both research and direct service efforts. Addressing researchers, Schaie (1993) pointed out that contemporary psychology should be concerned about ageism in contemporary psychology because (a) the rapid growth of older people in the 1990s has focused considerable research attention on this population; (b) the increased funding for research in this area has attracted researchers with little previous experience with research on aging, researchers whose ageist language may reinforce societal stereotypes; and (c) psychological research is playing an increasingly important role in developing public policy. Similarly, direct service psychologists should be concerned about how their ageist attitudes and behavior may impact older people as more and more services are targeted for this age group.

> Ageism may be manifested by psychologists in many ways, including (a) assumptions of restrictions on behavior due to age, (b) positive or negative stereotypes about the elderly, (c) belief that age is usually or always a relevant dimension to variables under study, and (d) the untested assumption that data from one age group generalize to others. (Schaie, 1993, p. 49)

In chapter 18 we discuss some of the steps that psychology must take to address the psychological needs of older people.

## CURRENT DISCRIMINATION

From the preceding overview of past treatment, it should be clear that older people have been both held in high esteem and stereotyped as worthless, depending on their role in society. Those attitudinal extremes still prevail today. Furthermore, older people are being victimized and discriminated against economically.

### Social Discrimination

Attitudes held toward aging and older people in contemporary U.S. culture are a complex mixture of negative and positive views (Kite & Wagner, 2002). On the one hand, even a cursory examination of the commercials appearing on television and in print reveals that a premium is placed on remaining youthful. On the other hand, more and more advertisements picture robust, attractive older people enjoying the good life in their "Golden Years." Miller, Miller, McKibbin, and Pettys (1999) examined the stereotypes of older persons appearing in print advertisements in magazines from 1956 to 1996 and found that only a small percentage depicted negative stereotypes. However, they also found a disturbing trend in that the percentage of negative stereotypes increased, and the percentage of positive stereotypes decreased, over that time period.

In their review of research on stereotypes of older people, Cuddy and Fiske (2002) found that there are multiple subtypes of older adults (e.g., grandmotherly, elder statesman, senior citizen) and that some of these subtypes have positive attributes and some negative attributes. They also concluded that older people in general are stereotyped as incompetent but warm (affectionate, good natured, trustworthy, etc.) and that older people experience a paternalistic form of prejudice, in that they are pitied but not respected. Furthermore, negative stereotypes may contribute to negative behavior:

> From workplaces to medical settings, stereotyping of elderly people manifests itself through discriminatory communication and treatment. . . . Believing older

people are incompetent leads others to treat them as if they are incompetent. Young people use baby talk—higher voices and simpler words—and sound more unpleasant when communicating with older people. . . . People are less willing to engage in challenging conversations with elderly people by asking them difficult questions. (p. 18).

Pasupathi and Lockenhoff (2002) found evidence of age-differentiated behavior toward older people in physician and patient communication, nursing homes, legal settings, work settings, and mass media and entertainment. They categorized age-differentiated behavior into three categories: (a) behaviors that distance, ignore, exclude older people; (b) behaviors that protect, positively portray, deferentially treat, or protect older people; and (c) behaviors that are negatively or overtly harmful of older people. Pasupathi and Lockenhoff contended that although the behaviors in categories (a) and (c) are clearly harmful, category (b) behaviors can also be ageist behaviors (behavior that is based on negative attitudes and harmful to older adults):

> Positive behaviors, such as more compassionate decision making by conservators, may fail to protect people who need protection. Deference and politeness may also deprive people of intimate connections, which they might prefer. . . . Even positive images in the mass media may provide unrealistic standards and implicitly suggest that those who are not "successful agers" have somehow failed and are responsible for their own ill health. (p. 229)

Nowhere are stereotypes of older people more extreme than in the arena of sexuality. Sexual stereotypes of older people include the perception that they are asexual, that their expressions of passion are gross and disgusting, that they are in danger of a heart attack when they engage in sex, and that sexually active older people are "dirty" old men and women (Campbell & Huff, 1995; Willert & Semans, 2000). Stereotypes of older women are particularly negative and can have a devastating effect on an older woman's feelings of self-worth.

Health practitioners may also hold stereotypes of older people that result in biased diagnoses and treatment. For example, Carmel (1998) found that medical students ranked the will to live of older people significantly lower than did older people themselves. Cohen (1990) pointed out that even the language of geriatric advocates tends to portray older adults with disabilities as incapable of exercising control over their lives. Cohen surveyed numerous earlier issues of the *Gerontologist, Generations,* and federal monographs and came up with the following terms used by mental health workers: "Elderly-at-risk, frail elderly, impaired elderly, institutionalized elderly, homebound elderly, chair-bound elderly, bedridden elderly, wheelchair bound elderly, vulnerable elderly, dependent elderly, patient (rather than consumer), and 'the Alzheimer' (referring to the person who has the disease)" (p. 14). He argued that terms like these rob older persons with disabilities of their motivation to assert themselves. Thus, even well-intentioned advocates may be contributing to a new ageism that restricts the capability of older people.

Perhaps the most destructive effect of negative stereotypes is the change in attitudes and behavior they have on the people against whom they are directed. Whitbourne and Sneed (2002) reviewed several recent experimental studies that demonstrate that subliminal priming of older people with negative stereotypes before and during a task reduces walking speed, gait, and memory performance. They suggested the fact that older people in the United States that are constantly bombarded with negative images of old age helps explain why they are outperformed by older people in cultures where more positive attitudes prevail (e.g., China).

## Economic Discrimination

Paradoxically, older people are currently among the most affluent and, at the same time, most poverty-stricken group in the United States. Due to rising salaries, the success of private and public pension plans, a growing economy in the 1990s, and the inflation of property values over the past five decades, many retirees are enjoying a higher standard of living than at any time in the history of the United States (Morris & Caro, 1995). Hess (1991) credited the decision by Congress to link changes in Social Security benefits to inflation and the introduction of health insurance for older people as reasons why "the incidence of poverty among America's aged has dropped from over one in three before 1960 to slightly under the national rate of 14% today" (p. 8).

Poverty rates below the national average have contributed to a new stereotype of older people as "greedy geezers" (Holstein, 1995), "fat cats living the good life at the expense of everybody else" (Lewis, 1992b, p. 14). As a result, entitlements for older people were being blamed for the growing federal deficit in the late 1980s and early 1990s. Furthermore, the rising federal deficit and the shrinking funds for programs that benefit children and adolescents were being blamed on the mandated increases in Social Security.

> Critics of Social Security and Medicare blamed the deteriorating condition of children and families on the "graying of the federal budget" (more than half of all federal domestic spending goes to the elderly) and raised the specter of intergenerational warfare between young and old. . . . The generational equity campaign continues to portray the elderly as selfish, politically powerful, and potentially dangerous. (Cole, 1991, pp. 23–24)

This theme is again reflected in the early part of the 21st century since these same economic conditions have returned after a period of budget surpluses in the 1990s. However, the view of older people as budgetary piranhas ignores the fact that the most costly entitlement programs are largely self-funded; many current retirees have been paying into Social Security since its inception. As Hess (1991) pointed out:

> It should also be realized that before the 1980s, the Social Security Trust Funds had never before been included in the regular federal budget, where they now serve to make the U.S. budget deficit appear *smaller* than it actually is. . . . If . . . one takes only the programs funded from general revenues (that is, excluding Medicare and Social Security), the elderly are not overly coddled, receiving a share of federal outlays considerably lower than their representation in the total population. The fact that assistance for poor children and their families is vastly under funded is an issue that should be addressed directly on its own merits and not made into a zero-sum situation in which the benefits available to one group must come at the cost of reducing programs for other needy populations. (p. 8)

According to Adams and Dominick (1995)

> efforts in the United States to promote a politics of generational equity are best un-
> derstood as part of a larger class struggle over the welfare state, an important aspect
> of which is the attempt to define the conflict in terms of age rather than class. (p. 41)

As has been suggested by Holstein (1995), the debate about disproportionate resources going to the older people has not led to proposed programs that would re-
distribute these resources to children and other needy groups. Rather, the focus
has been on budget reduction, a problem that could be addressed in other ways
without denying dignity and health care to the current and future generations of
older people. More recently, rising military and homeland defense budgets have
been taking resources away from programs for young and old alike.

The economic gains made by a minority of retired individuals are in direct
contrast to the experiences of many older persons, particularly single women, ethnic minorities, the seriously ill, and the old-old (people over 85). The most recent
Census Bureau report that provides extensive income data for older Americans is
a report by Hobbs and Damon (1996) based primarily on 1992 data. This report
documents the bimodal distribution of income levels for the older population and
demonstrates how being single and over age 75 affects income. For example,
52.8% of White married-couple households with a householder age 65 or older
had annual incomes of $25,000 and over, and 16.6% had annual incomes of
$50,000 and over in 1992. However, more than 1 out of every 2 people (54%) 75
years or older who lived alone had incomes below $10,000, and more than 4 out
of every 5 people (86%) 75 and older living alone had incomes below $20,000.
Married couples fared a little better; among those couples with at least one householder 75 years of age or older, 44% had incomes below $20,000. As indicated in
Figure 3.1, Black married-couple households with a householder 75 years of age
or older fared worse than their White counterparts.

**FIGURE 3.1**    Percentage of married-couple households with householder 75+ and
living below selected income levels.

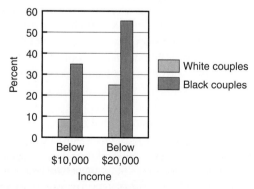

Based on data from Hobbs, F. B., & Damon, B. L. (1996). *65+ in the United States* (U.S. Bureau of the Census, Current Population Reports, P23-190). Washington, DC: U.S. Government Printing House. Retrieved November 7,
2002. from http://www.census.gov/prod/1/pop/p23-190/p23-190.pdf.

Given these income figures, it is not surprising that a sizable portion of older people live below or near the poverty level. Although as a group, fewer older people (12.9%) live below the poverty level than do younger people (14.7%; the number of children living below the poverty level boosts this number), more older people (27.6%) than younger people (23.6%) live below 150% of the poverty threshold. Furthermore, these percentages increase with age, being female, and ethnic minority status. For example, almost 1 in 5 (19.8%) women 75 years of age or older lived in poverty and more than 2 in 5 (41.7%) women 75 years of age or older lived below the 150% of poverty threshold in 1992. In 1992, 33.3% of Blacks and 22.0% of Hispanics ages 65 and older lived below the poverty level, compared with 10.9% of Whites ages 65 and older.

> Women made up 58.4 percent of the elderly population but 71.3 percent of the poor elderly population in 1992. Although Blacks were only 8.6 percent of the total elderly population, they made up 22.3 percent of all elderly poor. Black women were 5.1 percent of the elderly population and 15.0 percent of the elderly poor. (Hobbs & Damon, 1996, p. 4-19)

Also, the federal figures on older people and poverty are misleading in that figures to compute the poverty level are adjusted by age. Because older people are assumed to have lower nutritional requirements than younger people, the poverty threshold in 1992 for single older people was $6,729 compared with $7,299 for single people ages 15 to 64. Thus, if the poverty threshold used for younger people were applied to older people, the poverty rates cited in the preceding would be even higher.

Older people are often the first to lose their jobs in economic downswings. Although recent federal legislation increased the mandatory retirement age from 65 to 70, it did not eliminate occupational discrimination for those 70 and above, and people 65 to 70 are still pushed into retirement by unchallenging work (particularly among blue-collar jobs), company pressure, self-fulfilling prophecy, and economic incentives provided, ironically, by the government. Older workers are often given the choice to retire early or take a drop in rank and pay. The Age Discrimination in Employment Act was supposed to eliminate or greatly reduce employment discrimination against older workers. However, according to Morris and Caro (1995), enforcement of the act "has been uneven over the years, and discrimination based on negative attitudes toward older workers continues" (p. 33). For example, Caro and Motika (1992) found that only 15% of the discrimination cases filed in 1989 with the Massachusetts Commission Against Discrimination produced favorable outcomes for the worker, and for older workers with complaints about hiring practices the favorable outcome rate was even lower.

Once they lose their jobs older workers find it difficult to obtain new employment (Morris & Caro, 1995). Without jobs, many older people have to rely on Social Security benefits for their primary source of income. For a majority of the older population, Social Security benefits account for more than half of their income. Further, 1 in 5 of all older people (2 in 5 Blacks) receive 90% or more of their income from Social Security. Unemployment, low income, and poverty figures are most dismal for women and ethnic minorities as subgroups of the older population.

Although some older people retired in the 1980s and early 1990s with excellent pension plans that help account for the more affluent members of this population, the security of some of these pension plans is now threatened. According to Rappaport (1995), the "old social contract" between employers and employee that provided health care and fixed income for former employees in retirement is being replaced by the "new social contract" that views health care and retirement income as the responsibility of the employee. Defined-benefit pension plans (where a level of income is guaranteed at retirement) increasingly are being phased out by many major companies in favor of defined-contribution plans (retirement income is based on how the employee invests his or her pension funds). Since most employees lack both the training and the time to properly manage their pension funds and consequently invest them in secure but low-interest portfolios, future retirees are likely to have even less expendable income than current retirees (Krain, 1995). Also, as more and more large companies downsize, move to other countries, or simply shut down, a greater percentage of the population is employed by small companies that do not offer pension plans of any kind (Rappaport, 1995). Older workers who lose their jobs due to companies downsizing, leaving, or closing often use "contingent" jobs as an income bridge until they reach retirement (Lewis, 1992a). Contingent work consists of part-time, temporary, contract, and freelance jobs that pay less, provide fewer benefits, and offer less security than full-time jobs. According to Lewis:

> What is new about part-time, temporary and other contingent workers is the way they're being used by employers these days: as commodities to be plugged into the workplace on an "as-needed" basis, and then to be dispensed with very much like water cooler refills or Dixie cups. . . . Corporations are moving toward a new . . . job strategy that, in effect, cuts labor costs by converting full-time jobs to contingent jobs. (p. 2)

For workers over 50, this switch from full-time to contingent jobs means a loss of income, benefits, and security at a time in life when they should be most affluent and padding their pension funds for retirement years. The knowledge that they are "disposable" workers also threatens their self-esteem at a time when peers have moved to the top of their career ladders.

## Victimization

Victimization of older people occurs as the result of criminal activity, often by strangers, and abuse, often by family members.

**Crimes Against Older People**   Although some research suggests violent crimes against older people are not as common as they were thought to be earlier, they are often targeted for nonviolent crimes that have a particularly devastating effect on people with limited physical, intellectual, and financial resources. For example, McCabe and Gregory (1998) reported that older adults are more at risk than younger people for crimes of robbery, intimidation, vandalism, and forgery/fraud. Futhermore, according to Dr. Rosalie Wolf, president of the National Committee for the Prevention of Elder Abuse, policymakers often underestimate the prevalence of crimes against older people (U.S. Department of Justice, 2000).

> When older people are victimized, the impact on them is greater than on younger people: When elderly people are victimized, they usually suffer greater physical, mental, and financial injuries than other age groups. Elderly victims are twice as likely to suffer serious physical injury and to require hospitalization than any other age group. Furthermore, the physiological process of aging brings with it a decreasing ability to heal after injury—both physically and mentally. Thus, elderly victims may never fully recover from the trauma of their victimization. Also, the trauma that elderly victims suffer is worsened by their financial difficulties. Because many elderly people live on a low or fixed income, they often cannot afford the professional services and products that could help them in the aftermath of a crime. (U.S. Department of Justice, 2001, p. 1).

When older people are the victims of crime, they may be reluctant to report it because they worry (and rightly so) that their families and the authorities will question their competence. Worse yet, they may question their own competence and tend to blame themselves for letting the crime happen rather than blame the offender. Also, because they feel very vulnerable, they may fear retaliation by the offender for reporting the crime. If the offender is a family member, they may be reluctant to report the crime because it will be embarrassing to the family or may lead to the loss of the family member as a care provider (U.S. Department of Justice, 2000).

Older people are clearly the targets of criminals for selected types of crimes, particularly property crimes (Aiken, 1995; Doyle, 1990). Purse thieves often see older women as easy targets, and it is not uncommon that the victim is injured during the commission of the crime. Cashing a Social Security check can be a particularly dangerous event for an older person. Older adults are particularly vulnerable to financial exploitation, in part because they tend to be more trusting and less cynical than younger people (U.S. Department of Justice, 2000). Swindlers often prey upon older people, employing "pigeon drops" to filch their lifetime savings. Hearing aid, insurance, medical, work-at-home, home improvement, investment, and postal fraud are all examples of swindles directed at older people. Telemarketers are notorious for targeting older people. According to an AARP survey, although people 50 years of age or older only make up 26% of the population, they make up 56% of the telemarketing victims. Telemarketing scams include prize and sweepstake scams, slamming, pay-for call services, work-at-home sales, and magazine sales (U.S. Department of Justice, 2000). Older people are particularly vulnerable to home improvement scams if their home is their only large asset, their home is older and often in need of repair, they have diminished ability to perform home maintenance and repair themselves, and they have a strong desire to remain in their own home. Many such crimes go unreported due to the victim's embarrassment, and little solid information is available about their frequency.

Because they are often trusting and dependent on others, older people are vulnerable to financial exploitation. For example, predatory lenders often convince older people to take out home equity loans that, because of their low incomes, they cannot repay. Sometimes unsavory relatives, acquaintances, or even strangers manage to be appointed guardian, trustee, or power of attorney for incompetent older people and misuse their funds for personal gains as a result. Older people are also particularly vulnerable to identity theft in which a scam artist uses the victim's Social Security number and/or other personal information to run up debts or deplete assets. A survey by the AARP found that older adults rely heavily on investment brokers and advisers to make investments on their behalf and may end up being charged exorbitant fees or making poor investments. That same survey found that half of all older investors did not think that diversification of investments was a way of reducing financial risk, suggesting they do not have even the most basic knowledge needed to protect their own investments (U.S. Department of Justice, 2000).

Particularly pernicious is the health care fraud perpetuated by health care providers charged with looking after the physical and mental well-being of older people. Speaking to a national symposium on victimization of older people jointly sponsored by the Department of Justice (DOJ) and Department of Health and Human Services (DHHS), Barbara Harriman from the Office of Inspector General revealed that the Medicare Trust has lost billions of dollars to health care fraud (U.S. Department of Justice, 2000). Unethical health care providers also overcharge older patients or bill them for services not provided, in addition to defrauding Medicare. Although a law enacted by Congress in 1989 limits doctors not participating in Medicare from charging patients more than 20% over the Medicare rate, "thousands of Medicare patients are being overcharged by their doctors" (McLeod, 1992). These excessive charges affect older patients directly because they must make up the difference between what the doctor charges and what Medicare will pay; they also affect all Medicare patients and all taxpayers by draining Medicare resources.

Although older people may not experience more violent crimes than younger persons, fear of such crimes have a particularly debilitating effect on older adults. Furthermore, it is clear that older people are overrepresented as victims of many different types of crimes.

**Abuse of Older People**   Of all the forms of domestic abuse, abuse of older people remained obscure for the longest. According to Myers and Shelton (1987), the public first became aware of child abuse in the 1960s and spousal abuse in the 1970s but did not become aware of older people abuse until the 1980s. Even then it received little attention from mental health professionals, law enforcement officials, and legislators compared with the attention given to child abuse and spousal abuse. By the early 1980s, however, it became apparent that abuse of older people was common and widespread.

The House Select Committee on Aging, chaired by the late Representative Claude Pepper, began hearing testimony on abuse of older Americans by their family members and other care providers in 1978. After those initial hearings, the Committee issued three reports, the titles of which reflect how imbedded abuse of older people was in American culture: (a) *Elder Abuse: The Hidden Agenda,* published in 1980; (b) *Elder Abuse: A National Disgrace,* published in 1985; and

(c) *Elder Abuse: A Decade of Shame and Inaction,* published in 1990. (The U.S. House of Representatives allowed the House Select Committee on Aging to expire in 1993 after only a little more than a decade of serving as a forum for airing issues vital to older persons.) The first report revealed that abuse of older people was not an isolated or localized problem involving a few frail older people. Instead, the Committee characterized it as a full-scale national problem that existed at a frequency and rate similar to that of child abuse. The second report revealed that instead of diminishing, abuse of older people was increasing dramatically from year to year. The third and most recent report found further evidence that abuse of older people is on the increase. Whereas in 1980 the Committee reported that 1 out of every 25 (roughly 1 million) older Americans were abused annually, in 1990 investigators found that 1 out of every 20 (about 1.5 million) older Americans are victims of abuse each year, suggesting that the incidents of abuse were increasing at the time.

Currently it's believed that only 1 in 5 cases of abuse gets reported and that the incidence of abuse is rising (U.S. Department of Justice, 2000). Recent (1999) figures for reported cases of older adult abuse range from 443,000 official complaints of abuse, neglect, and exploitation (U.S. Department of Justice, 2001), to 551,011 reported cases (Administration on Aging, 2001). Based on these figures, it can be projected that there are 2.5 million incidents of older people abuse annually.

The most common type of abuse is neglect (60%), followed by emotional/psychological abuse (35.5%), physical abuse (25.6%), financial abuse (30.2%), and abandonment (3.6%; these figures add up to more than 100% and may seem counterintuitive because many substantiated abuse cases involve more than one type of abuse). Individuals 80 years of age and older receive a disproportionate share of the abuse: 51.8% of neglect; 41.3% of emotional/psychological abuse; 43.7% of physical abuse; 48.0% of financial abuse; and 19.8% of abandonment. Women are more likely to be the victims of all types of abuse except abandonment. Because women make up 57.6% of all people over age 60, whenever their representation exceeds that figure they are overrepresented. As can be seen in Figure 3.2, women are overrepresented for all types of abuse except abandonment. Whites make up 79.0% of neglect victims, 82.8% of emotional/psychological abuse victims, 86.0% of physical abuse victims, 83.0% of financial abuse victims, and 41.3% of abandonment victims. Blacks are overrepresented as victims in all forms of abuse except neglect; Hispanics are underrepresented in all forms of older adult abuse (Administration on Aging, 1998).

For all substantiated older adult abuse cases, men are more likely than women to be abusers (52.5% men vs. 47.5% women). This holds true across all categories of abuse except neglect (the most common form of abuse), where women constitute 52.4% of abusers. Approximately two thirds (65.8%) of all abusers are under age 60. However, 25% were over age 70. Across all forms of older adult abuse, 77% of abusers are White, 18% Black, 1% Hispanic, and 4% other ethnicity (Administration on Aging, 1998). Readers should keep in mind that racial bias and uneven distributions of resources may be factors in reporting and occurrence of older adult abuse.

Abuse occurs in all types of settings, including domestic homes, private nursing facilities, and public hospitals. However, in 90% of all abuse cases, the per-

**FIGURE 3.2**   Percentage of types of abuse by gender.

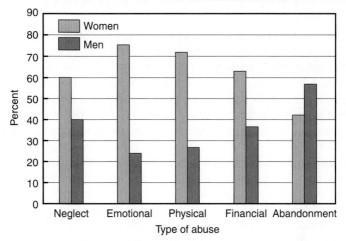

Based on data from Administration on Aging. (2001). *Elder abuse prevention.* Washington, DC: Author. Retrieved November 27, 2002, from http://www.aoa.gov/factsheets/abuse.html.

petrator is a family member; two thirds are adult children or spouses. Furthermore, abuse by relatives may be much higher because authorities report that abuse occurring in the victim's home is particularly hard to detect due to the privacy accorded private homes (mandated reporters are seldom in private homes, and when they are, care providers are on their best behavior). Contrary to stereotype, "rather than the victim being dependent on the abuser, in most instances the abused person describes the abuser as depending on him or her for finances, housing, transportation, cooking, cleaning, or other services" (Aiken, 1995). Those older people living with relatives are often treated as burdens on young families and made to feel guilty for their state of dependence. In recent years the stress on family care providers has led to "granny dumping," abandonment of older people with disabilities on hospital emergency room doorsteps in desperation. According to Hey and Carlson (1991), such abandonment is much more routine than had been thought and provides graphic evidence that our long-term care policies in this country are inadequate.

A number of factors combine to create the conditions under which an adult child will abuse his or her older parent:

> The likely abuser will usually be experiencing great stress. Alcoholism, drug addiction, marital problems and long-term financial difficulties all play a role in bringing a person to abuse his or her parents. The son of the victim is the most likely abuser, followed by the daughter of the victim. It is interesting to note that the abuser, in many cases, was abused by the parents as a child. (Select Committee on Aging, 1990, p. xii)

Furthermore, many adult children who are caregivers for aged parents are often facing problems associated with aging themselves (Schwiebert & Myers, 1994).

As a result, the responsibilities of care providing often come at a time when the adult children are preparing for or entering retirement and beginning to experience a loss of resources.

Those living in nursing homes are often ignored and isolated by staff who have neither the time nor inclination to interact with their charges in a constructive way. Vladeck and Feuerberg (1995–1996) concluded that although the quality of nursing home care has improved in recent years, "overall nursing home quality in 1995 still falls very short of what it should be" (p. 10). Furthermore, advocates for nursing homes point out that nursing home regulations that resulted in improvements in overall nursing home quality have come under siege from conservative members of Congress (Freeman, 1995–1996). Also, in recent years there has been a tremendous expansion of community-based services, a change that carries with it problems of its own. Although it was generally assumed that any home- and community-based services for older people would be better than nursing home care, "the development of quality standards and enforcement mechanisms for these services has lagged considerably behind the movement on the nursing home front" (Vladeck & Feuerberg, 1995–1996, p. 12).

Abuse in nursing homes, even when reported, is often not prosecuted:

> States have made laws and regulations to protect the rights of nursing home residents and assure a high quality of care. However, the sheer number of different agencies charged with safeguarding older adults makes it difficult to hold abusive institutions accountable for the harm they do. (U.S. Department of Justice, 2000, p. 57)

Abuse in institutional settings often takes the form of overmedication. "Older persons in institutions take an average of 10 to 12 drugs per day, in contrast to 4 to 7 per day for older persons living in communities" (Myers & Shelton, 1987). Cooper (1994) reported that a review of nursing home drug records by pharmacists revealed that medication errors or adverse drug reactions occurred each month for 2 out of 3 patients in surveyed nursing homes.

Most experts agree that reported cases are just the tip of the iceberg (as indicated earlier, only about 1 in 5 cases is reported). Abuse of older adults is often ignored by third parties due to our negative stereotypes of older people. Friends, relatives, and caretakers often ignore self-reports of violence and assume they are the result of a wandering mind. Bruises and cuts are often attributed to an aging body and ambulation problems. Also, older people are reluctant to report that their child is abusing them because of the shame it will bring to the family and because they are afraid of losing whatever support they do receive from the abusing child; over 70% of older-people-abuse cases are reported by third parties (Aiken, 1995).

Prior to 1980, only 16 states had adult protective service laws mandating that abuse of older people be reported. During the 10-year period from 1980 to 1990, mandatory reporting laws were passed in 26 additional states; reporting of abuse of older people is now mandatory for selected professionals in all 50 states and the District of Columbia (Administration on Aging, 2001). The California mandatory reporting law is typical of that in many states. The California law stipulates that "any person who has assumed full or intermittent responsibility for care or custody of an elder or dependent adult" who has observed or has knowledge of physical abuse, abandonment, isolation, financial abuse, or neglect *shall* report it to the proper authority. No one who is required to report known or suspected instances of abuse can be held liable for their report. However, failure to report an instance of older or dependent adult abuse can result in a fine of $1,000 or six months in jail or both. Individuals who make abuse reports even though they are not required to cannot be held liable unless it can be proven that they knowingly made a false report.

Abuse of older people is a national disgrace, and responsibility for this growing problem rests at a number of different levels. Funding for the prevention of older adult abuse is woefully inadequate. Federal funds for prevention have remained stable at $4–5 million per year for a number of years. By comparison, domestic violence services (spousal and partner abuse) currently receive about $200 million annually, and child abuse services receive $4 billion each year (U.S. Department of Justice, 2001).

At the local level, all of us can feel some share of the responsibility for ignoring the problem. In addition to the more obvious forms of discrimination against older people, benign neglect of our older citizens and their problems in living can be viewed as a form of discrimination and victimization. The United States clearly has the technology and resources to ease the life stresses placed on older people due to failing health, loss of income, lack of transportation, difficulty living independently, isolation, victimization, and other problems. The fact that we are unwilling to prioritize the needs of older people over military and defense spending, for example, is evidence of discrimination by benign neglect. The fact that when we do respond to the needs of older people, it is often with high-visibility material assistance rather than with low-visibility social assistance (personal involvement, emotional nurturing, respect) provides further evidence of discrimination by benign neglect.

## REFERENCES

Achenbaum, W. A. (1978). *Old age in the new land: The American experience since 1790.* Baltimore: Johns Hopkins University Press.

Adams, P., & Dominick, G. L. (1995). The old, the young, and the welfare state. *Generations, 19,* 38–42.

Administration on Aging. (1998). *The National Elder Abuse Incidence Study; Final Report September 1998.* Retrieved November 29, 2002, from www.aoa.gov/abuse/report/default.htm.

Administration on Aging. (2001). *Elder abuse prevention.* Washington, DC: Author. Retrieved November 27, 2002, from www.aoa.gov/factsheets/abuse.html.

Aiken, L. R. (1995). *Aging: An introduction to gerontology.* Thousand Oaks, CA: Sage Publications.

American Association of Retired People. (2002). *AARP facts.* Washington, DC: Author. Retrieved November 29, 2002, from www.aarp.org/what_is.html.

Birren, J. E. (1959). *Handbook of aging and the individual: Psychological and biological aspects.* Chicago: University of Chicago Press.

Birren, J. E. (1961). A brief history of the psychology of aging. *The Gerontologist, 1,* 69–77, 127–134.

Birren, J. E. (1964). *The psychology of aging.* Englewood Cliffs, NJ: Prentice Hall.

Campbell, J. M., & Huff, M. S. (1995). Sexuality in the older woman. *Gerontology and Geriatrics Education, 16,* 71–81.

Carmel, S. (1998). Medical students' attitudes regarding the use of life-sustaining treatments for themselves and for elderly persons. *Social Science and Medicine, 46,* 467–474.

Caro, F. G., & Motika, S. (1992). *Age discrimination in employment: A review of cases filed in the Massachusetts Commission against Discrimination.* Boston: Gerontological Institute, University of Massachusetts.

Cavaliere, F. (1995, December). Elderly deserve better mental health services. *APA Monitor, 26,* 11.

Cohen, E. S. (1990). The elderly mystique: Impediment to advocacy and empowerment. *Generations, 14* (Suppl.), 13–16.

Cole, T. (1991). The specter of old age: History, politics, and culture in an aging America. In B. B. Hess & E. W. Markson (Eds.), *Growing old in America* (4th ed., pp. 23–37). New Brunswick, NJ: Transaction Books.

Cooper, J. L. W. (1994). Drug-related problems in the elderly patient. *Generations, 28*(2), 19–27.

Covey, H. C. (1988). Historical terminology used to represent older people. *The Gerontologist, 28,* 291–297.

Cowgill, D. O., & Holmes, L. (1972). *Aging and modernization.* New York: Appleton-Century-Crofts.

Cuddy, A. J. C., & Fiske, S. T. (2002). Doddering but dear: Process, content, and function in stereotyping of older persons. Attitudes toward older adults. In T. D. Nelson (Ed.), *Ageism: Stereotyping and prejudice against older persons* (pp. 3–26). Cambridge, MA: MIT Press.

Doyle, D. P. (1990). Aging and crime. In K. F. Ferraro (Ed.), *Gerontology: Perspectives and issues* (pp. 294–315). New York: Springer.

Fein, R. (1992). Prescription for change. *Modern Maturity, 35*(4), 22–35.

Feinson, M. C. (1991). Reexamining some common beliefs about mental health and aging. In B. B. Hess & E. W. Markson (Eds.), *Growing old in America* (4th ed., pp. 125–135). New Brunswick, NJ: Transaction Books.

Fischer, D. H. (1977). *Growing old in America.* New York: Oxford University Press.

Freeman, I. C. (1995–1996). A contemporary advocacy agenda for nursing home consumers. *Generations, 19,* 52–54.

Gatz, M., Karel, M. J., & Wolkenstein, B. (1991). Survey of providers of psychological services to older adults. *Professional Psychology: Research and Practice, 22,* 413–415.

Hall, G. S. (1923). *Senescence: The last half of life.* New York: D. Appleton.

Hendricks, J., & Hendricks, C. D. (1981). *Aging in mass society: Myths and realities.* Cambridge, MA: Winthrop.

Hess, B. B. (1991). Growing old in the 1990s. In B. B. Hess & E. W. Markson (Eds.), *Growing old in America* (4th ed., pp. 5–22). New Brunswick, NJ: Transaction Books.

Hey, R. P., & Carlson, E. (1991). "Granny dumping": New pain for U.S. elders. *AARP Bulletin, 32*(8), 1, 16.

Hirshbein, L. D. (2001). Popular views of old age in America, 1900–1950. *Journal of American Geriatrics Society, 49,* 1555–1560.

Hobbs, F. B., & Damon, B. L. (1996). *65+ in the United States* (U.S. Bureau of the Census, Current Population Reports, P23-190). Washington, DC: U.S. Government Printing House. Retrieved November 7, 2002, from www.census.gov/prod/1/pop/p23-190/p23-190.pdf.

Holstein, M. (1995). The normative case: Chronological age and public policy. *Generations, 19,* 11–14.

Johnson, T. F. (1995). Aging well in contemporary society. *American Behavioral Scientist, 39,* 120–130.

Karlen, A., & Moglia, R. (1995). Sexuality, aging, and the education of health professionals. *Sexuality and Disability, 13,* 191–199.

Kebric, R. B. (1988). Old age, the ancient military, and Alexander's army: Positive examples for a graying American. *The Gerontologist, 28,* 298–302.

Kent, K. L. (1990). Elders and community mental health. *Generations, 14*(1), 19–21.

Kite, M. E., & Wagner, L. S. (2002). Attitudes toward older adults. In T. D. Nelson (Ed.), *Ageism: Stereotyping and prejudice against older persons* (pp. 129–161). Cambridge, MA: MIT Press.

Krain, M. A. (1995). Policy implications for a society aging well. *American Behavioral Scientist, 39,* 131–151.

Kunkel, M. A., & Williams, C. (1991). Age and expectations about counseling: Two methodological perspectives. *Journal of Counseling and Development, 70,* 314–320.

Levin, J., & Levin, W. C. (1980). *Ageism: Prejudice and discrimination against the elderly.* Belmont, CA: Wadsworth.

Lewis, R. (1992a). Disposable workers: New corporate policies put many older employees at risk. *AARP Bulletin, 33*(5), 2.

Lewis, R. (1992b). Ups and downs of the 1980s: New income data refutes "fat cat" age stereotype. *AARP Bulletin, 33*(2), 1, 14–16.

Margolis, R. J. (1990). *Risking old age in America.* Boulder, CO: Westview Press.

McCabe, K. A., & Gregory, S. S. (1998). Elderly victimization: An examination beyond the FBI's index crimes. *Research on Aging, 20,* 363–372.

McLeod, D. (1992). Overcharge . . . Critics: Feds slighting Medicare patients. *AARP Bulletin, 33*(2), 1, 4–5.

Miller, P. N., Miller, D. W., McKibbin, E. M., & Pettys. G. L. (1999). Stereotypes of the elderly in magazine advertisements 1956–1996. *International Journal of Aging and Human Development, 49,* 319–337.

Morris, R., & Caro, F. G. (1995). The young-old, productive aging, and public policy. *Generations,* Fall, 19(3), 32–37.

Moses, S. (1992). More clinicians needed to help a graying America. *Monitor, 23*(8), 34.

Myers, J. E. (1992). Competencies, credentialing, and standards for gerontological counselors: Implications for counselor education. *Counselor Education and Supervision, 32,* 34–42.

Myers, J. E., & Shelton, B. (1987). Abuse and older persons: Issues and implications for counselors. *Journal of Counseling and Development, 65,* 376–380.

Pasupathi, M., & Lockenhoff, C. E. (2002). Ageist behavior. Attitudes toward older adults. In T. D. Nelson (Ed.), *Ageism: Stereotyping and prejudice against older persons* (pp. 201–246). Cambridge, MA: MIT Press.

Rappaport, A. M. (1995). Employer policy and the future of employee benefits for an older population. *Generations, 19,* 63–67.

Rich, B. M., & Baum, M. (1984). *The aging: A guide to public policy.* Pittsburgh: University of Pittsburgh Press.

Robb, C., Chen, H., & Haley, W. E. (2002). Ageism in mental health and health care: A critical review. *Journal of Clinical Geropsychology, 8,* 1–12.

Schaie, K. W. (1993). Ageist language in psychological research. *American Psychologist, 48,* 49–51.

Schwiebert, V. L., & Myers, J. E. (1994). Midlife care givers: Effectiveness of a psychoeducational intervention for midlife adults with parent-care responsibilities. *Journal of Counseling and Development, 72,* 627–632.

Select Committee on Aging. (1990). *Elder abuse: A decade of shame and inaction* (Comm. Pub. No. 101-752). Washington, DC: U.S. Government Printing Office.

Simmons, L. W. (1945). *The role of the aged in primitive society.* New Haven, CT: Yale University Press.

Simonton, D. K. (1990). Creativity in the later years: Optimistic prospects for achievement. *The Gerontologist, 30,* 626–631.

U.S. Department of Justice. (2000). *Our aging population: Promoting empowerment, preventing victimization, and implementing coordinated interventions.* Washington, DC: Author. Retrieved November 27, 2002, from www.disability-abuse.com/cando/documents/AgingVic186256.pdf.

U.S. Department of Justice. (2001). *First response to victims of crime, 2001.* Washington, DC: Author. Retrieved November 26, 2002, from www.ojp.usdoj.gov/ovc/publications/infores/firstrep/2001/eldvic.html.

Vladeck, B. C., & Feuerberg, M. (1995–1996). Unloving care revisited. *Generations, 19*(4), 9–14.

Whitbourne, S. K., & Sneed, J. R. (2002). The paradox of well-being, identity process, and stereotype threat: Ageism and its potential relationships to the self in later life. In T. D. Nelson (Ed.), *Ageism: Stereotyping and prejudice against older persons* (pp. 247–273). Cambridge, MA: MIT Press.

Willert, A., & Semans, M. (2000). Knowledge and attitudes about later life sexuality: What clinicians need to know about helping the elderly. *Contemporary Family Therapy: An International Journal, 22,* 415–435.

# CHAPTER 4

Oppression
of Women: Past
and Present

This chapter describes the oppression of women, past and present. In order to understand current forms of discrimination against women, it is helpful to first examine past discrimination against this population.

## PAST DISCRIMINATION

The role of women in society has varied greatly, from egalitarian treatment in primitive societies to total subjugation by men in Ancient Greece and Rome to increasing women's rights in contemporary society.

### Society's Treatment of Women

Women have been largely neglected in historical texts, existing mostly in passing references or as the wives, mothers, or lovers of great men. Only in the latter part of the 20th century have historians begun to untangle the reality of women's lives throughout history from the fiction of myth and literature (Schulenburg, 1979). Virginia Woolf (1957) best summarized the problems in understanding women's place in history:

> If woman had no existence save in the fiction written by men, one would imagine her a person of utmost importance; very various; heroic and mean; splendid and sordid; infinitely beautiful and hideous in the extreme; as great as man, some think even greater. But this is woman in fiction. In fact, as Professor Trevelyan points out, she was locked up, beaten, and flung about the room. A very queer, composite being thus emerges. Imaginatively she is of the highest importance; practically she is completely insignificant. She pervades poetry from cover to cover; she is all but absent from history. . . . Some of the most inspired words, some of the most profound thoughts in literature fall from her lips; in real life she could hardly read, could hardly spell, and was the property of her husband. . . . It was certainly an odd monster that one made up by reading the historians first and the poets afterward—a worm winged like an eagle; the spirit of life and beauty in a kitchen chopping up suet. But these monsters, however amusing to the imagination, have no existence in fact. (pp. 45–46)

Women's actual status in society has varied tremendously across time and across cultures (Leavitt, 1971). However, the generalization that must be derived from any study of women through the ages is that women's status has usually been inferior to men's (Nielsen, 1978).

Leavitt (1971) argued that the key to understanding women's status anywhere is her degree of participation in the economy of the society, as well as her control over the products she produces. Every known society employs some type of sexual division of labor, but this segregation of tasks per se is not the cause of the inferior status of women. Rather, it is the *nature* of the division of labor by sex that affects the relative status of men and women and that influences their relationships within each society (Nielsen, 1978).

**Primitive Societies**    In early hunting and gathering societies in the Old Stone Age, and in the modern-day world where such societies still exist, women's status within the clan was roughly equal to men's (Leavitt, 1971). In primitive societies the division of labor by sex originated because of women's limited mobility due to child-bearing and -rearing responsibilities. Men ranged widely as hunters, whereas women's responsibilities included gathering vegetables and grains. Women, however, contributed equally to the subsistence of the clan; their contribution to the food supply was stable, and at least as important as men's. In fact, in some societies the clan depended primarily on the food gathered by women, with the meat provided by men being seen as a luxury (Martin & Voorhies, 1975).

With the domestication of animals and the agricultural advances in the New Stone Age, 10,000 to 12,000 years ago, came the beginnings of social changes that had a tremendous impact on women's status. Men are generally credited with the discovery of the domestication of animals, a development that evolved naturally from their earlier hunting activities (Deckard, 1983). Women's food-gathering activities also subsequently led to important cultural advances:

> It is generally accepted that owing to her ancient role as the gatherer of vegetable foods, woman was responsible for the invention and development of agriculture. Modern analogies indicate that so long as the ground was prepared by hoeing and not by ploughing women remained the cultivator. (Hawkes & Woolley, 1963, p. 265)

Women are also credited with the invention of pottery, weaving and the loom, and various tools related to their work activities, such as tools for grinding wheat (Deckard, 1983). Most early horticultural and herding societies maintained their dependence on vegetables and grains as their primary food source, and so women's status remained fairly high (Deckard, 1983).

In the clan societies of that time, women's status was probably the highest ever achieved. The existence of matrilineal clans, that is, communities in which kinship and descent were calculated through the women, were common in primitive agricultural societies (Deckard, 1983). More recent examples of this type of kinship system can be found among Native American tribes such as the Hopi (Leavitt, 1971).

Even in herding societies, where men's influence was greater and descent through the male line (i.e., patriliny) was typical, women were not necessarily demeaned or dominated in the ways they were later in history. Male dominance, or patriarchy, seems to have been stimulated by the increasing sexual division of labor and the decreasing importance of women's contribution to the economy of the community resulting from the invention of the plow (Leavitt, 1971). The plow changed agriculture from a female to a male occupation; women's hardest labor was ended, but women also lost control of the food supply; consequently their economic value diminished.

Increased agricultural productivity produced, for the first time in history, surpluses of food and thus wealth. These surpluses were then consolidated by individual chiefs who sought ways to transfer their wealth and authority to their descendants. In clan societies, especially matrilineal societies, children were community property and paternity was unimportant. With the accumulation of private as opposed to community property and the desire to preserve wealth through one's line came the tendency to regard women as property and the necessity of secluding women to ensure legitimate sons (Gough, 1975).

Not only women were treated as property. The development of private property and surplus wealth also produced slave societies (Deckard, 1983). As slaves provided more and more of the productive work, women's value to the economy declined further; both slave and free women were used for sexual pleasure.

**Ancient Greece and Rome**    In Athenian Greece, 80% of women were slaves, sometimes performing the hardest work in the fields but more often employed in the household; however, even the wives of the ruling class men were treated as property and had few rights (Childe, 1971). The golden era of Greek democracy applied only to the free male ruling class. Ruling-class women were secluded, prohibited from participating in the political system, required to have a legal guardian, usually father or husband, and could not obtain a divorce except under extreme circumstances (Childe, 1971).

The great Greek philosophers and writers held that women were inherently inferior and evil. The Pandora legend exemplifies the woman hatred (misogyny) that was widespread even among the intellectuals of ancient Greece. Aristotle, whose influence on religious and scientific thought, and on our culture generally, has been profound, felt that women were defective men. He classed women and children together, concluding that neither had a fully developed rationality; in his view, both women and children ought to be ruled by men (Schaffer, 1981). Women's status was slightly better within Roman culture; women were not excluded from political and social life, and their status was less obviously inferior (Hunter, 1976). However, women were still seen as the source of misery and suffering, and women's emancipation was viewed in Roman literature as a causal factor in the decline and fall of Rome (Hunter, 1976). These themes of women as inferior and woman as a source of evil and suffering appear throughout history in various forms.

**Medieval Societies**    In medieval times slavery was replaced by systems of serfdom. Serfs were slightly better off than the slaves of ancient times but were still bound to the land and their masters. Society was ordered into classes: king, greater nobility, lesser nobility, and the serfs, with women varying in status according to their husband's or father's place in society. Christian doctrine was a strong source of support for the views on the inferiority of women at this time. Christ himself demonstrated a high regard for women and nothing appeared in his original teachings denigrating women. But St. Paul was the major influence on the early and medieval church, and the Christian Church has historically held a low opinion of women as a result (Chafetz, 1978). "The head of the woman is the man . . . for a man is the image and glory of God. . . . I suffer not a woman to teach, nor to usurp authority over the man, but to be in silence." (St. Paul, quoted in Deckard, 1983, p. 197).

As in Ancient Greece, medieval women of the nobility had little freedom. Nunneries were one of the few places where women could get an education and find respite from men's oppression. Despite the glorification of the "weaker sex" within the medieval code of chivalry, female serfs worked as hard as their male counterparts.

In the late medieval period, some women of the growing middle class achieved a measure of independence as merchants and as weavers and spinners (thus the term "spinster" for older, unmarried women) (Deckard, 1983). As capitalistic economies evolved, upper-class women's lives improved, although they were still regarded as inferior to men. Women generally had a more significant role in feudal societies than indicated in most historical texts, even though they were legally subjugated. For example, female serfs played a leading role in peasant uprisings and rebellions, perhaps because of their double oppression. Rebellious peasants often met at night, and such night assemblies were claimed to be " 'witches' Sabbaths" because of women's roles in them. Both men and women were tortured and burned as witches, but women were persecuted in greater numbers and with more vigor; the terms *woman* and *witch* became virtually equivalent (Nelson, 1979). Women's so-called evil nature was a source of both hatred and fear by the male rulers and nobility. Women who refused to accept their subordinate status, or who obtained knowledge or power that was considered the domain of men (e.g., women who practiced the healing arts), were particularly vulnerable to charges of witchcraft and sorcery. Witch burnings were an effective means of social control (Nelson, 1979).

The Renaissance produced many advances in the status of upper-class women, including increased educational opportunities for women. Women of the lower classes did not fare as well. However, a considerable number of noblewomen of this time had a significant impact on history (e.g., Queen Isabella of Spain, Catherine de Medici, and Elizabeth I), and enlightened views on women were increasingly expressed. Thomas More, in *Utopia,* stated that women should receive an education equivalent to men's, although he added the caveat that some books are more appropriate to one sex than the other. The Protestant Reformation and the subsequent rise in religious bigotry cut short the progress stimulated by the Renaissance (Deckard, 1983).

**The Enlightenment**   The Age of Revolutions, generally regarded as a time when freedom and democracy began to flower in Western Europe and the United

States, was also a time of advances for women, but not because the major philosophers of the time advocated that equality be extended to women. In fact, most liberal philosophers still held reactionary positions on women. Rousseau, one of the French Enlightenment's most important theorists said:

> Nature herself has decreed that woman, both for herself and her children, should be at the mercy of man's judgement. . . . When the Greek women married, they disappeared from public life; within the four walls of their home they devoted themselves to the care of their household and family. This is the mode of life pre-scribed for women alike by nature and reason. (Rousseau, quoted in Hunter College Women's Studies Collective, 1983, p. 71)

"Liberty, equality, and brotherhood" meant just that—liberty and equality for men, usually only property-owning men.

The Enlightenment did stimulate the writings of the first feminist philoso-phers. In 1792 Mary Wollstonecraft, in *A Vindication of the Rights of Woman,* spoke out against the oppression of women and argued for equal educational op-portunities for upper-class, middle-class, and working-class women:

> Men, indeed, appear to me to act in a very unphilosophical manner when they try to secure the good conduct of women by attempting to keep them always in a state of childhood. . . . It is a farce to call any being virtuous whose virtues do not result from the exercise if its own reason. This was Rousseau's opinion re-specting men: I extend it to women. (Quoted in Hunter College Women's Stud-ies Collective, 1983, p. 71)

One of the few male liberal philosophers who spoke out in support of the equality of women was John Stuart Mill. Mill and his wife, Harriet Taylor, col-laborated on many works, including *On the Subjection of Women.* Mill argued that women were not innately inferior and ascribed women's inferior social sta-tus to environmental factors such as lack of educational opportunities.

The industrial era of the 19th and 20th centuries was again a time of advances for women. The women's movement in the United States arose out of the aboli-tionist movement, and the histories of both civil rights campaigns have been in-terconnected to the present day (Davis, 1981; Kessler-Harris, 2001).

**Women in America**   Prior to the first women's movement, women in the United States had few rights; many women came to the United States as indentured slaves. White women were sold from London prisons or kidnapped from the streets; Black women were kidnapped from Africa (Deckard, 1983). Married women did not "exist" legally apart from their husbands; they could not testify in court, their property belonged to their husband, and they did not even have a right to their own children. In frontier settlements in early America, women enjoyed the rough "equality" borne of economic and social necessity:

> Women were just as indispensable as men, since a household which lacked their homemaking skills, as well as nursing, sharpshooting and hunting when needed, was not to be envied. As colonial society became more complex this tradition be-came obscured, but its roots remained in American life and thinking; as the frontier

moved westward in a changing world, the idea that women were the equals of men traveled with it, with far-reaching results. (Flexner & Fitzpatrick, 1996, pp. 8–9).

Indeed, the western states have always been at the forefront of the fight for women's equality, with Wyoming the first state to give women the right to vote in 1869 (Flexner & Fitzpatrick, 1996).

Black female slaves in the southern states held a position very similar to the slaves in Athenian Greece; the same analogy could be extended to their White mistresses and the ruling-class women in Greece. The latter's status was higher but still subordinate to men. The paradox between the antebellum South's notions of chivalry and its beliefs about women's nature, the treatment of Black women in slavery, and the disadvantagement of free Black women and poor and working-class White women is captured in Sojourner Truth's famous statement. At a women's rights meeting in Ohio in 1851, a male clergy member ridiculed the demand for women's right to vote by arguing that women were weak, dependent, and helpless. Sojourner Truth responded:

> The man over there says women need to be helped into carriages and lifted over ditches, and to have the best place everywhere. Nobody ever helps me into carriages or over puddles, or gives me the best place—and ain't I a woman? Look at my arm! I have plowed and planted and gathered into barns and no man could lead me—and ain't I a woman? I could work as much and eat as much as a man—when I could get it—and bear the lash as well! And ain't I a woman? I have borne 13 children, and seen most of 'em sold into slavery, and when I cried out with my mother's grief, none but Jesus heard me—and ain't I a woman? (Quoted in Flexner & Fitzpatrick, 1996, p. 85).

The first Women's Rights Conference was held at Seneca Falls, New York, in 1848. The catalyst for this action was the refusal of male abolitionists to seat female delegates at the World Anti-Slavery Convention in London in 1840 (Flexner & Fitzpatrick, 1996). Although much disagreement arose over whether women should demand the right to vote (it was seen as too radical by many), the conference delegates did unanimously agree to use every means possible to end discrimination against women (Flexner & Fitzpatrick, 1996).

By the 1860s women had made progress in certain areas, such as securing the right to control the wages they earned. Progress in education and work came more slowly, and the right to vote for women was not won in the United States until the 19th Amendment became law in 1920 after decades of work and continuing frustration. Prior to the passage of the 19th Amendment, suffragists in the United States adopted some of the militant techniques of the British suffragists (Flexner & Fitzpatrick, 1996). The Equal Rights Amendment was originally brought before Congress in 1923 and then reintroduced every year until it passed in 1972, only to go down to defeat in 1982 (Deckard, 1983; Flexner & Fitzgerald, 1996; Kessler-Harris, 2001).

Despite the advances made by women in the 20th century in terms of their social roles, legal rights, and access to the political process, inequities persisted. The extreme disparity between what has been called the "happy housewife" myth and the reality of women's lives in the 1950s gave rise to the second women's movement (Amundsen, 1971). Betty Friedan, in her classic *The Feminine Mystique* (1963), gave voice to the dissatisfaction felt by many middle-class American women that reflected the gap between social ideology and social reality.

Dramatic legal progress was not obtained for women until the 1960s and 1970s. The Equal Pay Act of 1963, first introduced in 1945, required that women be paid at the same rate as men, but it did nothing to make job discrimination illegal (Kessler-Harris, 2001). Title VII of the comprehensive Civil Rights Bill of 1964 went much further and finally gave women legal recourse for discriminatory practices (Bird, 1971; Kessler-Harris, 2001). Even though the sex discrimination section of this bill was introduced as a way to kill the bill (opponents of civil rights for minorities assumed that the inclusion of women would cause the bill to be laughed off the floor), Title VII has had far-reaching effects (Kessler-Harris, 2001). Other legal "victories" for women's rights included the 1967 Executive Order 11246, prohibiting sex discrimination in employment by federal contractors, and the passage of Title IX in 1972, prohibiting sex discrimination in educational institutions (Kessler-Harris, 2001).

## Psychology's Treatment of Women

The academic discipline of psychology was slow to attend seriously to female psychology and women's experiences, and the psychological literature was so full of blatant sexism that, in 1971, Naomi Weisstein was prompted to write: "Psychology has nothing to say about what women are really like, what they need and what they want, essentially because psychology does not know" (p. 209). Weisstein's central thesis, indicated by the title of her article "Psychology Constructs the Female, or the Fantasy Life of the Male Psychologist" was that, due to the androcentric (i.e., male-centered) bias in the field, psychological research and theory had little connection to women's reality. Since that call to arms over 30 years ago much has changed, as evidenced by the voluminous research on the psychology of women. Nevertheless, many problems, subtle and not so subtle, remain, and counselors and psychologists must still be cognizant of the detrimental and ongoing effects of sexism on women (Enns, 1997, 2000).

At the dawn of the discipline, usually traced to the late 1870s, psychologists were concerned with establishing a "scientific" field of study of the individual. The "woman question" was regarded as a social issue and therefore outside the purview of the nascent field (Shields, 1975).

> The business of psychology was the description of the "generalized adult mind," and it is not at all clear whether "adult" was meant to include both sexes. When the students of German psychology did venture outside of the laboratory, however, there is no evidence that they were sympathetic to those defending the equality of male and female ability. (Shields, 1975, p. 739)

**The Search for Sex Differences** Although German psychology under Wundt chose to ignore women, the functionalist movement in the United States in the late 19th and early 20th centuries stimulated a great deal of research on sex differences in human functioning. Functionalists, heavily influenced by evolutionary theory, sought mainly to establish the superiority of White males; their attention was focused primarily on racial differences that supported White supremacy, but investigations of sex differences aimed at proving the subordinate role of women were a natural by-product of such thinking (Shields, 1975).

Researchers in the functionalist tradition first began to search for the "proof" of women's inferiority by examining sex differences in cranial capacity (Gould, 1996). Women's heads are on the average smaller than men's, and this was originally thought to be the physiological mechanism of women's diminished capacity (Shields, 1975). Broca, an early researcher on brain functioning and cranial capacity, said:

> In general, the brain is larger in mature adults than in the elderly, in men than in women, in eminent men than in men of mediocre talent, in superior races than in inferior races. . . . Other things being equal, there is a remarkable relationship between the development of intelligence and the volume of the brain. (Broca, 1861; quoted in Gould 1996, p. 115)

This avenue of research came to a dead end after several grand and notable failures. When adjusted for size of the body, women's brains were found to be *larger* than men's; no clear relationship could be established between achievement in life and cranial capacity after death; and repeatedly, the brains of highly eminent men (e.g., Walt Whitman and Anatole France) were found to be embarrassingly small (Gould, 1996).

Research on sex differences then proceeded through comparative examinations of whatever aspect of brain organization, structure, or functioning might provide the elusive evidence for the widely held assumption of female intellectual inferiority. The legacy of this androcentric, biased approach to the scientific study of women is with us today, manifested in studies of sex differences in cerebral dominance and laterality (Unger, 1979).

Functionalist psychologists also focused their attention on the purported biological mechanisms of sex differences in temperament, including the presumed biological complementarity of the sexes and the effects of "maternal instinct" on women's "nature." As to the former, men were seen as having different metabolisms than women, resulting in two different and complementary natures:

> The feminine passivity is expressed in greater patience, more open-mindedness, greater appreciation of subtle details, and consequently what we call more rapid intuition. The masculine activity lends a greater power of maximum effort, of scientific insight, or cerebral experiment with impressions, and is associated with an unobservant or impatient disregard to minute details, but with a more stronger [*sic*] grasp of generalities. (Geddes & Thomson, 1890, quoted in Shields, 1975, p. 746)

Functionalists' presuppositions about sex differences, though disproved repeatedly, continued to influence eminent psychological researchers, as did the concept of maternal instinct, an assumption strongly held in American society and predating the advent of formal psychology (Shields, 1975). In essence it was believed that "women's emotional nature (including her tendency to nurturance) was a direct consequence of her reproductive physiology" (Shields, 1975, p. 749).

This maternal tendency was seen as a significant detriment to women's development. The long-standing impact of these sexist and unproven assumptions are illustrated in the comments made by Bruno Bettelheim, over 100 years after the ideas had first been introduced: "as much as women want to be good scientists or engineers, they want first and foremost to be womanly companions of men and to be mothers" (1965, p. 15).

There were some oppositional voices "crying in the wilderness." In 1910, Helen Thompson Wooley characterized the extant research on sex differences as "logic martyred in the cause of supporting a prejudice, unfounded assertions, and even sentimental rot and drivel" (quoted in Shields, 1975, p. 739). Leta S. Hollingworth effectively dismantled the period's carefully constructed arguments on the intellectual inferiority of women in an article entitled "Social Devices for Impelling Women to Bear and Rear Children" (cited in Sherif, 1979). Nevertheless, the dominant sexist attitudes persisted within psychology.

The early functionalist influence on psychology, and the consequent search for the biological mechanisms of sex differences, was eventually supplanted by the behaviorist tradition in this country in the 1930s. Behaviorists, searching for the universal laws governing behavior, were not concerned with sex differences, and so there came a hiatus in the study of female psychology in the United States (Shields, 1975). However, psychoanalytic theory was in ascendance in Europe, and eventually Freudian theory dominated the study of women.

**Freud and His Followers**   Although some of Freud's most famous clients were women, he was far less certain about female than about male developmental processes. His theory of girls' development was presented fully 20 years after his more famous exposition of the Oedipal theory for boys; his writings on women reflect a trend common in psychological writings even today; that is, extending men's experiences to women's (Hare-Mustin, 1983; Schaffer, 1981). Psychoanalytic theory rests squarely on the dictum "anatomy is destiny" (for women but not men) and corresponding assumptions about the biological inferiority of women. Thus Freud, despite having written only three articles on women, has had a significant and negative impact on both past and contemporary psychological views of women (Rohrbaugh, 1979).

Freud's central thesis was that girls, lacking a penis, are never as motivated as boys by castration anxiety to resolve the central developmental dilemma of the Oedipal complex. Girls therefore tend to be more susceptible to psychological disturbances, as well as to lag behind boys developmentally (Rohrbaugh, 1979). On the consequences of these developmental differences, Freud had this to say in 1925:

> I cannot escape the notion (though I hesitate to give it expression) that for women the level of what is ethically normal is different from what it is in men. Their super-ego is never so inexorable, so impersonal, so independent of its emotional origins as we require it to be in men. (Quoted in Rohrbaugh, 1979, p. 87)

In other words, women generally fail to develop a strong superego, or conscience. Further, women are seen as developing various personality characteristics as a result of their differential development, penis envy in particular and also narcissism, vanity, jealousy, passivity, and masochism (Schaffer, 1981). Margaret Mead (1974) summarized one perspective on Freud when she commented that it was a pity that Freud, although contributing so much to psychology, understood so little about women.

Among Freud's followers were many critics: Helene Deutsch, Karen Horney, Alfred Adler, Clara Thompson, and Carl Jung all disagreed with various aspects of Freud's views on women (Schaffer, 1981). Adler, for example, posited that society requires men to assume positions of unnatural dominance over women. Karen Horney wrote extensively about the social and cultural biases in Freud's thinking and explicitly rejected the psychoanalytic notion of women as masochistic (Schaffer, 1981). In critiquing Freud, Horney also stressed his tendency to look at women from an exclusively male perspective; "like all sciences and all valuations, the psychology of women has hitherto been considered only from the point of view of men" (1926; quoted in Rohrbaugh, 1979, p. 108).

Such critiques of androcentric bias did not prevent later theorists, most notably Erik Erikson, from making the same mistakes. Erikson's (1968) schema outlining stages of identity development was developed out of boys' and men's experiences. The theory was later expanded to account for women's development, but women received attention primarily in terms of their perceived deviance from the male model of development (Erikson, 1968). Erikson hypothesized that a women's identity becomes clear only after her decision about a marriage partner; he saw a woman's role as a mother as crucial to her development of an identity. Moreover, women were seen as becoming neurotic and feeling deprived, lonely, and unfulfilled unless their "inner space" (i.e., womb) was filled (via motherhood) (Rohrbaugh, 1979).

**Bias in Psychology** Psychodynamic theory and its offshoots are not the only culprits behind the bias against women in psychology. Every research area within the field can be exposed in similar ways. One further example will suffice as an illustration of this "masculine bias" in scientific psychology. In research on achievement motivation, elaborate theories evolved detailing the factors predictive of educational and vocational success (Atkinson & Feather, 1966; McClelland, Atkinson, Clark, & Lowell, 1953). These theories, as with many other theories in different domains, have been presented as equally applicable to men and women. Yet studies on achievement motivation consistently yielded different results for women than men, and women's responses in such studies were not congruent with the hypothesized theories of achievement motivation (Rohrbaugh, 1979). Only upon careful reading of this literature can the reader determine the truth. The data on women were so confusing that they were consequently largely ignored by the major theorists and researchers.

Thus we can identify four main themes characterizing psychology's historical treatment of women: (1) neglect of female psychology entirely; (2) blatant sexism, including searches for the presumed mechanisms of women's inferiority; (3) ignorance of women's unique experiences and the consequent unthinking extension of theories of male functioning and development to women; and (4) feminist analyses geared toward understanding women's personality patterns, behavior, and male-female relationships in social context. The latter theme, as we will see in the next section, is unfortunately still not in ascendance in mainstream psychology, despite the recent explosion of research and writing by feminist psychologists (Brown, 1994; Enns, 2000; Worell & Remer, 2003).

## CURRENT DISCRIMINATION

"Americans are condescendingly sure that women in this country are much better off than women anywhere else" (Hewlett, 1986, p. 139). Despite being written almost 20 years ago, this statement probably still best captures mainstream opinion in the United States today. It is *assumed* that women have achieved equality; women now have only to sort out the problems and responsibilities that have come with that success. Some writers even referred to a "post-feminist era" beginning in the late 1980s and early 1990s (Faludi, 1991); nothing more need be done to advance women's rights. Unfortunately the reality in the new century is far different from long-held and common beliefs.

After the significant and far-reaching legal and social advances of the liberal 1960s and 1970s, women in the United States entered a regressive era in the 1980s and early 1990s. Conservative political groups became increasingly powerful politically, and some of the major goals of such groups were and are strongly antifeminist (Faludi, 1991). As a result of changes in the political climate, many of the advances in women's rights and civil rights programs were stalled or even reversed. For example, conservative forces successfully fought against the ratification of the Equal Rights Amendment (Kessler-Harris, 2001). Some conservative groups also opposed affirmative action, sex education, and interference with the family in the form of programs combating child abuse, battered women's shelters, and funding for child care programs—all issues intimately related to women's social status (Faludi, 1991). Republican administrations in the 1980s consistently opposed most women's rights issues. The Equal Employment Opportunity Commission (EEOC), the agency responsible for enforcing anti-sex-discrimination laws, was all but dismantled (Faludi, 1991), and Presidents Reagan and George H. Bush had poor records of appointing women to influential offices, despite some high-level and highly visible appointments of women, such as Reagan's appointment of the first female Supreme Court Justice. President Reagan, in particular, had a record of appointing antifeminists when his appointments were female (Deckard, 1983). Although the Clinton administration reversed this trend and was strongly committed to women's issues, the problems and setbacks of the 1980s require substantial and enduring redress. The following section documents the continuing problems faced by American women, despite the real and significant social advances that have been made in the latter half of the 20th century.

### Social Inequality

As we have seen, attitudes toward women and women's relative status within a given society fluctuate in response to social and economic trends. The 1970s were a time when it became less socially acceptable to espouse the sexist notion of women's inherent biological inferiority; yet at the beginning of a new century, at least in some sectors of society, sexist attitudes and behaviors remain strong; and, in some places, sexism is still actively promoted.

More commonly, people ascribe to the "different but equal" view. That is, women and men are social equals but have different roles, both equally valuable (Unger, 2001). On the surface this belief (and there are many variations of the theme) appears to be egalitarian. Upon closer inspection, another variant of sexist ideology is revealed. Women's special place and special roles invariably turn out to be inferior and devalued. For example, occupational segregation by sex is commonly justified on the basis of women's and men's different strengths or as a result of the "choices" made by women; yet feminine characteristics are often reframed to encourage women to participate in low-paid drudge work or to discourage women from pursuing advancement and attainment within occupations (Fassinger, 2000). In American society feminine characteristics lead women "naturally" to the "women's jobs" of beautician, secretary, child care worker, and waitress, and away from such "masculine work" as physician. Conversely in Russia, feminine characteristics lead women "naturally" to predominate in the medical specialty of general practitioner (women account for 74% of all physicians in Russia), a relatively low-paid, low-status area of medicine, while masculine characteristics lead Russian men naturally to the higher-status specialties. In the United States, women remain underrepresented in the physical sciences.

> Cross-cultural evidence supports the view that the dearth of women in science is due to culture, not biology. In the United States, 15% of B.S. degrees go to women. Among tenure track faculty in physics, women are only about 3%. In contrast, in France 21% of Ph.D.s in physics go to women and 23% of university faculty in physics are women. In Italy, the figures are identical to those in France: 21% and 23%. Even in Turkey, 23% of physics faculty members are women. Cross-culturally, the percentage does not approach an equitable 50% except in Hungary, where 47% of physics faculty in universities are women. (Hyde, 1997, p. 286).

We discuss occupational segregation in greater depth in the next section of this chapter; for now, it is important to note how social ideologies in the form of "women are not inferior, but . . ." are sexist at the core and serve to promote and maintain women's inferior status (Deckard, 1983; Gilbert & Sher, 1999).

The ongoing subtle and often not-so-subtle sexism that prevails in American culture manifests itself in many forms; "power differences permeate society and those power differences are detrimental to the mental and physical health of women and girls" (chapter 12, this text). Research has repeatedly demonstrated that even very young children have already acquired stereotypical views of masculine and feminine characteristics and of the occupational choices open to each gender (Enns, 2000; Gilbert & Sher, 1999). Overall, some loosening in traditional gender-role stereotypes has been observed, but we are still far from equality.

Attitudes toward women's roles, especially work roles, have been changing markedly (Worell & Remer, 2003), but certain other fundamental assumptions remain largely unchanged. We see in the next section how traditional assumptions about women's gender roles and responsibilities in the family continue to interact complexly with changing expectations for women, producing new problems for women, men, and society.

## Economic Disadvantagement

A major cause of the economic disadvantages for women is the differential pay they receive for similar work. Although women accounted for 46% of the labor force in 1998, American women earn, on the average, 76 cents on the dollar compared with men (Costello & Stone, 2001). "Even in traditionally female occupations where women outnumber, women still earn less than men" (U.S. Women's Bureau, 1996, p. 3). The wage disparity is even more severe for racial/ethnic minority women and women who are disadvantaged in other ways, such as the physically disabled (Faludi, 1991). "Earnings also vary by race and ethnicity, with white workers earning more, on average, than either Black or Hispanic workers regardless of gender" (Herz & Wootton, 1996, p. 67). For example, in 1998 African American women were earning 85.5% of what African American men earned, 86% of what White women earned, and 66% of what White men on the average earned (Costello & Stone, 2001). In that same year, Hispanic women were earning 56 cents on the dollar compared with men and 72% of what non-Hispanic women earned (Costello & Stone, 2001). Even college-educated women are not doing well; they continue to earn less than college-educated men (Costello & Stone, 2001).

Nevertheless,

> as of 1998, the typical working woman was earning more than ever before and her earnings were making an important difference to family income. . . . Compared with women workers of earlier generations, today's women have more to gain by continuing to work and more to lose by dropping out. (Costello & Stone, 2001, p. 225)

Between 1978 and 1998 the earnings gap between men and women narrowed considerably (15 percentage points). Conversely, although there has been some improvement in women's real earnings, this narrowing of the gender gap had more to do with men's real wages declining than with dramatic improvements in women's circumstances (Costello & Stone, 2001; Herz & Wootton, 1996).

What are the reasons for the continuing disparity in earnings? The explanation invoked most often historically has been that women work for *pin money* (the term refers to extra pocket money for trinkets, e.g., pins, rather than earnings necessary for survival) and are not seriously attached to the workforce (Farmer & Backer, 1977). In fact, most women work out of economic need, because they are single, divorced, or widowed, or if married because their earnings are required by the family for subsistence (Hewlett, 1986; U.S. Women's Bureau, 1996). Other explanations for the gender gap in earnings include the assumption that women freely choose to work in occupations that pay less, or that women simply are not as good as men. These explanations are inadequate to explain profound and long-standing earnings disparities by gender and ethnicity. Ongoing discrimination, even though illegal, continues; but the reasons for the wage gap are complex and extend beyond overt discrimination and simplistic and sexist views of women in the workforce, to include inadequate maternity benefits and child care, occupational segregation by sex, and devaluation of women's work as well as outright pay inequities.

**Maternity and Child Care Support**    One of the most significant social changes in the 20th century was the increasing entry of married women and mothers into the paid labor force (Costello & Stone, 2001; U.S. Women's Bureau, 1996). Currently, nearly 70% of all women are in the labor force, and women comprise 46% of all American workers (Costello & Stone, 2001). Over 78% of mothers with children under the age of 18 and 62% of women with children under 3 work outside the home (Costello & Stone, 2001). The overwhelming majority (nearly 95%) of all women will participate in the workforce at some time in their lives (Betz, 1994). Cultural variables complicate the picture as women of color participate at different rates than do White women; for example, African American women are more likely and Hispanic women are less likely to be in the paid workforce (Costello & Stone, 2001).

The failure of our society to provide adequate and affordable child care has been a significant drawback for working women and a formidable barrier to mothers of young children, often blocking participation in the paid labor force completely. High-quality private child care is very costly and can easily consume a substantial part of a working mother's earnings. Many single or divorced mothers of young children are virtually forced to go on welfare in order to survive, even when they would rather be working (Costello & Stone, 2001). Employed married women with children experience a double burden, working their paid job and also working as caretaker of their spouse, children, and home.

Our country has an extremely poor record on the issues of maternity and child care:

> The United States is the only industrialized country that has no statutory maternity leave. One hundred and seventeen countries (including every industrialized nation and many developing countries) guarantee a woman the following rights: leave from employment for childbirth, job protection while she is on leave, and the provision of a cash benefit, to replace all or most of her earnings. (Hewlett, 1986, p. 96)

Further, despite lip service given to Americans' priority on the family, all efforts at developing government programs for child care have failed. In 1971, President Nixon vetoed the Comprehensive Child Care Act, and subsequent administrations were unsupportive or even hostile toward any child care programs (Faludi, 1991). Some businesses and major corporations have been experimenting with work/life programs, such as flextime, parental leaves for fathers as well as pregnancy leaves for mothers, and child care programs for employees, but these efforts are not yet widespread despite the scope of the problem and findings that indicate these programs benefit employers as well as employees (Costello & Stone, 2001; Hewlett, 2002).

In stark contrast, most European countries provide subsidized child care, child allowances, and other sources of support for women and their families, with consequent beneficial effects on women's economic status (Hewlett, 1986):

> It is also no coincidence that the country with the most developed benefits and services for working women—Sweden—is also the country with the smallest wage gap, while the country with the least developed benefits and services—the United States—is also the country with one of the largest wage gaps. (p. 99)

The consequence of this scarcity in support services is that women must bear the full burden of their double duty as worker and mother, and this double burden is then reflected in their earnings and accomplishments (Hewlett, 1986, 2002). Women are forced to go on welfare, take part-time instead of full-time work, and lose wages due to maternity or child care responsibilities, drastically lowering their earnings and future earning power.

**Occupational Segregation and Comparable Worth**    Although lack of adequate child care services is certainly one factor in the wage gap, occupational segregation by sex is clearly a more significant contributor (Hewlett, 2002). In 1991 Faludi argued that occupational segregation by sex accounted for at least 45% of the wage gap; this remains an accurate estimate today. The extent of occupational segregation by sex was dramatic in the past; up through the mid-1980s, the majority of employed women were clustered into only 20 occupational areas (Faludi, 1991; Hewlett, 1986, 2002). Despite significant shifts in the gender composition of the entire range of occupations, in the 1990s "women and men still tend to be concentrated in different occupations; women are highly overrepresented in clerical, sales, and services occupations, for example, while men are disproportionately employed in craft and laborer jobs" (Herz & Wootton, 1996, p. 56). As the percentage of women in the total workforce grew in the 1990s and early 21st century, "the proportion of women workers holding managerial and professional jobs rose. . . . [although] black and Hispanic women are less well represented than white women in professional and managerial occupations" (Costello & Stone, 2001, p. 226).

We have already seen in the historical overview that job segregation by sex is common to almost all societies, but we have also seen that such segregation need not necessarily lead to gender inequality in society. The current sex segregation in our economy, coupled with the denigration of "women's work," is both a consequence and continuing cause of the social and economic disadvantagement of women. Traditionally female jobs, that is, jobs where the majority of workers are women, are almost always lower paying and lower status occupational pursuits. Howe (1977) employed the term *pink collar* to characterize the dead-end, low-status nature of such women's jobs as beautician, waitress, and secretary. In 1980, 97.6% of all secretaries were women; in 1983 women comprised 70% of all retail and personal sales workers and 80% of all administrative support workers (Kahn-Hut, Daniels, & Colvard, 1982). In 1998, more than a quarter of employed women but only 6% of employed men worked in sales and administrative support jobs. Administrative support, sales, and service categories accounted for twice the share of employed women as employed men (58% vs. 30%) (Costello & Stone, 2001).

In some occupations extreme segregation by gender continues. Women continue to be overrepresented in traditional female professions; for example, in 1998, 84% of elementary school teachers were women. In contrast, less than 2% of women in the workforce work in precision, craft, and repair jobs, whereas almost 20% of men work in these generally higher paying areas (Costello & Stone, 2001). In 1994, only 10% of engineers, 7% of construction inspectors, 2% of electricians, and 1% of carpenters were female (Herz & Wootton, 1996).

Even where women appear to be making significant inroads, the realities are discrepant with widely held perceptions. Despite dramatic increases in their absolute numbers in management positions in business and industry, White women and women and men of color have faced serious obstacles to advancement within the ranks of management (Costello & Stone, 2001; Morrison & Glinow, 1990). Overall, women constitute approximately 40% of all management positions (including entry-level and middle management) but are only 12% of corporate officers, 3% of the top earners of Fortune 500 companies, and less than one-tenth of 1% of CEOs of Fortune 500 companies (Costello & Stone, 2001). The "glass ceiling" in management, "a concept popularized in the 1980s to describe a barrier so subtle that it is transparent, yet so strong that it prevents women and minorities from moving up the management ladder" (Morrison & Glinow, 1990, p. 200) remains intact in the 21st century.

Further compounding women's economic status is that the legal mandate of "equal pay for equal work," even if it were being enforced, would not resolve the economic problems encountered by women. In 1980, registered nurses with over 14 years of education earned less than deliverymen; secretaries with 13+ years of education and comparably higher level job responsibilities earned less than truck drivers with an average of a ninth-grade education (Kahn-Hut, Daniels, & Colvard, 1982); these types of inequities persist today. The concept of equal pay for *comparable* work was introduced as an attempt to resolve some of these discrepancies (Kessler-Harris, 2001). Comparable work proponents advocated assessing the skills, education, and responsibilities required in various jobs and adjusting pay scales to reflect equal pay for work of comparable worth or social value but made little progress in implementing this concept (Kessler-Harris, 2001).

**Wage Discrimination**   Wage discrimination persists within fields as well; as indicated previously, women consistently earn less than men for the same work. In 1998, the median salary for men was $31,096 and the median salary for women was $24,180 (Costello & Stone, 2001). These wage differences are reflected in virtually all vocational areas, at all levels, but the size of the gap varies by occupational category; for example, women in managerial and professional specialties earn 72% of what men earn, women in precision production occupations earn 64% of what men in those occupations earn, and women in sales occupations earn only 60% of what men in sales earn. In addition to being paid less than men for the same jobs, women also tend to be clustered in the lower levels of even tradi-

tionally female occupations; for example, although women predominate in elementary school teaching positions, the majority of school administrators are
male, and men earn more than women even in female-dominated occupations
(Costello & Stone, 2001).

Women are now receiving the majority of bachelor's and master's degrees,
but, despite clear progress, significant gender differences persist in a number of
fields (Costello & Stone, 2001). For example, as of 1996, 27.5% of degrees in
computer and information sciences, 16% of degrees in engineering, and 36% of
degrees in the physical sciences were awarded to women (Costello & Stone,
2001). The most rapid progress has been made in areas traditional for women,
whereas progress in highly nontraditional majors and career areas, although
marked, is still fairly slow. Further, women receive only 5% of the engineering
doctorates, and although the wage gap between women and men is smaller in the
scientific/technological fields than in other vocational areas, women engineers
still earn less than men at comparable levels (Costello & Stone, 2001). Again,
racial/ethnic minority women and women with a disability experience a multiplicative burden of disadvantagement; the wage gap and unemployment figures
for these groups in scientific/technical career areas is worse than for White
women (Costello & Stone, 2001).

Statistics on female academics demonstrate the same pattern of wage discrimination and occupational segregation. Although the majority of instructors in
institutions of higher education are women, most of these women are "ghet-
toized" in a limited number of fields and in unstable, lower paying positions, a
situation that has not changed for years. Only 33% of full-time faculty overall are
women (14% of the faculty were women of color, up from 11% in 1972), and in
1998, 19% of the full professors were women (Costello & Stone, 2001). At every
level and in all fields women earn less than their male counterparts and are less
likely to be tenured. Female academic administrators are most likely to be concentrated in traditionally female areas such as education and nursing; female administrators in nonacademic areas are likewise concentrated in female-dominated
areas such as student affairs (Costello & Stone, 2001). Women are also likely, for
complex and varied reasons, to take longer to be promoted to associate and to full
professor than their male counterparts. Conversely, 45% of all leadership positions in higher education are held by women (although only 7% by women of
color), and 16% of university presidents are women.

**Economic Consequences of Unequal Treatment**   An alarming development in
the late 20th century, an upshot of the wage gap and discriminatory practices, has
been termed *the feminization of poverty* (Pearce, 1979). This term refers to the increasing percentage of women living below the poverty level due to their disadvantaged economic status. When women combine their relatively lower earnings
with a man's higher earnings, as in a marriage, their economic situation is
markedly better than when they must survive independently. When women are
the sole supporters of dependents, especially children, their economic situation is
precarious. The major factors in this dramatic rise in the number of female-
headed households subsisting below poverty level are occupational segregation

and the wage gap. In 1994, over 34% of all families with female heads of the household were below the poverty level (U.S. Women's Bureau, 1996). For women of color, the statistics are even more alarming; for example, nearly half of families headed by Hispanic women are below the poverty level (U.S. Women's Bureau, 1996).

In addition to women's economic circumstances, changes in the divorce laws in the late 20th century also contributed to the problem (Weitzman, 1985). The discrepancies in economic status of divorced men and divorced women (heavily in favor of men) result in negative social, interpersonal, and personal consequences and unsettling economic repercussions:

> When the downward change in the family standard of living followed the divorce and the discrepancy between the father's standard of living and that of the mother and children was striking, this discrepancy was often central to the life of the family and remained as a festering source of anger and bitter preoccupation. (Wallerstein & Kelly, 1980, p. 231, quoted in Weitzman, 1985, p. 353)

**Gender-Role Stereotyping**    The point of this discussion thus far has been to highlight the continuing effects of past discrimination on women's social and economic status and to emphasize that women have not yet attained equality in employment. But, as previously discussed, the present state of affairs is not entirely due to overt sex discrimination; it takes many years for increases in female graduates pursuing traditionally male careers to make an impact in the job market. Further, discrimination does not have to exist overtly to produce a situation where many women are still underutilizing their talents and abilities in career pursuits. As we have seen, there has been some loosening of the traditional gender-role stereotypes, and more female models in a wider range of occupational roles exist, but boys and girls continue to be trained in different ways (Worell & Remer, 2003). Although written long ago, Bem and Bem's (1970/1984) aptly articulated statement on the general issue remains compelling:

> Even if all discrimination were to end tomorrow, nothing very drastic would change. For job discrimination is only part of the problem . . . it does not, by itself, help us to understand why so many women "choose" to be secretaries or nurses rather than executives or physicians. Discrimination frustrates choices already made. Something more pernicious perverts the motivation to choose. That "something" is an unconscious ideology about the nature of the female sex, an ideology which constricts the emerging self-image of the female child and the nature of her aspirations from the very beginning; an ideology which leads even those Americans who agree that a black skin should not uniquely qualify *its* owner for a janitorial or domestic service to act as if possession of a uterus uniquely qualifies *its* owner for precisely such service. (p. 12)

It is important to note, however, that because race/ethnicity and gender interact in fairly complex ways, women of color experience sexism in its many forms very differently than White women (see chapter 14, this text). For a woman of color, "belonging to two groups whose positions are determined by oppression, her experience differs from that of her fellow victims, the man of color and the White woman, because her reality involves the dynamics of both racism and sexism" (Comas-Diaz & Greene, 1994, p. xi). "Women of color are not only exposed to oppression within the dominant group, but also experience sexism and oppression within their own ethnic and racial communities as well" (Comas-Diaz & Greene, 1994, p. 5).

Even when women of any racial/ethnic background are able to surmount their cultural gender-role conditioning to enter challenging and demanding educational programs, they are still in need of additional support and encouragement. Freeman (1979) identified the "Null Environment" as a major problem for women in academic and vocational pursuits. In academic situations when *neither* men nor women are actively encouraged or discouraged, women and minorities are inherently discriminated against because of the differential socialization and external environments experienced by women and men. Freeman (1979) felt that women enter higher education with a "handicap" that a "null" academic environment does nothing to minimize or decrease, resulting in the inadvertent discouragement of women because of lack of *encouragement.* Thus educators, and by extension counselors, may discriminate against women "without really trying." Women need active encouragement, not simply the absence of discrimination, to surmount the barriers posed by traditional feminine gender-role socialization.

## Victimization

One of the most damaging manifestations of sexism in any society is the physical, sexual, and emotional abuse of women that results from virulent misogynist attitudes intertwined with women's relative powerlessness. The long-term emotional, interpersonal, and social costs of violence against women are considerable. Sexual assault is a constant (and statistically real) fear for most American women, regardless of age, physical attractiveness, race, or class (Worrell & Remer, 2003). Some groups of women within society are more vulnerable to assault than others, but no woman is "safe." Rape, sexual harassment, childhood sexual abuse, and other forms of violence against women have little to do with sexuality; sexual assault is motivated by domination and power.

Current statistics indicate the widespread nature of the problem: Estimates of the probability of a woman being raped in her lifetime range from 14% to 25%, and a high number of women seeking mental health care have experienced some type of physical or sexual abuse (Koss, 1993); 1 in 2 women will be physically battered by her spouse or significant other; conservatively, 25% of women experience some form of sexual harassment on the job—the figures are much higher for women in highly nontraditional occupations; and 10–30% of women are survivors of child sexual abuse, the perpetrator usually being male and someone close to the child (Courtois, 1986; Enns, 2000; Fitzgerald, 1993; Muehlenhard, Highby, Phelps, & Sympson, 1997). Countless other women have suffered emotional abuse, often for years. Because crimes of violence against women are grossly underreported, these statistics may very well be on the low side. Although rape crisis centers, battered women's shelters, and support services for survivors of incest and child sexual abuse have done much to serve survivors of violence and inform the public, the root of the problem remains (Worrell & Remer, 2003).

The social myths that exist about the seven types of violence against women (i.e., battering, rape, girl-child incest, pornography, prostitution, sexual harassment on the job, and sexual harassment between client and professional, e.g., doctor or therapist) reveal the underlying sexism behind these actions (Walker, 1979). One of the core myths about sexual and physical assaults on women is that the "victim" was responsible for the assault. With rape we often see the false and mistaken accusation of a seductive appearance on the part of the rape victim, an assumption also made about children victimized by sexual assault; in the case of wife (woman) battering, we see the label "masochistic" placed on the victim to justify the assault (Collier, 1982; Worell & Remer, 2003). Victims (or, more positively, "survivors") of sexual harassment are accused of "sleeping their way to the top" or dressing too provocatively at work, and male therapists who sleep with their clients are often excused as having been "seduced" (Collier, 1982).

Another common myth (as false as the first) is that the abuser is mentally ill or, in the case of rape, has been overcome by a powerful sex drive (Collier, 1982; Enns, 1996). In fact, rapists have not been found to be different from nonrapists on measures of psychological functioning *except* in their tendency to act out their impulses via sexual assault; further, most rapes are premeditated (Collier, 1982). "The stereotype of the harasser is of the uneducated manual worker, the uncouth traveling salesman, the boorish office 'lech'. Professional individuals with impeccable credentials and multiple degrees are assumed to be beyond reproach, despite multiple examples to the contrary" (Fitzgerald, 1993).

All these forms of violence toward women and abuse of women are methods of establishing dominance and control over women. Controversy exists as to the exact reasons behind sexual and physical assaults. However, what can be said with some confidence is that women do not freely choose to be victimized, and women's and men's socialization, along with women's relative powerlessness in society, are central causative factors in violence toward women (Betz & Fitzgerald, 1993; Enns, 2000; Worell & Remer, 2003).

Interestingly, mental health professionals and the public at large were bombarded in the 1990s with claims that statistics such as those cited at the beginning of this section are grossly exaggerated (Enns, 1996). As part of the general social backlash against women over the past decade, two areas of research have been targeted: rape and sexual abuse statistics, relabeled "rape hype" and "false memory syndrome," respectively (Enns, 1996). The first series of claims, namely, that feminists have inflated rape statistics for political purposes, was ironically aimed at a very well designed and conducted series of studies by Mary Koss and her colleagues (e.g., Koss, Gidycz, & Wisniewski, 1987), funded by the National Institute of Mental Health, wherein the authors reported the now well-known figure that 1 of 4 women reported being raped. In addition to various distortions that appeared in the media, one of the crucial aspects of the debate was the finding by Koss and her colleagues (1987) that, although many women reported being treated in a manner that met the legal definition of rape,

73% of the women who were survivors of rape did not label their experience as rape, and critics have contended that this statistic invalidates the research. [However,] although the Koss et al. (1987) study is the most frequently cited and criticized, a substantial number of additional studies have examined rates of sexual assault and rape and have found similar prevalence rates. (Enns, 1996, p. 359).

It is common and solid scientific practice for researchers to develop operational definitions of the targeted behavior under study, in this case using the legal definition of rape. The fact that many women who have been raped do not recognize the experience as such is more a reflection on the status of women in our society than a negation of the 1-in-4 rape statistic (Muehlenhard et al., 1997).

Another area of intense debate has been taking place around the issue of "recovered memories" of child sexual abuse (Enns, 1996). "Critics of therapy for adult sexual abuse survivors charge that therapists create false memories of abuse. Critics who focus on the 'epidemic' of false memory often use sensational language that resembles the rape hype literature" (Enns, 1996, pp. 73–74). Although there certainly may be cases of poorly trained or unethical therapists persuading clients to remember false details about sexual abuse, the *false memory syndrome* (a popular, not a scientific term) movement advocates sought to deny that sexual abuse was and is a widespread problem. However, most of the evidence in support of therapists implanting memories is anecdotal and circumscribed (Enns, 1996).

On the other hand:

> During the past century, several cycles of awareness and denial of abuse have already occurred. Arguments that issues of abuse have been exaggerated are often compelling to a society that prefers to believe that this is a just world. Within this climate, counselors may begin to question the perceptions and reality of their clients, or even avoid dealing with these issues for fear of creating an issue that does not really exist. . . . To avoid the public amnesia that has already occurred several times in the past century, counselors must commit themselves to competent practice and outreach relevant to these issues. (Enns, 1996, p. 361)

Rather than embrace a reactionary standpoint, practitioners are advised to (1) educate themselves on the issues, rather than rely on sensational media accounts; and (2) follow the various professional guidelines that have been developed for working with survivors of sexual abuse (Enns, 1996).

## Women and the Mental Health System

As we have seen, the sexism embedded in society penetrated and influenced the development of scientific psychology. These biases within psychology have had profound consequences for the diagnosis and treatment of women by mental health practitioners.

**Bias in Diagnosis**   Women are much more likely than men to be treated for mental illness (Enns, 2000; Gove & Tudor, 1973; Williams, 1983); the sex ratio varies depending on the diagnosis and also on type of treatment facility, but women are clearly in the majority. Various explanations have been promulgated for this preponderance of women diagnosed as having mental problems: Women are weaker and therefore more susceptible to psychological disturbance than men; women's traditional gender roles are inherently mentally unhealthy; women are labeled as ill more often than men, but no genuine sex difference in the incidence of mental illness exists; and women subjected to excessive stress and tension manifest their disturbance via emotional symptoms congruent with their gender role, whereas men's disturbance is manifested in physical symptomology (Becker, 2001).

Phyllis Chesler (1972) in her classic book *Women and Madness,* for example, advanced the argument that mental illness in women is a result of underconformity or overconformity to the feminine sex role:

> Men do not usually seem as "sick" if they act out the male role fully—unless, of course, they are relatively powerless contenders for "masculinity." Women are seen as "sick" when they act out the female role (are depressed, incompetent, frigid, and anxious) and when they reject the female role (are hostile, successful, sexually active, and especially with other women). (p. 118)

A meta-analysis of 26 studies examining the relationships of gender roles to mental health produced results congruent with Chesler's thesis: "Masculinity," as measured by various gender-role inventories, is more consistently and significantly associated with psychological measures of mental health than is "femininity" (Basoff & Glass, 1982). Chesler (1997) contended that, 25 years after *Women and Madness,* gender bias in diagnosis and assessment continues to be problematic for women and men.

A different but related argument about the origins of gender bias in assessment has been advanced by writers who, taking note of the differences in rates of mental illness in married and unmarried men and women, have suggested that social roles are a significant factor in susceptibility to mental distress (Becker, 2001; Williams, 1983). Bernard (1971) demonstrated that men are happier when married than women; single women score higher than married women on various indices of psychological well-being than married women; and women make more adjustments in marriage than do men. These findings correspond with findings from psychological studies, indicating higher rates of mental illness for married women than for single women or married men (Gove, 1980). Marriage seems to have a disadvantageous effect on women (Gove, 1973).

As Enns (2000) has stated, "Studies continue to reveal that the gender and race of clients may influence assessments of their symptoms" (p. 617). In addition to bias in assessment, however, methodological weaknesses and bias in research methods may also be influencing common findings of gender differences in diagnoses. For example, Hartung and Widiger (1998) reviewed the research on gender and diagnosis and concluded that sampling biases in research studies, gender differences in help-seeking behaviors, biases within diagnostic criteria, and gender differences in referral patterns may all be contributing to observed gender differences within diagnostic categories. Specifically, attempts to describe disorders in gender-neutral ways fail to take into account the gender-role socialization that may result in different mental health problems (Hartung & Widiger, 1998).

Arguments about the reasons for gender differences in the prevalence of mental illness may be moot, and in recent years the literature has moved toward developing nonsexist and feminist approaches to therapy and counseling, rather than to continue focusing on gender differences (e.g., Brown, 1994; Enns, 2000; Worell & Remer, 2003). As Johnson (1980) pointedly argued:

> To speak of the overall mental health of two sexes is too sweeping a generaliza-
> tion. . . . Diagnoses are frequently of questionable reliability . . . often based on
> ambiguous symptoms, subject to a variety of interpretation. . . . Furthermore, a
> report of symptoms is not synonymous with mental illness; a person can ac-
> knowledge symptoms, but be coping with them. (pp. 363–364)

Johnson went on to argue that we must look at the complex confluence of female socialization, societal attitudes toward women and women's roles, and external stressors, including the treatment of women by clinicians, in order to understand and assist women therapeutically. The point here is not that sexism has waned in the new century; just that it is more productive to focus on what ought to be done rather than what is wrong.

Nevertheless, new controversies about gender bias have arisen over the past 10 to 15 years, revolving around new diagnoses affecting women. In the revised third edition of the *Diagnostic and Statistical Manual of Mental Disorders (DSM-III-R)*, the standard guide for the diagnosis of mental problems, "five areas of the DSM have been targeted as potentially harmful to women: Borderline Personality Disorder, Histrionic Personality Disorder, Dependent Personality Disorder, Self-Defeating Personality Disorder, and Premenstrual Dysphoria Disorder" (Walsh, 1997, p. 338). Two of these gender-related diagnoses, self-defeating personality disorder (originally titled "masochistic personality disorder") and premenstrual dysphoria disorder (i.e., premenstrual syndrome, originally labeled "late luteal phase disorder"), were included after considerable controversy, as unofficial diagnoses in the appendices of the *DSM-III-R*. Many feminist psychologists viewed the attempts to officially sanction such diagnoses as a major step backward for women:

> While the criteria for this diagnostic category [self-defeating personality disor-
> der] are couched in non-sexist language, the behaviors described reflect the cul-
> tural conditioning experienced by females, hence labeling as masochistic the so-
> cial and religious values taught women. Furthermore all the criteria reflect
> characteristics of women victims of violence. Therefore it is entirely possible
> that using such a diagnosis . . . will violate the civil rights of women by causing
> irreparable injury and undue hardship to women and victims of violence (most
> of whom are women). (Rosewater, 1985, p. 1)

To pathologize behaviors that reflect conformity to societal expectations and that are exhibited by a substantial majority of women is clearly problematic (Enns, 2000). Caplan (1991) exposed the underlying sexism behind this diagnosis by proposing a parallel diagnosis pathologizing conformity to the traditional masculine gender role: The diagnosis of "delusional dominating personality disorder" (or the John Wayne syndrome) is no more scientifically supportable than the self-defeating personality disorder diagnosis. Serious charges about blaming the victim subsequently led to the withdrawal of the diagnosis self-defeating personality disorder from the *DSM-IV* (American Psychiatric Association, 1994).

There were serious problems with the premenstrual dysphoria disorder as well, among them that the diagnosis is not supported by research, that symptoms associated with the premenstrual syndrome are adequately covered in existing diagnoses, and that possible psychological and emotional effects of a medical condition experienced by women will be pathologized (Caplan, 1991; Kupers, 1997). However, that diagnosis was retained in the *DSM-IV* (Enns, 2000; Walsh, 1997). Kupers (1997) phrased her continuing objections to that inclusion in this manner:

> In regard to Late Luteal Phase Dysphoric Disorder, the question was why pathologize the women's natural cycles? Why not pathologize instead men's need to avoid all signs of emotion and dependency while maintaining an obsessively steady pace . . . ? I coined the term "pathological arrythmicity" for this disorder in men. (p. 343)

**Bias in Treatment**    The classic study of bias on the part of mental health practitioners treating women was conducted by Broverman, Broverman, Clarkson, Rosenkrantz, and Vogel (1970). In this study, 79 clinicians were asked to rate the characteristics of mentally healthy adults, mentally healthy women, and mentally healthy men. Clinicians' ratings of the characteristics of mentally healthy men and mentally healthy adults were found to be virtually identical; ratings of the characteristics of "mentally healthy" women were significantly different from the ratings for mentally healthy men, tending toward the stereotypical feminine gender-role traits held by the dominant culture. That is, healthy women, as compared with healthy men and adults, were characterized as being "more submissive, less independent, less adventurous, more easily influenced, less aggressive, less competitive, more excitable in minor issues, having their feelings more easily hurt, being more emotional, more conceited about their appearance, less objective, and disliking math and science" (Broverman et al., 1970, p. 4). The Broverman et al. study has been interpreted to demonstrate a double standard in mental health for women; masculine gender traits are more closely associated with depictions of mental health, yet women are socialized to display "feminine," less "healthy" characteristics and may be deemed aberrant if they reject the feminine role (Collier, 1982; Sherman, 1980). A replication of the Broverman et al. (1970) research with a larger but similar sample yielded findings consistent with the earlier results; in 1985, males and females were still being described in gender-stereotypical ways (O'Malley & Richardson, 1985). However, O'Malley and Richardson also reported a "loosening" of stereotypes in that clinicians attributed *both* masculine and feminine traits to mentally healthy "adults."

The controversy stimulated by the landmark Broverman et al. (1970) study continues today. Although a number of investigations have yielded results supporting the contention that clinicians hold biased views toward women (e.g., Aslin, 1977; Dremen, 1978), are misinformed about women (e.g., Bingham & House, 1973), and actually respond in biased ways toward women (e.g., Abramowitz, 1977), other studies have failed to find such evidence of differential attitudes or treatment by gender (e.g., Davenport & Reims, 1978; Johnson, 1978). The two primary arguments against the existence of gender bias in counseling can be summarized as follows: (1) Some evidence for bias in attitudes may exist, but this is not evidence that these attitudes have a detrimental effect on women in counseling (e.g., Stricker, 1977); and (2) no empirical evidence of gender bias exists (e.g., Smith, 1980). Stricker (1977) argued that the research providing evidence for a double standard in mental health was itself biased and the conclusions about such a double standard were based on questionable data, while Smith's (1980) meta-analysis of the research literature revealed no demonstrable bias against women, or bias for stereotypical roles for women, on the part of counselors or psychotherapists.

One major problem with studies of gender bias is that, because the Broverman et al. (1970) study is so well known, the validity of therapists' responses in studies of bias is questionable. It is therefore increasingly difficult to disentangle real changes in counselor attitudes toward women from possible experimental demands for social desirability. Further, problems abound in performing methodologically sound investigations in this area. Richardson and Johnson (1984) concluded that there *is* a basis in the empirical literature for claims of gender bias, but they recommended that the nature of such research be modified. Farmer (1982) also concluded that, although weak, evidence does exist for gender bias in counseling. Other writers have documented instances of continuing, often subtle, biases against women in traditional forms of therapy (Brown, 1994; Worell & Remer, 2003) in developing arguments for adopting feminist perspectives in all aspects of counseling and therapy, beginning with assessment. Nevertheless, it will undoubtedly be far more productive if researchers focus attention on what *aspects* of counselor gender-role-related attitudes and behaviors influence female (and male) clients negatively, rather than continue with the past preoccupation with demonstrating (or disproving) the overall existence of gender bias. An example of this positive focus on what we should do versus what goes wrong is the updating of the guidelines for psychological practice with girls and women (Worell, 2002).

Chapters 12 through 14 cover issues that counselors need to know about, guidelines for counseling women, and many of the newly evolving approaches to working with female clients in "sex-fair" ways. Suggestions for training and ongoing professional development in this area are outlined in chapter 18.

## REFERENCES

Abramowitz, C. V. (1977). Blaming the mother: An experimental investigation of sex-role bias in countertransference. *Psychology of Women Quarterly, 2,* 25–34.

American Psychiatric Association. (1994). *Diagnostic and statistical manual of mental disorders* (4th ed.). Washington, DC: Author.

Amundsen, K. (1971). *The silenced majority.* Englewood Cliffs, NJ: Prentice Hall.

Aslin, A. L. (1977). Feminist and community mental health center psychotherapists' expectations of mental health for women. *Sex Roles, 3,* 537–544.

Atkinson, J. W., & Feather, N. T. (Eds.). (1966). *A theory of achievement motivation.* New York: Wiley.

Basoff, E. S., & Glass, G. V. (1982). The relationship between sex roles and mental health: A meta-analysis of twenty-six studies. *The Counseling Psychologist, 10,* 105–112.

Becker, D. (2001). Diagnosis of psychological disorders: DSM and gender. In J. Worell (Ed.), *Encyclopedia of women and gender* (pp. 333–343). San Diego: Academic Press.

Bem, S. L., & Bem, D. J. (1984). Homogenizing the American women: The power of an unconscious ideology. Reprinted in A. M. Jaggar & P. S. Rothenberg (Eds.), *Feminist frameworks* (2nd ed., pp. 10–22). New York: McGraw-Hill. (Originally published in 1970)

Bernard, J. (1971). The paradox of the happy marriage. In V. Gornick & B. K. Moran (Eds.), *Women in sexist society* (pp. 145–162). New York: New American Library.

Bettelheim, B. (1965). The commitment required of a woman entering a scientific profession in present-day American society. In J. A. Mattfield & C. G. Van Aken (Eds.), *Women and the scientific professions* (pp. 1–21). Cambridge, MA: MIT Press.

Betz, N.E. (1994). Basic issues and concepts in career counseling for women. In W. B. Walsh & S. H. Osipow (Eds.), *Career counseling for women* (pp. 1–42). Hillsdale, NJ: Erlbaum.

Betz, N. E., & Fitzgerald, L. F. (1993). Individuality and diversity: Theory and research in counseling psychology. *Annual review of psychology, 44,* 343–381.

Bingham, W. C., & House, E. W. (1973). Counselors view women and work: Accuracy of information. *Vocational Guidance Quarterly, 21,* 262–268.

Bird, C. (1971). *Born female.* New York: Pocket Books.

Broverman, I. K., Broverman, D. M., Clarkson, F. E., Rosenkrantz, P. S., & Vogel, S. R. (1970). Sex-role stereotypes and clinical judgments of mental health. *Journal of Consulting and Clinical Psychology, 34,* 1–7.

Brown, L. S. (1994). *Subversive dialogues: Theory in feminist therapy.* New York: Basic Books.

Caplan, P. (1991). Delusional dominating personality disorder (DDPD). *Feminism and Psychology, 1,* 171–174.

Chafetz, J. (1978). *Masculine, feminine, or human?* Itasca, IL: Peacock.

Chesler, P. (1972). *Women and madness.* New York: Avon.

Chesler, P. (1997). *Women and madness: Twenty-fifth anniversary edition.* New York: Four Walls Eight Windows.

Childe, G. (1971). *What happened in history?* Baltimore: Penguin.

Collier, H. V. (1982). *Counseling women.* New York: Free Press.

Comas-Diaz, L., & Greene, B. (Ed.). (1994). *Women of color.* New York: Guilford Press.

Costello, C. B., & Stone, A. J. (Eds.). (2001). *The American woman, 2001–2002: Getting to the top.* New York: W. W. Norton.

Courtois, C. A. (1986, April). *The new scholarship on child sexual abuse: Counseling adult survivors*. Paper presented at the annual meeting of the American Educational Research Association, San Francisco.

Davenport, J., & Reims, N. (1978). Theoretical orientation and attitudes toward women. *Social Work, 23,* 306–309.

Davis, A. Y. (1981). *Women, race and class*. New York: Vintage Books.

Deckard, B. S. (1983). *The women's movement: Political, socioeconomic, and psychological issues* (3rd ed.). New York: Harper & Row.

Dremen, S. B. (1978). Sex-role stereotyping in mental health standards in Israel. *Journal of Clinical Psychology, 34,* 961–966.

Enns, C. Z. (1996). Counselors and the backlash: "Rape hype" and "false memory syndrome." *Journal of Counseling and Development, 74,* 358–631.

Enns, C. Z. (1997). *Feminist theories and feminist psychotherapies: Origins, variations, and themes*. New York: Harrington.

Enns, C. Z. (2000). Gender issues in counseling. In S. D. Brown & R. W. Lent (Eds.), *Handbook of counseling psychology* (3rd ed., pp. 601–638). New York: Wiley.

Erikson, E. H. (1968). *Identity, youth, and crisis*. New York: Norton.

Faludi, S. (1991). *Backlash: The undeclared war against American women*. New York: Crown.

Farmer, H. S. (1982). Empirical evidence for sex bias in counseling weak. *The Counseling Psychologist, 10,* 87–88.

Farmer, H. S., & Backer, T. E. (1977). *New career options for women: A counselor's sourcebook*. New York: Human Science Press.

Fassinger, R. E. (2000). Gender and sexuality in human development: Implications for prevention and advocacy in counseling psychology. In S. D. Brown & R. W. Lent (Eds.), *Handbook of counseling psychology* (3rd ed., pp. 346–378). New York: Wiley.

Fitzgerald, L. F. (1993). The last great open secret: The sexual harassment of women in the workplace and academic. *Federation of behavioral, psychological, and cognitive sciences*. Washington, DC: Author.

Flexner, E., & Fitzpatrick, E. (1996). *Century of struggle: The women's rights movement in the United States*. Cambridge, MA: Belknap Press.

Freeman, J. (Ed.). (1979). *Women: A feminist perspective* (2nd ed.). Palo Alto, CA: Mayfield.

Friedan, B. (1963). *The feminine mystique*. New York: Dell.

Gilbert, L. A., & Sher, M. (1999). *Gender and sex in counseling and psychotherapy*. Boston: Allyn & Bacon.

Gough, K. (1975). The origin of the family. In R. R. Reither (Ed.), *Toward an anthropology of women* (pp. 62–83). New York: Monthly Review Press.

Gould, S. J. (1996). *The mismeasure of man* (Rev. ed.). New York: W. W. Norton.

Gove, W. R. (1973). Sex, marital status, and mortality. *American Journal of Sociology, 79,* 45–67.

Gove, W. R. (1980). Mental illness and psychiatric treatment among women. *Psychology of Women Quarterly, 4,* 345–362.

Gove, W. R., & Tudor, J. F. (1973). Adult sex roles and mental illness. *American Journal of Sociology, 78,* 812–835.

Hare-Mustin, R. T. (1983). An appraisal of the relationship between women and psychotherapy: 80 years after the case of Dora. *American Psychologist, 38,* 593–601.

Hartung, C. M., & Widiger, T. A. (1998). Gender differences in the diagnosis of mental disorders: Conclusions and controversies of the DSM-IV. *Psychological Bulletin, 123,* 260–278.

Hawkes, J., & Woolley, L. (1963). *Prehistory and the beginning of civilization.* New York: Harper & Row.

Hays, P. A. (1996). Addressing the complexities of culture and gender in counseling. *Journal of Counseling and Development, 74,* 332–338.

Herz, D. E., & Wootton, B. H. (1996). Women in the workforce: An overview. In C. Costello & B. K. Krimgold (Eds.), *The American woman, 1996–97* (pp. 44–78). New York: W. W. Norton.

Hewlett, S. A. (1986). *A lesser life: The myth of women's liberation in America.* New York: William Morrow.

Hewlett, S. A. (2002). *Creating a life: Professional women and the quest for children.* New York: Talk Miramax Books.

Howe, L. K. (1977). *Pink collar workers.* New York: Avon.

Hunter College Women's Studies Collective. (1983). *Women's realities, women's choices: An introduction to women's studies.* New York: Oxford University Press.

Hunter, J. (1976). Images of women. *Journal of Social Issues, 32,* 7–17.

Hyde, J. S. (1997). Gender difference in math performance. In M. R. Walsh (Ed.), *Women, men, and gender: Ongoing debates* (pp. 283–287). New Haven, CT: Yale University Press.

Johnson, M. (1978). Influence of counselor gender on reactivity to clients. *Journal of Counseling Psychology, 25,* 359–365.

Johnson, M. (1980). Mental illness and psychiatric treatment among women: A response. *Psychology of Women Quarterly, 4,* 363–371.

Kahn-Hut, R., Daniels, A. K., & Colvard, R. (1982). *Women and work: Problems and perspectives.* New York: Oxford University Press.

Kessler-Harris, A. (2001). *In pursuit of equity: Women, men, and the quest for economic citizenship in 20th century America.* Oxford, England: Oxford University Press.

Koss, M. P. (1993). Rape: Scope, impact, interventions, and public policy responses. *American Psychologist, 48,* 1062–1069.

Koss, M. P., Gidycz, C. A., & Wisniewski, N. (1987). The scope of rape: Incidence and prevalence of sexual aggression and victimization in a national sample of higher education students. *Journal of Consulting and Clinical Psychology, 55,* 162–170.

Kupers, T. A. (1997). The politics of psychiatry: Gender and sexual preference in DSM-IV. In M. R. Walsh (Ed.), *Women, men, and gender: Ongoing debates* (pp. 340–347). New Haven, CT: Yale University Press.

Leavitt, R. R. (1971). Women in other cultures. In V. Gornick & B. K. Morgan (Eds.), *Woman in sexist society* (pp. 393–427). New York: New American Library.

Martin, M. K., & Voorhies, B. (1975). *Female of the species.* New York: Columbia University Press.

McClelland, D. C., Atkinson, J. W., Clark, R. A., & Lowell, E. L. (1953). *The achievement motive.* New York: Appleton-Century-Crofts.

Mead, M. (1974). On Freud's view of female psychology. In J. Strouse (Ed.), *Women and analysis* (pp. 24–40). New York: Grossman.

Morrison, A. M., & Glinow, M. A. (1990). Women and minorities in management. *American Psychologist, 45,* 200–208.

Muehlenhard, C. L., Highby, B. J., Phelps, J. L., & Sympson, S. C. (1997). Rape statistics are not exaggerated. In M. R. Walsh (Ed.), *Women, men, and gender: Ongoing debates* (pp. 243–246). New Haven, CT: Yale University Press.

Nelson, M. (1979). Why witches were women. In J. Freeman (Ed.), *Women: A feminist perspective* (2nd ed., pp. 451–468). Palo Alto, CA: Mayfield.

Nielsen, J. (1978). S*ex in society: Perspectives on stratification.* Belmont, CA: Wadsworth.

O'Malley, K. M., & Richardson, S. (1985). Sex bias in counseling: Have things changed? *Journal of Counseling and Development, 63,* 294–299.

Pearce, D. (1979). Women, work and welfare: The feminization of poverty. In K. W. Feinstein (Ed.), *Working women and families* (pp. 103–124). Beverly Hills, CA: Sage.

Richardson, M. A., & Johnson, M. (1984). Counseling women. In S. D. Brown & R. W. Lent (Eds.), *Handbook of counseling psychology* (pp. 832–877). New York: Wiley.

Rohrbaugh, J. B. (1979). *Women: Psychology's puzzle.* New York: Basic Books.

Rosewater, L. B. (1985). *A critical statement on the proposed diagnosis of masochistic personality disorder.* Unpublished manuscript.

Schaffer, K. F. (1981). *Sex roles and human behavior.* Cambridge, MA: Winthrop.

Schulenburg, J. T. (1979). Clio's European daughters: Myopic modes of perception. In J. A. Sherman & E. T. Beck (Eds.), *The prism of sex: Essays in the sociology of knowledge* (pp. 33–54). Madison: University of Wisconsin Press.

Sherif, C. W. (1979). Bias in psychology. In J. A. Sherman & E. T. Beck (Eds.), *The prism of sex* (pp. 93–133). Madison: University of Wisconsin Press.

Sherman, J. A. (1980). Therapist attitudes and sex-role stereotyping. In A. M. Brodsky & R. Hare-Mustin (Eds.), *Women and psychotherapy* (pp. 35–66). New York: Guilford Press.

Shields, S. (1975). Functionalism, Darwinism, and the psychology of women: A study in social myth. *American Psychologist, 30,* 739–754.

Smith, M. L. (1980). Sex bias in counseling. *Psychological Bulletin, 87,* 392–407.

Stricker, G. (1977). Implications of research for psychotherapeutic treatment of women. *American Psychologist, 32,* 14–22.

Unger, R. K. (1979). Toward a redefinition of sex and gender. *American Psychologist, 34,* 1085–1094.

Unger, R. (Ed.) (2001). *Handbook of the psychology of women and gender.* New York: Wiley.

U.S. Women's Bureau (1996, September). *Fact sheet on women workers* (No. 96-2). Washington, DC: U.S. Department of Labor.

Walker, L. E. (1979). *The battered woman.* New York: Harper & Row.

Walsh, M. R. (Ed). (1997). *Women, men, and gender: Ongoing debates.* New Haven, CT: Yale University Press.

Weisstein, N. (1971). Psychology constructs the female, or the fantasy life of the male psychologist. In V. Gornick & B. K. Moran (Eds.), *Woman in sexist society* (pp. 207–224). New York: New American Library.

Weitzman, L. J. (1985). *The divorce revolution: The unexpected social and economic consequences for women and children in America.* New York: The Free Press.

Williams, J. H. (1983). *Psychology of women* (2nd ed.). New York: Norton.

Woolf, V. (1957). *A room of one's own.* New York: Harcourt, Brace Jovanovich. (Original work published 1929)

Worell, J. (2002). Guidelines for psychological practice with girls and women: Update. *The Feminist Psychologist, 29*(3), 8, 10.

Worell, J., & Remer, P. (2003). *Feminist perspectives in therapy: Empowering diverse women* (2nd ed.). New York: Wiley.

# CHAPTER 5

# Oppression of Sexual Minorities: Past and Present

As with the other diverse populations included in this book, lesbians, gay men, and bisexuals are oppressed by the larger society. To better understand contemporary forms of discrimination, it is helpful to first examine past discrimination.

## PAST DISCRIMINATION

Attitudes toward gay people have varied considerably throughout the history of Western culture from the ancient civilizations of Greece and Rome, where homo-eroticism was considered quite unremarkable, to the intolerance and persecution characteristic of both the Middle Ages and the Twentieth century. Regardless of opposition or tolerance, some group of people in every age turns out to be gay; the greatest difference between periods is not the proportion of the population that is gay, but in the way sexual preference is expressed. (Moses & Hawkins, 1982, p. 4)

### Society's Treatment of Lesbians, Gays, and Bisexuals

Lesbians and gay men, even more so than women, have been invisible in history; most of what we know about homosexuality and attitudes toward homosexuality is derived from religious and legal sanctions against homosexual behavior (Bullough, 1976). We know very little, for example, about the everyday experience of gay people in different historical periods, and what evidence exists largely concerns gay men (Bullough, 1979). The attitudes of society, as illustrated in the preceding quote, have ranged the gamut from tolerance to harsh oppression; the norm in Western societies has been hostility and condemnation. Further, bisexuals have not only been invisible in the historical record of the distant past but until very recently were absent from modern history as well; there is still very little research on bisexuals (Dworkin, 2000). In this chapter we generally include bisexuals in the discussion of gay men and lesbians because most of the historical record addresses homosexual behavior, not gay or bisexual identity; therefore, bisexuals often came to be grouped under the rubric "homosexuals" and undoubtedly share significant aspects of the gay experience in history.

Lesbian, gay, and bisexual (LGB) people in the past (and, to a great degree, in the present) have kept their sexual orientation a secret. When LGB people have surfaced in the historical record, it is often because of exposure and persecution, resulting in a distortion of the historical picture. For example, Oscar Wilde is one of the few "known" gay men in 19th-century England because of his prosecution and imprisonment as a result of his liaison with Lord Alfred Douglas (Bullough, 1979). His name and lifestyle have been equated with homosexuality, yet his life is undoubtedly unrepresentative. In this chapter we are therefore largely confined to a discussion of broad societal attitudes because of the furtive nature of gay life and the relative neglect and active avoidance of the topic by past historians.

Although LGB people have always been present as a significant minority, and at certain times homosexual behavior has been viewed with tolerance or even as an acceptable developmental stage for men, at no time has exclusive homosexuality been acceptable for the majority of the population. Societal views toward LGB people can be roughly categorized in terms of views of homosexual behavior as tolerable, as sin, as crime, and as sickness. The first three views are addressed in this section, the last in the section on psychology's attitudes toward homosexuality.

**Tolerant Attitudes Toward Homosexuality**    Before detailing the overwhelmingly negative societal attitudes toward LGB people, we focus on some examples of societal views of homosexuality as a normal variant of sexual behavior. Plato was one of the first writers to propose an explanation of the origins of homosexuality. In *Symposium,* he explained that people originally had four arms and four legs until the gods divided these individuals into two. The "double people" contained only male, only female, or both male and female elements, and sexual orientation could be explained as "trying to find one's other half" (Bullough, 1976). Plato's attitudes are more a reflection than a cause of the accepting and tolerant attitudes of the Ancient Greeks toward LGB people.

In classical Greek society homosexual or "homoerotic" attachments were viewed as a normal and acceptable stage of development, especially for men, and both exclusive homosexuality and bisexuality were regarded as appropriate sexual behavior, although no Greek equivalent to these modern terms existed. Evidently homophobia was also unknown in Ancient Greece (Fone, 2000).

> Many Greeks represented gay love as the only form of eroticism which could be lasting, pure, and truly spiritual. The origin of the concept "Platonic Love" (which postdates Plato by centuries) was not Plato's belief that sex should be absent from gay affairs but his conviction that only love between persons of the same gender could transcend sex. The Attic lawgiver Solon considered homosexual eroticism too lofty for slaves and prohibited it to them. In the idealistic world of the Hellenistic romances, gay people figured prominently as star-crossed lovers whose passions were no less enduring or spiritual than those of their non-gay friends. . . . Even among primitive peoples some connection is often assumed between spirituality or mysticism and homosexuality. Only in comparatively recent times have homosexual feelings come to be associated with moral looseness. (Boswell, 1980, p. 27)

Women in Ancient Greek society were not encouraged as men were to have homoerotic attachments; women of all classes led severely restricted lives. In fact, one rationale for the elevation of male homosexual love appears to be related to the inferior status of women in Greek society. Plato, in *Symposium,* argues that "love between males is not only different from love between men and women but superior to it, because it is discriminating, faithful, permanent, and because men are superior to women in both intelligence and strength" (Fone, 2000, p. 22).

Very little solid evidence exists about female homosexuality. The scraps of information that survive about gay and bisexual women in the ancient world take the form of the writings of Sappho, a 6th-century B.C. poet from the Greek island of Lesbos (thus the term *lesbian* for gay women and *sapphic* as a description of love between women). Sappho was the head of a school for girls on Lesbos, and her poetry clearly praises love between women (Bullough, 1979). Bullough (1979) pointed out that Sappho was married and described the parallel to the lives of many women today who do not "come out" as gay until sometime after their marriage. One of the reasons for the paucity of information about Sappho appears to be the purposeful destruction of most of her poetry later, in the Christian era, because of the antigay attitudes of the Christian church (Bullough, 1976). The term *lesbian,* however, did not achieve currency as a descriptor of homosexual women until the late 19th century (Rothblum, 2000). As we will see in the next section, the ascendancy of Christianity in the 3rd and 4th centuries A.D., influenced as it was by the decidedly antigay and virulently sexist writings of St. Paul and subsequent theologians, was a significant factor in the shift from relatively widespread tolerance of homosexuality in the ancient world to its condemnation (Fone, 2000).

The neglect of the topic of homosexuality throughout history, especially the systematic erasure of evidence (e.g., Sappho's poems) about gay people's lives or positive attitudes toward homosexuality, makes the discussion of tolerant attitudes difficult. However, some evidence does exist from cross-cultural research performed on supposedly "inferior" people that helps to illuminate the topic; discussions of the sexual customs of "heathens" or "primitive peoples," although blatantly racist, are much more candid than Western observers' descriptions of their own cultures (Bullough, 1979).

Ford and Beach (1951) published a classic, comprehensive survey of sexual activities across cultures and concluded that no absolute norms for sexual behavior could be identified; no one culture's attitudes toward homosexuality can be viewed as representative. Even though their data probably suffered from underreporting of homosexual activity, they found that, of the societies where data existed about attitudes toward homosexuality, fully 64% viewed it as normal, at least for some portion of the population (Ford & Beach, 1951). For example, some American Indian subcultures—but not all—fostered positive or tolerant attitudes toward gay men and lesbians (Fukuyama & Ferguson, 2000). "Many American Indian tribes had institutionalized homosexuality, at least of the male variety, into the role of the *berdache* (the male woman), while other primitive groups have chosen their Shamans from them" (Bullough, 1979, p. 2). The berdache was clearly a man dressed as a woman; American Indians typically confounded cross-dressing with "sodomy," or homosexual behavior, which was widely accepted (Fone, 2000). Gender-role expectations differ across cultures, and cross-gender behaviors were evidently not only tolerated but honored in many American Indian cultures (Fukuyama & Ferguson, 2000). Unfortunately, most of what we know about early Native American Indian attitudes and practice of homosexuality comes from the written accounts of European colonial observers, which were laced with western European homophobia and moral outrage (Fone, 2000).

Finally, some idea can be gained of the pervasiveness of homosexual behavior across time and societies, of the neglect and active avoidance of the subject by mainstream historians, and of the contributions made by gay men and lesbians to society by examining the lives of eminent individuals in Western civilization who were gay, lesbian, or bisexual. Because the lives of prominent politicians, royalty, soldiers, artists, and writers have been open to a scrutiny not focused on the "average" person, eminent gay men, lesbians, and bisexuals are hardly representative. Yet their exposure by recent historical writings allows LGB people today to gain a sense of their own history that has previously been unavailable to them (Duberman, Vicinus, & Chauncey, 1989).

Rowse's (1977) book, *Homosexuals in History,* describes in some detail the lives of famous gay and/or bisexual male artists, among them Leonardo da Vinci and Michelangelo; gay/bisexual kings and other royalty such as Richard the Lion Heart, Henri III of France, James I of England, Frederick the Great, and Ludwig II of Bavaria; military commanders such as Alexander the Great and Julius Caesar; scientists such as Erasmus and Francis Bacon; musicians such as Tchaikovsky; and other eminent gay/bisexual men such as T. E. Lawrence and John Maynard Keynes. Writers proliferate among known gay men, lesbians, and bisexuals, largely because their written work often contains references to or illuminates their personal lives. The philosophers George Santayana and Ludwig Wittgenstein, and the writers Jean Cocteau, Oscar Wilde, Marcel Proust, Andre Gide, Lytton Strachey, E. M. Forster, Walt Whitman, Hart Crane, Herman Melville, and W. H. Auden were all gay and/or bisexual (Bullough, 1979; Rowse, 1977). Prominent lesbian and bisexual women in history are harder to identify and largely consist of writers and poets, for example, Virginia Woolf, Collette, Elizabeth Bowen, Vita Sackville-West, Gertrude Stein, Alice B. Toklas, Willa Cather, and May Sarton (Foster, 1956; Rule, 1975). One of the few examples in the older historical record of the daily existence of two lesbians can be obtained from the intriguing story of "The Ladies of Llangollen," two Irish noblewomen who lived in Wales in the 18th century (Martin & Lyon, 1972). Despite the paucity of references and detail about the lives of LGB people in the historical record, it is clear that knowledge of same-sex love between women has been known for centuries (Rothblum, 2000).

**Homosexuality as Sin**   Some writers regard the Judeo-Christian religious tradition as the most significant force in determining Western attitudes about gay people (Bullough, 1979). "The church bears heavy responsibility for our present attitudes toward sex deviates and their problems, and for the severe penalties with which the law has requited them for their offenses" (Wysor, 1974, p. 65). Boswell (1980), however, refuted this stance and argued persuasively that religious beliefs merely served to justify the oppression and persecution of groups, especially LGB people, who are held in contempt because of personal hostility and prejudice. Regardless of the exact role, cause, or justification of intolerance, Western religious views are an important factor to explore in any discussion of LGB people in history.

The interpretation of scriptural references to homosexuality has been a source of ongoing controversy (Baird & Baird, 1995; Fone, 2000). Wysor (1974) noted, from extensive research:

> Exactly seven references in the entire Bible [refer] to what is interpreted by some as activity involving homosexuality. Six of these seem to refer to such activity among men, and one appears to refer to women. However, these have been quite sufficient to help generate over two thousand years of condemnation and judgment against persons who express their emotional and sexual natures man to man or woman to woman. (pp. 22–23)

The earliest reference in the Bible specifically condemning homosexuality (although not using the word) can be found in Leviticus: "Thou shalt not lie with mankind, as with womankind: it is an abomination" (quoted in Bullough, 1979, p. 19). However, the story of Sodom has had the greatest influence on attitudes toward gays; the term *sodomy,* referring to anal intercourse, was derived from this biblical passage. The destruction of Sodom and Gomorrah is commonly interpreted as resulting from the sin of homosexuality on the part of the townspeople. Yet many scholars have pointed out the following:

> None of the biblical condemnations of homosexuality refer to Sodom, nor, more important, do any of the biblical references to Sodom explain just exactly what crimes the residents were guilty of having committed. In fact, when the Bible does spell out the sins for which Sodom (and Gomorrah, Admah, and Zeboin) were destroyed, they are listed as pride, unwillingness to aid the poor and needy, haughtiness, and the doing of abominable things, all actions and attitudes which many other biblical peoples and cities demonstrated. Though the doing of abominable things might refer to sexual activities, their greatest sin was clearly pride, contentment, and ignoring the needy, none of which was unforgivable. (Bullough, 1979, pp. 20–21)

Bailey (1955) argued that the antihomosexual aspects of the story of Sodom were added much later than the original writing, probably as part of an anti-Greek campaign by the Jews in Palestine (since homosexuality was tolerated and even adulated in Greek culture). Evidence from early Talmudic writings indicates that the Jews, although hostile to homosexuality, were by no means actively and virulently antihomosexual (Bullough, 1979). And of course there is no mention in any of the Christian scriptures of Christ saying anything about homosexuality (Bullough, 1979). In fact, it is clear that Jesus of Nazareth did not view homosexuality as a sin; in various New Testament passages wherein Jesus lists Mosaic commandments to be upheld, he does not ever reinforce Old Testament prohibitions against homosexuality (Fone, 2000).

Nonetheless, various Christian theologians were virulently antigay, among them St. Paul, St. Augustine, and St. Thomas Aquinas. Only three passages in the New Testament condemn male homosexuality, and all three are found in the epistles of St. Paul (Fone, 2000). Interestingly, Paul, a misogynist of the first order, also condemned women who abandon their "natural roles" (Fone, 2000). This passage may not even refer to female homosexuality, as "abandoning the natural for the unnatural" could mean women taking on an active sexual role with men as well as referring to women engaging in sex with other women (Fone, 2000). However, later Christian writers, such as St. Ambrose, clearly took this passage in St. Paul to be a condemnation of female homosexual behavior (Fone, 2000).

Augustine, another misogynist, was particularly virulent in his denunciation of homosexuality and, in fact, all sexual behavior outside of marriage. He condoned sexual behavior exclusively for the purpose of procreation, decrying sexual pleasure of any sort—this despite his experience of a loving homosexual relationship in his youth (Fone, 2000).

> Augustine maintained that since "the body of man is as superior to that of a woman as the soul is to the body," for a man to "use his body like a woman" was to undermine masculine superiority as well as to commit the sin punished in Sodom's flames. "These foul offenses," he insisted, "which be against nature" ought to be "everywhere and at all times detested and punished, just as were those of Sodom." (Fone, 2000, p. 106)

In the medieval period, Aquinas made the definitive statement against homosexuality, including the proposal of a separate category of "sins against nature"; homosexuality figured prominently in a list of such sins, which also included bestiality, intercourse in an unnatural position, and masturbation (Bullough, 1979; Fone, 2000). Later, during the Reformation, Martin Luther and other Protestant theologians, while disagreeing with much of Catholic doctrine, continued the arguments of the early Church fathers against homosexuality (Bullough, 1979). Many of the same arguments, based on dubious scriptural interpretation, can still be heard today (e.g., Jones, 1995; Fone, 2000).

Boswell (1980), the author of a classic scholarly analysis of religious views on homosexuality, summarized his views on the matter of scriptural justification of antigay sentiment:

> In the particular case at issue, the belief that the hostility of the Christian Scriptures to homosexuality caused Western society to turn against it should not require any elaborate refutation. The very same books which are thought to condemn homosexual acts condemn hypocrisy in the most strident terms, and on greater authority; and yet Western society did not create any social taboos against hypocrisy, did not claim hypocrites were "unnatural," did not segregate them into an oppressed minority, did not enact laws punishing their sin with castration or death. No Christian State, in fact, passed laws against hypocrisy per se, despite its continual and explicit condemnation by Jesus and the church. In the very same list which has been claimed to exclude from the Kingdom of Heaven those guilty of homosexual practices, the greedy are also excluded. And yet no medieval states burned the greedy at the stake. (p. 27)

Reverend Troy Perry, a gay activist, made a thought-provoking response to those who base antigay sentiments on the Bible. According to Weinberg (1972), he felt that such persons

> are exercising considerable judgment over which Biblical teachings to accept and which to disregard. Perry often refers to Leviticus, where the recommendation is made that two men who engage in a homosexual act should be stoned. He observes that in the same book of the Bible, it is said to be wrong for a woman to wear a scarlet dress or for anyone to eat shrimp. And yet people who wear scarlet and eat shrimp continue to cite Leviticus as their authority for condemning homosexuality. (p. 10)

Many other and more recent examples of selective reading of the scriptures to support personal attitudes are readily available, and numerous examples of church endorsement of homophobic attitudes exist, despite progress within many religious denominations.

> The Roman Catholic Church continues to treat homosexuality as a violation of "moral" and "natural" law and most conservative Protestants . . . argue that practicing homosexuals, having willfully chosen perversion, stand outside the divinely created natural order. . . . While claiming to hate the sin but love the sinner, most conservative religious sects do the latter only if the homosexual agrees to reject the "homosexual lifestyle." (Fone, 2000, p. 412)

**Homosexuality As Crime**    Sin eventually became crime. Religious views influenced legal codes throughout history, but laws against LGB people have also, in turn, influenced attitudes toward homosexuality. Modern American and European legal systems have been profoundly influenced by early Roman laws, especially the laws of Christian Rome (Bullough, 1979).

Bullough (1979) identifies the key Roman law about homosexuality affecting succeeding generations, dating from about A.D. 390, as the law prescribing the death penalty for anal intercourse. The intention of this rarely enforced law was evidently to curb male prostitution and invoke sanctions for men acting out of role; it said:

> We shall not suffer the City of Rome . . . any longer to be defiled by the pollution of effeminacy in males. . . . Praiseworthy is your practice of seizing all who have committed the crime of treating their male bodies as though they were female, submitting them to the use becoming the opposite sex, and being in no wise distinguishable from women, the monstrosity of the crime demands, dragging them out of the brothels. . . . In the sight of the people shall the offender expiate his crime in the avenging flames, that each and every one may understand that the dwelling place of the male soul should be sacrosanct to all and that no one may without incurring the ultimate penalty aspire to play the part of the other sex by shamefully renouncing his own. (Quoted in Fone, 2000, pp. 114–115)

Later this mandate became codified in the 6th-century collection of Roman laws sponsored by the Emperor Justinian, and the *corpus juris civilis* served as the foundation for the laws of the Christian Church (canon law) as well as European and English civil law (Bullough, 1979; Fone, 2000). A curious twist to the original condemnation of homosexuality was added by Justinian in the 6th century A.D. "calling for repentance and confession by homosexuals, warning that God would condemn the sinner, and adding if they did not repent, society as a whole would be punished" (Bullough, 1979, p. 32). Such a warning naturally resulted in the scapegoating of gays; plagues, famines, and other disasters were commonly attributed to the "sin" of homosexuality, and gay men and bisexuals were sought out, castrated, and put to death in times of crisis.

Interestingly, the tendency to scapegoat LGB people is apparent throughout the historical record, from Ancient Roman times to today, and warrants a brief digression into the relationship between laws and social repression. Just as the emancipation of women was proposed as a cause for the decline and fall of Rome, so too was homosexuality, despite the fact that homosexual behavior was outlawed and severely punished during Roman times.

> The civilization of the Roman Empire was vitiated by homosexuality from its earliest days. A question, uncomfortable to our contemporary lax moralists, may be raised: Is not the common practice of homosexuality a fundamental debilitating factor in any civilization where it is extensively practiced, as it is a wasting spiritual disease in the individual? (Cantor, 1963, quoted in Bullough, 1979, p. 89)

In the medieval period accusations of witchcraft were often associated with claims of homosexual activity, and heretics were also usually charged with sodomy (Bullough, 1979). In essence, religious deviance became equated with sexual deviance, charges were leveled at enemies without regard to the truth, and accusations of sodomy or heresy became powerful political weapons (Fone, 2000). The term *faggot,* an epithet still employed for gay men, is derived from the term *fagot,* a bundle of twigs, sticks, or branches bound together; men accused of same-sex sexual activity were often used as kindling for burning witches (Grahn, 1984).

> Stigmatizing one's enemies with charges of homosexuality is a standard practice, and some in the past have raised it to great art. In his *Divine Comedy,* Dante describes many of the inhabitants of Hell as homosexual, most of them people who happened to be his political opponents. (Bullough, 1979, p. 92)

The Knights Templar, a powerful and wealthy organization in France in the 14th century whose primary goal was to protect pilgrims visiting the Holy Land, were destroyed through accusations of heresy and sodomy; the motives behind the accusations were envy, power, and greed (Fone, 2000). This practice of using accusations of homosexuality for political purposes continued and, in the 20th century, was evidenced in Nazi Germany and in the McCarthy-era Red-baiting in the 1950s in the United States (Bullough, 1979). In Nazi Germany, hundreds of thousands of homosexuals or men accused of homosexuality were incarcerated in the concentration camps and brutalized with special ferocity. Many of these homosexuals remained in jail after the war because West Germany did not eliminate antigay laws from the books until 1969 (Plant, 1986). Senator Joe McCarthy, in 1950, declared homosexuality as much of an issue as Communism and initiated a campaign to get 3,500 "sex perverts" out of jobs in the federal government (Bullough, 1979).

The tradition of antihomosexual laws continued from Roman through medieval times in the form of legal prescriptions against "sodomy" and "crimes against nature." Although homosexual activity was one of the activities clearly indicted, the laws themselves were vague and *sodomy* referred to a variety of sexual activities, including any form of heterosexual intercourse other than the position of a woman on her back. Only at the end of the Middle Ages did *sodomy* begin to refer more specifically to homosexual acts (Fone, 2000). These ambiguities of language produce problems in deciphering the historical record. For example, Havelock Ellis, an early sex researcher, equated *buggery* and *sodomy* when he happened upon these terms. *Buggery* is currently employed as a derogatory term for anal intercourse. Yet the word originally applied to members of a heretical group in the late medieval period who were often burnt at the stake for their heresy, not for homosexual activity (Bullough, 1979). Only later were the terms *buggery* and *sodomy* equated.

In the 16th century, at the height of the Reformation and the resulting conflicts between Protestants and Catholics, negative attitudes about sexual activity in general and homosexuality in particular again resulted in sanctions appearing in the civil laws. Sodomy laws enacted in the time of Henry VIII were renewed with vigor by his daughter Elizabeth I in 1563 and marked the progression of religious sanctions into civil law (Fone, 2000). These laws, specifying the death penalty for homosexual behavior between men, remained in effect until the 19th century, when the punishment was changed to penal servitude for life (Fone, 2000). Interestingly, homoerotic writings were in evidence throughout the European Renaissance, celebrating same-sex "friendships" and emotional attachments; yet people who acted on those feelings faced execution (Fone, 2000). Various cases of legal action against homosexual behavior appeared in England over the years, but, as in medieval times, often politics rather than antigay hostility was the compelling factor behind the prosecution. For example, in the reign of Charles I, the Earl of Castlehaven was charged with sodomy and rape and subsequently executed. The Earl was Catholic, and the jurors' anti-Catholic hostility was proposed as a more important reason for his conviction than the sodomy charges (Bullough, 1979).

The issue of homosexuality per se was revived in the 17th century. English legal commentators, for example, spent much time justifying antigay laws, usually drawing on biblical sources to support their views.

> Buggery is a detestable and abominable sin, amongst Christians not to be named, committed by carnal knowledge against the ordinance of the Creator, and order of nature, by mankind with mankind, or with brute beast, or by womankind with brute beast. (Bullough, 1979, p. 35)

This passage demonstrates the continuing view of homosexual behavior as a "crime against nature," the classification of homosexual behavior with various forms of "unnatural" heterosexual behavior, and also highlights the relative neglect of female homosexuality by the law. Women were, by definition, not considered capable of "buggery," except via anal intercourse with a man. The origins of this attitude seem to be the biblical injunction against a man "spilling his seed" except to procreate. Male semen, as the key to conception, was of vital importance; consequently, the sin was viewed as relatively minor when women engaged in lesbian activity (Bullough, 1979). Undoubtedly the low regard in which women were held also accounts for the lack of attention to lesbian activity.

In France, with the introduction of the Napoleonic code, came the view that any consenting sexual activity by adults in private was outside the purview of the law:

> Deviant sexual acts were treated as a crime only when they implied an outrage on public decency, when there was violence or absence of consent, or when one of the parties was under age or not regarded as able to give valid consent for one reason or another. (Bullough, 1979, p. 37)

Despite the legal changes, public opinion in France and all of Europe remained hostile to LGB people. Many countries in Europe and some Latin American countries adopted the Napoleonic code in whole or in part. The one notable exception was Germany, long an active antagonist of France. Germany, under Prussian leadership in the 19th century, maintained the harsh Prussian laws against homosexuality; the death penalty was kept on the books until the 20th century. By the late 19th century only England and Germany retained their repressive laws against homosexual behavior, although the legal changes elsewhere in Europe often did not reduce the oppression experienced by LGB people.

Yet in every country there were some proponents of more liberal attitudes toward homosexuality. In England, for example, Jeremy Bentham, the founder of English utilitarianism, wrote extensively in the 1800s against regarding any kind of sexual activity as evil in and of itself, and he outlined guidelines for judging the morality of sexual activity. His central thesis was that public opinion should not be used as the final arbiter of sexual conduct and he argued persuasively for changing the law (Bullough, 1979). Unfortunately, his writings were never published, probably due to the attitudes of the time. In the late 19th century, John Addington Symonds discovered Plato's *Symposium* and wrote *A Problem in Greek Ethics,* one of the classics in the gay studies literature, wherein he argued that contemporary society ought to reclaim the tolerant attitudes of the Greeks toward homosexuality (Fone, 2000).

In the late 1880s in England, Parliament hurriedly passed a series of laws originally designed to protect children from sexual abuse and prostitution. The wording of these laws inadvertently resulted in the prohibition of any sexual act between adult males, even if consenting and taking place in private. Oscar Wilde, as mentioned previously, was the first victim of this new act and spoke at his trial of "the love that dare not speak its name." "In the aftermath of Oscar Wilde's conviction [in 1895], a dark shadow descended on advocates of homosexual rights" (Fone, 2000, p. 309). Friedreich Krupp (1851–1902), the scion of the powerful armaments firm in Germany, also suffered because of his exposure as a homosexual at about the same time. Because accusations of sodomy were so difficult to prove, many gay and bisexual men escaped legal prosecution. But, as in the case of Krupp, who committed suicide because of the scandal, many people were ruined by the accusation alone (Bullough, 1979).

In the United States, actual convictions for sodomy were rare, but not unknown. Laws in the United States banning homosexual activity were largely instituted on the state or local level. In 1610 the Virginia Colony passed the earliest sodomy law; the first recorded conviction for homosexual activities in the colonies occurred in 1637 in Plymouth, Massachusetts; the first execution for sodomy occurred several years later (Bullough, 1979; National Museum and Archive of Lesbian and Gay History, 1996). State courts often had difficulties defining the exact meaning of "crimes against nature," and, for example, the Texas courts in the 1860s judged that sodomy could not be punishable until it was defined. Thereafter, numerous court decisions in Texas and in other states were focused on identifying the various definitions of punishable crimes under the sodomy laws and eventually included oral intercourse and heterosexual and homosexual anal intercourse as crimes. Iowa only explicitly introduced sodomy as a crime in 1897; California finally passed laws clarifying what was meant by "crimes against nature" in 1915, including fellatio and cunnilingus as well as anal intercourse (Bullough, 1979). California clearly prohibited lesbian activity as well as gay male activity but also included heterosexual oral-genital contacts as well. These types of laws remained on the books in California into the 1970s and can still be found in some states in the 21st century.

## Psychology's Treatment of Lesbians, Gays, and Bisexuals

Thomas Szasz pointed out that "what was defined as sin in the moral order became sickness in the evolution of the medical model and both definitions have equally destructive effects" (1970, quoted in Woodman & Lenna, 1980, p. 3). Essentially, the fields of psychology and psychiatry merely translated religious attitudes about homosexuality into medical terms, and these negative attitudes have long biased the "scientific" investigation of gay men and women.

**Studies of Sexual "Degenerates"**   The earliest social scientific studies of LGB people were conducted by sociologists studying criminal behavior and "degeneracy." Many of the sociological writings of the 19th century attempted to explain the causes of homosexuality, or as it is sometimes still called, "sexual deviance," in an attempt to discern whether it was "curable" (Bullough, 1976, 1979).

> Most of the early students of sexual behavior believed that homoerotic behavior and other "perversions of nature" were biological in origin, stemming from such things as degeneration of genes, abnormal or incomplete embryonic development, incomplete social evolution, and disorders of the brain or sex glands or both. In order to determine what had gone wrong with these people and to be able to identify possible degenerates, there were a number of attempts to isolate their distinctive features. (Moses & Hawkins, 1982, p. 7).

Attempts to distinguish sexual deviates from "normal" people included a wide variety of what now seem amusing tests, including skull measurement and examination of distribution patterns of body hair (Moses & Hawkins, 1982). A sexual degenerate was seen, in the popular evolutionary terms of the time, as a "throw-back"—

"degeneracy was a reversal of progressive evolution. . . . A sexual degenerate was thus a primitive, animal-like person who might do anything" (Bullough, 1979, p. 9).

Some challenges to the prevailing views did appear. Karl Ulrichs, a gay man himself, argued that homosexual urges were inborn, and therefore "natural," and posited a pattern of development for gay people whereby *inverts* as he called them (he created the term as a positive label for gays) had the physical features of one sex but were born with the sexual instincts of the other sex. He felt that the development of a "third sex" resulted in an "inversion" of sexual attraction for gay people, but that gays were not "degenerates" as a result (Bullough, 1979).

**Early Sex Researchers**    The most important of the early social scientific and medical studies of gay people were conducted by Richard von Krafft-Ebing in the late 19th century (Bullough, 1979). Krafft-Ebing combined several prevailing views on "sexual inversion" and collected over 200 case studies in his famous *Psychopathia Sexualis* of "abnormal" or "pathological" individuals to support his theses. He claimed that "frequent abuses of the sexual organs (masturbation) or . . . an inherited abnormal constitution of the nervous system" (quoted in Bullough, 1979, p. 11) produced a perversion of the sexual instinct and "unnatural practices" such as homosexuality. His views on homosexuality were directly related to his religious view that the purpose of sex was reproduction and, therefore, any other type of sexual activity was an "unnatural practice" (Bullough, 1979). Interestingly, the term *homo-sexuality* was first introduced to an English audience by one of Krafft-Ebing's translators, Charles Gilbert Chaddock (Halperin, 1989).

> Sexual inversion, the term used most commonly in the nineteenth century, did not denote the same conceptual phenomenon as homosexuality. "Sexual inversion" referred to a broad range of deviant gender behavior, of which homosexual desire was only a logical but indistinct aspect, while "homosexuality" focused on the narrower issue of sexual object choice. (Chauncey, 1982, quoted in Halperin, 1989, p. 38)

Havelock Ellis, the other prominent sex researcher of the period, worked from a premise very different from Krafft-Ebing's. Ellis, considered the forerunner of modern sex researchers, took a sympathetic and descriptive stance in relation to his subject. Ellis regarded homosexual behavior as a part of a spectrum of sexual activity and, although not a defender of gay people, he was a sex reformer who advocated repealing laws banning sexual activity between consenting adults in private (Bullough, 1979). Various other lesser known sexologists of the 19th century, including John Addington Symonds and Magnus Hirschfeld, also promoted the view that homosexuality was not a perversion (Bullough, 1979).

**Freud and His Followers**    Unlike his biased attitudes toward women and his subsequent negative impact on the psychology of women, Freud's views on homosexuality were fairly tolerant, certainly for his time, and he had a mixed influence on attitudes toward gay people (Rothblum, 2000). Freud felt that homosexual behavior was a normal aspect of development, although he also thought that most people moved beyond it to heterosexuality in adulthood (Bullough, 1979). A letter he wrote to a distressed mother of a gay son illustrates his views:

> Homosexuality is assuredly no advantage, but it is nothing to be ashamed of, no vice, no degradation, it cannot be classified as an illness; we consider it to be a variation of the sexual function produced by certain arrest of sexual development. (Quoted in Moses & Hawkins, 1982, p. 8)

Freud demonstrated this same tolerance toward other variants of sexual behavior but actually paid little attention to homosexuality in his writings (Bullough, 1979).

It was the work of Freud's followers, who developed his preliminary ideas on the environmental rather than biological causes of variant sexual behavior, that ultimately had a harmful effect on gays. The implication of the belief that gayness is environmentally caused and an immature stage of adult development led inevitably to attempts by analytically trained psychiatrists and psychologists to "cure" LGB people. The dynamic view, focused mostly on gay men, was that homosexuality was

> a flight from incest. In the absence of a father, or in the presence of a weak one, a boy child who fell in love with his mother and sought to become her lover repressed his desire most effectively by suppressing sexual feeling toward all women. . . . The boy, suppressing his desires for the father, sought to be like the woman who accepted his father, but, unable to reconcile the incestuous sin of a father love, sought the father in other roles. (Bullough, 1979, pp. 13–14)

The psychoanalytic approach toward homosexuality, promoted more by his followers than by Freud, has resulted in psychology's focus on curing rather than understanding gay and bisexual women and men. They were thus viewed, by various writers, as neurotic, mentally ill, "egocentric, . . . lonely, unhappy, tormented, alienated, sadistic, masochistic, empty, bored, repressed, and neurotic" (Moses & Hawkins, 1982, p. 8).

Weinberg and Williams (1974), in their study of research on homosexuality, pointed out the negative ramifications of the psychoanalytic case study approach to research on homosexuality. First, they criticized the psychoanalytic research as biased. Homosexual behavior was presumed from the start to be immature and productive of maladjustment, an assumption that was not subjected to empirical tests, at least by the psychoanalytically oriented psychiatrists and psychologists. Because pathology was presumed, only its possible causes were investigated. Second, the gay people who have been studied within this research tradition have been psychiatric patients who cannot be assumed to be representative of all gays any more than nongay psychiatric patients can be presumed to be representative of all nongays. And finally, Weinberg and Williams (1974) criticized the literature on homosexuality as culture bound. As we have previously seen, cross-cultural studies cast grave doubt on the assumptions made about the pathology of homosexual behavior (Ford & Beach, 1951). Maladjustment among LGB people is more likely caused by society's reactions to them than by inherent pathology. It was not until the Kinsey studies (Kinsey, Pomeroy, & Martin, 1948; Kinsey, Pomeroy, Martin, & Gebhard, 1953) that homosexual behavior was examined from a descriptive viewpoint and more representative, nonclinical samples of LGB people were obtained.

**Heterosexuals Versus Homosexuals**   When researchers within psychology and psychiatry finally approached the issue of *whether* LGB people differed from non-LGB people on measures of pathology (rather than *presuming* pathology), interesting results emerged. Research findings have often been directly influenced by the preexisting assumptions of the investigators.

Bieber et al. (1962), for example, in a psychoanalytic study of gay men, found that a "close-binding intimate mother" was much more common for gay than nongay men. This retrospective case study is, of course, open to methodological critique. More important, however, are the criticisms of the conclusions derived from Bieber et al.'s data. Because gay men were found to have come from homes differing in child-rearing practices, the assumption of the pathology of gay men was viewed as supported. Yet Davison (1977) noted that "one cannot attach a pathogenic label to a pattern of child-rearing unless one a priori labels the adult behavior pattern as pathological" (p. 198). This tautological thinking on the part of the researchers—that is, presuming pathology, looking for differences in early life experiences, and then using those demonstrated differences to support the original theory of pathology—is commonplace within the research literature on homosexual behavior.

Contrary to the preceding example, some psychologists conducted research on gay people from a nonpathological perspective, and their research has yielded results opposite of the views of the psychoanalysts. Evelyn Hooker (1957), in a landmark study, found no differences in mental health between gays and nongays and set a precedent of using matched control groups of heterosexuals when studying gay men and lesbians (Rothblum, 2000). Hammersmith and Weinberg (1973) found positive correlations between an acceptance of a gay identity and mental health, while Weinberg (1970), Evans (1970), and Dean and Richardson (1964) also found no evidence of pathology on the part of gay men as compared with nongay men. In research comparing gay men and women with their heterosexual counterparts, some studies actually found more positive personality characteristics along select dimensions among gay people (Rothblum, 2000). Only in the latter part of the 20th century did social scientists move from studying the presumed pathology of gay men and lesbians and begin focusing on the correlates and precursors of homophobia, in an attempt to understand the problems of gay people.

## CURRENT DISCRIMINATION

The long-standing historical pattern of social, legal, medical, psychological, and religious discrimination against gay people continues in various forms to this day. Many Americans still hold negative, homophobic attitudes toward gay people (Fone, 2000; Moses & Hawkins, 1982; National Museum and Archive of Lesbian and Gay History, 1996). Internalized homophobia remains with us, too. Nonetheless, research strongly suggests that the psychological problems experienced by LGB people are profoundly influenced by the hostile and derogatory societal attitudes and the internalization of those homophobic attitudes (Dworkin & Gutierrez, 1992; Fone, 2000).

Compared with those holding more favorable attitudes, people expressing negative attitudes toward gays generally (a) have had little personal contact with lesbians or gay men; (b) are less likely to have had any homosexual contact or to label themselves as gay; (c) are more likely to see their peers as holding homophobic attitudes; (d) are more likely to live in areas of the country where homophobia flourishes, especially the Midwest and South, and rural areas and small towns; (e) are older and less educated; (f) are more likely to subscribe to a conservative religious ideology; (g) hold more restrictive views about gender roles; (h) have more negative views about sexuality in general; and (i) are more authoritarian (Herek, 1984; Melton, 1989).

In 1986 Herek reported that surveys showed that only 25–30% of Americans claimed to know a lesbian or gay man. A subsequent *U.S. News & World Report* poll revised that figure upward: 53% of respondents reported that they "personally know someone who is gay and this familiarity makes them think more favorably about equal rights" (National Museum and Archive of Lesbian and Gay History, 1996, p. 104). Of course, given the large percentage of LGB people in the population, it is safe to assume that *everyone* knows at least one if not more lesbian or gay person (questions were not asked about bisexuals); the 53% figure undoubtedly represents those who are familiar with an *openly* gay man or woman. Further, in most surveys, the majority of respondents who knowingly have had contact with a gay person have positive attitudes about gays as a result of their contact (Herek, 1986; National Museum and Archive of Lesbian and Gay History, 1996). Conversely, in the *U.S. News & World Report* study, the 46% of respondents who did not know any gay people also opposed gay rights (National Museum and Archive of Lesbian and Gay History, 1996). Antigay sentiment is clearly based, to a large degree, on unfounded assumptions and untested stereotypes.

Homophobic individuals are more likely to hold racist and sexist attitudes, underscoring the common sources of all forms of oppression (Dunbar, Brown, & Amoroso, 1973). However, "homophobia remains nearly untouched by the other battles fought against social and religious hostilities, against racism, against sexism, against prejudice itself" (Fone, 2000, p. 420). Some evidence also suggests that nongay men are more homophobic than nongay women (Morin & Garfinkle, 1978). It is unclear whether these findings are related to fear of same-sex homosexuality (i.e., most research asks respondents for attitudes about homosexuality in general, which is usually taken as meaning gay males) or to a "horror of difference," fear of femininity, violation of the male gender role, and/or other gender-role issues (Fone, 2000; Morin & Garfinkle, 1978).

Herek (1984), in a review of the research on homophobia, also pointed out that people hold positive and negative views about gays for different reasons; understanding the complexity of these issues is important if efforts at attitude change are to be successful. Attitudes toward gays may develop out of personal experience with gay men or lesbians and the resultant generalization of these experiences because of defensiveness and the need to project some inner conflict or anxiety onto LGB people, or the attitudes may be symbolic, representing firmly held beliefs or convictions (Herek, 1984).

Finally, in addition to outright homophobia, researchers have identified "heterosexual bias" as a problem for LGB people. Even people who hold liberal attitudes about lesbians and gay men may believe, either subtly or overtly, that heterosexuality is inherently superior to or more "natural" than homosexuality (Morin, 1977). This "heterosexual bias," then, precludes a true commitment to the validity of the gay lifestyle and represents at best tolerance toward, rather than a proactive affirmation of, gay people. Thus, homophobic attitudes may range from repulsion through pity to tolerance; only when public and personal attitudes are truly *accepting* will gay people attain equality in this society.

## Social Discrimination

Surveys on public attitudes toward LGB people reveal both some trends toward tolerance as well as continuing negative attitudes. Levitt and Klassen (1974) conducted two attitude surveys in the early 1970s, one in 1970 and the other in 1974. In 1970 they found that over 75% of their sample of Americans believed that homosexual activity was wrong if no love was involved, and 70% felt homosexual activity was wrong even if the participants loved each other. The large majority of the respondents felt that gays should not be allowed to hold positions of responsibility and authority such as schoolteacher, minister, medical doctor, lawmaker, and judge (Levitt & Klassen, 1974). Other findings supported the existence of a hostile, destructive atmosphere for LGB people in our society. The overwhelming majority of people still believed that homosexuality was wrong and tended to agree with such statements as "Homosexuals are dangerous as teachers or youth leaders, because they try to get sexually involved with children"; and "Homosexuality is a social corruption that can cause the downfall of a civilization." Other widely held beliefs included the assumption that gay people act like members of the opposite sex, and that gay men and lesbians can be identified on the basis of their appearance (Levitt & Klassen, 1974).

Interestingly, this survey was conducted about the same time that the gay liberation movement began (Bullough, 1979). Homosexual rights organizations are not a recent phenomenon; the first organized gay rights organization was formed by Magnus Hirschfield in 1897 in Germany (Lauritsen & Thorstad, 1974). However, the work of the early homosexual rights movements achieved no lasting effect on antihomosexual attitudes, and the movement was ended by the Nazis in the 1930s (Lauritsen & Thorstad, 1974). Secret gay groups have existed in various countries and at different times; most notably in this country, the Mattachine Foundation, later the Mattachine Society, organized originally in 1950 (Bullough, 1979; Fone, 2000). The Daughters of Bilitis, a lesbian organization, was founded in 1955, published a magazine called *The Ladder*, and provided a beginning for much of the leadership of the lesbian movement of the 1970s (Bullough, 1979; Rothblum, 2000).

The contemporary gay rights movement grew out of the earlier secretive societies and was officially born in 1969 as a result of a spontaneous demonstration by gay men in reaction to police harassment at The Stonewall Inn, a popular gay men's bar in Greenwich Village (Fone, 2000; Rothblum, 2000). Out of the

"Stonewall riots" and succeeding demonstrations the Gay Liberation Front, a civil rights organization, was formed (National Museum and Archive of Lesbian and Gay History, 1996; Teal, 1971). Although parallels can be found between the movement for the civil rights of gay people and other civil rights movements, the meaning of the Stonewall confrontation for gay men and lesbians was also somewhat different than was, for example, the Watts riots of 1969 for Black people. Because of their stigmatized place in society, and their ability to remain hidden, few gay men or lesbians were willing to be public about their sexual orientation (Bullough, 1979). With the advent of the new wave of the gay rights movement and the resultant public support and affirmation of gays, many more gay people were willing to become visible, creating an overt, as opposed to the earlier covert, movement for social reform. However, as was the case with earlier movements, social progress has been slow (National Museum and Archive of Lesbian and Gay History, 1996).

In 1974 Levitt and Klassen conducted a follow-up to their 1970 survey on public attitudes about homosexuality (Levitt & Klassen, 1974). The results of the two surveys are similar, revealing limited social progress in this period despite the active and public work of the gay liberation movement. In 1974 the overwhelming majority of Levitt and Klassen's sample still believed that homosexuality was wrong, and the majority tended to agree that homosexuals should not be teachers or youth leaders and that homosexuality can cause the downfall of a civilization. Most of the sample also still believed that gay people act like members of the opposite sex, and that gay men and lesbians can be identified by their appearance (Levitt & Klassen, 1974).

A 1977 Gallup poll revealed somewhat more positive attitudes, with 56% of Americans agreeing that gay people should have equal rights in job opportunities. These more accepting attitudes did not extend to the employment of gay people in certain types of positions; 65% of the sample believed that gays should not be allowed to be elementary teachers, 54% thought gay men and lesbians should be denied jobs as members of the clergy, and 44% and 38%, respectively, agreed that gays should not be medical doctors or members of the armed forces (Gallup, 1977). Only 43% of this sample advocated legalization of homosexual activity, and 14% felt that gay people should be allowed to adopt children (Gallup, 1977). In a *Psychology Today* poll of a sample of liberals, 70% of the heterosexuals polled felt that "homosexual men are not fully masculine" (Tavris, 1977).

A national poll conducted in 1989 (reported in Fassinger, 1991) yielded more evidence of positive changes in attitudes toward gays, although not widespread acceptance:

> The overwhelming majority of the nongay public, 81%, is opposed to discrimination based on sexual orientation, but 57% disapprove of gays living together as a married couple and 18% think homosexuality should be illegal. Two thirds believe discrimination has decreased during the past 10 years, but almost one fifth reported that they would withdraw support for a gay candidate for political office, even if they agreed with everything the individual said. Nongays would more easily accept a gay friend than a gay child, and one third would "try to change" a gay child. (p. 163)

The previously mentioned 1993 *U.S. News & World Report* poll (National Museum and Archive of Lesbian and Gay History, 1996) revealed some interesting inconsistencies in public attitudes toward gays: while 65% of respondents stated that they "want to ensure equal rights for gay people," 50% opposed "extending civil-rights laws to cover homosexuals" (National Museum and Archive of Lesbian and Gay History, 1996, p. 105).

Despite some encouraging results from public opinion polls, the overall climate in the United States was noticeably more antigay in the 1990s:

> Gay bashing is our new national pastime. From the Republican presidential campaign to the state of Oregon, homophobia has taken center stage. It is the last prejudice, a bias that public officials and everyday citizens are displaying without fear of instant condemnation or repudiation. . . . Imagine if a candidate for president or vice president said Jews or Catholics should not be in the cabinet, that women or African-Americans do not deserve rights. That candidate would be forced to withdraw. Not so when the prejudice is against lesbians or gay men. (Rothschild, 1992, p. A9)

Several notable reversals in civil rights for gays occurred in the 1990s. Idaho and Oregon attempted to pass antigay measures in 1994, but the electorate voted both measures down (National Museum and Archive of Lesbian and Gay History, 1996). Similar laws have been proposed in other states, and in 1992 Colorado did, in fact, pass a statute forbidding gay antidiscrimination legislation. The statute has never been enforced, however, as the Colorado Supreme Court ruled that the measure violated the U.S. Constitution. It is virtually impossible to imagine any law *denying* basic civil rights to any other group in this society even being proposed, let alone passed. Furthermore, the antigay initiatives of the 1990s "mimic a rash of ballot measures targeted at African-American civil rights in the 1960s and 1970s" (National Museum and Archive of Lesbian and Gay History, 1996, p. 252).

In 1992, Bill Clinton was the first presidential candidate to ever mention gays in an acceptance speech (National Museum and Archive of Lesbian and Gay History, 1996), and shortly after his inauguration, President Clinton proposed ending the ban on gays in the military, a move that was applauded by gays and civil rights groups. The consequent uproar in response to his proposal, however, is reflective of a retreat from tolerance; the resulting compromise has been a failure. "Between 1998 and 1999, more than 1600 military careers were ended because of 'don't ask don't tell', and harassment of gay soldiers doubled" (Fone, 2000, p. 415). Despite overwhelming evidence to the contrary, the military and the majority of the public at large continue to argue against the suitability of gays for military service (Herek, 1993). One of the most dramatic episodes of this period of U.S. history was the opposing testimonies to the Senate Armed Services Committee by Marine Colonel Fred Peck, testifying on behalf of the current ban, and by his gay son, arguing for admitting gays into the military. The linchpin in Colonel Peck's reasoning for continuing discrimination was his concern for his son and other gay people, who, he argued, would be in mortal danger from fellow military personnel (Smolowe, 1993). The question of whose problem it was, gays or the virulently homophobic armed forces, was evidently never considered. Research indicates, however, that lesbians and gay men are not inherently less capable of military service than are heterosexual women and men; that prejudice in the military can be overcome; that heterosexual personnel can adapt to living and working in close quarters with lesbian and gay male personnel; and that public opinion will be influenced by the way this issue is framed. (Herek, 1993, p. 547)

The AIDS epidemic, too, has had a profound effect on attitudes toward LGB people (Rudolph, 1988, 1989). AIDS has been identified as the "gay plague," has been labeled by some as punishment for immoral behavior, and has exacerbated already existing biases about LGB people (Rudolph, 1989). Opposition to gay rights activities has also been justified by the AIDS epidemic. Black (1986) reported graffiti highlighting this tendency: Scrawled on a wall outside a New York University Conference on Gay/Lesbian Health was the slogan *Gay Rights = AIDS.*

Some methodological problems exist with both the research on correlates of homophobic attitudes and surveys about public attitudes toward gays. First, many surveys do not clearly differentiate between attitudes toward gay men and attitudes toward lesbians, and they usually do not address bisexuality at all. Second, questions are often phrased globally, reflecting general cultural beliefs and failing to reflect individual attitudes and the more specific ways in which gays are responded to negatively in everyday situations. And third, questions about the extent to which the survey data are representative abound (Morin, 1977; Morin & Garfinkle, 1978). Yet some conclusions can be drawn. Widespread disapproval and stigmatization of lesbians, gay men, and probably also bisexuals clearly exists in American society and these negative attitudes are strong and persistent. The AIDS epidemic undoubtedly contributed to justifying and maintaining such negative attitudes. Finally, cultural and social influences on the development of biased attitudes toward gays are as important to understanding the problems of gay men and lesbians as is the study of gay adjustment, behavior, and reactions.

Examples of the ongoing problem of virulently antigay attitudes and prejudices abound. A 1995 *New York Post* editorial, "Saying No to the Gay Crusade," went far beyond its intended purpose of applauding the exclusion of gay groups from the St. Patrick's Day parade to expose the social acceptance of antigay attitudes and homophobia: "In our view the goal of the homosexual litigants is to secure judicial affirmation of homosexuality as a morally valid alternative lifestyle. . . . There's only one kind of family society we should actively encourage: two-parent homes featuring a mother and father" (quoted in Fone, 2000, p. 417). Fulminations against LGB people from televangelists are commonplace, and even some of our national leaders have no compunction about openly flaunting their homophobia. For example, U.S. Senator Trent Lott likened homosexuals to "alcoholics, sex addicts, and kleptomaniacs" (Fone, 2000, p. 417).

## Legal Discrimination

The legal status of gay people in this country is largely dependent on local and state statutes, varying considerably depending on geographic location. No federal statutes protect lesbians and gay men from discrimination in employment, housing, or child custody, and half the states have laws prohibiting various types of consensual sexual behavior, which are used largely against gay people (Hunter, Michaelson, & Stoddard, 1992). Although some employers have voluntarily implemented antidiscrimination policies, gays are rarely legally protected from employment discrimination. In fact, in 1999, "40 states allowed known homosexuals to be summarily fired from their jobs" (Fone, 2000, p. 12).

In 1996, 21 states still had sodomy statutes on the books (National Museum and Archive of Lesbian and Gay History, 1996). Periodic state-by-state challenges to the so-called sodomy laws, which outlaw all consensual same-sex sexual relations, have met with some successes, causing the elimination of these restrictions (National Museum and Archive of Lesbian and Gay History, 1996). However, a 1986 Supreme Court decision served as a major setback for gay rights. In *Bowers v. Hardwick,* the Supreme Court made its first major ruling on a gay rights issue, overturning a federal appellate court decision in Georgia and refusing to extend constitutional protection to private homosexual acts between consenting adults (Jeffries, 1995). Essentially, this ruling denied the same protection enjoyed by nongays to gay people. The vote was close (5 to 4), and Justice Harry A. Blackmun vehemently chastised the Justices in the majority, calling the decision an opening for the state to "invade the houses, hearts and minds of citizens who choose to live their lives differently" (Hager, 1986, pp. 1, 13).

Because LGB people lack legal protection, they are vulnerable to many other types of discriminatory behavior. For example, in *Gaylor v. Tacoma School District,* the Supreme Court refused to hear a case involving the dismissal, solely on the grounds of being gay, of a public school teacher who had years of outstanding work performance behind him (Moses & Hawkins, 1982). Only eight statewide laws protecting employment discrimination against gays existed in 1996 (National Museum and Archive of Lesbian and Gay History, 1996). Though employment protection does exist for LGB people in some cities (a full listing is available from the National Gay Task Force), most gays are economically vulnerable. Likewise, housing discrimination against LGB people is legal in most states and cities (National Museum and Archive of Lesbian and Gay History, 1996). Further, because many financial benefits accrue from legally sanctioned marriages, gay couples experience profound disadvantages.

> Some states have domestic partner laws, but most gay and lesbian couples cannot assume the basic rights of non-gay couples (e.g., insurance benefits, filing joint income tax returns, next-of-kin rights when a partner is hospitalized, and legal custody of children). The combination of the AIDS epidemic (prompting the need for legally sanctioned medical decisions and wills) and the "gayby boom" of increasing numbers of gay and lesbian parents has led to a push for legal protection of family rights. (Fassinger, 1991, p. 162)

In 1993 the Supreme Court in Hawaii ruled

> that the refusal to issue marriage licenses to same-sex couples appeared to violate the state constitutional right to equal protection, and ordered a trial in which the state would either have to present "compelling" reasons for continuing to discriminate against gay and lesbian couples who want to marry, or stop discriminating. (National Museum and Archive of Lesbian and Gay History, 1996, p. 259)

That ruling was eventually overturned but prompted a spate of activity aimed at passing laws against gay marriages in states across the country.

Finally, gay men and lesbians have not had much success in court in attempts to retain custody of their children after a divorce. Because custody is decided on the basis of the "best interest of the child," and lesbianism and gayness are usually viewed as inherently unhealthy, gay people are vulnerable to losing their children solely on the basis of their sexual orientation (Falk, 1989; Fone, 2000).

## Violence Against LGB People

One of the alarming consequences of the rampant homophobia in our society is the relative impunity with which individuals can harass, assault, and persecute LGB people. Herek (1986, 1989) documented the prevalence of antigay violence and the ferocity and seriousness of these attacks. In statewide surveys, anywhere from 15% to 25% of the gay men and lesbians polled reported being survivors of physical violence directly related to their gayness (Herek, 1986); the overwhelming majority of lesbians and gay men have experienced antigay threats and verbal abuse (Herek, 1989, 1991).

The perpetrators of antigay violence are usually young men in groups; gay men are more likely to be the targets of physical assault, while lesbians are more often sexually assaulted and harassed. The seriousness of the problem is highlighted by the following:

> Attacks against gay people often are characterized by an intense rage on the part of the attackers; thus there tends to be more violence than other physical assaults. Commenting on this phenomenon, sociologists Brian Miller and Laud Humphreys observed, "Seldom is a homosexual [murder] victim simply shot. He is more apt to be stabbed a dozen times, mutilated, *and* strangled." (Herek, 1986, p. 3)

Herek (1991) also noted that violence against lesbians and gay men is increasing in frequency and attributes this increase to the public fears of gay people fueled by the AIDS crisis. Attacks on gay military personnel have received attention in tandem with the debates about gays in the military. In 1993, a U.S. Navy sailor was beaten to death by a shipmate because he was gay; he was bludgeoned so badly that his body could only be identified by his tattoos. On being sentenced, the murderer declared no remorse and said he would do it again because he was "disgusted by homosexuals" ("Sailor in Beating Death," 1993). The prevalence of attacks against gay men and lesbians appears to be continuing to rise; for example, antigay attacks increased 7% in 1998 compared with a 4% drop in the overall crime rate (Fone, 2000). After the shocking and nationally publicized murder of Matthew Shephard by two self-identified homophobes in 1999, a flurry of legislative activity designed to more strictly punish hate crimes was observed, but none of the bills passed (Fone, 2000).

In addition to their susceptibility to senseless assaults and violence, LGB survivors of violence must cope with the homophobic attitudes of medical personnel, police, and lawyers (Herek, 1989, 1991). The experience of these survivors is not unlike that of rape survivors. Often LGB people are "blamed by others for their assault, [and] accused of inviting the attack or deserving it" (Herek, 1986, p. 4). Furthermore, because of their vulnerability to arbitrary dismissal from jobs or eviction from their residences, gay men, lesbians, and bisexuals who have been assaulted are unlikely to report their assault to law enforcement officials, fearing public exposure of their sexual orientation; as many as 80% of antigay assaults go unreported (Herek, 1986).

## LGB People and the Mental Health System

After decades of discriminatory treatment of LGB people by the mental health system, there have been some important changes in the "official" status of homosexuality within psychology and psychiatry. Generally, in therapy and counseling, the movement has been toward the treatment of the *problems* of lesbians and gay men rather than the condition of homosexuality (Bieschke, McClanahan, Tozer, Grzegorek, & Park, 2000; Stein & Cohen, 1986), and toward gay-affirmative counseling (Dworkin, 1992, 2000; Dworkin & Gutierrez, 1992; Hunt, 1993). Although this trend is positive, it does not necessarily reflect the attitudes and behaviors of all practitioners; LGB clients are still often faced with subtle and even blatant homophobia, heterosexual bias, and misinformation about LGB people in counseling and therapy.

**Bias in Diagnosis**    A landmark in psychiatry's treatment of gay people occurred in 1973 when the American Psychiatric Association decided to remove homosexuality as a diagnosis from their *Diagnostic and Statistical Manual of Mental Disorders.* Although protesters of this decision accused the American Psychiatric Association of succumbing to political pressure by gay rights organizations, the reality was just the opposite (Krajeski, 1986). Bias in psychology and psychiatry had historically justified the assumption, never scientifically proven, that homosexuality per se was pathological. The 1973 decision to depathologize homosexuality, followed by a similar move by the American Psychological Association in 1975, simply corrected a long-existing and unscientific injustice (Krajeski, 1986).

The diagnosis of homosexuality was replaced, in the *Diagnostic and Statistical Manual Disorders III* (American Psychiatric Association, 1980), with the diagnosis "ego-dystonic homosexuality." This diagnostic label has been employed with individuals who express dissatisfaction with their homosexual behavior, and a desire to change their sexual orientation. It was grouped with other "Psychosexual Disorders" such as exhibitionism, masochism, and pedophilia in the *DSM-III.* Although an improvement over the previous diagnostic system, the inclusion of the diagnosis of ego-dystonic homosexuality in the *DSM-III* reinforced prevailing biases in society at large, shared by many mental health professionals. The emphasis on the individual rather than the social causes of distress remained, and gay people continued to be placed in a position inferior to that of nongays. An example of this perhaps subtle point is that there was never an official diagnosis of ego-dystonic heterosexuality. The very idea appears absurd, but only because of the cultural context of the stigmatization of gays.

The upshot of the ego-dystonic homosexuality diagnosis was that many professionals continued to "treat" gay clients for their gayness by promoting programs to change sexual orientation and thereby to encourage gay people to personalize and internalize their oppression rather than work through these issues with the goal of developing a positive gay identity. Ego-dystonic homosexuality was eliminated from the diagnostic nomenclature in the *DSM-III-R* and the *DSM-IV* (American Psychiatric Association, 1994). However, this has not prevented practitioners from continuing to use the diagnosis unofficially despite the American Psychological Association's policy statement that "homosexuality and bisexuality are not indicative of mental illness" (American Psychological Association, 2000, p. 3). The ethical issues related to sexual orientation change programs will be discussed more fully in the following section on bias in treatment.

**Bias in Treatment: Attitudes of Counselors and Therapists**   The research on homophobia indicates that professionals, including mental health professionals, generally hold more positive attitudes about gay men and lesbians than the public at large, but therapists' attitudes are not totally accepting (Bieschke et al., 2000; Moses & Hawkins, 1982). A large proportion of therapists and counselors appear to agree that homosexuality is not an illness, but attitude surveys also suggest that mental health professionals do see homosexuality, lesbianism, and bisexuality as signs of some type of disturbance or developmental arrest, and many view the goal of changing sexual orientation as valid (Garfinkle & Morin, 1978; Martin, 1982). Therapists are generally uninformed about gay and lesbian lifestyles and issues (Graham, Rawlings, Halpern, & Hermes, 1984), tend to hold many of the societal stereotypes about lesbians and gay men (Casas, Brady, & Ponterotto, 1983), and may exhibit distorted judgment about the clinical concerns of gay people (Davison & Friedman, 1981). Rudolph (1988) argued that inconsistency and ambivalence perhaps best describes the mental health establishment's perspective on counseling lesbians and gay men.

   It is of vital importance to effective counseling and therapy for mental health professionals to work on their own attitudes and inform themselves about gay lifestyles and related information. In fact, our professional organizations and ethical guidelines expect a proactive stance of counselors. For example,

> in 1987 the American Counseling Association (ACA) approved a Human Rights Position Paper stating that every member should "engage in [an] ongoing examination of his/her own attitudes, feelings, stereotypic views, perceptions and behaviors that might have prejudicial or limiting impact on . . . gay/lesbian persons . . . [and] advocate equal rights for all individuals through concerted personal, professional, and political activity." (Hunt, 1993, p. 2)

Likewise, the American Psychological Association's (2000) *Guidelines for Psychotherapy with Lesbian, Gay, and Bisexual Clients* encourages psychologists to examine their own attitudes and assumptions about LGB people.

   Gays seek counseling at a higher rate than nongays (Dworkin, 2000; Rudolph, 1988); no data exist for bisexuals. Therefore, some substantial percentage of any practitioner's client load will be gay, lesbian, and/or bisexual, whether the counselor or therapist knows it or not. Paulsen (1983) reported that former gay clients of therapists perceived as holding negative views toward lesbians and gay men often experienced greater psychological distress after therapy. Further, in one study, fully half of gay men and lesbians preferred working with a gay counselor; this statistic is no doubt related at least to some extent to client fears of homophobic reactions from counselors (McDermott, Tyndall, & Lichtenberg, 1989). Nonetheless, few research studies have investigated therapist homophobia; very little on the subject is available in the counseling and clinical literature; and the topic is rarely addressed in training programs (Graham et al., 1984; chapter 15, this text). This lack of introspection on the part of counselors and therapists is particularly striking in the psychodynamic literature, where Kwawer (1980) reported that not one article on "countertransference issues" with LGB clients appeared.

Results of one major survey of psychologists supports the need for greater attention to therapist attitudes toward, and treatment of, gay men and lesbians (Garnets, Hancock, Cochran, Goodchilds, & Peplau, 1991). Ninety-nine percent of the psychologists in the survey reported providing services to at least one lesbian or gay man; approximately 6% of the average caseload were gay men and 7% were lesbians (Garnets et al., 1991). A majority of the respondents provided critical incidents illustrating the treatment of gay men and lesbians in therapy. Examples of biased, inadequate, or inappropriate practice with LGB clients included the following: believing that homosexuality per se is pathological; attributing client problems to their sexual orientation; failing to recognize the effects of homophobia on gay clients; assuming that all clients are heterosexual; focusing on sexual orientation when it is not relevant; demanding that clients change their sexual orientation; trivializing or demeaning a client's gay identity; inappropriately terminating a client upon disclosure of the client's sexual orientation; lack of understanding about gay identity; gross insensitivity to the importance of a client's relationships; and numerous other examples of ignorance and bias.

In addition to misinformation, stereotyping, and homophobia, a more subtle but still damaging and widespread therapist bias is "compulsory heterosexuality" (Rich, 1980). Some of the negative examples provided in the last paragraph reflect this prejudice, especially when LGB clients presenting themselves for counseling or therapy do not immediately reveal their sexual orientation to their therapists. A form of heterosexual bias, compulsory heterosexuality is the implicit and unquestioned belief in the normality and inevitability of heterosexuality, resulting in the neglect in the literature and, by extension, in the minds of mental health practitioners of the very existence of gay people. Such an assumption can cause serious damage to gay clients who are still "in the closet" (Cohen & Stein, 1986). Lesbians have been more vulnerable to this lack of acknowledgment of their existence than gay men, as illustrated by an apocryphal tale about Queen Victoria. Upon being presented with a law criminalizing consenting adult homosexual activity, Victoria was unable to imagine that such a law had anything to do with "the ladies." She replied to her ministers: "Women don't do such things," and all references to lesbians were expunged from the law (Weintraub, 1987).

**Bisexuality**    Finally, some specific attention to bisexuality is in order. Bisexuality is not a well-understood phenomenon. The bisexual movement achieved visibility and momentum only in the 1990s but has already affected the research literature, for example, by fueling research into bisexual identity development (Reynolds & Hanjorgiris, 2000). Researchers have become more educated about bisexuality very recently, and research studies on bisexuals, theories of bisexuality, and bisexual identity development are in their infancy (Dworkin, 2000).

Traditionally, when it has been addressed at all, bisexuality has been viewed as a state of confusion, or as a transition point in the process of moving from a heterosexual to a homosexual identity (American Psychological Association, 2000; Wolf, 1992). That is, bisexuals were viewed simply as gay men or lesbians who have not yet accepted their identity. Among the gay community, bisexuality is sometimes viewed as a betrayal, where the bisexual enjoys "the privileges of heterosexual society while at the same time avoiding the stigma of homosexuality" (Zinik, 1985, p. 11). On the other hand, going all the way back to Kinsey, human sexuality has been defined on a continuum and as fluid across a lifetime, with very few individuals at either "extreme" of heterosexuality or homosexuality. Thus, the bisexual can be viewed as flexible rather than confused; in this view "bisexuality is characterized as the coexistence of heterosexual and homosexual feelings and behaviors, and an integration of homosexual and heterosexual identities" (Zinik, 1985, p. 11). Some of the confusion experienced by bisexuals may merely be the natural consequence of its "inherent complexity" (Wolf, 1992). Some authors believe that there may be some fundamental differences between homosexuality and bisexuality: "exclusive homosexuality tends to emerge from a deep-seated predisposition, while bisexuality is more subject to influence and sexual learning" (Bell, Weinberg, & Hammersmith, 1981, quoted in Wolf, 1992, p. 176).

"Bisexuals experience extreme marginalization from both the heterosexual and lesbian and gay communities, which can cause additional distress and make self-disclosure more risky" (Dworkin, 2000, p. 164). Thus, counseling issues of bisexuals

> are similar to those of gay and nongay people with the added stress that bisexuals feel "caught between two worlds" and belonging to neither. . . . The limited research in this area shows that bisexuals become aware of their sexual orientation later than gay or nongay people. . . . People who later identify themselves as bisexual may come into counseling to sort out feelings of confusion and anxiety related to the dichotomous model of sexual orientation. (Hunt, 1993, p. 1)

Professional guidelines address the need for practitioners to increase their understanding of and confront negative attitudes toward bisexuality (American Psychological Association, 2000).

**Bias in Treatment: Ethical Issues**    One of the overriding issues in the psychotherapeutic treatment of LGB people concerns treatments designed to change sexual orientation. The controversy applies to therapists and counselors of *all* theoretical orientations but has been particularly heated within the behavioral tradition. Therefore, the following discussion focuses mainly on behavioral interventions, but the reader should keep in mind the generalizability of the issues.

Traditionally, behaviorists, while disagreeing vehemently with psychoanalytic views in general, did agree with the Freudians about the environmental origin of homosexuality (although the mechanisms theorized to cause homosexual behavior were thought about very differently) and also focused on curing rather than studying LGB people (Bullough, 1979). The behaviorists stated that they ascribed to a "value-free" stance and focused on treating the client's presenting concern. Thus, the argument went, the *client* had control over the goals of treatment, and the therapist or counselor was not passing judgment on the client's problem. Numerous behavioral sexual-reorientation procedures were developed, mostly for gay men (Adams & Sturgis, 1977). These behavioral treatments took the form of aversive techniques, including the use of chemicals to produce noxious reactions and electrical shocks, geared to reduce sexual responses to same-sex stimuli, and positive conditioning techniques designed to increase heterosexual arousal (Adams & Sturgis, 1977). Social skills training programs to enhance heterosexual dating skills are another example of behavioral approaches to the modification of homosexuality (Adams & Sturgis, 1977).

In the 1970s some behaviorists raised serious questions about the behavioral treatment, or indeed any other treatment, of gays designed to change sexual orientation. Davison (1976, 1977) and Begelman (1975) were at the forefront of the debate over the ethics of behavioral reorientation treatment of gays.

> I believe that clinicians spend time developing and analyzing procedures only if they are concerned about a problem. This seems to be the case with homosexuality. And yet, consider our rhetoric that typically speaks of social labeling of behavior rather than viewing a given behavior as intrinsically normal or abnormal. Consider also the huge literature on helping homosexuals (at least males) change their sexual preference, and the paucity of literature aimed at helping the labelers change their prejudicial biases and encouraging the homosexual to develop as a person without going the change route. (Davison, 1977, p. 199)

Thus, one criticism of sexual reorientation treatments is that there is no cure without a disease. Second, the availability of procedures encourages their use in treatment. And, third, a charge of bias has been leveled (Davison, 1976, 1977; Begelman, 1975). "How can we honestly speak of non-prejudice when we participate in therapy regimes that by their very existence—and regardless of their efficacy—condone the current societal prejudice and perhaps also impede social change?" (Davison, 1977, p. 199).

Begelman (1975), arguing in much the same vein as Davison, also pointed out the countertherapeutic effects of treating gay people *for their gayness:*

> Behavior therapists contribute significantly to preventing the exercise of any *real* option in decision-making about sexual identity, by further strengthening the prejudice that homosexuality is a "problem behavior," since treatment may be offered for it. As a consequence of this therapeutic stance, as well as a wider system of social and attitudinal pressures, homosexuals tend to seek treatment *for being homosexuals.* Heterosexuals, on the other hand, can scarcely be expected to seek voluntary treatment for being "heterosexual," especially since all the social forces arrayed—including the availability of behavior therapy for heterosexuality—attest to the acknowledgment of the idea that whatever "problems" heterosexuals experience are not due to their sexual orientation. (p. 180)

Thus, despite the ostensibly "positive" view of behaviorally oriented therapists and counselors toward LGB people, *in fact* gay men, lesbians, and bisexuals have been treated differently within this theoretical tradition. Gay-affirmative writers and researchers stress that individuals presenting themselves with the desire to change their sexual orientation are actually going through a stage in the "coming out" process in the development of a positive gay identity (Cass, 1979).

More recently, proponents of conversion therapy have resurrected many of the old arguments about client choice and self-determination, despite the problematic methods of conversion therapy research and the poor success rates of most programs (Bieschke et al., 2000). Further, many proponents of conversion therapy for LGB people are motivated primarily by religious attitudes and beliefs (Bieschke et al., 2000). The American Psychological Association (1992) Ethics Code mandates that psychologists examine their own attitudes and beliefs and how these may affect their work with clients. "Yet inherent in conversion therapy is the premise that same-sex orientations are pathological, an arrest in development, or (less stigmatizing but still homophobic and harmful in nature) not as well accommodated in society as a heterosexual orientation" (Bieschke et al., 2000, pp. 312–313). We agree with Bieschke et al. (2000) that conversion therapy is both inappropriate and unethical.

Gay adolescents are especially at risk of being damaged by efforts to change sexual orientation (Coleman & Remafedi, 1989). Intense homophobia, both external and internal, and potential or actual rejection by their families profoundly complicates the developmental tasks of adolescence and enhances the difficulties associated with achieving a stable and mature personal and sexual identity on the part of teenagers; thus, gay teenagers may present with a desire "to be normal" (i.e., heterosexual) (American Psychological Association, 2000). Lack of sensitivity and inappropriate treatment can be equally damaging. The gravity of the matter can be seen in statistics indicating that confusion over sexual orientation is a significant contributor to teenage suicide (Gibson, 1988). Working with adolescents grappling with issues of sexual orientation is challenging enough, but the process is further confounded by ethical issues such as parental consent and confidentiality (Sobocinski, 1990). School counselors, who are the most likely mental health practitioners to be in a position to assist gay youths, may themselves be at risk of sanctions from school administrators for providing ethical, gay-affirmative counseling services. Readers are referred to Sobocinski's (1990) helpful overview of ethical issues and dilemmas in counseling gay and lesbian adolescents.

## Conclusion

Most of the problems experienced by LGB people are a direct result of societal oppression and the internalization of homophobia, and homophobic attitudes have parallels with other prejudicial attitudes such as sexism, racism, and ageism (American Psychological Association, 1997, 2000; Dworkin, 2000). Further, there is an intimate connection between antigay attitudes and gender-role beliefs, underscoring the relationship of homophobia and sexism. And finally, to be effective, counselors and therapists must not only inform themselves about gay lifestyles and treatment issues but must also address their own homophobia and heterosexual biases in order to work therapeutically with gay clients (American Psychological Association, 2000).

Chapters 15, 16, and 17 specifically address some of the counseling issues most relevant to LGB people generally and to lesbians and gay men specifically. Chapter 18 contains further information on education, training and supervision, and research related to counseling LGB people.

## REFERENCES

Adams, H. E., & Sturgis, E. T. (1977). Status of behavioral reorientation techniques in the modification of homosexuality: A review. *Psychological Bulletin, 84,* 1171–1188.

American Psychiatric Association. (1980). *Diagnostic and statistical manual of mental disorders* (3rd ed.). Washington, DC: Author.

American Psychiatric Association. (1994). *Diagnostic and statistical manual of mental disorders* (4th ed.). Washington, DC: Author.

American Psychological Association. (1992). Ethical principles of psychologists and code of conduct. *American Psychologist, 47,* 1597–1611.

American Psychological Association. (1997). *Resolution on appropriate therapeutic responses to sexual orientation* [adopted by the American Psychological Association Council of Representatives, August 14]. Washington, DC: Author.

American Psychological Association. (2000). *Guidelines for psychotherapy with lesbian, gay, and bisexual clients.* Washington, DC: Author.

Bailey, D. S. (1955). *Homosexuality and the Western Christian tradition.* London: Longman's.

Baird, R. M., & Baird, M. K. (1995). *Homosexuality: Debating the issues.* Amherst, NY: Prometheus Books.

Begelman, D. A. (1975). Ethical and legal issues of behavior modification. In M. Hersen, R. Eisler, & P. M. Miller (Eds.), *Progress in behavior modification* (pp. 175–199). New York: Academic Press.

Bieber, I., Dain, H. J., Dince, P. R., Diellich, M. G., Grand, H. G., Gandlach, R. H., Kremer, M. W., Rifkin, A. H., Wilbur, C. G., & Bieber, T. B. (1962). *Homosexuality: A psychoanalytic study.* New York: Random House.

Bieschke, K. J., McClanahan, M., Tozer, E., Grzegorek, J. L., & Park, J. (2000). Programmatic research on the treatment of lesbian, gay, and bisexual clients: The past, the present, and the course for the future. In R. M. Perez, K. A. DeBord, & K. J. Bieschke (Eds.), *Handbook of counseling and psychotherapy with lesbian, gay, and bisexual clients* (pp. 309–335). Washington, DC: American Psychological Association.

Black, D. (1986). *The plague years.* New York: Simon & Schuster.

Boswell, J. (1980). *Christianity, social tolerance, and homosexuality.* Chicago: University of Chicago Press.

Bullough, V. L. (1976). *Sexual variance in society and history.* New York: Wiley.

Bullough, V. L. (1979). *Homosexuality: A history.* New York: New American Library.

Casas, J. M., Brady, S., & Ponterotto, J. G. (1983). Sexual preference biases in counseling: An information processing approach. *Journal of Counseling Psychology, 30,* 139–145.

Cass, V. C. (1979). Homosexual identity formation: A theoretical model. *Journal of Homosexuality, 4,* 219–235.

Cohen, C. J., & Stein, T. S. (1986). Reconceptualizing individual psychotherapy with gay men and lesbians. In T. S. Stein & C. J. Cohen (Eds.), *Contemporary perspectives on psychotherapy with lesbians and gay men* (pp. 27–56). New York: Plenum Press.

Coleman, E., & Remafedi, G. (1989). Gay, lesbian, and bisexual adolescents: A critical challenge to counselors. *Journal of Counseling and Development, 68,* 36–40.

Davison, G. C. (1976). Homosexuality: The ethical challenge. *Journal of Consulting and Clinical Psychology, 44,* 157–162.

Davison, G. C. (1977). Homosexuality and the ethics of behavioral intervention. *Journal of Homosexuality, 2,* 195–204.

Davison, G., & Friedman, S. (1981). Sexual orientation stereotype in the distortion of clinical judgment. *Journal of Homosexuality, 6,* 37–44.

Dean, R. B., & Richardson, H. (1964). Analysis of MMPI profiles of 40 college-educated overt role homosexuals. *Journal of Consulting Psychology, 28,* 483–486.

Duberman, M. B., Vicinus, M., & Chauncey, G., Jr. (Eds.). (1989). *Hidden from history: Reclaiming the gay and lesbian past.* New York: New American Library.

Dunbar, J., Brown, M., & Amoroso, D. (1973). Some correlates of attitudes toward homosexuality. *Journal of Social Psychology, 89,* 271–279.

Dworkin, S. H. (1992). Some ethical considerations when counseling gay, lesbian, and bisexual clients. In S. H. Dworkin & F. J. Gutierrez (Eds.), *Counseling gay men and lesbians: Journey to the end of the rainbow* (pp. 325–334). Alexandria, VA: American Association for Counseling and Development.

Dworkin, S. H. (2000). Individual therapy with lesbian, gay, and bisexual clients. In R. M. Perez, K. A. DeBord, & K. J. Bieschke (Eds.), *Handbook of counseling and psychotherapy with lesbian, gay, and bisexual clients* (pp. 157–181). Washington, DC: American Psychological Association.

Dworkin, S. H., & Gutierrez, F. J. (Eds.). (1992). *Counseling gay men and lesbians: Journey to the end of the rainbow.* Alexandria, VA: American Association for Counseling and Development.

Evans, R. B. (1970). Sixteen personality factor questionnaire scores of homosexual men. *Journal of Consulting and Clinical Psychology, 34,* 212–215.

Falk, P. J. (1989). Lesbian mothers: Psychosocial assumptions in family law. *American Psychologist, 44,* 941–947.

Fassinger, R. E. (1991). The hidden minority: Issues and challenges in working with lesbian women and gay men. *The Counseling Psychologist, 19,* 157–176.

Fone, B. (2000). *Homophobia: A history.* New York: Picador.

Ford, C. S., & Beach, F. A. (1951). *Patterns of sexual behavior.* New York: Harper.

Foster, J. H. (1956). *Sex variant women in literature.* New York: Vantage Press. [Reprinted: Baltimore: Diana Press, 1975]

Fukuyama, M. A., & Ferguson, A. D. (2000). Lesbian, gay, and bisexual people of color: Understanding cultural complexity and managing multiple oppressions. In R. M. Perez, K. A. DeBord, & K. J. Bieschke (Eds.), *Handbook of counseling and psychotherapy with lesbian, gay, and bisexual clients* (pp. 81–105). Washington, DC: American Psychological Association.

Gallup, G. (1977, July 18). Gallup poll on gay rights: Approval with reservations. *San Francisco Chronicle,* pp. 1–18.

Garfinkle, E. M., & Morin, S. F. (1978). Psychologists' attitudes toward homosexual psychotherapy clients. *Journal of Social Issues, 34,* 101–112.

Garnets, L., Hancock, K. A., Cochran, S. D., Goodchilds, J., & Peplau, L. A. (1991). Issues in psychotherapy with lesbians and gay men. *American Psychologist, 46,* 964–972.

Gibson, P. (1988). Gay male and lesbian youth suicide. In *Report of the secretary's [Department of Health and Human Services] task force on youth suicide* (pp. 3–110 to 3–142). Washington, DC: U.S. Government Printing Office.

Graham, D. L. R., Rawlings, E. I., Halpern, H. S., & Hermes, J. (1984). Therapists' needs for training in counseling lesbians and gay men. *Professional Psychology, 15,* 482–496.

Grahn, J. (1984). *Another mother tongue: Gay words, gay worlds.* Boston: Beacon Press.

Hager, P. (1986, July 1). Ruling upholds ban on homosexual conduct. *Los Angeles Times,* pp. 1, 13.

Halperin, D. M. (1989). Sex before sexuality: Pederasty, politics, and power in classical Athens. In M. B. Duberman, M. Vicinus, & G. Chauncey, Jr. (Eds.), *Hidden from history: Reclaiming the gay and lesbian past* (pp. 37–53). New York: New American Library.

Hammersmith, S. K., & Weinberg, M. S. (1973). Homosexual identity: Commitment, adjustment, and significant others. *Sociometry, 36,* 56–79.

Herek, G. M. (1984). Beyond "homophobia": A social psychological perspective on attitudes toward lesbians and gay men. *Journal of Homosexuality, 10,* 1–21.

Herek, G. M. (1986, October 9). *Violence against lesbians and gay men.* Statement presented to the United States House of Representatives, Committee on the Judiciary, Subcommittee on Criminal Justice.

Herek, G. M. (1989). Hate crimes against lesbians and gay men: Issues for research and policy. *American Psychologist, 44,* 948–955.

Herek, G. M. (1991). Stigma, prejudice, and violence against lesbians and gay men. In J. Gonsiorek & J. Weinrich (Eds.), *Homosexuality: Research implications for public policy* (pp. 60–80). Newbury Park, CA: Sage.

Herek, G. M. (1993). Sexual orientation and military service: A social science perspective. *American Psychologist, 48,* 538–549.

Hooker, E. (1957). The adjustment of the male homosexual. *Journal of Projective Techniques, 21,* 18–31.

Hunt, B. (1993). What counselors need to know about counseling gay men and lesbians. *Counseling and Human Development, 26,* 1–12.

Hunter, N. D., Michaelson, S. E., & Stoddard, T. B. (1992). *The rights of lesbians and gay men: The basic ACLU guide to a gay person's rights.* Carbondale: Southern Illinois University Press.

Jeffries, J. C., Jr. (1995). Changing times: Gay rights. In R. M. Baird & M. K. Baird (Eds.). *Homosexuality: Debating the issues* (pp. 103–118). Amherst, NY: Prometheus Books.

Jones, S. L. (1995). The loving opposition. In R. M. Baird & M. K. Baird (Eds.), *Homosexuality: Debating the issues* (pp. 243–253). Amherst, NY: Prometheus Books.

Kinsey, A. C., Pomeroy, W. B., & Martin, C. E. (1948). *Sexual behavior in the human male.* Philadelphia: Saunders.

Kinsey, A. C., Pomeroy, W. B., Martin, C. E., & Gebhard, P. H. (1953). *Sexual behavior in the human female.* Philadelphia: Saunders.

Krajeski, J. P. (1986). Psychotherapy with gay men and lesbians. In T. S. Stein & C. J. Cohen (Eds.), *Contemporary perspectives on psychotherapy with lesbians and gay men* (pp. 9–26). New York: Plenum Press.

Kwawer, J. S. (1980). Transference and countertransference in homosexuality—Changing psychoanalytic views. *American Journal of Psychotherapy, 34,* 72–80.

Lauritsen, J., & Thorstad, D. (1974). *The early homosexual rights movement.* New York: Times Change Press.

Levitt, E., & Klassen, A., Jr. (1974). Public attitudes toward homosexuality: Part of a 1970 national survey by the Institute of Sex Research. *Journal of Homosexuality, 1,* 29–43.

Martin, A. (1982). Some issues in the treatment of gay and lesbian patients. *Psychotherapy: Theory, research and practice, 19,* 341–348.

Martin, D., & Lyon, P. (1972). *Lesbian/woman.* New York: Bantam.

McDermott, D., Tyndall, L., & Lichtenberg, J. W. (1989). Factors related to counselor preference among gays and lesbians. *Journal of Counseling and Development, 68,* 31–35.

Melton, G. B. (1989). Public policy and private prejudice: Psychology and law on gay rights. *American Psychologist, 44,* 933–940.

Morin, S. F. (1977). Heterosexual bias in psychological research on lesbianism and male homosexuality. *American Psychologist, 32,* 629–637.

Morin, S. F., & Garfinkle, E. M. (1978). Male homophobia. *Journal of Social Issues, 34,* 29–47.

Moses, A. E., and Hawkins, R. O. (1982). *Counseling lesbian women and gay men.* St. Louis: Mosby.

National Museum and Archive of Lesbian and Gay History. (1996). *The gay almanac.* New York: Berkeley Books.

Paulsen, J. (1983, April). *Homophobia in American psychiatrists.* Paper presented to the Group for the Advancement of Psychiatry, Philadelphia.

Plant, R. (1986). *The pink triangle: The Nazi war against homosexuals.* New York: New Republic.

Reynolds, A. L., & Hanjorgiris, W. F. (2000). Coming out: Lesbian, gay, and bisexual identity development. In R. M. Perez, K. A. DeBord, & K. J. Bieschke

(Eds.), *Handbook of counseling and psychotherapy with lesbian, gay, and bisexual clients* (pp. 35–55). Washington, DC: American Psychological Association.

Rich, A. (1980). Compulsory heterosexuality and lesbian existence. *Signs: Journal of Women in Culture and Society, 5,* 631–660.

Rothblum, E. D. (2000). "Somewhere in Des Moines or San Antonio": Historical perspectives on lesbian, gay, and bisexual mental health. In R. M. Perez, K. A. DeBord, & K. J. Bieschke (Eds.), *Handbook of counseling and psychotherapy with lesbian, gay, and bisexual clients* (pp. 57–80). Washington, DC: American Psychological Association.

Rothschild, M. (1992, September 21). Gay bashing becomes new national pastime. *Arizona Republic,* p. A9.

Rowse, A. L. (1977). *Homosexuals in history.* New York: Carroll & Graf.

Rudolph, J. (1988). Counselors' attitudes toward homosexuality: A selective review of the literature. *Journal of Counseling and Development, 67,* 165–168.

Rudolph, J. (1989). The impact of contemporary ideology and AIDS on the counseling of gay clients. *Counseling and Values, 33,* 96–108.

Rule, J. (1975). *Lesbian images.* New York: Doubleday.

Sailor in beating death of gay would "do it again." (1993, May 26). *Arizona Republic,* p. A5.

Smolowe, J. (1993, May 24). Hearts and minefields. *Time,* pp. 41–42.

Sobocinski, M. R. (1990). Ethical principles in the counseling of gay and lesbian adolescents: Issues of autonomy, competence, and confidentiality. *Professional Psychology: Research and Practice, 21,* 240–247.

Stein, T. S., & Cohen, C. J. (Eds.). (1986). *Contemporary perspectives on psychotherapy with gay men and lesbians.* New York: Plenum Press.

Tavris, C. (1977, January). Men and women report their views on masculinity. *Psychology Today, 35.*

Teal, D. (1971). *The gay militants.* New York: Stein & Day.

Weinberg, G. (1972). *Society and the healthy homosexual.* New York: Anchor.

Weinberg, M. S. (1970). The male homosexual: Age-related variations in social and psychological characteristics. *Social Problems, 17,* 527–537.

Weinberg, M. S., & Williams, C. J. (1974). *Male homosexuals: Their problems and adaptations.* New York: Oxford University Press.

Weintraub, S. (1987). *Victoria: An intimate biography.* New York: E. P. Dutton.

Wolf, T. J. (1992). Bisexuality: A counseling perspective. In S. H. Dworkin & F. J. Gutierrez (Eds.), *Counseling gay men and lesbians: Journey to the end of the rainbow* (pp. 175–187). Alexandria, VA: American Association for Counseling and Development.

Woodman, N. J., & Lenna, H. R. (1980). *Counseling with gay men and women.* San Francisco: Jossey-Bass.

Wysor, B. (1974). *The lesbian myth.* New York: Random House.

Zinik, G. (1985). Identity conflict or adaptive flexibility: Bisexuality reconsidered. In F. Klein & T. Wolf (Eds.), *Bisexualities: Research and theory* (pp. 7–19). New York: Haworth.

# Part II THE CLIENT WITH A DISABILITY

CHAPTER 6 Counseling Families and Children With Disabilities

Timothy R. Elliott, University of Alabama at Birmingham, and Larry L. Mullins, Oklahoma State University

The occurrence of a physical disability has practically always had repercussions within the family system. A physical disability may be congenital or acquired; in both scenarios the occurrence may be best construed as an *off-time* life event in terms of the normative developmental expectations for the family and the child with the condition (Neugarten, 1979). Although a physical disability is not a welcomed occurrence, the ramifications of the condition vary considerably among families, and there is no set pattern that typifies family reactions and subsequent adjustment. Many children with severe physical disability may have considerable difficulty living independently, and a parent may be compelled to assume assistive duties at the expense of their personal career goals, social activities, and interpersonal relationships. Due to tremendous advances in medical technology, individuals who incur severe physical disability often have considerable life expectancy, and thus the need for assistance from family members may exist throughout a lifetime.

Counselors need at their disposal a working knowledge of the family and a useful model that can guide assessment and intervention strategies. In this chapter, we focus on the epidemiology of physical disability and the specific issues and task demands experienced by these families, and we provide a working model to organize relevant information about factors that facilitate the adjustment of family members.

## WHAT COUNSELORS NEED TO KNOW ABOUT CHILDREN WITH DISABILITIES AND THEIR FAMILIES

Children with disabilities constitute a large, heterogeneous group of individuals, with varying degrees of physical limitations and cognitive development. Collectively, it is estimated that approximately 4 million children in the United States have a significant disability (Wenger, Kaye, & LaPlante, 1996). Prevalence rates vary, but somewhere between 10% and 20% of children in the United States appear to evidence some form of disability at any given point in time (Gortmaker &

Sappenfield, 1984). Children from lower socioeconomic backgrounds are at higher risk to have a severe condition that limits their daily functioning (Perrin & McLean, 1988).

Children with disabilities often contend with various sensory and mobility impairments, endure recurrent hospitalizations and medical procedures, and adhere to complex therapy regimens. The nature of their disabilities also affects interpersonal relationships by reducing social contacts and the number of individuals in their social network (Lyons, Sullivan, Ritvo, & Coyne, 1995). Children with developmental disabilities are at high risk for manifesting significant behavior problems at a rate 5 times greater than that of children without health problems (Wallander, Varni, Babani, Banis, & Wilcox, 1989). Research also indicates that having a disability places a child at significantly greater risk for abuse and neglect by a parent compared with a child without a disability (National Center on Child Abuse and Neglect, 1993). Indeed, up to one third of all children with disabilities have experienced some form of maltreatment (Sullivan & Knutson, 2000). Thus, substantial evidence indicates that children with disabilities constitute a population at risk for various medical, psychological, and social problems.

The task demands of caring for and parenting a child with a disability can be substantial. Parents are confronted with complicated medical regimens and health crises, and financial resources are often strained, especially when only one parent can work, or only one parent is present. Many researchers have commented on the considerable stress placed on parents of these children (e.g., Kazak & Simms, 1996), and although many appear to cope well, some clearly do not. Overall, the extant research indicates that parents of children with disabilities are at risk for adjustment problems, which in turn may place their children at even greater risk for behavioral problems and possibly maltreatment.

To understand the wealth of information concerning family and child adjustment following disability, it is imperative that we recognize that disability does not occur in a vacuum. Disability is always defined by the immediate environment, and by the historical and temporal context in which it occurs. At its intellectual core, rehabilitation psychology embraces a Lewinian field-theory perspective to understand observed behavior associated with a disability, as expressed in the classic equation, $B = f(P, E)$. As succinctly conveyed in this statement, any observed behavior associated with a disability is a product of the interaction between the person and the environment. For our purposes, it is essential that we recognize the many facets of the environment and the behavioral processes of the different family members that contribute to the family experience of disability.

Second, it is critical that we recognize that adjustment can be defined in positive and negative terms. Historically, the study of adjustment following physical disability was restricted to negative indicators of adjustment. Much of this work was conducted in clinical settings in which the attention was directed to serviceable activity to facilitate the detection and treatment of problems presented by children and families. This context resulted in a pathological model of adjustment, so that there was little—if any—recognition of the ways in which families might benefit or experience positive growth following the occurrence of a physical disability in a child. Indeed, behaviors that could be construed as serving a useful or adaptive function for the family were often routinely construed in a pathological manner. Furthermore, this historical perspective placed a disproportionate emphasis on personal and medical factors implicated in adjustment, as these characteristics fit conveniently within the traditional scope (and comfort zone) of serviceable activity provided by professionals in educational, medical, and mental health institutions.

For our purposes, we rely on a conceptualization of family adjustment following disability that encompasses relevant elements in several broad-based domains, each of which has considerable impact on areas of adjustment that subsume positive and negative outcomes. This model, as first described in an essay on positive growth following disability (Elliott, Kurylo, & Rivera, 2002), owes much to the "disability-stress-coping" models that were designed to explain why some children fare better following chronic illness than others (Thompson & Gustafson, 1996; Wallander et al., 1989). Essentially, these models argue that chronic illness or disability serves as a stressor to which the individual and the family attempt to adapt.

The present model differs from these previous conceptualizations in a number of important ways. As depicted in Figure 6.1, the model is designed in such a way to understand issues that may affect adjustment over the life span, taking into account development, ecological, and temporal factors that occur as people age, as relationships change, and as significant technological advancements occur. This model is not specific to the understanding of child adjustment per se but is meant to be useful in appreciating adjustment of people with chronic disease and disability across the life span.

**FIGURE 6.1**   Model for understanding positive growth following disability.

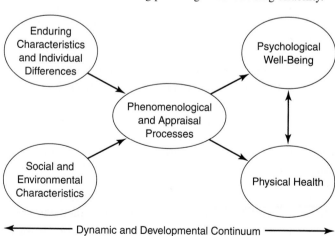

Additionally, the concept of stress is not a centerpiece of this model; rather, it emphasizes the pivotal role of phenomenological appraisals and personal experience of events, and the dynamic processes that occur as people respond to the ambiguity, banality, and occasional urgency of everyday life. The model recognizes that certain aspects of living with a disability will impose specific activities as a part of health maintenance and self-care regimens for optimal adjustment. However, the degree to which these will be experienced as stressful or incorporated into everyday routines will depend on the phenomenological ways in which people process information, accommodate change, and develop new behaviors. The model also recognizes that problems are associated with disability and disease outside the realm of personal volition. These can include a variety of social, institutional and service-related issues (e.g., school placement, support from public health service programs). These problems vary in valence and impact at any point in time, and each individual should be consulted to determine the degree to which these are problematic.

Thus, the model recognizes that individuals (and a family) operate as active stakeholders in their health and well-being, and many factors can promote or undermine the degree to which individuals can operate as active and informed consumers in their health care. Families who have a member living with a chronic disease or disability are best viewed as competent yet dynamic entities that are influenced by an array of societal systems (Aneshensel, Pearlin, Mullan, Zarit, & Whitlatch, 1995).

In the present model, the phenomenological experience of children living with a condition is influenced by not only the enduring characteristics of the condition but also the individual differences that pertain to their developing personality characteristics and learned patterns of behavior. Their experience, perceptions, and appraisals are also influenced by factors in their social environment, which can serve to ameliorate, buffer, or exacerbate their day-to-day life. This aspect—the phenomenological perspective—stands as a separate component in the model. The components and the major outcomes that encompass the major aspects of adjustment in both positive and negative terms are described in the following sections.

## ENDURING CHARACTERISTICS
## AND INDIVIDUAL DIFFERENCES

This component of the model includes the specific demographic characteristics of the family and its members, disability-related characteristics (e.g., the type of disability), and various behavioral patterns and personality characteristics of the family members.

### Demographic Characteristics

The extant literature is inundated with descriptive differences between children with disabilities (of any kind) and those without disabilities; similarly, there is considerable work documenting differences between families living with a child's disability and families that do not. To a great extent, this work was not grounded in any a priori theory, and the focus of the work was decidedly negative, largely disinterested in any positive outcomes or comparisons. Research essentially assumed that the presence of a disability in a family is sufficient to cause disruptions in the person and the family and development of subsequent "psychopathology" (Harper, 1991). For example, some early research guided by this premise reported that siblings of a child with a disability were at risk for behavioral and emotional problems (Breslau & Prabucki, 1987).

However, many demographic characteristics may exert considerable influence on family adjustment, including the socioeconomic status of the family. A disproportionate percentage of families with children with disabilities live below the poverty line throughout the United States. This situation translates into restricted access to health care, fewer resources for therapy and other adjunctive services (e.g., respite care, vocational rehabilitation), and fewer opportunities for acquiring assistive devices. There is a greater likelihood that these families will live in neighborhoods that have physical barriers that impede mobility and schools districts that are inadequately funded and thus unprepared to educate children with complex needs. Under such circumstances, families living in poverty face incredible obstacles that conspire against the best interests and well-being of the child.

Concepts of gender and ethnicity share considerable overlap with the social and environmental component of this model because these are often socially defined constructs; thus, gender and ethnicity are discussed in a later section that addresses social and environmental influences on adjustment.

## Disability-Related Characteristics

Among children with disability it is essential that counselors understand the complex nature of a disability and its concomitant characteristics, and the ensuing ramifications on the other components within the model. To understand family and child adjustment following disability, counselors should explore the following issues in a thorough assessment:

- Does the child experience alterations in the typical brain-behavior relationships as a feature or consequence of the disability?
- What are the prerequisite requirements (i.e., task demands) for maintaining and promoting the optimal health and well-being of the child?
- To what extent does the disability pose particular physical limitations?
- To what extent does illness intrusiveness exist (Devins, Cameron, & Edworthy, 2000)? In other words, to what degree does the disability limit the child's ability to engage in desired activities?

Disabilities associated with impairments in higher cortical functions (e.g., cerebral palsy, epilepsy, traumatic brain injury) may result in permanent brain-behavior alterations that adversely affect learning ability and social behavior. In some cases a child may have limited or restricted intellectual capacities; among children with brain injuries, behavioral disruptions such as agitation, impulsivity, or emotional lability may be present independent of intellectual impairments. Some chronic conditions (e.g., narcolepsy, idiopathic hyposomnia) may have fluctuating and unpredictable effects on alertness and awareness.

For many children with disability, optimal health may be contingent upon successful completion of a daily array of medical and behavioral activities. Some medications may be necessary to maintain alertness or facilitate appropriate social behavior. Many disabilities that impair central nervous system function require adults to assist the child in movement (turning, stretching, transferring, etc.), toileting, and other activities of daily living (eating, clothing, grooming). In these situations, the concomitants of the disability (e.g., motor paralysis) interact with the qualities of the social and interpersonal environment to directly affect the health and well-being of the child. Parents vary considerably in their propensity to adhere to behavioral regimens for care and in having access to appropriate services from medical, educational, and public institutions.

Certain disabilities also result in significant physical limitations, which in turn may or may not impinge on the ability to engage in valued life activity. Numerous studies now point out that disease severity in and of itself is not as predictive of adjustment as is the extent to which the condition intrudes on one's ability to engage in pleasurable life activities (Devins et al., 2000).

## Personality Characteristics of Family Members

Personality characteristics or traits are often related in predictable ways to family adjustment following disability. Although many different constructs have been studied in this area, variables that are grounded in cognitive-behavioral models appear particularly promising. These models often feature a logical framework with testable hypotheses, a supportive literature base, psychometrically sound measures, and clear directions for interventions. Exemplary research has been guided by a model of social-problem-solving abilities (D'Zurilla & Nezu, 1999). Mothers of children with disabilities who report a greater sense of confidence in their problem-solving ability report higher levels of adjustment than mothers who lack this confidence (Noojin & Wallander, 1997). These beneficial effects appear independent of stress levels reported by the mothers. Effective social-problem-solving abilities are predictive of family caregiver depression, anxiety, and ill health over the first year of the caregiver role (Elliott, Shewchuk, & Richards, 2001).

Parents who have more effective written and verbal problem-solving skills adhere more to complex self-care regimens for their children than parents of children noted for poor compliance (Fehrenbach & Peterson, 1989). Families that exhibit effective problem-solving strategies in interpersonal interactions report less distress, and these benefits can be observed up to 3 years later (Rivara et al., 1996). These skills may be a major determinant of child behavioral outcomes over the first year of traumatic brain injury (Kinsella, Ong, Murtagh, Prior, & Sawyer, 1999).

Children also vary in the degree to which they possess adaptive personality characteristics, some of which reflect specific cognitive patterns or styles. Children may have hopeful beliefs about themselves, their goals, and ways to achieve these goals, and these beliefs have been inversely related to distress reported by children with sickle-cell disease (Lewis & Kliewer, 1996) and burns (Barnum, Snyder, Rapoff, Mani, & Thompson, 1998). Higher levels of hope are uniquely associated with improved maternal adjustment, and this effect seems to be most pronounced under conditions of high stress specific to the condition (Horton & Wallander, 2001). Children with Type 1 diabetes who exhibit a negative attributional style (i.e., learned helplessness) are at risk for adjustment problems and difficulty in adherence to their medical regimen (Kuttner, Delameter, & Santiago, 1990). Similarly, perceived control has been linked to adjustment in children with Type 1 diabetes (Band & Wiesz, 1990). Collectively, these studies underscore the importance of attending to the cognitive-behavioral characteristics of children with disability and of their parents.

## SOCIAL AND ENVIRONMENTAL FACTORS

This component of the model encompasses the social and environmental factors that can have a tremendous impact on a child's behavior, including stigma, social relations, family interactional patterns, social support, gender-related issues, parental modeling, and issues of ethnicity.

### Stigma, Competence, and Social Relations

The special education literature is replete with evidence demonstrating the deleterious effects of social stigma on children with disabilities, as it is encountered in educational institutions from peers and adults. Stigma may occur in reaction to the physical features of the disability or its treatment, but it may also be in reaction to a diagnostic label for an "invisible" disability (e.g., attention-deficit disorder). Stigma is associated with decreased expectations for performance, lowered accountability, and increased expectations for failure.

Less obvious has been the experience of stigma perpetrated by helping professionals toward the family and child. Many health-related professionals anticipate negative outcomes, and positive behaviors will often be construed in a negative light. For example, an adolescent with an outstanding history of scholastic achievement and personal adjustment was criticized by rehabilitation staff for stating her optimistic goal to return to school as soon as possible following her discharge from an inpatient program for traumatic brain injury (Elliott & Kurylo, 2000). Her goals were interpreted by staff as "pathological denial," and the neuropsychologist recommended the girl should miss a year of school. The team did not recommend any assistive devices to support her pursuits. The parents were forced to choose between their daughter's stated goals and the team's recommendations. The family supported their daughter over the objections of the team; the daughter successfully met her goal to graduate on time with her high school class (and has since earned her bachelor's degree from a major state university).

This case may not be representative of many outcomes following brain injury. Nevertheless, it illustrates the difficulties families must navigate in their interactions with health care professionals—who may pressure families to discount their personal experience and the opinions of the child—in order to pursue an agenda that may be more suitable to professional bias than the family.

## Social Relations

Children with disabilities that affect the central nervous system (e.g., cerebral palsy, epilepsy, spina bifida) may experience significant difficulties with social competence and peer relations. In part, the cognitive impairments associated with these conditions may blunt the learning, understanding, and recognition of social cues and interpersonal relationships (Nassau & Drotar, 1997). Low cognitive ability is associated with diminished social skills (Bellanti & Bierman, 2000). Children with cancerous brain tumors may also demonstrate difficulties with social competence. Such problems may be related to treatment procedures, to the time spent away from school in lengthy and time-consuming treatments, and to parental overprotectiveness (Fuemmeler, Elkin, & Mullins, 2001). Thus, children with disabilities may experience considerable disruption in their social relationships.

## Family Interactional Patterns

For many years, clinical lore concerning family dynamics in the wake of a chronic health condition was driven by Minuchin's conceptualization of rigid, overprotective, and enmeshed family interaction patterns that contribute to the development and exacerbation of physical symptoms in children (Minuchin et al., 1975). Subsequent research has not supported the basic tenets of this model (Coyne & Anderson, 1989), and alternative models have been suggested that involve biobehavioral formulations (Wood, 1993) or transactional stress and coping approaches (Thompson & Gustafson, 1996). Such contemporary approaches have empirical support and lend themselves to continued research on family interaction. For example, recent evidence indicates that some of these interactive patterns in which a child's input is recruited into dyadic discussions may be related to marital quality and may be useful in long-term coping, monitoring, and management of a chronic condition (Northey, Griffin, & Krainz, 1998). Increased family cohesion and high quality of mother-child interactions are predictive of positive growth in socialization, daily living skills, and communication among young children with Down's syndrome (Hauser-Cram et al., 1999).

## Social Support

Despite the usually unquestioned premiums associated with social support, the extant literature does not provide clear implications for counselors in search of therapeutic direction for clinical practice. For many mothers who provide care to a child with a disability or chronic disease, social support once at hand erodes with the passage of time (Quittner, Glueckauf, & Jackson, 1990). Social support also seems to depend on personal characteristics: Mothers who have more personal resources (e.g., self-esteem, mastery), more intimate personal resources, and lower discomfort in seeking support report more support over a year of caregiving for a child with chronic illness (Hobfoll & Lerman, 1989).

Other research indicates that mothers of children with physical disability may experience a lack of positive reinforcement (or opportunities for such) in pleasant interactions with the world outside the family. Quittner and colleagues have found that mothers of children with chronic disease have fewer leisure activities, as they are preoccupied with caregiving tasks (Quittner, Opipari, Regoli, Jacobsen, & Eigen, 1992). Time spent in recreation might mediate the relation between role strain of parents and their distress (Quittner et al., 1998). This dearth of meaningful, rewarding leisure time may deny family members the opportunity to experience positive reinforcement and positive moods associated with these activities.

## Issues of Gender

Research to date indicates distinct parent gender differences in the context of children's disability. Women are more likely to assume the role of primary caregiver for a child with a disability (Moen, Robison, & Dempster-McClain, 1995). Women in caregiving roles report more distress than men in similar roles, but these differences may be attributable to the willingness of women to report distress and the different appraisal processes between men and women (Burman & Margolin, 1992).

Children's adjustment is often associated with the mother's adjustment, but maternal caregiver adjustment is influenced more by stress, family support, and personal resources than the severity of the condition or functional abilities of the child (Wallander, Pitt, & Mellins, 1990; Wallander et al., 1989). Although mothers often encounter social isolation as they care for a child with a chronic disease or disability, fathers report more strains associated with financial obligations and work-related activities that affect the care and well-being of the child (Frank, Brown, Blount, & Bunke, 2001).

The emotional needs of men and women may also vary considerably while parenting a child with a disability. As an example, although fathers and mothers of children with spina bifida reported less parental satisfaction than those in a comparison group, the mothers—and not the fathers—of these children reported higher levels of social isolation and lower levels of perceived parental competence (Holmbeck et al., 1997). These mothers were also more likely to rely on avoidant coping behaviors, implying a possible association between palliative coping behaviors, lower competence, and distress. Other longitudinal research indicates that spouses' use of avoidance coping is predictive of poorer parental adjustment 1 year later among parents of children with juvenile rheumatoid disease (Timko, Stovel, & Moos, 1992).

Although the impact of fathers on child adjustment has been largely overlooked in past research, accumulating evidence now demonstrates that fathers have a considerable impact on adjustment of a child with a chronic health condition, even when the father does not assume the role of family caregiver per se. For example, fathers' drinking problems and parental strain were predictive of child adjustment over a 4-year period (Timko, Baumgartner, Moos, & Miller, 1993). Chaney, Mullins, Frank, and Peterson (1997) found child adjustment over a year was directly related to increases in fathers' distress, and not the mothers' distress.

A decline in fathers' adjustment was inversely related to mothers' adjustment. Such research clearly demonstrates the need to attend differentially to fathers and mothers as it concerns their specific response to child disability.

## Modeling Influences From Parent to Child

Parents can model effective coping skills for their children, who in turn may use similar strategies (Kliewer & Lewis, 1995). Parental support and coping behavior are positively associated with a child's compliance with self-care regimens (Chaney & Peterson, 1989). In contrast, behavioral problems and health complaints of adolescents with chronic disease are more likely in families lower in family competence (Kell, Kliewer, Erickson, & Ohene-Frempong, 1998) and in marriages characterized by poor adjustment and interactional strain between husbands and wives (Clay, Wood, Frank, Hagglund, & Johnson, 1995; Frank et al., 1998). Numerous studies now document a clear pattern; one of the single best predictors of child adjustment to illness is parent adjustment (Mullins & Chaney, 2001). What remains to be determined are the specific processes by which this modeling occurs.

## Issues of Ethnicity

Research to date has yet to systematically address issues associated with minority status and ethnic backgrounds in this area (Drotar, 1997). The very constitution of family in minority ethnic groups can differ from the majority in American society. For many European American families, the close family consists of mother, father, and children; in many minority families this can include grandparents, aunts, and uncles (Basic Behavioral Science Task Force, 1996). Pickett, Vraniak, Cook, and Bertram (1993) observed that African American parents of children with disabilities had higher feelings of self-worth and lower levels of depression than European American parents with children who had disabilities. Importantly, the extended family structure and the collectivist spirit characteristic of many minority families suggests that these families might be able to cope better with a disabling condition of a family member than European American families.

However, such conclusions should be made cautiously. Errors in judgment about cultural groups are frequently based on such stereotypes. Because families of color are often depicted as being close-knit and supportive of their kin, for example, social service agencies may not take the time to assess the actual needs of this population. Such assumptions may lead to *less* allocation of resources, personnel, and finances for outreach to those communities (Valle, 1981), which in turn, may help perpetuate the misconception that they underutilize social services because they are taken care of by their own families (Henderson & Gutierrez-Mayka, 1992).

## PHENOMENOLOGICAL PROCESSES IN ADJUSTMENT

Cognitive appraisals reflect personal experience and interpretations of events, and because they are influenced by personal and social factors, they are dynamic and complex. Generally, clinicians encounter phenomenological appraisals as they are expressed in times of duress as individuals search for meaning and avenues for coping. Clinicians are then vigilant for manifestations of denial, assuming family members are unconsciously unable to accept the fact that a loved one may be permanently affected by a diagnosis. However, clinicians often fail to appreciate that many people are generally unaware or uninformed about specific health problems and their concomitants and thus may have legitimate difficulty in understanding the meaning and ramifications of a specific condition. Denial is not a single, simplistic entity: Families may not deny the factual existence of a particular disabling condition, but in turn they also may not accept the implications of the condition as promulgated by clinical staff. Families that maintain positive goals and expectations and that express optimism in the wake of an acquired disability are often labeled by staff and treated with disregard and condescension when in fact a family may express nothing more than a difference of opinion with staff.

Phenomenological perspectives are also expressed in terms of personal values and goals. Goals of personal importance are more likely to be attained in rehabilitation programs than goals imposed by a treatment team (Webb & Glueckauf, 1994). Family members may experience positive shifts in their values and reconsider goals that were altered in the face of disability, and these shifts are indicative of stress-related growth and subjective well-being (King & Patterson, 2000; King, Scollon, Ramsey, & Williams, 2000).

Furthermore, families are quite capable of identifying the specific problems they experience in facing their child's disability and in recommending ways to address these problems and meet their needs. Families are not usually seen as active stakeholders in their health care, so decisions about problems to be addressed and services to be provided are often made by institutional staff with no input from these consumers (Elliott & Shewchuk, in press). We have learned in focus groups, for example, that mothers of adolescents with cerebral palsy report specific problems with finances, patience, worries about outliving their child (and the child's subsequent welfare), and difficulties with public resources, sources of assistance and support, and other relationships. These are problems that can be actively addressed in intervention programs for the family. Such problems also have implications for public and social policy that affects these families. Other researchers have developed instruments that are oriented toward identifying specific areas of concern for intervention, which can be more useful than a global index of stress for diagnostic or research purposes (e.g., Noojin & Wallander, 1996).

In this model, we recognize the need to understand and appreciate the individual experience as it is expressed in the report of problems, concerns, and stress, and in terms of personal meaning, values, goals, and attributions. In this fashion we avoid a top-down approach in which we assume the nature of stress or the types of problems "typically" experienced. This permits a more strategic tailoring of interventions to meet the unique needs of the family and the child and incorporates these individuals as active participants in their health and well-being. It also allows us to respect the development and dynamic process of adjustment and accompanying changes that may occur for the individuals over time, without being confined to condescending and demeaning language that emphasizes pathology (conveyed, e.g., in the term *relapse*).

## DEFINING ADJUSTMENT AND QUALITY OF LIFE

Optimal adjustment, as depicted in Figure 6.1, entails physical health and personal well-being, and these broad concepts are often related. Difficulties and personal setbacks in health, which often result in secondary complications specific to a condition (e.g., pressure sores associated with a spinal cord injury), usually occur at great expense to the child, the family, and service institutions and health care programs. These are often understandably associated with distress and discouragement. However, maintenance of health and optimal adjustment is also associated with a greater sense of well-being and satisfaction.

Although researchers and clinicians usually focus on the adjustment problems experienced by families following disability and disease, some families experience positive changes (Perlesz, Kinsella, & Crowe, 1999). Acquired disability can force family members to directly confront issues of trust, mortality, and values, which in turn compel members to develop deeper commitments and restructure the meaning of marriage or kinship (Olkin, 1999). Some family members report a greater sense of closeness, a greater emphasis on family and personal relationships, and positive changes in shared family values (Crewe, 1993). Many studies appear to overreport or misrepresent distress experienced by siblings of children with disability, and these issues seem to be adversely slanted by methodological and theoretical approaches that perpetrate negative views and ignore positive aspects of this experience (Perlesz et al., 1999; Summers, White, & Summers, 1994). Indeed, some studies actually indicate that siblings of children with developmental disabilities report a number of positive consequences of growing up in such a family (McHale, Sloan, & Simeonsson, 1986).

## INTERVENTIONS

Working with families and children with disability requires a more expanded role than is typical in many settings. Because by definition intervention therapeutic efforts are often interdisciplinary and multisystemic (Mullins & Chaney, 2001) counselors will often serve as individual therapist, family counselor, case manager, advocate, and systems consultant in almost simultaneous fashion. Clearly, the family remains the centerpiece of the intervention effort. The role of family members is routinely acknowledged as a major focus of psychological intervention for a child with a disability or chronic disease (Kazak, Segal-Andrews, & Johnson, 1995). Counselors should first and foremost develop interventions that best meet the needs of the child and family, as they are experienced and reported by these individuals. Interventions that address the specific needs of families and their members—as they perceive them—may be more likely to succeed (Burman & Margolin, 1992). Parents will need education about the nature of a particular disabling condition, its course, and the likely effects it may have on their child's development. Moreover, they will need continued support at strategic times in the developmental course of a given condition. Shifting role responsibilities within the family system may also be a concern, not to mention financial stress. Counselors should also be mindful of the impact different social, educational, and medical agencies have on the well-being of parents and children living with a disability and should advocate for the need to intervene with these systems on behalf of the family (Kazak et al., 1995). In this regard, the counselor must be knowledgeable of both local public education law as well as the Individuals with Disability Education Act (IDEA) and the implications for the child with whom they are working. Finally, the counselor must be cognizant of medical systems and culture, as frequent contact with health care professionals is an essential part of many intervention efforts.

There are times when counselors will intervene to provide specific skill-building activities so that a child may be better equipped to negotiate the realities of his or her social and interpersonal world; social skills training is an effective intervention for these children (Varni, Katz, Colegrove, & Dolgin, 1993). Children can be taught to recognize social cues, develop social competency, and engage in assertive responding through the use of role plays and modeling. In recent years, empirically supported treatments have also been developed for promoting treatment adherence (e.g., Lemanek, Kamps, & Chung, 2001) and for managing acute and chronic pain (e.g., Walco, Sterling, Conte, & Engel, 1999). Each of these problems is particularly common in children with disabilities. And, because many children with disabilities are often targets for teasing and bullying, efforts can also be extended to teaching specific adaptive responses to taunting and threats. Finally, cognitive behavioral interventions developed for nondisabled children can be readily adapted and utilized for helping children cope with anxiety and depression.

In other situations, it may be more strategic to directly address the needs of the parents, and this may at times involve some nontraditional accommodations to circumvent barriers in transportation and mobility. This is particularly true for parents who live in geographically remote areas. One multisite, randomized trial of face-to-face problem-solving training sessions for mothers of children with cancer offered some telephone sessions for participants if they were unable to make the designated site and if they had attended at least one session with the trainer (Sahler et al., 2002). After an 8-week intervention, mothers assigned to the treatment group had significantly lower distress and higher problem-solving skills in comparison with control group participants.

Computer-based technologies can be used to conduct family counseling sessions, and these modalities have been used successfully with families that have a teenage child with seizure disorders (Hufford, Glueckauf, & Webb, 1999). Home-based video counseling and speaker phone counseling, and face-to-face office-based counseling appear to be equally effective in reducing problem severity experienced by families and preadolescents with epilepsy; moreover, these respondents preferred the two home-based modalities over the traditional office visit (Glueckauf et al., 2002). Virtual-reality technologies have also been developed to help children and adolescents learn specific skills (e.g., cope with intense pain; Hoffman, Doctor, Patterson, Carrougher, & Furness, 2000) and attain greater mobility and independence (learn activities of daily living, driving skills; Schultheis & Rizzo, 2001). Counselors should be aware of alternative interventions and assistive technologies that can promote behavioral change and enhance quality of life.

Other less traditional forms of intervention may also be initiated by the counselor for families of children with disability. In recent years, respite care has become an increasingly popular form of care offered as a means of alleviating caregiver burden or stress. Respite care can be offered on an outpatient, inpatient, or in-home basis according to the desires of the family and available resources. Recent evidence suggests that short-term inpatient respite stays (3–7 days) can result in significant decreases in psychological distress experienced by parents of children with severe disability (Mullins, Aniol, Boyd, Page, & Chaney, 2002). Importantly, these benefits were maintained over a 6-month period.

Counselors will invariably be in a position to consult with educational and other service institutions on appropriate interventions for children. Well-intentioned but misguided efforts have often assumed that increased contact between children with and without disability will dispel stigma and foster peer acceptance, but research presents a very different picture. The quality of the contact and the experience of achievement and the emphasis on ability (rather than the disability) will have ameliorating effects on stigma. In other cases, counselors may need to advocate on behalf of the family for certain and specific services to increase the likelihood of achievement or may need to suggest appropriate accommodations that promote access and independence in an environment.

# Cases and Questions

1. You are a university counselor at a major university and you also direct the Employees Assistance Program. A staff member calls and seeks your help in dealing with his 7-year-old son's adjustment to Type 1 diabetes. Diagnosed approximately 3 years ago, he is refusing to take his insulin shots, test his blood sugar, or adhere to his diet. He displays a defiant attitude, and in his father's words, now "runs the family." The parents apparently disagree over ways to discipline the child, and the father sounds bitter and angry in describing their arguments. The school is threatening to recommend a home school program if he cannot get his blood sugar under control in the school environment.

    (a) What family systems factors might be operating to perpetuate these behavior problems?

    (b) How might you go about assessing the parent's phenomenological perspective on their son's difficulties?

    (c) How might you empower these parents to enhance their role as stakeholders in their child's health?

2. A local school counselor calls you expressing his concerns about a 13-year-old African American boy who was diagnosed at birth with cerebral palsy. Although he uses a wheelchair, he is quite mobile and has little difficulty negoti-

ating the school environment. He has no known cognitive impairments and typically has performed well in his classes. The school counselor, who has known this adolescent and his mother for the past 4 years, has noticed distinct changes in his behavior in recent months. He has appeared withdrawn, his grades have dropped, and he seems to be hanging out with a "rougher" crowd. A teacher also reported that he was no longer taking care of his personal hygiene, and that his mother uncharacteristically did not attend a parent-teacher meeting earlier this year, as she has apparently taken a second job.

(a) What approach might you take in consulting with this school counselor? What issues would you want the counselor to further assess?

(b) What issues might emerge as it concerns the adolescent's African American background? Would this influence how you might conceptualize the change in his behavior, or not?

(c) How might you go about differentiating between how this client's problems are influenced by his disability versus other factors at home and at school?

## AUTHOR NOTE

This chapter was supported by grants to the first author from the National Institute on Child Health and Human Development (1 R01 HD37661-01A3), and from the National Institute on Disability and Rehabilitation Research, Office of Special Education and Rehabilitative Services, U.S. Department of Education (grant numbers H133B90016 and H133A021927), and from the National Center for Injury Prevention and Control and the Disabilities Prevention Program, National Center for Environmental Health (grant number R49/CCR412718-01). Its contents are solely the responsibility of the authors and do not necessarily represent the official views of the funding agencies.

## REFERENCES

Aneshensel, C. S., Pearlin, L. I., Mullan, J. T., Zarit, S. H., & Whitlatch, C. J. (1995). *Profiles in caregiving: The unexpected career.* San Diego, CA: Academic Press.

Band, E. B., & Weisz, J. R. (1990). Developmental differences in primary and secondary control coping and adjustment to juvenile diabetes. *Journal of Clinical Child Psychology, 19,* 150–158.

Barnum, D. D., Snyder, C. R., Rapoff, M. A., Mani, M., & Thompson, R. (1998). Hope and social support in the psychological adjustment of children who have survived burn injuries and their matched controls. *Children's Health Care, 27,* 15–30.

Basic Behavioral Science Task Force. (1996). Basic behavioral science research for mental health: Sociocultural and environmental processes. *American Psychologist, 51,* 722–731.

Bellanti, C. J., & Bierman, K. L. (2000). Disentangling the impact of low cognitive ability and inattention on social behavior and peer relationships. *Journal of Clinical Child Psychology, 29,* 66–75.

Breslau, N., & Prabucki, K. (1987). Siblings of disabled children: Effects of chronic stress in the family. *Archives of General Psychiatry, 44,* 1040–1046.

Burman, B., & Margolin, G. (1992). Analysis of the association between marital relationships and health problems: An interactional perspective. *Psychological Bulletin, 112,* 39–63.

Chaney, J. M., Mullins, L. L., Frank, R. G., & Peterson, L. (1997). Transactional patterns of child, mother, and father adjustment in insulin-dependent diabetes mellitus: A prospective study. *Journal of Pediatric Psychology, 22,* 229–244.

Chaney, J. M., & Peterson, L. (1989). Family variables and disease management in juvenile rheumatoid arthritis. *Journal of Pediatric Psychology, 14,* 389–403.

Clay, D., Wood, P. K., Frank, R. G., Hagglund, K., & Johnson, J. (1995). Examining systematic differences in adaptation to chronic illness: A growth modeling approach. *Rehabilitation Psychology, 40,* 61–70.

Coyne, J. C., & Anderson, B. J. (1989). The "psychosomatic family" reconsidered II: Recalling a defective model and looking ahead. *Journal of Marital and Family Therapy, 15,* 139–148.

Crewe, N. (1993). Spousal relationships and disability. In F. P. Haseltine, S. Cole, & D. Gray (Eds.), *Reproductive issues for persons with physical disabilities* (pp. 141–151). Baltimore, MD: Paul H. Brookes.

D'Zurilla, T. J., & Nezu, A. (1999). *Problem-solving therapy* (2nd ed.). New York: Springer.

Devins, G. M., Cameron, J., & Edworthy, S. (2000). Chronic disabling disease. In C. Radnitz (Ed.), *Cognitive-behavioral interventions for persons with disabilities* (pp. 105–140). New York: Jason Aronson.

Drotar, D. (1997). Relating parent and family functioning to the psychological adjustment of children with chronic health conditions: What have we learned? What do we need to know? *Journal of Pediatric Psychology, 22,* 149–165.

Elliott, T., & Kurylo, M. (2000). Hope over disability: Lessons from one young woman's triumph. In C. R. Snyder (Ed.), *The handbook of hope: theory, measures, and applications* (pp. 373–386). New York: Academic Press.

Elliott, T., Kurylo, M., & Rivera, P. (2002). Positive growth and adjustment following acquired physical disability. In C. R. Snyder & S. Lopez (Eds.), *Handbook of positive psychology* (pp. 687–699). London: Oxford.

Elliott, T., & Shewchuk, R. (in press). Family adaptation in illness, disease, and disability: Implications for research, policy, and practice. In J. Racynski, L. Bradley, & L. Leviton (Eds.), *Health and behavior handbook* (Vol. II). Washington, DC: American Psychological Association Press.

Elliott, T., Shewchuk, R., & Richards, J. S. (2001). Family caregiver problem solving abilities and adjustment during the initial year of the caregiving role. *Journal of Counseling Psychology, 48,* 223–232.

Fehrenbach, A. M., & Peterson, L. (1989). Parental problem-solving skills, stress, and dietary compliance in phenylketonuria. *Journal of Consulting and Clinical Psychology, 57,* 237–241.

Frank, N. C., Brown, R. T., Blount, R. L., & Bunke, V. (2001). Predictors of affective responses of mothers and fathers of children with cancer. *Psycho-Oncology, 10,* 293–304.

Frank, R. G., Thayer, J., Hagglund, K., Veith, A., Schopp, L., Beck, N., Kashani, J., Goldstein, D., Cassidy, J. T., Clay, D., Chaney, J., Hewett, J., & Johnson, J. (1998). Trajectories of adaptation in pediatric chronic illness: The importance of the individual. *Journal of Consulting and Clinical Psychology, 66,* 521–532.

Fuemmeler, B., Elkin, T. D., & Mullins, L. L. (2001). Survivors of childhood brain tumors: Behavioral, emotional, and social adjustment. *Clinical Psychology Review, 22,* 1–39.

Glueckauf, R. L., Fritz, S., Ecklund-Johnson, E., Liss, H., Dages, P., & Carney, P. (2002). Videoconferencing-based family counseling for rural teenagers with epilepsy: Phase 1 findings. *Rehabilitation Psychology, 47,* 49–72.

Gortmaker, S. L., & Sappenfield, W. (1984). Chronic childhood disorders: Prevalence and impact. *Pediatric Clinics of North America, 31,* 3–18.

Harper, D. C. (1991). Paradigms for investigating rehabilitation and adaptation to childhood disability and chronic illness. *Journal of Pediatric Psychology, 16,* 533–542.

Hauser-Cram, P., Warfield, M., Shonkoff, J., Krauss, M., Upshur, C., & Sayer, A. (1999). Family influences on adaptive development in young children with Down's syndrome. *Child Development, 70,* 979–989.

Henderson, J. N., & Gutierrez-Mayka, M. (1992). Ethnocultural themes in caregiving to Alzheimer's Disease patients in Hispanic families. *Clinical Gerontologist, 11*(3/4), 59–74.

Hobfoll, S. E., & Lerman, M. (1989). Predicting receipt of social support: A longitudinal study of parents' reactions to their child's illness. *Health Psychology, 8,* 61–77.

Hoffman, H. G., Doctor, J., Patterson, D., Carrougher, G., & Furness, T. (2000). Use of virtual reality for adjunctive treatment of adolescent burn pain during wound care: A case report. *Pain, 85,* 305–309.

Holmbeck, G. N., Gorey-Ferguson, L., Hudson, T., Seefeldt, T., Shapera, W., Turner, T., & Uhler, J. (1997). Maternal, paternal, and marital functioning in families of preadolescents with spina bifida. *Journal of Pediatric Psychology, 22,* 167–181.

Horton, T., & Wallander, J. L. (2001). Hope and social support as resilience factors against psychological distress of mothers who care for children with chronic physical conditions. *Rehabilitation Psychology, 46,* 382–399.

Hufford, B. J., Glueckauf, R. L., & Webb, P. M. (1999). Home-base, interactive videoconferencing for adolescents with epilepsy and their families. *Rehabilitation Psychology, 44,* 176–193.

Kazak, A. E., Segal-Andrews, A. M., & Johnson, K. (1995). Pediatric psychology research and practice: A family/systems approach. In M. C. Roberts (Ed.), *Handbook of pediatric psychology* (pp. 84–104). New York: Guilford Press.

Kazak, A. E., & Simms, S. (1996). Children with life-threatening illnesses: Psychological difficulties and interpersonal relationships. In F. W. Kaslow (Ed.), *Handbook of relational diagnosis and dysfunctional family patterns* (pp. 225–238). New York: Wiley.

Kell, R. S., Kliewer, W., Erickson, M. T., & Ohene-Frempong, K. (1998). Psychological adjustment of adolescents with sickle cell disease: Relations with demographic, medical and family competence variables. *Journal of Pediatric Psychology, 23,* 301–312.

King, L. A., & Patterson, C. (2000). Reconstructing life goals after the birth of a child with Down's syndrome: Finding happiness and growing. *International Journal of Rehabilitation and Health, 5,* 17–30.

King, L. A., Scollon, C., Ramsey, C., & Williams, T. (2000). Stories of life transition: Subjective well-being and ego development in parents of children with Down's syndrome. *Journal of Research in Personality, 34,* 509–536.

Kinsella, G., Ong, B., Murtagh, D., Prior, M., & Sawyer, M. (1999). The role of the family for behavioral outcome in children and adolescents following traumatic brain injury. *Journal of Consulting and Clinical Psychology, 67,* 116–123.

Kliewer, W., & Lewis, H. (1995). Family influences on coping processes in children and adolescents with sickle cell disease. *Journal of Pediatric Psychology, 20,* 511–525.

Kuttner, M. J., Delamater, A. M., & Santiago, J. V. (1990). Learned helplessness in diabetic youths. *Journal of Pediatric Psychology, 15,* 581–594.

Lemanek, K. L., Kamps, J., & Chung, N. B. (2001). Empirically supported treatments in pediatric psychology: Regimen adherence. *Journal of Pediatric Psychology, 26,* 253–276.

Lewis, H. A., & Kliewer, W. (1996). Hope, coping, and adjustment among children with sickle cell disease: Tests of mediator and moderator models. *Journal of Pediatric Psychology, 21,* 25–41.

Lyons, R. F., Sullivan, M. J. L., Ritvo, P. G., & Coyne, J. C. (1995). *Relationships in chronic illness and disability.* Thousand Oaks, CA: Sage.

McHale, S. M., Sloan, J., & Simeonsson, R. J. (1986). Sibling relationships of children with autistic, mentally retarded, and nonhandicapped brothers and sisters. *Journal of Autism and Developmental Disorders, 16,* 399–413.

Minuchin, S., Baker, L., Rosman, B., Liebman, R., Milman, L., & Todd, T. (1975). A conceptual model of psychosomatic illness in children. *Archives of General Psychiatry, 32,* 1031–1038.

Moen, P., Robison, J., & Dempster-McClain, D. (1995). Caregiving and women's well-being: A life course approach. *Journal of Health and Social Behavior, 36,* 259–273.

Mullins, L. L., Aniol, K., Boyd, M., Page, M., & Chaney, J. (2002). The influence of respite care on psychological distress in parents of children with developmental disabilities: A longitudinal study. *Children's Services: Social Policy, Research, and Practice, 5,* 123–138.

Mullins, L. L., & Chaney, J. (2001). Pediatric psychology: Contemporary issues. In C. E. Walker & M. C. Roberts (Eds.), *Handbook of clinical child psychology* (pp. 910–927). New York: Wiley.

Nassau, J. H., & Drotar, D. (1997). Social competence among children with central nervous system-related chronic health conditions: A review. *Journal of Pediatric Psychology, 22,* 771–793.

National Center on Child Abuse and Neglect. (1993). *A report on the maltreatment of children with disabilities* (DHHS Contract No. 15-89-1630). Washington, DC.: National Clearinghouse on Child Abuse and Neglect Information.

Neugarten, B. L. (1979). Time, age, and the life cycle. *American Journal of Psychiatry, 36,* 887–894.

Noojin, A. B., & Wallander, J. L. (1996). Development and evaluation of a measure of concerns related to raising a child with a physical disability. *Journal of Pediatric Psychology, 21,* 483–498.

Noojin, A. B., & Wallander, J. L. (1997). Perceived problem-solving ability, stress, and coping in mothers of children with physical disabilities: Potential cognitive influences on adjustment. *International Journal of Behavioral Medicine, 4,* 415–432.

Northey, S., Griffin, W. A., & Krainz, S. (1998). A partial test of the psychosomatic family model: Marital interaction patterns in asthma and non-asthma families. *Journal of Family Psychology, 12,* 220–235.

Olkin, R. (1999). *What psychotherapists should know about disability.* New York: Guilford Press.

Perlesz, A., Kinsella, G., & Crowe, S. (1999). Impact of traumatic brain injury on the family: A critical review. *Rehabilitation Psychology, 44,* 6–35.

Perrin, J. M, & McLean, W. E., Jr. (1988). Children with chronic illness: The prevention of dysfunction. *Pediatric Clinics of North America, 35,* 1325–1337.

Pickett, S. A., Vraniak, D. A., Cook, J. A., & Bertram, J. (1993). Strength in adversity: Blacks bear burden better than Whites. *Professional Psychology: Research and Practice, 24,* 460–467.

Quittner, A. L., Espelage, D., Opipari, L., Carter, B., Eid, N., & Eigen, H. (1998). Role strain in couples with and without a child with a chronic illness: Associations with marital satisfaction, intimacy, and daily mood. *Health Psychology, 59,* 1266–1278.

Quittner, A. L., Glueckauf, R., & Jackson, D. (1990). Chronic parenting stress: Moderating versus mediating effects of social support. *Journal of Personality and Social Psychology, 59,* 1266–1278.

Quittner, A. L., Opipari, L., Regoli, M., Jacobsen, J., & Eigen, H. (1992). The impact of caregiving and role strain on family life: Comparisons between mothers of children with cystic fibrosis and matched controls. *Rehabilitation Psychology, 37,* 275–290.

Rivara, J., Jaffe, K., Polissar, N., Fay, G., Liao, S., & Martin, K. (1996). Predictors of family functioning and change 3 years after traumatic brain injury in children. *Archives of Physical Medicine and Rehabilitation, 77,* 754–764.

Sahler, O., Varni, J. W., Fairclough, D., Butler, R., Noll, R., Dolgin, M., Phipps, S., Copeland, D., Katz, E., & Mulhern, R. (2002). Problem-solving skills training for mothers of children with newly diagnosed cancer: A randomized trial. *Journal of Developmental and Behavioral Pediatrics, 23,* 77–86.

Schultheis, M. T., & Rizzo, A. A. (2001). The application of virtual reality technology for rehabilitation. *Rehabilitation Psychology, 46,* 296–311.

Sullivan, P. M., & Knutson, J. F. (2000). Maltreatment and disabilities: A population-based epidemiological study. *Child Abuse and Neglect, 24,* 1257–1273.

Summers, C. R., White, K. R., & Summers, M. (1994). Siblings of children with a disability: Review and analysis of the empirical literature. *Journal of Social Behavior and Personality, 9*(5), 169–184.

Thompson, R. J., Jr., & Gustafson, K. E. (1996). *Adaptation to chronic childhood illness.* Washington, DC: American Psychological Association.

Timko, C., Baumgartner, M., Moos, R. H., & Miller, J. J. (1993). Parental risk and resistance factors among children with juvenile rheumatoid disease: A four-year predictive study. *Journal of Behavioral Medicine, 16,* 571–588.

Timko, C., Stovel, K. W., & Moos, R. H. (1992). Functioning among mothers and fathers of children with juvenile rheumatic disease: A longitudinal study. *Journal of Pediatric Psychology, 17,* 705–724.

Valle, R. (1981). Natural support systems, minority groups and late life dementias: Implications for service delivery, research, and policy. In N. E. Miller & G. D. Cohen (Eds.), *Aspects of Alzheimer's disease and senile dementia* (pp. 277–354). New York: Raven Press.

Varni, J. W., Katz, E. R., Colegrove, R., & Dolgin, M. (1993). The impact of social skills training on the adjustment of children with newly diagnosed cancer. *Journal of Pediatric Psychology, 18,* 751–767.

Walco, G. A., Sterling, C. N., Conte, P. M., & Engel, R. (1999). Empirically supported treatments in pediatric psychology: Disease-related pain. *Journal of Pediatric Psychology, 24,* 155–167.

Wallander, J. L., Pitt, L. C., & Mellins, C. A. (1990). Child functional independence and maternal psychosocial stress as risk factors threatening adaptation in mothers of physically or sensorially handicapped children. *Journal of Consulting and Clinical Psychology, 58,* 818–824.

Wallander, J. L., Varni, J., Babani, L., Banis, H., & Wilcox, K. (1989). Family resources as resistance factors for psychological maladjustment in chronically ill and handicapped children. *Journal of Pediatric Psychology, 14,* 157–173.

Webb, P. M., & Glueckauf, R. L. (1994). The effects of direct involvement in goal setting on rehabilitation outcome for persons with traumatic brain injuries. *Rehabilitation Psychology, 39,* 179–188.

Wenger, B. L., Kaye, S., & LaPlante, M. P. (1996, March). *Disabilities among children. Disability Statistics Abstract (15).* Washington, DC: National Institute for Disability and Rehabilitation Research.

Wood, B. L. (1993). Beyond the "psychosomatic family": A biobehavioral family model of pediatric illness. *Family Process, 32,* 261–278.

# CHAPTER 7

# Navigating the Road to Independent Living

Margaret A. Nosek
and Rosemary B. Hughes, Baylor
College of Medicine

Just as pilots have navigators to help them get their crafts through storms, so do people with disabilities benefit from counseling on the rocky road to independent living. For most, this road is fraught with barriers and disincentives, both physical and emotional, coming from society and the family, and within oneself. The role of mental health counselors, therefore, is not just one of helping clients with disabilities plan the logistics of moving toward a self-determined lifestyle, but also helping them develop the self-confidence, social skills, and advocacy mindset that will ensure their success.

This chapter describes the context of disability. We draw largely on the example of the experiences of women with physical disabilities because that is our specific area of expertise. We also describe some of the physical, emotional, and environmental barriers that people with disabilities encounter as they emerge from nonindependent living situations. Taking into account the myriad of definitions given to the concept of independence, we define independence and give an overview of the skills that individuals need to acquire, across the life span, in order to successfully navigate the road to independence. Finally, we offer recommendations on how counselors can be maximally effective as they assist people in determining the lifestyle that best suits their needs and ambitions and in developing a plan to reach their independent living goals.

## UNDERSTANDING THE CONTEXT OF DISABILITY

The world of people with disabilities is truly in another plane of reality. Some have super high-tech elevating and reclining wheelchairs, others have wheelchairs constructed of salvaged parts held together with duct tape. Some have had their hearing or vision restored with the most recent advances in microsurgery, others live their lives with hearing or vision impairments that could be corrected very easily. It is not unheard of to see individuals with very severe physical limitations with upwardly mobile careers in major corporations. This lifestyle, however, is not the norm for this population. Unemployment runs around 75% among women with moderate to severe impairments. It is a world of contradictions, anomalies, and absurd juxtapositions, such as the world-renowned theoretical astrophysicist who struggles to find someone to get him out of bed every morning. The essential reality is that the majority of people with disabilities (and, disproportionately, women) are poor, socially isolated and unmarried, and lack access to education, health care services, and barrier-free environments. This reality prohibits the resources needed to reach anything resembling the independence taken for granted by the general population. Highlights of research studies addressing some of the life situations and the barriers to independent living experienced by women with physical disabilities may offer counselors important insights into the world of this population.

## Demographics

The Americans with Disabilities Act (ADA) of 1990 defines disability as a substantial limitation in a major life activity (McNeil, 1993). Substantial limitation is operationalized in various ways. An individual with a disability may have difficulties with activities of daily living such as dressing and eating. She may use certain assistive devices including wheelchairs and canes. Those who have functional limitations experience difficulties performing activities such as lifting, carrying, using stairs, walking, bending, standing for several minutes, reaching, and grasping or handling small objects.

In the 1997 census, over 52 million women and men (19.7% of the population) in this country had some level of disability (McNeil, 1997), with more than half having a severe disability. According to this report, age plays a role in disability status. In the younger population (15–24 years of age), the prevalence of disability was lower among women (9.8%) compared with men (11.6%). This relationship was reversed in those who were 45–54 years of age, with 24.2% of the women having a disability compared with 20.9% of the men. In terms of race, people who were Black or non-Hispanic White had a greater likelihood of disability than those in other racial groups. More women (18.2 million) than men (14.8 million) had severe disabilities, with more women having a need for personal assistance. Women comprise the majority of people with disabilities.

According to the 1995 Survey of Income and Program Participation, 28 million women have disability-related work limitations, comprising 21% of the population of women as a whole (McNeil, 1997). The most prevalent disabling condition in women is back disorder (15.3%), followed by arthritis (13.3%), heart diseases (9.7%), asthma (5.3%), orthopedic impairment of lower extremity (4.2%), mental disorders (3.3%), diabetes (3.3%), and learning disability and mental retardation (2.5%) (Jans & Stoddard, 1999).

One of the most notable problems among women with physical disabilities is low economic status, which often translates into lack of medical insurance and/or access to medical care and health services. A woman's health and well-being can be unnecessarily compromised by a lack of access to services, inaccessible medical equipment, and inadequate public transportation (Nosek, 2000). Notably, mental health professionals and health care and other service providers often fail to receive disability-related training, leaving them unprepared to address the independent living needs of this population. Later on, we address the issue of training in more detail.

Women with disabilities share the work-related problems of women in general, including low wages and occupational segregation (Schaller & DeLaGarza, 1995). They may, however, also experience restricted career aspirations as a result of the nature of their disabilities, gender plus disability socialization experiences, and a lack of role models or mentors (Patterson, DeLaGarza, & Schaller, 1998). There is a significant gender disparity in poverty status, which is further compounded by women's lower disability benefits from public programs. This difference is related to women becoming disabled at a younger age, having fewer years in the workforce, and being compensated at lower levels (Kutza, 1985).

Analysis of data from the 1994 and 1995 National Health Interview Survey Disability Panel showed that roughly 16% of the population of women had at least one functional limitation (Nosek, 2000). Of the women with at least one functional limitation, 77% were White, non-Hispanic; 13% were Black, non-Hispanic; 7% were Hispanic; and 3% were non-Hispanic of other races. This racial/ethnic distribution is similar to that for women with no functional limitations, with a slightly higher rate of disability among African American women in the 45–64 age range. Compared with women in general, women with three or more functional limitations were less likely to be married (40% vs. 63%), more likely to be living alone (35% vs. 13%), more likely to have a high school education or less (78% vs. 54%), less likely to be employed (14% vs. 63%), more likely to be living in households below the poverty level (23% vs. 10%) particularly in the 18–44 age range, and less likely to have private health insurance (55% vs. 74%). The majority (56%) of women with three or more functional limitations did not receive disability or other government income.

## Physical Health Problems

Disability is not the only source of limitation. The secondary health conditions that accompany disability over time compound the initial effect (Nosek, 2000). Decades of propelling manual wheelchairs can result in repetitive motion injuries such as carpal tunnel syndrome. Scoliosis often results from muscular weakness and leads to respiratory problems that may become life threatening. Decades of infrequent urination and/or bowel and bladder management programs result in numerous genitourinary problems. The ability to control these basic bodily functions is crucial for maintaining independence (Krotoski & Bennett, 1996). The thinning of skin with age increases the tendency for pressure ulcers, not only in spinal cord injury, but also in postpolio and other disorders that do not affect sensation. Such disorders do affect mobility, hence one's ability to weight shift to relieve pressure on bony prominences. Increased muscle weakness that accompanies aging with disability can seriously diminish physical and social functioning. Very early in life, osteoporosis results from reduced weight bearing. It may or may not increase after menopause; that research has not yet been conducted. There also seems to be a high rate of endocrine disorders in persons with disabilities, such as diabetes, which demands further examination. A lifetime of taking prophylactic antibiotics and other medications can lead to immune system problems. Other common problems that are pervasive among people with disabilities are pain, fatigue, and obesity.

These secondary conditions certainly can diminish a person's ability to live an independent lifestyle. Although they are often highly preventable, these health conditions are all too often the cause of death in this population. Rehabilitation and disability research is just beginning to recognize the problem and offer effective prevention strategies for both men and women with disabilities.

Significant gaps exist in knowledge about the course of health problems in people with disabilities. In terms of general health, many live in robust health, including some who use a ventilator and can only move one finger. Statistics show, however, that there is a strong inverse relationship between self-rated health status and number of functional limitations. Only 12% of women with three or more limitations across all age groups rated their health as excellent or very good, compared with 66% of women with no impairments. Census data confirm that weight control is indeed a problem of women with disabilities in middle age, with 42% of those with three or more limitations being overweight. Hypertension increases substantially with age and severity of impairment (National Center for Health Statistics, 2002). This may be related to the physical and emotional stress associated with living with disability. More thorough research is needed on these conditions, particularly as they relate to men with disabilities. Health maintenance practices, such as exercise, suffer from the environmental and personal barriers mentioned earlier. These compounding physical health problems add to the complexity of establishing and maintaining independence.

## Mental Health Problems

Low self-esteem, stress, and depression appear to be disproportionately common among people with disabilities, particularly women, compared with the general population. (Hughes, Taylor, Robinson-Whelen, & Nosek, 2002). Mental health is extremely important for living an independent lifestyle.

**Self-esteem**   In our national study of women with physical disabilities, more than three quarters of the sample had high self-esteem and a positive body image, regardless of the severity of their disability (Nosek, Howland, Rintala, Young, & Chanpong, 2001). For the remainder, however, high rates of unemployment and abuse and lack of intimate relationships seemed to exert a serious toll on self-esteem. Research findings suggest that it is not disability itself, but rather the contextual, social, physical, and emotional factors associated with disability that may influence self-esteem and other aspects of the self (Barnwell & Kavanagh, 1997; Brooks & Matson, 1982). We become who we are based, in part, on our interpretations of how others see us, similar to the phenomenon that Cooley (1902) called the "looking glass self." Self-esteem is linked to external feedback or affection from important others. (Adler, 1979; Bednar & Peterson, 1995; Mead, 1934).

In a qualitative study of 31 women with disabilities, Nosek (1996) concluded that negative messages, such as being a burden to the family, or positive expectations regarding women's potential profoundly influenced their self-esteem. Women with disabilities frequently confront assaults on their self-esteem associated with attitudes that they are "ill, ignorant, without emotion, asexual, pitiful, and incapable of employment" (Perduta-Fulginiti, 1996, p. 298). Women's self-worth may be compromised by internalizing the negative devaluation that society often equates with physical impairment. Goffman (1963) referred to this devaluing phenomenon as "stigma."

Diminished self-esteem has been associated with increased pain and fatigue (Cornwell & Schmitt, 1990) and greater functional limitation (Nosek, Hughes, Swedlund, Taylor, & Swank, in press). Losing the ability to perform activities of daily living can threaten one's sense of self. On the other hand, social connection and support can validate the sense of self-worth in people with disabilities (Crisp, 1996). Connectedness serves as the foundation for autonomy, competence, and self-esteem in women (Jordan, Kaplan, Miller, Stiver, & Surrey, 1991). In our experience, these resources are often unavailable due to problems with mobility and environmental barriers including public transportation. Weather can be another barrier to social participation. Consider a woman who uses a wheelchair and the difficulties she might experience in dealing with snow and slippery conditions. Many of the women in our studies tell us that they are simply unable to get out of their homes to visit friends and family and participate in community activities. Such loss of support can lead to serious problems with social isolation. Widely associated with health problems and mortality (Berkman & Syme, 1979), social isolation is a common secondary condition associated with a primary disability (Coyle, Santiago, Shank, Ma, & Boyd, 2000; Ravesloot, Seekins, & Walsh, 1997).

We investigated self-esteem as a mediator between disability and contextual factors on pro-self-esteem behaviors, specifically, intimate relationships, employment, and health-promoting behaviors, among a sample of women with physical disabilities compared with women without disabilities (Nosek, Hughes, et al., in press). The findings suggested that women with disabilities had significantly lower self-esteem, greater social isolation, less education, more overprotection during childhood, poorer quality of intimate relationships, and lower rates of salaried employment than women without disabilities. Self-esteem was significantly related to intimacy, health-promoting behaviors, and employment. The women who were older, less disabled, less educated, and less overprotected and had more affection shown in the home tended to feel that others saw them more positively. Women who had experienced positive school environments, less overprotection, and more affection reported less social isolation. Age, education, and disability severity were not significantly related to social isolation. These findings illustrate the importance of self-esteem in the independence and quality of life of women with physical disabilities.

**Stress** Disability is a major stress factor in the lives of persons with disabilities. Although for years researchers have been investigating stress and its effects on physical and psychological health (Taylor, 1999), stress in the context of disability has only recently received consideration and empirical attention (Hughes et al., 2002). According to chapter 6 in *Healthy People 2010,* increased stress represents a health-related disparity between people with and those without disabilities (U.S. Department of Health and Human Services, 2000). Having a physical disability, in and of itself, appears to constitute a chronic life strain (Turner & Wood, 1985). Women are more likely than men to experience stress related to social isolation, poverty, violence and other victimization, and chronic health problems (McGrath, Keita, Strickland, & Russo, 1990). We believe the situation may be even more serious for women with disabilities.

One of our recent studies of 415 women with physical disabilities revealed that women experienced greater stress if they had low levels of social support, high levels of pain, and/or disclosed experiences with abuse in the previous year (Hughes et al., 2002). We know from years of personal and clinical experience, plus the relevant literature, that the sources of stress are numerous for women with disabilities. These stressors include interruption of ordinary activities, inability to independently carry out self-care activities, changes in appearance, increased need for personal assistance, and dealing with everyday unrelenting life hassles such as increased time, planning, and effort to do things (Crewe & Clarke, 1996). Other sources of stress are poverty with resulting inadequate nutrition, lower levels of fitness, pain, illness, vulnerability to abuse, environmental barriers, and lack of social support (Nosek, 1995). Rintala and coworkers (Rintala, Hart, & Fuhrer, 1996) reported that, in a study of people with spinal cord injury, women reported significantly more perceived stress than men. These authors found that life satisfaction, depressive symptomatology, self-assessed health rating, and severity of pressure ulcers were all significantly related to perceived stress. Many of the secondary conditions that are attributed to disability are more the result of the stress of living in an unsupportive environment rather than due to the disability itself.

**Depression**   Depression is a complicated phenomenon in the context of disability (Coulehan, Schulberg, Block, Madonia, & Rodriguez, 1997). Making an accurate diagnosis is difficult given that symptoms of depression (such as fatigue or sleep problems) may indicate mental disorder in most people, but the same symptoms may suggest a secondary condition for men and women with physical disabilities. This situation can result in depression being either underdetected or overdiagnosed in persons with disabilities. Depression appears to be more common for persons with physically disabling health conditions compared with people in general (Berlly, Strauser, & Hall, 1991; Turner & Noh, 1988; Williamson & Walters, 1996; Yelin & Callahan, 1995), possibly 3 times so (Turner & Beiser, 1990), including a greater risk for suicide (Flachenecker & Hartung, 1996).

Depression is at least twice as common among women as among men (McGrath et al., 1990; Stotland & Stotland, 1999). Women face a multitude of biological, social, economic, and psychological factors increasing their vulnerability for depression (McGrath et al., 1990). Compared with people in general, women and men with physical disabilities appear to be at greater risk for depression (Noh & Posthuma, 1990; Turner & Noh, 1988; Turner & Wood, 1985). Membership in an ethnic minority group introduces another dimension related to depression in the general population (Munoz, Hollon, McGrath, Rehm, & VandenBos, 1994).

*Healthy People 2010* (U.S. Department of Health and Human Services, 2000) reports racial and ethnic disparities in the prevalence of depressive symptoms among adults with disabilities, including Hispanic or Latino (40%), Black or African American (31%), and White (28%).

Chronic pain is frequently associated with higher rates of depressive symptoms. Romano and Turner (1985) acknowledged that depression and pain may coexist, that depression may follow the onset of pain, and that pain may be a symptom of depression mediated by biochemical changes and/or other factors. Social isolation also has been associated with increased risk for depression (Roberts, Kaplan, Shema, & Strawbridge, 1997) and other negative health outcomes (Berkman & Syme, 1979). Pope and Tarlov (1991) emphasized that depression and neglect of self-care are consequences of isolation among persons with disabilities who "often live an isolated existence, depending on others to initiate social contact" (p. 237).

Depression is highly prevalent among women with physical disabilities (Coyle et al., 2000). Younger women with three or more functional limitations have been found to be more frequently depressed (30%) than women without disabilities (4%) and were 8 times more likely to report having experienced major depression in the past year (National Center for Health Statistics, 2002).

We recently conducted a study involving 64 women with spinal cord injury whose high prevalence (59.4%) of clinically significant depressive symptomatology was linked primarily with perceived stress and social isolation. Other contributing factors included social support, vitality, mobility, pain, unemployment, and current abuse (Hughes, Swedlund, Petersen, & Nosek, 2001).

The concept of "depletion depression" (McGrath et al., 1990) typifies the depression of women who experience the stress-related consequences of "being chronically tired, overwhelmed, stressed, and drained by role demands and role conflicts confronting contemporary women" (p. 199). Like other women, contemporary women living with disabilities confront these factors plus disability-related stressors such as access problems and the multiple social, interpersonal, physical, and emotional demands of being women living with disabilities.

Elevated depression has been observed among women who are experiencing current abuse (Cascardi & O'Leary, 1992). Abuse appears to be a common experience for women with physical disabilities, with more than 50% experiencing physical or sexual abuse in their lifetimes (Nosek, Howland, & Young, 1997; Young, Nosek, Howland, Chanpong, & Rintala, 1997). Although estimates vary widely on the prevalence of lifetime and current abuse experienced by women with disabilities, there is general agreement that disability introduces additional vulnerability for abuse in women's lives (Nosek, Foley, Hughes, & Howland, 2001). We found that compared with able-bodied women, women with disabilities tend to experience longer duration and more intense types of abuse (Nosek, Walter, Young, & Howland, in press).

**Access to Health Care**   Access to health care is a significant problem for women with physical disabilities. According to the National Health Interview Survey, younger women with impairments were much more likely to delay seeking medical care (33% vs. 11%) or to be unable to get medical care at all (18% vs. 3%) than women without disabilities or all women over age 65 (Nosek, 2000). We can only assume that this situation is increasingly exacerbated given the country's current national crises, such as those related to Social Security and health coverage. Even for those people with disabilities who have insurance coverage for health care, the problem intensifies as insurance companies are forced to increase health premiums to overcome the rising costs of health care. Problems with finances or insurance were the reasons cited for being unable to get medical care by more than three quarters of women in all three groups. Younger women with more severe disabilities have the most difficulty obtaining mental health care, dental care, prescription medicine, and eyeglasses (National Center for Health Statistics, 2002). These facts aptly illustrate the extent of access barriers experienced by individuals with disabilities who seek an independent lifestyle.

Beneath the major barrier of lack of health insurance coverage lie many more obstacles that are more transparent but none the less insidious. For many women, just getting from their house to a doctor's office is a major effort. Inadequate accessible public transportation, lack of attendant services to accompany the woman on the visit, lack of child care, and long waiting periods for appointments in overcrowded public health care systems all serve to discourage women from tending to health problems at early and more easily treatable stages. Many women with disabilities know from experience that specialists are the type of health care provider who can best meet their needs, but strict gate-keeping regulations in managed care organizations restrict access to these providers. In our national study, 31% of the women with disabilities reported that a doctor had refused to see them because of their disability. Just getting in the front door or using the restroom, not to mention getting up on the table, are serious barriers to health care in many physicians' offices. The medical establishment seems to be the last bastion of resistance to full compliance with the Americans with Disabilities Act (Nosek, 2000).

## DEFINITION OF INDEPENDENT LIVING

We define independent living in terms of having control over one's life. An independent lifestyle encourages persons with disabilities to make choices that minimize their reliance on others, especially when making decisions or performing activities of daily living. To live independently means being able to fulfill various roles and participate fully in community activities. It means managing daily affairs and making decisions leading to self-determination. Persons with severe disabilities may require assistance with personal care and other support systems to achieve an independent lifestyle. Exercising power and control in one's life maximizes a person's physical and psychological independence and autonomy.

The common notion of independence revolves around self-determination, doing what you want to do, but also having the resources with which to do it. For men, this is often expressed in terms of finances and autonomous goal achievement. For women, although finances and other resources are certainly a primary concern, there are two other equally important components of independence, social connectedness and freedom from those forces that would restrain their social activities and limit their personal and career advancement.

When it comes to applying the concept of independence to people with disabilities, however, definitions of independence traditionally have been formulated in very medical and insurance-driven terms. The rehabilitation perspective has traditionally conceptualized independence in narrow terms, that is, indicators such as medical recovery and employability (Nosek, 1992). This approach has focused on independence in self-care activities. Being able to tie your own shoes without help has been more important to educators, medical professionals, and, too often, families, than being able to make sound decisions without help. This has been a rallying cry for the disability rights movement and a point of contention between more progressive rehabilitation researchers and their more traditional colleagues. For example, Kerr and Meyerson (1987) noted, "By definition, a person with a physical disability lacks adequate tools for certain physical behaviors, but there is no necessary relationship between those missing or impaired physical tools and the ability to meet the demands of higher social, psychological, and cognitive tasks" (p. 175). Corbett (1989) added that "a narrow focus upon basic skills impedes the quality of life and inhibits self-expression" (p. 159).

Clearly, we concur with Rock's (1988) belief that independence should speak to control and choice. She conducted interviews of six people with physical disabilities who talked about independence in terms of risk taking, privacy, decision making, organization and control, and encouragement. We agree with those participants who defined independence in terms such as being able to go out alone; lock one's door; decide what, how, and when money would be spent; determine how their own personal care tasks would be completed; and obtain encouragement to develop individual interests and talents. These areas are about choice, and the participants felt that independence was meaningless without it. Brown and Lehr (1989) concurred: "Choosing how to live one's life is the 'catalytic trigger' of independence" (p. 269).

Whereas some researchers emphasize interaction with the environment rather than control as a determinant of independence (Mathews & Seekins, 1987), others examine only behaviors and do not consider cognitive or emotional processes. For example, Kerr and Meyerson (1987) questioned the value of independence as a goal of rehabilitation, stating that the mature person should be equally satisfied to be dependent, interdependent, independent, or dependable at various times in their lives. This "four-corner" rather than continuous model restricts independence to behavior. It simply disregards independence as a state of mind, attitude, trait, or general approach to life. People with disabilities are not perceived as creating, altering, or controlling a situation; instead, they find themselves in a situation, then adapt by acting dependently, interdependently, independently, or dependably, as required by the circumstances.

Nosek and Fuhrer's (1992) heuristic model of independent living draws on a definition adopted early in the independent living movement that focuses on controlling one's life, having options, making decisions, performing daily activities, and participating in the life of the community (Frieden, Richards, Cole, & Bailey,

1979). In their model, Nosek and Fuhrer identified and defined four essential components of independence: (1) perceived control of one's life, (2) physical functioning, (3) psychological self-reliance, and (4) characteristics of the physical and social environment. They then discussed these components in relation to a quasi-Maslovian hierarchy of four levels: (1) basic survival, (2) material well-being, (3) productivity, and (4) self-actualization. They operationalized this model by developing an assessment tool, the Personal Independence Profile (Nosek, Fuhrer, & Howland, 1992). Counselors may consider using this tool in working with clients in clarifying their specific needs for achieving independence, assessing their need for personal assistance for activities of daily living, and overcoming barriers in their environment. Clients who are nonindependently minded may benefit from self-management skills training and empowerment techniques. They may also benefit from interventions designed to improve their sense of personal control, self-efficacy, and problem-solving abilities. For those who score high on independence, counselors might work with them to overcome barriers to their career success and participation in community activities. Group counseling interventions for this group might involve self-development programs focusing on topics such as assertiveness and effective communication, healthy relationships, and advocacy.

We have been incorporating self-management in our group interventions on depression, stress, and self-esteem—all grounded in strategies for improving self-efficacy and social connectedness. Counselors may intervene to help their clients improve their decision-making skills, and it is especially important that counselors are prepared to respond to their clients' needs to increase their independence regarding social and community roles and self-management of daily affairs. This type of counseling can help maximize a person's physical and psychological independence and autonomy.

## BARRIERS TO INDEPENDENT LIVING

With its meaning so highly individualized, independent living is somewhat difficult to define; however, it is not hard to conceptualize what it is not. Within the disability rights movement, living in an institution, parental home, or any other residential setting where control is essentially in the hands of someone else is not considered conducive to independent living. In the culture of the United States, restrictive barriers go beyond the residential setting to include poverty, lack of education, unemployment, lack of health insurance or adequate health care, lack of affordable housing, lack of transportation, geographic isolation, and, some would add, excessive governmental restrictions on civil rights. Limiting factors in the community and family culture may include restrictive gender roles, religious beliefs and prescribed behaviors, dysfunctional family dynamics, and the most damaging of all, sexual, physical, and emotional abuse. Personal factors include low self-esteem and self-efficacy, lack of a supportive family or community, and symptoms of a disabling condition that limit mobility, self-care, endurance, cognition, communication, emotional stability, or socially acceptable behaviors. All of these factors could limit anyone's independence; however, there is a separate list of factors that disproportionately affect people with disabilities.

The strongest force that limits the ability of people with disabilities to achieve self-determined lifestyles is attitudes toward disability. Much has been written about the negative effects of devaluing, stigmatizing, and prejudicial attitudes toward disability (Goffman, 1963; Suris, Resnick, Cassuto, & Blum, 1996), but the tendency to ascribe these to society in general fails to track the problem to its roots. Certainly, the power of tradition holds much of the blame for the perpetuation of negative, limiting attitudes and assumptions, but they attain their strongest destructive force when they are internalized by families and individuals.

Other factors that specifically limit the independence of people with disabilities include the dearth of affordable attendant care (personal assistance) services, inaccessibility of the built and natural environments, lack of affordable assistive devices and adaptive technology, lack of information about products and services that might be available, lack of health care that is informed and relevant to disability-related health maintenance needs, and organizational policies that prohibit or restrict the participation of people with disabilities. The vignettes in the Cases and Questions section will clarify these limitations. For further understanding of clients' potential for, and barriers to, independent living, it is helpful to know more about the reality of their life situations.

## RECOMMENDATIONS FOR COUNSELING PERSONS WITH DISABILITIES

So far in this chapter, we have highlighted key issues surrounding the context of disability, independent living, and research on persons with disabilities. When discussing various studies, we have drawn largely from our professional expertise, which currently focuses on research on women with physical disabilities. The chapter also relies heavily on our combined clinical experience and expertise in psychotherapy and counseling and rehabilitation counseling. As researchers, we know that we have cited only a small fraction of the studies on people with disabilities. As practitioners, we must remember that we are not "superhumans redolent with benevolence and devoid of prejudices" (Olkin, 1999, p. 75). While considering our suggestions and information we advise our clinical colleagues to embrace both their clients' freedom and self-determination and their own clinical expertise and judgment, cross-cultural counseling skills, and resources for self-evaluation and consultation, especially regarding any countertransference with persons with disabilities.

### General Recommendations

We invite you to consider the following suggestions when working with individuals with disabilities:

1. *Examine your own assumptions and attitudes toward the individual sitting in front of you.* Although you may assume that the disability is part of the pre-

senting problem, the client may not even identify as a person with a disability nor identify with the disability community in any way. Nevertheless, the person's experience may be influenced by membership in a minority culture with its potential for discrimination, stereotyping, and prejudices. Or, as Olkin (1999) pointed out, the disability serves as the context from which the individual's core issues, such as abandonment or powerlessness, have been enacted. An example would be the young, recently married woman whose father left the family during her infancy and now presents to you with distressful symptoms that she attributes to the rapid progression of her disabling health condition.

2. *Ask the clients what they hold as short- and long-term goals.* Although it is important that clients set their own goals, the counselor and client together can evaluate how realistic they are for a particular person. Say, for example, that the client wants to learn to be independent and yet has severe functional limitations. What are the possibilities for working with the person to develop ways for attaining that goal of independence? Encourage the person to consider all options. For example, the short-term goal might involve talking with others about ways they self-manage their disabilities or reading about how others have accomplished the goal of an independent lifestyle. It might be helpful to explore together and with peers the idea of interdependence and specific ways to remain the agent of control and decision making and to manage one's life while receiving assistance from someone else.

3. *Offer information about services, training opportunities, assistive devices, or whatever resources might support clients in achieving their goals.* The counselor might invite clients to ask for suggestions rather than ask what they should do (Lorig et al., 2000). Understanding the community of people with disabilities is critical to successful outcomes in counseling with them. Again, we encourage counseling professionals to visit independent living centers and read their literature, ask for a tour of a multiservice center for people with disabilities, participate in town meetings on disability, become familiar with websites offering information on training opportunities and assistive technology, and visit a nursing home or other residential institutions providing care for this population. Develop a list of resources, and be prepared to offer sound disability-related information for clients with disabilities, or better yet collaborate with them to identify and become acquainted with such resources themselves.

4. *Explore strengths and past successes with the individual and with family members, if available and appropriate.* To help clients strengthen their independent living skills, it is important first to know what has worked well for them in the past. Counselors may formally or informally conduct an assessment with clients regarding sources of inner strength and personal resources. It may be helpful to evaluate factors such as their motivations, abilities, values and spirituality, feelings about sexuality, attitudes about disability, personality and interpersonal styles, sense of identity, self-esteem, and coping styles. Identifying and evaluating external resources is important, too. It should prove beneficial to identify and process clients' experiences with environmental barriers such as those related to

transportation, societal attitudes, employment, or personal assistance. All of this information may help to develop appropriate counseling goals and productive strategies for a positive outcome to the counseling process.

Understanding the client's family dynamics and strengths, and involving this system in the counseling process, can be beneficial. We cannot assume that the families and individuals are necessarily accepting of disability and thus empowered to move beyond the attitudinal barriers to independence, self-advocacy, and control. Olkin (1999) talked about the importance of exploring the effects of the family on the person with disability, not just the effects of disability on the family. Counselors can work with client and family together to recognize and, if necessary, change their expectations regarding important issues such as living an independent lifestyle, career aspiration, and self-advocacy. Together they can develop realistic perceptions about the client's ability to function and can clarify and process their expectations for the future. Finally, it is important to remember that disability is a family experience. When one's partner is diagnosed with a disabling health condition, "Couples need direct and honest information in simple language . . . considered a team, not a patient and caregiver, and treated as such" (Olkin, 1999, p. 116). When planning interventions, counselors may consider involving not only the family but also other individuals such as personal assistants, rehabilitation physician, roommates, and friends.

5. *Identify barriers to achieving clients' goals.* This counseling task involves identifying and processing feelings about prejudice, discrimination, and negative attitudes, including internalized negativity toward disability; economic dependence; lack of social support; unemployment or underemployment; lack of role models; substance abuse; and lack of disability pride. This is to name just a few of the potential barriers to attaining independence and other life goals. A counselor may consider facilitating a group of persons with disabilities. Group members offer one another ways to overcome barriers such as the attitudinal, economic, and social examples already stated. For example, women who use wheelchairs and who are interested in having children may pick up important information from other group members on pregnancy, childbirth, and adaptive equipment for parenting. Managing or overcoming these barriers is essential to maintaining independence and goal attainment.

6. *Develop a plan for action with steps that will lead clients toward their goals.* Talk with clients about the key components of an action plan or short-term plans: something they want to accomplish, something reasonable and behavior-specific, a plan that answers the questions "what?," "when?," "how often?," and "how much?". Encourage them to write or type it, keep track of progress, problem-solve when setbacks occur, and make midcourse changes if necessary (Lorig et al., 2000).

7. *Assess clients' confidence level for completing these steps.* When a client has created the action plan, the counselor may assess her confidence for completing it by working with the client to ask, "On a scale of 0 to 10, with 0 being *completely unsure* and 10 being *completely confident,* how confident am I that I will be able to complete this action plan?" If the confidence level

is 7 or greater, the plan is probably a realistic one. If the confidence level is below 7, then it may not be realistic; and, the person may need to consider the barriers and solve the problems beforehand or modify the plan to increase her confidence in successfully completing the action plan (Lorig et al., 2000).

8. *Together, create incentives (self-rewards) that could motivate clients along the way.* Counselors may want to work with their clients to identify positive reinforcers, noting that what is a reward for one person may serve as a disincentive for another. It might be helpful to create a reward menu and invite a discussion on healthy versus unhealthy rewards (i.e., taking time to visit with a friend versus indulging in a high caloric dessert).

9. *Link clients with other people with disabilities who have similar goals or life situations.* Invite the client to visit the local center for independent living, or to look in the telephone book or on the Internet for other ways to join organizations whose goal is to assist people with disabilities in connecting with one another. Remember, "Empowerment, hopefulness, meaning, and value cannot survive without support . . . persons with disabilities need a safe and secure place to be disabled" (Olkin, 1999, p. 179). Other people with disabilities frequently offer safety and a sense of being understood. Given the importance of role models to successful independent living (Nosek, 1992), counselors might implement peer-led group interventions to offer role models of self-determination, problem-solving and assertiveness training, discussions about dating and sexuality, and opportunities for developing and actualizing the goal of maximal independence. Moreover, these group experiences would offer participants opportunities for greater integration in the disability community and shared empowerment for self-advocacy.

10. *Keep in touch to assess progress.* An occasional "check-in" or "maintenance visit" with the counselor might be a way for the client to evaluate progress toward long-term goals. Even just scheduling an occasional telephone contact may be effective for maintaining change and working effectively toward goals. We have received feedback that when women in our group intervention studies are asked to pair up with buddies, they occasionally continue with the action-planning process for years after the study has ended, but they more typically stay in touch about their progress by telephone visits and lunch get-togethers with one another.

Olkin (1999, pp. 154–155) offered the following seven guidelines for clinical work with persons with disabilities: (1) Have a framework for therapy that is based on models such as the minority model of disability, family, and larger systems theories, and an expansion of the biopsychosocial model; (2) demonstrate knowledge of the bicultural nature of disability and your ability to conduct competent cross-cultural counseling; (3) conduct systemic work with the family system; (4) realize that disability is a social construct (personal *is* political); (5) acquire disability-specific education, training, practice, and skills; (6) work beyond reduction of deficits to mitigate the pathologizing of persons with disabilities and to work with disability as a long-term experience; and (7) show, not just tell, that you can work effectively with this population.

## Recommendations for Counseling: Issues Across the Life Span

Finally, we urge counselors to consider developmental issues when working with people with disabilities. Although we have focused most of this chapter on adult women with physical disabilities, counselors may employ specific stage-related techniques when working with children and adolescents, or elderly clients.

**Children and Adolescents With Disabilities**   Price (1990) lamented that children with severe disabilities in special education programs have few opportunities to make choices that would prepare them for independent living in the community after graduation. Sutkin (1984) addressed the need for both teachers and parents to recognize the importance of what the school-age child can do and to encourage the child's efforts to develop autonomy. Counselors may facilitate this process, too, by intervening with the families and school with the goal of raising their expectations for the child's self-determination and decision making. These children "have very little control over their lives. They are taught, transported, assessed, and evaluated with little possibility of input or understanding" (Sutkin, 1984, p. 16). As a result, studies have shown that special education graduates who did not fail in special education programs nevertheless did fail once they were on their own (Mithaug, Martin, Agran, & Rusch, 1988).

For adolescents to be prepared to meet the occupational and social goals of young adulthood, they require opportunities to develop a sense of self. Parents of adolescents with disabilities may have provided loving and protective physical care, and teachers may have taught academic subjects and skills. Nevertheless, these same caring adults may have failed to provide an ever-increasing independent environment supportive of healthy, adolescent-appropriate experimentation. Counselors and peer groups may offer opportunities for self-expression, goal setting and attainment, peer interactions, and experiences with control and its consequences.

**Elderly People With Disabilities**   Although only a few mental health professionals have developed expertise in the field of gerontology, most will have ample opportunity to respond to the needs of a population living longer and with chronic, disabling health conditions. Are mental health professions required to prescribe a distinct counseling and psychotherapy approach with this population? Schienle and Eiler (1984) addressed this question and concluded that assuming a "life-span continuity in psychological style" would be the most productive approach. Counselors could work with older clients to come to an understanding of their lifetime psychological resources, including their coping styles and self-management skills, and to help them develop and practice strategies for maintaining those resources consistently throughout the remainder of their lives. Counselors can also be very helpful in assisting older individuals in accessing available community services when their need for assistance with activities of daily living increases.

Examples of other issues that may be salient for older clients with disabilities include concerns about the development of secondary conditions and other new health problems, issues related to death and dying, and losses of many kinds. Informal feedback from participants in our health promotion group program for women aging with disability suggests that the social connectedness and sharing with others like them is experienced as particularly helpful. Meeting with clients and their families and scheduling sessions at home, the hospital, or other settings may be especially important for this population. Schienle and Eiler (1984) reminded counselors that the "intervention that is least disruptive of usual functioning in the usual setting should be the treatment of choice" (p. 259) while emphasizing the importance of assessment to ensure that older clients' needs are met.

Elderly residents of nursing homes who are no longer allowed to practice the independent behaviors they were accustomed to performing in the community are at risk of losing these abilities (Avorn & Langer, 1982; Booth, 1986; Kiernat, 1987). They may feel that the decision to relocate to a nursing home was executed without adequately involving them. Since nursing homes are not typically focused on rehabilitation, decreased function often ensues (Schienle & Eiler, 1984). When the "environment encourages independence in activities such as dressing . . . then people will tend to function at or near optimum levels" (Zarit & Zarit, 1984, p. 274). Depriving residents of those functions prematurely will compromise their abilities and often hard-earned skills in independent living. Counselors can work with their clients to maintain their independent lifestyle by encouraging them to assert their rights and needs, to continue to use their coping and self-management skills, and to help them to become socially integrated in the residential setting but to maintain their lifetime connections as much as possible.

## CONCLUDING REMARKS

Mental health professionals may serve as admirable pilots to help persons with disabilities navigate the choppy waters that they encounter in their voyage toward independence. In this brief overview, we focused our attention primarily on information we believe is critical for counselors who are working with people with disabilities. We have illustrated many of the concepts and pressing issues surrounding independence by drawing on our current professional activities and expertise involving research on women with disabilities. Our personal and clinical experience has heightened our awareness that training programs for mental health professionals do not adequately address the specific needs of persons with disabilities. Perhaps this chapter will help to fill in any disability-related gap in the diversity training of counselors and other mental health professionals.

# Cases and Questions

1. Sarah is a 23-year-old Hispanic woman with cerebral palsy that moderately impairs her speech and mobility. She lives with her large family in an urban trailer park. Sarah attended special education classes in the local public school, even though she has no cognitive impairment, but has stayed at home since ninth grade when she had an operation to correct muscle contractures in her ankles. After her recovery, her parents found that it helped family finances if she took care of the two youngest children who were preschoolers, so they did not encourage her to resume classes. For the past 8 years, Sarah has stayed primarily in and around the trailer park and knows few people outside her family and close neighbors. She was taken to the emergency department of the city's charity hospital for what appears to be a miscarriage.
   (a) List your assumptions about Sarah's pregnancy.
   (b) What helping agencies would you refer her to?
   (c) What would be your approach to discussing Sara's situation with her family, pursuant to a suspicion of domestic violence?
2. Ethel just turned 75. As a homemaker, she has excellent management skills. Her husband passed away 2 years ago, and between his retirement pension from the steel plant and Social Security, she has been able to make ends meet. Now their two-story house, which was paid for years ago, needs some repairs. Ethel's vision and hearing are diminishing and the arthritis in her knees is making it too painful to walk up stairs. Her daughter lives about 45 minutes away and has a very sick husband, so she is unable to help her mother as much as she would like. All of Ethel's four children are concerned for their mother's safety, and one has suggested that she go into a nursing home. Ethel loves her home and her wide circle of friends and is distraught about being forced to leave.
   (a) What are the factors that make Ethel a good candidate for maintaining her independence in her own home?
   (b) What are the barriers she'll have to deal with as her physical functioning diminishes?
   (c) How would you advise Ethel to communicate with her family about her desire for independence?

## REFERENCES

Adler, A. (1979). *Superiority and social interest.* New York: Norton.
Avorn, J., & Langer, E. J. (1982). Induced disability in nursing home patients: A controlled trial. *Journal of the American Geriatric Society, 30,* 397–400.
Barnwell, A. M., & Kavanagh, D. J. (1997). Prediction of psychological adjustment to multiple sclerosis. *Social Science and Medicine, 45,* 411–418.

Bednar, R. L., & Peterson, S. R. (1995). *Self-esteem: Paradoxes and innovations in clinical theory and practice* (2nd ed.). Washington, DC: American Psychological Association.

Berkman, L. F., & Syme, S. L. (1979). Social networks, host resistance, and mortality: A nine-year follow-up study of Alameda County residents. *American Journal of Epidemiology, 109,* 186–204.

Berlly, M. H., Strauser, W. W., & Hall, K. M. (1991). Fatigue in postpolio syndrome. *Archives of Physical Medicine and Rehabilitation, 72,* 115–118.

Booth, T. (1986). Institutional regimes and induced dependency in homes for the aged. *The Gerontologist, 26,* 418–423.

Brooks, N. A., & Matson, R. R. (1982). Social-psychological adjustment to multiple sclerosis. *Social Science and Medicine, 16,* 2129–2135.

Brown, F., & Lehr, D. H. (1989). *Persons with profound disabilities: Issues and practices.* Baltimore, MD: Paul H. Brookes.

Cascardi, M., & O'Leary, K. D. (1992). Depressive symptomatology, self-esteem, and self-blame in battered women. *Journal of Family Violence, 7,* 249–259.

Cooley, C. H. (1902). *Human nature and the social order.* New York: Scribner's.

Corbett, J. (1989). The quality of life in the 'independence' curriculum. *Disability, Handicap and Society, 4,* 145–163.

Cornwell, C. J., & Schmitt, M. H. (1990). Perceived health status, self-esteem, and body image in women with rheumatoid arthritis or systemic lupus erythematosus. *Research in Nursing and Health, 13,* 99–107.

Coulehan, J. L., Schulberg, H. C., Block, M. R., Madonia, M. J., & Rodriguez, E. (1997). Treating depressed primary care patients improves their physical, mental, and social functioning. *Archives of Internal Medicine, 157,* 1113–1120.

Coyle, C. P., Santiago, M. C., Shank, J. W., Ma, G. X., & Boyd, R. (2000). Secondary conditions and women with physical disabilities: A descriptive study. *Archives of Physical Medicine and Rehabilitation, 81,* 1380–1387.

Crewe, N. M., & Clarke, N. (1996). Stress and women with disabilities. In D. Krotoski, M. A. Nosek, & M. A. Turk (Eds.), *Women with physical disabilities: Achieving and maintaining health and well-being* (pp. 193–202). Baltimore, MD: Paul H. Brookes.

Crisp, R. (1996). Community integration, self-esteem, and vocational identity among persons with disabilities. *Australian Psychologist, 31,* 133–137.

Flachenecker, P., & Hartung, H. P. (1996). Course of illness and prognosis of multiple sclerosis: I: The natural illness course. *Nervenarzt, 67,* 435–443.

Frieden, L., Richards, L., Cole, J. A., & Bailey, D. (1979). *ILRU sourcebook: A technical assistance manual on independent living.* Houston, TX: The Institute for Rehabilitation and Research.

Goffman, E. (1963). *Stigma: Notes on management of spoiled identity.* Englewood Cliffs, NJ: Prentice-Hall.

Hughes, R. B., Swedlund, N., Petersen, N., & Nosek, M. A. (2001). Depression and women with spinal cord injury. *Topics in Spinal Cord Injury Rehabilitation, 7,* 16–24.

Hughes, R. B., Taylor, H. B., Robinson-Whelen, S., & Nosek, M.A. (2002). *Perceived stress and women with physical disabilities.* Manuscript submitted for publication.

Jans, L., & Stoddard, S. (1999). *Chartbook on women and disability in the United States: An InfoUse report.* Washington, DC: U.S. Department of Education, National Institute on Disability and Rehabilitation Research.

Jordan, J. V., Kaplan, A. G., Miller, J. B., Stiver, I. P., & Surrey, J. L. (1991). *Women's growth in connection.* New York: Guilford Press.

Kerr, N., & Meyerson, L. (1987). Independence as a goal and a value of people with physical disabilities: Some caveats. *Rehabilitation Psychology, 32,* 173–180.

Kiernat, J. M. (1987). Promoting independence and autonomy through environmental approaches. *Topics in Geriatric Rehabilitation, 3*(1), 1–6.

Krotoski, D. M., & Bennett, C. J. (1996). Section IV: Managing bladder and bowel function. In D. M. Krotoski, M. A. Nosek, & M. A. Turk (Eds.), *Women with physical disabilities: Achieving and maintaining health and well-being* (pp. 283–285). Baltimore, MD: Paul H. Brookes.

Kutza, E. A. (1985). Benefits for the disabled: How beneficial for women? In M. J. Deegan & N. A. Brooks (Eds.), *Women and disability: The double handicap* (pp. 68–86). New Brunswick, NJ: Transaction.

Lorig, K., Holman, H., Sobel, D., Laurent, D., Gonzalez, V., & Minor, M. (2000). *Living a healthy life with chronic conditions: Self-management of heart disease, arthritis, diabetes, asthma, bronchitis, emphysema and others* (2nd ed.). Palo Alto, CA: Bull.

McGrath, E., Keita, G. P., Strickland, B. R., & Russo, N. F. (1990). *Women and depression: Risk factors and treatment issues: Final report of the American Psychological Association's National Task Force on Women and Depression.* Washington, DC: American Psychological Association.

McNeil, J. M. (1993). *Americans with Disabilities 1991–1992. U.S. Bureau of the Census: Current Populations Report, P70-33,* U.S. Government Printing Office, Washington, DC.

Mathews, R. M., & Seekins, T. (1987). An interactional model of independence. *Rehabilitation Psychology, 32,* 165–172.

Mead, G. H. (1934). *Mind, self, and society.* Chicago: University of Chicago Press.

Mithaug, D. E., Martin, J. E., Agran, M., & Rusch, F. R. (1988). *Why special education graduates fail.* Colorado Springs, CO: Ascent.

Munoz, R. F., Hollon, S. D., McGrath, E., Rehm, L. P., & VandenBos, G. R. (1994). On the AHCPR depression in primary care guidelines: Further considerations for practitioners. *American Psychologist,* January, 42–61.

National Center for Health Statistics. (2002). *Healthy women with disabilities: Analysis of the 1994–1995 National Health Interview Survey: Series 10 Report* [forward by F. Chevarley, J. Thierry, M. Nosek, & C. Gill]. Unpublished manuscript.

Noh, S., & Posthuma, B. (1990). Physical disability and depression: A methodological consideration. *Canadian Journal of Occupational Therapy, 57,* 9–15.

Nosek, M. A. (1992). Independent living. In R. M. Parker (Ed.), *Rehabilitation counseling: Basics and beyond* (2nd ed., pp. 103–133). Austin, TX: Pro-Ed.

Nosek, M. A. (1995). Sexual abuse of women with physical disabilities. *Physical Medicine and Rehabilitation: State of the Art Reviews, 9,* 487–502.

Nosek, M. A. (1996). Wellness among women with physical disabilities. In D. M. Krotoski, M. A. Nosek, & M. A. Turk (Eds.), *Women with physical disabilities: Achieving and maintaining health and well-being* (pp. 17–33). Baltimore, MD: Paul H. Brookes.

Nosek, M. A. (2000). Overcoming the odds: The health of women with physical disabilities in the United States. *Archives of Physical Medicine and Rehabilitation, 81,* 135–138.

Nosek, M. A., Foley, C. C., Hughes, R. B., & Howland, C. A. (2001). Vulnerabilities for abuse among women with disabilities. *Sexuality and Disability, 19,* 177–189.

Nosek, M. A., & Fuhrer, M. J. (1992). Independence among people with disabilities: I. A heuristic model. *Rehabilitation Counseling Bulletin, 36,* 6–20.

Nosek, M. A., Fuhrer, M. J., & Howland, C. A. (1992). Independence among people with disabilities: II. Personal Independence Profile. *Rehabilitation Counseling Bulletin, 36,* 21–36.

Nosek, M. A., Howland, C. A., Rintala, D. H., Young, M. E., & Chanpong, G. F. (2001). National study of women with physical disabilities: Final report. *Sexuality and Disability, 19,* 5–39.

Nosek, M. A., Howland, C. A., & Young, M. E. (1997). Abuse of women with disabilities: Policy implications. *Journal of Disability Policy Studies 8,* 157–176.

Nosek, M. A., Hughes, R. B., Swedlund, N., Taylor, H. B., & Swank, P. (in press). Self-esteem and women with disabilities. *Social Science and Medicine.*

Nosek, M. A., Walter, L. J., Young, M. E., & Howland, C. A. (in press). Lifelong patterns of abuse experienced by women with physical disabilities. *Journal of Interpersonal Violence.*

Olkin, R. (1999). *What psychotherapists should know about disability.* New York: Guilford Press.

Patterson, J. B., DeLaGarza, D., & Schaller, J. (1998). Rehabilitation counseling practice: Considerations and interventions. In R. M. Parker & E. M. Szymanski (Eds.), *Rehabilitation counseling: Basics and beyond* (3rd ed., pp. 269–302). Austin, TX: Pro-Ed.

Perduta-Fulginiti, P. S. (1996). Impact of bladder and bowel dysfunction on sexuality and self-esteem. In D. M. Krotoski, M. A. Nosek, & M. A. Turk (Eds.), *Women with physical disabilities: Achieving and maintaining health and well-being* (pp. 287–298). Baltimore, MD: Paul H. Brookes.

Pope, A. M., & Tarlov, A. R. (Eds.). (1991). *Disability in America: Toward a national agenda for prevention.* Washington, DC: National Academy Press.

Price, E. B. (1990). *Independence and the individual with severe disabilities. Journal of Rehabilitation, 56,* 15–18.

Ravesloot, C., Seekins, T., & Walsh, J. (1997). A structural analysis of secondary conditions experienced by people with physical disabilities. *Rehabilitation Psychology, 42,* 3–16.

Rintala, D. H., Hart, K. A., & Fuhrer, M. J. (1996). Perceived stress in individuals with spinal cord injury. In D. Krotoski, M. A. Nosek, & M. A. Turk (Eds.), *Women with physical disabilities: Achieving and maintaining health and well-being* (pp. 223–242). Baltimore, MD: Paul H. Brookes.

Roberts, R. E., Kaplan, G. A., Shema, S. J., & Strawbridge, W. J. (1997). Prevalence and correlates of depression in an aging cohort: The Alameda County Study. *Journal of Gerontology: Social Sciences, 52B,* S252–S258.

Rock, P. J. (1988). Independence: What it means to six disabled people living in the community. *Disability, Handicap and Society, 3*(1), 27–35.

Romano, J. M., & Turner, J. A. (1985). Chronic pain and depression: Does the evidence support a relationship? *Psychological Bulletin, 97,* 18–34.

Schaller, J., & DeLaGarza, D. (1995). Issues of gender in vocational testing and counseling. *Journal of Job Placement, 11,* 6–14.

Schienle, D. R., & Eiler, J. M. (1984). Clinical interventions with older adults. In M. G. Eisenberg, L. C. Sutkin, & M. A. Jansen (Eds.), *Chronic illness and disability through the life span: Effects on self and family* (pp. 245–268). New York: Springer.

Stotland, N. L., & Stotland, N. E. (1999). Focus on primary care: Depression in women. *Obstetrical and Gynecological Survey, 54,* 519–525.

Suris, J. C., Resnick, M. D., Cassuto, N., & Blum, R. W. (1996). Sexual behavior of adolescents with chronic disease and disability. *Journal of Adolescent Health, 19,* 124–131.

Sutkin, L. C. (1984). Introduction. In M. G. Eisenberg, L. C. Sutkin, & M. A. Jansen (Eds.), *Chronic illness and disability through the life span: Effects on self and family* (pp. 1–19). New York: Springer.

Taylor, S. E. (1999). *Health psychology* (4th ed.) Boston, MA: McGraw-Hill.

Turner, R. J., & Beiser, M. (1990). Major depression and depressive symptomatology among the physically disabled: Assessing the role of chronic stress. *Journal of Nervous Mental Disorders, 178,* 343–350.

Turner, R. J., & Noh, S. (1988). Physical disability and depression: A longitudinal analysis. *Journal of Health and Social Behavior, 29,* 23–37.

Turner, R. J., & Wood, D. W. (1985). Depression and disability: The stress process in a chronically strained population. *Research in Community and Mental Health, 5,* 77–109.

U.S. Department of Health and Human Services. (2000). Disability and secondary conditions. In *Healthy People 2010.* Washington, DC: Author.

Williamson, G. M., & Walters, A. S. (1996). Perceived impact of limb amputation on sexual activity: A study of adult amputees. *Journal of Sex Research, 33,* 221–230.

Yelin, E., & Callahan, L. F. (1995). The economic cost and social and psychological impact of musculoskeletal conditions. *Arthritis and Rheumatism, 38,* 1351–1362.

Young, M. E., Nosek, M. A., Howland, C., Chanpong, G., & Rintala, D. H. (1997). Prevalence of abuse of women with physical disabilities. *Archives of Physical Medicine and Rehabilitation, 78,* S-34–S-38.

Zarit, S. H., & Zarit, J. M. (1984). Psychological approaches to families of the elderly. In M. G. Eisenberg, L. C. Sutkin, & M. A. Jansen (Eds.), *Chronic illness and disability through the life span: Effects on self and family* (pp. 269–288). New York: Springer.

CHAPTER 8 # Counseling and Psychotherapy With Clients With Disabilities

John F. Kosciulek, Michigan State University

Clients with disabilities present counselors with both unique challenges and opportunities in the counseling process. Most individuals with disabilities will present in the counseling situation similar or identical to all other individuals. However, similar to ethnicity, gender, age, and sexual identity, disability can be viewed as an individual difference. Persons with disabilities may come to counselors with unique presenting problems, developmental issues, and adjustment needs. As such, disability is an important diversity characteristic that counselors must consider.

This chapter is intended to help you extend and expand your counseling repertoire to include those skills and techniques necessary to effectively serve people with disabilities. To this end, the chapter initially addresses the process of response to disability and potential client presenting problems. The importance of the four "common factors" that contribute to positive therapeutic outcomes when counseling clients with disabilities are then discussed. Readers are next provided with a description of the major counseling intervention strategies that may be particularly effective when working with individuals with disabilities. These strategies include social support development, family systems counseling, and facilitating client self-determination. In the next section, general principles to guide the counseling process with clients with disabilities and specific counseling etiquette suggestions are discussed. The final section of the chapter presents case studies for enabling reader application of the theory and techniques described in this chapter.

## ADAPTATION AND RESPONSE TO DISABILITY

To provide effective services to clients with disabilities, counselors must understand the theory, models, and clinical reports regarding the definition, process, and outcome of a client's response to disability. In this section, the stage model of adaptation to disability is presented as a theoretical framework that counselors will find useful for conceptualizing the client disability experience. Prior to describing the stage model, it is important to briefly discuss the contemporary terminology and conceptualization of response to disability as it is being espoused in the theoretical and clinical disability literature.

## Contemporary Notions of Response to Disability

The terms *adjustment, adaptation,* and *acceptance* have been used to describe the end result of coping with a disability and successfully integrating the disability into the individual's life and identity (Lindemann, 1981; Linkowski & Dunn, 1974; Livneh & Antonak, 1997; Smart, 2001). As described in the following section, in the early stages of disability scholarship, adjustment to disability was conceptualized as a series of stages through which the individual passed, ending with the acceptance of the disability. Current models of coping with a disability use the term *the individual's response to disability* (Livneh; 2001; Livneh & Antonak, 1997). The word *response* is more appropriate and accurate because, according to Smart (2001), it communicates the following more fully:

- It is not the disability itself, but the meaning that the individual ascribes to the disability that will determine the response to the disability.
- There are many types of responses or adjustments to disability in addition to the psychological adjustment, including occupational and social adjustment or response.
- The words *adjustment, adaptation,* and *acceptance* pathologize the experience of a disability, meaning a disability is automatically assumed to be an undesirable state.
- The individual copes with disability and makes adjustments throughout his or her lifetime, including those with stable disabilities, and therefore *acceptance* is not a onetime event.

## Stage Model of Adaptation to Disability

The stage theory of adaptation to disability provides useful guidelines for understanding and predicting the course and outcome of the individual's response process. This process is a gradual assimilation of an altered identity and is a process, not a onetime event (Livneh, 2001). The stages of adaptation to disability include shock or initial impact, defensive retreat or denial, depression or mourning, personal questioning and anger, and integration and growth. Prior to describing each of the stages, it is important to note that not all disabilities have a sudden, acute, traumatic onset (Smart, 2001). For example, disabilities such as diabetes and lupus have an insidious onset, and therefore it is more accurate to speak of the time of diagnosis rather than the time of onset (Moos, 1984). Further, Smart (2001) noted that moving through the stages of adaptation requires goal-directed changes in attitude and behavior, but this does not imply that the onset/diagnosis of every disability is thought to be tragic. A final important point regarding the stages of adaptation to disability for counselors to be aware of is that the stage theory is based on theories of adaptation to loss, especially Kübler-Ross's theories of acceptance of one's death (Kübler-Ross, 1969).

**Shock or Initial Impact**   In this stage, the individual's thinking is often disorganized, and he or she may be feeling overwhelmed and confused. A disability may present as totally unexpected and devastating, such as in the case of a traumatic brain injury resulting from a motor vehicle accident. Individuals in the shock stage often feel that more is happening to them than they can understand or absorb (Livneh & Antonak, 1997; Smart, 2001).

**Defensive Retreat or Denial**   Denial can take three forms: (1) denial of the presence of the disability, (2) denial of the implications of the disability, or (3) denial of the permanence of the disability (Smart, 2001). Denial allows the individual to maintain his or her self-identity. The word *defensive* implies that this stage is often considered to be a therapeutic, adaptive strategy on the part of the person with a disability. Defensive retreat or denial can prevent what is called "emotional flooding" and allows the individual to assimilate both the permanence and the full implications of the disability. For this reason, denial is considered to be therapeutic if it does not continue too long. Individuals in this stage, in an attempt to guard against the trauma, may refuse to accept information, insist there has been a mistake, and may seek out other service providers.

**Depression or Mourning**   Whereas denial is considered to be past oriented, in that the individual is trying to regain his or her former identity (Smart, 2001), depression is considered to be future oriented because the individual now struggles with questions of an uncertain future and an uncertain identity (Marshak & Seligman, 1993; Olkin, 1999). In this stage, the person with a disability does not have energy or motivation to invest in a rehabilitation program. The individual may withdraw from others and have trouble sleeping, eating, and concentrating. Smart (2001) aptly described how it is often typical for the person with a disability to experience a cycle of loss of hope, apathy, and depression that includes feelings of guilt and self-blame.

**Personal Questioning or Anger**   In this stage, the individual may ask, "Why did God allow this to happen to me?" The onset of disability seems unfair. Anger is often a combination of feeling helpless, frustrated, afraid, and irritated. Other types of personal questioning may take the form of the person with a disability "replaying" the accident or prediagnosis period, in an attempt to find ways in which the disability could have been avoided. For example, a counselor may hear an individual who has sustained a brain injury as a result of a motor vehicle accident state, "If I just hadn't driven to the store that night when I knew it was snowing and icy out on the roads." If carried on for too long, compulsive, obsessive questioning and search for cause and meaning can delay the treatment and rehabilitation process (Livneh & Antonak, 1997; Smart, 2001). Counselors can be facilitative in this stage by helping the individual to understand the difference between the causes of the disability and the meaning and purpose of the disability.

**Integration and Growth**   The individual with a disability reaches this stage when he or she (1) understands and accepts the reality and implications of the disability, (2) establishes new values and goals that do not conflict with the disability, and (3) explores and utilizes his or her strengths and abilities (Marshak & Seligman, 1993; Smart, 2001). Integration and growth may necessitate changes in the environment such as assistive technology, changes in role functioning (e.g., the individual no longer serving as the primary breadwinner in a family system), and assuming responsibility for the management of the disability such as attending to regular medical needs. Vash (1981) termed this stage "transcendence," in which the individual feels that the disability is an opportunity for growth and learning. Upon reaching this stage, some persons with disabilities may begin advocacy and support work with other individuals with disabilities and their families. Further, they may view their advocacy, service, and political activity as a means of bringing meaning and purpose to their own disability experience (Kosciulek, 1995; Smart, 2001).

## POTENTIAL CLIENT PRESENTING PROBLEMS

Most clients with disabilities will present counselors with adjustment and developmental issues similar to all other clients. However, four presenting problem areas may be more prevalent among clients with disabilities. These areas include discrimination and stigma, depression, substance abuse, and career/vocational issues. Counselors must be aware of the increased possibility of these areas as the primary reason a client is seeking counseling services. In addition, counselors must be skilled at assessing and assisting clients with successfully managing these four challenging life situations.

### Discrimination and Stigma

The literature is clear that individuals with disabilities experience discrimination and stigma at a higher rate than the population in general (Smart, 2001). Persons with disabilities are disproportionately discriminated against in such major and important life areas as education and employment (Kosciulek, 1999). In addition, as aptly described by Marshak and Seligman (1993), stigma in the form of negative attitudes and irrational fears toward persons with disabilities may exist that limit an individual's access to social and leisure activities.

Society generally holds diminished expectations for people with disabilities (Schroeder, 1995). These attitudes are pervasive; they influence all of us to some degree. As a class, people with disabilities have suffered discrimination. Individuals with disabilities, similar to members of racial and ethnic minority groups, face common social problems of stigma, marginality, and discrimination (Fine & Asch, 1988; Trueba, 1993).

A factor that has not been fully addressed in relation to the individual's response to disability is the degree of prejudice and discrimination toward the type and severity of disability. The degree of stigma and prejudice the individual experiences will influence his or her response to the disability (Smart, 2001). Further, the outcome of long-term exposure to prejudicial attitudes may be negative self-appraisal. Clients with disabilities may present to counselors with much anxiety in relation to these potential life situations and experiences. Counselors must be prepared to assist such individuals with managing the stress associated with ongoing negative stigma and successfully combating discriminatory practices.

## Depression

Depression was previously described as one of the theoretical stages in the process of adaptation to disability. The diagnosis and treatment of depression in a client with a disability merits special attention for several reasons. First, the clinical literature indicates that sizable minorities of persons who acquire a physical disability become depressed after the injury. Estimates vary but are roughly 30% plus or minus 5% (Heinrich & Tate, 1996; Lichtenberg, 1997). Second, depression is a common coexisting disability among individuals who are diagnosed with a major mental disorder (Sammons & Schmidt, 2001). A third reason to explore the potential presence of depression in a client with a disability in particular is that depression has been shown to complicate the recovery and rehabilitation process, increase length of hospital stay, and reduce independence (Olkin, 1999). Fourth, there is a correlation between degree of insight and depression, at least in persons with traumatic brain injuries (Campodonico & McGlynn, 1995). These researchers detected a positive correlation between depression and awareness of brain injury deficits. This can be explained in both directions: Those with greater awareness of deficits became more depressed, and those with more depression focused more on their deficits. This supports the idea that depression per se is an important aspect of the rehabilitative process and must not be overlooked. Given such data, Olkin (1999) recommended that depression be viewed as a primary medical condition, and its diagnosis and treatment a high priority in the counseling process.

## Substance Abuse

The rates of alcoholism and other drug abuse for people with disabilities are estimated to be twice as high of those of the general population (Rehabilitation Research and Training Center on Drugs and Disability [RRTCDD], 1996). Substance abuse may exist as a primary disability for an individual. In such situations, counselors must be skilled in the assessment and treatment of substance abuse as a presenting problem. Such skills include counselor ability to assist clients with identifying and using community support services and systems such as aftercare programs and Alcoholics Anonymous groups.

Substance abuse also may exist as a coexisting disability. In these situations, a client may present with both a primary disability and substance abuse problems. It is important to note that alcohol and drug use rates are particularly high among people with spinal cord injuries, brain injuries, mental illness, blindness, and learning disabilities (RRTCDD, 1996).

Counselors must be aware of the cause and effect relation between specific disability conditions and substance abuse. Several examples may provide counselors with useful starting points for considering when developing treatment plans for clients with substance abuse as a coexisting disability. First, mental illness conditions are compounded by the use of substances (e.g., depression and the use of alcohol and other chemical depressants). Individuals may seek out illegal drugs for symptom management. This is referred to as self-medication. Second, for individuals with blindness and visual impairments, isolation and inaccessibility are critical factors that may lead to substance abuse. In addition, substance abuse may compound visual impairments and contribute to the acceleration of their symptoms through neglect of deteriorating health. Third, there appears to be a strong correlation between substance abuse and early, undiagnosed learning disabilities. A sense of failure and early rejection by peers may lead an individual to turn to drugs or alcohol for a social life and feelings of acceptance, or for withdrawal from the challenges of life (Stevens & Smith, 2001). A primary challenge to the counselor in the situation of a client with substance abuse as a coexisting disability is in meeting the need for additional and more coordinated medical and rehabilitation services.

## Career Development Issues

Providing career-related counseling services to people with disabilities presents an additional unique challenge to counselors. Assisting people with disabilities to find suitable employment is becoming an increasingly difficult task due to the ever-changing nature of work. Major trends such as globalization of the American economy, technology, and population shifts are changing the nature of work and worker skill requirements (Ryan, 1995). Despite rehabilitation efforts, a majority of Americans with disabilities between the ages of 16 and 64 are not employed and their numbers have not changed since 1986, despite the fact that a majority of nonemployed people with disabilities in the working-age population want to work (National Organization on Disability, 2000). In general, the vocational adjustment of people with disabilities has been characterized by limited salable work skills, low income, underemployment, and unemployment (Curnow, 1989). In addition, according to Harrington (1997), students with disabilities frequently leave school without marketable skills or the ability to function independently. Given that work is a central force in peoples' lives, dramatically high rates of unemployment and underemployment can adversely affect not only the economic and social status of individuals with disabilities but also their self-image. A distinct set of career challenges encountered by many people with disabilities that can be used as a reference point for counselors includes: (a) limitations in early life experiences, (b) career decision-making difficulties, and (c) a negative worker self-concept (Kosciulek, 1998).

## COMMON THERAPEUTIC FACTORS

The potential client presenting problems described in the last section coupled with the process of client response to disability pose a significant challenge to counselors in the therapeutic process. As such, it is imperative that counselors are equipped with the knowledge and skills regarding what works in therapy with clients with disabilities. Despite the fact that counselors have many therapy models from which to choose, 40 years of psychotherapy outcome research have demonstrated that although most models effect change, no one approach is significantly more effective than another (Bertolino & O'Hanlon, 2002; Lambert & Bergin, 1994). The contemporary counseling and psychotherapy outcome literature concludes that it is more efficacious for counselors to focus on commonalities or similarities that occur across all modalities when the end result is positive change, rather than comparing models to determine what makes one approach more effective than another (Hubble, Duncan, & Miller, 1999).

Lambert (1992) and Miller, Duncan, and Hubble (1997) argued that the research evidence makes it clear those similarities rather than differences between therapy models account for most of the positive change that clients experience in treatment. These researchers stated that what emerges from examining these similarities are a group of consistent, non-theory-based commonalities that account for that change. Clinicians and researchers have learned that when positive change does occur in therapy that these commonalities are present regardless of the model being used. Thus, in relation to counseling clients with disabilities, it is important for counselors to be aware that the clinical effectiveness of different therapies may depend more on their common elements than their theoretical differences (Miller et al., 1997). The core group of factors responsible for similar outcomes with different therapy models was referred to by Lambert (1992) as the four therapeutic factors and later by Hubble et al. (1999) as the common factors. These factors, which provide counselors a guide for how to approach the therapeutic relationship, conduct assessment, utilize interventions, and create change in clients with disabilities, are extratherapeutic, relationship, placebo, and model and technique.

## Extratherapeutic Factors: The Contribution of Clients and Chance Events

Extratherapeutic factors account for much of the improvement that occurs in any form of psychotherapy. Lambert (1992) estimated that these factors account for 40% of the variance in outcome. Extratherapeutic factors are the resources that clients with disabilities bring to therapy, including their strengths, abilities, resources, and social support systems. The research clearly indicates that the client is the single, most potent contributor to outcome in therapy (Bohart & Tallman, 1999).

Extratherapeutic factors also include external influences, such as spontaneous or chance events that occur outside therapy. These are events that occur during the course of therapy but that typically have little or no correlation to the treatment itself. By identifying and amplifying positive, spontaneous changes, counselors can help clients with disabilities see that change is constant in their lives. Further, counselors can explore with clients the significance of such changes and work with them to expand and build on them in the future (Bertolino & O'Hanlon, 2002).

## Relationship Factors: The Contribution of the Therapeutic Alliance

The therapeutic relationship is a central factor in successful therapy. Researchers estimate that as much as 30% of the variance in counseling outcome can be attributed to relationship factors (Lambert, 1992). Perhaps the two most significant factors in this realm are the quality of the client's participation and the degree to which the client is motivated, engaged, and joined in the therapeutic work (Lustig, Strauser, Rice, & Rucker, 2002; Prochaska, 1995).

Both general psychotherapy (Horvath, 1994) and disability-focused (Chan, Shaw, McMahon, Koch, and Strauser, 1997) researchers have expanded the therapeutic relationship to a broader concept known as the *therapeutic alliance,* a more encompassing term that emphasizes collaborative partnership between clients and therapists. Counselors can promote the therapeutic alliance by adjusting treatment to fit the client's motivational level or stage of change, goals and preferred outcomes for therapy, and view of the therapeutic relationship.

Clients with disabilities who are engaged and connected with counselors may benefit most from therapy. In contrast, the strength of the therapeutic bond is not highly correlated with the length of treatment (Horvath, 1994). In other words, there can be an instant bond between the counselor and client. Essential here are clients' perceptions of the therapeutic relationship. In fact, client ratings of therapists as empathic, trustworthy, and nonjudgmental are better predictors of positive outcome than therapist ratings, diagnosis, approach, or any other variable (Hubble et al., 1999; Lambert & Bergin, 1994). Overall, the therapeutic alliance can be most beneficial and an excellent predictor of outcome for clients with disabilities when

- counselors agree with clients on goals and preferred outcomes,
- counselors collaborate with clients on tasks to accomplish those goals and preferred outcomes (Lustig et al., 2002), and
- clients have a favorable view of the therapeutic relationship (Bertolino & O'Hanlon, 2002).

## Placebo Factors: The Role of Hope and Expectancy

Placebo factors relate to the role of hope and expectancy in therapy and contribute approximately 15% of the variance in therapeutic outcome (Lambert, 1992). This class of therapeutic factors refers to the portion of improvement deriving from clients' knowledge of being treated, the installation of hope, and how credible the client perceives therapy's rationale and techniques (Hubble et al., 1999). Marrone (1997) identified hope as a primary resource that counselors can bring to the therapeutic relationship when working with individuals with disabilities. Hope, according to Marrone, is not ill-informed optimism, but rather a positive outlook from the counselor's perspective that a current stressful life situation will be resolved.

Expectancy corresponds to the expectations that clients with disabilities have when beginning therapy. It also relates to both the client and counselor's belief in the restorative power of the treatment, including its procedures. A client's expectation that therapy will help can serve as a placebo and counteract demoralization, activate hope, and advance improvement. Bertolino and O'Hanlon (2002) provided a useful guide for enhancing the therapy process with clients with disabilities in relation to the placebo factors. These researchers have recommended that counselors

- show interest in the results of the therapeutic procedure or orientation,
- make sure the procedure or orientation is credible from the client's frame of reference,
- make sure the procedure or orientation is connected with or elicits previously successful experiences of the client,
- have a future focus in treatment,
- work in a way that enhances or highlights the client's feeling of personal control, and
- be sure to depersonalize the client's problems, difficulties, or shortcomings.

## Model and Technique Factors: The Role of Structure and Novelty

Model and techniques are the last of the four common factors. Like hope and expectancy, Lambert (1992) estimated that they account for 15% of improvement in counseling. Counseling techniques and procedures include, but are not limited to, asking particular questions, using specific interventions, assigning tasks, making interpretations, and teaching skills. Most techniques or procedures are designed to get clients to do something different, such as experience emotions, face fears, change patterns of thinking or behavior, and develop new understandings or meanings (Bertolino & O'Hanlon, 2002). Counselors can work to improve the effectiveness of therapeutic techniques with clients with disabilities by considering whether the orientation, techniques, and strategies

- fit with, support, or complement the client's worldview as a person with a disability (Smart, 2001);
- fit with or complement the client's expectations for treatment;
- capitalize on client strengths, abilities, and resources;
- utilize the client's environment and existing support network, a particularly important consideration with clients with disabilities (Szymanski, 2000);
- increase the client's sense of hope, expectancy, or personal control; and
- contribute to the client's sense of self-esteem, self-efficacy, and self-mastery.

## COUNSELING INTERVENTION APPROACHES

Application of the "common factors" conceptual framework will enable counselors to identify, develop, and successfully implement specific intervention skills and techniques useful for counseling clients with disabilities. Strategic counseling interventions for persons with various types of disabilities typically have the therapeutic goal of providing clients and their families with emotional, cognitive, and behavioral support and with adaptive coping skills for use during and after the rehabilitation process (Livneh & Antonak, 1997). The counseling approaches discussed in this section include social support development, family systems counseling, and facilitating client self-determination. Successful implementation of these three approaches will lead to optimal counseling outcomes for clients with disabilities. In other words, these three areas provide a useful structure for "what works" when counseling clients with disabilities.

## Social Support Development

A key ingredient in successful client response to disability and positive therapy outcomes is meaningful social support. Thus, in addition to direct counseling, counselors may affect positive client outcomes by helping clients with disabilities to develop support networks. Strong social supports may alleviate psychological difficulties related to client social isolation (Kosciulek, 1995).

A primary resource for developing long-term client social supports is the various national and state organizations that provide information and support for individuals with disabilities and their families. Examples of such organizations include the National Brain Injury Association and the National Alliance for the Mentally Ill. Clients can contact such organizations at the national, state, or local level and receive information and guidance about resources in their geographic area related to their specific needs, such as information on educational and rehabilitation programs; support groups for the member with the disability and family unit; federal, state, and local financial assistance programs; and related community-based services (Berry & Hardman, 1998). The client's participation in support groups and contact with other individuals in similar disability-related situations are important supplements to professional counseling. The education and emotional support provided by support groups complements that provided by the counselor.

There are some things that clients may appreciate or understand only in communicating with other individuals who have had similar experiences. For example, clients may more readily make decisions about treatment alternatives and difficult stages in rehabilitation processes if they have discussed the issues with individuals who have made similar decisions (Sachs, 1991). Further, support groups in which individuals with disabilities are afforded the opportunity to share their fears, concerns, and needs enable clients with disabilities to gain acknowledgment of their unique life situation and social support from the remaining group members (Livneh & Antonak, 1997). Kosciulek (1995) reported that many counselors in the rehabilitation field view this client-to-client support as a crucial element in helping clients work through the adaptation process. More important, clients themselves find this type of mutual support and information exchange extremely valuable (Muir, Rosenthal, & Diehl, 1990).

In addition to encouraging client participation, counselors may benefit from actual participation in family support groups. Listening and interacting with clients in a support group environment will provide the counselor a larger view of the individual's experience. With this experience, the counselor can be more sensitive and effective in his or her work with clients with disabilities.

## Family Systems Counseling

Disability affects not only the person who is born with or acquires a disability but also his or her entire family system. In fact, Brooks (1991) and Kosciulek (1995) have suggested that the impact of disability is at least as great for families, and that family members often are more distressed than the person with the disability. Thus, coping with the impact of disability is one of the most difficult tasks that can confront a family (Power, 1995). Ongoing challenges families of individuals with disabilities may encounter include: (a) emotional, personality, behavioral, and physical changes in the family member with the disability; (b) lack of information and appropriate services; (c) financial burden as a result of disability-related medical, rehabilitation, education, and independent living needs; and (d) emotional strain from prolonged caregiving. Functional consequences of such difficulties for families include marital discord, psychological distress, substance abuse, depletion of family finances, and the social isolation of families (Berry & Hardman, 1998; Williams, 1991).

In most of the services that deal with individuals with disabilities, the perception of the family is that of a resource for helping in the rehabilitation of the person with the disability. However, family members themselves are a group at high risk for physical, emotional, and social difficulties. Families require help in their own right and not only as a by-product of the counseling or rehabilitation process with the member with the disability. In consideration of the ongoing family life challenges that families of persons with disabilities may experience, the number of families who may seek and benefit from the services of counselors is substantial. Counselors working with families in a variety of settings, including medical facilities, vocational rehabilitation agencies, community mental health centers, family clinics, and private practice, can expect to serve families of persons with disabilities. An increased awareness of the impact of disability on families will enable counselors to meet the needs of individual family members and entire family systems. Thus, in addition to specific intervention strategies with clients with disabilities, counselors must be prepared to provide effective family system counseling services.

Marshak and Seligman (1993) presented a guide particularly useful for conceptualizing the intensity of counselor interface with the family depending on family needs and preferences. These authors noted that the intervention of counselors with families who have a member with a disability could occur at any of the following five levels:

- Level 1—Focus on the individual client (emphasis on the needs of the client, especially his or her problems; no direct involvement with the client's family).
- Level 2—Provide information for the family (minimum involvement with the client's family, restricted to "fact" or "information" communication).
- Level 3—Provide emotional support for the family (encourage family members to disclose their feelings; seek to show sympathy and emotional support to family members).
- Level 4—Provide structured assessment and intervention (provide well-planned support in reducing family stress and tension; empower the family through changing the family patterns associated with the disability).

- Level 5—Provide family therapy (professional intervention for families that become dysfunctional due to disability).

Many counselors are able to provide high-quality intervention with families at Levels 1 through 3 with relative ease. However, according to Roessler, Chung, and Rubin (1998), in order for effective family counseling to occur at Levels 4 and 5, counselors must possess both structural and relationship skills. Structural skills refer to the counselor's ability to identify problems or needs, define outcomes and alternatives, and confront family members' resistance. Relationship skills include the capacities to build rapport with and express empathic understanding to families.

Dell Orto and Power (1994) provided an additional perspective on counseling families of persons with disabilities by differentiating between the family intervention role of the counselor at the acute and extended phases of adjustment to disability. According to these authors, during the acute phase, the individual with the disability and his or her family encounter and cope with the onset of the impact of disability. During this initial phase, the family may be experiencing fear, shock, and distress. The role of the counselor at this stage is congruent with crisis intervention, with an emphasis on listening, understanding, observing, supporting, and encouraging. Dell Orto and Power (1994) reported that counseling objectives during the acute phase include the following:

1. Establishing a trusting relationship with the family
2. Learning early in family intervention the meaning of the disability to the family members, their expectations for the client and for each other, and family goals
3. Attempting to build self-esteem among the family members
4. Observing the communication patterns among the family members

During the extended phase of counseling, the client and his or her family members are in the process of gradually adapting to the disability. The roles of the counselor are to be an advocate and resource person, emphasizing a proactive intervention approach (Dell Orto & Power, 1994). Counseling objectives in the extended phase include: (a) providing information, (b) identifying and prioritizing presenting problems, (c) improving family interaction, and (d) developing and implementing treatment plans.

Muir et al. (1990) also have provided clinical guidelines useful for structuring the counseling process with families who have a member with a disability. These authors stated that counseling should help families deal with the anxiety, guilt, and other emotional reactions to disability and should reinforce their feelings of adequacy, self-worth, and competence. According to Muir et al. (1990), counselors should assist individual family members with learning how to draw on their own strengths while using the family unit as a source of support. Further, counselors must encourage families to explore their concerns regarding changing roles, sibling relationships, marital issues, and community reactions to disability onset within a family. Counseling should also help families adjust to the daily disruptions caused by disability, work to restore relationships, and approximate a normal family lifestyle. To achieve these objectives, counseling must be designed to meet such long-term family needs as maintaining a social support network, respite, obtaining services for the member with the disability, and managing legal and financial matters.

Given the potential complexity of the disability and its deleterious effect on families, a team approach, in which one cofacilitator specializes in family issues and the other specializes in disability sequelae (e.g., impact of psychiatric disability on a family), may be a very effective intervention format (Kosciulek, 1995). Another issue facing the counselor is whether to include the person with the disability in family counseling sessions. Muir et al. (1990) indicated that counselors must exercise caution when considering whether to involve the family member with the disability, particularly in the situation of a cognitive or emotional disability, as the individual must be able to participate in a meaningful way. DePompei and Zarski (1991), however, believe that severity of disability is not a reason to exclude the person with the disability from counseling sessions. These authors stated that if the therapist has reasons to believe that the person with the disability can learn and profit from the experience, family counseling could be a meaningful intervention for the entire family.

In situations in which family members feel uncomfortable or unable to express their feelings and concerns in the presence of the family member with the disability, counseling with individual members or family subgroups may be necessary. Spouses, parents, and siblings may express, or otherwise demonstrate, the need for individual counseling sessions. Muir et al. (1990) pointed out that this may occur for a variety of reasons, such as greater acceptance of professional counseling help by one individual than by the rest of the family, the need to express feelings that would be too uncomfortable to express in the presence of other family members, or simply greater comfort with individual counseling than with the group process.

The family systems and disability literature suggests several additional counseling approaches that may be particularly effective with families of persons with disabilities. One approach involves emphasizing the mutuality of responsibility for family problems and shifting the burden of causality from the member with the disability to the dysfunctional areas of the family system. A second approach focuses on strengthening the positive aspects of the family system (e.g., coping styles and communication patterns). Another potentially effective counseling approach may involve exploring dysfunctional interaction patterns by reenacting family conflicts and assisting family members in substituting conflict resolution strategies that are acceptable within their family system. Finally, prescribing homework assignments for the family to practice outside counseling sessions may foster generalization of behavior change.

## Facilitating Client Self-Determination

A strengths-based approach to counseling clients with disabilities focuses on goals related to the optimization of functioning. Such an approach is preferable to counseling that focuses on deficit reduction, or only goals related to the amelioration of negative symptoms such as depression and anxiety. Counseling that counteracts negative messages about self-limitations and conversely focuses on increasing positive aspects is desirable because disability is oftentimes a long-term condition, and enhancement of personal resources provides long-term insurance of well-being (Olkin, 1999).

*Self-determination,* a concept and process that has emerged from the fields of rehabilitation counseling, special education, and disability studies, provides the basis for a strengths-based approach to counseling clients with disabilities. Field, Hoffman, and Spezia (1998) have defined self-determination as a multidimensional concept that includes

- attitudes, abilities, and skills that lead people with disabilities to define goals for themselves and to take the initiative to reach these goals;
- the capacity to choose and to have those choices be the determinants of one's actions;
- determination of one's own fate or course of action without compulsion; and
- the ability to define and achieve goals based on a foundation of knowing and valuing oneself.

Promoting client self-determination should be a primary effort of counselors working with clients with disabilities. Client self-determination can be enhanced by helping clients develop the knowledge, skills, and beliefs that will allow them to exercise greater control during the counseling process by providing opportunities to develop greater self-awareness and by teaching decision-making, goal-setting, and negotiation skills (Kosciulek, Bruyere, & Rosenthal, 2002). The steps in the self-determination development process include clients knowing and valuing themselves, client planning, client action, experiencing outcomes and learning, and making adjustments. Client self-knowledge can be facilitated by encouraging clients to expand their thinking about the possibilities in their life, deciding what is truly important to them, having a keen sense of his or her strengths, limitations, and preferences, and knowing what options are available. Counselors can promote client self-valuing by assisting clients with accepting themselves as they are, admiring their strengths that come from uniqueness, and recognizing and respecting their rights and responsibilities.

The third step in the client self-determination process is the development of effective planning skills. Effective planning involves a process of setting goals; identifying action steps to meet goals and anticipate results; and visually and orally rehearsing potentially stressful events such as job interviews. In addition to planning, counselors can facilitate client self-determination by encouraging clients to act. Client self-determined action may include dealing directly with conflict and criticism (e.g., with a family member or coworker) and accessing resources and supports such as assistive technology devices and vocational rehabilitation services.

As a result of planning and acting, clients with disabilities will have the opportunity to experience positive outcomes and learn more about themselves. Counselor facilitation of the client self-determination process can enable individuals to compare performance and outcomes to their expectations and realize successes. In the final step toward enhancing client self-determination, counselors can help clients with disabilities make adjustments relative to self-perception and expected outcomes from future planning and actions.

## THE COUNSELING PROCESS: PRINCIPLES AND ETIQUETTE

As discussed throughout this chapter, a unique array of counselor knowledge and skills are required for effective counseling with clients with disabilities. Counselors must have a philosophical and attitudinal approach to therapy that is consistent with the needs and goals of clients with disabilities. In addition, effective communication and interaction between the counselor and client are necessary to facilitate the attainment of counseling goals. This section of the chapter provides counselors guiding principles and suggestions for etiquette useful for facilitating an optimal counseling process with clients with disabilities.

### Principles to Guide Counseling

The following principles provide counselors with a structure for an effective treatment approach with clients with disabilities:

1. *A framework for counseling.* According to Olkin (1999), in order to provide effective counseling services to clients with disabilities, counselors should "be familiar with the minority model of disability, family systems theory, larger systemic theory (e.g., interface with medical service system), and an expanded biopsychosocial model that includes legal, political, economic, and cross-cultural elements as essential components of treatment" (p. 154).
2. *Biculturalism.* Given the fact that many persons with disabilities are essentially bicultural, going back and forth between the disabled community and nondisabled larger society, counselors must be aware of disability culture to avoid problems inherent in cross-cultural counseling, such as premature termination, insufficient rapport, or negative outcomes (Olkin, 1999).
3. *A family systems method to counseling.* As was discussed earlier in this chapter, disability affects not only the person who is born with or acquires a disability but also his or her entire family system. Effective counselors will possess an understanding of the interplay between the disability and family system.
4. *The need for additional clinical skills.* Counselors must understand the reciprocal influences of disability and typical presenting problems. This means knowledge of how to modify the diagnosis, case formulation, and treatment to integrate the disability (Olkin, 1999).
5. *A strengths-based approach.* In counseling clients with disabilities, a focus on goals related to optimization of functioning (e.g., quality of life) is always necessary. A strengths-based approach to counseling is especially important for people with disabilities, who may, because they have so frequently been viewed in terms of what they cannot or should not attempt, have learned to

define themselves in terms of their limitations and inabilities. The "Facilitating Client Self-Determination" section of this chapter is an excellent example of a strengths-based approach to counseling individuals with disabilities.

## Counseling Etiquette With Clients With Disabilities

It is important that counselors be sensitive to the feelings as well as the needs of clients with disabilities from their first contact onward. Counselors who may never have worked with a client with a visible physical disability or obvious emotional or cognitive disability may feel awkward, unsure of what to say, or what help to offer. Sensitivity and openness will help ease any potential discomfort on the part of the counselor and client.

In planning and providing counseling services to clients with disabilities, the importance of asking questions cannot be overemphasized. Disability etiquette involves maintaining an awareness of intrusion into an individual's personal physical and/or emotional/cognitive space. Olkin (1999) stated that a key area of counseling behavior relates to the small, but important, interaction between the counselor and new client with a disability: the etiquette of interchange. Guidelines for disability etiquette presented by Olkin provide counselors with helpful suggestions for facilitating effective communication and interaction with clients with disabilities. These guidelines include the following:

1. Don't stare. As stated by Olkin (1999), this guideline may seem obvious, but in practice it may be hard to do. Disabilities often contain oddities, assistive devices, and unusual mannerisms that draw our attention.
2. Don't assume a client with a physical disability needs your help. Asking before providing any physical assistance is a basic principle important to remember.
3. Be clear about who is the client. As aptly stated by Olkin (1999), if the client with a disability has a personal assistant, interpreter, or family member who accompanies him or her to therapy, it is vitally important to be clear, direct, and explicit about that person's role in the treatment process.
4. If a client with a disability presents with a speaking impairment, don't be afraid to say you don't understand either the words themselves or the meaning.
5. Don't be overly concerned about word choices that seem counter to the disability. It is perfectly appropriate to use such words as *see* with a person with a visual impairment and *walk* with an individual who uses a wheelchair for mobility purposes.
6. Don't touch a client's assistive device (e.g. wheelchair, prosthetic) without permission.
7. Nonverbal cues may be altered by disability. For example, individuals who communicate with sign language use their faces and bodies to change meaning of hand signs. Counselors must be aware of the interaction among specific disabilities, their severity, and body movements.
8. Be aware of the temperature of the counseling setting. Some individuals with disabilities may be sensitive to heat (e.g., multiple sclerosis) or cold (e.g., arthritis).

## CONCLUDING REMARKS

This chapter focused on providing information and techniques to help counselors effectively serve clients with disabilities. The discussion of the concept of response to disability and stage model of adaptation to disability that was presented may aid counselors in understanding a client's disability experience. Further, the description of the four common factors that contribute to positive therapeutic outcomes will enable counselors to focus on what works when counseling clients with disabilities. The counseling intervention strategies of social support development, family systems counseling, and facilitating client self-determination provide counselors with major therapeutic approaches for addressing client presenting problems such as discrimination, depression, substance abuse, and career issues. Finally, counselors can use the principles to guide the counseling process and specific counseling etiquette suggestions presented in this chapter to develop effective therapeutic relationships and enhance counseling outcomes for clients with disabilities.

# Cases and Questions

1. You are a counselor at a 4-year college who provides mental health counseling for students. A freshman female African American student with an obvious physical disability requests your assistance with the adjustment to classes and college life in general. Her specific disability limitations include mobility and fatigue. The student presents with anxiety regarding her ability to succeed in course work. During your initial counseling session, she also described a situation surrounding independence and separation from her parents. She lives in a residence hall on campus and feels that her parents are being overly intrusive and protective of her. This student also revealed that she is concerned about her ability to interact effectively and develop fulfilling social relationships with costudents and, in particular, with her roommate.
   (a) How would you characterize this client's process of response to disability?
   (b) What are the major factors you would need to consider for developing an effective therapeutic alliance with this client?
   (c) What family system variables would you need to address in the counseling process?
2. As a counselor working in a community-based rehabilitation program, you provide services to individuals with chronic and persistent mental illness. A 25-year-old male client presents to you in a weekly outpatient counseling session with issues related to his ability to successfully perform work tasks and keeping his job. Your client is employed as a computer operator at a payroll-processing firm. He expresses anxiety related to being able to interact effectively with coworkers and his supervisor. His primary concerns are that he feels isolated and underappreciated in the workplace. He fears that he

will one day soon be terminated and requests your assistance with developing the skills to communicate in a more natural and comfortable manner with his coworkers. In addition, your client is seeking help with developing appropriate assertiveness and communication skills so he can confidently approach his supervisor with his concerns.

(a)   What are your observations regarding the self-determination skill development needs of this client?

(b)   How would you approach assisting this client with social skill development?

(c)   Which of the *Principles to Guide Counseling* presented in this chapter would you most need to incorporate in the therapeutic process with this client?

## REFERENCES

Berry, J. O., & Hardman, M. L. (1998). *Lifespan perspectives on the family and disability.* Boston: Allyn & Bacon.

Bertolino, B., & O'Hanlon, B. (2002). *Collaborative, competency-based counseling and psychotherapy.* Boston: Allyn & Bacon.

Bohart, A., & Tallman, K. (1999). *What clients do to make therapy work.* Washington, DC: American Psychological Association.

Brooks, D. N. (1991). The head-injured family. *Journal of Clinical and Experimental Neuropsychology, 13,* 155–188.

Campodonico, J., & McGlynn, S. (1995). Assessing awareness of deficits: Recent research and applications. In L. Cushman & M. Scherer (Eds.), *Psychological assessment in medical rehabilitation* (pp. 393–418). Hyattsville, MD: American Psychological Association.

Chan, F., Shaw, L. R., McMahon, B. T., Koch, L., & Strauser, D. (1997). A model for enhancing rehabilitation counseling-consumer working relationships. *Rehabilitation Counseling Bulletin, 41,* 122–137.

Curnow, T. C. (1989). Vocational development of persons with disability. *Career Development Quarterly, 37,* 269–278.

Dell Orto, A. E., & Power, P. W. (1994). *Head injury and the family: A life and living perspective.* Winter Park, FL: PMD Publishers Group.

DePompei, R., & Zarski, J. J. (1991). Assessment of the family. In J. M. Williams & T. Kay (Eds.), *Head injury: A family matter* (pp. 101–120). Baltimore: Paul H. Brookes.

Field, S., Hoffman, A., & Spezia, S. (1998). *Self-determination strategies for adolescents in transition.* Austin, TX: Pro-Ed.

Fine, M., & Asch, A. (1988). Disability beyond stigma: Social interaction, discrimination, and activism. *Journal of Social Issues, 44,* 3–21.

Harrington, T. F. (1997). *Handbook of career planning for students with special needs.* Austin, TX: Pro-Ed.

Heinrich, R., & Tate, D. (1996). Latent variable structure of the Brief Symptom Inventory in a sample of persons with spinal cord injuries. *Rehabilitation Psychology, 41,* 131–148.

Horvath, A. (1994). Research on the alliance. In A. Horvath & L. Greenberg (Eds.), *The working alliance: Theory, research, and practice* (pp. 259–286). New York: Wiley.

Hubble, M. A., Duncan, B. L., & Miller, S. D. (1999). *The heart and soul of change: What works in therapy.* Washington, DC: American Psychological Association.

Kosciulek, J. F. (1995). Impact of head injury on families: An introduction for family counselors. *The Family Journal: Counseling and Therapy for Couples and Families, 3,* 116–125.

Kosciulek, J. F. (1998). Empowering the life choices of people with disabilities through career counseling. In N. C. Gysbers, M. J. Heppner, & J. A. Johnston (Eds.), *Career counseling: Process, issues, and techniques* (pp. 109–122). Boston: Allyn & Bacon.

Kosciulek, J. F. (1999). Implications of consumer direction for disability policy development and rehabilitation service delivery. *Journal of Disability Policy Studies, 11,* 82–94.

Kosciulek, J. F., Bruyere, S. M., & Ph.D., Rosenthal, D. A. (2002, July). *Career development and people with disabilities.* Paper presented at the National Career Development Annual Conference, Chicago, IL.

Kübler-Ross, E. (1969). *On death and dying.* New York: Macmillan.

Lambert, M. J. (1992). Implications of outcome research for psychotherapy integration. In J. C. Norcross & M. R. Goldfried (Eds.), *Handbook of psychotherapy integration* (pp. 94–129). New York: Basic.

Lambert, M. J., & Bergin, A. E. (1994). The effectiveness of psychotherapy. In A. E. Bergin & S. L. Garfield (Eds.), *Handbook of psychotherapy and behavior change* (4th ed., pp. 143–189). New York: Wiley.

Lichtenberg, P. (1997). The DOUR project: A program of depression research in geriatric rehabilitation minority inpatients. *Rehabilitation Psychology, 42,* 103–114.

Lindemann, J. I. (1981). *Psychological and behavioral aspects of physical disability.* New York: Plenum Press.

Linkowski, D. C., & Dunn, M. A. (1974). Self-concept and acceptance of disability. *Rehabilitation Counseling Bulletin, 17,* 28–32.

Livneh, H. (2001). Psychosocial adaptation to chronic illness and disability: A conceptual framework. *Rehabilitation Counseling Bulletin, 44,* 151–160.

Livneh, H., & Antonak, R. F. (1997). *Psychosocial adaptation to chronic illness and disability.* Gaithersburg, MD: Aspen.

Lustig, D. C., Strauser, D. R., Rice, N. D., & Rucker, T. F. (2002). The relationship between working alliance and rehabilitation outcomes. *Rehabilitation Counseling Bulletin, 46,* 25–33.

Marrone, J. (1997, May). *Job placement for individuals with psychiatric disabilities.* Paper presented at the Utah State Office of Rehabilitation 75th Anniversary Conference, Provo, Utah.

Marshak, L. E., & Seligman, M. (1993). *Counseling persons with physical disabilities: Theoretical and clinical perspectives.* Austin, TX: Pro-Ed.

Miller, S. D., Duncan, B. L., & Hubble, M. A. (1997). *Escape from Babel: Toward a unifying language for psychotherapy practice.* New York: Norton.

Moos, R. H. (Ed.). (1984). *Coping with physical illness. Volume 2: New perspectives.* New York: Plenum Press.

Muir, C., Rosenthal, M., & Diehl, L. N. (1990). Methods of family intervention. In M. Rosenthal, E. R. Griffith, M. R. Bond, & J. D. Miller (Eds.), *Rehabilitation of the adult and child with traumatic brain injury* (2nd ed., pp. 433–448). Philadelphia: Davis.

National Organization on Disability. (2000). *Survey of the status of people with disabilities in the United States: Employment.* Washington, DC: Author.

Olkin, R. (1999). *What psychotherapists should know about disability.* New York: Guilford Press.

Power, P. W. (1995). Family. In A. E. Dell Orto & R. P. Marinelli (Eds.), *Encyclopedia of disability and rehabilitation* (pp. 321–326). New York: Macmillan.

Prochaska, J. O. (1995). Common problems: Common solutions. *Clinical Psychology: Science and Practice, 2,* 101–105.

Rehabilitation Research and Training Center on Drugs and Disability. (1996). *Substance abuse, disability, and vocational rehabilitation.* Wright State University: Author.

Roessler, R. T., Chung, W., & Rubin, S. E. (1998). Family-centered rehabilitation case management. In R. T. Roessler & S. E. Rubin, *Case management and rehabilitation counseling: Procedures and techniques* (3rd ed., pp. 231–254). Austin, TX: Pro-Ed.

Ryan, C. P. (1995). Work isn't what it used to be: Implications, recommendations, and strategies for vocational rehabilitation. *Journal of Rehabilitation, 61*(4), 8–15.

Sachs, P. R. (1991). *Treating families of brain-injury survivors.* New York: Springer.

Sammons, M. T., & Schmidt, N. B. (Eds.). (2001). *Combined treatments for mental disorders: A guide to psychological and pharmacological interventions.* Washington, DC: American Psychological Association.

Schroeder, F. K. (1995, November). *Philosophical underpinnings of effective rehabilitation.* Sixteenth Mary E. Switzer Lecture, Worcester, MA.

Smart, J. (2001). *Disability, society, and the individual.* Gaithersburg, MD: Aspen.

Stevens, P., & Smith, R. L. (2001). *Substance abuse counseling: Theory and practice* (2nd ed.). Upper Saddle River, NJ: Prentice-Hall.

Szymanski, E. M. (2000). Disability and vocational behavior. In R. G. Frank & T. R. Elliott (Eds.), *Handbook of rehabilitation psychology* (pp. 499–517). Washington, DC: American Psychological Association.

Trueba, H. T. (1993). Castification in multicultural America. In H. T. Trueba, C. Rodriguez, Y. Zou, & J. Contron, *Healing multicultural America: Mexican immigrants rise to power in rural California* (pp. 29–51). Philadelphia: Falmer.

Vash, C. L. (1981). *The psychology of disability.* New York: Springer.

Williams, J. M. (1991). Family reaction to head injury. In J. M. Williams & T. Kay (Eds.), *Head injury: A family matter* (pp. 81–99). Baltimore: Paul H. Brookes.

# Part III    THE OLDER CLIENT

CHAPTER 9   # What Counselors Can Do to Facilitate Successful Aging

Eve H. Davison, National Center
for Post-Traumatic Stress Disorder,
Veterans Administration's Boston
Health Care System

In 2000, there were approximately 35 million adults aged 65 and older in the United States; by the year 2030 there will be over 70 million—more than twice that number—and older adults will comprise approximately 20% of the U.S. population. This "elder boom" is due in large part to the baby-boom generation; baby boomers will be entering old age in unprecedented numbers over the next few decades. The boom is also due to rising life expectancies and better health care.

Counselors and other mental health professionals can play a proactive role in primary prevention and early intervention to help ensure that our older clients age as successfully as possible given the vicissitudes of contemporary U.S. society. To be effective with our older clients, however, counselors must first arm themselves with information about aging in the United States; this chapter presents an overview of many of the important issues.

What is "successful aging"? In their recent book of the same name, Rowe and Kahn draw upon data from the large MacArthur Foundation Study of Aging and define *successful aging* as "the ability to maintain three key behaviors or characteristics: low risk of disease and disease-related disability; high mental and physical function; and active engagement with life" (Rowe & Kahn, 1998, p. 38). Others' definitions may vary somewhat, but most agree that aging successfully is indeed a combination of the preceding interrelated factors, and that intertwined throughout these domains must be the ability to adjust to inevitable change and the ability to continue to grow. Indeed, a recent study in the Netherlands found that the oldest-old—those 85 and older—define successful aging as a process of adaptation, and they ranked a sense of well-being and social functioning more highly than physical and cognitive functioning (von Feber et al., 2001).

*Subjective well-being* appears to be closely linked to the notion of successful aging. Evidence suggests that a person's subjective perception of well-being is more predictive of life satisfaction than are objective measures of health or status, such as physical health or economic situation. Burnside pointed out that it is not health per se that is important for older adults' sense of well-being, but rather "the attitude, the stance they take toward their own health problems and their ability to cope, their finesse in meeting and adapting to new situations and crises" (Burnside, 1993, p. 22). In a study that looked at both African American and European American older adults, Johnson (1994) found that subjective perception, rather than economic status, was more predictive of morale and well-being. Andrews and Robinson (1991) pointed out that people who seem objectively better off—for example, people who own better houses—often report lower levels of subjective well-being than people who appear less objectively well off; they stated that one explanation for this phenomenon is that "although the well-housed individuals may be 'better off', their aspirations may be much higher than those of people living in the modest homes" (Andrews & Robinson, 1991, p. 64).

The emerging concept of *positive aging* can be tied to the study of successful aging. The term *positive aging* grew out of the positive psychology movement and is exemplified by the research and trends discussed in Kenneth and Mary Gergen's monthly e-newsletter, *The Positive Aging Newsletter* (www.healthandage.com/html/res/gergen/entrance.htm). In a recent newsletter, the Gergens wrote, "Challenging the longstanding view of aging as decline, we strive to create a vision of life in which aging becomes an unprecedented period of human enrichment" (Gergen & Gergen, 2002, Commentary section, para. 1). They went on to say that by focusing on strengths and resiliencies, researchers and practitioners alike can empower older adults to action and change.

As people age, they become more and more different from each other. Enormous variability exists in the financial, social, physical, cognitive, and psychological status of older Americans. Thus, it is crucial to consider the sociocultural context in which your older client lives when designing your intervention; a poor, widowed 83-year-old African American woman will bring a vastly different worldview—and different strengths, resiliencies, and needs—to the table than will an upper-middle-class, recently retired, married 72-year-old European American man. A *social gerontological* approach proves quite useful when working with older adults. A social gerontological approach to the study of old age "enables us to understand the ways in which what is occurring within the larger society shapes the life course of individuals . . . [and] allows us to see the link between history and biography" (Stoller & Gibson, 2000, p. 1). Many authors in gerontology underscore the utility of taking a *life course perspective* (also called a *life span perspective*) to the study of aging. Stoller and Gibson (2000) describe the life course perspective as a framework that "emphasizes the ways in which people's location in the social system, the historical period in which they live, and their unique personal biography shape their experience of old age" (p. 19).

In the year 2000, racial and ethnic minority elders represented 16.4% of the U.S. population aged 65 and older; by the year 2030, their numbers are projected to reach 25.4%. Throughout the following sections of this chapter, cultural factors are highlighted and discussed, and considerations for counselors are proposed. These cultural factors are by necessity painted with a broad brush, and it is essential to remember that within-group differences—particularly among older adults—are far greater than between-group differences, and it is vital to honor the uniqueness of each client.

## PROMOTING A HEALTHY LIFESTYLE

With aging come physical and cognitive changes—this much is certain. However, it is now known that much of the decline previously believed to be intrinsic to the aging process can be greatly influenced by lifestyle choices and changes. To empower their clients, counselors need to know both about normative aging changes and about the lifestyle choices their older clients can make to prevent unnecessary disability and decline and promote successful aging.

### Physical Activity

The salubrious effect of physical activity upon almost all domains of well-being is well known and has been empirically demonstrated (Christmas & Anderson, 2000; Stathi, Fox, & McKenna, 2002; Tryon, 1998). Exercise is now known to influence not only physical health status but to improve psychological well-being and even cognitive functioning. (Counselors interested in learning more about specific recommendations are referred to Christmas and Anderson, 2000, for exercise guidelines for geriatricians.) Physical activity—in particular, weight-bearing activity—can slow and in some cases even reverse bone density loss, which can in turn prevent osteoporosis. Exercise can also reduce the risk of falling in older adults. Falls, and the resultant injuries such as hip fractures, are a substantial problem and a significant source of morbidity and mortality in the older adult population. Recently, practitioners working with older adults have noted the benefits of tai chi. An ancient martial art characterized by slow, graceful, deliberate movement sequences, tai chi has been shown to greatly increase balance and flexibility and to reduce falls in older adults.

Counselors can inform their older clients about the considerable benefits of exercise and can work with them to identify and challenge some of the obstacles to exercising that their clients may be experiencing. For example, a counselor might encourage low-income clients to take advantage of the free exercise classes that many senior and community centers now offer. Or a counselor might help clients who have a history of previous falls to overcome their fear of falling and encourage them to consult with a physician as to a safe and healthy exercise plan.

### Nutrition

A basic knowledge of nutritional issues in older adults is very important for the mental health practitioner (Bortz & Bortz, 1996); nutritional needs change as one grows older, and nutritional deficiencies can lead to serious health problems. For example, vitamin $B_{12}$ deficiency can cause cognitive deficits that mimic an early dementing process; it can also cause "pernicious anemia," which leads to extremity parasthesias that can cause tingling sensations and numbness, weight loss, abnormal reflexes, and difficulty walking in a straight line. And older adults are at greater risk for dehydration, which is more likely to cause serious problems (such as delirium) in older versus younger adults. Counselors can provide education on the importance of good nutrition to their older adult clients and connect them to services—transportation to congregate meal sites, transportation for grocery shopping, Meals on Wheels—that will facilitate their getting proper nutrition.

## Medical and Medication Issues

Counselors can educate their clients as to the importance of regular health screens, such as regular blood testing to screen for such problems as diabetes and $B_{12}$ deficiency; PSA levels to screen for prostate problems; mammograms to screen for breast cancer; cardiovascular testing to screen for coronary artery and heart disease. Many medical advances have occurred in the past several decades, and early detection of illness and disease can often mean the difference between a life riddled with disability and one relatively unencumbered by illness. Significant ethnic and racial differences exist in risk levels for certain problems—for example, there is a higher incidence of stroke, hypertension, and vascular dementia in African Americans, and higher rates of diabetes in American Indians and African Americans. Additionally, African American men evidence an earlier age of onset of prostate problems; consequently, African American men should begin screening for prostate problems earlier than European American men. Gender differences also exist in risk levels for certain problems. For example, women are at higher risk for crippling osteoporosis; smoking, poor diet, and physical inactivity all increase this risk. In contrast, women are at equal risk for certain ailments that have traditionally been thought of as men's ailments. For example, post-menopausal women are at equal risk for heart attack and heart disease as are men—indeed, heart disease is the leading cause of death in postmenopausal women. Counselors can help additionally by talking to their clients about the benefits of quitting smoking and limiting alcohol intake, no matter how old one is.

If we are lucky to live long enough, most of us will sooner or later develop one or more chronic medical conditions: hypertension, Type II diabetes, and cerebrovascular disease, to name a few. Nowadays, these conditions can be managed in part by prescription medications, and older adults are more likely than younger adults to be taking several prescription medications. As a consequence, older adults are at higher risk for adverse medication interactions and medication mismanagement. Some medication side effects or interactions can cause dizziness or lightheadedness, leading to greater risk of falls; as mentioned earlier, falls are a significant source of morbidity and mortality in older adults. Also, there is a potential for interactions with over-the-counter medications, including many "all natural" herbal supplements. Counselors can help prevent problems by talking with their older clients about any medications they are taking, providing them with information about the potential for adverse interactions, and encouraging them to speak to their primary care providers.

## Sleep

The architecture of sleep changes as we grow older, and older clients often complain of sleep difficulties to their health care providers. Many of these changes are normative. For example, older adults generally sleep more lightly than they did when they were younger, and although they sleep about the same length of time, they may spend more time awake in bed than they used to. Counselors can educate older clients about normal versus problematic changes in sleep, and about the importance of good sleep hygiene. Even small behavioral changes—going to bed at the same time every night, instituting a "no-television" rule for the bedroom, and avoiding caffeine after midday—can have a significant impact. Other sleep difficulties may represent more significant problems that can in turn lead to serious medical and psychological problems (e.g., sleep apnea, a respiratory disorder, causes significant fatigue in the short run and is now known to contribute to hypertension in the long run), and counselors should be prepared to refer older clients to sleep specialists when necessary. At the same time, counselors need to be aware that older adults are more likely to be prescribed sedatives and hypnotics and to take over-the-counter sleep aids; these medications are potentially addictive and, additionally, can have unwanted side effects, such as falls. Research has also demonstrated that the long-term use of benzodiazepines can cause mild cognitive problems in older adults (Gagne & Morin, 2000). Counselors should let their clients know that nonpharmacological interventions have been found to be more effective and enduring than have pharmacological ones in treating sleep problems in older adults (Morin, Blais, & Mimeault, 1998),

## Sexuality and HIV/AIDS

The topic of sexuality and sexual behavior is explored in detail in a later chapter, but a mention of the rise of HIV and AIDS in the older adult population is made here to underscore the urgency of this issue. The proportion of people over 50 with HIV and AIDS has been rising steadily for the past several years, and as the baby boomers move into older adulthood, this trend will no doubt continue. Researchers have found that the older one is, the less likely it becomes that one has an accurate knowledge of HIV and AIDS (Wright, Drost, Caserta, & Lund, 1998). Some have raised the possibility that the increasingly widespread use of Viagra is leading to more sexual risk taking in older adults (Paniagua, 1999). Counselors can play an integral role in providing basic yet much-needed information on HIV and AIDS to their older clients. (See Strombeck & Levy, 1998, for a useful discussion of strategies for HIV prevention and intervention with older adults.)

## Cognitive Activity

As we age, we experience some cognitive changes—for example, most older adults demonstrate a decline in "fluid intelligence" such as processing speed, although "crystallized intelligence" remains basically the same. A certain level of cognitive decline in old age is expected and most likely inevitable for most of us; however, quite often an older adult will interpret normative cognitive changes as signs of a dementing process such as Alzheimer's disease. Counselors working with older adults should familiarize themselves with normative cognitive changes so that they will be in a position to provide education and reassurance to their clients. Additionally, we now know that there are behaviors that can slow, and even stop or reverse, certain types of cognitive losses. For example, a recent study found that cognitive retraining techniques, such as memorization strategies, reversed some age-related decline (Logan, Sanders, Snyder, Morris, & Buckner, 2002). And much evidence indicates that keeping the mind active through reading, crossword puzzles, and other intellectual activity ("use it or lose it") helps maintain cognitive ability. Of course, counselors must also be prepared to refer those older clients who are evidencing impairment due to cognitive changes to neuropsychological and/or medical services.

## Social Activity and Interaction

The protective quality of social interaction is discussed in greater detail in a later section. Here, a mention must be made of a fascinating trend: Adults aged 60 and older are now the fastest-growing group of Internet users in the United States (National Institute on Aging [NIA], 2001). The Internet is an invaluable resource for older adults, both to obtain helpful health- and benefits-related information and to maintain existing social contacts and form new ones. Many older adults are hesitant to try computers and mistakenly believe they are "too old" to begin learning. Counselors can help dispel these erroneous beliefs and can encourage their older clients to take advantage of the free computer classes for seniors at local libraries and community centers. (See both Morrell, Dailey, Feldman, Mayhorn, & Echt, 2002, and NIA, 2001, for comprehensive guidelines on older adults and information technology.)

## Attitudes Toward Aging

Older adults hold many of the same ageist beliefs and misconceptions as do people of other ages; as with other oppressed groups, this internalized prejudice can have deleterious effects. A remarkable finding from a large longitudinal study of aging underscores the significance of internalized ageism: Older adults with positive self-perceptions of aging lived an average of 7.5 years longer than did adults with less positive self-perceptions (Levy, Slade, Kunkel, & Kasl, 2002). And this was after controlling for the effects of age, gender, functional health, and socioeconomic status! Counselors can explore their clients' attitudes toward aging and can actively work in collaboration with their clients to challenge and change ageism.

## Spirituality and Religion

Spirituality and involvement with religion have both been found to contribute to well-being in older adults. (For excellent discussions of spiritual development across the life course, see both Koenig, 2000, and Wotherspoon, 2000.) Researchers have uncovered an association between spirituality and perceived health and well-being (e.g., Wotherspoon, 2000) and have found that active religious participation—particularly of the sort that involves increased social support and social interaction—contributes significantly to well-being in older adults (Koenig, 2000). There is evidence that, for some, spirituality becomes more central to their lives as they grow older, perhaps as they reflect on their life story and contemplate death. The role of organized religion may be greater among certain racial and ethnic groups (e.g., the role of the church in many African American communities). Counselors can ask their older adults about the role of spirituality and religion in their lives and, when appropriate, can encourage clients to become reconnected with their religious communities.

## FACILITATING LIFE TRANSITIONS

Old age brings with it inevitable transitions and losses. Friends and family members pass away, paid work often ceases, health problems multiply, housing needs change. The ability to successfully navigate these transitions is one of the central components of successful aging. Counselors can play an important role in assisting older clients with the transitions of aging. As with clients of any age, it is important to consider the cultural, social, and familial context in which the older adult client exists. It becomes even more crucial to assess the familial context in particular with older adult clients, as older adults may come into more contact—and conflict—with their family system around many of the transitions that are normative to the aging process, and they may of necessity rely on family and community members for more support than they have in the past. Counselors should consider bringing in family members to counseling. Additionally, they should attend to such factors as the role of elders in their clients' particular cultures.

### The Role of Coping

Why do some older adults age more "successfully" than others and adapt more effectively to the changes, transitions, and losses of old age? Coping appears to play an important role. Coping refers to the manner in which a person handles stressors in her or his life. In keeping with the recent trend of studying positive aging, an examination of the strengths and resiliencies women bring to aging proves particularly useful. It has been noted that women cope more effectively than men with some aspects of the aging process. But given their double minority status, why is this the case? Older women's coping skills may be enhanced due to their frequent role changes and multiple roles across their lifetimes. Some have hypothesized that women may also be better equipped than men to cope with discrimination resulting from ageism because they have learned to cope with other forms of discrimination, such as sexism, long before they reach old age. Canetto (1992) pointed out that "men may come to late life with unrealistic expectations and a limited range of coping strategies" (pp. 92–93); when they reach old age and experience discrimination and marginalization for perhaps the first time, many are unprepared.

Coping skills learned across the life span may play a significant role in successful aging for oppressed groups in general. In a review of the literature on older gay men and lesbians, Friend (1991) identified a subset that he named "Affirmative Lesbian and Gay People." He described these older adults as people who have reconstructed the meaning of homosexuality into something positive, and he wrote that the majority of older gay men and lesbians who have been studied seem to fall in this group. This group of older adults is consistently described in the literature as psychologically well adjusted, happy, and adapting well to aging. Friend suggested that "as a result of managing what it means to be lesbian and gay in a heterosexist world, many lesbian and gay adults develop skills for managing their lives which facilitate their adjustment to the aging process" (Friend, 1991, p. 109). Turk-Charles, Rose, and Gatz (1996) reported that several researchers have found that gay men and lesbians may adapt better to the aging process because difficulties (homophobia, prejudice) faced throughout their lives "have fostered coping skills that may be beneficial in old age. . . . [and] Older gay men and lesbians often have a sense of competence from early life crises surrounding the coming out process" (p. 119).

Other studies have examined the role of race and ethnicity in adaptability to aging. A study that looked at African American women from the ages of 60 to 94—a group holding triple minority status—found that direct instrumental coping skills were significantly positively related to adaptation in aging. The researchers suggested that these adaptive strategies, acquired by the women throughout a lifetime of experience with racism, served as resources that they were able to apply as they adapted to old age (Hill, Colby, & Phelps, 1983, cited in Stoller & Gibson, 2000). Padgett (1989) wrote of minority women's ability to draw on previously acquired psychological, social, and cultural strengths in navigating the transition to old age: "They have spent their lives as strategists, marshalling scarce resources to cope with everyday demands and these coping strategies 'pay off' later on . . ." (pp. 218–219). It is reasonable to assume that many older ethnic minority men also benefit from similar experiences. Regardless of their older clients' backgrounds, counselors can work with their clients to build on effective coping mechanisms honed during difficult experiences earlier in life, and they can draw on the experiences of minority elders to teach their clients new ways of coping.

## Changes in Health Status

One of the most common issues older people bring to counseling is coping with changes in health status: medical problems, vision and hearing loss, memory changes, and the like. Because health problems can lead to functional impairment, these problems often go hand in hand with other losses. For example, vision loss may necessitate that an older adult give up driving; this in turn may bring a sense of loss of autonomy and control. A counselor can help both by processing these feelings with an older client and by providing practical assistance in working with the client to come up with alterative transportation options.

## Work and Retirement Issues

The topic of retirement has received a great deal of attention from gerontologists during the past several years. Findings have been mixed: Some studies find retirement to positively impact well-being, and others find it to impact well-being negatively or not at all (Kim & Moen, 2001, 2002; Shaw, Patterson, Semple, & Grant, 1998). Retirement may be an easy transition for some and quite difficult for others. Some have postulated that women may find retirement less stressful because they have filled multiple roles throughout their lives (see "Multiple Roles and Resilience" in following section). Kim and Moen (2001) stressed that retirement decisions are shaped by the social and developmental contexts of a person's life, and that, consequently, retirement adjustment must be examined within an ecological, life course framework. Counselors are better off not making assumptions about the personal or cultural meaning of retirement for a particular client. Also, counselors should be aware that work and retirement patterns are changing, and many older adults now see retirement as an opportunity to begin a new career. Still other older adults continue working either full- or part-time long after traditional retirement age out of financial necessity.

Myths and misconceptions about finances in retirement abound (e.g., the belief that Social Security income will keep pace with cost of living increases and will be enough to subsist upon). Counselors can talk to their clients about the importance of financial planning both long before and during retirement and can alert them to resources (often free) in their area that can assist them in their planning. (For a comprehensive overview of health and well-being in retirement see Shaw et al., 1998.)

## Housing Issues

Housing challenges are considerable for many older Americans, particularly lower-income and fixed-income elders. Counselors can provide valuable consultation and assistance in the exploration of housing options and can support their clients in coping with housing changes. We can provide our older clients with information about alternate living for seniors (such as retirement communities, assisted living, and elderly subsidized housing). We can work with our clients together with their family members to facilitate discussions on housing. We can connect clients and their families with the resources and benefits in the community that will help enable them to "age in place." Our lesbian, gay, bisexual, and transgender (LGBT) older clients may have special considerations when it comes to housing choices, due to issues of comfort and safety (see link named "Directory" on the Senior Action in a Gay Environment [SAGE] website for housing and other resources for LGBT elders; www.sageusa.org); counselors need to be sensitive to and knowledgeable about these issues in order to adequately assist LGBT clients with housing decisions.

Counselors should be aware that more and more older adults, often widowed or divorced, are living together without getting married. Although this trend is no doubt in part due to changing social norms, the reason many couples are moving in together appears to be financial.

## Widowhood and Bereavement

The loss of a spouse or partner is, unfortunately, a normative late-life event for many older adults, particularly women; in the year 2000, 45% of women 65 and older were widowed, compared with 14% of men. These numbers increase with increasing age. The transition through bereavement into widowhood is one of the most challenging to navigate. Bereavement refers to the suffering resulting from the loss of a partner or spouse by death. One issue that has been of interest in the study of bereavement in older adults has been the question of survivability—in other words, the likelihood that the partner left behind will not die soon after her or his partner dies. Some of the bereavement and survivability data tie in with the suicide data (to be discussed further in "Suicide Prevention" in the following section). Older adults whose spouses have died are more likely to commit suicide than those whose spouses have not died. The risk is greater for men than for women, however, despite the fact that women aged 65 and over are much more likely to be widowed than are their male counterparts (Canetto, 1992).

Canetto (1992) linked these findings to the research on differential mental health and happiness of single and married women and men. Much research has demonstrated that being married is a better predictor of mental health and life satisfaction for men than for women, and a better protection against suicide for men than for women (Canetto, 1992). Additionally, as Spacapan and Oskamp (1989) pointed out, as a result of adherence to traditional gender roles, men may be more dependent on their wives for their emotional and interpersonal needs; consequently, the loss of a life partner may impact men in different ways than it does women.

## Death and Dying

A part of successful aging can be considered the navigation of the biggest transition of all: dying. To be effective, counselors working with older adults need to be aware of their own feelings and reactions when speaking to clients about end-of-life decisions and about dying. Mental health practitioners are uniquely positioned to play an extremely helpful and important role in clients' end-of-life care and decision making and have valuable contributions to make, both through listening and talking openly with their clients about these issues and through advocacy (see last chapter section).

## Building on Past Successes

To support the successful navigation of all late-life transitions, counselors can encourage their older clients to draw on strengths and coping skills learned previously in their lives. They can talk with clients about difficult and challenging experiences they have had in the past, and they can explore ways that clients can transfer what they have learned to present challenges. In this task, recognition of individual and cultural variability, and the strengths and weaknesses that clients bring to the table, is crucial. In particular, when working with clients who are members of oppressed groups, counselors can encourage them to think about life-long coping with discrimination and marginalization.

## PREVENTING MENTAL HEALTH PROBLEMS

In this section, issues germane to the prevention of serious mental health problems are the focus of discussion. The significance of trauma in the lives of older adults is given special attention, as is the issue of suicide prevention and what can be learned from certain groups' relative resiliencies. (Treatment considerations for mental health problems in older adults is addressed in detail in chapter 10.) Findings from a recent study underscore the importance of preventing even mild mental health problems in older adults: Even mild, chronic depressive symptoms were found to weaken the immune system of older adults, and the relationship between symptoms and immunity to illness grows stronger with advancing age (McGuire, Kiecolt-Glaser, & Glaser, 2002).

## Caregiver Burden

Many older adults are the primary caregivers for others in their family; often the care recipients have dementia or other extremely challenging illnesses. It is important for counselors to have an awareness of caregiver burden in the lives of their clients; to provide education, support, and referral for caregivers (Gallagher-Thompson, Coon, Rivera, Powers, & Zeiss, 1998); and to educate themselves as to caregiver diversity issues (see Gallagher-Thompson et al., 1998, for a detailed description of interventions for culturally diverse caregiving populations). As life expectancies continue to swell and as the baby boomers move into old age, counselors also need to be alert to what has been dubbed the "coming generation of caregiving" (Laditka & Laditka, 2000, p. 191): aging children caring for their even more elderly, often frail parents.

Another, often overlooked, source of caregiver burden is that of older adults who are the primary or secondary caregivers for grandchildren (Musil & Ahmad, 2002). Additionally, a phenomenon that may be seen in increasing numbers in coming years is that of elderly clients providing care for elderly children with dementia: Morlino, Milan, De Bonis, and Postiglione (2002) presented the example of an 86-year-old woman caring for her 57-year-old daughter with advanced Alzheimer's disease. (For a thorough discussion of caregiver considerations, see Schulz, 2000.)

## Alcohol and Substance Use

Alcohol, drug, and prescription medication abuse is an issue often overlooked in older adults, in part due to providers' beliefs that "old people just don't do that." The risks of medication mismanagement in older adults were mentioned earlier in this chapter. Counselors can assist their older clients by gaining an awareness of the potential for prescription drug misuse, abuse, and dependence, and by providing needed information to clients. Older adults are prescribed drugs such as benzodiazepines for sleep and anxiety problems in proportions far greater than younger adults. Likewise, counselors can aid in the prevention of alcohol and substance abuse and dependence problems through educating both themselves and their clients as to the warning signs of substance abuse and dependence, risk factors and prevalence rates in older adults, adverse effects of alcohol and substance use, and the like.

## Trauma in the Lives of Older Adults

The study and treatment of long-term and/or delayed effects of trauma in older adults are receiving increasing amounts of attention of late. Military service has been called the "hidden variable" in aging research (Spiro, Schnurr, & Aldwin,

1994): In 1996, 76% of men aged 70–74 were military veterans (American Psychological Association Working Group on the Older Adult, 1998), many of whom saw heavy combat. Additionally, many older adults—particularly older women—are survivors of childhood sexual abuse and/or of early adulthood rape or assault.

Long-term and/or delayed effects of trauma, and later-life exacerbation of trauma-related symptoms, have been documented in such populations as aging combat veterans (Buffum & Wolfe, 1995; Falk, Hersen, & Van-Hasselt, 1994; Hunt & Robbins, 2001; Macleod, 1994; Spiro et al., 1994), former prisoners of war (Engdahl, Harkness, Eberly, Page, & Bielinski, 1993; Port, Engdahl, & Frazier, 2001), and Holocaust survivors (Danieli, 1997; Kellermann, 2001). In their discussion of older combat veterans, Buffum and Wolfe (1995) suggested that common losses associated with the aging process (loss of physical health, loss of loved ones), and the concomitant feelings of powerlessness and helplessness, may trigger memories and feelings associated with combat-related trauma and loss. The term *late-onset stress symptomatology,* or *LOSS,* was coined by a research team at a VA medical center (King, King, Bachrach, Spiro, & Davison, 2001) to describe "a condition among older veterans who: (1) were exposed to highly stressful war-zone events in their early adult years; (2) have functioned successfully with no long-term history of chronic stress-related disorders; but (3) begin to register combat-related complaints commensurate with the changes and challenges of the aging process (e.g., retirement, loss of spouse, or physical illness)" (King et al., 2001, p. 1).

Even more recent writings have examined the prevalence and sequelae of interpersonal trauma and violence in the histories of older adults, particularly older women. Rates of interpersonal trauma are higher in the lives of older women and have been demonstrated to have a deleterious effect on later-life physical health and psychological functioning (Higgins & Follette, 2002). The writings on the older adult population of sexual trauma survivors are particularly compelling. For example, in their psychotherapy case accounts of elderly survivors of childhood sexual abuse, Gagnon and Hersen (2000) documented presenting issues of depression, anxiety, helplessness, shame, and decreased functioning that improved substantially once their patients disclosed and addressed their histories of childhood trauma. These authors described how the normative developmental challenges and losses of old age exacerbated their clients' unresolved childhood sexual abuse, and they stressed the importance of inquiring after trauma history rather than attributing older patients' struggles to "normal aging." McInnis-Dittrich (1996) also presented several case studies of older women grappling with the effects of childhood sexual abuse and noted that these women reported recent onset of increased thoughts and memories of their abuse. Somer (2000) posited, "Later-life experiences, such as loss of autonomy, can operate as retrieval cues for traumatic memories" (p. 56) in survivors of childhood sexual abuse. A tendency to engage in life review—a drive originally identified in older adults by Erikson (1968)—may increase the likelihood that traumatic memories will gain salience. Many geropsychologists—this writer included—have treated older women in psychotherapy who disclose, often for the first time in their lives, the sexual abuse they experienced in childhood or the assault they suffered in early adulthood.

Often these individuals have recently experienced one or more significant late-life stressors such as medical problems, role loss, or the illness or death of a relative and are reporting recent onset of stress symptomatology.

## Elder Abuse and Neglect

Every year, between 1.5 and 2 million older adults are abused or neglected by family members (Adelman, Siddiqui, & Foldi, 1998); some of these cases represent abuse carried over from earlier in the relationship, and others are new. Counselors working with older adults must be aware of the warning signs of abuse and must not be hesitant to address their concerns with clients. (See Nagpaul, 2001, for a description of an effective elder abuse screening and referral protocol.) Having experienced trauma earlier in life puts one at higher risk for revictimization in old age (Sadavoy, 1997); indeed, Allers, Benjack, and Allers (1992) noted that one of the most common manifestations of unresolved trauma in older adults with histories of childhood sexual abuse is revictimization, such as elder abuse.

## Suicide Prevention

Adults aged 65 and over comprise the age group with the highest rates of suicide in the United States, with the highest rates found in the oldest-old (those over 85); additionally, older adults use more lethal methods and are more likely to complete a suicide attempt than younger cohorts (McIntosh et al., 1994). Risk factors for suicide in old age include male sex, European American descent, recent widowhood, social isolation, physical illness and impairment, feelings of hopelessness, and a history of psychiatric illness (Conwell, 2001). Counselors who are alert to these risk factors can intervene early.

When taken as a group, adults evidence a steady rise in suicide rates across the life span. However, when the sexes are examined separately, it emerges that the suicide rate for men rises more or less steadily throughout their lives, whereas the rate for women peaks in middle age—in their 50s—and then slightly yet steadily declines across the rest of their life span (Conwell, 2001; McIntosh et al., 1994). In 1998, the U.S. suicide rate for all adults 65 and older was 16.88 per 100,000; when the sexes in this age group were separated, the rate was 34.15 per 100,000 for men and 4.73 for women. In addition, differences exist along racial lines: Among older adults, the 1998 suicide rate for elderly White men was by far the highest (33.1 per 100,000), followed by elderly African American men (11.7), then elderly White women (4.85), then elderly African American women (number too small for reliable rate estimate) (Cook, Pearson, Thompson, Black, & Rabins, 2002).

Much effort is under way to ascertain the reasons behind the significantly higher rate of suicide among older White males; recently, the U.S. Department of Health and Human Services included a mental health objective specifically for this group in its Healthy People 2000 project (McIntosh, 1995). Some researchers, however, suggest that instead of looking for the causes of older White male suicide, an examination of the possible reasons behind women's relatively *low* rates of suicide in later life might be more enlightening. Canetto (1992) noted that examining the factors behind "women's resilience rather than men's vulnerability" (p. 81) might prove more useful. Similarly, other researchers (e.g., Alston et al., 1995) are interested in probing the relatively lower suicide rates of the non-White elderly of both sexes.

Theories have been advanced to address the possibility that, again, learned coping can help explain the differences in suicide rates among subpopulations of older adults. As mentioned earlier, it is possible that women and other minority groups have had more experience with marginalization and discrimination before they reach old age and therefore have had to develop adaptive coping mechanisms in response in order to survive and thrive. Some older White men, in contrast, may experience what it is like to be devalued by society for the first time as they reach old age; this loss of status may come as a shock for which they are not psychologically or socially prepared. Older women, on average, suffer from more chronic health problems and more debilitating symptoms than do men, are more likely to live in poverty than are men, and are more discriminated against by social and public policy—and yet they live longer, their suicide rates are lower, and they seem more able to adapt to some of their changing life circumstances, such as bereavement. Canetto (1992) suggested that as a result of prior life experiences that required complex coping strategies, women "may be capable of more complex and flexible coping than men" (p. 84) once they reach old age.

## Multiple Roles and Resilience

As mentioned earlier in this chapter, multiple roles have been hypothesized to contribute to greater well-being and help stave off mental illness. Gerontological researchers have noted that women are required to change roles frequently over the course of their lives (from maternal and spousal roles to possible career-related roles to postparental and widowhood roles), whereas men often remain in a more stable role (the career- or work-dominated role of the provider) up until they reach old age and retirement (Sinnott, 1986). Kline (1979, cited in Sinnott, 1986) documented role inconstancies throughout the lives of women and theorized that these very inconstancies contribute to women's relative resilience in old age, the implication being that women have practice in navigating major role changes in their lives before they reach old age. A man's primary and most reinforcing role during his life is often his work role; in old age this role is frequently lost, necessitating a sudden shift without the benefit of practice with role change earlier in life (Sinnott, 1986). In contrast, women may have more practice with changing roles—and consequently more resilience—by the time they reach old age.

## Social Support and Resilience

The importance of social support and social interaction in promoting mental health and preventing mental illness in all age groups is unequivocal. In older adults, the link between social support and mental health is also well established (Nezlek, Richardson, Green, & Schatten-Jones, 2002). (However, researchers have also noted that it is natural for many older adults to become more selective in their social behavior in an effort to conserve emotional resources in the face of limited time; see Fredrickson and Carstensen, 1990.) As mentioned earlier in this chapter, family relationships may also gain influence and play a greater role in people's lives as they grow older. Older adults often lose relationships through death and relocation and may need to make a greater effort than in the past to avoid social isolation. Counselors can encourage their older clients both to maintain the relationship ties they already have and, when appropriate, to forge new ones. They can encourage clients to participate in activities and organizations—adult learning such as Elderhostel, community and senior centers, political organizations such as AARP and Older Women's League, religious organizations—that may lead to increased social support. Counselors need to attend to their clients' cultural context when making recommendations; for example, extended family members may have greater influence and importance in some clients' lives. And for LGBT elders, the concept of "family" may be quite different from biological relatives; some LGBT elders may have fewer ties to biological family members and may consider a chosen community their family.

## ADVOCATING FOR OLDER CLIENTS

As the baby boomers head inexorably into old age, societal attitudes toward older adults are slowly but surely changing for the better. However, ageism and neglect—on societal, institutional, and personal levels—still exist, and older Americans continue to be marginalized. The problem is particularly acute for older minority Americans, who were members of oppressed groups long before reaching old age. We as counselors can play an active role in combating the effects of neglect, unfair treatment, and oppression by advocating for our older clients at all levels. In addition, counselors can advocate for those clients who, due to loss of physical or cognitive functioning, may not be able to advocate as effectively on their own behalf as they once did.

### Facilitating Access to Resources

Counselors can help clients to access community and other resources for older adults and their families. At minimum, a basic knowledge of local, state, and national agencies and organizations that work for older adults is invaluable. For example, every state has several Area Agencies on Aging, which were established under the Older Americans Act in 1973. Area Agencies on Aging provide a wide range of services, often based on need, to older adults; their services include such things as case management, health insurance counseling, retirement planning, senior centers, meal sites, transportation to medical appointments, Meals on Wheels, and some in-home services. Also, counselors can alert older clients to the existence of numerous advocacy organizations such as the American Association for Retired Persons (AARP), the Older Women's League, and the Gray Panthers.

## Prevention of Elder Victimization and Abuse

Counselors can fight for greater recognition of elder abuse and victimization. We can be aware that older adults are often the targets of financial schemes and of fraud. We can educate our clients as to the warning signs of exploitation and abuse, and we can advocate for legislation that criminalizes this activity. (See AARP's website, www.aarp.org, for helpful information on how to identify and prevent scams.) Counselors can work at the local, state, and national levels to increase awareness of the scope of the problem, and we can work together with agencies in our area that are combating elder abuse and victimization.

## End-of-Life Advocacy

Counselors can educate older clients on the importance of living wills and health care proxies and can alert clients of the existence of such living will documents as *Five Wishes* (legal in 33 states so far—see www.agingwithdignity.org). Counselors can talk to clients about their feelings regarding these often difficult matters and can encourage and facilitate frank communication between clients and their families and loved ones. A counselor's advocacy efforts can be particularly valuable for older LGBT clients for whom "spouse" and "family" may not be legally defined or recognized by an institution such as a hospital. Counselors can advocate for clients if they become hospitalized and/or incapacitated. The counselor who has already been working with an older client is in a uniquely qualified position to speak to end-of-life issues; one very important way we can advocate for our clients is to participate, along with family members and other health care personnel, in this difficult decision-making process. Also, we can fight to keep older couples—for example, couples where one member has become quite incapacitated—from being separated if at all possible, and we can advocate for the support and services they need to stay together.

## Education and Consultation

Counselors can provide education, consultation, and supervision to other health care providers working with our older adult clients, and (with our clients' permission) we can educate families as to the need for certain medical or psychological services. More generally, we can provide education, consultation, and outreach to private and public institutions and to the public at large in an effort to advance the welfare of older people. We can speak to the needs of older adults at public forums such as town meetings; we can write newspaper op-ed pieces or letters to the editor to increase public awareness of age discrimination and other challenges that older adults face; we can educate about the need for culturally aware services for our increasingly diverse older population. Those of us in academia can work to ensure that courses in gerontology, geropsychology, and geriatrics are added to the offerings of graduate professional programs in counseling, psychology, education, and medicine.

## Research

Counselors can conduct applied research that advances the interests of older adults, and we can be sure to include older women and older minority adults in our research. For example, we can survey diverse older populations to uncover the types of services they find most useful and are most likely to access. And we can test the efficacy of existing programs for older adults and develop and pilot new programs and interventions (for a recent example of a successful test of a community-based early intervention program for low-income older adults, see Shapiro & Taylor, 2002). Researchers (e.g., James & Haley, 1995) have demonstrated that clinicians tend to rate older clients as less appropriate for mental health services and as having a poorer prognosis; we can expand upon this body of research and work to disseminate the results to practitioners. More generally, we can challenge the inherent age bias that exists in much psychological research (see Polizzi & Millikin, 2002).

## Political Activism and Lobbying

Counselors can lobby on the local, state, and national levels for fair and equitable funding and can fight cuts in Medicare, Medicaid, and Social Security. (For example, mental health professionals recently lobbied for Medicare coverage for psychological interventions with Alzheimer's patients, and Medicare adjusted its policies.) We can use the media (radio, Internet, local access television) to increase awareness of the needs of older adults and to advocate for needed services. We can participate in the activities of state and national professional organizations such as the Gerontological Society of America, the American Counseling Association, and the American Psychological Association. Also, counselors can advocate for greater funding for graduate training in geropsychology and geriatrics (VandenBos & DeLeon, 1998).

## CONCLUSION

As the number and proportion of older adults grow in this country, and as baby boomers with more accepting attitudes toward counseling and mental health issues join the ranks of the older population, counselors can expect to see increasing numbers of older clients in the years ahead. Consequently, we need to be prepared to address the unique needs of this remarkably diverse population. In addition to providing counseling and psychotherapy for existing problems (see chapter 10), counselors can help prevent some problems from developing in the first place and can facilitate successful aging in their older clients. Counselors can promote healthy lifestyles through encouraging physical activity, proper nutrition, sleep, and social activity; through providing information on basic medical and cognitive issues; and through an ability and readiness to refer clients for more specialized services should the need arise. We can facilitate the successful navigation of normative late-life transitions such as changes in health status, retirement, housing, bereavement, and dying, and we can both bolster existing coping mechanisms and help clients develop new ones. We can help prevent major mental health problems in our clients by recognizing early warning signs such as caregiver burden, alcohol and substance use, trauma history, signs of abuse or neglect, and risks for suicidality; and we can intervene early to capitalize on the strengths our clients bring to the table.

Older adults are by definition survivors. Through honoring the unique experiences, strengths, and resiliencies that have brought them through to old age, and by supplementing these strengths with additional knowledge and skills, counselors play a valuable role in the promotion of successful aging in their older clients.

# Cases and Questions

1. Ms. Higgins, an 83-year-old twice-widowed European American woman, a retired nurse, living by herself on a fixed income, in fairly good physical health, is brought to your office by her 57-year-old adult daughter. The daughter explains that although her mother has many friends in her building, she has become a bit more isolated since the death of her second husband last year; she adds that sometimes when she telephones her mother in the evenings her speech seems a little slurred.
   (a) What are some of your initial concerns about Ms. Higgins? What additional questions might you have for her regarding her daughter's observations?
   (b) What experiences might Ms. Higgins have had as a working woman during her lifetime? What strengths and resiliencies might Ms. Higgins bring to the table?
   (c) What community resources might you suggest to Ms. Higgins and her daughter?
2. Mr. Adams, a 76-year-old married African American man, World War II veteran of the army, comes to your office because he has recently begun having nightmares at night and some mild anxiety during the day. Mr. Adams worked for the railroads for 46 years. Physically healthy throughout the majority of his life, Mr. Adams was recently obliged to retire from his railroad job because of increased disability from a leg injury incurred in combat during his time in the war.
   (a) What follow-up questions might you have for Mr. Adams regarding his feelings about retirement and about his nightmares and anxiety?
   (b) How might Mr. Adams's life experiences have been different from those of an older European American man? What strengths and resiliencies might Mr. Adams bring to the table?
   (c) Would your concerns for Mr. Adams be different if he were a widower?

# REFERENCES

Adelman, R. D., Siddiqui, H., & Foldi, N. (1998). Approaches to diagnosis and treatment of elder abuse and neglect. In M. Hersen & V. B. Van Hasselt (Eds.), *Handbook of clinical geropsychology* (pp. 557–567). New York: Plenum Press.

Allers, C. T., Benjack, K. J., & Allers, N. T. (1992). Unresolved childhood sexual abuse: Are older adults affected? *Journal of Counseling and Development, 71,* 14–17.

Alston, M. H., Rankin, S. H., & Harris, C. A. (1995). Suicide in African American elderly. *Journal of Black Studies, 26,* 31–35.

American Psychological Association Working Group on the Older Adult. (1998). What practitioners should know about working with older adults. *Professional Psychology: Research and Practice, 29*(5), 413–427.

Andrews, F. M., & Robinson, J. P. (1991). Measures of subjective well-being. In J. P. Robinson, P. R. Shaver, & L. S. Wrightsman (Eds.), *Measures of personality and social psychological attitudes* (pp. 61–114). San Diego, CA: Academic Press.

Bortz, W. M., & Bortz, S. S. (1996). Prevention, nutrition, and exercise in the aged. In L. L. Carstensen, B. A. Edelstein, & L. Dornbrand (Eds.), *The practical handbook of clinical gerontology* (pp. 36–53). Thousand Oaks, CA: Sage.

Buffum, M. D., & Wolfe, N. S. (1995). Posttraumatic stress disorder and the World War II veteran. *Geriatric Nursing, 16*(6), 264–270.

Burnside, I. (1993). Healthy older women—in spite of it all. *Journal of Women and Aging, 5*(3/4), 9–24.

Canetto, S. S. (1992). Gender and suicide in the elderly. *Suicide and Life-Threatening Behavior, 22,* 80–97.

Christmas, C., & Anderson, R. A. (2000). Exercise and older patients: Guidelines for the clinician. *Journal of the American Geriatrics Society, 48,* 318–324.

Conwell, Y. (2001). Suicide in later life: A review and recommendations for prevention. *Suicide and Life-Threatening Behavior, 31,* 32–47.

Cook, J. M., Pearson, J. L., Thompson, R., Black, B. S., & Rabins, P. V. (2002). Suicidality in older African Americans: Findings from the EPOCH Study. *American Journal of Geriatric Psychiatry, 10*(4), 437–446.

Danieli, Y. (1997). As survivors age: An overview. *Journal of Geriatric Psychiatry, 30,* 9–26.

Engdahl, B. E., Harkness, A. R., Eberly, R. E., Page, W. F., & Bielinski, J. (1993). Structural models of captivity trauma, resilience, and trauma response among former prisoners of war 20 to 40 years after release. *Social Psychology and Psychiatric Epidemiology, 28,* 109–115.

Erikson, E. H. (1968). *Identity: Youth and crisis.* New York: W. W. Norton.

Falk, B., Hersen, M., & Van-Hasselt, V. B. (1994). Assessment of posttraumatic stress disorder in older adults: A critical review. *Clinical Psychology Review, 14*(5), 383–415.

Friend, R. A. (1991). Older lesbian and gay people: A theory of successful aging. *Journal of Homosexuality, 20*(3/4), 99–118.

Fredrickson, B. L., & Carstensen, L. L. (1990). Choosing social partners: How old age and anticipated endings make people more selective. *Psychology and Aging, 5*(3), 335–347.

Gagne, A. M., & Morin, C. M. (2000). Effets des benzodiazepines sur la performance cognitive et psychomotrice des personnnes agees soufrant d'insomnie [Effects of benzodiazepines upon cognitive and psychomotor performance in older people suffering from insomnia]. *Canadian Journal on Aging, 19*(4), 479–493.

Gagnon, M., & Hersen, M. (2000). Unresolved childhood sexual abuse and older adults: Late-life vulnerabilities. *Journal of Clinical Geropsychology, 6*(3), 187–198.

Gallagher-Thompson, D., Coon, D. W., Rivera, P., Powers, D., & Zeiss, A. M. (1998). Family caregiving: Stress, coping, and intervention. In M. Hersen & V. B. Van Hasselt (Eds.), *Handbook of clinical geropsychology* (pp. 469–493). New York: Plenum Press.

Gergen, K., & Gergen, M. (2002, January). Positive aging: Renewing the vision. *The Positive Aging Newsletter.* Retrieved April 4, 2002, from http://www.healthandage.com/html/res/gergen/entrance.htm.

Higgins, A. B., & Follette, V. M. (2002). Frequency and impact of interpersonal trauma in older women. *Journal of Clinical Geropsychology, 8*(3), 215–226.

Hunt, N., & Robbins, I. (2001). The long-term consequences of war: The experience of World War II. *Aging and Mental Health, 5*(2), 183–190.

James, J. W., & Haley, W. E. (1995). Age and health bias in practicing clinical psychologists. *Psychology and Aging, 10*(4), 610–616.

Johnson, C. L. (1994). Differential expectations and realities: Race, socioeconomic status and health of the oldest-old. *International Journal of Aging and Human Development, 38,* 13–27.

Kellermann, N. P. F. (2001). The long-term psychological effects and treatment of holocaust trauma. *Journal of Loss and Trauma, 6,* 197–218.

Kim, J. E., & Moen, P. (2001). Is retirement good or bad for subjective well-being? *Current Directions in Psychological Science, 10*(3), 83–86.

Kim, J. E., & Moen, P. (2002). Retirement transitions, gender, and psychological well-being: A life-course, ecological perspective. *Journal of Gerontology: Psychological Sciences, 57B*(3), P212–P222.

King, D. W., King, L. A., Bachrach, P. S., Spiro, A., & Davison, E. H. (2001). *Characterizing LOSS: Late-Onset Stress Symptomatology among aging combat veterans: Proposal for a series of three pilot studies.* Interim report submitted to the Normative Aging Study. Boston, MA: VA Boston Healthcare System.

Koenig, H. G. (2000). Religion, well-being, and health in the elderly: The scientific evidence for an association. In J. A. Thorson (Ed.), *Perspectives on spiritual well-being and aging* (pp. 84–97). Springfield, IL: Charles C Thomas.

Laditka, J. N., & Laditka, S. B. (2000). Aging children and their older parents: The coming generation of caregiving. *Journal of Women and Aging, 12*(1/2), 189–204.

Levy, B. R., Slade, M. D., Kunkel, S. R., & Kasl, S. V. (2002). Longevity increased by positive self-perceptions of aging. *Journal of Personality and Social Psychology, 83*(2), 261–270.

Logan, J. M., Sanders, A. L., Snyder, A. Z., Morris, J. C., & Buckner, R. L. (2002). Under-recruitment and nonselective recruitment: Dissociable neural mechanisms associated with aging. *Neuron, 33,* 827–840.

Macleod, A. D. (1994). The reactivation of post-traumatic stress disorder in later life. *Australian and New Zealand Journal of Psychiatry, 28*(4), 625–634.

McGuire, L., Kiecolt-Glaser, J. K., & Glaser, R. (2002). Depressive symptoms and lymphocyte proliferation in older adults. *Journal of Abnormal Psychology, 111,* 192–197.

McInnis-Dittrich, K. (1996). Adapting life-review therapy for elderly female survivors of childhood sexual abuse. *Families in Society: The Journal of Contemporary Human Services, 77*(3), 166–173.

McIntosh, J. L. (1995). Suicide prevention in the elderly (age 65–99). In M. M. Silverman & R. W. Maris (Eds.), *Suicide prevention toward the year 2000* (pp. 180–192). New York: Guilford Press.

McIntosh, J. L., Santos, J. F., Hubbard, R. W., & Overholser, J. C. (1994). *Elder suicide: Research, theory, and treatment.* Washignton, DC: American Psychological Association.

Morin, C. M., Blais, F. C., & Mimeault, V. (1998). Sleep disturbances in late life. In M. Hersen & V. B. Van Hasselt (Eds.), *Handbook of clinical geropsychology* (pp. 273–299). New York: Plenum Press.

Morlino, M., Milan, G., De Bonis, S., & Postiglione, A. (2002). A mother as caregiver of a patient with Alzheimer disease. *American Journal of Geriatric Psychiatry, 10*(2), 220–221.

Morrell, R. W., Dailey, S. R., Feldman, C., Mayhorn, C. B., & Echt, K. V. (2002). *Older adults and information technology: A compendium of scientific research and web site accessibility guidelines.* Bethesda, MD: National Institute on Aging.

Musil, C. M., & Ahmad, M. (2002). Health of grandmothers: A comparison by caregiver status. *Journal of Aging and Health, 14,* 96–121.

Nagpaul, K. (2001). Application of elder abuse screening tools and referral protocol: Techniques and clinical considerations. *Journal of Elder Abuse and Neglect, 13*(2), 59–78.

National Institute on Aging. (2001). *Making your web site senior friendly: A checklist.* PDF document retrieved April 4, 2002, from http://www.nln.nih.gov/pubs/checklist.pdf.

Nezlek, J. B., Richardson, D. S., Green, L. R., & Schatten-Jones, E. C. (2002). Psychological well-being and day-to-day social interaction among older adults. *Personal Relationships, 9,* 57–71.

Padgett, D. (1989). Aging minority women: Issues in research and health policy. In L. Grau & I. Susser (Eds.), *Women in the later years: Health, social, and cultural perspectives* (pp. 213–225). New York: Harrington Park Press.

Paniagua, F. A. (1999). Commentary on the possibility that Viagra may contribute to transmission of HIV and other sexual diseases among older adults. *Psychological Reports, 85,* 942–944.

Polizzi, K. G., & Millikin, R. J. (2002). Attitudes toward the elderly: Identifying problematic usage of ageist and overextended terminology in research instructions. *Educational Gerontology, 28,* 367–377.

Port, C. L., Engdahl, B., & Frazier, P. (2001). A longitudinal and retrospective study of PTSD among older prisoners of war. *American Journal of Psychiatry, 158*(9), 1474–1479.

Rowe, J. W., & Kahn, R. L. (1998). *Successful aging.* New York: Pantheon Books.

Sadavoy, J. (1997). Survivors: A review of the late-life effects of prior psychological trauma. *American Journal of Geriatric Psychiatry, 5*(4), 287–301.

Schulz, R. (Ed.). (2000). *Handbook on dementia caregiving: Evidence-based interventions for family caregivers.* New York: Springer.

Shapiro, A., & Taylor, M. (2002). Effects of a community-based early intervention program on the subjective well-being, institutionalization, and mortality of low-income elders. *The Gerontologist, 42*(3), 334–341.

Shaw, W. S., Patterson, T. L, Semple, S., & Grant, I. (1998). Health and well-being in retirement. In M. Hersen & V. B. Van Hasselt (Eds.), *Handbook of clinical geropsychology* (pp. 383–409). New York: Plenum Press.

Sinnott, J. D. (1986). *Sex roles and aging: Theory and research from a systems perspective.* Contributions to Human Development, Vol. 15. Basel, Switzerland: Karger.

Somer, E. (2000). Effects of incest in aging survivors: Psychopathology and treatment issues. *Journal of Clinical Geropsychology, 6,* 53–61.

Spacapan, S., & Oskamp, S. (1989). Introduction to the social psychology of aging. In S. Spacapan & S. Oskamp (Eds.), *The social psychology of aging* (pp. 9–24). Newbury Park, CA: Sage.

Spiro, A., III, Schnurr, P. P., & Aldwin, C. M. (1994). Combat-related post-traumatic stress disorder symptoms in older veterans. *Psychology and Aging, 9,* 17–26.

Stathi, A., Fox, K. R., & McKenna, J. (2002). Physical activity and dimensions of subjective well-being in older adults. *Journal of Aging and Physical Activity, 10,* 76–92.

Stoller, E. P., & Gibson, R. C. (2000). *Worlds of difference: Inequality in the aging experience* (3rd ed.). Thousand Oaks, CA: Pine Forge Press.

Strombeck, R., & Levy, J. A. (1998). Educational strategies and interventions targeting adults age 50 and older for HIV/AIDS prevention. *Research on Aging, 20*(6), 912–936.

Tryon, W. W. (1998). Physical activity. In M. Hersen & V. B. Van Hasselt (Eds.), *Handbook of clinical geropsychology* (pp. 523–555). New York: Plenum Press.

Turk-Charles, S., Rose, T., & Gatz, M. (1996). The significance of gender in the treatment of older adults. In L. L. Carstensen, B. A. Edelstein, & L. Dornbrand (Eds.), *The practical handbook of clinical gerontology* (pp. 107–128). Thousand Oaks, CA: Sage.

VandenBos, G. R., & DeLeon, P. H. (1998). Clinical geropsychology and U.S. federal policy. In M. Hersen & V. B. Van Hasselt (Eds.), *Handbook of clinical geropsychology* (pp. 19–28). New York: Plenum Press.

Von Faber, M., Bootsma-van der Wiel, A., van Exel, E., Gussekloo, J., Lagaay, A. M., van Dongen, E., Knook, D. L., van der Geest, S., & Westendorp, R. G. (2001). Successful aging in the oldest old: Who can be characterized as successfully aged? *Archives of Internal Medicine, 161*(22), 2694–2700.

Wotherspoon, C. M. (2000). The relationship between spiritual well-being and health in later life. In J. A. Thorson (Ed.), *Perspectives on spiritual well-being and aging* (pp. 69–83). Springfield, IL: Charles C Thomas.

Wright, S. D., Drost, M., Caserta, M. S., & Lund, D. A. (1998). Older adults and HIV/AIDS: Implications for educators. *Gerontology and Geriatrics Education, 18*(4), 3–21.

# CHAPTER 10

# Psychotherapy with Older Clients

## Sara Honn Qualls, University of Colorado at Colorado Springs

Unique aspects of psychotherapy or counseling with older clients primarily relate to the specific life contexts in which they live. The biopsychosocial model of well-being points us to three primary contexts: biological, psychological, and social. Environmental contexts also warrant attention because of the importance of person-environment fit to maximize function (Lawton, 1982). In this chapter, we consider some of those contexts, some of the unique mental health concerns that arise because of those contexts, available treatment approaches to address them, and ethical concerns that arise in the course of psychotherapy with older persons.

## BIOPSYCHOSOCIAL ASPECTS OF AGING

Among the more challenging aspects of later life are the biological changes that accompany aging (Masoro & Austad, 2001). Although most of later adulthood is characterized by relatively robust health, with advancing age the likelihood of experiencing chronic health conditions increases significantly. Chronic illnesses have their primary impact on well-being through the functional impairments that they produce. In addition, medications that manage those disease processes also commonly impact well-being by affecting mood, cognition, energy, or other aspects of functional well-being.

Psychological aging consists of normal changes in cognition, changes in perspective on life because of longevity and mortality salience, and for some, changes in personality that are essentially accommodations to changes in biological or social contexts. The aging brain experiences significant losses in function, most notable of which is in processing speed (Salthouse, 1996). The age at which various cognitive functions decline varies, but ultimately almost all functions show some deterioration by the late 80s. Considerable research is now available to document which specific functions decline at which point in later life (e.g., Schaie & Willis, 1993). On a more positive note, evidence of the joys of grandparenthood and the higher prevalence of wisdom in later life suggest there are uniquely positive aspects of later life as well (Baltes & Baltes, 1990; Ryff & Keyes, 1996).

The social world of older adults is characterized by both stability and change (Rook, 2000). The salient members of the social network of older adults tend to be long-term members of the "convoy" of people who have accompanied them throughout their lives (Antonucci & Akiyama, 1995). Family takes on increasing salience, and core friendships continue to influence positive well-being, but peripheral social relationships are lost. Social changes that receive the most attention are losses in the social network due to death of members of the network (Rook, 2000). Particularly challenging is the death of a spouse, deaths of close friends and family, or loss of contact with family members following divorce. Although the networks of older adults are smaller than those of younger adult cohorts, some of the shrinkage is due to a selectivity process that places more value on close members of the network who can affirm the self (Carstensen, Isaacowitz, & Charles, 1999). Older adults who lack close family members fare less well in later adulthood than those with strong family structures (Antonucci & Akiyama, 1995). Although friends are important to psychological well-being, family members are the persons who provide assistance, a safety net.

In contrast to mythical images of a placid old age, later life is an eventful time that requires significant adjustment. Common events in later life include retirement, restructuring of daily life to include meaningful activities, onset of physical health problems, initiation of caregiving responsibilities, death of friends and family, deterioration of functional health, changes in lives of adult children or grandchildren (e.g., divorce, illness, business success or failure), and changes in social roles (e.g., onset of elder role within family and community organizations). Daily hassles have even more influence on well-being of older adults than do life events, and neither appear to have the rate of influence on well-being that occurs in younger years. Indeed, most older adults adapt well despite the prevalence of life events (Gatz, Kasl-Godley, & Karel, 1996).

## MENTAL HEALTH AND AGING

What is mental health in later life? The McArthur Foundation Study of Aging in America defines successful aging as "the ability to maintain three key behaviors or characteristics: Low risk of disease and disease related disability, high mental and physical function; and active engagement with life" (Rowe & Kahn, 1998, p. 38). Ryff and colleagues (Ryff & Keyes, 1996) demonstrated that six distinct dimensions of wellness emerged from very large factor-analytic studies of nationally representative samples: autonomy, environmental mastery, personal growth, positive relations with others, purpose in life, and self-acceptance. Their research demonstrated that these same core factors frame well-being for adults across the life span.

As is evident from the brief preceding discussion of age-related changes in the contexts of life, later life is a period of both gains and losses. With advancing age, the balance between losses and gains tips toward losses (Baltes & Baltes, 1990). However, older adults are active agents who adjust to the changes in later life by drawing on their strengths to compensate for losses. Baltes and Baltes

(1990) offered a theory of "selective optimization with compensation" to describe the active coping strategies used by older adults. Thus, although the domains of competence shrink with declining physical or mental capacity, older adults remain amazingly independent by optimizing reliance on domains of competence to compensate for deterioration or loss.

A recent definition of a mentally healthy elderly person is "one who accepts the aging self as an active being, engaging available strengths to compensate for weaknesses in order to create personal meaning, maintain maximum autonomy by mastering the environment, and sustain positive relations with others" (Qualls, 2002, p. 12).

## MENTAL DISORDERS IN LATER LIFE

Despite the impressive adaptation that most older adults exhibit, about 20% of older adults are experiencing mental disorders at any given point in time (Gatz & Smyer, 2001). Generally, the prevalence of diagnosable mental disorders is slightly lower in older adults than in other adults, with two exceptions. Low-level, chronic disorders that lack sufficient intensity to meet diagnostic criteria (e.g., minor depression) appear to be highly prevalent in older adults. Also, the rates of cognitive impairment increase significantly in advanced old age, inflating the overall prevalence of mental disorder substantially.

Three of the more common mental disorders of later life are often referred to as the three D's: delirium, dementia, and depression. These disorders are often discussed together because they represent one of the more challenging differential diagnostic problems for mental health professionals due to their overlapping presentations.

### Delirium

*Delirium* refers to acute confusional states that typically have a rapid onset. The person usually shows signs of compromised cognitive abilities that include problems common in dementia, such as memory problems and problem-solving difficulties. In addition, delirium usually compromises attention, resulting in difficulty processing information available in the immediate environment. Common causes of delirium include physical illness, medication toxicity or interaction, nutritional deficits, and substance abuse. Delirium may be discriminated from more chronic sources of cognitive impairment by careful history taking related to the onset and progression of symptoms, and through brief cognitive assessments. One reason that evaluation of cognitive impairment always involves a careful history and physical examination is that causes of delirium are usually identified in the course of careful medication examination and laboratory tests. Treatment is targeted at the underlying medical cause of the delirium state and is typically successful unless the underlying problem goes untreated too long. Psychotherapy is not useful during a delirium state because cognition is typically too impaired for psychotherapy to be effective.

## Dementia

*Dementia* is the term applied to a range of diseases that produce chronic, irreversible, deteriorating patterns of cognitive impairment due to brain disease. Alzheimer's disease is the most prevalent dementia (comprising 50–80% of dementia), occurring in about 5–6% of adults over age 65 (Evans et al., 1989). Vascular dementias are produced by permanent deterioration in the vascular system that results in increasing damage to the brain. Other diseases that produce dementia include Pick's disease, Huntington's chorea, Parkinson's disease, and Creutzfeldt-Jakob disease.

Dementias are identified through a procedure of ruling out alternative hypotheses for deteriorating cognition. A thorough medical history and physical are needed, followed often by neurological examination. Neuropsychological testing is helpful to identify the specific pattern of deterioration in functioning that characterizes the specific disease process. Recent data suggest that PET scans have a high rate of positive identification of Alzheimer's dementia, but these machines are not readily available for use outside of medical research settings.

For many, the first signs of cognitive impairment due to dementia are changes in personality or behavior. For example, social withdrawal or paranoia represent a person's effort to cope with memory loss but may easily be viewed by family and friends as a change in personality, motivation, or mood. Thorough multidisciplinary evaluations are required to rule out all possible alternative explanations for the subtle and often ambiguous changes that result from dementia. Neuropsychological testing and neuroimaging are used to identify structural and functional changes in the brain and in cognitive performance that are consistent with specific types of dementia. Brief screening tests, such as mental status exams, provide only gross indications of the presence or absence of significant cognitive impairment and are thus useful primarily for screening but not for diagnostic purposes.

Current treatments for dementia are often successful in slowing the progression of the disease and assisting caregivers in the daily environment with management of the impact of the disease. Psychotherapy is useful only in the early stages of the disease and only if the person clearly has capacity to benefit from talk therapy. Most interventions rely on persons in the environment (e.g., family or formal providers) to alter the environment or behavior patterns in ways that improve mood (Teri, Logsdon, Uomoto, & McCurry, 1997). Current pharmacological treatments primarily slow the progression of dementia; none of the dementing diseases are yet fully curable.

## Depression

Clinical *depressions* (major depressive disorders and dysthymia) are slightly less prevalent in older adults than in younger adults, but they are still a significant mental health challenge. In contrast to the myth that aging would make anyone depressed, most older adults are not depressed. However, rates of subclinical levels of depression symptoms (sometimes referred to as minor depression) are higher in older adults (Blazer, 1999). Older adults often report their depression in terms that are not recognized as indicative of a mood disorder. For example, rather than reporting emotional sadness and crying, older adults may report loss of interest or pleasure in their lives. They may downplay the importance of those losses, attributing them to predictable, normal parts of aging. Thus, older adults often do not identify themselves as depressed (attributing the difficulty to old age or laziness), nor do their families or physicians (Wells, Schoenbaum, Unützer, Lagomasino, & Rubenstein, 1999).

Depression is typically assessed in interview, although self-report depression instruments are very useful, quick, and inexpensive to use. The Geriatric Depression Scale (Yesavage et al., 1983) is frequently recommended because it is simple to use in either the 15- or 30-item version (yes-no response format), has norms for several age groups, does not inflate the score with symptoms of physical illnesses, and is readily available (http://www.stanford.edu/~yesavage/GDS.html).

Depression treatment efficacy is now well demonstrated in older adults (Gerson, Belin, Kaufman, Mintz, & Jarvik, 1999). As is the case with many disorders, several brands of therapy have been shown to work well, and all work at least as well as pharmacotherapy (Cuijpers, 1998; Gerson et al., 1999). Cognitive behavioral therapies (CBT) show somewhat stronger maintenance rates over a 2-year period (Cuijpers, 1998). A recent controlled trial suggests that medication alone may not do as well as either CBT or combined medication-CBT (Thompson, Coon, Gallagher-Thompson, Sommer, & Koin, 2001). The primary adaptations made in these therapeutic strategies to increase effectiveness with older adults are the addition of a few more sessions to allow for a slightly slower pace and use of multiple learning modalities (e.g., visual as well as verbal).

## Differential Diagnostic Issues

The differential diagnosis among the three D's is particularly challenging because older adults who are depressed often report concerns about their memory and concentration. Thus, self-reported memory loss is important and meaningful and must be evaluated to determine whether it represents depression, dementia, or delirium. On the other hand, family members of persons experiencing cognitive impairment may report behavior or personality changes that they attribute to aging, depression, or personality difficulties. Failure to accurately recognize any of these disorders leads to ineffective treatment, unnecessary deterioration in functioning, and distress for family and friends who must deal with the psychosocial consequences regardless of the cause.

## Anxiety Disorders

Anxiety disorders have received far less attention but turn out to be more prevalent than depressive disorders across the life span. The 1-month prevalence rate is approximately 5.5%, but approximately 10–20% of older persons experience significant anxiety symptoms (Regier et al., 1988; Stanley & Beck, 1998). Anxiety has high rates of comorbidity with depression, dementia, and illness, which leaves counselors and researchers struggling for a tool that is useful in differential diagnosis. Anxiety disorders may also present as physical disorders (e.g., cardiac difficulties), adding to the complexity of differential diagnosis. Some self-report instruments are now available, but none have the empirical base of norms as is available with the various depression assessment instruments.

Treatment research is now emerging, with inconsistent evidence for the efficacy of psychotherapy with anxiety disorders (Scogin, Floyd, & Forde, 2000). Stanley, Beck, and Glassco (1996) reported on the successful use of CBT and supportive psychotherapy for generalized anxiety disorder. Psychodynamic and eclectic approaches have also been described as useful for anxiety disorders (Knight, 1992; Verwoerdt, 1981).

## Substance Abuse Disorders

Substance abuse disorders also warrant the attention of professionals working with older adults. Two characteristics of substance abuse patterns in older adults are especially noteworthy. The most common drugs that are used by elderly are prescription and over-the-counter medications. Indeed, older adults consume 30% of all prescribed medications and 40% of over-the-counter medications (HHS Inspector General, 1989). Usage does not imply abuse, but several factors make this usage rate concerning. First, chemicals are metabolized quite differently with increasing age, leading to considerable variation in the therapeutic and unintended consequences of medications (including mental health effects). Second, the common use of multiple health providers increases the chances of adverse drug reactions or interactions under the best of conditions. Self-determined adherence patterns (e.g., "I'd rather take two pink ones in the morning than at night because they upset my stomach" can easily lead to substance abuse patterns. Abuse of these medications may occur because of ignorance, poor communication with health providers, or due to purposeful intent.

Alcohol abuse in older adults occurs in two quite distinct patterns: lifelong abuse and late-onset abuse. Lifelong abusers are usually recognized by those around them as having difficulty, and they typically begin to experience poor health as a consequence of the long-term abuse. Late-onset abusers, however, often ingest alcohol in a more private ingestion pattern that is harder to detect. The prevalence rate is estimated to be as high as 10–12% in community populations (Segal, Van Hasselt, Hersen, & King, 1996).

## Personality Disorders

Personality disorders have a particularly powerful impact on aging adults' well-being when aging losses result in increased dependence on others whose tolerance for the unpleasant aspects of the defensive style wears thin over time. Community prevalence rates and the effects of aging on prevalence have been difficult to establish due to widely varying estimates that emerge from various methods of assessing these disorders (Segal, Coolidge, & Rosowsky, 2000). However, persons with personality disorders are particularly visible in long-term care settings, family caregiving arrangements, and senior housing facilities. Caregivers describe frustration with manipulative strategies for meeting needs that undermine the care plans. Furthermore, the efficacy rates for psychotherapy for any condition are lower when personality disorders are present (Gradman, Thompson, & Gallagher-Thompson,

1999). Little empirical research is available to examine the emerging array of treatment approaches, although a growing body of descriptive research is now available (Rosowsky, Abrams, & Zweig, 1999).

## PSYCHOTHERAPY PROCESSES WITH OLDER ADULTS

In general, psychotherapy processes are quite similar regardless of the adult client's age (Hinrichsen & Dick-Siskin, 2000), although a limited set of differences have been identified (Knight, 1996). Older adults respond to the same modalities of therapy as do younger adults, at approximately the same rate. As mentioned above, the contexts of aging must be understood and, at times, require accommodation in therapy. For example, the site and frequency of sessions may be influenced by limitations in ambulation, or the choice of assessment tools may be influenced by visual impairments. The basic framework for conceptualizing change and the intervention strategies are similar, however.

Knight (1996) has provided the most comprehensive framework for conceptualizing psychotherapy with older adults. The long title of his model illustrates the multiple components of the framework: contextual, cohort-based, maturity, specific challenge model. The life *contexts* of older persons are unique in Western culture, which tends to organize services and lifestyles in age-segregated ways. Therapists counseling older clients need to understand the organizational structures for housing, social services, and health care for older persons. For example, nursing homes and assisted living facilities offer vastly different social, physical, and psychological milieus that are critical to counseling. Medical information is more salient in this type of work, as are issues related to decision-making competence. Legal contexts for decision making, guardianship, conservatorship, and self-determination also are commonly part of psychotherapy with later-life clients. Members of birth *cohorts* differ in their belief and value structures, coping styles, biomedical influences, and historical perspectives. All of these factors influence clients' willingness to use psychotherapy and their modes of engaging in therapy processes. Longevity affords the opportunity for advanced maturity that may result in wisdom, enhanced emotion regulation, or simply a wider range of experiences on which to draw. The personal experiences of a lifetime provide strengths and resiliency that provide a base for building within psychotherapy that is not available in young adulthood. Specific challenges that characterize the last phase of the life cycle are often linked to the reason a client seeks therapy. In particular, biomedical aging concerns that result from normal aging and age-correlated diseases shape the life structures and daily concerns of many older adults, particularly the old-old (age 85+). Grief work is quite common in therapy in later life, regardless of the initial presenting concern, simply by virtue of the commonness of loss experiences.

### Younger Therapists and Older Clients

A distinct aspect of counseling or psychotherapy with aged clients is that most therapists are younger than their clients, yielding a unique interpersonal context for psychotherapy that warrants attention. Younger therapists are inevitably dealing with clients' life challenges off-time to their own development, a factor that can lead them to idealize, deny, or otherwise distort their empathy for the real challenges described by the client. My training experience suggests that many young therapists are hesitant to label psychopathology or character difficulties in older clients that they would be quick to recognize in a young adult. Younger therapists may also hesitate to require significant change efforts because of their belief that the older person's medical difficulties, or even simply age, render such efforts too demanding. Work with older clients requires significant self-examination of one's own family of origin issues and propels therapists into differentiation from the family of origin sooner than might occur naturally due to family development tasks.

Older clients working with younger therapists are also faced with the reality of their place in the life cycle in a unique way. Clients and therapists may fear that younger therapists cannot understand or relate to their life concerns, or that the older clients will not choose to trust someone who has not yet been in their life phase. As I commonly remind my clients and my students, there are too few 80-year-old therapists available to meet the mental health needs, so we have to figure out a way to compensate for our different life stages through empathy, collaboration, and mutual exploration. After the first few sessions, rarely are these fears an issue any longer. Elderly clients may adopt a mildly paternalistic attitude toward their younger therapists while engaging in a meaningful therapeutic process. Stronger parental or grandparental reactions are, of course, interesting content for the therapeutic process.

## Other Therapy Modalities

Modalities other than individual psychotherapy or counseling are also very appropriate to consider with older clients. Group therapy is a particularly helpful tool for older adults who have relocated or become widowed and are in the process of reconstructing a social life. Although most older persons rely on their lifelong convoy of social contacts, some older people become increasingly selective across the life span (Antonucci & Akiyama, 1995; Carstensen et al., 1999), and some find themselves uprooted from familiar contexts and are bereft of ideas or skills for building new relationships. Group therapy is a perfect laboratory for building relationship skills while working on other life challenges.

Marital or family therapy is most appropriate when structural or functional aspects of the marriage or family have shifted in ways that leave family members vulnerable to not having their needs met (Qualls, 1995, 1999). Not only is later life a time of tremendous transition and challenge, but marital and family relationships also are altered by significant events in the lives of individual members who are intricately interwoven in a "life event web" (Pruchno, Blow, & Smyer, 1984). Although the process of marital therapy is similar in many ways to work with couples of any age, the longevity of marriages (commonly 40–60 years) provides a familiarity that relies less on words than on shared (mis-)understandings. The key question for marital therapy is "why now," the answer to which is often that someone's functional capacity has changed because of medical illness or dementia.

Family therapy differs more significantly because typically the participants are all adults whose positions in the intergenerational hierarchy are often in conflict with their legal positions as adult peers (Qualls, 1999). A common reason for engaging the family in therapy is the need for the entire family system to adapt to the altered capacity of one member, whose deterioration forces renegotiation of roles and rules within the family. Family therapists may simply provide information about the family consequences of various illnesses or may need to guide the family through the renegotiation. Families with a history of poor attachment or significant conflict require more significant intervention, whereas families with a positive developmental history may need only information or minimal guidance (Shields, King, & Wynne, 1995). Family interventions with caregiving families are among the unique approaches to family therapy that have emerged in the gerontology literature (Schulz, 2000; Zarit, Orr, & Zarit, 1985). Family mediation is an emerging practice opportunity that engages families in collaborative problem solving to address the appropriate legal solutions for a cognitively impaired elder rather than relying on the adversarial process of probate court.

## ETHICAL ISSUES IN COUNSELING OLDER ADULTS

An overarching ethical concern is that psychologists limit their practice to clients and problems for which they have received training. The difficult differential diagnostic issues described earlier require particular sensitivity to the *scope of practice* ethical principle. For example, a highly competent psychologist who lacks training in the recognition and assessment of cognitive impairment in later life may well interpret the highly similar presentations of depression, dementia, and delirium in the same way as with a younger client, yielding a plan for treating depression without recognition of the high risks related to the other possible problems.

As losses become more salient than gains in advanced old age, clients are increasingly vulnerable to exploitation, fraud, and abuse. Therapists must be particularly conscientious to set high standards of professional conduct with a vulnerable population that cannot be presumed able to advocate on its own behalf. Recent efforts to set standards of practice with residents in long-term care settings were intended to establish criteria for appropriate and effective treatment (Lichtenberg et al., 1998).

### Working With the Provider Team

A key consequence of the constraint to practice within the scope of professional expertise is that most geriatric care involves a team of providers. The team may never meet, but the roles of the various professionals must be taken into account by each person on the implicit team. Mental health providers must regularly interact with the primary health care provider and likely should have at least intermittent contact with other relevant providers (e.g., home health agency, social services agency, family, residence staff). Providing care in an isolated framework is not appropriate with clients whose problems require the attention of multiple disciplines and agencies.

## Monitoring for Abuse

The potential for abuse by other persons in the environment of the older adult (e.g., nursing assistants in nursing homes, family caregivers) warrants careful monitoring by mental health professionals. Most states require reporting of abuse to older adults, but responses to more subtle forms of exploitation are often not specified in the law. Psychologists must be prepared to work closely with staff in other systems (e.g., adult protection units within the county social services units) to address problems related to abuse, exploitation, and fraud.

## Protecting Legal Rights

Professionals must protect the legal rights of older adults to make the same bad decisions that younger adults are allowed. The ethical principles of autonomy and beneficence often come into direct conflict when dealing with frail older adults with the legal capacity to make decisions but whose decisions appear not in their best interest. For example, legally competent older adults may choose to stay with an adult child caregiver despite apparent excessive financial costs to the elder or may choose to engage in very unhealthy behaviors such as excessive sugar intake while on insulin treatment for diabetes or abuse of alcohol. Of course, there are boundaries to these rights that are defined primarily by decision-making capacity and the responsibility to not engage in behaviors that result in imminent harm to self or others. Counseling older adults will inevitably require education and skill in working through ethical dilemmas in this domain.

Legal decision-making capacity is determined by the courts, drawing upon data from health professionals among others. Specific standards and strategies for assessing capacity are now available as a clinical standard (Grisso, 1994). A considerable challenge is posed by persons who demonstrate diminishing cognitive capacity but for whom no guardian has been appointed legally. State laws provide guidelines for how protective decisions can be made for such persons (including temporary guardianship). Mental health professionals working with older adults need more than a cursory understanding of the ethical and legal aspects of decision-making capacity, advanced directives, and surrogate decision making.

## Setting Confidentiality Boundaries

Finally, confidentiality issues can become quite tricky in psychotherapy with older clients. Family members often desire and need involvement in the therapy to ensure implementation of treatment strategies. Indeed, family caregiver involvement is key to many therapists (e.g., Teri et al., 1997). Furthermore, family members may seek consultation with a therapist to provide guidance about whether they should in fact be concerned about their loved one's mental health, and if so, how to proceed. The boundaries of confidentiality need to be carefully specified in the process of providing informed consent, and carefully followed in the provision of feedback on assessment or treatment. Key issues in specifying the limits of confidentiality are whether the older adult has a court-appointed guardian or is documented to be sufficiently incapacitated that a durable health power of attorney has been invoked. Either legal circumstance requires that evaluation of decision-making capacity has been made (Grisso, 1994).

## CONCLUSION

The demographic aging revolution currently happening worldwide has brought increasing attention to the need for more mental health professionals to address the needs of older adults (Halpain, Harris, McClure, & Jeste, 1999; Qualls, 1998; Qualls, Segal, Normans, Niederehe, & Gallagher-Thompson, 2002). While most counselors have the skill to work with difficult adjustments to the life events and challenges of later life, those who lack specialized training to work with older adults will struggle with some of the differential diagnostic issues that emerge in later life. A growing literature on epidemiology, assessment, and treatment offers significant guidance and standards for mental health services. An important unique aspect to work with older adults is that multiple disciplines are typically needed to address the highly complex interactions among the biological, psychological, and social spheres of well-being in later life. Thus the counselor to older adults must gain expertise in many systems of service delivery, interdisciplinary work, and systems level intervention as well as one-to-one interaction in order to provide the highest standard of services to older persons.

# Cases and Questions

1. John Jones is a 75-year-old man who has cared for his wife with Alzheimer's disease for the past 4 years. She has deteriorated rapidly in the past 6 months, and he now faces the necessity of placing her in a nursing home. Currently, she cannot manage her basic self-care routines without assistance (bathing, bathrooming, dressing). She gets days and nights confused and often keeps him awake at night wandering around the house. He is afraid she will fall because her balance is declining. Even with all of the problems, he has always managed. He cannot imagine living alone, seeing her in an institution, or even telling the children. His doctor has told him that he essentially has no choice, so he knows he has to deal with it, but maybe tomorrow.
   (a) What sources of stress are obvious in this case?
   (b) What sources are worth investigating but not obvious?
   (c) What coping strategies might be most useful to him as he takes the next steps in caring for his wife?
2. Suzann Norwood believes she has had a hard life during her 76 years. Her family was dirt poor when she grew up because her father was an alcoholic. She worked in a factory to support her three children after her husband left following the third birth. She retired at 65 and lives on a very modest pen-

sion in a small apartment in a questionable neighborhood. She spends much of her time watching television and crocheting. The children visit only occasionally. The youngest daughter often needs financial help, a situation that frustrates Suzann but she ends up helping her anyway. Her only living sister, who lives 300 miles away, seems to be doing great—always has some kind of activity happening. Recently, when Suzann's dog died, Suzann's apartment manager noticed that she wasn't getting dressed or leaving her apartment. The apartment manager encouraged her to seek some help from you.

(a) What signs of depression can you identify in this story of Suzann?
(b) What symptoms are not noted but warrant further inquiry?
(c) What approach would you advocate for treatment, and what steps in that approach do you believe would be key to its effectiveness for Suzann?

## REFERENCES

Antonucci, T. C., & Akiyama, H. (1995). Convoys of social relations: Family and friendships in a life span context. In R. Blieszner and V. Bedford (Eds.), *Handbook of aging and family* (pp. 355–371). San Diego, CA: Academic Press.

Baltes, P. B., & Baltes, M. M. (1990). Psychological perspectives on successful aging: The model of selective optimization with compensation. In P. B. Baltes & M. M. Baltes (Eds.), *Successful aging* (pp. 1–34). Cambridge: University of Cambridge Press.

Blazer, D. G. (1999). Depression. In W. R. Hazzard, J. P. Blass, W. H. Ettinger, Jr., D. B. Halter, & J. G. Ouslander (Eds.), *Principles of geriatric medicine and gerontology* (4th ed., pp. 1331–1339). New York: McGraw-Hill.

Carstensen, L. L., Isaacowitz, D. M., & Charles, S. T. (1999). Taking time seriously: A theory of socioemotional selectivity. *American Psychologist, 54,* 165–181.

Cuijpers, P. (1998). Psychological outreach programs for the depressed elderly: A meta-analysis of effects and dropout. *International Journal of Geriatric Psychiatry, 13,* 41–48.

Evans, D. A., Funkenstein, H. H., Albert, M. S., Scherr, P. A., Cook, N. R., Chown, M. J., Hebert, L. E., Hennekens, C. H., & Taylor, J. O. (1989). Prevalence of Alzheimer's disease in a community population of older persons: Higher than previously reported. *Journal of the American Medical Association, 262,* 2551–2556.

Gatz, M., Kasl-Godley, J. E., & Karel, M. J. (1996). Aging and mental disorders. In J. E. Birren & K. W. Schair (Eds.), *Handbook of the psychology of aging* (4th ed., pp. 365–382). San Diego, CA: Academic Press.

Gatz, M., & Smyer, M. A. (2001). Mental health and aging at the outset of the twenty-first century. In J. E. Birren & K. W. Schaie (Eds.), *Handbook of the psychology of aging* (5th ed., pp. 523–544). San Diego, CA: Academic Press.

Gerson, S., Belin, T. R., Kaufman, A., Mintz, J., & Jarvik, L. (1999). Pharmacological and psychological treatments for depressed older patients: A meta-analysis and overview of recent findings. *Harvard Review of Psychiatry, 7,* 1–28.

Gradman, T., Thompson, L., & Gallagher-Thompson, D. (1999). Personality disorders and treatment outcome. In E. Rosowsky, R. Abrams, & R. Zweig (Eds.), *Personality disorders in older adults: Emerging issues in diagnosis and treatment* (pp. 69–94). Mahwah, NJ: Erlbaum.

Grisso, T. (1994). Clinical assessments for legal competence of older adults. In M. Storandt & G. Vandenbos (Eds.), *Neuropsychological assessment of dementia and depression in older adults: A clinical guide* (pp. 119–139). Washington, DC: American Psychological Association.

Halpain, M. C., Harris, M. J., McClure, F. S., & Jeste, D. V. (1999). Training in geriatric mental health: Needs and strategies. *Psychiatric Services, 50,* 1205–1208.

HHS Inspector General, U.S. Department of Health and Human Services. (1989). *Expenses incurred by Medicare beneficiaries of prescription drugs.* Washington, DC: U.S. Department of Health and Human Services.

Hinrichsen, G. A., & Dick-Siskin, L. P. (2000). General principles of therapy. In S. K. Whitbourne (Ed.), *Psychopathology in later adulthood* (pp. 323–353). New York: Wiley.

Knight, B. (1992). *Older adults in psychotherapy: Case histories.* Newbury Park, CA: Sage.

Knight, B. (1996). *Psychotherapy with older adults* (2nd ed.). Thousand Oaks, CA: Sage.

Lawton, M. P. (1982). Competence, environmental press, and the adaptation of older people. In M. P. Lawton, P. G. Windley, & T. O. Byerts (Eds.), *Aging and the environment: Theoretical approaches* (pp. 33–59). New York: Springer.

Lichtenberg, P. A., Smith, M., Frazer, D., Molinari, V., Rosowsky, E., Crose, R., Stillwell, N., Kramer, N., Hartman-Stein, P., Qualls, S., Salamon, M., Duffy, M., Parr, J., & Gallagher-Thompson, D. (1998). Standards for psychological services in long term care facilities. *Gerontologist, 38,* 122–127.

Masoro, E. J., & Austad, S. N. (2001). *Handbook of the biology of aging* (5th ed.). San Diego, CA: Academic Press.

Pruchno, R. A., Blow, F. C., & Smyer, M. A. (1984). Life events and interdependent lives: Implications for research and intervention. *Human Development, 27,* 31–41.

Qualls, S. H. (1995). Marital therapy with later life couples. *Journal of Geriatric Psychiatry, 28,* 139–163.

Qualls, S. H. (1998). Training in geropsychology: Preparing to meet the demand. *Professional Psychology: Research and Practice, 29,* 23–28.

Qualls, S. H. (1999). Family therapy with older adult clients. *In Session: Psychotherapy in Practice, 55,* 1–14.

Qualls, S. H. (2002). Defining mental health in later life. *Generations, 26,* 9–13.

Qualls, S. H., Segal, D. L., Normans, S., Niederehe, G. W., & Gallagher-Thompson, D. (2002). Psychologists in practice with older adults: Current patterns, sources of training, and need for continuing education. *Professional Psychology, 33,* 435–442.

Regier, D. A., Boyd, J. H., Burke, I. D., Rae, D. S., Myes, J. K., Kramer, M., Robins, L. N., George, L. K., Karno, M., & Locke, B. Z. (1988). One-month prevalence of mental disorders in the United States: Based on five epidemiologic catchment area sites. *Archives of General Psychiatry, 45,* 977–986.

Rook, K. S. (2000). The evolution of social relationships in later adulthood. In S. H. Qualls & N. Abeles (Eds.), *Psychology and the aging revolution* (pp. 173–191). Washington, DC: American Psychological Association.

Rosowsky, E., Abrams, R., & Zweig, R. (Eds.). (1999). *Personality disorders in older adults: Emerging issues in diagnosis and treatment.* Mahwah, NJ: Erlbaum.

Rowe, J. W., & Kahn, R. L. (1998). *Successful aging.* New York: Pantheon.

Ryff, C., & Keyes, C. L. (1996). The structure of psychological well-being revisited. *Journal of Personality and Social Psychology, 69,* 719–727.

Salthouse, T. A. (1996). The processing-speed theory of adult age difference in cognition. *Psychological Review, 103,* 403–428.

Schaie, K. W., & Willis, S. L. (1993). Age difference patterns of psychometric intelligence in adulthood: Generalizability within and across ability domains. *Psychology and Aging, 8,* 44–55.

Schulz, R. (Ed). (2000). *Handbook on dementia caregiving: Evidence-based interventions for family caregivers.* New York: Springer.

Scogin, F., Floyd, M., & Forde, J. (2000). Anxiety in older adults. In S. K. Whitbourne (Ed.), *Psychopathology in later adulthood* (pp. 117–140). New York: Wiley.

Segal, D. L., Coolidge, F. L., & Rosowsky, E. (2000). Personality disorders. In S. K. Whitbourne (Ed.), *Psychopathology in later adulthood* (pp. 89–115). New York: Wiley.

Segal, D. L., Van Hasselt, V. B., Hersen, M., & King, C. (1996). Treatment of substance abuse in older adults. In J. R. Cautela & W. Ishaq (Eds.), *Contemporary issues in behavior therapy: Improving the human condition* (pp. 69–85). New York: Plenum Press.

Shields, C. G., King, D. A., & Wynne, L. C. (1995). Interventions with later life families. In R. H. Mikesell, D. Lusterman, & S. H. McDaniel (Eds.), *Integrating family therapy: Handbook of family psychology and systems theory* (pp. 141–158), Washington, DC: American Psychological Association.

Stanley, M. A., & Beck, J. G. (1998). Anxiety disorders. In M. Hersen & V. B. Van Hasselt (Eds.), *Handbook of clinical geropsychology* (pp. 217–238). New York: Plenum Press.

Stanley, M. A., Beck, J. G., & Glassco, J. D. (1996). Treatment of generalized anxiety in older adults: A preliminary comparison of cognitive-behavioral and supportive approaches. *Behavior Therapy, 27,* 565–581.

Teri, L., Logsdon, R., Uomoto, J., & McCurry, S. M. (1997). Behavioral treatment of depression in dementia patients: A controlled clinical trial. *Journal of Gerontology, 52B,* P159–P166.

Thompson, L. W., Coon, D. W., Gallagher-Thompson, D., Sommer, B. R., & Koin, D. (2001). Comparison of desipramine and cognitive/behavioral therapy in the treatment of elderly outpatients with mild-to-moderate depression. *American Journal of Geriatric Psychiatry, 9,* 225–240.

Verwoerdt, A. (1981). *Clinical geropsychiatry* (2nd ed.). Baltimore: Williams & Wilkins.

Wells, K. B., Schoenbaum, M., Unützer, J., Lagomasino, I. T., & Rubenstein, L. V. (1999). Quality of care for primary care patients with depression in managed care. *Archives of Family Medicine, 8,* 529–536.

Yesavage, J. A., Brink, T. L., Rose, T. L., Lum, O., Huang, V., Adey, M., & Leirer, V. O. (1983). Development and validation of a geriatric depression screening scale: A preliminary report. *Journal of Psychiatric Research, 17,* 37–49.

Zarit, S. H., Orr, N. K., & Zarit, J. M. (1985). *The hidden victims of Alzheimer's disease: Families under stress.* New York: New York University Press.

CHAPTER 11 # Sexuality and Older Adults: What Counselors Need to Know

Audrey U. Kim, University
of California-Santa Cruz,
and Donald R. Atkinson, University
of California-Santa Barbara

By the year 2020, the older adult population (age 65 and over, also referred to as seniors in this chapter) in the United States is expected to grow to more than 54 million people, representing 1 out of every 6 Americans (U.S. Bureau of the Census, 2000). By 2050, the growth rate of older adults is expected to be double that of the general population as a result of longer life spans, better access to health care, and the increasing numbers of aging baby boomers (Hillman, 2000). Nonetheless, mental health practitioners and researchers have tended to ignore this population. In particular, there has been a paucity of research and writing to date in the professional counseling literature about older adults and sexuality. However, as this country's population ages and people live longer, it is important for counselors to become more knowledgeable about and responsive to the needs of seniors, including their sexual concerns.

In part, the topic of older adult sexuality has been overlooked because of the negative attitudes associated with both sexuality and older people in our society. Although idealized and exaggerated images of sexuality abound in the media and popular culture, sex remains a taboo topic in most families, schools, churches, and other socializing institutions. Moreover, the youth cult in Western society assumes that sex is appropriate only for the young, healthy, and physically attractive, and accordingly older persons are often treated as nonsexual beings (Kellett, 1993; Kennedy, Hague, & Zarankow, 1997; Willert & Semans, 2000). Practitioners may also experience negative countertransference about their own fears of aging or dying, or embarrassment about discussing sexual issues with older clients (Hillman, 2000). This chapter provides therapists with information about sexuality that is pertinent to older adults and suggests ways to address these issues with older clients.

## COMMON PERCEPTIONS OF AGING
## AND SEXUALITY

Before reviewing the facts about aging and sexuality, it is informative to examine some common perceptions regarding the intersection of these two human qualities. Historically, sexuality for men and women over age 65 has been considered to be an inappropriate, immoral, and foolish attempt to regain lost youth (Covey, 1989). Common myths about seniors are that they are not interested in sex (or considered to be abnormal if they do express such interest), not able to feel sexual, not sexually desirable, and not physically capable of sexual activity (McDougall, 1993).

Several authors have speculated about the origins of these negative attitudes about aging and sexuality. Hodson and Skeen (1994) suggested that, by ignoring the sexuality of older adults, younger people are trying to avoid the inevitability of their own aging. Adult children may also be reluctant to think of their parents as sexual beings because they are uncomfortable with the thought of their parents having sex (Rose & Soares, 1993). Along these lines, Kernberg (1991) posited that aversion to sexuality among older adults may be a defense against the child's Oedipal desires and represents the adult child's unconscious need to renounce any sexual activity even loosely connected with parental sexuality. Furthermore, cultural attitudes that revere reproductiveness and youth contribute to the expectation that seniors are, or should be, asexual (Deacon, Minichiello, & Plummer, 1995).

However, the reality is that sexuality is not just for the youthful nor is it exclusively about human reproduction. Although the importance of sexual behavior for reproductive purposes decreases with age, sexual expression and physical contact continue to satisfy important human needs for love, intimacy, pleasure, and individual expression throughout the life span. Moreover, a healthy sex life provides an important source of reinforcement and pleasure that helps to maintain an individual's psychological and physical well-being, thereby reducing physical and mental health problems (Trudel, Turgeon, & Piché, 2000). Kaplan (1990) has even suggested that since sexual capacity is among the last of the biological functions to deteriorate with age, sex may become more important for adults as they age. In addition, as the baby boomers age, it is anticipated that they will continue to expect sexual satisfaction, and, since they are more familiar with the therapy culture than previous generations, they are more likely to seek counseling for sexual problems (Kingsberg, 2000; Hillman, 2000). Thus, it is increasingly important for counselors to become more knowledgeable about this issue.

While recognizing that older adults continue to remain sexual throughout the life span, counselors also should be aware of the physiological and psychological changes that occur with age and be careful not to promote unrealistic expectations (Segraves & Segraves, 1995). Therapists who work with older adults may be overly optimistic about aging and sexuality, perhaps in an effort to appease their own fears of aging (Rose & Soares, 1993). However, overly optimistic attitudes or neglecting to educate seniors about the effects of aging on sexual functioning may promote unrealistic standards and gloss over important realities, which may lead to frustration and disappointment for older adults (Rose & Soares, 1993;

Willert & Semans, 2000). At the same time, counselors should recognize that, although sexual functioning is affected by age, these changes are not necessarily pathological (Metz & Miner, 1998). In short, although it is important for counselors to counteract the common misperceptions that desexualize seniors, they also should educate themselves and older adults about the realities of sexuality and the aging process.

## RESEARCH ON SEXUALITY AND AGING

Although the body of research on aging and sexuality has grown since the seminal work of Kinsey and his colleagues (Kinsey, Pomeroy, & Martin, 1948; Kinsey, Pomeroy, Martin, & Gebhard, 1953) and Masters and Johnson (1966), the methodological limitations inherent in many of these studies must be recognized so as not to misinterpret the data derived from them. For one, many studies have utilized cross-sectional rather than longitudinal designs. Many authors have noted that cross-sectional methodology confounds cohort and time of measurement effects and that the results of these studies cannot be interpreted independently of cohort experiences (Avina, O'Donohue, & Fisher, 2000). For example, Allgeier and Allgeier (1984) observed that previous studies reporting decreased sexual interest and activity with age are more attributable to generational differences than to the aging process. Along these lines, Kellett (2000) noted that longitudinal studies conducted at Duke University (George & Weiler, 1981; Pfeiffer, Verwoerdt, & Wang, 1968) found the decline in sexual activity among older adults to be significantly less than shown in previous cross-sectional studies.

Another limitation with the available research is the use of inconsistent and unclear definitions and categories; in particular, the definitions of sexual behavior used by researchers have lacked consistency. In addition, older adults have usually been lumped into one demographic category, even though this age group includes an extremely broad age range, and people of different generational cohorts. Pedersen (1998) noted that it is more useful when older adults are divided into subgroups in order to provide more meaningful data. He suggested the use of "young old (55–65)," "middle old (66–75)," and "old old (76 and above)." However, most research samples do not utilize these types of subgroupings, resulting in samples that are heterogeneous. At the same time, samples of seniors may also be limited by their lack of diversity. Older adults who agree to participate in research about sexuality may not be demographically representative of seniors as a whole and may be more willing to talk about this subject than those who have more conservative attitudes or have less active sex lives (Mulligan & Moss, 1991; Pedersen, 1998). It is also important to consider that most of the limited research on sexuality and aging has been conducted on heterosexual European Americans (Zeiss & Kasl-Godley, 2001). Accordingly, the results may have limited application to gay, lesbian, and bisexual seniors and to older adults from ethnic minority cultures, as well as those from diverse socioeconomic backgrounds.

In short, it is important to consider both the paucity and limitations of the research available on older adult sexuality as well as the need to interpret these results with extreme caution. In our review of the research, we found that many of the same older studies (e.g., Kinsey et al., 1948, 1953; Pfeiffer et al., 1968) continued to be cited and analyzed by recent authors, because there has been relatively little new research on this subject. However, attitudes toward sex and sexual behavior have changed dramatically since the 1960s, coincidental with improved contraception methods and more liberal abortion legislation (Pedersen, 1998). Also, some of these original studies are being reexamined and their results reinterpreted. For example, Kellett (2000) pointed to the small numbers of older participants included in early studies of sexuality, including those of Kinsey and his colleagues (1948, 1953). Although the Kinsey researchers interviewed 2,800 men and 1,800 women aged 16–20, they only interviewed 26 men and 10 women over the age of 70. Thus, Kinsey's notable conclusion that 75% of men aged 80 and older were impotent was based on a sample size of only four men! Finally, it is important to consider that research is embedded in conceptual frameworks about sexuality that are biased by the preconceived ideas of younger researchers, who are themselves influenced by cultural standards that are largely insensitive to the older person's sexual needs (Deacon et al., 1995).

## SEXUAL BEHAVIOR

In contrast to common perceptions, research indicates that seniors continue to maintain an interest in sex and engage in sexual activities throughout life (e.g., Kennedy et al., 1997; Mulligan & Palguta, 1991). Kinsey and his colleagues (1948) found that men over the age of 60 continued to engage in intercourse with no sudden decline in sexual activity related to aging. Similarly, women over the age of 60 continued to engage in patterns of sexual behavior like that in their late teenage years (Kinsey et al., 1953). In a longitudinal study of older husbands and wives, George and Weiler (1981) found that the frequency of sexual activity remained constant among participants over the 6-year study period. More recent studies have also concluded that older men and women continue to enjoy satisfying sexual relations in later life (Janus & Janus, 1993; Matthias, Lubben, Atchison, & Schweitzer, 1997). In her review of the research on aging and sexuality, Hillman (2000) concluded that an abundance of data contradicts the common stereotypes of older adults as asexual. A number of studies have found that declines in sexual activity are related to factors other than age, such as cohort effects, availability of a partner, or physical health (Johnson, 1996; Matthias et al., 1997; Trudel et al., 2000).

### Decrease in Sexual Activity

At the same time, some researchers have noted a decline in sexual activity with age (Kinsey et al., 1948, 1953; Marsiglio & Donnelly, 1991; Roughan, Kaiser, & Morley, 1993), although it is difficult to distinguish whether such changes are related specifically to aging or to other factors, such as past sexual activity, availability of a partner, and physical health (Hillman, 2000). A few researchers have found a decrease in sexual activity even when accounting for health and availability of a partner (Call et al., 1995; Marsiglio & Donnelly, 1991). Thus, conflicting data exist about the effects of aging on sexual activity.

It is also important to consider how the results of this type of research might be skewed by the limited and conflicting definitions of sexual activity. Researchers have typically used frequency of sexual intercourse as the benchmark measure. However, when Adams (1980) expanded the definition of sexual activities beyond just heterosexual intercourse, the results actually indicated an increase in sexual functioning among seniors. Sexuality needs to be understood in a context that is broader and more inclusive than heterosexual intercourse. Older adults may engage in sexual intercourse less frequently than they did in their younger years or in comparison to younger cohorts. However, this does not necessarily mean that they have become less sexual or that their level of sexual satisfaction has diminished.

Nonetheless, mental health professionals should also be knowledgeable about the factors that might contribute to a decline in sexual activity among older adults. Lack of a partner or the illness of a spouse are commonly cited reasons (Matthias et al., 1997; Mulligan & Palguta, 1991; Pfeiffer et al., 1968). Along these lines, research indicates that the male partner's attitudes or physical condition is often responsible for the cessation of sexual activity among older women (Kaiser, 1991). Negative stereotypes and internalized societal proscriptions may also be related to the decline in sexual activity for some seniors (Roughan et al., 1993). Conversely, positive attitudes toward sexuality have been linked to the maintenance of sexual activity in later life (Persson, 1990). Practitioners should note that past history, rather than the aging process, seems to be most predictive of sexual interest and behavior for individuals in later life (George & Weiler, 1981; Persson, 1990). Although sex may not be important to some older people, for those who have been sexually active in their youth, sex is likely continue to play an important role as they age (Hodson & Skeen, 1994).

## Satisfaction With Sexual Activity

More important, research indicates that, although the frequency of sexual behavior may decrease with age, older people manage to maintain satisfying sexual lives. Crose and Drake (1993) concluded that even though the incidence of sexual activity declined for older women, their overall satisfaction with sex remained the same or even increased with age. Schiavi, Mandelli, and Schreiner-Engel (1994) also found no age differences in terms of sexual enjoyment and satisfaction among older men, even though they showed a decline in sexual desire, arousal, and activity. The results of the study conducted by Matthias and colleagues (1997) were particularly interesting. These researchers surveyed 1,126 older adults and found that almost 30% had participated in some sexual activity in the past month; however, an even greater number (67%) were satisfied with their current level of sexual activity. These results suggest that current sexual involvement may not necessarily be related to satisfaction with one's level of sexual activity. Such views run counter to the pervasive messages in our highly sexualized and youth-oriented society that suggest sexual satisfaction is a function of frequency of sexual intercourse.

In summary, a review of the literature indicates that there may be some decrease in interest and decline in frequency of sexual behavior with age, but that most older adults continue to remain sexually interested, active, and satisfied. In addition, we must broaden the way in which sexuality is defined and understand that quality and satisfaction with one's sexual life may be more significant than the frequency of specific sexual behaviors. Moreover, sexual activity needs to be understood as encompassing more than just heterosexual intercourse. Finally, we must recognize that older adults are a diverse group and that it would be misleading to generalize the results of the limited research to date to all seniors.

## PHYSIOLOGICAL FACTORS

Notwithstanding the studies that point to the decline in sexual activity among older adults, there is no physiological reason why a healthy man or woman cannot continue to engage in and enjoy sexual activity throughout the entire life span. Although an older adult may have some degree of physical impairment that may affect sexual activity, the impact of physical limitations is typically exacerbated by a variety of cultural, intrapsychic, and relationship stressors, which often transform minor limitations into full-fledged sexual disability (Kaplan, 1990). For example, an older couple's lack of knowledge about normal, age-related physiological changes in their bodies can lead to frustration, anxiety, and even avoidance of sex (Willert & Semans, 2000). In short, although age may be accompanied by physiological changes that can impact sexual activity, the aging process itself does not abolish the need or capacity for sexual activity.

### Age-Related Changes in Men

However, physiological changes do take place for both men and women that can affect sexual functioning. Counselors must be aware of, and also educate, older clients about these developments. It is still unclear whether and how older men are affected by hormonal changes (Morley, 1996). Specifically, it is unclear whether or not differences exist in the levels of testosterone and androgen, and how these changes might affect sexual interest and capacities for erection (Segraves & Segraves, 1995). Regardless of the specific causes, a number of age-related changes have been observed in older men, including decreased sexual desire, increased time needed to achieve erection, decreased penile sensitivity, more time required for orgasm and ejaculation, and less semen expelled at orgasm (Avina et al., 2000; Metz & Miner, 1998). In addition to needing more time than they did in their youth, older men may require physical stimulation to produce an erection. These changes may not only be alarming to the older male client but also to his partner, who may be questioning his or her own sexual attractiveness and performance. It is important for therapists to educate clients and their partners about these changes and to normalize these developments.

On a positive note, many older men find that once an erection is achieved, it can be maintained for an extended period of time without ejaculation. In addition, the older male may not always experience a demand for orgasm and ejaculation during intercourse. Although older men may have erections that are less firm, and ejaculate with less force than when they were younger, for most healthy men, the pressure within the penis remains sufficient for vaginal or anal penetration. As men age, the orgasm is of shorter duration and the refractory period (time between ejaculation and next erection) increases substantially; at age 17, the refractory period may be as brief as a few minutes but at age 70, it can be as long as 48 hours (Kaplan, 1990). Although these physiological changes do not necessarily impact the subjective enjoyment of the sexual experience, it is important for counselors to educate seniors about them, since this slowing of the sexual response cycle can lead to performance anxiety for older men (Bretschneider & McCoy, 1988).

## Age-Related Changes in Women

For women, the onset of menopause brings on significant changes in the body that can, in turn, affect sexual functioning. After menopause, women experience a decline in the circulating levels of estrogen and progesterone. As a result, the rate and amount of vaginal lubrication are decreased, and a general atrophying of vaginal tissue occurs, making the vagina more sensitive. There is some controversy as to the importance of these hormonal changes on a woman's sexuality. For example, menopause has been connected to changes in sexual desire for some women (Gelfand, 2000). However, Pedersen (1998) noted that although a minority of women do report a decline in sexual activity after menopause, the majority do not, which suggests that changes in hormonal levels are not the only factor related to sexual interest and activity after menopause. Along these lines, Cole and Rothblum (1990) observed that women with serious menopausal problems are overrepresented in the research literature, which may distort the negative impacts of menopause. Many women do seem to experience some slowing of the sexual response cycle, requiring more time to become sexually aroused and for the vagina to become lubricated. However, once a woman is adequately aroused and lubricated, she can experience the same kind of sexual pleasure and satisfaction as prior to menopause. It is important to provide information about these kinds of physical changes in order to prevent misunderstandings. For example, a woman might interpret these physiological changes inaccurately as a sign that she is no longer feminine or that she is no longer interested in her partner. Similarly, because the woman takes longer to arouse, her partner may feel sexually inadequate and unattractive (Hillman, 2000).

Therapists should also be aware that as women age, they experience other physiological changes, such as a reduction in the size of the cervix and uterus. In addition, some older women may become more sensitive to touch, so that breast, nipple, and clitoral stimulation may feel irritating instead of arousing (Galindo & Kaiser, 1995). Older women may also be prone to dyspareunia (discomfort during intercourse due to thinning of the vaginal walls) and vaginismus (difficult or uncomfortable sexual intercourse due to involuntary vaginal contractions) as a result of decreased vaginal lubrication (Croft, 1982; Gelfand, 2000). Another common sexual problem experienced by older women is female orgasmic disorder, which describes a woman who can become sexually aroused but is unable to achieve orgasm (Croft, 1982). Unfortunately, there is sparse literature that addresses how clinicians can help older women with these types of dysfunctions (Willert & Semans, 2000). However, counselors can begin by acknowledging and normalizing such difficulties. Kegel exercises, which consist of contracting and relaxing the pubococcygeal muscles, may be suggested to help restore tone to vaginal muscles and tissue. Therapists also can inform older women about the availability of topical lubricants (e.g., Astroglide, KY Jelly) to counteract vaginal dryness.

## Impotence

For men, the most commonly cited cause of sexual dysfunction and dissatisfaction is impotence (National Institutes of Health, 1993). Impotence is characterized by the inability to achieve an erection or one that is firm enough for masturbation or penetration. The causes of impotence are usually multifactorial and may include a combination of medical and psychological factors (e.g., vascular disease, diabetes, substance dependence, neurological disorders). Although sexual intercourse may not be an important form of sexual expression for some older adults, it would be presumptuous for counselors to assume that intercourse is not important for the older male client.

Since broaching the topic of impotence can be embarrassing for some clients, counselors may have to initiate this type of discussion and help the client explore the psychological issues that may contribute to this disorder. For example, individual psychotherapy and support groups may help men with widower's syndrome, a temporary impotence related to unresolved feelings of guilt, grief, and loss that some men experience after the death of their spouse (Hillman, 2000). In addition, mental health professionals can encourage clients to talk to their physicians about impotence in order to address any underlying medical causes.

In recent years, treatments for impotence have garnered much media attention, specifically with the introduction of the drug Viagra. Viagra is a physician-prescribed oral treatment taken 1 hour before sexual intercourse, which has been shown to be effective for 60–80% of people suffering from erectile dysfunction (Dunea, 1998). Although Viagra has been touted as a new miracle drug, it is important to acknowledge the medical risks and side effects. Moreover, Viagra is not a cure-all; it should be administered with caution and preferably as an adjunct to sex therapy or couples therapy (Willert & Semans, 2000). It is also important to consider that for heterosexual couples who have settled into a relationship that does not include sexual intercourse, the use of Viagra and resumption of sexual intercourse may require some adjustment for both partners. Specifically, for the older female partner, whose aging vagina has narrowed and atrophied, it may be difficult to resume sexual intercourse suddenly without some pain or risk of injury. In these cases, the woman may want to prepare by slowly stretching and exercising her vagina (e.g., with a finger or dilator) to accommodate the penis (Kingsberg, 2000). Practitioners should also be aware that other treatments for impotence include vacuum devices, penile implants, and vasoactive drugs (Galindo & Kaiser, 1995).

## Effects of Illness

When considering the effects of aging on sexuality, it is crucial not to confuse the aging process with the illnesses that often accompany old age. Although the incidence of sexual dysfunction rises with age, age is also associated with a general increase in medical problems and the use of medications. Physical health has been related to sexual activity; for example, older adults who suffer from arthritis, high blood pressure, heart disease, stroke, diabetes, and kidney problems were found to be less sexually active than seniors who suffered from fewer of these chronic ailments (Matthias et al., 1997). Accordingly, it is often difficult to determine whether sexual problems are attributable to increased age, to specific diseases, or to medications used to treat the diseases (Spence, 1992). Although counselors are not medical professionals, those working with older adults should be familiar with common medical problems that can interfere with clients' sexual functioning. Studies indicate that the majority of patients fail to receive any information about sexuality in relation to their acute or chronic illness (Walker, Osgood, Richardson, & Ephross, 1998). Mental health professionals can help to educate clients as well as make referrals to physicians and other professionals as necessary.

Arthritis is a common ailment among the older population; up to 48% of older adults suffer from arthritis (Dorgan, 1995). Arthritis can cause difficulties in flexion of the hips, knees, and back, resulting in restriction of movement as well as pain. Even though sexual intercourse may be more painful than enjoyable for some seniors with arthritis, they may feel guilty about not continuing to engage in sexual activity. In such instances, it may be helpful for counselors to give permission to their clients to refrain from sexual activity or to make necessary adjustments. For example, heterosexual seniors with severe arthritis may find it more comfortable to have intercourse from the vaginal rear entry position rather than the traditional missionary position. Other adjustments may reduce the arthritic pain and enhance sexual adjustment. Warm baths may help to loosen muscles, and, since pain and stiffness are generally more pronounced during the evenings and nighttime, couples may prefer to have sex in the mornings after a period of rest. Using analgesics and experimenting with positioning pillows to support the body can also be helpful for arthritis sufferers (Hillman, 2000).

A common misperception is that patients should abstain from sexual intercourse after cardiac arrest or a stroke. Yet research indicates that a patient's psychological response, rather than the severity of the heart attack, is a better predictor of sexuality disability (Thompson, 1990). The misguided fear that sex will lead to another, possibly fatal incident, may inhibit the patient and his or her partner from engaging in sex. However, the anxiety and tension related to the restriction of sex pose greater risks than the physical risks associated with intercourse (Butler &

Lewis, 1988). Many people erroneously interpret the breathlessness of orgasm as evidence of a strain on the heart or lungs, when, in fact, the orgasm causes the over-breathing (Kellett, 2000). The danger of a coronary attack is slight, and resumption of intimacy may even reduce the risk of a recurrence (Kellett, 2000).

Similar to the misunderstandings about the effects of a coronary attack on a patient's sexuality, a common belief is that stroke sufferers are not interested in sex. Although strokes, which are brain injuries caused by a decrease in blood flow to parts of the brain, can result in some loss of sexual interest, this change is usu-ally slight and short-lived (Kellett, 1991). However, disabilities resulting from the stroke may affect sexual expression, such as hugging, embracing, fondling, and intercourse, as well as verbal communication (Deacon et al., 1995). Fortunately, no association has been found between sexual activity and recurrence of subse-quent strokes (Badeau, 1995).

Diabetes is another common illness among older adults, one that affects nearly 1 in 10 older men and women (Dorgan, 1995). It is also recognized as the primary organic cause of impotence and can be related to ejaculatory problems for men (Deacon et al., 1995). The effect of diabetes on female sexuality has largely been ignored; moreover, the myth exists that diabetes has little impact on women (Badeau, 1995). However, diabetes can result in lack of blood flow to the clitoris and vagina during sexual arousal, and atrophying of the uterine and ovar-ian tissue may occur. In addition, some women may experience some decrease in the frequency of orgasms and may need additional manual stimulation to reach orgasm (Hillman, 2000).

Alzheimer's and other forms of dementia associated with advanced age have been found to alter the sexual behavior of older adults; these diseases can also take a toll on the patient's spouse or caregiver. Patients with dementia experience cog-nitive deficits, including decreased impulse control, and may behave in sexually inappropriate ways (Duffy, 1995; Spence, 1992). Changes in libido also have been noted, with some patients showing an increased, and others a decreased, interest in sex (Duffy, 1995; Kellett, 1993). Partners may become confused, frightened, or anxious about such changes. Sexual functioning for the caretaking partner also may be affected, partly because of difficulties redefining the role as both caregiver and lover (Ballard, 1995). For example, the caregiver can start to feel like a parent and may feel ambivalent about engaging in sexual relations with a partner who represents a childlike figure (Duffy, 1995). Being a caregiver may also breed feel-ings of anger or resentment, or the caregiver may just be too tired to even consider sexual contact (Hillman, 2000). Counselors can help both the dementia patient and the partner by educating them about the illness and its impact on the relationship, and by allowing them to articulate and process their feelings.

Many older persons also undergo surgery that can affect both their feelings and behaviors related to sexuality. For example, some surgeries (e.g., prostate sur-gery) can damage parasympathetic nerves and inhibit physiological arousal (Kel-lett, 1991). A prostatectomy can also affect the amount of ejaculate or ejaculatory sensation (Kellett, 2000). For women, surgeries for hysterectomy or mastectomy can impact how they feel about their sexuality, even if there are no direct physio-logical consequences (Gelfand, 2000). In general, any operation that disfigures the body can affect body image and attitudes toward intimacy (Kellett, 2000). Most amputees are seniors; more than 85% of amputations are performed on patients over the age of 60 (Schultz, Williamson, & Bridges, 1991). Yet physicians rarely initiate a discussion with patients about how amputation will affect their sexuality (Williamson & Waters, 1996). When a surgery patient returns home with scars, stitches, and new medications, he or she may be unclear about the appropriateness of sexual activity, and these doubts may be reinforced if they are not addressed by a clinician. Thus, it may be important for mental health professionals to initiate these kinds of discussions and to help clients express their feelings and concerns about how surgery might affect sexual feelings and behaviors (Kellett, 2000).

## Effects of Medications

In addition to being knowledgeable about the natural physiological changes that occur with aging, therapists working with older clients should also be aware of the effects that medications can have on sexual functioning, since older adults are the largest consumers of prescription and nonprescription drugs (Montamat, Cusack, & Vestal, 1989). Moreover, many prescription and over-the-counter medications have been associated with a decrease in sexual desire and function (Galindo & Kaiser, 1995). Specifically, studies indicate that antihypertensives, diuretics, and antidepressants may cause male erectile dysfunction (Avina et al., 2000; Segraves & Segraves, 1993). For women, antidepressants, antihypertensives, and antipsychotics have been linked to disruptions in the female sexual response cycle, including decreased libido, less vaginal lubrication, and inability to achieve orgasm (Gelfand, 2000). Therapists should advise their clients to consult with a physician if they are experiencing sexual discomfort or problems while using a medication. However, both counselors and their clients should be aware that the most common cause of sexual failure for older adults is also the most popular aphrodisiac—alcohol (Kellett, 2000).

## Health Benefits of Sexual Activity

On a positive note, research indicates that sexual activity may actually provide psychological and physiological benefits that counteract the effects of aging (Trudel et al., 2000). Some research suggests that sex helps to stimulate natural production of endorphins and corticosteroids that serve as natural pain relievers and can remain in effect for hours after sexual activity has ended (Badeau, 1995). Regular coitus also appears to reduce the physiological effects of menopause and preserve vaginal functioning (Kellett, 2000). Sexual activity may also help to relax the musculoskeletal system and reduce pain (Butler, Lewis, Hoffman, & Whitehead, 1994).

## PSYCHOLOGICAL ISSUES

It is important to consider psychological as well as physiological factors as they relate to the sexual functioning of older adults. For example, relationship concerns, depression, anxiety, identity, and self-esteem issues may manifest in the older person as sexual difficulties. In particular, because depression is one of the more common ailments among older people, it is important for clinicians to rule out the possibility of depression or the effects of antidepressants as contributors to sexual dysfunction (Hillman, 2000). Research also indicates that there is a significant relationship between knowledge about sexual issues, positive attitudes about sexuality, and sexual behavior in later years (Hillman & Stricker, 1994). Thus, psychological and attitudinal factors are just as important, if not more important, than physiological ones, in explaining sexual behavior among seniors. It is critical for counselors to educate older adults about sexual issues, although changing such beliefs, which are often linked with values, morals, and religious beliefs developed over a lifetime, may not be an easy task (Steinke, 1988). Otherwise, seniors may internalize the ageist stereotypes that prevail in our society, leading them to believe that they should not feel sexual or act in a sexual manner (Deacon et al., 1995).

## Relationship Issues

The landmark studies by Kinsey and his colleagues (1948) and by Masters and Johnson (1966) found that decline in sexual activity was attributable more to psychological factors such as fatigue, unsatisfying relationships, boredom, career worries, and performance anxiety than to age-related physiological changes. In addition, relationship issues may be exacerbated in old age and manifest as sexual difficulties (Deacon et al., 1995; Kaplan, 1990). Older couples can be at various stages of a relationship; some have just begun dating while others have been together for many years. A couple may be facing the stresses of a blended family or negotiating conflicts with adult children. Some couples who have been together for a long time may feel bored in their relationship, whereas others may find that their long history together has created the foundation for a more loving partnership. In short, counselors need to explore how relationship issues may be impacting sexual functioning for the older client—just as they do for younger clients—rather than assuming that sexual problems for older people are physiologically and age based.

## Self-Esteem and Appearance Issues

Issues related to performance and self-esteem may also be salient for older adults and, in turn, affect sexual functioning. In particular, older adults moving through retirement may be faced with a transitional period of redefining their identity, which may result in feelings of anxiety and insecurity (Deacon et al., 1995). As men age, many become increasingly vulnerable to the psychological effects of performance anxiety; this anxiety is heightened for those who already feel insecure about their sexuality (Kaplan, 1990). For example, an older man's feelings of insecurity related to his retirement might feed his anxieties about his sexual performance, impeding him from achieving an erection. Willert and Semans (2000) noted that it is not uncommon for couples with some sexual difficulty to feel anxious and begin to avoid sex altogether, which they may then generalize to avoidance of all physical affection. Practitioners can help couples to recognize this type of pattern and to communicate their needs and feelings to each other in order to break this kind of cycle.

Notwithstanding the lack of clear scientific evidence about the negative effects of menopause on women's sexual functioning, and the fact that a healthy woman can continue to engage in and enjoy sexual activities throughout her life span, menopause and the aging process can influence how older women feel about themselves and their own sexuality. For some women, the onset of menopause may have cultural, social, or religious meanings. For example, sexual intercourse without the possibility of pregnancy can have prohibitive meanings for some women. At the same time, some women may feel freer to explore and enjoy their sexuality without the fear of pregnancy (Hillman, 2000).

Menopause and the aging process also affect a woman's appearance; for example, many women tend to gain weight at the onset of menopause (Rodin, Silberstein, & Streigel-Moore, 1984). For women, who have generally been socialized to place a high value on their appearance, an aging body can also impact their feelings about their sexuality (Hillman, 2000). Women's sexuality has generally been associated with reproduction, marriage, or prostitution, which are dependent on beauty and youthfulness (Nay, 1992). Although older men are still considered to be sexually attractive in our society, mature women are not widely viewed as attractive or sexual. Thus, an older woman, whose body is no longer youthful or reproductive, may question her femininity and attractiveness to her partner. It is also important to recognize that men are not altogether exempt from concerns about their body image and appearance. As men age, they may experience hair loss as well as increased fatty tissue in their breasts, which can affect their feelings about their own masculinity and attractiveness (Hillman, 2000).

Counselors need to be sensitive to the fact that although the physiological changes related to aging may not have a direct effect on sexual functioning, how older men and women feel about the aging process can significantly influence their sense of self and feelings about their sexuality (Hillman, 2000). However, therapists and their older adult clients might also take note of the results of Starr and Weiner's (1981) study, which found that both men and women preferred sexual partners their own age.

## Attitudes About Sex

On a positive note, for some older adults, the sexual experience may actually improve with age. The majority of women in Crose and Drake's (1993) study noted that their attitudes toward sex had become more positive over time; they felt less pressured and were more aware of their own needs. Similarly, women in another study reported that they believed that sex had become better for them with age and that they associated sex in later life with pleasure and release of tension (Nay, 1992). For older men, the changes in erectile functioning enable them to gain ejaculatory control and maintain erection for longer periods compared with their youth. Thus, the older heterosexual male is better able to coordinate his pleasure cycle with his partner, and the increased time needed to achieve sexual arousal can help couples prolong the period of sensual enjoyment prior to orgasm (Whitbourne, 1990). Research also points to the emotional as well as the physical benefits of sex. For example, Brecher (1984) reported that those who enjoyed an active sex life and intimate relationships were more likely to note a higher level of life satisfaction. In contrast, repressing sexuality can lead to problems such as emotional distress (Starr & Weiner, 1981).

## IMPLICATIONS FOR PRACTICE

Sexual problems for older adults are often multifactorial and multidetermined, with a combination of physiological, psychological, and sociocultural factors. Seniors tend to present more commonly in a medical setting for sexual problems rather than to a psychotherapist (Hirst & Watson, 1996). Thus, it is crucial for mental health professionals to be able to work in an interdisciplinary way with professionals from disciplines such as geriatric medicine, social work, psychiatry, nursing, and occupational and physical therapy (Hillman, 2000). Counselors can serve as important advocates for their older clients, making referrals and encouraging seniors to obtain more information and follow-up with other clinicians as necessary. It is also useful for therapists to distinguish between educating older adults about the aging process and sexual functioning versus treating older clients for sexual dysfunctions; most older adults do not suffer from sexual dysfunction per se. The principles of sex therapy are the same for clients of any age but should be adjusted to suit the physical capacity of older clients (Kennedy et al., 1997). In particular, cognitive behavioral therapy and sensate focus are acknowledged to be effective treatments for sexual dysfunction, including impotence (Avina et al., 2000; Kellett, 2000).

   Many older adults today grew up in an era when sex was not openly discussed and accurate information about sex was not widely available. Yet practitioners might erroneously assume that older adults are sufficiently experienced and don't need to be educated about sexual matters (Kellett, 2000). Given the preponderance of myths and stereotypes about sexuality and aging and the discomfort that older adults may have in broaching this topic, it may be necessary for the counselor to initiate such a discussion and educate older clients about sexual issues. In fact, the counselor's mere acknowledgment of an older client's sexuality may be a relief to the client and open the door for a frank discussion of sexual issues (Rose & Soares, 1993).

### Information Gathering

The counselor can begin by gathering information about the client's sexual history and current behaviors. Older clients are often accompanied by family members to the initial interview. In such cases, it is usually preferable to talk alone with the client in order to maintain privacy and confidentiality about these sensitive issues (Hillman, 2000). Therapists should be aware that health problems and changes in memory and information processing may affect the clinical interview with older clients. It is important for the therapist to consider and assess the client's comfort level about discussing sexual issues; it may be helpful to first assess other relevant factors, such as the client's cultural and religious values, and their partner status. Since the older adult may be reticent about discussing such matters, it may be helpful for the therapist to acknowledge that these issues might be sensitive, and to ask the client's permission. For example, the interviewer might first ask "May I ask you some questions about your love and sex life?" in order to show respect for the client and to give that person control in a potentially anxiety-provoking situation. The therapist might also normalize the client's discomfort by stating "Some people find it difficult to discuss these issues at first" or ask "What is it like for me to ask you these questions about your sex life?" (Hillman, 2000). Using open-ended questions and questions that assume the presence of difficulties rather than making them the exception may also facilitate information gathering (Hillman, 2000). Galindo and Kaiser (1995) provided a useful list of questions that can be used in a clinical interview. Finally, when talking about sexual matters, counselors should try to use terminology consistent with the client's vocabulary; thus, it may be appropriate at first to use medical terminology but then to shift to the vernacular depending on the client's comfort level (Hillman, 2000).

## Education

Education and normalization are key to addressing issues of sexuality with older clients. Hillman and Stricker (1994) reviewed the literature regarding the link between knowledge and attitudes about aging and sexuality. Their review found a positive linear relationship between knowledge and attitudes about sexuality and aging in health care workers, children of older adults, and older adults themselves. Pedersen (1998) noted that it is important to educate older people to expect similar changes in their sexual functioning as in other areas (e.g., psychomotoric or cognitive development). Specifically, older adults can expect a reduction in frequency with age, a slowing down in reaction time or responsivity, diminished strength and endurance, and a need for stronger sensory stimuli to elicit reaction. Thus, seniors need to adjust their expectations and not expect the same kind of sexual response that they remember from their youth (Metz & Miner, 1998).

Lack of information or openness about sex can prevent couples from adapting to age or illness-related changes in sexual response (Kennedy et al., 1997). Mental health professionals can be instrumental, not only in providing facts and information, but also in encouraging and giving permission to older couples to make adaptations in their sexual practices (Kingsberg, 2000). For example, counselors might advise older couples to shift their lovemaking from lengthy intercourse toward experimentation with alternative forms of sexual gratification (Kaplan, 1990). Making sure that seniors have accurate information and are knowledgeable about sexual issues is also important; one instrument that has been used extensively to both assess and educate is the Aging Sexual Knowledge and Attitudes Scale (White, 1982). For example, a counselor might ask a couple to separately complete the 35-item knowledge subtest of this instrument and then have them score the answers together to facilitate discussion of a taboo topic. Education should also include instruction on anatomy and physiology of genital functioning; partners can even use each other as models (Kellett, 2000).

As part of the education process, counselors should also broaden the definition of sexuality to encompass all forms of intimacy, such as touching, caressing, and kissing, as well as masturbation and oral sex. Our society primarily equates sex with intercourse, and many older adults grew up in a time when being sexual meant having genital contact. However, this provides a very limited view of sexual expression. Although noncoital activities can provide an important source of sexual expression and even provide more comfortable ways of meeting intimacy needs for seniors, these expressions of sexuality are not as valued in our society as intercourse (Hodson & Skeen, 1994). Yet research suggests that as people age, their expressions of sexuality become more varied and less emphasis is placed on intercourse. For example, Starr and Weiner (1981) found in their survey of 800 respondents that older people defined and expressed sexuality in more diffuse and varied ways than did younger cohorts, indicating that modifications in sexual expression and preferred sexual activity may be prevalent with advanced age. Similarly, Bretschneider and McCoy (1988) found that the three most common forms of sexual activity among healthy, upper-middle-class residents in retirement facilities were (a) touching and caressing without sexual intercourse, (b) masturbation, and (c) intercourse.

Thus, many older adults appear to have developed a wider repertoire of sexual expression and find satisfaction with their sexuality through means other than intercourse (e.g., masturbation, massage, kissing) (Hillman, 2000). It is important for therapists to validate these expressions of sexuality and convey that an individual's sexuality is more global than just genital functioning. Counselors can do this by asking questions that reflect a broader conceptualization of sexuality and by helping clients to assess the nature and quality of their sex life, rather than measuring specific behaviors against a clinical benchmark (Hillman, 2000). Therapists also can encourage couples to express their sexuality in diverse ways, such as mutual masturbation or exploration of sexual fantasies and erotica with each other (Kaplan, 1990; Kellett, 1991).

Finally, when addressing sexual issues with older adults, it is crucial for counselors to educate them about AIDS and HIV. Along with the assumption that seniors do not engage in sexual behavior follows the supposition that older adults are not affected by AIDS. Yet, according to the Centers for Disease Control (1995), more than 11% of all new AIDS cases in the United States occur in people over the age of 50, and AIDS is now the 15th leading cause of death among those over age 65 (Kaye & Markus, 1997). Although most cases of infection have been associated with blood transfusions or intravenous drug use, older adults have also contracted the AIDS virus through unsafe sexual practices. In fact, because seniors are less likely to use condoms to prevent pregnancy, they may be more at risk to contract the AIDS virus (Hillman, 2000). It may be difficult for counselors to ask older clients about high-risk sexual behavior, but it is our professional responsibility not to overlook older adults in this respect by making age-biased assumptions.

# CONCERNS OF SPECIAL GROUPS

Differences in social context affect opportunities for and attitudes about the expression of sexuality. The following are specific groups within the older adult population that may require special attention by counselors.

## Single, Heterosexual, Older Adults

Another important point to keep in mind when working with seniors is that there are significantly more older women than men. According to the 2000 census data, the ratio of men to women steadily decreases beyond age 55: 92.2 for ages 55–64; 82.3 for ages 65–74; 65.2 for ages 75–84; and 40.7 for ages 85 and older (Smith & Spraggins, 2001). This has implications for heterosexual women's opportunities for relationships and sexual activity in later years. Women typically live to an older age than men and tend to marry older men; thus, many heterosexual women are left without partners in their later years (Kellett, 2000). At the same time, cultural attitudes make it more difficult for older women than men to find new sexual partners (Segraves & Segraves, 1995). Research indicates that lack of a suitable partner is one of the most common reasons for decline in sexual activity; due to current demographics, this problem is more pronounced for older women than for older men (Matthias et al., 1997; Trudel et al., 2000). Thus, counselors should be sensitive to how the increased competition for the few available single men might affect a single older woman's self-esteem or leave her feeling discouraged (Hillman, 2000). Moreover, most older women today were raised in a culture in which they were evaluated as dating prospects primarily on the basis of their looks, and they waited to be approached by men who were interested. The reality today for the single older woman is different; her appearance may not be her primary asset, and she may need to be assertive in approaching prospective male partners (Hillman, 2000).

Thus, counselors may want to suggest alternative ways in which single older men and women might meet their sexual needs, including sexual activities and expressions that do not require a partner. However, seniors may be averse to alternative expressions of sexuality, such as sexual fantasizing, masturbation, sex outside marriage, polygamy, or intimate relations with a person of the same sex, because of their historically and culturally influenced lifelong beliefs and values (Steinke, 1988). Yet, although older adults may hold negative feelings about masturbation because of its stigma when they were growing up, an increasing number seem to be using masturbation as a sexual outlet. For example, Hodson and Skeen (1994) found that 66% of men and 47% of women in their 50s, and 43% of men and 33% of women age 70 and over masturbate. Older heterosexual women, for whom the issue of partner availability is most pressing, may find that they can meet their intimacy needs through an attachment to or living arrangement with another older woman. Although these relationships are not sexual in the conventional sense, they can still provide an important source of support and emotional intimacy (Capuzzi & Friel, 1995).

Some authors have also speculated that, because of the lack of male partners, single heterosexual women may begin to adopt a gay or bisexual orientation in later life in order to meet their intimacy and sexual needs (McDougall, 1993). Although many anecdotes of such cases seem to exist, little empirical research indicates that this phenomenon is real. It is more likely that when they were younger, these women were not able to openly express their lesbian or bisexual identity because of societal prohibitions. However, as these women have aged, and in today's somewhat more tolerant society, they have found it easier to express their underlying sexual identity (Hillman, 2000). Hodson and Skeen (1994) also hypothesized that, in some cases, the death of the heterosexual partner may allow the surviving partner to acknowledge his or her own homosexuality.

## Older Sexual Minorities

In working with older adults, counselors need to be particularly sensitive to the needs of older lesbian, gay, bisexual, and transgendered individuals (please note that the terms *queer* and *LGBT* are also used as general terms for this population). The first step for most counselors is to address and overcome their own biases about LGBT people. It is important to consider that the literature on sexual function and dysfunction has largely been approached from a heterosexual and masculine perspective focusing on sexual intercourse (Deacon et al., 1995). Also, the research to date on queer issues has neglected older populations, and studies of older ethnic minority LGBT people are virtually nonexistent (Jacobson & Grossman, 1996). Although in recent years there has been growing interest in studying the sexuality of older gay men and lesbians (e.g., Dorfman et al., 1995; Slusher, Mayer, & Dunkle, 1996), the needs of bisexual and transgendered seniors has not really begun to be addressed. Moreover, the research that has been conducted with gay and lesbian older adults has generally sampled from financially secure, well-educated and urban populations. Thus, it is hard to generalize the results of these studies to people from lower socioeconomic status or rural backgrounds, or to bisexual and transgendered people (Hillman, 2000). Finally, counselors should keep in mind that older clients who are queer may have values and beliefs that are very different from their younger counterparts, since they grew up before the sexual revolution and gay liberation (McDougall, 1993).

Just as there are myths about aging and sexuality, there are inaccurate perceptions about older sexual minorities. Although common notions are that older gay and lesbian people are lonely and depressed, these myths have not been supported by empirical research (Dorfman et al., 1995; Slusher et al., 1996). In fact, the research indicates that older gay men and lesbians are moderately involved in gay culture, are moderately to highly interested in sexual relations, and highly satisfied with their current sexual relations (Hillman, 2000). Generally, older LGBT people seem to face many of the same challenges as older heterosexuals.

At the same time, queer older adults are somewhat different from their heterosexual peers. Queer seniors have had to develop a variety of coping mechanisms to survive in a world that is generally hostile and oppressive toward sexual minorities, and they are more likely to rely on friends rather than family members for social support (Dorfman et al., 1995; Jacobson & Grossman, 1996). Some authors have hypothesized that the aging process may compound the feelings of stigmatization already present for sexual minorities (Hillman, 2000). Other authors have suggested that the adjustment to old age and facing ageism may actually be easier for sexual minorities who have had to combat homophobia all their lives (Berger, 1982). Heterosexual seniors, by comparison, may be less prepared to deal with society's ageist biases. Interestingly enough, our society also seems to be less suspicious and more accepting of older same-sex couples; for example, it is more acceptable for two older persons of the same sex to live together or to walk arm in arm than it is for younger people (McDougall, 1993). The literature, in fact, suggests that adjustment to aging varies according to the individual and is dependent on the person's satisfaction with being gay and the pattern of early gay developmental events (Aldeman, 1991). Thus, for an older person who is still struggling with sexual orientation issues, such difficulties may indeed be exacerbated with old age.

## Older Adults in Institutions

Older adults living in nursing homes and other institutions constitute another population that requires special attention from counselors. Unfortunately, little research has been conducted to date on the sexual needs and concerns of this population (Walker & Ephross, 1999). One study did find that residents believed that little sexual activity was taking place in the nursing home, but that they also continued to be interested in sexual expression (Walker & Ephross, 1999). Sexual behaviors of nursing home residents are most likely affected by the attitudes of staff and provisions made by these facilities. Although health care providers seem to hold relatively permissive views about aging sexuality (e.g., Glass & Webb, 1995), nursing home staff are likely to harbor the same kinds of biases evidenced in the larger society. When confronted with specific sexual situations and behaviors, some staff members express discomfort and respond negatively. For example, in Wallace's (1992) study, nursing home staff reported that incidents of sexuality among older residents were more common than uncommon in their workday and that they found these to be among the most disturbing "problem behaviors" they encountered. In particular, staff, as well as residents, found it difficult to deal with masturbation (Walker & Ephross, 1999). In these settings, normal expressions of sexuality are often regarded as age-related behavioral problems or the result of senility; a resident who behaves in a sexual manner may even be reprimanded (Hodson & Skeen, 1994).

Counselors who work in nursing homes can educate both staff and residents that expressions of sexuality by older residents are healthy and normal. Walker and Ephross (1999) proposed a curriculum for staff based on (a) providing factual information, (b) fostering positive and tolerant attitudes, and (c) engaging in appropriate practices and responses. Research also suggests that residents themselves harbor negative attitudes about sexuality and older adulthood (Adams, Rojas-Camero, & Clayton, 1990), indicating that they may also benefit from education about this topic. Since lack of privacy can be a deterrent to sexual intimacy, counselors can encourage nursing homes to provide privacy rooms if residents do not have individual private rooms. However, practitioners should also note that some sexual behaviors are actually inappropriate in these settings (Hodson & Skeen, 1994). For example, the impact of dementias or personality disorders can lead to lowered impulse control and manifest as inappropriate sexual behaviors. It may not always be clear if an older adult who is suffering from illness or cognitive deficits is competent to make clear, rational decisions for him- or herself. Thus, although staff need to be accepting and encouraging of sexual expression among residents, they also need to assess whether these activities are consensual (Hillman, 2000).

## Ethnic Minority Older Adults

If little attention has been focused on the sexuality of older adults in general, there is truly a dearth of literature about the sexuality of seniors from diverse cultures. In part, this may have to do with difficulties recruiting participants for such studies (Hillman, 2000). The research on aging and sexuality has focused almost exclusively on European American samples, whereas research on the sexuality of ethnic minorities has concentrated on teenagers. Yet to fully understand the sexuality of older adults, counselors must consider factors such as race, ethnicity, and culture, since sexual attitudes are sociocultural products. Moreover, the variability found in people's sexual behavior can often be attributed to cultural differences (Abramson & Imai-Marquez, 1982). Along these lines, in their review of the research on women, ethnicity, and sex, Rushton and Bogaert (1987) noted a number of differences in sexual behaviors and attitudes based on race and ethnicity, especially in terms of sexual restraint and precocity.

In one of the few cross-cultural studies of older adult sexuality, Winn and Newton (1982) analyzed data from 106 cultures gathered by anthropologists, sociologists, and psychologists. These researchers found that in most of these traditional cultures, sexual activity among older men and women is accepted and commonplace. Specifically, 70% of these cultures reported sexual activity among their older men, and more than 84% reported sexual activity among their older women. In the majority of these societies, menopause was not associated with a decrease in sexual activity for women but rather seen as another "point in a woman's life." In many Eastern and Middle Eastern cultures, men were found to engage in sexual relations well beyond the age of 80. Obviously, it is hard to generalize the findings of one international study conducted 20 years ago to older ethnic minorities in the United States today. However, these results do point to the influence of culture on the sexual attitudes and behaviors of older adults. Since there is no directly relevant research on the sexuality of American ethnic minorities, some of the research on older ethnic minorities and general studies of ethnic minority sexuality are discussed next.

Older ethnic minority populations are growing at a faster rate than are non-Hispanic Whites. Between 2000 and 2050, the non-Hispanic White population age 65 and older will not quite double in number, whereas for Blacks it will increase threefold, Asian Americans over sixfold, and Hispanics over sevenfold (U.S. Bureau of the Census, 1996). Although ethnic minority seniors comprise a diverse group, including African American, Asian American, Hispanic, and Native American peoples, they also seem to share some common characteristics. For one, many ethnic minority older adults live on Social Security, perhaps because of poor-paying jobs in their youth. There is also variation by ethnic group in terms of common health problems, and ethnic minorities have more limited access to professional health care, relying more on family caregivers. Thus, compared with European American older adults, ethnic minority seniors may experience higher levels of stress and psychological distress, which would also impact their sexual functioning. Ethnic minority older adults also tend to live with family members for financial and cultural reasons (Primas & Harper, 1991). Such living arrangements could also impact their freedom to engage in sexual activities. Although this cursory overview of ethnic minority seniors is insufficient to even begin to understand this diverse group, it does suggest how characteristics specific to ethnic minority seniors (e.g., lack of financial resources, dependence on family members) might affect sexual behaviors.

General studies of ethnic minority sexuality might also help to inform our understanding of sexual issues for older ethnic minority adults. For example, in their analysis of Japanese Americans, Hirayama and Hirayama (1986) noted that compared with non-Asians, Japanese Americans are less physically demonstrative. However, they also cited ethnographic evidence indicating that traditional Japanese society was relatively uninhibited about sexual matters, and that Japanese Americans have overaccommodated to more inhibited Judeo-Christian attitudes about sex prevalent in mainstream American society. Along these lines, Abramson and Imai-Marquez (1982) found that in a comparison study of Japanese Americans and European Americans, Japanese Americans evidenced more guilt about sex. This finding was true even for highly acculturated Japanese American participants and even more pronounced for Japanese American women. The authors noted that this is in keeping with the tendency of Japanese American families to de-emphasize and suppress sexuality. The results of this study also suggest that there may be an interaction between sex and ethnicity in determining sexual attitudes. In a recent review of research, Okazaki (1999) concluded that Asian Americans in general have more conservative sexual attitudes and behaviors than other ethnic groups and that larger society misinterprets this conservatism as disinterest in sex.

In contrast, the literature seems to indicate that African Americans may be less constricted than European Americans in terms of some sexual attitudes and behavior, and more constricted in terms of others. For example, Weinberg and Williams (1988) found that both African American men and women reported more liberal attitudes about pre- and extramarital sex, thought about sex more often, and had fewer sexual problems than the European Americans sampled. In Houston's (1981) study of college students, African American men and women reported looking at erotic materials more than did their European American counterparts. Another study conducted by Oggins, Leber, and Veroff (1993) of African American and European American newlyweds found that sexual enjoyment had different meanings for African American and European American men and women, but they also noted that socioeconomic class may be a mediating variable. However, Wyatt and Dunn's (1991) study of women found that African

American participants evidenced higher levels of sex guilt than did their European American peers. Also, Wyatt et al. (1998, cited in Zeiss & Kasl-Godley, 2001) reported that African American older women felt less comfortable with and were less likely to engage in oral sex and masturbation than their European American counterparts.

None of the just-discussed studies with ethnic minorities was conducted with an older adult population. However, the research cited does indicate that ethnic minority seniors may exhibit different sexual attitudes and behaviors compared with European Americans, on whom most of the sex research has been conducted. In their study of adolescents, Davis and Harris (1982) found that ethnicity was significantly related to participants' sexual knowledge, sexual interests, and sources of information, and the authors noted the importance of considering ethnicity in planning a sex education program. The same suggestion can be applied to those working with older adults. At the same time, therapists should keep in mind that although ethnicity may be an important factor in understanding an individual's sexuality, there are diverse attitudes about sexuality and other topics *within* various cultural groups.

## SUMMARY

With the growing older adult population, there is increased need for counselors to be more knowledgeable about older adult sexuality and to incorporate these competencies into their work with older clients. Since sexual problems for older clients are often multifactorial, mental health professionals need to be able to work with providers from other disciplines, such as medical professionals and physical therapists. For example, it may be necessary to make referrals to a physician or coordinate care with nursing home staff. Counselors can serve an important function by educating both older clients and other professionals about the realities of aging and sexuality to counteract myths and false information. Normalizing the effects of aging on the sexual response cycle and providing suggestions for modifications to sexual practices can also be important for seniors. However, counselors need to be mindful that older adults may have values about sexuality that are different from their own, and that it is important to respect these differences (Spence, 1992). In particular, older adults from various ethnic, cultural, lifestyle, and religious backgrounds may have different views of sexuality and appropriate sexual behavior. In the coming years, as the baby boomers join the ranks of older adults, it will be interesting to see how attitudes and behaviors related to older adult sexuality are redefined and changed.

# Cases and Questions

1. A 68-year-old Hispanic woman comes to see you about feelings of depression she has experienced since her husband died two years earlier. She reports a lingering sense of despair over the loss of companionship and emotional intimacy. In disclosing her feelings, she touches on the loss of a close sexual relationship.
   (a) What are some questions you might ask to help you and your client explore this aspect of her depression further?
   (b) What more do you need to know about the woman before you could begin to address this aspect of her depression?
   (c) What information might you provide your client that could be helpful to her?
   (d) How might your client attempt to satisfy her sexual needs at this point in her life?

2. A 54-year-old woman and her 62-year-old husband (both European Americans) come to see you about their shared sense of boredom with their relationship. They have been married for 30 years, and their three children are themselves married and living in other parts of the country. One married daughter has two children but lives far away, so your clients only see their grandchildren occasionally.
   (a) What contribution might sexual intimacy, or lack thereof, be playing in the sense of boredom with their relationship that this couple is feeling?
   (b) How might you introduce and explore the sexual aspect of their relationship?
   (c) How might you assess this couple's knowledge of sexuality and aging?
   (d) Assuming the lack of sexual intimacy in recent years is contributing to their sense of boredom with their relationship, how might you help your clients address this aspect of their marriage?

3. A 75-year-old gay man self-refers for feelings of loneliness and despair and thoughts about suicide. He has had two long-term relationships over his lifetime but has lived the last 10 years without a partner. He also reports that his most recent partner terminated the relationship when he (your client) developed impotence during the last year they were together.
   (a) What special issues might this man face that would not likely affect a 75-year-old heterosexual man?
   (b) What factors might have contributed to your client's impotence? What role could this dysfunction be playing in your client's reporting problem?
   (c) Assuming that lack of an intimate relationship is an underlying cause of your client's reporting problem, what actions might you encourage him to take to address this need?

# REFERENCES

Abramson, P. R., & Imai-Marquez, J. (1982). The Japanese-American: A cross-cultural, cross-sectional study of sex guilt. *Journal of Research in Personality, 16,* 227–237.

Adams, C. (1980). *Sexuality and the older adult.* Unpublished doctoral dissertation, University of Massachusetts.

Adams, M. A., Rojas-Camero, C., & Clayton, K. (1990). A small-group sex education/intervention model for the well elderly: A challenge for educators. *Educational Gerontology, 16,* 601–608.

Aldeman, M. (1991). Stigma, gay lifestyles and adjustment to aging: A study of later life gay men and lesbians. In J. Lee (Ed.), *Gay midlife and maturity* (pp. 7–32). New York: Haworth Press.

Allgeier, E., & Allgeier, A. (1984). *Sexual interactions.* Lexington, MA: D. C. Heath.

Avina, C., O'Donohue, W. T., & Fisher, J. E. (2000). Sexual dysfunctions in later life. In S. K. Whitbourne (Ed.), *Psychopathology in later adulthood* (pp. 173–187). New York: Wiley.

Badeau, D. (1995). Illness, disability, and sex in aging. *Sexuality and Disability, 13,* 219–237.

Ballard, E. L. (1995). Attitudes, myths, and realities: Helping family and professional caregivers cope with sexuality in the Alzheimer's patient. *Sexuality and Disability, 13,* 255–270.

Berger, R. M. (1982). The unseen minority: Older gays and lesbians. *Social Work, 27,* 236–242.

Brecher, E. M. (1984). *Love, sex, and aging.* Boston: Little, Brown.

Bretschneider, J. G., & McCoy, N. L. (1988). Sexual interest and behavior in healthy 80- to 102-year-olds. *Archives of Sexual Behavior, 17,* 109–129.

Butler, R. N., & Lewis, M. I. (1988). *Love and sex after 60.* New York: Harper & Row.

Butler, R. N., Lewis, M. I., Hoffman, E., & Whitehead, E. D. (1994). Love and sex after 60: How physical changes affect intimate expression. *Geriatrics, 49,* 20–27.

Call, V., Sprecher, S., & Schwartz, P. (1995). The incidence and frequency of marital sex in a national sample. *Journal of Marriage and the Family, 57,* 639–653.

Capuzzi, D., & Friel, S. E. (1995). Current trends in sexuality and aging: An update for counselors. In D. R. Atkinson & G. Hackett (Eds.), *Counseling diverse populations* (pp. 207–216). Dubuque, IA: Wm. C. Brown.

Centers for Disease Control. (1995). Acquired immunodeficiency syndrome. *MMWR, 34,* 583–589.

Cole, E., & Rothblum, E. (1990). Commentary on "Sexuality and the midlife woman." *Psychology of Women Quarterly, 14,* 509–512.

Covey, H. C. (1989). Perceptions and attitudes toward sexuality of the elderly during the Middle Ages. *The Gerontologist, 29,* 93–100.

Croft, L. (1982). *Sexuality in later life: A counseling guide for physicians.* Boston: PSG.

Crose, R., & Drake, L. K. (1993). Older women's sexuality. *Clinical Gerontologist, 12,* 51–56.

Davis, S. M., & Harris, M. B. (1982). Sexual knowledge, sexual interests, and sources of sexual information of rural and urban adolescents from three cultures. *Adolescence, 17,* 471–492.

Deacon, S., Minichiello, V., & Plummer, D. (1995). Sexuality and older people: Revisiting the assumptions. *Educational Gerontology, 21,* 497–513.

Dorfman, R., Walters, K., Burke, P., Hardin, L., Karanek, R., Raphael, J., & Silverstein, E. (1995). Old, sad, and alone: The myth of the aging homosexual. *Journal of Gerontological Social Work, 24,* 29–44.

Dorgan, C. A. (Ed.). (1995). *Statistical record of health and medicine.* New York: Gage Research.

Duffy, L. M. (1995). Sexual behavior and marital intimacy in Alzheimer's couples: A family theory perspective. *Sexuality and Disability, 13,* 239–254.

Dunea, G. (1998). Say no to Viagra. *British Medical Journal, 136,* 1755–1756.

Galindo, D., & Kaiser, F. E. (1995). Sexual health after 60. *Patient Care, 29,* 25–35.

Gelfand, M. M. (2000). Sexuality among older women. *Journal of Women's Health and Gender-Based Medicine, 9,* S15–S20.

George, L., & Weiler, S. (1981). Sexuality in middle and late life. *Archives of General Psychiatry, 38,* 919–923.

Glass, J. C., & Webb, M. L. (1995). Health care educators' knowledge and attitudes regarding sexuality in the aged. *Educational Gerontology, 21,* 713–733.

Hillman, J. L. (2000). *Clinical perspectives on elderly sexuality.* New York: Kluwer Academic/Plenum.

Hillman, J. L., & Stricker, G. (1994). A linkage of knowledge and attitudes toward elderly sexuality: Not necessarily a uniform relationship. *The Gerontologist, 34,* 256–260.

Hirayama, H., & Hirayama, K. K. (1986). The sexuality of Japanese Americans. *Journal of Social Work & Human Sexuality, 4,* 81–98.

Hirst, J. F., & Watson, J. P. (1996). Referral aged 60+ to an inner-city psychosexual dysfunction clinic. *Sexual and Marital Therapy, 11,* 131–147.

Hodson, D. S., & Skeen, P. (1994). Sexuality and aging: The hammerlock of myths. *Journal of Applied Gerontology, 13,* 219–235.

Houston, L. N. (1981). Romanticism and eroticism among Black and White college students. *Adolescence, 16,* 263–272.

Jacobson, S., & Grossman, A. H. (1996). Older lesbians and gay men: Old myths, new images, and future directions. In R. C. Savin-Williams & K. M. Cohen (Eds.), *The lives of lesbians, gays, and bisexuals* (pp. 345–367). Forth Worth, TX: Harcourt Brace.

Johnson, B. (1996). Older adults and sexuality: A multidimensional perspective. *Journal of Gerontological Nursing, 22,* 6–15.

Kaiser, F. E. (1991). Sexuality and impotence in the aging man. *Clinical Geriatric Medicine, 7,* 63–72.

Kaplan, H. S. (1990). Sex, intimacy, and the aging process. *Journal of the American Academy of Psychoanalysis, 18,* 185–205.

Kaye, R. A., & Markus, T. (1997). AIDS teaching should not be limited to the young. *USA Today Magazine, 126,* 50.

Kellett, J. M. (1991). Sexuality of the elderly. *Sexual and Marital Therapy, 6,* 147–155.

Kellett, J. M. (1993). Sexuality in later life. *Reviews in Clinical Gerontology, 3,* 309–314.

Kellett, J. M. (2000). Older adult sexuality. In L. T. Szuchman & F. Muscarella (Eds.), *Psychological perspectives on human sexuality* (pp. 355–379). New York: Wiley.

Kennedy, G., Hague, M., & Zarankow, B. (1997). Human sexuality in late life. *International Journal of Mental Health, 26,* 35–46.

Kernberg, O. F. (1991). Aggression and love in the relationship of the couple. In G. I. Fogel & W. A. Myers (Eds.), *Perversions and near-perversions in clinical practice: New psychoanalytic perspectives* (pp. 153–175). New Haven, CT: Yale University Press.

Kingsberg, S. A. (2000). The psychological impact of aging on sexuality and relationships. *Journal of Women's Health and Gender-Based Medicine, 9,* S33–S38.

Kinsey, A. C., Pomeroy, W. B., & Martin, C. E. (1948). *Sexual behavior in the human male.* Philadelphia: W. B. Saunders.

Kinsey, A. C., Pomeroy, W. B., Martin, C. E., & Gebhard, P. H. (1953). *Sexual behavior in the human female.* Philadelphia: W. B. Saunders.

Marsiglio, W., & Donnelly, D. (1991). Sexual relations in later life: A national study of married persons. *Journal of Gerontology, 46,* 338–344.

Masters, W. H., & Johnson, V. E. (1966). *Human sexual response.* Boston: Little, Brown.

Matthias, R. E., Lubben, J. E., Atchison, K. A., & Schweitzer, S. O. (1997). Sexual activity and satisfaction among very old adults: Results from a community-dwelling Medicare population survey. *The Gerontologist, 37,* 6–14.

McDougall, G. J. (1993). Therapeutic issues with gay and lesbian elders. *Clinical Gerontologist, 14,* 45–57.

Metz, M. E., & Miner, M. H. (1998). Psychosexual and psychosocial aspects of male aging and sexual health. *Canadian Journal of Human Sexuality, 7,* 245–259.

Montamat, S. C., Cusack, B. J., & Vestal, R. E. (1989). Management of drug therapy in the elderly. *New England Journal of Medicine, 321,* 303–308.

Morley, J. E. (1996). Update on men's health: Progress in geriatrics. *Generations, 4,* 13–19.

Mulligan, T., & Moss, C. R. (1991). Sexuality and aging in male veterans: A cross-sectional study of interest, ability, and activity. *Archives of Sexual Behavior, 20,* 17–25.

Mulligan, T., & Palguta, R. (1991). Sexual interest, activity, and satisfaction among male nursing home residents. *Archives of Sexual Behavior, 20,* 199–204.

National Institutes of Health. (1993). NIH Consensus Development Panel on Impotence. *Journal of the American Medical Association, 270,* 83–90.

Nay, R. (1992). Sexuality and aged women in nursing homes. *Geriatric Nursing, 13,* 312–314.

Oggins, J., Leber, D., & Veroff, J. (1993). Race and gender differences in Black and White newlyweds' perceptions of sexual and marital relations. *Journal of Sex Research, 30,* 152–160.

Okazaki, S. (1999). Influences of culture on Asian Americans' sexuality. *Journal of Sex Research, 39,* 34–42.

Pedersen, J. B. (1998). Sexuality and aging. In I. H. Nordhus, G. R. VandenBos, S. Berg, & P. Fromholt (Eds.), *Clinical geropsychology* (pp. 141–145). Washington, DC: American Psychological Association.

Persson, G. (1990). Sexuality in a 70-year-old urban population. *Journal of Psychosomatic Research, 24,* 335–342.

Pfeiffer, E., Verwoerdt, A., & Wang, H. (1968). Sexual behavior in aged men and women. *Archives of General Psychiatry, 19,* 753–923.

Primas, M. E., & Harper, M. S. (1991). Psychosocial care for racial and ethnic minority elderly. In M. S. Harper (Ed.), *Management and care of the elderly: Psychosocial perspectives* (pp. 157–174). Newbury Park, CA: Sage.

Rodin, J., Silberstein, L., & Streigel-Moore, R. (1984). Women and weight: A normative discontent. In *Nebraska Symposium on Motivation 1984* (pp. 267–304). Lincoln: University of Nebraska Press.

Rose, M. K., & Soares, H. H. (1993). Sexual adaptations of the frail elderly: A realistic approach. *Journal of Gerontological Social Work, 19,* 167–178.

Roughan, P. A., Kaiser, F. E., & Morley, J. E. (1993). Sexuality and the older woman. *Clinics in Geriatric Medicine, 9,* 87–106.

Rushton, J. P., & Bogaert, A. F. (1987). Race differences in sexual behavior: Testing an evolutionary hypothesis. *Journal of Research in Personality, 21,* 529–551.

Schiavi, R. C., Mandelli, J., & Schreiner-Engel, P. (1994). Sexual satisfaction in healthy aging men. *Journal of Sex and Marital Therapy, 20,* 3–13.

Schultz, R., Williamson, G. M., & Bridges, M. (1991). *Limb amputation among the elderly: Psychosocial factors influencing treatment.* Washington, DC: AARP Andrus Foundation.

Segraves, R. T., & Segraves, K. B. (1993). Medical aspects of orgasm disorder. In W. O'Donohue & J. H. Greer (Eds.), *Handbook of sexual dysfunctions: Assessment and treatment* (pp. 225–252). Needham Heights, MA: Allyn & Bacon.

Segraves, R. T., & Segraves, K. B. (1995). Human sexuality and aging. *Journal of Sex Education and Therapy, 21,* 88–102.

Slusher, M. P., Mayer, C. J., & Dunkle, R. E. (1996). Gays and lesbians older and wiser (GLOW): A support group for older gay people. *The Gerontologist, 36,* 118–123.

Smith, D. I., & Spraggins, R. E. (September, 2001). *Gender 2000* (Census 2000 Brief). U.S. Census Bureau. Retrieved July 31, 2002, from http://www.census.gov/prod/2001pubs/c2kbr01-9.pdf.

Spence, S. H. (1992). Psychosexual dysfunction in the elderly. *Behavior Change, 9,* 55–64.

Starr, B. D., & Weiner, M. B. (1981). *The Starr-Weiner report on sex and sexuality in the mature years.* New York: McGraw-Hill.

Steinke, E. E. (1988). Older adults' knowledge and attitudes about sexuality and aging. *Journal of Nursing Scholarship, 20,* 93–95.

Thompson, D. (1990). Intercourse after myocardial infarction. *Nursing Standard, 4,* 32–33.

Trudel, G., Turgeon, L., & Piché, L. (2000). Marital and sexual aspects of old age. *Sexual and Relationship Therapy, 15,* 381–406.

U.S. Bureau of the Census. (1996, February). *Population projections of the United States by age, sex, race, and Hispanic origin: 1995–2050* (Current population reports, P25-1130). Retrieved July 31, 2002, from http://www.census.gov/prod/1/pop/p25-1130/.

U.S. Bureau of the Census. (2000). *Projections of the resident population by age, sex, race, and Hispanic origin: 1999–2100.* Retrieved July 30, 2002, from http://www.census.gov/population/www/projections/natdet-D1A.html.

Walker, B. L., & Ephross, P. H. (1999). Knowledge and attitudes toward sexuality of a group of elderly. *Journal of Gerontological Social Work, 31,* 85–107.

Walker, B. L., Osgood, N. J., Richardson, J. P., & Ephross, P. H. (1998). Staff and elderly knowledge and attitudes toward elderly sexuality. *Educational Gerontology, 24,* 471–489.

Wallace, M. (1992). Management of sexual relationships among elderly residents of long term care facilities. *Geriatric Nursing, 13,* 308-311.

Weinberg, M. S., & Williams, C. J. (1988). Black sexuality: A test of two theories. *Journal of Sex Research, 25,* 197–218.

Whitbourne, S. K. (1990). Sexuality in the aging male. *Gender and Aging, 14,* 28–30.

White, C. B. (1982). A scale for the assessment of attitudes and knowledge regarding sexuality in the aged. *Archives of Sexual Behavior, 11,* 491–502.

Willert, A., & Semans, M. (2000). Knowledge and attitudes about later life sexuality: What clinicians need to know about helping the elderly. *Contemporary Family Therapy, 22,* 415–435.

Williamson, G. M., & Walters, A. S. (1996). Perceived impact of limb amputation on sexual activity: A study of adult amputees. *Journal of Sex Research, 33,* 221–235.

Winn, R. L., & Newton, N. (1982). Sexuality in aging: A study of 106 cultures. *Archives of Sexual Behavior, 11,* 283–298.

Wyatt, G. E., & Dunn, K. R. (1991). Examining predictors of sex guilt in multiethnic samples of women. *Archives of Sexual Behavior, 20,* 471–485.

Zeiss, A., & Kasl-Godley, J. (2001). Sexuality in older adults' relationships. *Generations, 25*(2), 18–25.

# Part IV THE FEMALE CLIENT

# CHAPTER 12

# Counseling Girls and Women: Attitudes, Knowledge, and Skills

## Carolyn Zerbe Enns, Cornell College

In 1968, Naomi Weisstein (1968/1993) stated: "Psychology has nothing to say about what women are really like, what they need and what they want, essentially, because psychology does not know" (p. 197). She described three major flaws within psychology: (1) psychologists' use of theory without evidence, including the practice of applying "clinical insight" to validate sexist biases about women; (2) psychologists' tendency to decontextualize human experience, or to explain behavior in terms of inner traits rather than activities occurring in a complex social context; and (3) psychologists' reliance on reductionist biologically based theories of sex and gender differences that propose that men and women are essentially different.

Four years later, Phyllis Chesler (1972) published *Women and Madness,* which described a variety of "treatments" that were purported to help women but often exacerbated their problems. She proposed that mental health professionals and theorists tended to (a) notice signs of illness and pathology and ignore clients' positive coping patterns and resources, (b) view "masculine" behaviors as more healthy than "feminine" behaviors, (c) conceptualize "real" women as mothers but to also blame mothers for various "pathologies" manifested by their children, and (d) believe that "certain women" were promiscuous (e.g., rape and child sexual abuse victims) and, thus, responsible for their emotional pain. Chesler concluded that therapy reinforced sexism, bias, heterosexism, and racism, and she contended that "the psychotherapeutic encounter is just one more instance of an unequal relationship, just one more opportunity to be rewarded for expressing distress and to be "helped" by being (expertly) dominated" (p. 140). She argued that the counseling relationship approximated or mirrored women's traditional experience in the patriarchal family—one in which they were trained to be helpless, dependent, and "unreasonable." In this relationship, women were "diagnosed" for both overconforming or underconforming to traditional "feminine" behavior.

During the 30 years since Weisstein and Chesler voiced these criticisms, mental health practitioners and researchers have collected voluminous amounts of data about women's lives and published a wide range of documents regarding gender-fair practice that have dramatically altered women's experiences in psychotherapy. This chapter summarizes major attitudes, domains of knowledge, and skills that are necessary for working effectively with women in the 21st century. The primary framework for this brief summary is the Principles Concerning the Counseling and Psychotherapy with Women (American Psychological Association [APA], 1979), and recent revisions (in progress) of these guidelines (Worell, 2002). The chapter begins with a discussion of four major assumptions that provide a foundation for working with women and is followed by brief sections that discuss counselor awareness, counselor knowledge, and counselor skills.

## BASIC ASSUMPTIONS AND FOUNDATIONS FOR WORKING WITH GIRLS AND WOMEN

This section summarizes four foundations for working with gender-related issues, including the assumptions that (a) gender is socially constructed, (b) gender socialization practices shape the realities of girls' and women's lives, (c) the social identities and social locations of girls and women are diverse, and (d) power dynamics within relationships and society influence girls' and women's realities.

### Gender as Socially Constructed

Psychological theories have tended to either minimize or exaggerate differences between groups of men and women, and to frame gender as characteristics that are lodged within persons rather than created and modified within relationships and social structures. These approaches can perpetuate the notion that "the categories of 'man' and 'woman' are natural, self-evident," and unitary (Marecek, 1995, p. 162) and encourage individuals to draw conclusions about "generic" men and women in isolation from other important aspects of social position and identity, such as race, culture, ethnicity, sexual orientation, and social class.

To emphasize the variability within and between genders and the importance of many social identities and locations that contribute to a person's sense of maleness or femaleness, most feminist counselors and psychologists view gender as socially constructed. Gender is not represented as a noun or a set of traits that describe permanent internal characteristics, but as a verb that involves "doing" or engaging in behavior (West & Zimmerman, 1987) and that is manifested differently in a variety of social encounters (Deaux & Stewart, 2001). For example, rather than describing a woman as "feminine," and assuming that she exhibits traditional "feminine" traits across contexts, counselors who operate from a social constructionist framework are attentive to how different situations may elicit or require specific behaviors. At home a woman may show executive authority; however, in close relationships with other women, her behaviors may be marked primarily by empathy, caring, and a love for fun. In her secretarial role at work, a woman may follow orders, acquiesce, and rarely offer suggestions; as a community volunteer, she may implement her organizational and advocacy skills. Gendered behaviors are complex and are often enacted at an individual level as gender roles and personal characteristics, at the interpersonal level as cues that shape reactions and perceptions of those in the social environment, and at the social structural level as a system of power relations between and among men and women (Crawford & Unger, 2000). At the individual level, a woman may tend to show a distinctive style of dress, to smile when uncomfortable, and to use unique hand gestures to mark her points. At the interpersonal level, her partner may or may not interpret her hand gestures and smiles as manifestations of traditional femininity. At a structural level, her "passive" behavior represents her method of coping with a powerful and authoritarian supervisor.

## Gender Socialization

Considerable evidence reveals that the socialization, interpersonal experiences, and institutional experiences of girls and women are different from those of most men. Although gender socialization varies by culture and class, cultural influences reinforce stereotyped beliefs about boys and girls and men and women through multiple avenues such as clothing, toys, books, language, television, gendered play experiences, the beliefs of adults, religious organizations, and schools (Gilbert & Scher, 1999; Worell & Remer, 2003). These experiences become the foundation for complex cognitive schemas that individuals use to organize the world into gendered categories. Gender schemas often represent powerful, automatic, and unconscious mechanisms that become shortcuts for processing information and the foundation for perceptual distortions of behavior (Bem, 1993). For example, persons with traditional gender schemas may see gender difference even when objective measures reveal no difference, or they may pay attention to another person's behavior when it conforms to one's gendered expectations but ignore behavior that is not consistent with gender stereotypes and that might disconfirm traditional gender beliefs. Counselors seek to be aware of clients' internalized gender-related beliefs and how they intersect with beliefs about other social identities, as well as the gender-related beliefs of those in clients' environments that may limit the perspectives and options of girls and women.

## Diversity Among Girls and Women

Women's lives are influenced by multiple social locations and social identities that interact in complex ways (Deaux & Stewart, 2001; Worell & Remer, 2003). In many cases, it is impossible to separate one aspect of identity from others. Some aspects of girls' and women's identities may be a part of the foreground in some situations but move to the background in other situations. For example, a woman of 50 may be especially conscious of her age when in a classroom with students who are of traditional college age; however, in a group with many 50-year-old women, her age may become part of the background, and some other aspect of her identity (e.g., race or class) may feel especially salient because it marks her uniqueness in that setting. Although gendered aspects of identity are characteristic of all persons, these identities may be modified substantially by other identities that intersect with gender (e.g., race, sexual orientation, professional status)

(Deaux & Stewart, 2001). For some individuals, gender may only rarely become the most significant marker of identity but may be filtered through other social identities such as race, ethnicity, or class. It is important for counselors to explore how women define themselves in multiple situations and how these constructions influence their daily interactions and self-concepts.

Counselors and psychologists are also aware that some social identities that intersect with gender are associated with power and privilege, and others are associated with oppression or discrimination. The degree of privilege and oppression that one experiences also varies in different situations and contexts (Worell & Remer, 2003). For example, a White middle-class woman may experience sexual harassment that is perpetrated by a male coworker in the workplace, but she may in turn show subtle forms of racism in her interactions with a woman of color who works as her secretary. As noted by Spelman (1988), although "all women are women, there is no being who is only a woman" (p. 102). Speaking about the diversity of women, Baber and Allen (1992) added: "There is no women's voice, no woman's story, but rather a multitude of voices that sometimes speak together but often must speak separately" (p. 19). Gender cannot be isolated from other complex aspects of identity and viewed as the sole or primary source of women's concerns but must be understood in its multiple manifestations and as it is modified by individual difference, cultural values, class, race, and sexual orientation.

## Power Dynamics and Personal Experience

Counselors recognize that power differences permeate society and that these power differences are detrimental to the mental and physical health of women and girls (Wyche & Rice, 1997). Gender-related power differences are present at interpersonal, institutional, and social structural levels and are evidenced in domains associated with economic power, legal and political power, organizational power, and personal power (Goodwin & Fiske, 2001). The uses of power that damage individuals range from structural power differences that reinforce economic disparities and poverty, to interpersonal violence, to various forms of more subtle bias and "isms" that may permeate the experiences of women in interpersonal relationships, the work world, and institutional interactions.

Goodwin and Fiske (2001) noted that "[p]ower differences persist despite the narrowing of gender gaps and changes in attitudes that have characterized the past century" (p. 358). The literature on racism and sexism also indicates that although blatant forms of sexism, racism, and negative attitudes toward women have decreased substantially during recent decades (Campbell, Schellenberg, & Senn, 1997), contemporary sexism and racism often assume more subtle and clandestine forms, which have been labeled by terms such as (a) *modern sexism and racism* (Swim, Aikin, Hall, & Hunter, 1995), (b) *unintentional or symbolic racism and sexism* (Dovidio & Gaertner, 1996), and (c) *ambivalent sexism* (Glick & Fiske, 1997). Ambivalent sexism is characterized by both hostile sexism, which is marked by negative and competitive attitudes toward women, as well as benevolent sexism, which is marked by paternalistic attitudes and the belief that men and women should play complementary roles. Hostile sexism is more likely to be directed at competent but disliked women (e.g., career women and feminists), and benevolent sexism is more frequently directed at women who are perceived as less competent but likable (e.g., homemakers and women who fulfill traditional roles) (Goodwin & Fiske, 2001).

Glick and Fiske (1997) labeled current forms of gender bias as "kinder and gentler justifications of male dominance and prescribed gender roles" (p. 121) and argued that they may be no less virulent than blatant biases and abuses of power that were evident in the past. Given the subtle and contradictory nature of much contemporary sexism and racism, it may be more difficult for individual men and women to recognize their presence in their lives. They may also be more likely to internalize subtly sexist, racist, or homophobic attitudes and have greater difficulty resisting the effects of bias.

## ATTITUDES AND VALUES OF THE COUNSELOR

The Principles Concerning the Counseling and Psychotherapy with Women (APA, 1979) as well as revisions in progress indicate that self-knowledge and self-awareness are essential for working with the concerns of girls and women. Competent counselors develop awareness of their own socialization experiences, sociodemographic identities (e.g., class, race, culture), values, stereotypes, and biases. They also explore how their own positions of oppression and/or privilege may influence their practice with women and girls. Self-reflection, professional education and development, supervision, self-care, and consultation represent important aspects of ongoing self-examination. Self-care is also an essential aspect of self-awareness because it helps ensure that counselors will not be distracted by their own stresses and unexamined assumptions. Self-care increases the likelihood that counselors will maintain positive attitudes and engage in ongoing reflection about additional blank spots they may need to address (Feminist Therapy Institute [FTI], 2000; Wyche, 2001).

### Awareness of Privilege, Ethnocentrism, and Bias

Even well-intentioned counselors are not immune from subtle and modern forms of bias and ethnocentrism. Within contemporary counseling practice, sexism, racism, and heterosexism may be most frequently manifested by lack of acknowledgment of the realities and experiences of persons who are often marginalized within society. For example, *omission bias*, or lack of attention to relevant circumstances and experiences relevant to lesbians, contributes to their invisibility. Heterosexuality is considered a "given" in society, and the lives of lesbians are judged according to the "normative" experiences of heterosexual women. A second negative attitude may take the form of *connotation bias*, which involves using phrases with negative meanings or implications when referring to a nondominant group in society (Chernin, Holden, & Chandler, 1997). Morton (1998) noted that lesbian relationships are often characterized as fused or enmeshed when compared with heterosexual relationships. More appropriate and positive characterizations of these relational styles include "ability for empathic relating" or "self-boundary flexibility."

Counselors are often unaware of their subtle ethnocentric, heterosexist, racist, or androcentric beliefs unless they examine carefully their own experiences of privilege and marginalization/oppression and become educated about the lives, histories, strengths, and oppressions of diverse groups of people. McIntosh (1989) described White privilege as the "invisible package of unearned assets which I can count on cashing in each day, but about which I was 'meant' to remain oblivious" (p. 10). These unearned privileges resemble a "weightless knapsack" or "blank checks" that are available to people who hold significant social and economic power. As a result, counselors who work with women educate themselves about the unearned entitlements or statuses that they may hold on the basis of their class, race, sexual orientation, or ability. Antiracism, antiheterosexism, or anticlassism consciousness-raising groups represent crucial opportunities for increasing awareness.

Another problematic bias occurs when counselors have been attentive to sexism and gender bias but are unaware of the intersections of these biases with other aspects of identity. Too frequently, the lives of White women have been viewed as identical or relevant to the experiences of "women in general," or as the normative group to which all other groups of women are compared (Espin, 1995). For many women of color, racism or class-related oppression may be far more visible, virulent, and frequent than sexism or heterosexism (Comas-Diaz & Greene, 1994). If the counselor assumes, for example, that women of color have more in common with other women than men who experience a shared oppression (e.g., related to racism or classism), the counselor may deny the relevance of important bonds and sources of support that ethnic minority women form with men who experience racism and other forms of common oppression. Although gender oppression is a common experience of women, and although women of color may experience both sexism and heterosexism within their racial/ethnic communities, women's experiences of oppression and privilege are shaped by individual economic, social, historical, and ecological realities (Greene & Sanchez-Hucles, 1997; Worell & Remer, 2003; Wyche, 2001).

## Personal Functioning and Self-Care

The Feminist Therapy Institute's (2000) Code of Ethics identifies self-care activities as an important foundation for working with women. It also emphasizes the importance of recognizing one's personal and professional needs; engaging in self-reflection, personal support and/or therapy; and consulting with colleagues about difficult issues.

Coster and Schwebel (1997) found that psychologists rated the following items as most central to well-functioning: self-awareness and self-monitoring, a clear personal value system, balance between one's personal and professional lives, relationships with family members and partners, vacations, relationships with friends, and personal therapy. Mahoney (1997) found that emotional exhaustion or fatigue was the most frequently cited personal problem encountered by psychotherapists (43%), and roughly one-third of respondents reported anxiety or depression during the past year. A recent survey of counseling psychologists revealed that 62% identified themselves as having experienced depression (Gilroy, Caroll, & Murra, 2002). Another survey of members of the Association for Women in Psychology revealed that 76% of the 220 respondents had experienced some type of depressive illness, and 85% had participated in personal therapy (Gilroy, Carroll, & Murra, 2001). These statistics underline the stressful nature and personal costs associated with counseling, as well as the importance of self-care activities.

Special challenges to personal functioning may be associated with working with clients who have experienced violence or abuse, or working with clients whose concerns may remind the therapist of painful aspects of her or his life history. The phrase *vicarious traumatization* has been used to convey "the experience of a transformation in the self of a treatment provider as a result of empathic engagement with trauma survivors and their material, in the context of feeling responsible or committed to help the survivor" (Deiter, Nicholls, & Pearlman, 2000, p. 1188). Research reveals that compared with counselors with typical caseloads, counselors who work with a high proportion of survivors of violence experienced more symptoms of post-traumatic stress disorder (PTSD) (Brady, Guy, Poelstra, & Brokaw, 1999; Schauben & Frazier, 1995) and more disrupted cognitions related to basic schemas such as safety, self-trust, and self-esteem (Schauben & Frazier, 1995). Pearlman and MacIan (1995) found that therapists who were new to trauma work reported higher levels of distress and greater disruptions of basic schemas than did seasoned professionals. In addition, compared with those with no trauma history, counselors with a trauma history reported more distress and disruptions related to basic schemas such as safety, self-trust, and self-esteem.

Studies reveal that roughly one-third of mental health practitioners report experiencing sexual or physical abuse as a child or an adolescent (Little & Hamby, 1996; Polusny & Follette, 1996; Pope & Feldman-Summers, 1992). These surveys suggest that a therapist's abuse history is not related to a therapist's competence and practices; however, therapists with abuse histories articulated more concerns about countertransference issues such as making boundary mistakes or crying with clients, and they reported the use of more personal coping strategies to support their practice as therapists (Little & Hamby, 1996). Counselors with similar trauma histories as their clients may experience increased compassion and commitment to clients with trauma histories, but they may also be vulnerable to restimulation of their own pain and, thus, are likely to benefit from regular self-monitoring and self-care (Pearlman & Saakvitne, 1995).

## KNOWLEDGE FOUNDATION
## FOR COUNSELING WOMEN

This section introduces three foundations of counselor knowledge, including the importance of (1) gaining understanding of the specific life experiences and worldviews of diverse groups of women and girls, (2) applying personality and counseling theories that support girls' and women's growth and development, and (3) acquiring knowledge of high-prevalence problems and issues girls and women experience.

## Knowledge of Diversity

Comprehensive preparation for effective counseling with women involves educating oneself about the plurality of human experience, and not assuming that clients from diverse backgrounds will provide this education for the counselor. Counselors of women must strive to learn about the diverse traditions and values of their clients and seek out experiences and educational opportunities that sensitize them to important themes, issues, and concerns in their clients' lives. The knowledgeable counselor also seeks to be aware of how individual differences modify the impact of culture, race, class, religion, and sexual orientation (FTI, 2000).

## Theories About Women's Lives

It is beyond the scope of this brief chapter to review and identify specific theories that may be both useful and detrimental for conceptualizing women's lives. However, Lerman's (1986) criteria for feminist theoretical models provide a useful metaframework for assessing the adequacy of theoretical models. Woman-affirming models (a) view women positively and centrally and do not omit important aspects of their life experiences that may not be reflected in men's lives; (b) avoid particularistic or exclusionary language that is associated with traditional roles and that imply that specific roles are more relevant for one gender or sex (e.g., by substituting terms such as caregiving or parenting for more narrowly defined terms such as mothering); (c) encompass the diversity and complexity of women's lives; (d) recognize the intersections and inextricable connections between the internal and external worlds of women and girls; (e) attend to the intersections of gender, sexual orientation, race, ethnicity, age, ability, and other social identities for shaping women's and girls lives and self-concepts; and (f) support nonsexist, feminist, and multicultural approaches to counseling.

Bem (1993) acknowledged that although psychology has made substantial progress in developing gender-sensitive models, it continues to adhere to three hidden assumptions or "lenses of gender" that reproduce limited theoretical models of gender. She argued that androcentrism, or the notion that the "male experience" is still the neutral standard against which all other behavior is compared, is still pervasive. Thus, for example, women are often described as having lower self-esteem than men; in contrast, men are not usually described as holding unrealistic levels of self-esteem in comparison to women. The second lens of gender polarization "superimposes a male-female dichotomy on virtually every aspect of human experience" (p. 233), and notions of gender difference remain a major basis on which behavior is classified. The third lens of biological essentialism is, at least in part, a consequence of gender polarization. Because maleness and femaleness are often seen in polarized terms, human beings tend to assume that any difference that does exist is the consequence of "the intrinsic biological natures of women and men" (p. 233). Counselors seek to be aware of the subtle ways in which these biases may permeate theory and conceptual models and strive to use models that avoid these problems.

## Knowledge of High-Prevalence Issues Encountered by Girls and Women

This section briefly summarizes three high-prevalence problems that are intertwined with the culture and stereotypes about women and that contribute to many of the psychological difficulties women experience. They include violence against women, career and work-family life balance, and body image and objectification.

**Violence Against Women**   Violence against girls and women occurs throughout the life span and includes child sexual and physical abuse, dating violence, sexual assault and rape, domestic violence, and violence toward elderly women. Studies reveal that between 40% and 60% of patients seeking psychiatric care have experienced physical or sexual abuse of some kind (Koss, 1993). Rape prevalence rates for women ranging from 14% to 25% have been reported in eight major studies (Koss, 1993). Acute PTSD symptoms are experienced by up to 95% of rape survivors within 2 weeks after rape, and about 50% continue to meet the diagnostic criteria of PTSD 3 months after rape (Foa & Riggs, 1995). Within their relationships with male intimates, between 22% and 31% of women experience physical and/or sexual violence (Collins et al., 1999; Tjaden & Thoennes, 1998). High rates of intimate violence are present in both heterosexual and gay and lesbian relationships, and issues of power and dependency are associated with violence in both heterosexual and gay/lesbian relationships (White, Donat, & Bondurant, 2001). Studies also estimate that between 35% and 50% of women have experienced sexual harassment during their working lives (Gutek & Done, 2001). In general, women are 13 times more likely to be victims of violence than are men, and girls are twice as likely to experience sexual abuse than are boys (APA, 1996). The interconnections between forms of violence are complex, and individuals may be victims of multiple forms of violence over a lifetime. The effects of violence can also be cumulative, with childhood violence increasing the risk that one may experience violence later in life.

One of the original concerns raised by Chesler (1972) was the labeling of victims of violence as promiscuous. A major issue that remains today is the denial of many women's experiences of trauma or the belief that women exaggerate the emotional consequences of trauma. Rape myths are pervasive in our culture and reinforce the blaming of victims (Worell & Remer, 2003), even when victims of stranger rape do nothing to "ask for" rape. Rape myths vary somewhat by who the victim is. For example, stereotypes of African American women as "Mammys," "Jezebels," or "Sapphires," influence perceptions of rape and the willingness of victims to disclose violence (McNair & Neville, 1996; West, 2000). For many women of color and poor women, rape must also be understood in context of sexual exploitation associated with slavery, colonization, and immigration (Holzman, 2000). Societal messages that women deserve the sexual coercion they experience, that they didn't do enough to protect themselves, that they have been demeaned and are of lesser value because they have been abused, and that they should accept blame for sexual violence are often internalized by women and may contribute to long-term physical and psychological problems (Neville & Heppner, 1999).

Although substantial data attest to the extensive negative consequences of intimate violence, therapists sometimes underplay the seriousness of such violence or do not address the violence (Harway & Hansen, 1993). As a foundation for working with interpersonal violence, it is important for counselors to be knowledgeable about violence statistics, research findings regarding the dynamics and types of interpersonal violence (including variations by sexual orientation, race, and culture), the diverse and variable psychological consequences of violence, and methods for assessing violence and trauma. Given the multidimensionality of violence, counselors must also attend to a range of influences, including intrapsychic factors, developmental factors, family influences, power dynamics, and the social context in which violence occurs. They should be familiar with crisis intervention procedures, methods for addressing posttraumatic symptoms and reactions, methods for working with perpetrators, and the costs and benefits of couples therapy for working with partners in violent relationships (APA, 1996).

**Career and Work-Family Convergence**    Equality for women in the work world is still elusive. Even with substantial gains in wage equities between 1978 and 1998, women earn approximately 76% of men's pay. Furthermore, the wage gap between White women and Black and Hispanic women has widened during the past 20 years (Costello & Stone, 2001). Women are seen more frequently in professions and high-status jobs, but most women remain clustered in lower-status jobs that are associated with limited financial benefits. Even when women's incomes at early stages of their careers approach the income levels of men, institutional power structures, values, and promotion policies still limit the likelihood that women will achieve equal power with men over the course of a career (Crawford & Unger, 2000).

A majority of American households are built on a dual-earner model, and the balancing of work and family roles is a crucial component of women's mental health and well-being. Although employed married women report higher levels of mental and physical mental health than women who are not employed (Barnett & Rivers, 1996), the benefits of marriage are still greater for men than they are for women, and the balance of labor for men and women in the home remains uneven. Barnett and Hyde's (2001) expansionist theory of work-family convergence hypothesizes that multiple roles enhance physical and mental health by buffering persons from the negative effects of stressful roles, enhancing social support, increasing opportunities for success, expanding one's frame of reference and sense of self-complexity, facilitating positive interaction with a significant other because of the shared nature of work and family roles, and increasing financial resources. However, Steil (2001) concluded that although there is greater endorsement of egalitarian intimate relationships than in the past, and although those who share household responsibilities report fewer feelings of dysphoria, less stress, and a higher sense of fairness, "relationships remain unequal" (p. 350). Although men have increased their participation in household work and women have decreased the amount of time they devote to household responsibilities, women continue to perform roughly two times as much housework as their spouses and approximately 80% of the time-consuming and ongoing tasks associated with food preparation, house cleaning, and laundry (Steil, 2001).

Counselors also need to have knowledge of diversity among women (e.g., by class, race, sexual orientation, age, single status) with regard to career and work-personal life balance. Most research on multiple roles and home-career issues has focused on role distributions in White, middle-class households (Crawford & Unger, 2000; Gilbert & Rader, 2001), limiting the generalizability of many conclusions about work salience and work-personal life balance. Levels of workforce participation have often been higher for women of color compared with White women, and the need to balance work and personal life has been a "given" (Gilbert & Rader, 2001). A recent study of blue-collar families found that despite their adherence to traditional gender-role ideologies, the behaviors of partners conveyed a "real egalitarianism" (Deutsch & Saxon, 1998, p. 359). Research on lesbian couples reveals that, compared with heterosexual partners, they more typically reject traditional roles, achieve more egalitarianism in relationships, believe that both partners should work for pay, and share more social/leisure interest. Thus, despite few cultural supports and social disapproval, lesbian couples may be better prepared to negotiate balanced lifestyles (Steil, 2001). Finally, single women generally experience less serious psychological distress than their married counterparts and enjoy higher levels of education and occupational status, suggesting some significant benefits associated with this lifestyle choice (Crawford & Unger, 2000). Each of these findings points to the necessity of knowledge about the diversity of women's working lives.

Given the centrality of work to women's lives throughout the life span, counselors strive to help girls and women explore and transcend restrictive gender-role messages about careers, expand their frames of reference and increase self-efficacy, develop skills for challenging workplace and home inequities, and consider methods for achieving a satisfying balance between work and personal roles (Bingham & Ward, 1994; Brooks & Forrest, 1994; Gilbert & Rader, 2001; Hackett & Lonborg, 1994).

**Body Image and Body Objectification**    Body discontent has been described as normative among North American women (Crawford & Unger, 2000). Cultural beliefs and stereotypes about beauty and women's bodies contribute to many of women's problems, including eating disorders, anxiety, depression, sexual dysfunction, fragmented identity, a distorted linkage between sexual experience and beauty, and lowered self- and body-esteem (Fredrickson & Roberts, 1997; Travis, Meginnis, & Bardari, 2000). Objectification theory (Fredrickson & Roberts, 1997) proposes that women learn to assume an observer's point of view and apply internalized cultural stereotypes of beauty when they view and evaluate their own bodies. This internalization of the culture may lead to habitual body monitoring or surveillance and a "looking glass self," which contributes to women's shame and anxiety, the reduction of peak motivational states or "flow," and decreased awareness of internal signals of hunger and satiation. Women may become objects rather than agents, a condition that manifests itself in the search for beauty through cosmetic surgery as well as body manipulations and behaviors that have long-term detrimental effects on women's physical and mental health (Travis et al., 2000).

A number of other models seek to explain the connection between cultural mandates and women's problems with body image and eating. The culture of thinness perspective suggests that society puts forth thinness as the major precursor to having a happy and successful life, and that eating disturbances become a method for securing this attractive life. The "weight as power and control" perspective suggests that controlling one's weight is a method of gaining control in a world in which much is uncontrollable, and that body image issues and preoccupations represent a form of coping that distracts women from difficult issues of major importance in their lives. Yet another approach proposes that achieving the perfect body may be a way to avoid negative stereotypes of high-achieving women as lonely, ruthless, unfeminine, or unattractive. Finally, preoccupation with the physical self may help compensate for having an underdeveloped psychological self (Gilbert & Thompson, 1996).

As with other concerns discussed in this section, issues related to body satisfaction, body image, and eating may be experienced in somewhat different ways by women of color (e.g., Thompson, 1994) and lesbians (Bergeron & Senn, 1998). Although there is substantial overlap between lesbian and heterosexual women's body image attitudes, lesbian women may internalize oppressive societal norms about the body to a lesser degree and may be more adept at resisting these attitudes (Bergeron & Senn, 1998). For women of color, skin color consciousness and the internalization of White standards of beauty may represent additional beauty pressures (Travis et al., 2000). In addition, Thompson (1994) found that for women of diverse backgrounds, eating issues were not only associated with cultural pressures and ideals about thinness and beauty, but often emerged as coping mechanisms at times of significant emotional strain of many kinds. Thus, they represented active survival mechanisms when other mechanisms of coping were not available.

## Knowledge for Conceptualizing Problems Experienced by Girls and Women

Some of the high-prevalence disorders experienced by women include depression, eating disorders, and many of the anxiety disorders, and these forms of distress are often exhibited by women who encounter problems described in the previous section. Eating disorders are sometimes referred to as culture-bound syndromes in that 90% of those experiencing eating disorders are women and they are closely tied to standards of femininity and the social structure of contemporary North American society (Marecek, 2001). In contrast, substance use and abuse are less frequently diagnosed in women than men, and mental health practitioners may underestimate the presence of these problems in women (Marecek, 2001; Roades, 2000). As noted by Hartung and Widiger (1998), some problems may be expressed differently in men and women, even though diagnostic criteria present symptoms as though they are experienced in identical ways by men and women. It is difficult to apply gender-neutral descriptions of problems when the manifestations of and symptoms associated with these problems, such as substance use and abuse, are influenced by gender-role socialization. Thus, competent counselors are attentive to the unique ways in which individual women express distress.

Given that a substantial number of women's high-prevalence disorders are linked to cultural learning and gender-related experiences, it is important for counselors to use conceptual frameworks that link personal distress to the communicative function of symptoms and the contexts in which they arise. For example, when conceptualizing the complicated symptoms that are often associated with long-term interpersonal violence, the labels of PTSD or complex PTSD may convey the logic or contextual foundation for distress and can be used to emphasize the adaptive role of symptoms (Brown, 1994; Herman, 1992). However, the category PTSD does not adequately conceptualize many potential triggers and consequences of traumatic reactions and can also be used to "create" disorders out of experiences that involve normal reactions to trauma; thus, it should be used cautiously (Becker, 2001; Worell & Remer, 2003). In contrast to efforts to contextualize symptoms, the label borderline personality disorder (BPD), which is often applied to survivors of interpersonal and sexual violence, conceptualizes problems in intrapsychic terms and is associated with pejorative meanings that may detract from the client's sense of dignity (Becker, 2001; Brown, 1994). In addition, compared with categories of disorders such as depression and anxiety, the diagnostic categories referred to as personality disorders are more frequently associated with gender bias in that they label exaggerations of feminine stereotypes as disorders (e.g., dependent and histrionic personality disorder) (Kaplan, 1983).

Roughly 60% of those who seek help from a mental health professional experience problems that do not fit categories of formal diagnosis that are represented in the *DSM-IV* (Wylie, 1995), and it is not always necessary for counselors to use formal diagnosis as represented by the *Diagnostic and Statistical Manual-IV (DSM-IV;* American Psychiatric Association, 1994). Marecek (2001) argued that the *DSM* conforms to a disease model that "ignores everyday identities and social categories—such as gender, race/ethnicity, and social class—that shape experience" (p. 306) and describes problems in such a way that the personal meaning of clients' concerns is often lost. A narrative overview of the client's pattern of relationships, self-perceptions, and behaviors may often convey most effectively the meaning of the client's concerns and a foundation from which to construct counseling goals.

Although substantial progress has been made toward eliminating bias in assessment, diagnosis, and conceptual frameworks, subtle forms of gender bias remain an area of concern to feminist counselors. Subtle gender bias in assessment and diagnosis may include lack of attention to environmental factors, the presence of gender bias within assessment instruments, the use of different labels for similar behaviors in men and women, and therapist misjudgments about diagnosis due to stereotyped beliefs about gender and its intersections with other aspects of identity (Santos de Barona & Dutton, 1997).

## SKILLS FOR COUNSELING GIRLS AND WOMEN

Over the past three decades, counselors have worked toward and arrived at consensus about optimal counseling practices for enhancing the growth and development of girls and women. The practices discussed in this section include: (a) methods for building collaborative relationships, (b) skills for supporting clients' strengths and empowerment, and (c) skills for facilitating ethical, respectful practice.

### Building Collaborative Relationships

Developing a sound therapeutic alliance based on a collaborative partnership is an important predictor of positive counseling outcomes. Collaborative relationships convey to clients that they are respected as active participants and also convey the value of egalitarian relationships (Horvath, 2000). Egalitarian counseling relationships communicate to women and girls that they are competent, knowledgeable, and have the necessary resources for taking an active role in their own healing.

The effective counselor models communication skills such as genuineness, confrontation, empathy, and congruence as methods for establishing collaborative relationships. In addition, the counselor communicates with the client about her or his assumptions and approaches to counseling and provides information about the costs and benefits of counseling, what the client can expect from the counselor, and what the therapist will expect of the client (FTI, 2000). Whenever possible, the counselor and client specify the issues they will address, the goals they will work toward, and the time frame in which they will seek to accomplish these goals.

Research reveals that a counselor's relationship skills are crucial for forming a therapeutic bond; however, the gender of the therapist and the therapist's level of androgyny appear to have very limited impact on the quality of counseling relationships and counseling outcomes (Horvath, 2000; Nelson, 1993). More crucial is the counselor's ability to explore empathically a client's issues that are related to gender and other social identities that intersect with gender. Being sensitive to occasions when women and girls may prefer to work with women is also important, especially when the client's presenting issues are related to issues of male-to-female violence such as rape, sexual abuse, domestic violence, and sexual harassment.

### Identifying Client Strengths and Empowering Girls and Women

Traditional approaches to working with girls and women tend to define problems in terms of "pathology," focus on removing "symptoms," and view problems as lodged in the individual personality of the distressed person. Counselors who emphasize the strengths and resources of women and girls consider the following questions: "What do my client's symptoms tell me about her strengths and coping skills?" and "How can I help my client redirect ineffective coping efforts in productive ways so she is not just surviving but also meeting positive goals for herself?" This redefinition of problems is a powerful antidote for undoing a "patient identity" and turning perceived weaknesses into strengths (Greenspan, 1993). By focusing on positive coping, counselors can help clients transcend self-blame, view their distress in more positive terms, and adopt action-oriented strategies to change their conditions (Worell & Remer, 2003).

Empowerment involves (a) examining power dynamics that influence a person's life and the ways in which women and girls have been socialized to feel powerless; (b) developing skills for achieving control, influence, and well-being in personal, interpersonal, and institutional domains; and (c) using advocacy skills on behalf of girls and women (Hawxhurst & Morrow, 1984). Tools for implementing the first component of empowerment include gender-role analysis, power analysis, reframing, and other consciousness-raising experiences (Worell & Remer, 2003). Worell (2001) proposed 10 components of personal empowerment in girls and women, and these themes are especially important to the second and third components of empowerment. They include self-esteem and self-affirmation; a positive comfort-distress ratio as exhibited in daily functioning; self-sustaining behaviors informed by knowledge of gender, culture, and power issues; personal efficacy and control beliefs; the ability to engage in self-nurturance; access to problem-solving skills; flexibility of gender-related behaviors and thinking; assertiveness; the ability to access and use community and personal resources; and the ability to engage in social justice activity. Counselors who work with girls and women seek to develop a wide variety of skills and techniques that assist girls and women in achieving these goals.

Advocacy roles and social change skills are addressed infrequently in counselor training but represent crucial skills for supporting the empowerment of girls and women. These skills may include providing active support when a client needs external intervention to help her reach goals or counteract the negative impact of community systems. They may also involve helping a client negotiate the complexities of a local social service network or mental health system, or advocating for the client when institutional policies are blocking her growth. Many of the high-prevalence problems that affect the mental health concerns of women represent major social problems that need to be addressed within communities, at regional levels, and at national levels. The counselor's involvement in local community efforts (e.g., grassroots community organizations and sexual assault coalitions) and regional/national efforts (e.g., working for legislation and services that support the mental health of girls and women) are important for ensuring the empowerment and mental health of women and challenging institutional and systemic power dynamics that limit the potential of girls and women.

## Ethical Practice

Each of the areas of awareness, knowledge, and skills discussed in this chapter are crucial foundations for ethical practice (Brabeck, 2000). However, several issues related to boundary management merit additional attention. Although the counselor and client work toward establishing a relationship of equality, the counselor avoids a stance of "undifferentiated egalitarianism," which can lead to the blurring of boundaries between counselor and client, inappropriate role reversals, and lapses of attention on the part of the counselor regarding her or his professional responsibility to the client. Counselors bring skills, professional preparation, and the power of expertise and position to the counseling relationship, and these factors are associated with power and role differences. The open discussion of power and role differences in the counseling relationship assists the client in becoming aware of how power dynamics influence counseling and other relationships, provides an opening for the counselor and client to explore ways to reduce power differentials when it is appropriate, and helps clients understand how roles can be negotiated effectively in contexts other than counseling (FTI, 2000).

Boundary violations and power imbalances represent some of the more common forms of unethical behavior and can assume many forms, ranging from blatant forms of sexual misconduct to less invasive but problematic behaviors such as using touch or self-disclosure inappropriately. Both counselor self-disclosure and counselor-initiated touch can provide reassurance, increase trust, and decrease anxiety, but both can also be experienced as unwanted or intrusive, especially by clients who have experienced boundary violations in the past. Thus, decisions to use either tool must be used for specific purposes, rather than haphazardly, and in the best interests of clients. The counselor should consider the meanings self-disclosure and touch hold for clients, the degree to which they reinforce counseling goals, and the degree to which a client's unique history may influence her perceptions of these tools. Sexualized and sexual relationships with clients are the most blatant of boundary violations and are unacceptable under any circumstances (APA, 1979).

## CONCLUDING THOUGHTS

During the past 30 years, substantial progress has been made in addressing the concerns raised by Weisstein (1968/1993) and Chesler (1972). In her 25-year reassessment of the state of psychotherapy, Chesler (1997) cautioned that (a) gender bias and mother blaming have decreased, but subtle stereotyping is still an issue; (b) some of women's medical problems are mislabeled as psychological problems; (c) inadequate progress has been made in addressing issues of diversity and concerns of people of color; (d) those with limited resources have limited access to psychological services; (e) victims of sex discrimination and violence are still pathologized within both clinical and legal systems; and (f) therapist-client sex abuse remains a significant issue. Because of the presence of these ongoing issues, attention to specific awareness, knowledge, and skills is as important in the 21st century as it was 30 years ago.

During the 1990s, some of the most important advancements in conceptualizations about counseling women emphasized the centrality of diversity and multicultural awareness (Worell & Remer, 2003). Espin and Gawelek's (1992) list of core assumptions represent key features for an inclusive multicultural feminist practice: (a) all women's experiences must be explored, valued, and understood; (b) optimal theory and practice are based on an appreciation and valuing of pluralism and difference; (c) cultures and contexts are powerful influences on behavior, and (d) egalitarian relationships are a key to effective practice, and include the understanding that women of diverse statuses can create theory and shape knowledge on their own behalf.

# Case and Questions

Sharon, a 21-year-old African American college student, reported difficulty concentrating on her courses, conflicts with her parents, depressed feelings, anxiety, and nightmares. Other issues included difficulties trusting others, feelings of inadequacy, dysfunctional eating, and alcohol use. During the second session, Sharon reluctantly revealed experiences of sexual harassment in high school and sexual assault 2 months ago. She tearfully blamed herself for being gullible and stupid and was attempting to avoid thinking about the assault by "forgetting" about it and moving on.

(a) How might you go about forming a collaborative relationship with Sharon? In what ways might your own experiences, social identities, privileges, and encounters with oppression enhance or detract from your capacity to form a strong working alliance with Sharon?

(b) The initial information described in the case provides minimal information about Sharon's various social identities. What types of questions might you formulate to help her explore these social identities?

(c) In what ways might Sharon's symptoms represent active survival mechanisms when other methods of coping are not available? How might you go about ensuring that Sharon's symptoms are seen in context rather than as symptoms that merely need to be treated and removed?

(d) What types of societal stereotypes about violence against women may influence Sharon's hesitancy to disclose abuse? To pursuing legal options (e.g., filing rape charges with local authorities)? (See Holzman, 2000; McNair & Neville, 1996; Neville & Heppner, 1999; West, 2000.)

(e) What type of information can you give to Sharon (e.g., about the counseling process) that is likely to enhance your working relationship and support progress toward specific goals?

(f) Assume that your counseling agency operates on a brief therapy model and you will need to work within a 10-session limit. How will you prioritize your goals?

(g) What empowerment goals and skills (see section on skills) seem especially important? In what ways might these empowerment goals be pursued at the level of individual change? Through advocacy? What experiences/activities outside of counseling are likely to support Sharon's empowerment?

# REFERENCES

American Psychiatric Association. (1994). *Diagnostic and statistical manual of mental disorders* (4th ed.). Washington, DC: Author.

American Psychological Association. (1979). Principles concerning the counseling and psychotherapy of women. *The Counseling Psychologist, 8,* 21.

American Psychological Association. (1996). *Violence and the family: Report of the American Psychological Association Presidential Task Force on Violence and the Family.* Washington, DC: Author.

Baber, K. M., & Allen, K. R. (1992). *Women and families: Feminist reconstructions.* New York: Guilford Press.

Barnett, R. C., & Hyde, J. S. (2001). Women, men, work, and family: An expansionist theory. *American Psychologist, 56,* 781–796.

Barnett, R. C., & Rivers, C. (1996). *She works/he works: How two-income families are happier, healthier, and better off.* New York: HarperCollins.

Becker, D. (2001). Diagnosis of psychological disorders: DSM and gender. In J. Worell (Ed.), *Encyclopedia of women and gender* (pp. 333–343). San Diego: Academic Press.

Bem, S. L. (1993). *The lenses of gender: Transforming the debate on sexual inequality.* New Haven, CT: Yale University Press.

Bergeron, S. M., & Senn, C. Y. (1998). Body image and sociocultural norms. *Psychology of Women Quarterly, 22,* 385–401.

Bingham, R. P., & Ward, C. M. (1994). Career counseling with ethnic minority women. In W. B. Walsh & S. H. Osipow (Eds.), *Career counseling for women* (pp. 165–195). Hillsdale, NJ: Erlbaum.

Brabeck, M. (Ed.). (2000). *Practicing feminist ethics in psychology.* Washington, DC: American Psychological Association.

Brady, J. L., Guy, J. D., Poelstra, P. L., & Brokaw, B. F. (1999). Vicarious traumatization, spirituality, and the treatment of sexual abuse survivors: A national survey of women psychotherapists. *Professional Psychology: Research and Practice, 30,* 386–393.

Brooks, L., & Forrest, L. (1994). Feminism and career counseling. In W. B. Walsh & S. H. Osipow (Eds.), *Career counseling for women* (pp. 87–134). Hillsdale, NJ: Erlbaum.

Brown, L. S. (1994). *Subversive dialogues.* New York: Basic Books.

Campbell, B., Schellenberg, E. G., & Senn, C. Y. (1997). Evaluating measures of contemporary sexism. *Psychology of Women Quarterly, 21,* 89–102.

Chernin, J., Holden, J. M., & Chandler, C. (1997). Bias in psychological assessment: Heterosexism. *Measurement and Evaluation in Counseling and Development, 30,* 68–76.

Chesler, P. (1972). *Women and madness.* New York: Doubleday.

Chesler, P. (1997). *Women and madness: Twenty-fifth anniversary edition.* New York: Four Walls Eight Windows.

Collins, K. S., Schoen, D., Joseph, S., Duchon, L., Simantov, E., & Yellowitz, M. (1999). *Health concerns across a woman's lifespan: The Commonwealth Fund 1998 survey of women's health.* New York: Commonwealth Fund.

Comas-Diaz, L., & Greene, B. (Eds.). (1994). *Women of color: Integrating ethnic and gender identities in psychotherapy.* New York: Guilford Press.

Costello, C. B., & Stone, A. J. (Eds.). (2001). *The American woman: 2001–2002.* New York: Norton.

Coster, J. S., & Schwebel, M. (1997). Well-functioning in professional psychologists. *Professional Psychology: Research and Practice, 28,* 5–13.

Crawford, M., & Unger, R. (2000). *Women and gender: A feminist psychology* (3rd ed.). Boston: McGraw-Hill.

Deaux, K., & Stewart, A. J. (2001). Framing gendered identities. In R. Unger (Ed.), *Handbook of the psychology of women and gender* (pp. 84–97). New York: Wiley.

Deiter, P. J., Nicholls, S. S., & Pearlman, L. A. (2000). Self-injury and self capacities: Assisting an individual in crisis. *Journal of Clinical Psychology, 56,* 1173–1191.

Deutsch, F. M., & Saxon, S. E. (1998). Traditional ideologies, nontraditional lives. *Sex Roles, 38,* 331–362.

Dovidio, J. F., & Gaertner, S. L. (1996). Affirmative action, unintentional racial biases, and intergroup relations. *Journal of Social Issues, 52,* 51–75.

Espin, O. (1995). On knowing you are the unknown: Women of color constructing psychology. In J. Adleman & G. Enguidanos (Eds.), *Racism in the lives of women: Testimony, theory and guides to practice* (pp. 127–136). New York: Harrington Park Press.

Espin, O., & Gawelek, M. A. (1992). Women's diversity: Ethnicity, race, class, and gender in theories of feminist psychology. In L. S. Brown & M. Ballou (Eds.), *Personality and psychopathology: Feminist reappraisals* (pp. 88–107). New York: Guilford Press.

Feminist Therapy Institute (2000). *Feminist therapy code of ethics* (revised, 1999). San Francisco: Feminist Therapy Institute.

Foa, E. D., & Riggs, D. S. (1995). Posttraumatic stress disorder following assault: Theoretical considerations and empirical findings. *Current Directions in Psychological Science, 4,* 61–65.

Fredrickson, B. L., & Roberts, R. A. (1997). Objectification theory: Toward understanding women's lived experiences and mental health risks. *Psychology of Women Quarterly, 21,* 173–206.

Gilbert, L. A., & Rader, J. (2001). Current perspectives on women's adult roles: Work, family, and life. In R. Unger (Ed.), *Handbook of the psychology of women and gender* (pp. 156–169). New York: Wiley.

Gilbert, L. A., & Scher, M. (1999). *Gender and sex in counseling and psychotherapy.* Boston: Allyn & Bacon.

Gilbert, S., & Thompson, J. K. (1996). Feminist explanations of the development of eating disorders: Common themes, research findings, and methodological issues. *Clinical Psychology: Science and Practice, 3,* 183–202.

Gilroy, P. J., Caroll, L., & Murra, J. (2001). Does depression affect clinical practice? A survey of women psychotherapists. *Women and Therapy, 23*(4), 13–30.

Gilroy, P. J., Carroll, L., & Murra, J. (2002). A preliminary survey of counseling psychologists' personal experiences with depression and treatment. *Professional Psychology, 33,* 402–407.

Glick, P., & Fiske, S. T. (1997). Hostile and benevolent sexism: Measuring ambivalent sexist attitudes toward women. *Psychology of Women Quarterly, 21,* 119–136.

Goodwin, S. A., & Fiske, S. T. (2001). Power and gender: The double-edged sword of ambivalence. In R. Unger (Ed.), *Handbook of the psychology of women and gender* (pp. 358–366). New York: Wiley.

Greene, B., & Sanchez-Hucles, J. (1997). Diversity: Advancing an inclusive feminist psychology. In J. Worell & N. G. Johnson (Eds.), *Shaping the future of feminist psychology* (pp. 173–202). Washington, DC: American Psychological Association.

Greenspan, M. (1993). *A new approach to women and therapy.* New York: McGraw-Hill.

Gutek, B. A., & Done, R. S. (2001). Sexual harassment. In R. Unger (Ed.), *Handbook of the psychology of women and gender* (pp. 367–387). New York: Wiley.

Hackett, G., & Lonborg, S. D. (1994). Career assessment and counseling for women. In W. B. Walsh & S. H. Osipow (Eds.), *Career counseling for women* (pp. 43–85). Hillsdale, NJ: Erlbaum.

Hartung, C. M., & Widiger, T. A. (1998). Gender differences in the diagnosis of mental disorders: Conclusions and controversies of the DSM-IV. *Psychological Bulletin, 123,* 260–278.

Harway, M., & Hansen, M. (1993). Therapist perceptions of family violence. In M. Hansen & M. Harway (Eds.), *Battering and family therapy: A feminist perspective* (pp. 1–12). Newbury Park, CA: Sage.

Hawxhurst, D. M., & Morrow, S. L. (1984). *Living our visions: Building feminist community.* Tempe, AZ: Fourth World.

Herman, J. L. (1992). *Trauma and recovery: The aftermath of violence.* New York: Basic Books.

Holzman, C. G. (2000). Counseling adult women rape survivors: Issues of race, ethnicity, and class. *Women and Therapy, 19*(2), 47–62.

Horvath, A. O. (2000). The therapeutic relationship: From transference to alliance. *Journal of Clinical Psychology, 56,* 163–173.

Kaplan, M. (1983). A woman's view of DSM-III. *American Psychologist, 38,* 786–792.

Koss, M. P. (1993). Rape: Scope, impact, interventions, and public policy responses. *American Psychologist, 48,* 1062–1069.

Lerman, H. (1986). *A mote in Freud's eye.* New York: Springer.

Little, L., & Hamby, S. L. (1996). Impact of a clinician's sexual abuse history, gender, and theoretical orientation on treatment issues related to childhood sexual abuse. *Professional Psychology: Research and Practice, 27,* 617–625.

Mahoney, M. J. (1997). Psychotherapists' personal problems and self-care patterns. *Professional Psychology, 28,* 14–16.

Marecek, J. (1995). Gender, politics, and psychology's ways of knowing. *American Psychologist, 50,* 162–163.

Marecek, J. (2001). Disorderly constructs: Feminist frameworks for clinical psychology. In R. Unger (Ed.), *Handbook of the psychology of women and gender* (pp. 303–316). New York: Wiley.

McIntosh, P. (1989, July/August). White privilege: Unpacking the invisible knapsack. *Peace and Freedom,* 10–12.

McNair, L. D., & Neville, H. A. (1996). African American women survivors of sexual assault: The intersection of race and class. *Women and Therapy, 18*(3/4), 107–118.

Morton, S. B. (1998). Lesbian divorce. *American Journal of Orthopsychiatry, 68,* 410–419.

Nelson, M. L. (1993). A current perspective on gender differences: Implications for research in counseling. *Journal of Counseling Psychology, 40,* 200–209.

Neville, H. A., & Heppner, M. J. (1999). Contextualizing rape: Reviewing sequelae and proposing a culturally inclusive ecological model of sexual assault recovery. *Applied and Preventive Psychology, 3,* 41–62.

Pearlman, L. A., & MacIan, P. S. (1995). Vicarious traumatization: An empirical study of the effects of trauma work on trauma therapists. *Professional Psychology, 26,* 558–565.

Pearlman, L. A., & Saakvitne, K. W. (1995). *Trauma and the therapist.* New York: Norton.

Polusny, M. A., & Follette, V. M. (1996). Remembering childhood sexual abuse: A national survey of psychologists' clinical practices, beliefs, and personal experiences. *Professional Psychology: Research and Practice, 27,* 41–52.

Pope, K. S., & Feldman-Summers, S. (1992). National survey of psychologists' sexual and physical abuse history and their evaluation of training and competence in these areas. *Professional Psychology: Research and Practice, 23,* 353–361.

Roades, L. A. (2000). Mental health issues for women. In M. Biaggio & M. Hersen (Eds.), *Issues in the psychology of women* (pp. 251–272). New York: Kluwer Academic/Plenum.

Santos de Barona, M. S., & Dutton, M. A. (1997). Feminist perspectives on assessment. In J. Worell & N. G. Johnson (Eds.), *Shaping the future of feminist psychology* (pp. 37–56). Washington, DC: American Psychological Association.

Schauben, L. J., & Frazier, P. A. (1995). Vicarious trauma: The effects on female counselors of working with sexual violence survivors. *Psychology of Women Quarterly, 19,* 49–64.

Spelman, E. V. (1988). *Inessential woman.* Boston: Beacon Press.

Steil, J. M. (2001). Family forms and member well-being: A research agenda for the decade of behavior. *Psychology of Women Quarterly, 25,* 344–363.

Swim, J. K., Aikin, K. J., Hall, W. S., & Hunter, B. A. (1995). Sexism and racism: Old fashioned and modern prejudices. *Journal of Personality and Social Psychology, 68,* 199–214.

Thompson, B. W. (1994). *A hunger so wide and so deep.* Minneapolis, MN: University of Minnesota Press.

Tjaden, P., & Thoennes, N. (1998). *Prevalence, incidence, and consequences of violence against women: Findings from the National Violence Against Women Survey.* Washington, DC: U.S. Department of Justice, Office of Justice Programs, National Institute of Justice.

Travis, C. B., Meginnis, K. L., & Bardari, K. M. (2000). Beauty, sexuality, and identity: The social control of women. In C. B. Travis & J. W. White (Eds.),

*Sexuality, society, and feminism* (pp. 237–272). Washington, DC: American Psychological Association.

Weisstein, N. (1968/1993). Psychology constructs the female; or the fantasy life of the male psychologist. *Feminism and Psychology, 3,* 195–210.

West, C. M. (2000). Developing an "oppositional gaze" toward the images of Black women. In J. C. Chrisler, C. Golden, & P. D. Rozee (Eds.), *Lectures on the psychology of women* (2nd ed., pp. 221–233). Boston: McGraw-Hill.

West, C., & Zimmerman, D. G. (1987). Doing gender. *Gender and Society, 1,* 125–151.

White, J. W., Donat, P. L. N., & Bondurant, B. (2001). A developmental examination of violence against girls and women. In R. Unger (Ed.), *Handbook of the psychology of women and gender* (pp. 343–357). New York: Wiley.

Worell, J. (2001). Feminist interventions: Accountability beyond symptom reduction. *Psychology of Women Quarterly, 25,* 335–343.

Worell, J. (2002). Guidelines for psychological practice with girls and women: Update. *The Feminist Psychologist, 29*(3), 8,10.

Worell, J., & Remer, P. (2003). *Feminist perspectives in therapy: Empowering diverse women* (2nd ed.). New York: Wiley.

Wyche, K. F. (2001). Sociocultural issues in counseling for women of color. In R. Unger (Ed.), *Handbook of the psychology of women and gender* (pp. 330–340). New York: Wiley.

Wyche, K. F., & Rice, J. K. (1997). Feminist therapy: From dialogue to tenets. In J. Worell & N. G. Johnson (Eds.), *Shaping the future of feminist psychology* (pp. 57–71). Washington, DC: American Psychological Association.

Wylie, M. S. (1995, May/June). Diagnosing for dollars. *Family Therapy Networker,* 23–34, 65–69.

# CHAPTER 13

# Approaches to Counseling and Psychotherapy with Women

## Laura U. Forrest, California State University, Long Beach

Although women are the primary recipients of counseling and psychotherapy, the field of counseling and psychotherapy with women is relatively new (Worell & Remer, 2003). Because of the inadequacies of past counseling theories to address the unique problems of women and attend to the influence of gender-role socialization (see chapter 12, "Counseling Girls and Women: Attitudes, Knowledge, and Skills"), feminist therapy arose to provide alternative approaches to conceptualizing women's issues and to design appropriate interventions.

Developing out of the consciousness-raising movement of the 1960s, feminist therapy has gone from relative anonymity to become a pervasive force within counseling and therapy, influencing other theories and schools of thought. During its relatively brief existence, feminist therapy has grown rapidly in scope and acceptance as an effective treatment and is an increasingly prominent approach to therapy today. Popular theories texts now regularly include sections within each theoretical orientation explicating the theory's application to women and persons of color (Sharf, 2000) as well as whole chapters on feminist theory (Prochaska & Norcross, 2003; Sharf, 2000).

Teasing out what is uniquely feminist in therapy has become problematic because feminist critiques and ideas have become incorporated into other theories. Most schools of therapy grew out of psychological theories, and their practices can be traced to the principles derived from these theories. As Brown (1994) pointed out, feminist therapy arose out of practice, rather than from a coherent theoretical framework. Unlike other counseling theories, feminist therapy was not created by one famous person; many women, both practitioners and academics, felt that existing models of therapy were inadequate for women, and their ideas converged to form the field of feminist therapy (Unger & Crawford, 1996). Many of its adherents were initially trained in diverse theoretical orientations. Consequently, there has been a wide variety of viewpoints on what the core tenets of feminist therapy should be (Enns, 1992b, 1993). Feminist therapy also developed out of feminist philosophy, which is itself diverse (Brown, 1994; Enns, 1992b). This lineage has resulted in diverse approaches to and definitions of feminist therapy, with many disparate theoretical orientations subsumed under its broad umbrella. However, important theorists are beginning to delineate and differentiate what feminist therapy is and, more importantly, what it is not (Brown, 1994). By trying to be as inclusive as possible and respect differences of opinion among its adherents, feminist therapy runs the risk of becoming yet another school of eclecticism. Indeed, many feminist therapists (Dutton-Douglas & Walker, 1988; Enns, 1997; Worell & Remer, 1992) do not see feminist therapy as a single, unified approach but refer to "feminist therapies." However, recent attempts at defining feminist therapy, such as those articulated at the Conference on Education and Training in Feminist Practice (Brown, 1986, 1994, Wyche & Rice, 1997), have identified some common areas of agreement among diverse groups of practitioners.

## CORE TENETS OF FEMINIST THERAPY

Several authors have attempted to summarize the core tenets of feminist therapy (Brown, 1994; Enns, 1997; Worell & Remer, 2003; Wyche & Rice, 1997) (see Table 13.1). These ideas can be summarized under four broad doctrines of feminist therapy: (1) attention to diversity of women's multiple identities; (2) utilization of a consciousness-raising approach; (3) development of egalitarian relationships; and (4) encouragement of a woman-valuing and self-validating process. Specific counseling techniques for each principle are explained in the "Special Skills/Treatment Strategies" section.

### Attention to Diversity of Women's Multiple Identities

The first principle, *attention to the diversity of women's multiple identities,* focuses on personal and social identities (Wyche & Rice, 1997) that women may or may not be aware of and their influences on the client's outlook, behavior, and her experience of privilege or oppression (or both). As chapters 12 and 14 point out, feminist therapy has become aware of its past mistake of primarily focusing on gender oppression for all women instead of acknowledging the diversity of women's lives and the intersections of racism, classism, and homophobia with sexism (Greene & Sanchez-Hucles, 1997). By recognizing the interdependence of women's multiple social and personal identities, gender is no longer presumed to be the primary source of oppression in all women's lives. Instead, "the meaning of gender . . . varies in its social construction across cultural contexts" (Worell & Remer, 2003, p. 67). For example, Greene and Sanchez-Hucles (1997) pointed out the historical differences in the meaning of work and career for diverse women. Women who have had to work in low-wage or -status occupations for generations have a very different experience from their counterparts who have focused on the rights of women to work and break through the "glass ceiling" in relatively satisfying and economically rewarding career fields.

### Utilization of Consciousness-Raising Approach

The second principle uses *a consciousness-raising approach,* helping clients distinguish between sexist, racist, or homophobic social and political systems (external structures) that affect women and internal influences that can cause problems

**TABLE 13.1**   Core Tenets of Feminist Therapy

1. Feminist therapy recognizes that being female always occurs in a cultural, social, political, economic, and historical context and affects development across the life span.
2. Feminist therapy focuses on the cultural, social, political, economic, and historical factors of women's lives as well as intrapsychic factors across the life span.
3. Feminist therapy includes an analysis of power and its relationship to the multiple ways women are oppressed; factors such as gender, race, class, ethnicity, sexual orientation, age, and ablebodiness, singly or in combination, can be the basis for oppression.
4. Feminist therapy acknowledges that violence against women, overt and covert, is emotionally, physically, and spiritually damaging.
5. Feminist therapy acknowledges that misogyny exists in all women's lives and is emotionally, physically, and spiritually damaging.
6. Feminist therapy's primary focus is on strengths rather than deficits. Therefore, women's behaviors are seen as understandable efforts to respond adaptively to oppressive occurrences.
7. Feminist therapy is committed to social change that supports equality for everyone.
8. Feminist therapy is based on the constant and explicit monitoring of the power balance between therapist and client and pays attention to the potential abuse and misuse of power within the therapeutic relationship.
9. Feminist therapy strives toward an egalitarian and nonauthoritarian relationship based on mutual respect.
10. Feminist therapy is a collaborative process in which the therapist and client establish the goals, direction, and pace of therapy.
11. Feminist therapy helps girls and women understand how they have incorporated societal beliefs and values. The therapist works collaboratively with them to challenge and transform those constructs that are destructive to the self and helps them create their own perspectives.
12. Feminist therapy empowers girls and women to recognize, claim, and embrace their individual and collective power as girls and women.
13. Feminist therapy expands girls' and women's alternatives, options, and choices across the life span.
14. Feminist therapy is a demystification process that validates and affirms the shared and diverse experiences of girls' and women's lives.
15. Feminist therapy involves appropriate types of self-disclosure. However, because self-disclosure may be harmful, it must be both value and theory driven and always in the client's best interest. Therapists must develop methods of continually monitoring their level of self-awareness.
16. Feminist therapists are committed to continually monitoring their own biases, distortions, and limitations, especially with respect to cultural, social, political, economic, and historical aspects of girls' and women's experiences.

From Wyche & Rice, 1997, p. 69.

for women. This principle is often referred to as "the personal is political" (Enns, 1997; Worell & Remer, 1992, 2003), a rallying cry from the early feminist political movement that refers to the fact that problems women experience in their personal lives often have common social or political roots, such as institutionalized sexism, racism, or homophobia. "Women's behaviors are seen as understandable efforts to respond adaptively to oppressive occurrences" (Wyche & Rice, 1997, p. 67). From this viewpoint, symptoms are often seen as methods of coping with external sources of oppression that no longer work for the client (Enns, 1997). By becoming aware of how they were socialized to conform to gender-role stereotypes, clients can replace their internalized oppressive messages with schemas that are freely chosen and more flexible. An example of this process would be an exploration of the messages that women get about unrealistic ideal female bodies. This body image distortion often results in disordered eating and unhealthy self-concepts. As clients become aware of the societal messages they have received from advertising and media about what their bodies should look like, they can replace these messages with positive, healthy images of realistic women.

By helping clients separate the internal versus external sources of distress, feminist therapy does not ignore individual responsibility for change. Rather, feminist therapists help clients take responsibility for changing themselves, which might include changing their internalized messages about gender roles, and for changing their environment as another step in taking back power. The critical difference in feminist therapy is that clients are not encouraged to adjust to the "dysfunctional environment"; the focus is on changing both the unhealthy internalized messages and the environment that created them (Worell & Remer, 2003). Clients are helped to identify ways in which they have developed coping mechanisms in response to an oppressive system of patriarchy, how these coping mechanisms no longer work well for them, and how they might develop new, healthier strategies (Enns, 1997).

Feminist therapy does not stop at changing women's internalized messages. There is a unique emphasis within feminist therapy on initiating and participating in social change, on the part of both clients and therapists (Wyche & Rice, 1997). An example of this might be a sexual abuse survivor who has undergone successful feminist therapy consolidating her gains and giving back through psychoeducational efforts in the schools aimed at preventing sexual abuse among children. For feminist counselors, this might include advocating not only for their specific clients but becoming active in social change movements (Wyche & Rice, 1997) that emphasize women's issues, such as abortion rights. Feminist therapy's emphasis on social change has been criticized for bringing politics into therapy. Feminist therapists believe that all theoretical orientations are political and that none are value-free and objective; it is important to be up front with our clients about our values so that they can judge for themselves whether or not we are trying to unduly influence them.

## Development of Egalitarian Relationships

The third principle encourages the *development of egalitarian relationships,* including the therapeutic relationship (Enns, 1997; Worell & Remer, 1992, 2003; Wyche & Rice, 1997). Although they acknowledge the inherent power differentials that exist between the client and the counselor, feminist therapists strive to minimize this and explain the therapeutic process, eventually translating this into ways in which the client can practice self-help. Feminist therapists are up front about their values and beliefs and use self-disclosure when it is appropriate and beneficial to the client. Feminist therapists emphasize a collaborative process between counselor and client, where the client is seen as the expert on her own life and the counselor contributes counseling skills and knowledge (Enns, 1997; Wyche & Rice, 1997). Feminist therapists are especially aware of their own positions of power and privilege, and also of domination and oppression, in relation to students they supervise (Brown, 1994).

By modeling an egalitarian relationship and balancing power between the client and the counselor, feminist therapy invites women to extend the notion of equality beyond the therapy hour to all interpersonal relationships. Clients are taught to analyze the balance of power in their relationships and make informed choices about changing power imbalances in their lives by assessing the costs and benefits (Worell & Remer, 2003). An example of analysis of power and equality in a woman's personal relationship might entail reframing a client's complaints about her spouse's lack of equal sharing of household responsibilities. Information about this documented inequality between dual-career couples, also known as "the second shift" (Hochschild, 1989), can help a client analyze the power imbalance in her own relationship and its result in terms of inequities in household chores. The therapist would help the client analyze who has the power in her relationship, what that means to her, and how she can make informed choices about the types of relationships she wants to engage in, including a cost/benefit analysis of planned changes she wishes to implement.

## Encouragement of a Woman-Valuing and Self-Validating Process

The last principle promotes a *woman-valuing and self-validating process,* respecting traditional female traits such as emotional expressiveness, cooperation and communication, nurturance, and interdependence that are often devalued by society (Enns, 1997; Worell & Remer, 1992, 2003). One common misconception about feminist therapy is that its objective is to make women more like men; however, the goal is to recognize that the preceding characteristics can be beneficial for both women and men. These traits are often devalued in society at the same time that women are reinforced for possessing them (or punished for not possessing them), creating a classic double bind. The notion of codependency is an excellent example of this; women are faulted for becoming enmeshed with significant others while they are expected to put other's needs before their own (Worell & Remer, 2003). The second part of this principle focuses on women learning to trust their inner perceptions and life experiences. Learning to identify their personal strengths, valuing themselves, and taking care of their own needs are all goals of this principle. An example of this would be to build on the knowledge of socially defined ideals of physical attractiveness (applying the example in the second principle discussed) by learning to enjoy and accept their own bodies (Worell & Remer, 2003).

Other important issues in feminist therapy theory include critiques of diagnosis, biased measurement instruments, and traditional diagnostic categorization (Enns, 1993). Although feminist therapy was created to address the concerns of women, it has also been applied to the gender-role concerns of men, such as the socialized gender-role expectation that men must be the primary breadwinners in heterosexual families (the ancillary of women's stereotypic role of being the primary caregivers of offspring and elders). There is a debate within the feminist therapy literature about the legitimacy of men as practitioners of feminist therapy (Enns,

1997; Szymanski, Baird, & Kornman, 2002). Some feminist therapists proclaim that only women can practice feminist therapy, and some recommend that male therapists whose work is informed by feminist principles refer to themselves as *profeminist* therapists (Ganley, 1988).

## MULTICULTURAL ISSUES

Current feminist counseling pays more attention to multicultural issues in counseling than most other theories due to its focus on external sociological influences that affect the individual. However, feminist therapy has been justifiably criticized by women of color (Espin, 1995; hooks, 2000) as focusing on the perspectives of middle-class White women and generalizing these concerns to all women. Indeed, in its beginning stages, feminist therapy often equated sexism with racism and ignored the multiple oppressions that women of color must endure. Currently the field of feminist therapy has begun to acknowledge its own shortcomings in this area (Comas-Diaz & Greene, 1994; Greene & Sanchez-Hucles, 1997) and to examine the notion of White privilege (Hobgood, 2000) as part of its continual effort at analysis of power in relationships. Greene and Sanchez-Hucles (1997) pointed out that feminist theorists have also traditionally overlooked the concerns of women with disabilities, older women, lesbians, and poor women. Attention to diversity issues and becoming more inclusive have become relatively recent focal points of feminist therapy (Enns, 1997; Landrine, 1995; Worell & Remer, 2003).

In an effort to rectify past omissions, feminist therapists are currently formulating recommendations for including diversity issues in their analyses of oppression. Some authors have suggested that, ideally, an *ethnospecific* feminist approach should be employed in therapy with women of color (Espin, 1994). An ethnospecific feminist approach in therapy is distinguished by a therapeutic dyad in which the client and counselor share the same background. As mentioned previously, many feminist therapists feel that women counselors have a deeper empathic understanding of women's concerns because they share many of the same gender experiences (Enns, 1997; Szymanski et al., 2002). In her seminal book *Women and Madness,* Chesler (1972) criticized the then common male therapist/female client dyad as duplicating the injurious social norm of male dominance and female submission; by extension, a White woman therapist/woman-of-color client dyad replicates the larger culture's power imbalance of privilege/oppression. However, when the counselor and client are both women of the same ethnic or racial background, they understand each other's values, culture, and belief systems on a deeper level (Espin, 1994). Also, in an ethnospecific dyad, the counselor can serve as a role model for the client, and the power differentials between the therapist and client can be further minimized due to the absence of privilege and power dynamics that mirror society at large. Espin (1994) acknowledged that this ideal situation is seldom possible in reality due to the lack of feminist therapists who are women of color. She cautioned White feminist therapists to avoid relying on the client to educate them about culture, class, and ethnic or racial differences, which puts the burden on the client and takes the focus off the client's needs. Indeed, many majority culture therapists remain unaware of oppression and the effects of their own position of privilege while clients of color are intimately familiar with the customs and culture of majority culture out of necessity (Collins, 1991, as cited in Enns, 1997). Espin (1994) further advocated that majority culture therapists acknowledge not only the deleterious effects of racism from the larger society on the client's experience but also how those effects may be unwittingly played out in the therapeutic dyad. Espin urged the White feminist therapist to adopt a nondefensive attitude, realizing that clients of color may bring a healthy adaptive "cultural paranoia" to the therapeutic relationship.

## SPECIAL SKILLS/TREATMENT STRATEGIES

Although the issues that women bring to counseling should not be separated into compartmentalized categories (Worell & Remer, 2003), several client concerns are particularly prevalent among women, including depression and anxiety, eating disorders and body image, sexual abuse and assault, and domestic violence and interpersonal abuse. Many authors have recognized the interaction effects between, for instance, depression and experiences of physical and sexual abuse (McGrath, Keita, Strickland, & Russo, 1990). The following sections review some of the most common concerns women bring to therapy and general recommendations for treatment. Then, the primary techniques of feminist therapy are outlined, with suggestions for practice.

### General Counseling Techniques for High-Prevalence Problems

Across all factors (such as age, ethnicity, marital status, etc.) depression affects twice as many women as men (American Psychological Association, 2002). Three major sources are often conceptualized as contributing to women's disproportionate rates of depression: biological influences, societal status, and gender-role socialization (Worell & Remer, 2003). Cognitive behavioral and interpersonal psychotherapy treatments for depression have been shown to be effective (Elkin, Shea, Watkins, & Imber, 1989), but special attention to women's issues is warranted. Worell and Remer (2003) advocated including psychoeducation about the possible biological influences on depression, an analysis of the influence of women's disadvantaged social status, and an examination of the gender-role messages women receive that become translated into self-blame, withdrawal from challenges, and feelings of incompetence.

Eating disorders, including anorexia, bulimia, and binge eating, are often acknowledged as culturally bound syndromes that are primarily experienced by women (Marecek, 2001). There is great debate about the cause of disordered eating, with some authors tracing it to the "culture of thinness," some blaming the sexual objectification of women, and others reporting research findings conceptualizing disordered eating as a response to severe emotional stress (Frederickson & Roberts, 1997, and Thompson, 1995, as cited in Marecek, 2001). Irving (2002) described effective components of eating disorder prevention programs, including encouraging a healthy body image, psychoeducational efforts that confront unhealthy media messages, and supporting acceptance of diverse body shapes.

Women are also disproportionate victims of sexual abuse and assault. Post-traumatic stress disorder (PTSD; American Psychiatric Association, 2000) does locate the cause of the disorder in external traumatic events but has been criticized for not including all common reactions to trauma in its criteria, ignoring cultural contexts that increase the risk of exposure to trauma (Sanchez-Hucles & Hudgins, 2001). Because the reactions to sexual abuse and assault include psychological, physical/somatic, and sociocultural responses (Koss, Heise, & Russo, 1994), they are often complex. Specific treatment strategies recommended for counselors working with survivors of incest and sexual assault include discussing the effects of traumatic events, the recovery process, challenging the victim's self-blame, developing support networks, and helping survivors understand how their symptoms can be seen as a form of communication (Brown, 1994; Worell & Remer, 2003). Beyond the effects of sexual abuse and assault on its direct victims, the threat of violence serves to intimidate all women (Rozee, 1996). All initial intakes and assessment interviews with women should include screening for possible depression, disordered eating, and interpersonal violence and abuse (Worell & Remer, 2003).

## Feminist Therapy Techniques

How do the theoretical tenets of feminist therapy translate into practice? The practice of feminist therapy begins before the client ever crosses the counselor's threshold. It starts with counselors' self-awareness of their own gender-role socialization (Brown, 1986, 1990, as cited in Hackett & Lonborg, 1994) and extends to their pursuit of cultural competence (Wyche, 2001) and adaptation of an antiracist stance, rejecting the privileges they might unwittingly possess due to their race and class (Brown, 1994). Including gender issues as a primary area of assessment in the initial intake interview sets feminist therapy apart from many other approaches. Indeed, everything about traditional assessment and diagnosis has been set on its head by feminist therapists, from criticism of traditional diagnostic labels à la the *Diagnostic and Statistical Manual of Mental Disorders* (American Psychiatric Association, 2000) as being sexist and culturally bound (Caplan, 1995; Lerman, 1996) to analysis of assessment instruments for biased items, inappropriate norm groups, and interpretation instructions (Hackett & Lonborg, 1994; Worell & Remer, 2003). Feminist counselors advocate not only the use of culture- and gender-fair tests and inventories but also consideration of gender implications when interpreting results and sharing them with clients. For instance, Hackett and Lonborg (1994) encouraged counselors who are counseling a client with career concerns to explore the gender-role messages clients have received about success and gender-appropriate occupations.

The primary technique of feminist therapy is *gender-role analysis,* which is the practical application of all of the principles named in the preceding discussion (Brown, 1986; Hackett & Lonborg, 1994; Worell & Remer, 2003). Clients are taught to identify the traditional gender-role messages they have received throughout their lives and examine the sources of these messages (parents, media, educational institutions, peer pressure). Examples of these messages about how women should and shouldn't act include dressing in certain ways, playing with particular toys, choosing selected occupations, and so on. Then clients are invited to weigh the costs and benefits of these messages to themselves and to women in general. Hackett and Lonberg (1994) offered an example of a client weighing the possible costs and benefits of both traditional feminine behaviors (such as nurturance and dependence) and nontraditional behaviors (such as self-care and independence). By recognizing how they have internalized these messages and deciding whether or not they want to change them, clients are able to modify messages that negatively influence their self-perception, beliefs, and behavior. Clients realize they have a wider range of behaviors available to choose from and can make better informed decisions about how they choose to behave (Hackett & Lonberg, 1994). Clients strategize plans for implementing these changes, prepare for possible resistance to these changes from others in their lives, and finally put their new choices into action. Group counseling can be a particularly effective modality for gender-role analysis (Worell & Remer, 2003).

Related to gender-role analysis are the techniques of *cultural and power analyses* (Worell & Remer, 2003). These techniques translate the first three principles (attention to the diversity of women's multiple identities, a consciousness-raising approach, and the development of egalitarian relationships) into practice. Cultural analysis attends to the multiple social locations, or cultural contexts, that affect the client's concerns. By considering clients' problems within their sociocultural context, the counselor and client collaborate in examining the influence of external injustices and multiple sources of oppression. Worell and Remer (2003) provided a useful list of questions to explore with clients, including examining the perhaps disparate incidence of clients' particular issues among various microcultural groups that clients may belong to as part of their identity (low or high SES levels, sexual identity, male or female, Whites or persons of color, persons with disabilities, etc.). Dissimilar rates of occurrence might indicate the disproportionate consequence of oppression. Helping clients understand their cultural and gender identity development might also shed light on contextual considerations specific to the issues they bring to therapy. For instance, women of color are disproportionately represented among victims of relationship violence; this is often attributed to the "displaced anger of oppressed men" of color (Espin, 1994, p. 266), who are denied outlets for success and appropriate expressions of assertiveness. Without condoning this inappropriate expression of frustration and labeling it as the injustice that it is, exploring the root causes may help women of color to understand their disproportionate victimization without accepting or justifying it.

Another related feminist therapy technique is power analysis. By examining the notion of power in relationships and societal institutions, women can begin to distinguish the kinds of power they currently possess and to which they have access (Worell & Remer, 2003), as well as to identify the kind of power they want to wield in their private lives and in the world at large. Again, the emphasis is on looking at the internalized messages they have received about power and its usage, both in positive and negative ways. Clients and counselors look at the obstacles women face in accessing power and employing a wider variety of choices in how they exercise their power. An example of this might be raising clients' awareness of the resiliency of gender-based power differentials between men and women (Goodwin & Fiske, 2001) and helping them look at the effects of this social inequity in their own lives. For example, women are often accused of being manipulative in relationships; a feminist therapist might help a client analyze her actions in light of the traditional power inequities between genders and ways in which women creatively cope with this situation by finding other avenues to power. Growing up in our society, what did the client learn about whether or not women have access to power, if it is acceptable for women to be powerful, how women get power, or if they are "allowed" to display power in social relationships? By looking at ways in which women acquire interpersonal power as a coping mechanism because of constrained avenues to power, the client can experiment with new ways of equalizing the power within her interpersonal relationships.

Assertive communication is one method of establishing women's power in interpersonal relationships. By giving their rights up to others, women often become frustrated, angry, and depressed or feel helpless in relationships with others. Assertion training (AT) has behavioral roots but has been widely used with women, both individually and in groups. Jakubowski's (1977) classic four-phase AT program is designed for groups of 6 to 10 women who meet for 2-hour sessions over 6 to 10 weeks. Teaching clients the difference between passive, aggressive, and assertive behavior and communication is the first step in AT. Next, clients examine their right to stand up for themselves without infringing on the rights of others. Clients scrutinize internal obstacles to behaving assertively, such as socialized gender-role schemas (Bem, 1981), and then role-play new ways of communicating assertively. The program is designed for flexibility in tailoring the interventions to clients' individual needs.

However, several authors (Enns, 1992a; Fodor & Epstein, 1983; Kahn, 1981; Linehan & Egan, 1979; Stere, 1985) have criticized AT for overemphasizing individual change over social change, the implied assumption that women's communication patterns are faulty and should reflect the male, "healthy" model of assertive communication, and that there are often real costs to women when they stand up for themselves. AT may encourage women to accommodate themselves to cultural mandates of success and individual achievement. In response, Enns (1992a) developed a powerful feminist therapy group intervention combining AT and consciousness-raising methods.

Consciousness-raising (CR) groups are the womb from which feminist therapy itself emerged, so it is not surprising that CR techniques are still very useful in feminist therapy. Early CR groups were unstructured self-help groups that emphasized the commonalities among women and the power of social change. These groups were leaderless by design, with members sharing responsibility for what happened in the groups. Although the importance of social change was stressed, members often reported that the groups' greatest benefits were providing them with emotional support (Kravetz, 1980; Lieberman & Bond, 1976; Weitz, 1982). As they spoke about their personal problems, they realized "that what each thought was individual is in fact common, that what each considered a personal problem has a social cause and probably a political solution" (Freeman, 1984). Over the years, these groups became an integral part of feminist therapy with several modifications. The CR groups retained the emphasis on shared commonalities among women that were based on external social factors and their supportive atmosphere for both personal growth and collective action. Although the importance of egalitarian relationships was retained, problems arose due to lack of leadership and structure, such as lots of talk but not much change or action (Kirsch, 1987; Phillips, 1997). In the newest versions of CR groups, trained leaders often lead groups with planned interventions and activities (Enns, 1992a).

## CONCLUSION

Growing out of the social movements of the 1960s, feminist therapy developed into a strong movement that has transformed counseling and psychotherapy, changing the way that all counselors and therapists viewed their clients in terms of gender. Feminist therapy has continued to evolve as a powerful means of looking at external influences on clients' internal realities, such as sexism, racism, and homophobia. The philosophy that *the personal is political,* or advocacy for social change and an emphasis on looking at the external causes of women's oppression, and the principle of *egalitarian relationships,* which refers to looking for power differentials in relationships, are both important contributions of feminist therapy. Feminist therapy also *values the female perspective,* transforming traditionally female qualities, such as nurturance and caring, into attributes that are celebrated and honored.

# Cases and Questions

1. You are a school counselor at a large public high school and receive a referral from a teacher for a 16-year-old student, Molly. She shows definite signs of disordered eating and disturbed body image; she is seriously underweight (she weighs less than 85% of the weight that is considered normal for her height and age); reports dieting, fasting, and excessively exercising regularly; and perceives herself as "fat." Molly does not feel that her weight is an issue as she is a cheerleader and a member of the gymnastics team who needs to "stay fit." She reports that her family supports her efforts to lose weight and that she and her mother often exercise together and share diet meals. She also mentions that her friends also share her values about weight loss and fitness.

   (a) How will you bridge the gap between the client's values and what you know about healthy body weight and unrealistic cultural expectations about women's bodies? What if the client feels that you are trying to impose your values on her?

(b) What are some of the gender-role messages that she might have received at home and at school? What are some of the socializing influences from the larger culture that you might identify about women's bodies to help her understand where she might have received these messages?

(c) Would you consult with or refer Molly to the school nurse or a nutritionist or a medical professional? If so, how? If not, why not? After securing Molly's permission (through a release of information), would you discuss her weight loss with her parents, especially her mother? Why or why not?

2. As a marriage and family therapist, you begin seeing a young couple, David and Diana, who report that they have been happily married for 5 years but are recently experiencing conflict due to Diana's pregnancy, which they are both pleased about. However, Diana, who is Latina, states that she was puzzled when David expressed his hope that she would quit her job once the baby is born. David, who is African American, acknowledges that his reaction also surprised him but states that he feels strongly that children need their mothers as primary caregivers during the first few years of life. Upon exploration of their family backgrounds, you learn that although Diana's mother was a stay-at-home mother, she encouraged Diana to pursue a fulfilling career, which Diana reports has happened; she loves her work at a large public relations firm. David reports that although his mother had to work during his childhood, members of his extended family always cared for him and he never resented his mother's need to work, understanding that it was necessary to the family's economic well-being. He states, "My mother never had a choice, and I understand that. However, we can afford for Diana to stay at home for a few years."

(a) How might your own background and beliefs influence your work with this couple? Would you feel a need to self-disclose your background or beliefs before working with them? Why or why not?

(b) What issues of power and gender-role constraints do you see in this dilemma? How can you value both clients' perspectives if you are a man or a woman? Do you see any social or political implications in this couple's impasse?

(c) From your understanding of the intersections of gender, culture, and socioeconomic class, what type of feminist approach might you take in working with this family? Please provide a rationale for your approach.

## REFERENCES

American Psychiatric Association, A. P. (2000). *Diagnostic and statistical manual of mental disorders* (text revision). Washington, DC: American Psychiatric Association.

American Psychological Association. (2002). *Proceedings: Summit on women and depression.* Washington, DC: Author.

Bem, S. L. (1981). Gender schema theory: A cognitive account of sex typing. *Psychological Review, 88,* 354–364.

Brown, L. S. (1986). Gender-role analysis: A neglected component of psychological assessment. *Psychotherapy, 23,* 243–248.

Brown, L. S. (1994). *Subversive dialogues.* New York: Basic Books.

Caplan, P. J. (1995). *They say you're crazy: How the world's most powerful psychiatrists decide who's normal.* Reading, MA: Addison-Wesley.

Chesler, P. (1972). *Women and madness.* New York: Doubleday.

Comas-Diaz, L., & Greene, B. (1994). *Women of color: Integrating ethnic and gender identities in psychotherapy.* New York: Guilford Press.

Dutton-Douglas, M. A., & Walker, L. E. A. (1988). *Feminist psychotherapies: Integration of therapeutic and feminist systems.* Westport, CT: Ablex Publishing.

Elkin, I., Shea, M. T., Watkins, J. T., & Imber, S. D. (1989). National Institute of Mental Health Treatment of Depression Collaborative Research Program: General effectiveness of treatments. *Archives of General Psychiatry, 46*(11), 971–982.

Enns, C. Z. (1992a). Self-esteem groups: A synthesis of consciousness-raising and assertiveness training. *Journal of Counseling and Development, 71*(1), 7–13.

Enns, C. Z. (1992b). Toward integrating feminist psychotherapy and feminist philosophy. *Professional Psychology: Research and Practice, 23*(6), 453–466.

Enns, C. Z. (1993). Twenty years of feminist counseling and therapy: From naming biases to implementing multifaceted practice. *Counseling Psychologist, 21*(1), 3–87.

Enns, C. Z. (1997). *Feminist theories and feminist psychotherapies: Origins, themes, and variations.* New York: Harrington Park Press/Haworth Press.

Espin, O. (1994). Feminist approaches. In B. Greene (Ed.), *Women of color: Integrating ethnic and gender identities in psychotherapy* (pp. 265–286). New York: Guilford Press.

Espin, O. (1995). On knowing you are the unknown: Women of color constructing psychology. In J. Adleman & G. Enguidanos (Eds.), *Racism in the lives of women: Testimony, theory and guides to practice* (pp. 127–136). New York: Harrington Park Press.

Fodor, I. G., & Epstein, R. (1983). Assertiveness training for women: Where are we failing? In P. Emmelkamp (Ed.), *Failures in behavior therapy* (pp. 132–154). New York: Wiley.

Freeman, J. (1984). The women's liberation movement: Its origins, structure, activities, and ideas. In J. Freeman (Ed.), *Women: A feminist perspective* (pp. 543–556). Palo Alto, CA: Mayfield.

Ganley, A. L. (1988). Feminist therapy with male clients. In L. E. Walker (Ed.), *Feminist psychotherapies: Integration of therapeutic and feminist systems* (pp. 186–205). Norwood, NJ: Ablex.

Goodwin, S. A., & Fiske, S. T. (2001). Power and gender: The double-edged sword of ambivalence. In R. Unger (Ed.), *Handbook of the psychology of women and gender* (pp. 358–366). New York: Wiley.

Greene, B., & Sanchez-Hucles, J. (1997). Diversity: Advancing an inclusive feminist psychology. In J. Worell & N. G. Johnson (Eds.), *Shaping the future of feminist psychology* (pp. 173–202). Washington, DC: American Psychological Association.

Hackett, G., & Lonborg, S. D. (1994). Career assessment and counseling for women. In E. W. Bruce Walsh & E. Samuel H. Osipow (Eds.), *Career counseling for women* (pp. 43–85). Hillsdale, NJ: Erlbaum.

Hobgood, M. E. (2000). *Dismantling privilege: An ethics of accountability.* Cleveland, OH: Pilgrim Press.

Hochschild, A. (1989). *The second shift.* New York: Viking.

hooks, b. (2000). *Feminist theory: from margin to center.* Cambridge, MA: South End Press.

Irving, L. M. (2002). Prevention of eating disorders: Problems, pitfalls, and feminist possibilities. In L. H. Collins, M. R. Dunlap & J. C. Chrisler (Eds.), *Charting a new course for feminist psychology* (pp. 255–281). Westport, CT: Praeger/Greenwood.

Jakubowski, P. A. (1977). Self-assertion training procedures for women. In E. I. Rawlings & D. K. Carter (Eds.), *Psychotherapy for women* (pp. 168–190). Springfield, IL: Charles C Thomas.

Kahn, S. E. (1981). Issues in the assessment and training of assertiveness with women. In M. D. Smye (Ed.), *Social competence* (pp. 346–367). New York: Guilford Press.

Kirsch, B. (1987). Evolution of consciousness-raising groups. In C. M. Brody (Ed.), *Women's therapy groups: Paradigms of feminist treatment* (pp. 43–54). New York: Springer.

Koss, M. P., Heise, L., & Russo, N. F. (1994). The global health burden of rape. *Psychology of Women* Quarterly, *18,* 509–537.

Kravetz, D. (1980). Consciousness-raising and self-help. In R. T. Hare-Mustin (Ed.), *Women and psychotherapy: An assessment of research and practice* (pp. 268–284). New York: Guilford Press.

Landrine, H. (Ed.). (1995). *Bringing cultural diversity to feminist psychology: Theory, research, and practice.* Washington, DC: American Psychological Association.

Lerman, H. (1996). *Pigeonholing women's misery: A history and critical analysis of the psychodiagnosis of women in the twentieth century.* New York: Basic Books.

Lieberman, M. A., & Bond, G. R. (1976). The problem of being a woman: A survey of 1,700 women in consciousness-raising groups. *Journal of Applied Behavioral Science, 12,* 363–379.

Linehan, M., & Egan, K. (1979). *Assertion training for women: Square peg in a round hole?* Paper presented at the Symposium on Behavior Therapy for Women, Association for Advanced Behavior Therapy, San Francisco, CA.

Marecek, J. (2001). Disorderly constructs: Feminist frameworks for clinical psychology. In R. K. Unger (Ed.), *Handbook of the psychology of women and gender* (pp. 303–316). New York: Wiley.

McGrath, E., Keita, G. P., Strickland, B. R., & Russo, N. F. (1990). *Women and depression.* Washington, DC: American Psychological Association.

Phillips, A. (1997). Paradoxes of participation. In J. Squires (Ed.), *Feminisms* (pp. 96–100). Oxford: Oxford University Press.

Prochaska, J. O., & Norcross, J. C. (2003). *Systems of psychotherapy: A transtheoretical analysis* (5th ed.). Pacific Grove, CA: Brooks/Cole.

Rozee, P. D. (1996). Freedom from fear of rape: The missing link in women's freedom. In J. C. Chrisler & C. Golden & P. D. Rozee (Eds.), *Lectures on the psychology of women* (pp. 309–324). New York: McGraw-Hill.

Sanchez-Hucles, J., & Hudgins, P. (2001). Trauma across diverse settings. In J. Worell (Ed.), *Encyclopedia of women and gender: Sex similarities and differences and the impact of society on gender* (Vol. 2, pp. 1151–1168). San Diego, CA: Academic Press.

Sharf, R. S. (2000). *Theories of psychotherapy and counseling: concepts and cases* (2nd ed.). Belmont, CA: Wadsworth.

Stere, L. K. (1985). Feminist assertiveness training: Self-esteem groups as skill training for women. In L. E. A. Walker (Ed.), *Handbook of feminist therapy* (pp. 51–61). New York: Springer.

Szymanski, D. M., Baird, M. K., & Kornman, C. L. (2002). The feminist male therapist: Attitudes and practices for the 21st century. *Psychology of Men and Masculinity, 3*(1), 22–27.

Unger, R. K., & Crawford, M. (1996). *Women and gender: A feminist psychology* (2nd ed.). New York: McGraw-Hill.

Weitz, R. (1982). Feminist consciousness raising, self-concept, and depression. *Sex Roles, 8,* 231–241.

Worell, J., & Remer, P. (1992). *Feminist perspectives in therapy: An empowerment model for women.* Oxford, England: John Wiley & Sons.

Worell, J., & Remer, P. (2003). *Feminist perspectives in therapy: Empowering diverse women* (2nd ed.). New York: Wiley.

Wyche, K. F. (2001). Sociocultural issues in counseling for women of color. In R. K. Unger (Ed.), *Handbook of the psychology of women and gender* (pp. 330–340). New York: Wiley.

Wyche, K. F., & Rice, J. K. (1997). Feminist therapy: From dialogue to tenets. In N. G. Johnson (Ed.), *Shaping the future of feminist psychology* (pp. 57–71). Washington, DC: American Psychological Association.

# CHAPTER 14

# Culture-Centered Counseling with Women of Color

Angela M. Byars-Winston, University of Wisconsin-Madison

Once we realize that all women are not White, and once we understand the implications of this realization, we see immediately the importance of race, ethnicity, and class when considering gender. (Butler, 2001, p. 177)

The preceding quote underscores that culture matters in understanding the lives of women of color. Women of color are not merely ". . . a variation of a more general model of American womanhood" (Zinn & Dill, 1994, p. 10). The contexts of their lives are shaped by both macro and micro forces that influence how they are socially constructed and in turn, how they socially construct personal identities and a sense of self and understand the worlds in which they live. To successfully counsel women of color, counselors need to attend to cultural issues, integrating their knowledge of psychological, biological, and social factors with cultural processes. These dynamic processes influence the client and therapists' views of presenting concerns, the nature of those concerns, desired interventions, and the therapeutic relationship.

Given the wide range of cultural variables and related dimensions that typify women of color's experiences, what do mental health practitioners need to know when counseling these groups? This chapter synthesizes guiding principles identified as critical for conducting culturally relevant interventions with women of color in the United States.

The intent of this chapter is not to offer prescribed modes of and approaches to intervention. Rather, the chapter reviews foundational issues related to the psychological functioning of U.S. women of color as it is influenced by cultural processes and considers the implications of these processes for counseling. Counseling guidelines common to both feminist therapy approaches and the emerging literature on multicultural counseling competencies are used to organize this discussion.

Prior to continuing, the use of the terms *women of color* and *culture* is clarified. For the purposes of this chapter, the umbrella term *women of color* refers to U.S.-born women who identify as Black or African American, American Indians, Asian and Pacific Islanders, and Latinas. The diversity among these groups is not negated. Clearly, behavioral variability among individuals within an ethnic, gender, or sociocultural group is always greater than the variability between these groups. Instead, the term is used as described by Bandarage (1986), who asserted that *women of color* is a transitional term used for political mobilization. She stated that it

> is especially popular among those who are feminists but who have fundamental disagreement with the White, middle class women's movement. For women who are oppressed by both patriarchy and White supremacy, women of Color—mujeres de color—provides a unifying conceptual formula and a direction for political organizing . . . it is a term of celebration calling us to find pride and power in ourselves as women and as people of Color. (p. 8)

*Culture* is used as defined in the American Psychological Association's (APA) multicultural guidelines (2002):

> the embodiment of a worldview through learned and transmitted beliefs, values, and practices, including religious and spiritual traditions. It also encompasses a way of living informed by the historical, economic, ecological, and political forces on a group. These definitions suggest that culture is fluid and dynamic, and that there are both cultural universal phenomena as well as culturally specific or relative constructs. (p. 11)

The chapter begins with a discussion of shared features across feminist and multicultural counseling theories, stressing points of commonality in counseling women of color. Next, several models for conducting multicultural counseling are reviewed. Finally, specific multicultural counseling competencies are summarized across three domains of counselors' knowledge, awareness, and skills, with attention to their relevance for interventions with women of color.

## "SHIFTING THE CENTER": FEMINIST AND MULTICULTURAL PERSPECTIVES ON WOMEN OF COLOR

Despite the acknowledgment of cultural influences on emotional and mental health, Hall (1997) asserted that the field of psychology is guilty of "cultural malpractice" with visible racial/ethnic minorities, stemming from unintentional bias as a result of cultural ignorance or misinformation. The long-term consequences of cultural malpractice have resulted in misdiagnoses and pathologizing of culturally diverse groups often due to reliance on prevailing stereotypes and social myths (e.g., view of poor women of color as having low self-esteem and an external locus of control). Countering this cultural malpractice requires a change in perspective, "shifting the center" (Collins & Andersen, 2001) so that previously held knowledge that was based on exclusionary paradigms can instead be reconstructed to use a cultural lens to understand the client's frame of reference.

Feminist counseling and multicultural counseling theories have provided shifts in the center of how women of color are viewed in therapy. For instance, original feminist theories pointed out that women's psychological distress does not stem solely from individual factors (Raja, 1998) but may result from restricted gender roles, social expectations, and sexism. Despite the reconstructed view of women's mental health from a dynamic person-environment transaction perspective, several scholars called attention to ways in which multiculturalism poses challenges to feminist therapy in its application to women of color (cf. Comas-Díaz, 1991; Espín, 1993, 1995). That is, feminist therapies were criticized for their emphasis on gender and sexism over ethnicity and other cultural variables. Indeed, Boyd (1990) stated, "Women of color view feminism as yet another system in which they have to define and justify their reality" (p. 162). On the other hand, multicultural perspectives explicitly extend the focus of cultural variables beyond race and gender to include socioeconomic status, sexual orientation, and physical ability status for example, as well as call attention to the impact of historical and social contexts on psychological functioning. Coupled with the inclusion of historical legacies on current emotional well-being, multicultural perspectives also consider the influence and consequences of cultural stereotypes and cultural adaptive processes like biculturalism and acculturation.

Feminist therapies commonly encourage collaboration throughout the counseling process, recognition of multiple oppressions, client advocacy and empowerment, use of avenues in addition to therapy for personal growth, therapists' continual examination of their own values, and attention to social contexts and power in the counseling relationship (Espín, 1994). Taken together, feminist and multicultural counseling theories converge on several shared principles relative to clinical interventions: (a) emphasis on client-in-context, (b) collaborative counseling relationships (attention to power and privilege), and (c) an expanded view of counselor roles, including that of an advocate. The common characteristics from these counseling perspectives are reflected in several models for conceptualizing and approaching multicultural counseling.

## MULTICULTURAL COUNSELING MODELS

Currently, there is no singular, agreed upon way to conduct multicultural counseling (Fuertes & Gretchen, 2001). Instead, extant models provide variables and processes to consider in understanding the complex interaction of cultural dynamics on the identification, recognition, diagnosis, and treatment of psychological problems. Four models are presented in this section to highlight a few of the domains identified as important to include in culturally relevant counseling. The reader is referred to Ponterotto, Fuertes, and Chen (2000) for a more extensive review of multicultural counseling models and theories.

Atkinson, Thompson, and Grant (1993) proposed a three-dimensional model to assist counselors in expanding their helping roles and appropriately selecting strategies for intervention with racial/ethnic minority clients. The three dimensions include assessing at a minimum the level of the client's acculturation, the locus of the client's problem (internal or external to the individual), and the focus or goals of counseling (e.g., prevention, rehabilitation). Depending on the resulting assessment of the client's status across these three dimensions, the counselor assumes varying roles (e.g., counselor, consultant, advocate, etc.). The model does not include factors for self-assessment of the counselor regarding his or her competence to assume the appropriate roles, although the authors noted that counselors should continuously engage in "self-examination" and receive extensive training in assessing the three dimensions identified.

The multicultural counseling model proposed by Atkinson, Morten, and Sue (1998) focused on factors that aid counselors in conceptualizing ethnic minority clients' needs. Specifically, they identified four factors affecting the counseling process: acculturation, racial/ethnic identity, cultural mistrust, and socioeconomic differences. They suggested that ethnicity, as one instance of cultural variables, plays a significant role in the emergence and experience of one's identity over a lifetime. The authors proposed a five-stage model of minority identity formation for racial/ethnic minorities in relation to their referent ethnic group, the dominant culture, and the relationship between the two: conformity, dissonance, resistance and immersion, introspection, and synergetic articulation and awareness. Cultural identity is viewed as a process that can moderate behavioral and psychological outcomes (Cuellar & Gonzalez, 2000). Thus, these models encourage counselors to examine the cultural identity development and cultural formulation processes for the clients with whom they work.

In an attempt to provide a model for conceptualizing work with culturally diverse clients, the fourth edition of the *Diagnostic and Statistical Manual of Mental Disorders* (*DSM-IV*, American Psychiatric Association, 1994) included a cultural formulation model. This model provides a framework for interweaving culture variables throughout clinical interventions. It consists of the following five considerations: (1) cultural identity of the individual, (2) cultural explanations of the individual's illness, (3) cultural factors related to psychosocial environment and levels of functioning, (4) cultural elements of the relationship between the individual and the clinician, and (5) overall cultural assessment for diagnosis and care. Although the inclusion of such a model within the *DSM-IV* is laudable, this model does not include culture-specific information and represents only an outline for attending to cultural influences on clients and their effect on the counseling relationship (Hays, 2001).

Based on a review of existing counseling literature, the only model identified for specifically counseling women of color was the culturally appropriate career counseling model synthesized by Fouad and Bingham (1995). This seven-step model advances a cyclical, dynamic approach to examining the impact of cultural factors with women of color throughout all phases of career counseling interventions. The first four steps are focused on preparation for counseling and culturally appropriate appraisal of career concerns. Steps 5 and 6, determination and implementation of culturally appropriate interventions, and culturally appropriate decision making, respectively, attend to the cooperative client-counselor relationship that facilitates mutually agreed upon courses of action in addressing the client's career concerns. Finally, Step 7 focuses on implementation of the client's plans and follow-up. Fouad and Bingham suggested that this model be flexible as clients may recycle through various stages of this counseling model to clarify their career issues.

Despite the absence of a unifying multicultural counseling theory or model for counseling women of color, many themes in that body of literature are consistent with social constructionist theories. They share in common a view of all people as having varying experiences with multiple social identities (e.g., ethnicity/race, social class, gender, sexual orientation, etc.), which are socially constructed through complex interactions between individuals and their immediate and distal sociocultural environments, and these dynamics, in turn, influence their worldviews. Such themes align with those in feminist psychology scholarship, indicating that women of color's psychologies, then, are contextual, socially constructed, and simultaneously expressed (Weber, 1998).

The points raised in the aforementioned conceptual frameworks and models argue for cultural variables and related processes to occupy a central role in counseling; this viewpoint captures the core of culture-centered counseling. Culture-centered counseling means putting at the center of our thinking the cultural experiences of women of color heretofore excluded. Culture-centered counseling is not a model of counseling per se, but an approach in which counselors "recognize that all individuals including themselves are influenced by different contexts, including the historical, ecological, sociopolitical, and disciplinary" (APA, 2002, p. 13). The remainder of this chapter considers clinical implications of the multicultural counseling competence literature and issues raised in the psychology of women of color for conducting culture-centered counseling with these groups.

## CULTURALLY RELEVANT COUNSELING SKILLS

A central ethical principle psychologists hold is that they should be competent to work with a diversity of populations (APA, 2002a). This tenet has sparked much work on identifying and operationalizing what counselor characteristics typify and promote cultural competence. Initial discussions emphasized the role of three competency domains—culturally related knowledge, awareness, and skills—that mental health professionals should possess about the groups with which they work in order to deliver more effective interventions (cf. Sue, Arredondo, & McDavis, 1992). The quest to specify and articulate what proficiencies mental health professionals need to improve the quality of counseling services to culturally diverse groups resulted in the Association for Multicultural Counseling and Development's (AMCD) publication *Operationalization of the Multicultural Counseling Competencies* (Arredondo et al., 1996). This publication builds on the previously identified competency domains by incorporating a multidimensional view of cultural variables beyond ethnicity and race (e.g., sexual orientation and ability status) and includes strategies to achieve these competencies. Arredondo (1999) noted that articulating such competencies was motivated by "the need to address racism and other forms of interpersonal and institutional oppression in the profession" (p. 45).

The 1996 AMCD competencies rest on four premises that build on the work of Arredondo and Glauner (1992): (1) all people are multicultural individuals; (2) all people have a personal, political, and historical culture; (3) all people are affected by sociocultural, political, environmental, and historical events; and (4) there is an intersection between multiculturalism and multiple dimensions of individual diversity (Arredondo et al., 1996). These premises are subsumed under three skill domains, which have defining characteristics organized across attitudes, knowledge/awareness, and skills as well as explanatory statements that provide examples of these competencies.

Recently, the APA (2002) approved the *Guidelines on Multicultural Education, Training, Research, Practice, and Organizational Change for Psychologists.* Out of the six guidelines proposed, three specifically apply to clinical practice. Three focus topics were specified for counselors as they develop cultural sensitivity to conduct effective clinical interventions: viewing clients within their context, culturally appropriate assessment tools, and a broad range of diverse interventions. Following is a summary of the AMCD competencies, integrating the three clinically relevant APA guidelines, with consideration of their relevance to counseling women of color and organized within the three multicultural counseling competency domains of knowledge, awareness, and skills.

## Knowledge

The first domain is *counselor's awareness of personal cultural values, attitudes, and biases.* This is consistent with the first APA guideline indicating that psychologists recognize that their attitudes and beliefs may be detrimental in their perceptions of and interactions with those who are ethnically different from themselves. An attitude under this domain is holding the belief that counselors' cultural self-awareness and sensitivity to one's own cultural heritage is essential. An indicator of knowledge or awareness is that counselors know and understand how oppression, racism, discrimination, and stereotypes affect them personally and in their work. This also means recognizing the subtle racism underlying many psychological theories (Raja, 1998). One representative skill competency in this domain states that counselors are committed to a constant understanding of themselves as cultural and racial beings, seeking a nonracist identity. Hays (2001) suggested that counselors especially pay personal attention to such dynamics as cognitive defensiveness, fear, and ignorance (e.g., internalizing dominant societal images of Chinese American women as passive) that may hinder their developing compassion for their client. Given that all individuals are predisposed to prejudice and stereotypes (Stephan, 1989), introspection is required for counselors to monitor their dissonance in their cross-cultural interactions and process through newly encountered experiences and information (Robinson & Howard-Hamilton, 2000).

A counselor may personally reflect on the following questions:

- What are my social biases and stereotypes?
- How is my view of the client's life situation influenced by my personal background, experiences, and contexts (Hays, 2001)?

- To what aspects of new information or experiences am I reacting? When am I most uncomfortable?

These competencies suggest that counselors working with women of color engage in intentional reflection on how their views about psychological processes have been informed by their own personal background and recognize that others have differing views. By attending to how the social and cultural contexts in their lives (e.g., family of origin background, socioeconomic status[es], educational background, etc.) have shaped their perspectives on psychological health and well-being, they can be more conscious of their biases and stereotypes, such as a lack of personal experiences with a diversity of individuals, that may constrain a fuller conceptualization of mental health.

## Awareness

The second domain is *counselor awareness of the client's worldview.* An attitude indicative of this domain is awareness of stereotypes and preconceived notions held about other racial and ethnic minority groups. Similarly, the second APA guideline encourages psychologists to recognize the importance of knowledge, understanding, and multicultural sensitivity and responsivity related to ethnically diverse clients. Related knowledge includes having an understanding of the sociopolitical factors influencing the lives of racial and ethnic minorities. A relevant skill under this domain is familiarity with current and relevant mental health research on issues affecting ethnic and racial groups.

**Beyond Gender and Sexism as Central Constructs**   Although multiple systems of oppression are acknowledged to impact the lives of women, sexism as one instance of oppression is often situated as the central construct against which other forms of oppression interact. This view erroneously presupposes the primacy of gender oppression relative to other systems of oppression, a view for which feminist therapy theories have often been criticized in application to women of color (Greene, 1994; Vandiver, 2002). Further problems have been identified with the use of the terms *double jeopardy* or *triple jeopardy* in referring to membership in two or three marginalized social groups (e.g., race, gender, and class).

King (1988) argued that concepts such as double and triple jeopardy oversimplify the relationships among these forms of discriminations and further the interpretation that the effects of these variables are additive. That is, variables of race, gender, and class are interpreted as having direct, separate, and independent effects on the status of African American women. King instead proposed the term *multiple jeopardy,* highlighting the interdependent and dynamic processes among multiple forms of discrimination. The effects of racism, sexism, and classism are viewed instead as multiplicative, with no one variable superseding the other. This view of race, gender, and class as interdependent variables acknowledges them as partially separate social hierarchies that uniquely position people to the distribution of power, privilege, and prestige (Ransford & Miller, 1983). Racial oppression, sexual exploitation, and class domination operate in distinct ways to constrain the life chances and choices of women affected by them. Consistent with King's proposition, Zinn and Dill (1994) suggested that how women of color experience race, gender, and class depends on the intersection of these variables with all forms of discrimination and inequalities (e.g., homophobia). The following example illustrates this intersectionality, highlighting the salience and multiplicative impact of ethnic identity, gender, and sexual orientation that must be explored with women of color who identify as lesbians or bisexuals.

**Example of Multiplicative Social Identity Influences**   Greene (2000) emphasized the need to pay special attention to the developmental challenge of "coming out" for African American lesbian women, which rings true for other lesbian women of color. In particular, she discussed the need to work with the client to explore the anticipated reactions to and consequences for coming out to various family members, noting the additional dynamic of often having a non-African-American partner (e.g., often White). The challenge of confronting homophobic responses from significant family and friends is confounded for some lesbian women of color who must additionally address issues of racial essentialism (e.g., constructions of what it means to "Be down" as an authentic Black person), which may not include accepting interracial relationships, let alone lesbian women for some ethnic group members. In this case, the counselor must consider the client's meaning and reality of being a lesbian woman of color. How might issues of internalized homophobia as well as racist stereotypes be evident for the client? At the interpersonal level, the experience of racism and homophobia may manifest for the client as anger and defensiveness, as she may feel the constant need to be ready to defend herself against judgment. A significant contribution of feminist therapy to counseling women is the validation of women's anger, especially in viewing it as a source of strength in reaction to oppressive social environments (Espín, 1994). From this perspective, a woman of color client's experience and expression of anger and frustration may be an indirect consequence of membership in a socially devalued, oppressed, and stigmatized cultural minority group, as may be true for the woman in the preceding example. In sum, this example illustrates the need for counselors to explore the client's multiple self-conceptions. Actively attending to the client's various social identities facilitates the counselor's understanding of the evolution and emergence of such identities within the context of multiple social oppressions for a woman of color.

**Conceptions of the Self Within Cultural Frames of Reference**   In exploring social identities and statuses, it is important to recognize that individuals are often assigned to various social groups, without the option of self-definition (Weinrach & Thomas, 2002). As such, the power of self-definition for women of color cannot be overstated. An examination of the salient aspects of cultural identity for a woman of color is necessary to understand how she has defined herself and been defined based on social group memberships. Cuellar and Gonzalez (2000) defined the cultural self as a subset of the self-concept regarding thoughts and feelings related to social and ethnic identities. It is critical that counselors facilitate the development of an accurate picture of self for women of color that is not based on cultural misinformation and stereotypes. Explore with the client what cultural stereotypes have potentially influenced her behavior and worldview, distinguishing whether a client is acting against cultural stereotypes versus acting out on them (Greene, 1996). To frame the exploration of multiple cultural identities and backgrounds, counselors may consider using the ADDRESSING model proposed by Hays (1996). The term ADDRESSING forms an acronym to organize the following variables: age/generational factors, developmental or acquired disabilities, religion and spiritual orientation, ethnicity, socioeconomic status, sexual orientation, indigenous heritage, national origin, and gender. This framework may help guide counselors in understanding the values, beliefs, and behaviors of their clients as well as formulating questions under each of the cultural variables.

Principles within the APA guidelines outline several cultural lenses through which to explore the constructions of self and seem especially poignant for women of color. Counselors are encouraged to understand the potential consequences of membership in a stigmatized, devalued cultural group—often experienced as being the "other"—and to learn about the historical experiences of women of color and the unique cultural practices of these groups that have emerged within and from their histories, paying particular attention to gender-related concerns within these groups. For example, counselors should be aware of the consequences of cultural and geographic dislocation, genocide, and forced acculturation in the histories of indigenous nations in North America and how an American Indian woman may cope with bicultural demands and roles. Counselors are also urged to become familiar with ethnic and racial identity developmental processes and statuses and how they affect worldview, cognitions, affect, and behavior, considering the intersectionality of these identity statuses with gender and other social identity constructions. Racial identity, for instance, may be a powerful lens through which to view the consequences of ethnic minorities' social and historical reality in the United States (cf. Cross, Parham, and Helms, 1998).

**Assessing Racial Trauma**  The confluence of "microaggressions" (Pierce, 1988), or daily insults stemming from racism and sexism at the institutional level, are important to assess. Daniel (2000) noted the impact of racialized traumas stemming from a myriad of oppressive experiences (e.g., economic, educational, judicial, and sexual) exacerbated by the racism underneath or tacked onto such experiences. An exploration of the woman of color client's experience with institutional and systems-level oppression is warranted, as racial trauma is a stressful event (Smith, 1985). For instance, Fordham's (1993) research on African American female adolescents found persistent, subtle and not-so-subtle stereotypes that operated against them in school. They were often overobserved and perceived to be loud and aggressive in their daily interactions with others, consistent with strongly held societal images of African American women as "bossy" and "emasculating" (Mullings, 1994). These stereotyped perceptions were exacerbated by the juxtaposed ideology of femaleness as being quiet and passive, and not necessarily because this was an accurate evaluation of the young women's displayed behavior. This example illustrates how social institutions become "conduits for oppression" (Andersen & Collins, 1992, p. 172). The consequences of such experiences for African American women and other women of color may surface in feelings of powerlessness, internalized anger, or externalized depression. Thus, the counselor may need to provide psychoeducation in helping the client understand how external and social factors influence a person's psychological functioning.

Counselors need to consider the interactions between clients' worldviews and their cultural and family backgrounds with individual concerns. For instance, the experience of shame for a Latina who survived incest may be compounded by her desire not to confirm the prevailing stereotypes of Latinos and other men of color as being violent and sexual predators. In attending to the consequences of sexual trauma for this individual, the counselor may also attend to the partial impact of institutional and/or societal forms of prejudice and discrimination, as well as family roles and expectations, in better understanding the range of complex feelings and thoughts that the client may have. The preceding examples underscore the potential value of seeking to understand the intersections among women of color clients' various cultural identities and other systems of oppression in understanding their psychological experiences.

**Attending to the "Superwoman" Complex**   Cultural dictums often place women of color in the role of being "all-suffering" for the sake of their community's survival at the expense of themselves (Jackson, 2000). Indeed, historical survival for many women of color has required their personal suffering as a function of economic, occupational, and sexual exploitation. The fact that they survived the suffering of such dehumanizing experiences and are "still here" (Greene, 1992) also bred a certain perceived internal and communal legacy of strength. Robinson (1983) wrote the following of African American women's legacy of strength:

> We have been forced by society, oppression, our position, and our tradition to be responsible for the economic, social, and physical survival of our families and communities, regardless of socioeconomic status, age, geographic location, or educational attainment. Our adaptability to varied roles, while transcending societal barriers, illustrates significant coping abilities. (p. 136)

This excerpt highlights the historical resistance and social agency of African American women. It also illustrates the self-sacrificing beliefs and extreme self-reliance that many women of color hold, two dynamics that may prevent women of color from seeking counseling. The icon of "the strong Black woman" has been discussed in the literature as one who often deals with issues of self-reliance to the point of not being interdependent, with internal pressure to always emotionally "have it together," ignoring personal challenges and weaknesses and not asking for or seeking support (Jackson, 2000).

It is important to explore dynamics around intimacy, control, and how a woman of color seeks out support. Emphasis should be on emotional flexibility, finding a balance between her personal needs and the needs of others, and acknowledging where her self-reliance skills and behavior benefit and do not benefit her. For example, it may be important for a woman of color to look at how self-reliance in work or educational settings are helpful but may hinder her personal relationships with significant others. Consider using bibliotherapy to help elicit a client's life experiences on multiple levels, paying attention to characters, themes, and story lines that are most salient for her (Byars, 2000). With what struggles and strengths does the client resonate? How does she understand the nature of relationships and intimacy among the characters? How does this help uncover her vulnerabilities? Counselors should be aware of cultural variations of this complex. For example, some American Indian cultures emphasize the enduring of life difficulties (LaFromboise, Choney, James, & Running Wolf, 1995). Attending to the dynamics discussed in this section may clarify how a woman of color experiences and copes with the demands of cultural roles and expectations. Overall, it is important to use culturally appropriate role models for coping with her problems.

The following questions may be pondered to examine cultural issues discussed under this domain:

- What does she consider to be the most important aspects of herself?
- What primary sources of information and experiences has this client used to construct her sense of self?
- To what degree are these sources based on cultural misinformation and/or cultural stereotypes?
- How does the client see the significance or role of culture in her issues?
- How salient is the influence from her referent ethnic group?
- How salient is the influence from the dominant Anglocentric culture?
- What experiences have been particularly racialized for her?
- In what ways is she marginalized in her life contexts?
- What are her experiences with and reactions to multiple forms of oppression (e.g., based on racial, gender, sexual, class, ability, etc., factors)?
- What self-generated definitions does the client want to guide her life?
- How does she experience emotional vulnerability? How does she define emotional strength? From what sources does she draw emotional strength?
- How does she experience and cope with bicultural demands (e.g., differing roles and behaviors between referent and dominant groups)?

The counselor's full understanding of the woman of color client is reliant upon knowledge of her immediate (e.g., personal, lived experiences) and sociopolitical and cultural contexts (e.g., the impact of U.S. internment camps on a Japanese American woman's national identity). Such knowledge informs the counselor of important social identities for the client and their impact on her personality formation, psychological functioning, and emotional expression, and it encourages the counselor to identify cultural sources of strength. Finally, counselors should allow for individual differences, taking care not to overfocus on cultural variables to the exclusion of an individual's unique socialization processes, life experiences, and person-specific factors (APA, 2002).

## Culture-Centered Counseling Competence

The third domain is *development of culturally appropriate intervention strategies* and is consistent with the fifth APA guideline (APA, 2002). An attitude reflective of this domain is a respect for indigenous helping practices and help-giving networks in diverse communities. One knowledge competency is awareness of institutional barriers that impede ethnic minorities' access to and use of mental health services. A skill indicated in this domain is counselors' responsibility for educating their clients about the processes involved in psychological services, including the counselors' counseling orientation, legal rights, and expectations. An implication of the competency domain is that focus should be on examining the cultural variables salient for that person, identifying the cultural strengths, and using them deliberately in counseling. A culturally skilled counselor has the ability to make "culture-centered adaptations" (APA, 2002) in counseling practices to be more effective.

**Collaborative Counseling Relationship**   The explicit sharing of power is key in conducting culturally competent counseling. A collaborative therapeutic relationship allows clients and counselors to actively participate in the counseling processes without presuming the power of the counselor over the client to define the course of counseling. From this perspective, Raja (1998) stated that the client is an "expert" on her given life circumstances and the counselor is seen as an "expert" on what techniques will assist in promoting change. She cautions that some cultural values for women of color may make them reluctant to share power in counseling, which may manifest as deference or the client's resistance to voicing her input on the progress of counseling. Raja suggested that a negotiation of shared power in a collaborative relationship might have to be repeatedly discussed as counseling progresses. Another related dynamic in promoting collaborative counseling relationships is the counselor's use of his or her power and privilege to benefit the client (Raja, 1998). As such, counselors may use their professional influence to advocate on behalf of a client and help her to access community resources (e.g., connecting her to educational or vocational opportunities).

**Discussing Issues of Cultural Variables in Therapy**   One challenge to many counselors is knowing when it is the right time to introduce culture in counseling, especially issues of race and ethnicity. Although cultural variables are ubiquitous and thus are important to include in working with the client from the onset of counseling, several factors must be considered. Attention must be given to the existing counseling rapport and how discussion of these variables will promote a more solid client-counselor relationship. Introducing cultural variables in counseling may enhance the working alliance in that the client sees the counselor as competent to "go there" with her and the counselor's skill to do so. Also, consider the client's readiness and ability to explore cultural explanations for her concerns. Indeed, cultural sensitivity is likely to promote the counseling relationship, whereas cultural insensitivity is detrimental to it and may result in cultural mistrust (cf. Evans & Larrabee, 2002; Fischer, Jome, & Atkinson, 1998). Liu and Clay (2002) cautioned that the most salient cultural issues might not be the most relevant in working effectively with a client. Counselors must be attuned to how important culture is to the client, especially in her understanding of her psychological concerns. For example, does she experience her depression as influenced by her perceived opportunities (e.g., barriers) as a woman of color, as having a genetic component (e.g., her mother also struggled with depression), as the manifestation of the cumulative stress of multiple life roles, or some combination of these factors?

When counseling a woman of color, it is especially important for counselors to let her know that they are aware that she has or will have experiences in her life revolving around race and ethnicity. This may mean that the counselor has to explore both shame and guilt around racism with women of color (Boyd-Franklin, 1991; Gainor, 1992). They may have to assist in helping a client to forgive herself and others (e.g., individuals and institutions) by whom she feels wronged as well as feeling okay about not addressing oppression all of the time (Greene, 1996). Given that the multiple social identities of women of color give them differential status depending on the context (e.g., at work vs. in the community where they live), clients may need to understand where they fit along the continuum of privilege and disadvantage and how those varying statuses have shaped their view of self and coping behaviors in dealing with both the benefits and challenges afforded by their multiple identity statuses. As a caveat, Jackson (2000) emphasized the need for counselors to distinguish between intrapsychic, cultural variables, and social constructions as they influence the overall psychological development, functioning, and coping mechanisms of African American women. These distinctions are key in not overlooking underlying psychological or psychiatric issues due to an overemphasis on cultural variables, which may contribute to the manifestation and management of presenting issues.

**Identify Forms of Resistance**    The experience of multiple forms of oppression also yields multiple forms of resistance to such oppression and multiple lenses through which to view one's world. King (1988) termed this psychological resistance *multiple consciousness,* a critical awareness about and understanding of the social and institutional dynamics producing the oppression. Social agency perspectives recognize that women of color are not just passive recipients of oppressive social relations but also shape their own lives. Their lives reflect an interaction between structured external inequalities and personal agency to cope with and resist these forces. There are often significant, yet subtle, forms of resistance at the community and familial levels. For example, research done by Joe and Miller (1994) illustrated how American Indian mothers from the Tohono O'odham and Yaqui tribes in Tucson, Arizona, promoted cultural heritage in their children as a way to help them cope with racism, poverty, and discrimination. This act helped to counteract the forced (economic) assimilation of American Indians that threatened their cultural autonomy. Promoting cultural pride and healthy ethnic identity can buffer against the experience and impact of cultural stressors in women of color.

**Use of Indigenous Cultural Supports**    The focus on sources of resistance for women of color encourages counselors to look for cultural strengths they exhibit that can be incorporated into the counseling interventions. Those cultural strengths may stem from a client's indigenous community or cultural institutions. Counselors must recognize and use additional sources of culturally relevant supports for a woman of color client in her cultural communities (e.g., religious, spiritual, ethnic, civic organizations, book clubs, etc.). These may be critical components in facilitating emotional healing and well-being (Raja, 1998).

In working with a woman of color, several questions are posed for counselors to consider in their counseling interventions:

- What did she learn or what was she told to do in reaction to oppressive or discriminatory experiences?
- What did she observe others do in reaction to such experiences?
- What are her patterns of personal agency and resistance?
- What indigenous or community resources are salient for her and available?
- How can the client's resources be built upon in the counseling context?

## Summary

Counseling guidelines, competencies, and principles are not without criticism. For instance, in examining the AMCD competencies, Weinrach and Thomas (2002) noted such shortcomings as the generation of these competencies based largely on input from academics, the lack of substantial empirical support for the superior efficacy of counselors who possess such competencies over those who do not, and the generalizability of competencies acquired in simulated settings to real-life situations. The merits and "bona fide" status of these competency statements and other multicultural guidelines and principles are beyond the scope of this chapter. However, few would argue that one benefit of the existence of such statements on culturally competent professional practice is the attention given to the impact of clients' cultural background and social contexts on their psychological functioning. Collectively, they emphasize the need for both preparation and practices that integrate culturally relevant knowledge, awareness, and skills into counseling processes (Arredondo et al., 1996).

In the delivery of culturally competent mental health services, these professional practice statements overlap in the recognized need for counselors to (1) gain knowledge of themselves relative to their cultural heritage and social identities and (2) gain knowledge of other cultures. Such guidelines and principles are consistent with Aponte's (1994) description of two interdependent roads counselors should travel to promote competent multicultural work, "reaching within to understand" and "reaching out to understand" (pp. 188–189).

Although there is a diversity of views regarding exactly what is multicultural counseling, McFadden's (1993) definition seems broadest to encompass all of them, asserting that it is "an approach to facilitating client insight, growth, and change through understanding and perpetuating multiple cultures within a psychosocial and scientific-ideological context" (p. 6). His definition suggests that multiculturally competent counselors appreciate and value cultural differences and multiple sources of diversity, understand the influence of these differences on worldviews/philosophical beliefs, and use the knowledge and awareness of culture to formulate scientific inquiries and approaches to intervening in the counseling. Finally, cultural competency is not an end point, but rather an ongoing process (APA, 2002; Arredondo et al., 1996).

## CONCLUSION

Culture-centered counseling approaches provide counselors with a conceptual rationale for addressing cultural variables and related processes in working with women of color. Such approaches put at the center of counselor interactions the cultural lives of women of color instead of viewing them as cultural variations of White women. The potential psychosocial issues that may be salient for these groups based on the literature reviewed stress themes of resistance and resilience in the lives of women of color. It is rather daunting and may be impossible to know and understand the myriad of cultural variables and dynamics that influence the lives of women of color. What does this mean for counselors working with these groups? Fischer et al. (1998), in response to the challenges of succinct theoretical formulations for multicultural counseling, argued for a universal approach to this counseling. They emphasized the common factors found to be facilitative of effective clinical interventions, such as the therapeutic relationship and a shared worldview with the client. The authors suggested that these common factors provide the basic foundation for successful multicultural counseling upon which knowledge of specific cultural factors rests. Their universal perspective highlights the fact that knowing all there is to learn of one's client is insufficient if that knowledge is not acted upon within the context of the identified universal therapeutic factors.

# Cases and Questions

1. Julie is a 33-year-old African American woman and one of only two African American students in a business doctoral program. She is the mother of one preschool-aged daughter and is experiencing difficulty in her marriage. The challenges from these multiple roles have converged to the point that Julie is having trouble sleeping and experiencing some physical problems with her blood pressure. Because it is difficult to keep up with her coursework, she has several grades of incomplete, is not making progress in her doctoral program, and is under a threat of dismissal from the program. She has a strong and salient faith, which helps her to emotionally cope; but she often questions her spiritual strength, feeling that if she had more faith she could manage things

better. Julie has always been seen by others and herself as "strong" and having it all together. She is coming to you as a counselor in the university counseling center at the urging of close friends.

(a) Given the multiple presenting concerns, what issues seem most critical to address?

(b) How might Julie's coping skills be examined? What cultural issues might affect how she expresses her needs and concerns?

(c) How might her sense of personal self-reliance affect your establishing a working alliance with her?

2. Tracy is a 19-year-old Filipina American undergraduate attending a midwestern college. She is originally from California and is having difficulty adjusting to the campus, especially in her classes where she is typically the only woman of color. She often feels overobserved when she speaks in class and feels like how well she does academically is being seen as representative of all Filipina women, making her more self-conscious and hesitant about participating in classes. This is especially true for Tracy in her American History class, where she often disagrees with how historical events and the accuracy of how people of color are portrayed but has not voiced her disagreements for fear of being stereotyped as the "angry woman of color." Tracy is not sure how long she can tolerate her feelings of isolation. She has come to the university counseling center on referral from her resident hall adviser in whom she has confided her frustrations.

(a) How will you explore the topics of race, gender, ethnicity, and so on with Tracy?

(b) What dynamics are important to address with Tracy in managing others' perceptions of her as a woman of color?

(c) How will you facilitate the identification and implementation of effective coping skills for her?

## REFERENCES

American Psychiatric Association. (1994). *The diagnostic and statistical manual of mental disorders* (4th ed.). Washington, DC: Author.

American Psychiatric Association. (2002a). Ethical principles of psychologists and code of conduct. *American Psychologist, 57,* 1060–1073.

American Psychological Association. (2002b). *Guidelines on multicultural education, training, research, practice, and organizational change for psychologists.* Washington, DC: Author.

Andersen, M. L., & Collins, P. H. (1992). *Race, class, and gender: An anthology.* Belmont, CA: Wadsworth.

Aponte, H. J. (1994). *Bread and spirit: Therapy with the new poor.* New York: Norton.

Arredondo, P. (1999). Multicultural counseling competencies as tools to address oppression and racism. *Journal of Counseling and Development, 77,* 102–108.

Arredondo, P., & Glauner, T. (1992). *Personal dimensions of identity model.* Boston, MA: Empowerment Workshops.

Arredondo, P., Toporek, R., Brown, S., Jones, J., Locke, D. C., Sanchez, J., & Stadler, H. (1996). *Operationalization of the multicultural counseling competencies.* Alexandria, VA: Association for Multicultural Counseling and Development.

Atkinson, D. R., Morten, G., & Sue, D. W. (1998). *Counseling American minorities* (5th ed.). New York: McGraw-Hill.

Atkinson, D. R., Thompson, C. E., & Grant, S. K. (1993). A three-dimensional model for counseling racial/ethnic minorities. *The Counseling Psychologist, 21,* 257–277.

Bandarage, A. (1986). Women of color: Toward a celebration of power. *Women of Power, 4,* 8–14.

Boyd, J. A. (1990). Ethnic and cultural diversity: Keys to power. *Women and Therapy, 9,* 151–167.

Boyd-Franklin, N. (1991). Recurrent themes in the treatment of African-American women in group psychotherapy. *Women and Therapy, 11,* 25–40.

Butler, J. E. (2001). Transforming the curriculum: Teaching about women of color. In J. Banks & C. McGhee Banks (Eds.), *Multicultural education: Issues and perspectives* (4th ed., pp. 174–193). New York: Wiley.

Byars, A. M. (2000). Rights-of-way: Affirmative career counseling with African American women. In W. Walsh, R. Bingham, M. Brown, & C. Ward (Eds.), *Career counseling for African Americans* (pp. 113–137). Mahwah, NJ: Erlbaum.

Collins, P. H., & Andersen, M. L. (2001). R*ace, class, and gender: An anthology* (4th ed.). Belmont, CA: Wadsworth.

Comas-Díaz, L. (1991). Feminism and diversity in psychology: The case of women of color. *Psychology of Women Quarterly, 15,* 597–609.

Cross, W. E., Jr., Parham, T. A, & Helms, J. E. (1998). (Eds.). Nigrescence revisited: Theory and research. In R. Jones (Ed.), *African American identity development* (pp. 3–71). Hampton, VA: Cobb & Henry.

Cuellar, I., & Gonzalez, G. (2000). Cultural identity description and cultural formulation for Hispanics. In R. Dana (Ed.), *Handbook of cross-cultural and multicultural personality assessment. Personality and clinical psychology series* (pp. 605–621). Mahwah, NJ: Erlbaum.

Daniel, J. H. (2000). The courage to hear: African American women's memories of racial trauma. In L. Jackson & B. Greene (Eds.), *Psychotherapy with African American women: Innovations in psychodynamic perspectives and practice* (pp. 126–144). New York: Guilford Press.

Espín, O. (1993). Feminist therapy: Not for or by White women only. *The Counseling Psychologist, 21,* 103–108.

Espín, O. (1994). Feminist approaches. In L. Comas-Díaz, & B. Greene (Eds.), *Women of color: Integrating ethnic and gender identities in psychotherapy* (pp. 265–286). New York: Guilford Press.

Espín, O. (1995). On knowing you are the unknown: Women of color constructing psychology. In J. Adleman & G. Enguídanos (Eds.), *Racism in the lives of women* (pp. 127–136). New York: Harrington Park Press.

Evans, K. M., & Larrabee, M. J. (2002). Teaching the multicultural counseling competencies and revised career counseling competencies simultaneously. *Journal of Multicultural Counseling and Development, 30,* 21–39.

Fischer, A. R., Jome, L. M., & Atkinson, D. R. (1998). Reconceptualizing multicultural counseling: Universal healing conditions in a culturally specific context. *The Counseling Psychologist, 26,* 525–588.

Fordham, S. (1993). "Those loud black girls": (Black) women, silence, and gender "passing" in the academy. *Anthropology and Education Quarterly, 24,* 3–32.

Fouad, N. A., & Bingham, R. P. (1995). Career counseling with racial and ethnic minorities. In W. Walsh & S. Osipow (Eds.), *Handbook of vocational psychology: Theory, research, and practice* (2nd ed., pp. 331–365). Hillsdale, NJ: Erlbaum.

Fuertes, J. N., & Gretchen, D. (2001). Emerging theories of multicultural counseling. In J. Ponterotto, J. Casas, L. Suzuki, & C. Alexander (Eds.), *Handbook of multicultural counseling* (2nd ed., pp. 509–541). Thousand Oaks, CA: Sage.

Gainor, K. A. (1992). Internalized oppression: A barrier to effective group work with Black women. *Journal for Specialists in Group Work, 17,* 235–242.

Greene, B. (1992). Still here: A perspective on psychotherapy with African-American women. In J. Chrisler, & D. Howard (Eds.), *New directions in feminist psychology: Practice, theory, and research. Springer series: Focus on women* (Vol. 13, pp. 13–25). New York: Springer.

Greene, B. (1994). Diversity and difference: The issue of race in feminist therapy. In M. Mirkin (Ed.), *Women in context: Toward a feminist reconstruction of psychotherapy* (pp. 333–351). New York: Guilford Press.

Greene, B. (1996, March). *Psychotherapy with African American women.* Training seminar presented at the annual conference of the Association for Women in Psychology, Portland, OR.

Greene, B. (2000). African American lesbian and bisexual women in feminist-psychodynamic psychotherapies: Surviving and thriving between a rock and a hard place. In L. Jackson & B. Greene (Eds.), *Psychotherapy with African American women: Innovations in psychodynamic perspectives and practice* (pp. 82–125). New York: Guilford Press.

Hall, C. I. (1997). Cultural malpractice: The growing obsolescence of psychology with the changing U.S. population. *American Psychologist, 52,* 642–651.

Hays, P. A. (1996). Addressing the complexities of culture and gender in counseling. *Journal of Counseling and Development, 74,* 332–338.

Hays, P. A. (2001). *Addressing cultural complexities in practice: A framework for clinicians and counselors.* Washington, DC: American Psychological Association.

Jackson, L. C. (2000). The new multiculturalism and psychodynamic theory: Psychodynamic psychotherapy and African American women. In L. Jackson &

B. Greene (Eds.), *Psychotherapy with African American women: Innovations in psychodynamic perspectives and practice* (pp. 1–14). New York: Guilford Press.

Joe, J. R., & Miller, D. L. (1994). Cultural survival and contemporary American Indian women in the city. In M. Baca Zinn & B. Thornton Dill (Eds.), *Women of color in U.S. society* (pp. 185–202). Philadelphia: Temple University Press.

King, D. K. (1988). Multiple jeopardy, multiple consciousness: The context of a Black feminist ideology. *Signs, 14,* 42–72.

LaFromboise, T. D., Choney, S. B., James, A., & Running Wolf, P. R. (1995). American Indian women in psychology. In H. Landrine (Ed.), *Bringing cultural diversity to feminist psychology* (pp. 197–239). Washington, DC: American Psychological Association.

Liu, W. M., & Clay, D. L. (2002). Multicultural counseling competencies: Guidelines in working with children and adolescents. *Journal of Mental Health Counseling, 24,* 177–187.

McFadden, J. (1993). *Transcultural counseling: Bilateral and international perspectives.* Alexandria, VA: American Counseling Association.

Mullings, L. (1994). Images, ideology, and women of color. In M. Baca Zinn & B. Thornton Dill (Eds.), *Women of color in U.S. society* (pp. 265–289). Philadelphia: Temple University Press.

Pierce, C. M. (1988). Stress in the workplace. In A. Conner-Edwards & J. Spurlock (Eds.), *Black families in crisis* (pp. 27–33). New York: Brunner/Mazel.

Ponterotto, J. G., Fuertes, J. N., & Chen, E. C. (2000). Models of multicultural counseling. In S. Brown & R. Lent (Eds.), *Handbook of counseling psychology* (3rd ed., 639–669). New York: Wiley.

Raja, S. (1998). Culturally sensitive therapy for women of color. *Women and Therapy, 21,* 67–84.

Ransford, H. E., & Miller, J. (1983). Race, sex, and feminist outlooks. *American Sociological Review, 48,* 46–59.

Robinson, C. R. (1983). Black women: A tradition of self-reliant strength. *Women and Therapy, 2,* 135–144.

Robinson, T. L., & Howard-Hamilton, M. F. (2000). *The convergence of race, ethnicity, and gender: Multiple identities in counseling.* Upper Saddle River, NJ: Prentice-Hall.

Smith, E. J. (1985). Ethnic minorities: Life stress, social support, and mental health issues. *The Counseling Psychologist, 13,* 537–579.

Stephan, W. G. (1989). A cognitive approach to stereotyping. In D. Bartal & C. Graumann (Eds.), *Stereotyping and prejudice* (pp. 37–57). New York: Springer-Verlag.

Sue, D. W., Arredondo, P., & McDavis, R. J. (1992). Multicultural counseling competencies and standards: A call to the profession. *Journal of Counseling and Development, 70,* 477–486.

Vandiver, B. J. (2002). What do we know and where do we go? *The Counseling Psychologist, 30,* 96–104.

Weber, L. (1998). A conceptual framework for understanding race, class, gender, and sexuality. *Psychology of Women Quarterly, 22,* 13–32.

Weinrach, S. G., & Thomas, K. R. (2002). A critical analysis of the multi-cultural counseling competencies: Implications for the practice of mental health counseling. *Journal of Mental Health Counseling, 24,* 20–35.

Zinn, M. B., & Dill, B. T. (1994). Difference and domination. In M. Zinn & D. Dill (Eds.), *Women of color in U.S. society* (pp. 3–12). Philadelphia, PA: Temple University Press.

# Part V    THE SEXUAL
MINORITY CLIENT

# CHAPTER 15 What Counselors Need to Know About Working with Sexual Minority Clients

Tania Israel, University of California-Santa Barbara

Lesbian, gay, and bisexual (LGB) individuals have been victims of societal oppression, as well as suffering from negative experiences with mental health providers (see chapter 5 of this book). Many LGB individuals experience undue stress and may exhibit high-risk behaviors at an elevated rate due to their marginalized status (Division 44/Committee on Lesbian Gay & Bisexual Concerns Joint Task Force, 2000); therefore, it is not surprising that they use counseling at a higher rate and participate in a greater number of therapy sessions than do heterosexual clients (Bieschke, McClanahan, Tozer, Grzegorek, & Park, 2000). These patterns attest to a compelling need for counselors to provide competent psychotherapy services for LGB clients. Because of the history of heterosexist practices within the mental health field, it is particularly important for therapists to acquire accurate information about LGB individuals and the factors that can affect their experiences in counseling.

This chapter focuses primarily on information related to LGB individuals. The term *LGBT* (lesbian, gay, bisexual, and transgender) is used when it is appropriate to signify the inclusion of transgender with LGB concerns, and a section toward the end of the chapter identifies some of the areas of commonality and distinction between LGB and transgender populations. The term *LGBTQ* expands this inclusiveness to incorporate those individuals who are questioning their gender or sexual orientation. For the purposes of this chapter, the term *sexual minority* is used as a broad-based term to encompass all those individuals who experience discrimination and oppression based on their affectional or gender orientation.

This chapter provides an overview of information that counselors need to know in order to work effectively with LGB clients. The first two sections discuss foundational knowledge for counselors regarding heterosexism and its impact, models of sexual orientation, and development of sexual orientation identity. These sections do not necessarily address specific issues that may arise in therapy with LGB clients; rather, they contextualize the experiences of individuals who present in counseling with issues related to sexual orientation. The section on professional

**347**

standards delineates ethical, professional, and accreditation guidelines related to counseling LGB clients. Finally, the chapter addresses variables that may affect counseling, including counselor characteristics; counseling process and skills; and within-group differences, such as concerns for ethnic minority, bisexual, and transgender clients.

## HETEROSEXISM AND MONOSEXISM

Negative attitudes toward LGB individuals are well documented (Herek, 1984; Kite & Whitley, 1996), and certain patterns in those attitudes are common. For example, individuals hold more negative attitudes toward gay men than toward lesbian women, and researchers have documented more negative attitudes toward LGB individuals on the part of men than women (Herek, 1988; Kite & Whitley, 1996). People with negative attitudes are also generally older, less educated, more religious, express traditional values about sex roles, and are less likely to have personal contact with lesbians or gay men (Herek, 1984; Herek & Glunt, 1993).

Negative attitudes toward LGB individuals may be referred to alternatively as "homophobia" (Weinberg, 1972),"homonegativism" (Hudson & Ricketts, 1980), or "heterosexism" (Neisen, 1990). When directed specifically toward bisexual women and men, these attitudes are similarly called "biphobia" (Ochs, 1996), "binegativity" (Eliason, 2001), or "monosexism" (Nagle, 1995), although the latter two have not yet been used widely in the professional literature.

The social context of heterosexism creates a situation in which people with same-sex attractions and sexual experiences face greater challenges than those who have attractions and sexual experiences exclusively with people of the other sex. Heterosexism and monosexism produce a context of hostility for LGB individuals that can affect many areas of their lives. LGB women and men experience the impact of heterosexism in terms of discrimination, alienation from family of origin, and violence (Division 44/Committee on Lesbian Gay & Bisexual Concerns Joint Task Force, 2000). Such experiences with negative attitudes may adversely affect the mental health and well-being of sexual minorities. Furthermore, internalization of such negative attitudes by LGB individuals may create a barrier to developing a positive LGB identity (Fox, 1991; Malyon, 1981; Ochs, 1996).

Although heterosexism can be understood in part as similar to racism, some key differences affect how heterosexism operates. Whereas ethnic minority individuals typically are raised by ethnic minority parents, people who are LGB usually grow up in heterosexual families and communities. Consequently, sexual minority identity development and connection with LGB communities often starts in adolescence or later. LGB individuals may, therefore, lack exposure to skills for coping with target group membership that ethnic minority parents and communities impart to their children.

Awareness of heterosexism and monosexism can help counselors understand some of the mental health concerns of LGB clients. Even if they have not directly experienced overt violence or discrimination themselves, counselors should strive to comprehend the fear, anger, and shame that are outgrowths of living in a heterosexist society as an LGB individual. Such awareness may help counselors develop empathy for LGB clients that can further the therapeutic relationship. Furthermore, knowledge about heterosexism and monosexism can help counselors identify and combat clients' internalized homophobia and biphobia.

## MODELS AND DEVELOPMENT OF SEXUAL ORIENTATION IDENTITY

Conceptual models of sexual orientation provide a foundation for understanding the identities and experiences of LGB individuals. Kinsey, Pomeroy, and Martin (1948) provided evidence that sexual behavior can be best represented, not as a dichotomy, but rather as a continuum between people who have sex exclusively with the same sex and people who have sex exclusively with the other sex. Since then others have expanded on Kinsey's continuum to include multiple dimensions of sexuality beyond behavior. For example, the Klein Sexual Orientation Grid (Klein, Sepekoff, & Wolf, 1985) takes into account multiple dimensions of sexual attraction, sexual behavior, sexual fantasies, emotional preference, social preference, self-identification, and gay/straight lifestyle. Furthermore, each dimension can be assessed along a continuum and evaluated at various points in development (e.g., past, present, and ideal).

The various models of sexual orientation may help counselors conceptualize their clients and can provide clients with tools for understanding themselves. Clients who are questioning their sexual identity may be limited by viewing their situation as a binary quandary of "am I gay or am I straight?" These models give such clients more complex ways of thinking about their sexual orientation, acknowledging multiple dimensions of self rather than feeling constrained by perceptions of "gay" and "straight," especially since sexual orientation is not always clearly one or the other. Although some people experience their sexuality as fluid and multidimensional, others seek a more stable sense of identity that enables them to affiliate with existing lesbian and gay male communities (Broido, 2000). Counselors may be able to best assist clients by assessing the clients' perceptions of their own sexual orientation, presenting multiple conceptual models, and affirming clients' own sense of their sexual orientation.

Models of lesbian and gay identity development describe the process of integrating same-sex attractions and experiences into a lesbian or gay identity. Cass presented a six-stage model that described the development of identity for lesbian and gay men as originating in identity confusion and ideally resulting in identity synthesis (Cass, 1979). McCarn and Fassinger (1996) described parallel processes of individual sexual identity development and group membership identity development that account for complex development of individual sense of self and relationship with community.

The coming-out process is an aspect of identity development unique to sexual minority individuals. One manifestation of heterosexism is that people are assumed to be heterosexual until they identify themselves otherwise. This presumption of heterosexuality necessitates an internal and external process by which individuals come to terms with their nonheterosexual identity. This process, known as *coming out,* is not a singular event. Coming out happens over time and may manifest in distinct ways in various contexts. For example, people may choose to disclose their sexual orientation to LGB-identified friends, but not to heterosexual friends, or they may be open about their same-sex relationship at family gatherings, but not in the workplace. Concealing sexual identity in certain circumstances is not necessarily negative. Rather, the complex decisions about where to conceal and where not to conceal may be adaptive, particularly for ethnic minority LGB individuals (Dworkin, 2000).

Although conceptual models of sexual orientation represent the experiences of people who are attracted to both women and men, models of identity development and the coming-out process have not been clearly articulated for these individuals. There is considerable variation in how people develop a bisexual identity, with some people identifying as bisexual prior to coming out as lesbian or gay, some people coming out as bisexual after identifying as lesbian or gay, and some people developing a lasting bisexual identity when they initially realize they are not heterosexual (Fox, 1996). Coming out also presents unique challenges for bisexual individuals, as the visibility of sexual minorities tends to be based on the sex of their partner. Whereas lesbian women and gay men may come out by introducing their partner or by using a same-sex pronoun to refer to their partner, bisexual individuals tend to be seen as heterosexual if they have an other-sex partner and lesbian/gay when they have a same-sex partner; thus, the bisexual identity tends to remain invisible (Ochs, 1996).

Counselors can benefit from knowledge about identity development and the coming-out process. These models may help the counselor to determine what type of support the client needs at various stages of identity development. Furthermore, counselors can assist clients in making decisions about how to identify their sexual orientation to themselves and to others.

## PROFESSIONAL STANDARDS

Adequate preparation to work with LGB clients is mandated by the ethical and accreditation standards of the American Psychological Association (1992, 2000) and the American Counseling Association (1997; Council for Accreditation of Counseling and Related Educational Programs [CACREP], 2001). The American Psychological Association's Ethical Standards (1992) and the American Counseling Association's Standards of Practice (1997) prohibit unfair discrimination based on sexual orientation. Furthermore, psychologists are required to "obtain the training, experience, consultation, or supervision necessary to ensure the competence of their services" with regard to individual differences, including sexual orientation (American Psychological Association, 1992).

Recently, the American Psychological Association reaffirmed its commitment to serving the LGB community by approving guidelines for working with LGB clients (Division 44/Committee on Lesbian Gay & Bisexual Concerns Joint Task Force, 2000). Similarly, the Association for Gay, Lesbian, and Bisexual Issues in Counseling has developed competencies for counseling LGBT clients (Association for Gay Lesbian and Bisexual Issues in Counseling [AGLBIC], n.d.). These guidelines identify the goals to which mental health professionals should aspire in working with LGB clients. The APA document outlines 16 guidelines in areas of attitudes toward homosexuality and bisexuality, relationships and family, issues of diversity, and education. These guidelines encourage psychologists to develop awareness of LGB issues and understand the impact that their attitudes and knowledge have on assessment and treatment of LGB clients. Each guideline is supported with empirical evidence and citations from the professional literature, making this document an excellent resource to help counselors develop a knowledge base about LGB individuals.

In addition to formulating guidelines for therapeutic practice, professional organizations have developed policy statements outlining their perspectives on a variety of issues related to sexual orientation. For example, the American Psychological Association has authored policy statements supporting the legal rights of same-sex couples, protesting discrimination against LGB teachers, and condemning antigay violence (American Psychological Association, n.d.). These policy statements are supported by research and can provide guidance for psychologists who engage in advocacy for LGB individuals.

Counselors should familiarize themselves with professional guidelines related to counseling LGB clients in order to conduct ethical counseling, research, supervision, and training on LGB issues. In addition, it is useful for counselors to know that professional organizations have not been neutral on LGB issues, instead consistently supporting the rights and interests of LGB individuals.

## VARIABLES THAT MAY AFFECT COUNSELING

Counseling experiences and outcomes for LGBT clients vary based on characteristics of the counselor, the counseling process, and the client. Theory, research, and professional guidelines specify aspects of these variables that enhance or diminish benefits of counseling for LGBT clients.

### Counselor Characteristics

Characteristics of the counselor may affect LGBT clients' counseling experiences. It may be possible to alter some of these characteristics (e.g., knowledge and attitudes) through educational interventions. Understanding the role of other characteristics, such as sexual orientation and gender, can guide counselor assignment and encourage exploration of the possible impact of these variables on the counseling relationship.

**Attitudes**  Despite professional standards calling for sensitivity and preparation for working with sexual orientation issues (American Counseling Association, 1997; American Psychological Association, 1992; National Association of Social Workers, 1996), counselors report antigay biases (Casas, Ponterotto, & Gutierrez, 1986; Glenn

& Russell, 1986; Graham, Rawlings, Halpern, & Hermes, 1984; Rudolph, 1988). Studies found that counselors make more errors in processing information related to lesbian and gay clients than other clients (Casas, Brady, & Ponterotto, 1983), that male therapists' homophobia predicted their behavioral avoidance with gay male clients (Hayes & Gelso, 1993), and that therapists' attitudes affected their anticipated reactions to a bisexual client and their perception of the client's presenting concerns (Mohr, Israel, & Sedlacek, 2001). The biases reported by therapists are typically less negative than those reported by the general public. Social desirability, however, may have a significant impact on therapists' self-report of attitudes, as evidenced by attitude assessments that use less obvious means of evaluation (Bieschke et al., 2000).

APA's guidelines for working with LGB clients stated that, ideally, counselors should hold the belief that homosexuality and bisexuality are not indicative of mental illness and should recognize the effects of their own and society's attitudes on their clients and the counseling process (Division 44/Committee on Lesbian Gay & Bisexual Concerns Joint Task Force, 2000). To be consistent with ethical standards and professional guidelines, counselors therefore need to explore their own attitudes and attempt to reduce bias toward LGB individuals. Educational interventions have effectively altered counselors' homonegative attitudes (Gilliland & Crisp, 1995; Rudolph, 1989), so counselors may benefit from seeking out specialized training, supervision, and consultation.

**Knowledge**   Researchers have identified counselors' lack of education about homosexuality as problematic in working with LGB clients (Garnets, Hancock, Cochran, & Goodchilds, 1991; Liddle, 1996). One study empirically identified specific areas of knowledge that experts believed were necessary to work effectively with LGB clients (Israel, Ketz, Detrie, Burke, & Shulman, in press). The authors enumerated 33 such topic areas, including oppression, heterosexism, mental health concerns, developmental issues, identity development, psychological bias, and ethical issues. Typically, LGB issues are covered only as a component of broader diversity courses (Phillips & Fischer, 1998), but the comprehensive information identified in this study cannot be covered in such a brief time. Thus, specialized training in LGB-specific information may be needed to adequately prepare counselors to work with LGB clients.

Although extensive specialized training is preferable, brief informational interventions should not be dismissed. One study demonstrated success in increasing counselors' knowledge about LGB issues in a 2½ hour intervention (Israel, 1998). Thus, counselor educators can have an impact on the knowledge level of their students, even if this topic is addressed in a single class session. Counselor knowledge may improve effectiveness with LGB clients by helping to establish counselor credibility and guiding the counselor to provide appropriate resources. In addition, knowledge may serve as a precursor to development of positive attitudes and effective skills in working with LGB clients (Phillips, 2000).

**Sexual Orientation**   Counselors do not need to identify as lesbian, gay, or bisexual in order to be perceived as effective in working with LGB clients. Several studies have investigated the effect of therapist-client matching on sexual orientation and gender. Lesbian women and gay men both report a preference for lesbian and gay counselors, although heterosexual female counselors are seen as equally helpful as LGB counselors (Atkinson, Brady, & Casas, 1981; Brooks & Kahn, 1990; Liddle, 1997). Several studies have suggested that counselor sexual orientation is likely more important if the client is seeking therapy for issues related to sexual orientation (Kaufman et al., 1997; McDermott, Tyndall, & Lichtenberg, 1989; Moran, 1992). Other factors found to be related to client preference for counselors include gender (Kaufman et al., 1997; Liddle, 1997), similarity of counselor to client's attitudes toward gay advocacy (Atkinson et al., 1981), and counselor's level of experience (Moran, 1992).

Particular issues may arise for LGB- and non-LGB-identified counselors in working with LGBT clients. LGB-affirming heterosexual counselors may experience stigma, and their sexual orientation may be called into question (Morrow, 2000), and such counselors may experience their own stages of coming out as allies of LGB individuals (Gelberg & Chojnacki, 1995). LGB counselors, too, lack immunity to the effects of sexual orientation on counseling and need to be aware of the way that their own experiences or perspectives may affect their work with LGB clients. For example, they may not be prepared to work with LGB individuals whose gender, sexual orientation, or experiences are different from their own (e.g., a lesbian counselor working with a bisexual male client). Furthermore, LGB counselors may be reluctant to acknowledge negative aspects of LGB experiences, such as domestic violence in same-sex relationships, for fear of further stigmatizing LGB individuals (Morrow, 2000). Self-exploration of beliefs, biases, and feelings can be beneficial for LGB and non-LGB counselors alike and may help counselors gain sufficient clarity about their own sexual orientation to use disclosure in ways that will benefit the client (Morrow, 2000).

## Counseling Process and Skills

Counselor actions and interactions with an LGBT client can affect therapeutic process and progress. Counselors can assist clients by knowing which practices clients consider helpful and harmful, understanding the ethical and professional considerations regarding conversion therapy, and creating LGBT-affirming counseling environments.

**Helpful and Harmful Practices**   Studies have attempted to identify harmful and beneficial counseling practices with lesbian and gay clients. One study asked psychologists to identify professional practices that they considered especially harmful or beneficial to lesbian and gay clients (Garnets et al., 1991). Detrimental practices identified included: assessment (e.g., assuming a client is heterosexual); intervention (e.g., abruptly transferring a client following disclosure of LGB orientation); identity (e.g., underestimating the consequences of client's disclosure of LGB orientation to others); relationships (e.g., encouraging the dissolution of a client's relationship because it is with a member of the same sex); family (e.g., opposing child custody for LGB parents); and therapist expertise and education (e.g., relying on a client to educate the counselor about LGB issues).

Exemplary practices included assisting in the development of a positive lesbian or gay identity; not attempting to change the client's sexual orientation; and demonstrating accurate knowledge about a range of LGB issues. Liddle (1996) provided further support for these helpful and harmful counseling practices by investigating them from the perspective of lesbian and gay clients.

A study discussed earlier that empirically identified areas of knowledge for counseling LGB clients also identified skills that experts deemed necessary to work effectively with LGB clients (Israel et al., in press). The authors enumerated 31 skills, including using ethical behavior, helping clients with the coming-out process, setting appropriate boundaries, seeking consultation and supervision, and not assuming that sexual orientation is the focus of therapy. Counselors can benefit from developing these skills, using the exemplary practices, and avoiding the biased, inadequate, or inappropriate practices.

**Conversion Therapy**   Interventions intended to change LGB clients' sexual orientation, known as sexual orientation conversion therapy, represent a controversial intersection of psychology, gay rights, religion, and public policy (Haldeman, 2002). Although the American Psychological Association declassified homosexuality as a mental illness in 1975, some counselors continue to engage in attempts to change LGB clients' sexual orientation, initiated either by the client or the therapist (Haldeman, 2000; Shidlo & Schroeder, 2002). Although the opportunity to talk with a counselor regarding struggles about sexual orientation may provide some relief for clients, conversion therapy may cause significant psychological harm, including depression, suicidality, internalized homophobia, sexual dysfunction, social isolation, and loss of spiritual faith (Shidlo & Schroeder, 2002). Furthermore, the very premise of conversion therapy reinforces antigay prejudice, and the heterosexist societal context may undermine clients' ability to freely seek or agree to conversion therapy (Haldeman, 2000). A client's request for conversion therapy may provide an ideal opportunity to explore the client's perceptions of his or her own sexual orientation, motives for seeking change, internalized homophobia, and access to LGB-affirming resources. If a counselor considers conducting conversion therapy, treatment should include provision of accurate information; informed consent about risks and benefits of conversion therapy; and attention to ethical concerns (Schneider, Brown, & Glassgold, 2002; Shidlo & Schroeder, 2002).

**Counseling Environment**   Very little research has investigated ecological variables related to counseling LGBT clients. One study found a correlation between career counselors' self-reported behaviors with LGB clients and the counselors' perceptions of their organizational climates as nonheterosexist (Bieschke & Matthews, 1996). This finding suggests that counselors and administrators can support LGB clients by creating LGB-affirming counseling settings.

**LGBT Within-Group Variation**   Mental health needs and services differ for lesbian women, gay men, bisexual women, bisexual men, and transgender individuals (Division 44/Committee on Lesbian Gay & Bisexual Concerns Joint Task

Force, 2000). For example, gay men have experienced the greatest impact of the AIDS epidemic, and they may present with related issues of illness and grief (Bohan, 1996). Whereas lesbian women have often been in primarily parenting roles, only a small percentage of gay men have traditionally lived with their children (Bohan, 1996; Patterson, 1994). Bisexual men may find little support from gay men, and bisexual women may feel ostracized from lesbian communities (Ochs, 1996). Furthermore, relationship concerns differ for male-male and female-female couples (Ossana, 2000). Although LGB individuals face decisions about coming out, these differ from the disclosure concerns of transgender individuals (Israel & Tarver, 2001). Moreover, differences in age, physical abilities, culture, and ethnicity affect the experiences of LGB individuals (Division 44/Committee on Lesbian Gay & Bisexual Concerns Joint Task Force, 2000).

Not only do LGB clients vary in terms of demographics, they differ with regard to their reasons for seeking counseling. Some clients present with concerns that non-LGB clients also face, such as career indecision (Croteau, Anderson, Distefano, & Kampa Kokesch, 2000), relationship conflict (Ossana, 2000), and grief (Kimmel, 1993). LGB clients also present in counseling with issues unique to this population. For example, LGB clients may seek assistance with coming-out issues (Reynolds & Hanjorgiris, 2000), coping with workplace discrimination (Croteau et al., 2000), internalized heterosexism (Shidlo, 1994), and hate crime victimization (Garnets, Herek, & Levy, 1993). Counselors should neither assume that LGB clients want to focus on sexual orientation issues, nor should they avoid these issues (Liddle, 1996). Rather, counselors should keep in mind the range of concerns that bring LGB clients to counseling.

Very little research has investigated individual differences related to mental health services for LGBT clients. "Researchers have been unsuccessful for the most part at obtaining samples of LGB individuals who are racially, ethnically, and geographically diverse" (Bieschke et al., 2000, p. 326), thus making it difficult to compare client experiences and outcomes on these dimensions. One notable exception is a study that found White and Latina lesbians used counseling at a slightly higher rate than did African American lesbians, and women with advanced degrees saw mental health care providers at a higher rate than did those with less than a high school degree (Bradford, Ryan, & Rothblum, 1994).

**Ethnic Minority LGB Clients Managing Multiple Oppressions**   Heterosexism is supported by the gender-role expectations, religious beliefs, and social sanctions of various cultures. In addition, ethnic minority individuals who view the family as a key defense against a racist society may perceive same-sex orientation as a betrayal of cultural values and loyalties (Garnets & Kimmel, 1993). Furthermore, racism exists within some LGB communities, and ethnic minority LGB individuals can lack visibility within these communities. As a result, ethnic minority LGB clients may have limited support for dealing with the internalized racism and heterosexism and external prejudice and discrimination that they are likely to experience.

In terms of ethnic and sexual identity development, existing models may not describe the complex situation of individuals who are members of both ethnic minority and sexual minority communities (Fukuyama & Ferguson, 2000). To accommodate intersections among gender, ethnicity, and sexual orientation, ethnic minority LGB individuals may prioritize identities, loyalties, and communities by choosing one as primary. Alternatively, they may synthesize them by developing an identity that encompasses multiple dimensions of self (Garnets & Kimmel, 1993).

Ethnic minority LGB individuals may face alienation from their cultural communities due to heterosexist cultural beliefs and practices, and they may also experience discrimination and dismissal of their values and perspectives by the primarily European American LGB community. Such marginalization of ethnic minority LGB people includes absence of ethnic minority individuals in event planning and requests for excessive identification to enter gay bars (Bohan, 1996). Thus, individuals may seek refuge from one type of prejudice in a community that harbors intolerance for another aspect of their identity.

To create a safe haven for such multiply oppressed ethnic minority LGB clients, counselors can examine their own assumptions about LGB individuals. For example, counselors may find they typically picture only European American individuals as being lesbian, gay, or bisexual. Counselors can also familiarize themselves with literature that describes how particular cultural backgrounds interact with specific sexual orientations so that they can address the unique needs of Latina lesbians (Espin, 1993), African American gay men (Loiacano, 1993), and bisexual women and men of color (Rust, 1996), to name a few. Finally, counselors can assist ethnic minority LGB clients by identifying sources of support within family and community, evaluating advantages and disadvantages of concealing LGB identity in various circumstances, overcoming internalized racism and heterosexism, and examining multiple layers of oppression to address the unique circumstances of clients who are faced with complex intersections of ethnicity and sexual orientation (Fukuyama & Ferguson, 2000).

**Bisexuality**   Bisexual individuals face unique stressors due to limited societal understanding of bisexuality and lack of acceptance in both lesbian/gay and heterosexual communities. Attitudes toward bisexual women and men reflect misconceptions and confusion about bisexuality. Although current conceptual models present sexual orientation as multidimensional and nondichotomous, personal beliefs, coming-out models, and much of the professional literature are based on dichotomous views of sexual orientation. Consequently, bisexual individuals may be viewed as nonexistent, sexually obsessed, and personally and politically disloyal (Israel & Mohr, in press).

Bisexual individuals have reported lack of validation, isolation, and ostracism from both heterosexual and lesbian/gay communities (Hutchins & Ka'ahumanu, 1991). Although rejection by heterosexual individuals can be understood in the context of heterosexism, ostracism from lesbian/gay communities is based on a variety of assumptions, personal experiences, and political motivations (Israel & Mohr, in press). The possibility of being bisexual may threaten the sense of self and community for individuals who have based their social identity on a lesbian or gay sexual orientation. Bisexuality may present such individuals with the possibility that the pain of being lesbian or gay in a homophobic society could have been avoided (Udis-Kessler, 1990) or fear that they would need to go through the difficulty of coming to terms with a new identity all over again if they were actually bisexual. Furthermore, lesbian women and gay men may fear that bisexual individuals are not committed to the lesbian and gay community and politics (Mohr & Rochlen, 1999; Ochs, 1996; Udis-Kessler, 1990).

Because bisexuality has been misunderstood and underrepresented in the professional literature, counselors may inadvertently conduct lesbian-gay-affirming therapy at the expense of bisexuality. For example, in an attempt to assist clients in developing a stable lesbian or gay identity, counselors may overlook the possibility that a bisexual identity might be a better fit for the client. Counselors can attend to concerns of bisexual clients by obtaining accurate information about bisexuality and about clients, focusing on clients' presenting concerns without getting distracted by their bisexual orientation, refraining from imposing one's own political beliefs on clients, and remaining aware of the impact of the counselor's own sexual orientation on clients (Matteson, 1996).

**Transgender Issues**   An emerging area for counselors to address is working with transgender clients. The term *transgender* is an umbrella term that includes persons whose perceived, identified, or lived gender is incongruent with their biological or assigned sex, encompassing such groups as cross-dressers, transvestites, transsexuals, drag queens/kings, and other persons who self-identify as transgendered (Cole, Denny, Eyler, & Samons, 2000; Gainor, 2000; Hunter & Mallon, 2000; Israel & Tarver, 2001). Not all people who fit this description identify themselves as transgender—some may simply identify as male or female or neither. Although the term *transgender* refers to a diverse community, the individuals in these groups share adjustment and discrimination patterns associated with incongruence between gender expression and physiology.

The counseling profession has started to include transgender individuals in discussions of LGB psychology (Carroll & Gilroy, 2002; Carroll, Gilroy, & Ryan, 2002; Gainor, 2000). Although there are differences between these populations, overlap exists that merits the inclusion of transgender clients in discussions of mental health services for sexual minority individuals. Although gender identity and sexual orientation are distinct constructs, the negative societal responses to both groups are based, in part, on the perceived transgression of traditional gender roles. Additionally, both LGB and transgender individuals grapple with identity development, the coming-out process, workplace discrimination, and hate crimes. Transgender individuals are "increasingly being considered members of the LGB community" (Bieschke et al., 2000, p. 328), and so counselors are encouraged to become knowledgeable about transgender mental health concerns.

Transgender clients may present with issues directly related to gender identity (e.g., seeking support for gender reassignment surgery), issues indirectly related to gender identity (e.g., workplace discrimination due to perceived gender-inappropriate presentation), or with concerns unrelated to gender identity (Gainor, 2000). Counselors can prepare themselves for working with transgender clients by seeking out specialized training and obtaining information about working with transgender clients (e.g., Ettner, 1999; Israel & Tarver, 2001).

## CONCLUSION

To prepare themselves to work with lesbian, gay, bisexual, and transgender (LGBT) clients, counselors should be familiar with the basic concepts of heterosexism, models of sexual orientation, and sexual identity development. Knowledge of professional standards can guide mental health professionals in maintaining ethical practices with LGBT clients. Moreover, understanding the variables that affect counseling can help therapists implement this knowledge to maximize the quality of services for LGBT clients. Ongoing training and supervision are recommended to help counselors gain the knowledge, attitudes, and skills necessary to work effectively with sexual minority clients.

# Cases and Questions

1. You are working with a 39-year-old male European American client. He recognized his same-sex attractions at age 14 and has identified as gay since age 22. Since that time he has had little contact with his family of origin who sees his lifestyle as "immoral" and "irresponsible." He typically meets men in gay bars, and his longest relationship lasted 2 months. He states that he does not find the "gay lifestyle" satisfying and requests that you help him "become heterosexual."
   (a) How do you respond to his request? How would you determine whether or not conversion therapy is appropriate for this client?
   (b) What information would you share with him about the lives of LGB individuals? about conversion therapy? about your values, beliefs, and sexual orientation?
   (c) What ethical guidelines would you consider relevant to your work with this client?
2. Your client is a 16-year-old Latina woman. She initially presented for counseling with concerns about self-esteem, particularly dissatisfaction with her body image. Three months into your work together, she shares her concern that she may have "feelings" for her female best friend. She feels "ashamed" of her feelings and has not told anyone else about them, fearing that people would think she's a "lezzie."
   (a) What questions would you ask her in order to gain a multidimensional perspective of her sexual orientation?
   (b) What information would you share with her about models of sexual orientation? about identity development? about the lives of LGB individuals?
   (c) How would you encourage her to view her feelings toward her friend (a phase, a crush, the first step in the development of a lesbian identity, etc.)?

# REFERENCES

American Counseling Association. (1997). *ACA Code of Ethics and Standards of Practice.* Alexandria, VA: Author.

American Psychological Association. (1992). Ethical Principles of Psychologists and Code of Conduct. *American Psychologist, 47*(12), 1597–1611.

American Psychological Association. (2000). *Guidelines and principles for accreditation of programs in professional psychology.* Washington, DC: Author.

American Psychological Association. (n.d.). *Lesbian, gay, and bisexual concerns policy statements.* Retrieved November 16, 2002, from http://www.apa.org/pi/lgbc/policy/statements.html.

Association for Gay Lesbian and Bisexual Issues in Counseling (AGLBIC). (n.d.). *Competencies for counseling gay, lesbian, bisexual and transgendered (GLBT) clients* [Website]. Retrieved April 22, 2002, from http://www.aglbic.org/competencies.html.

Atkinson, D. R., Brady, S., & Casas, J. M. (1981). Sexual preference similarity, attitude similarity, and perceived counseling credibility and attractiveness. *Journal of Counseling Psychology, 28*(6), 504–509.

Bieschke, K. J., & Matthews, C. (1996). Career counselor attitudes and behaviors toward gay, lesbian, and bisexual clients. *Journal of Vocational Behavior, 48*(2), 243–255.

Bieschke, K. J., McClanahan, M., Tozer, E., Grzegorek, J. L., & Park, J. (2000). Programmatic research on the treatment of lesbian, gay, and bisexual clients: The past, the present, and the course for the future. In R. M. Perez, K. A. DeBord, & K. J. Bieschke (Eds.), *Handbook of counseling and psychotherapy with lesbian, gay, and bisexual clients* (pp. 309–335). Washington, DC: American Psychological Association.

Bohan, J. S. (1996). *Psychology and sexual orientation: Coming to terms.* New York: Taylor & Francis/Routledge.

Bradford, J., Ryan, C., & Rothblum, E. D. (1994). National Lesbian Health Care Survey: Implications for mental health care. *Journal of Consulting and Clinical Psychology, 62*(2), 228–242.

Broido, E. M. (2000). Constructing identity: The nature and meaning of lesbian, gay, and bisexual identities. In R. M. Perez, K. A. DeBord, K. J. Bieschke (Eds.), *Handbook of counseling and psychotherapy with lesbian, gay, and bisexual clients.* (pp. 13–33): American Psychological Association.

Brooks, G. S., & Kahn, S. E. (1990). Evaluation of a course in gender and cultural issues. *Counselor Education and Supervision, 30*(1), 66–76.

Carroll, L., & Gilroy, P. J. (2002). Transgender issues in counselor preparation. *Counselor Education and Supervision, 41,* 233–242.

Carroll, L., Gilroy, P. J., & Ryan, J. (2002). Counseling transgendered, transsexual, and gender-variant clients. *Journal of Counseling and Development, 80,* 131–139.

Casas, J. M., Brady, S., & Ponterotto, J. G. (1983). Sexual preference biases in counseling: An information processing approach. *Journal of Counseling Psychology, 30*(2), 139–145.

Casas, J. M., Ponterotto, J. G., & Gutierrez, J. M. (1986). An ethical indictment of counseling research and training: The cross-cultural perspective. *Journal of Counseling and Development, 64*(5), 347–349.

Cass, V. C. (1979). Homosexual identity formation: A theoretical model. *Journal of Homosexuality, 4*(3), 219–235.

Cole, S. S., Denny, D., Eyler, A. E., & Samons, S. L. (2000). Issues of transgender. In L. T. Szuchman & F. Muscarella (Eds.), *Psychological perspectives on human sexuality* (pp. 149–195). New York: Wiley.

Council for Accreditation of Counseling and Related Educational Programs (CACREP). (2001). *The 2001 Standards* [Website]. Retrieved April 24, 2002, from http://www.counseling.org/CACREP/.

Croteau, J. M., Anderson, M. Z., Distefano, T. M., & Kampa Kokesch, S. (2000). Lesbian, gay, and bisexual vocational psychology: Reviewing foundations and planning construction. In R. M. Perez, K. A. DeBord, K. J. Bieschke (Eds.), *Handbook of counseling and psychotherapy with lesbian, gay, and bisexual clients* (pp. 383–408). Washington, DC: American Psychological Association.

Division 44/Committee on Lesbian Gay & Bisexual Concerns Joint Task Force. (2000). Guidelines for psychotherapy with lesbian, gay, and bisexual clients. *American Psychologist, 55*(12), 1440–1451.

Dworkin, S. H. (2000). Individual therapy with lesbian, gay, and bisexual clients. In R. M. Perez, K. A. DeBord, & K. J. Bieschke (Eds.), *Handbook of counseling and psychotherapy with lesbian, gay, and bisexual clients* (pp. 157–181). Washington, DC: American Psychological Association.

Eliason, M. (2001). Bi-negativity: The stigma facing bisexual men. *Journal of Bisexuality, 1*(2/3), 137–154.

Espin, O. M. (1993). Issues of identity in the psychology of Latina lesbians. In E. Linda D. Garnets & E. Douglas C. Kimmel (Eds.), *Psychological perspectives on lesbian and gay male experiences* (pp. 348–363). New York: Columbia University Press.

Ettner, R. (1999). *Gender loving care: A guide to counseling gender-variant clients.* New York: W. W. Norton.

Fox, A. (1991). Development of a bisexual identity: Understanding the process. In L. Hutchins & L. Ka'ahumanu (Eds.), *Bi any other name: Bisexual people speak out* (pp. 29–39). Boston: Alyson.

Fox, R. C. (1996). Bisexuality in perspective: A review of theory and research. In E. Beth A. Firestein (Ed.), *Bisexuality: The psychology and politics of an invisible minority* (pp. 3–50). Thousand Oaks, CA: Sage.

Fukuyama, M. A., & Ferguson, A. D. (2000). Lesbian, gay, and bisexual people of color: Understanding cultural complexity and managing multiple oppressions. In R. M. Perez, K. A. DeBord, & K. J. Bieschke (Eds.), *Handbook of counseling and psychotherapy with lesbian, gay, and bisexual clients* (pp. 81–105). Washington, DC: American Psychological Association.

Gainor, K. A. (2000). Including transgender issues in lesbian, gay, and bisexual psychology: Implications for clinical practice and training. In B. Greene & G. L. Croom (Eds.), *Education, research, and practice in lesbian, gay, bisexual, and transgendered psychology: A resource manual* (Vol. 5, pp. 131–160). Thousand Oaks, CA: Sage.

Garnets, L., Hancock, K. A., Cochran, S. D., & Goodchilds, J. (1991). Issues in psychotherapy with lesbians and gay men: A survey of psychologists. *American Psychologist, 46*(9), 964–972.

Garnets, L., Herek, G. M., & Levy, B. (1993). Violence and victimization of lesbians and gay men: Mental health consequences. In E. Linda D. Garnets & E. Douglas C. Kimmel (Eds.), *Psychological perspectives on lesbian and gay male experiences* (pp. 579–597). New York: Columbia University Press.

Garnets, L. D., & Kimmel, D. C. (Eds.). (1993). *Psychological perspectives on lesbian and gay male experiences.* New York: Columbia University Press.

Gelberg, S., & Chojnacki, J. T. (1995). Developmental transitions of gay/lesbian/bisexual-affirmative, heterosexual career counselors. *Career Development Quarterly, 43*(3), 267–273.

Gilliland, B., & Crisp, D. (1995, August). *Homophobia: Assessing and changing attitudes to counselors-in-training.* Paper presented at the 103rd Annual Meeting of the American Psychological Association, New York, NY.

Glenn, A. A., & Russell, R. K. (1986). Heterosexual bias among counselor trainees. *Counselor Education and Supervision, 25*(3), 222–229.

Graham, D. L., Rawlings, E. I., Halpern, H. S., & Hermes, J. (1984). Therapists' needs for training in counseling lesbians and gay men. *Professional Psychology: Research and Practice, 15*(4), 482–496.

Haldeman, D. C. (2000). Therapeutic responses to sexual orientation: Psychology's evolution. In E. Beverly Greene & E. Gladys L. Croom (Eds.), *Education, research, and practice in lesbian, gay, bisexual, and transgendered psychology: A resource manual* (Vol. 5, pp. 244–262). Thousand Oaks, CA: Sage.

Haldeman, D. C. (2002). Gay rights, patient rights: The implications of sexual orientation conversion therapy. *Professional Psychology: Research and Practice, 33*(3), 260–264.

Hayes, J. A., & Gelso, C. J. (1993). Male counselors' discomfort with gay and HIV-infected clients. *Journal of Counseling Psychology, 40*(1), 86–93.

Herek, G. M. (1984). Attitudes toward lesbians and gay men: A factor analytic study. *Journal of Homosexuality, 10*(1/2), 39–51.

Herek, G. M. (1988). Heterosexuals' attitudes toward lesbians and gay men: Correlates and gender differences. *Journal of Sex Research, 25*(4), 451–477.

Herek, G. M., & Glunt, E. K. (1993). Interpersonal contact and heterosexuals' attitudes toward gay men: Results from a national survey. *Journal of Sex Research, 30*(3), 239–244.

Hudson, W. W., & Ricketts, W. A. (1980). A strategy for the measurement of homophobia. *Journal of Homosexuality, 5*(4), 357–372.

Hunter, J., & Mallon, G. P. (2000). Lesbian, gay, and bisexual adolescent development: Dancing with your feet tied together. In B. Greene & G. L. Croom (Eds.), *Education, research, and practice in lesbian, gay, bisexual, and transgendered psychology: A resource manual* (Vol. 5, pp. 226–243). Thousand Oaks, CA: Sage.

Hutchins, L., & Ka'ahumanu, L. (1991). *Bi any other name: Bisexual people speak out.* Boston: Alyson.

Israel, G. E., & Tarver, D. E., II. (2001). *Transgender care: Recommended guidelines, practical information and personal accounts.* Philadelphia: Temple University Press.

Israel, T. (1998, August). *Training counselors to work with lesbian, gay, and bisexual clients.* Paper presented at the American Psychological Association annual convention, San Francisco, CA.

Israel, T., Ketz, K., Detrie, P. M., Burke, M. C., & Shulman, J. L. (in press). Identifying counselor competencies for working with lesbian, gay, and bisexual clients. *Journal of Gay and Lesbian Psychotherapy.*

Israel, T., & Mohr, J. J. (in press). Attitudes toward bisexual women and men—current research, future directions. *Journal of Bisexuality.*

Kaufman, J. S., Carlozzi, A. F., Boswell, D. L., Barnes, L. L. B., Wheeler-Scruggs, K., & Levy, P. A. (1997). Factors influencing therapist selection among gays, lesbians and bisexuals. *Counseling Psychology Quarterly, 10*(3), 287–297.

Kimmel, D. C. (1993). Adult development and aging: A gay perspective. In E. Linda D. Garnets & E. Douglas C. Kimmel (Eds.), *Psychological perspectives on lesbian and gay male experiences* (pp. 517–534). New York: Columbia University Press.

Kinsey, A. C., Pomeroy, W. B., & Martin, C. E. (1948). *Sexual behavior in the human male.* Philadelphia: Saunders.

Kite, M. E., & Whitley, B. E., Jr. (1996). Sex differences in attitudes toward homosexual persons, behaviors, and civil rights: A meta-analysis. *Personality and Social Psychology Bulletin, 22*(4), 336–353.

Klein, F., Sepekoff, B., & Wolf, T. J. (1985). Sexual orientation: A multivariable dynamic process. *Journal of Homosexuality, 11*(1/2), 35–49.

Liddle, B. J. (1996). Therapist sexual orientation, gender, and counseling practices as they relate to ratings on helpfulness by gay and lesbian clients. *Journal of Counseling Psychology, 43*(4), 394–401.

Liddle, B. J. (1997). Gay and lesbian clients' selection of therapists and utilization of therapy. *Psychotherapy: Theory, Research, Practice, Training, 34*(1), 11–18.

Loiacano, D. K. (1993). Gay identity issues among black Americans: Racism, homophobia, and the need for validation. In E. Linda D. Garnets & E. Douglas C. Kimmel (Eds.), *Psychological perspectives on lesbian and gay male experiences* (pp. 364–375). New York: Columbia University Press.

Malyon, A. K. (1981). Psychotherapeutic implications of internalized homophobia in gay men. *Journal of Homosexuality, 7*(2/3), 59–69.

Matteson, D. R. (1996). Counseling and psychotherapy with bisexual and exploring clients. In E. Beth A. Firestein (Ed.), *Bisexuality: The psychology and politics of an invisible minority* (pp. 185–213). Thousand Oaks, CA: Sage.

McCarn, S. R., & Fassinger, R. E. (1996). Revisioning sexual minority identity formation: A new model of lesbian identity and its implications. *Counseling Psychologist, 24*(3), 508–534.

McDermott, D., Tyndall, L., & Lichtenberg, J. W. (1989). Factors related to counselor preference among gays and lesbians. *Journal of Counseling and Development. Special Issue: Gay, Lesbian, and Bisexual Issues in Counseling, 68*(1), 31–35.

Mohr, J. J., Israel, T., & Sedlacek, W. E. (2001). Counselors' attitudes regarding bisexuality as predictors of counselors' clinical responses: An analogue study of a female bisexual client. *Journal of Counseling Psychology, 48*(2), 212–222.

Mohr, J. J., & Rochlen, A. B. (1999). Measuring attitudes regarding bisexuality in lesbian, gay male, and heterosexual populations. *Journal of Counseling Psychology, 46*(3), 353–369.

Moran, M. R. (1992). Effects of sexual orientation similarity and counselor experience level on gay men's and lesbians' perceptions of counselors. *Journal of Counseling Psychology, 39*(2), 247–251.

Morrow, S. L. (2000). First do no harm: Therapist issues in psychotherapy with lesbian, gay, and bisexual clients. In R. M. Perez, K. A. DeBord, & K. J. Bieschke (Eds.), *Handbook of counseling and psychotherapy with lesbian, gay, and bisexual clients* (pp. 137–156). Washington, DC: American Psychological Association.

Nagle, J. (1995). Framing radical bisexuality: Toward a gender agenda. In N. Tucker, L. Highleyman, & R. Kaplan (Eds.), *Bisexual politics: Theories, queries, and visions* (pp. 305–314). Binghamton, NY: Harrington Park Press.

National Association of Social Workers. (1996). *NASW code of ethics.* Washington, DC: Author.

Neisen, J. H. (1990). Heterosexism: Redefining homophobia for the 1990s. *Journal of Gay and Lesbian Psychotherapy, 1*(3), 21–35.

Ochs, R. (1996). Biphobia: It goes more than two ways. In B. A. Firestein (Ed.), *Bisexuality: The psychology and politics of an invisible minority* (pp. 217–239). Thousand Oaks, CA: Sage.

Ossana, S. M. (2000). Relationship and couples counseling. In R. M. Perez, K. A. DeBord, & K. J. Bieschke (Eds.), *Handbook of counseling and psychotherapy with lesbian, gay, and bisexual clients* (pp. 275–302). Washington, DC: American Psychological Association.

Patterson, C. J. (1994). Children of the lesbian baby boom: Behavioral adjustment, self-concepts, and sex role identity. In E. Beverly Greene & E. Gregory M. Herek (Eds.), *Lesbian and gay psychology: Theory, research, and clinical applications* (pp. 156–175). Thousand Oaks, CA: Sage.

Phillips, J. C. (2000). Training issues and considerations. In R. M. Perez, K. A. DeBord, & K. J. Bieschke (Eds.), *Handbook of counseling and psychotherapy with lesbian, gay, and bisexual clients* (pp. 337–358). Washington, DC: American Psychological Association.

Phillips, J. C., & Fischer, A. R. (1998). Graduate students' training experiences with lesbian, gay, and bisexual issues. *Counseling Psychologist, 26*(5), 712–734.

Reynolds, A. L., & Hanjorgiris, W. F. (2000). Coming out: Lesbian, gay, and bisexual identity development. In R. M. Perez, K. A. DeBord, & K. J. Bieschke

(Eds.), *Handbook of counseling and psychotherapy with lesbian, gay, and bisexual clients* (pp. 35–55). Washington, DC: American Psychological Association.

Rudolph, J. (1988). Counselors' attitudes toward homosexuality: A selective review of the literature. *Journal of Counseling and Development, 67*(3), 165–168.

Rudolph, J. (1989). Effects of a workshop on mental health practitioners' attitudes toward homosexuality and counseling effectiveness. *Journal of Counseling and Development. Special Issue: Gay, Lesbian, and Bisexual Issues in Counseling, 68*(1), 81–85.

Rust, P. C. (1996). Managing multiple identities: Diversity among bisexual women and men. In E. Beth A. Firestein (Ed.), *Bisexuality: The psychology and politics of an invisible minority* (pp. 53–83). Thousand Oaks, CA: Sage.

Schneider, M. S., Brown, L. S., & Glassgold, J. M. (2002). Implementing the resolution on appropriate therapeutic responses to sexual orientation: A guide for the perplexed. *Professional Psychology: Research and Practice, 33*(3), 265–276.

Shidlo, A. (1994). Internalized homophobia: Conceptual and empirical issues in measurement. In E. Beverly Greene & E. Gregory M. Herek (Eds.), *Lesbian and gay psychology: Theory, research, and clinical applications* (pp. 176–205). Thousand Oaks, CA: Sage.

Shidlo, A., & Schroeder, M. (2002). Changing sexual orientation: A consumers' report. *Professional Psychology: Research and Practice, 33*(3), 249–259.

Udis-Kessler, A. (1990). Bisexuality in an essentialist world: Toward an understanding of biphobia. In T. Geller (Ed.), *Bisexuality: A reader and sourcebook* (pp. 51–63). Ojai, CA: Times Change Press.

Weinberg, G. (1972). *Society and the healthy homosexual.* New York: St. Martin's Press.

# CHAPTER 16 Finding the "Yes" Within Ourselves: Counseling Lesbian and Bisexual Women

Susan L. Morrow, University of Utah

> We have been raised to fear the yes within ourselves, our deepest cravings. . . .
> Only now, I find more and more woman-identified women brave enough to risk
> sharing the erotic's electrical charge without having to look away. . . . Recog-
> nizing the power of the erotic within our lives can give us the energy to pursue
> genuine change within our world, rather than merely settling for a shift of char-
> acters in the same weary drama. For not only do we touch our most profoundly
> creative source, but we do that which is female and self-affirming in the face of
> a racist, patriarchal, and anti-erotic society. (Lorde, 1978)

How can counselors provide affirmative and empowering counseling to women
who love women and help them to find the "yes" within themselves? In the midst
of a larger society that denies women the full expression of their sexuality and
erotic potential, what are the values, perspectives, knowledge, skills, and training
that counselors need to help women-loving women love themselves and other
women fearlessly?

This chapter addresses how counselors and therapists can work with lesbian
and bisexual women to resolve problems of living and enhance mental health, as
well as ways to think about working with clients to empower them, foster their resilience, and support their liberation. The chapter is based on the assumption that
women's biology and socialization create unique sociocultural and psychological
issues that should be addressed in unique ways. Most of the literature on counseling women-loving women has been oriented toward lesbians, with a focus on bisexual women emerging more recently. This chapter includes both lesbian and bisexual women. Thus, the terms *lesbian* or *lesbian woman* and *bisexual woman* are
used to address women's identities; and *women-loving women* or *women who are
same-sex attracted* are terms that describe lesbian and bisexual women as well as
nonidentified women who love or are attracted to other women. Same-sex relationships between women are referred to as lesbian relationships, even though the
women involved may not be lesbian-identified. Unless stated otherwise, all references to bisexual women in relationships refer to relationships with women.

At the risk of neglecting the very real and important relationship issues of bisexual (and, indeed, lesbian) women who relate intimately with men, this chapter

**366**

focuses deliberately on issues of women whose attractions and relationships are primarily oriented to women. In that context, it first outlines a range of counseling traditions and approaches that have been used with lesbian and bisexual women, starting with more conventional perspectives and moving to those that are more ideological or sociopolitical in nature. Then, the principles and strategies of feminist counseling and psychotherapy that can be used to empower lesbian and bisexual women clients are explored in some depth. After that, issues across the life span that confront women-loving women and ways the counselor may work with clients dealing with these issues are addressed. Finally, additional comments about advocacy and activism are made, concluding with two short vignettes for consideration and discussion.

## WE'VE COME A LONG WAY, BABY! MODELS OF COUNSELING AND PSYCHOTHERAPY FOR LESBIAN AND BISEXUAL WOMEN

From viewing same-sex relationships between women as a sin, to as a crime, to as a mental illness, it would seem that mental-health professions have evolved over time. Though there are still those who hope to convert lesbians from what they see as a sinful or unhealthy—or at the very least unsatisfying—orientation, counselors and therapists for the most part have adopted the view that lesbian and bisexual women's orientations, attractions, and behaviors are natural points on a continuum of sexual orientation. From an era when lesbianism was treated by removing female sexual organs; performing lobotomies; administering hormones, LSD, and sexual stimulants or depressants; and subjecting patients to electroshock treatments and aversion therapies (Falco, 1991), counselors find themselves currently in a milieu where same-sex attractions per se are not viewed as a problem. Instead, there is a rich and varied literature on counseling lesbian and bisexual women about the real issues in their lives: relationships, identities, careers, parenting, and a host of concerns that confront human beings in general. In addition, the counseling profession's legacy from feminist, lesbian/gay/bisexual (LGB), and civil rights movements include rich and varied perspectives, counseling modalities, and techniques.

Various counseling and psychotherapeutic approaches have taken different views of same-sex relationships and attractions of women. Approaches to counseling lesbian and bisexual women may be categorized into traditional, nonsexist, affirmative, and feminist models of counseling.

### Traditional Counseling Approaches

Traditional therapies include the moral/religious paradigm, psychodynamic psychotherapies, Jungian therapy, cognitive and cognitive-behavioral approaches, and humanistic counseling. In many instances, the particular approach is based primarily on theories derived from men; thus, a particular focus on women has been traditionally absent.

**Moral/Religious Paradigm**    Religion has not always opposed homosexuality; however, the influence of Christianity in the West, with its historic prohibitions of sex in general and nonreproductive marital sex in particular, has had significant impact on psychology and psychotherapy. Today, the most prevalent forms of religious counseling for homosexuality include "reparative" or "conversion" therapies, predominantly the psychodynamically oriented approaches promoted by Socarides (1978) and Nicolosi (1991). Such approaches are based on the idea that male homosexuality arises as a result of a boy's unfulfilled desires for his presumably absent father, which become sexualized. Therapy consists of providing experiences in which same-sex-attracted men are encouraged to form nonsexual intimate relationships with other (presumably straight) men and to become competent in so-called masculine activities such as sports. Theory for the conversion of lesbians to a heterosexual orientation has not been as well developed as that for men; however, an important component of reparative therapy for lesbians is learning to dress and wear makeup in an "appropriate" feminine way. Lesbian invisibility in this case may be an advantage, as there has not been as systematic an effort to "cure" women of their same-sex attractions as there has been for men.

**Psychodynamic Psychotherapy**    Despite current applications of psychodynamic constructs to the "conversion" or "reparation" of same-sex-attracted individuals, Freud himself was scornful of Christian sexual ethics (Horrocks, 1998), seeing them as a reaction formation to repressed sexual (including homosexual) feelings. He viewed homosexuality as "assuredly no advantage," but noted that "it cannot be classified as an illness" (Abelove, 1993). He did, however, express considerable ambivalence about male homosexuality and virtually ignored women. Psychodynamic theory related to women has assumed that lesbians have feelings of inadequacy, bitterness toward men, and excessive masculinity (McDougall, 1985). Ryan (1998) argued that a fatal shortcoming in psychodynamic theory for women is the confusion of homosexuality with gender identity, noting that lesbians express a wide range of gendered behaviors and identities. Freud did not see lesbianism as a disorder; however, lesbians were basically invisible in psychoanalytic thought (Irigaray, 1977/1985).

Psychodynamic therapies have been applied more to gay men than lesbians (Fassinger, 2000), both because of the invisibility referred to in the last subsection and likely because lesbians have consciously sought out nonsexist or feminist therapies. It is probably fortunate for lesbian and bisexual women that they have been neglected in the psychodynamic approaches, as those approaches are based on paternalistic and heterosexist underpinnings and have a history of abuse (Fassinger, 2000). Downing (1996) further criticized psychodynamic approaches because they tend to lump together lesbians and gay men, assuming "that female experience can adequately be understood in relation to a model based on a male paradigm" (p. 7).

Like Freud, Jung appeared to have experienced considerable ambivalence about homosexuality (Kulkarni, 1998). To Jung's credit, he viewed female homosexuality as an impetus toward social and political organizing of women. However, despite his claim that the animus (masculine archetype) and *anima* (feminine archetype) are part of all humans, he privileged heterosexuality as the ideal form of sexual and intimate relating. He "tended . . . to genderize everything" (Kulkarni, 1998, p. 106). Kulkarni proposed a "radicalized" Jungian theory in which lesbian women and gay men are viewed as on a "legitimate path to individuation" (p. 101). Critiquing Jung as a product of the patriarchal culture in which he lived, Kulkarni viewed same-sex relationships between women as a participation in the postmodern (ad)venture of questioning dichotomous views of gender. She proposed removing heterosexuality from a privileged position, developing new theories and language that are inclusive of multiple sexualities, and questioning knowledge derived from counseling practice.

**Cognitive Approaches**   Cognitive approaches include cognitive, behavioral, cognitive behavioral (including rational-emotive), social learning, and related approaches. Albert Ellis, the founder of rational-emotive behavior therapy (REBT), was progressive in many areas of love and sex, including fighting censorship and insisting that sex was not reducible to mere sexual intercourse. He also was an early champion of the rights of homosexuals; however, he held that homosexuality was an emotional disturbance from which people could be cured. In later years, he revised his position, acknowledging the social construction of sexual orientation and defining sexual pathology as independent of sexual orientation. Notably, though, "if, for non-neurotic and non-coerced reasons" a client wanted to move from a lesbian to heterosexual orientation, some REBT therapists "would help the client to realize her goal" (Velten, 1998). Fassinger (2000) noted some of the possibilities of cognitive approaches in working with LGB clients. First, clients may be steeped in myths and misinformation that may be corrected via cognitive therapies. The didactive aspects of cognitive therapy can provide education and information, and psychoeducational and referral roles of the cognitive counselor are critical where clients may have few available resources. In addition, the client takes an active role in cognitive therapy, a necessary component of challenging internalized homophobia and forming a positive identity (Fassinger, 2000). Desensitization, relaxation, and other coping strategies can help the client handle anxiety. The coming-out process can be facilitated through reframing and stress inoculation training. However, cognitive approaches fail to emphasize the importance of the client-counselor relationship, which may be crucial for the lesbian or bisexual woman client. Finally, cognitive approaches tend to be largely ahistorical, ignore sociopolitical context, and fail to conduct a gender analysis. Even more than psychodynamic approaches, cognitive approaches have ignored issues specific to lesbian and bisexual women.

**Humanistic and Existential Approaches**   Some of the advantages of humanistic and existential approaches include a nonpathologizing model of homosexuality, a strong value of antidiscrimination, a view by many that a humanistic approach supports a gay-affirmative stance, a focus on fulfilling human potential, and a positive value on individual differences (Milton, Coyle, & Legg, 2002). In addition, person-centered, Gestalt, existential, and transactional-analysis approaches may be useful for clients experiencing life transitions or developmental crises, which may characterize LGB people. Fassinger (2000) recommended a person-centered approach as a foundation for all work with LGB clients, especially with regard to the importance of the therapeutic relationship. Humanistic and existential approaches may provide a corrective emotional experience for people who have been hurt by prejudice and discrimination. Clients may learn self-acceptance through the unconditional positive regard of therapists. Gestalt therapy can be used to address polarities and internal conflicts. However, these approaches may not be challenging or confronting enough for clients who have developed dysfunctional dynamics and behavior. Lesbian, gay, and bisexual clients may seek information and direction, and the nondirective therapist may seem too passive (Fassinger, 2000). In addition, the value of self-determination may conflict with the cultural values of more collectivist clients. Finally, like other traditional approaches to counseling, little has been written about the unique issues of women (and therefore of lesbian and bisexual women).

## Nonsexist Counseling

Traditional therapies have been criticized for inherent sexism and heterosexism. Nonsexist counseling consists of working to eliminate gender bias in counseling and psychotherapy. Nonsexist therapies avoid pejorative or stereotyping labels; but these approaches do not help women understand the impact of sexism, heterosexism, or other "isms" in their lives (Mowbray, 1995). Walker (1990) differentiated nonsexist therapy from feminist therapy by characterizing nonsexist therapy as having a neutral (vs. activist) stance toward social action. Nonsexist therapists acknowledge oppression but do not become advocates or activists. Mowbray (1995) criticized nonsexist approaches, saying that by not actively opposing sexism, counselors "may actually violate ethical guidelines for women's treatment—albeit in a more subtle fashion than their predecessors" (p. 11). She continued, "To ignore sexism is to implicitly promote it; therapy which does this is *not* therapeutic" (p. 28).

## Lesbian/ Gay/ Bisexual Affirmative Counseling

LGB-affirmative counseling "affirms a lesbian, gay, or bisexual identity as an equally positive human experience and expression to heterosexual identity" (Davies, 1996, p. 25). Sexuality and sexual orientation per se are not viewed as problematic (Milton, Coyle, & Legg, 2002). LGB-affirmative therapy acknowledges that traditional therapeutic approaches are inherently heterosexist and stresses that the core condition of counseling must be one of respect for the client's sexual orientation, personal integrity, lifestyle, and culture. Davies (1996) identified values and beliefs that make it impossible to work respectfully with an LGB client, including religious, moral, or medical views that homosexuality is sinful, unnatural, or sick; not seeing LGB parents or families as "real" or valid; or holding stereotypic views of gays as child molesters or bisexuals as really gay. Davies (1996) suggested that the counselor should be comfortable with her or his own homosexual feelings. In addition, the counselor should beware agreeing to help clients eliminate same-sex feelings and behaviors, as doing so implies that these feelings and behaviors are unacceptable or pathological. He emphasized the importance of assisting clients to appreciate their bodies and bodily impulses; in this context, the careful and ethical use of physical contact may be encouraged to combat the belief that the client is untouchable. In addition, it is essential to encourage the development of a lesbian, gay, and/or bisexual support system and to support consciousness raising and participation in community.

Affirmative LGB counseling forms a base, as do many therapeutic approaches, for providing counseling for lesbian and bisexual women. However, affirmative LGB counseling is based on the common oppression of lesbian and bisexual women, gay and bisexual men, without acknowledging that oppression is different across genders. For example, gay men experience extremes of antipathy across environments that is less common for lesbians. Lesbian women, on the other hand, are as likely to be victims of gender-related violence and harassment as to be threatened because of their sexual orientation. Browning, Reynolds, and Dworkin (1991) proposed affirmative psychotherapy for lesbian women. They noted that the identity-development process for lesbians differs from that of heterosexual women (and presumably gay men), in that some lesbians may reject a stereotypic feminine role early in their development; and that even those who are characterized by a more feminine role are subject to homophobia. Lesbians (and increasingly, bisexual women) have a social context in which to define themselves, and many lesbian and bisexual women have been more comfortably situated in the feminist than the gay and bisexual communities. Faderman (1984) proposed that lesbian identity development may follow a very different path from that of gay men, notably that, for some lesbians, sociopolitical awareness may precede sexual experiences. The uniqueness of lesbian and bisexual women's experiences as both women and sexual minorities may warrant an even more proactive counseling approach than is offered by LGB-affirmative therapies. Mowbray (1995) suggested that feminist therapy may be the only appropriate therapy for lesbian and bisexual women. Using feminist principles in counseling can be an empowering approach for counselors of any theoretical orientation or gender.

## Feminist Therapy With Lesbian and Bisexual Women

Feminist therapy is both a philosophical position as well as a model for conducting counseling and psychotherapy. As a philosophical stance, it is grounded in particular foundational concepts and counseling processes (Abousleman, Morrow, & University of Utah Women's Resource Center, 2002; Wyche & Rice, 1997). These foundations include a commitment to the liberation of women, the belief that the personal experience has political underpinnings, political analysis of the issues brought into the counseling setting, a focus on power in client's lives as well as the counseling relationship, an understanding of the social construction of gender, a holistic perspective, an understanding of the self in relation with others, and envisioning a future that is both personally and socially supportive of empowerment (Abousleman et al., 2002). Feminist therapy is more thoroughly described elsewhere (Brown, 1994; Enns, 1997; Espín, 1994; Morrow & Hawxhurst, 1998; Worell & Remer, 2003;

chapter 13, this volume) and these resources are essential reading for the counselor who hopes to incorporate a feminist perspective. Abousleman et al. (2002), based on a recursive review of the feminist therapy literature and ongoing focus groups of experienced feminist activists and therapists, described the climate, work, and goals of feminist therapy, which are used as a framework here to address feminist therapy with lesbian and bisexual women. The climate of feminist counseling is determined by the client-counselor relationship, a view that symptoms are coping strategies as opposed to pathology, and characteristics of the counselor.

**Client-Counselor Relationship**   Aspects of the client-counselor relationship of importance when counseling lesbian and bisexual women include client-counselor "fit" and choice, the therapist as a role model for the client, and power and collaboration in assessment and counseling. Under certain circumstances, it is valuable for a lesbian or bisexual woman to work with a lesbian or bisexual counselor (Milton et al., 2002). In particular, trust, safety, and rapport may be more easily built if the client senses that the counselor understands the challenges and rewards of being a woman-loving woman; and the counselor can more easily serve as a role model for the client under these circumstances (Milton et al., 2002). From both a lesbian-affirmative and a feminist-therapy perspective, the counselor's sexual orientation (regardless of what it is) should be disclosed to the client with the purpose of establishing an honest basis for the therapeutic relationship as well as (in the case of a lesbian or bisexual counselor) modeling being "out" (Falco, 1991). This disclosure also helps to establish equality in the counseling relationship (Enns, 1997). It may be that lesbian and bisexual women clients expect a more egalitarian relationship with their counselors because of the influence of feminism and their own experiences in relationships that offer the potential for equality. Thus, feminist therapy's emphasis on a collaborative counseling relationship is appropriate in working with lesbian and bisexual women clients.

**Positive Coping**   Feminist therapy views client "symptoms" as coping strategies rather than as pathology (Morrow & Hawxhurst, 1998). In a context that frequently pathologizes women, especially those with same-sex orientations, identifying the ways lesbian and bisexual clients have coped with oppression and discrimination can place the counseling relationship on firm grounding to examine those coping strategies; evaluate their effectiveness; and experiment with new, more effective ones. Closely related to seeing symptoms as coping rather than pathology is the feminist therapist's perspective on politicizing client issues rather than "psychologizing" them (Kitzinger & Perkins, 1993; Oppenheimer, 1998; Weiner, 1998). For example, a client's depression may have biochemical or psychological components; however, a feminist counselor working with a depressed lesbian or bisexual woman client will be more likely to begin by assuming that the client's distress is related to the experience of growing up "not fitting in," of being isolated, of experiencing prejudice or discrimination, or of not feeling free to exercise the same degree of openness at work about her family and social activities as her heterosexual colleagues.

**Counselor Characteristics**    The feminist therapist is multiculturally competent, is a social activist and client advocate, and evaluates and challenges her or his own assumptions and biases. Multicultural competence includes the knowledge, awareness, and skills to work both with clients who are lesbian and bisexual as well as with the wide variety of clients within lesbian and bisexual populations (Brown, 1994). Social activism and client advocacy are often discouraged in the training of counselors; thus, many counselors must break ingrained habits of noninvolvement in order to take a stand about injustice against women or LGB people. However, doing so models empowering action to clients as well as giving the message that client problems are not merely intrapsychic but are part of a much larger sociopolitical reality (Hill & Ballou, 1998).

In addition to the climate that undergirds the feminist counseling relationship, feminist therapy is based on the specific work of empowerment (Morrow & Hawxhurst, 1998). The work of feminist therapy includes oppression awareness and political analysis, skill development, holistic tools for healing, and visioning new possibilities.

**Oppression Awareness and Political Analysis**    At the heart of feminist counseling is the notion that "the personal is political" (Enns, 1997). This means that all personal problems have a contextual, sociopolitical component. The counselor using a feminist approach can work with the client to understand both the dynamics of her oppression as a lesbian or bisexual woman as well as the specifics of her life that demonstrate that oppression (Barrett, 1998). Lesbian and bisexual women live with the continual awareness that they are different from the norm, and often repeated assaults on their psyches become internalized as shame, guilt, or the feeling that "there is something wrong with me." By helping the client understand and externalize these assaults, the counselor assists the client to become aware of feelings of sadness or anger, thereby placing responsibility for oppression where it belongs (Morrow & Hawxhurst, 1998). The consequences of this important work are reduction in feelings of shame and self-blame, enhanced self-esteem, and a greater sense of efficacy to manage oppression. Using consciousness-raising strategies to help the client identify the sociopolitical aspects of her personal experience, the counselor raises questions about the cultural messages that have contributed to the client's current distress (Weiner, 1998). The counselor also works to help the client develop new skills (such as assertiveness, communication skills, and conflict resolution), pursue holistic and alternative tools for healing (e.g., indigenous healing and feminist forms of spirituality), and develop a positive vision of what the client desires and a map of how to get there (Abousleman et al., 2002).

Feminist therapy is distinct from other therapies that claim to empower clients in that empowerment is seen to occur on the sociopolitical dimension as well as intra- and interpersonally (Morrow & Hawxhurst, 1998). In fact, counseling that neglects social action and advocacy, even when conducted from a prowoman stance, is not feminist therapy. Mowbray (1995) insisted that political and social change were the only ways to achieve positive mental health. Thus, the unique set of skills involved in addressing the sociopolitical dimension of empowerment is integrated into the following section on counseling concerns and special issues across the life span of lesbian and bisexual women.

## COUNSELING CONCERNS AND SPECIAL ISSUES ACROSS THE LIFE SPAN

Lesbian and bisexual women encounter particular developmental and life span issues and concerns throughout their lives for which they may seek counseling. Although many of these issues are common to people regardless of gender or sexual orientation, some are impacted by the identities, experiences, and socialization of women who love women. These women may be further affected by multiple identities and oppressions. This section examines selected counseling issues for lesbian and bisexual women, including coming out across generations; multiple identities; counseling bisexual women; relationships with women; sexuality; partner abuse; and violence in women's relationships.

### Coming Out Across Generations

Being a woman-loving woman can be a very different experience depending on the age at which she becomes aware of her same-sex attractions (or even simply of being "different" from other girls) and the time and place in which she comes out. The very terminology associated with being same-sex attracted varies across generations and in different sociopolitical contexts. Women currently in their 70s and older may have come out prior to the gay or feminist movements at a time when the word *homosexual* was commonly used to describe their attractions (Dunker, 1987). One older lesbian psychiatrist wrote, "What I feel today is the result of what my yesterdays were like" (Schoonmaker, 1993, p. 21), and she identified a burden of triple shame induced by sexism, homophobia, and ageism. Older lesbian and bisexual women came out when secrecy was the rule; thus, they may find it difficult to disclose their orientations to counselors (Falco, 1991). Because of stereotypes in the early 1900s that loving women meant that lesbians really wanted to be men, many women, particularly from the working class, adopted male behaviors and dress (Falco, 1991) and took on butch-femme roles (Dunker, 1987). These women were also subject to extremes of persecution (Dunker, 1987), which were exacerbated by being women of color or poor women (Smith & Smith, 1981). These women also have developed strengths as a result of surviving persecution and being economically independent from men (Dunker, 1987). Thus, counseling women in this age range (or even younger women who were raised in rural or conservative environments) involves building on those strengths as well as helping them to understand the impact of oppression on their lives and assisting them in finding support systems—including activist organizations—to help transform shame to consciousness to action. Many cities have organizations for LGB elders, and web resources abound.

Many lesbian and bisexual women who are currently considered middle-aged became aware of their attractions to women during the apex of the women's liberation movement in the late 1960s and early 1970s. The feminist lesbian movement eschewed the butch-femme roles of the past, along with the traditional trappings of heterosexual femininity such as makeup, high heels, and dresses (Loulan, 1991). Bisexuality was (and still is among many lesbian-identified women in this age group) considered a cop-out. Bisexual women were seen as sitting on the fence, preserving their heterosexual privilege while "experimenting" sexually with being lesbian (Shuster, 1987). Some of the new lesbians who had formerly been heterosexually identified joined with newly activist women who had been lesbians for most of their lives, and the lesbian feminist movement was born (Pearlman, 1987). These women conducted a political analysis of sexist and heterosexist aspects of their lives, were and are avid consumers of counseling and psychotherapy services, and demanded feminist approaches to their counseling (preferably by lesbian feminist therapists). Many lesbians of color who rightly saw the feminist movement as racist and exclusionary maintained their primary support systems with other women of color (and sometimes gay men); others challenged white privilege in lesbian and feminist organizations with varying success (Pearlman, 1987; Smith & Smith, 1981). In addition, transgendered people, who were previously an integral part of the LGB community, found themselves excluded from the feminist lesbian community (Gainor, 2000). This was the best of times and the worst of times when many women-identified women found a political home while others still bear the scars of exclusion. This historical (or herstorical) context is important in counseling lesbian and bisexual women in middle age, and it is important to be aware of these multiple contexts of coming out as lesbian or bisexual. In addition, midlife lesbians (and presumably bisexual women) report greater self-confidence, self-acceptance, and self-directedness, a focus on creativity and fun, and a focus on change and integration (Sang, 1993). Thus, an exploration of existential concerns such as meaning in life may be a fruitful direction in counseling for these women.

Coming out has in many ways become less problematic over time since the 1970s. The legitimacy given to LGB lives and relationships is reflected in the proliferating number of books for the professional and lay public; increasing numbers of sport, entertainment, and media figures coming out; lesbian and gay film; and services for LGB people in cities, communities, and college and university campuses. Yet LGB youth of today continue, as did their foremothers and forefathers, to create themselves anew. Many have reclaimed and transformed the formerly pejorative term *queer*. Increasing numbers of young people refuse to adopt a label, and this has little to do with fear of being "out." There may be a wider discrepancy between the label one chooses to adopt and actual sexual behavior. The body of scholarship in "queer theory" postulates that there are no fixed identities (Esterberg, 1997); and young gay, lesbian, bisexual, transgendered, and questioning people exemplify this notion. In many ways, this is a return to an earlier time when a supportive community of people who did not "fit" societally prescribed gender roles was more important than an identity or label. A "queer" identity is highly political, and queer-identified young women may be sexually— in behavior, fantasy, or desire—lesbian, bisexual, heterosexual, celibate, or asexual. Recent research has supported the notion that women's sexual orientation is more fluid than was previously suspected (Kinnish & Strassberg, 2002). Though many young women identify themselves clearly as lesbian or bisexual, others express their sexual orientations more within a queer paradigm, complicating the counselor's understanding of what their identities—or lack thereof—mean to them. Recognizing that gender and sexuality are socially constructed (Kitzinger, 1988), counselors can follow the client's lead in the use of language, using a narrative or constructivist approach to understand the stories and meanings of their clients' lives.

## Multiple Identities of Lesbian and Bisexual Women

The flexibility of identities described in the preceding sections is even more apparent when looking at the many ways that gender, sexual orientation, race/ethnicity, culture, socioeconomic status, and ability/disability intersect. No one has just one fixed, singular identity; rather, identities may be seen as shifting, depending on context, with some aspects more or less salient at different times (Constantine, 2002). Thus, being a woman who loves women will have different meanings depending on the cultural group to which she belongs. Same-sex-attracted women of color may not be comfortable with the labels typically embraced by European American lesbian and bisexual women. In part, these labels may force meanings that do not fully express the experience of women of color. For example, the term *two-spirited* has come to be a better descriptor for many Native (Native American, American Indian, and aboriginal people of Canada and Central and South America) people, as it is more expressive of a spiritual/social identity, not just a sexual one (Tafoya, 1997). In addition, Native cultures appear to include a higher incidence of bisexuality and a "more fluid concept of gender relations and sexual expression" (Tafoya, 1997, p. 7). It is important to note that the concept of an identity based on sexual behavior or attraction is extremely culture-bound; thus, a lesbian or bisexual identity may be a foreign construct in many cultures (Rust, 1996).

It is common in many families and communities of color, particularly Latina/o cultures, to tacitly accept homosexual behavior but to have trouble if it is overtly acknowledged (Greene, 1997). Being an openly lesbian Latina may be seen as a threat to male dominance in Latino communities as well as violating Catholic teachings (Fukuyama & Ferguson, 2000; Greene, 1997). African American cultures have been characterized as having more fluid gender roles than other cultures, including European American cultures. However, African American communities have been characterized by their lesbian and gay members as extremely homophobic. African American lesbians typically retain strong bonds with their families and communities, have children, and look to other African American lesbians for support (Greene, 1997). Among many Asian American cultures, women have not been perceived by themselves or others as sexual beings; therefore sexual relations between women have not been taken seriously unless their invisibility is challenged by being acknowledged. Because of the potential loss of family and community support that may result from being openly lesbian or bisexual in many communities, lesbian and bisexual women may place less emphasis on coming out than their White counterparts. Counselors should not assume that this lack of openness implies confusion about clients' attractions, orientations, or even identities. In addition, a strong emphasis on family that characterizes many cultures of color can create a paradoxical situation in which, on the one hand, the lesbian or bisexual individual risks being ostracized if she is "out"; but the family bond may also overcome the stigma of being lesbian or bisexual (Fukuyama & Ferguson, 2000). This may be true especially if the woman has children. Thus the counselor should be aware of the importance of family in the lives of lesbian and bisexual clients. Counselors also need to be aware of these multiple stressors in their clients' lives, along with the reality that people of color are less likely to seek counseling for a number of reasons.

## Counseling Issues for Bisexual Women

In similar ways as for women of color, bisexual women's dual identities create unique issues that may emerge in the counseling setting. Because bisexual women have not received full acceptance in either heterosexual or lesbian communities, the dual marginalization and invisibility they experience may lead to isolation and to being in the closet about one part of their experience and identity (Dunker, 1987). Because counselors frequently have little training or knowledge about bisexuality, they often ground their work in stereotypes or assume that the bisexual woman is simply a hybrid of lesbian and heterosexual. However, as Weasel (1996) noted, "bisexuality is not just 'one part gay, one part straight, and mix'" (p. 8). A woman's identity as lesbian or bisexual may or may not correspond with her sexual attractions or behavior; and, given the fluidity of women's sexual orientation and identity, a woman may identify as lesbian at one time and as bisexual later in her life (Kinnish & Strassberg, 2002).

The intersections of race/ethnicity, socioeconomic status, and bisexuality are particularly salient. The relative invisibility of bisexuality in many cultures, despite the isolation that may result, also may provide a measure of protection. In addition, a community orientation where all members are valued may result in bisexuality being overlooked (Weasel, 1996). When women are dually or multiply marginalized or oppressed (e.g., women of color, lesbians), isolation compounds their oppression (Fukuyama & Ferguson, 2000). For bisexual women, who may not fit anywhere, the counselor can serve as an advocate and resource to find or create bi-friendly support systems. Finding these resources may not be difficult in large, progressive metropolitan areas; however, they may be nonexistent in smaller or more conservative environs. Creative efforts on the counselor's part, such as helping the client explore web resources and questioning the traditional stance of not introducing clients to one another may be helpful to reduce isolation and provide support.

## Women Loving Women: Lesbian and Bisexual Women's Relationships

What distinguishes women's relationships with women from those of heterosexuals and gay men? For starters, both partners are women, with similar gender socialization (Falco, 1991). Many factors may contribute to merging (or fusion), characterized by "psychic unity" (Burch, 1986), crossing of individual ego boundaries, and a sense of oneness. On the one hand, merging may be deeply satisfying for one or both women; on the other, it may threaten autonomy (Burch, 1986). It is important to validate, not pathologize, merging in women's relationships with one another; however, certain risks accompany this diffusion of boundaries. First, one or both partners may feel smothered. Relationships characterized by nonstop fusion frequently become boring, as eventually partners cease bringing novel experiences into the relationship (Falco, 1991). Differences may become problematic and smoothed over to prevent conflict, thereby inhibiting individual and couple growth; or the couple may find itself in constant conflict (Falco, 1991). Sexual desire may drop in one or both partners. Partners may feel guilty if they act independently or even want different things in the relationship (Falco, 1991). Thus, the counselor needs to validate the strengths of fusion in woman-to-woman relationships, supporting an emphasis on connection while validating partners' autonomy.

At first glance, it may appear that women's relationships with one another have many benefits that are not available elsewhere: Women who love women do not have to deal with the inequality inherent in male-female relationships in patriarchy, and lesbian relationships have the advantage of two partners who have been socialized to nurture relationships. In fact, these are two of the advantages often cited and appreciated by women who relate to women as their primary partners (Blumstein & Schwartz, 1983; Falco, 1991; Schneider, 1986). However, it is important to recognize that gender is not the only form of power imbalance in relationships, and other differences in status can and do create hierarchies of privilege and oppression in all relationships (Falco, 1991). Race/ethnicity, culture, socioeconomic status, physical condition and appearance, education, and other variables are issues that must be addressed to establish the egalitarian relationships that are so valued by lesbian and bisexual women. Thus, the counselor will want to be alert for manifestations of these power differences in relationship counseling.

## Sexuality in Lesbian and Bisexual Women's Relationships

A central issue in lesbian relationships is sexuality and sexual expression. Lesbian and bisexual women are defined for the most part—by the larger society and often by their own communities—by whom they relate to sexually. Sexuality in lesbian relationships carries both its own baggage and baggage from the larger culture. At the heart, women's sexuality as a whole, and women's sexual relationships with each other, have either been assumed to be an extension of or a complement to male sexuality, resulting in silence or invisibility. Masters and Johnson's (1966) models of human sexual response stemmed from the assumption that women's sexual biology and function mimic those of men (Hall, 2001). Loulan (1984), in her groundbreaking, classic, and timeless book *Lesbian Sex*, remodeled the then-popular sexual response cycle by introducing the concept of "willingness" into lesbian (and women's) response. This book continues to be an indispensable part of the library of many lesbian and bisexual women and those who counsel them.

Naturally, findings such as those by Blumstein and Schwartz (1983) that lesbian long-term relationships are characterized by sharply decreased sexual activity over time compared with heterosexual and gay male relationships have met with controversy. The term *lesbian bed death* has been embraced by couples who want to feel normal as well as challenged by feminists for its genital focus (Fassinger & Morrow, 1995). What constitutes sexual behavior? In a culture where heterosexual women admittedly engage in genital sex more often than they would like to in order to receive affection from their male partners, what does it mean for two women to "have less sex" as the years go by? Frye (1992) argued that what counts as sex for heterosexual couples is focused on male orgasm in an act that takes about 8 minutes to complete (Fassinger & Morrow, 1995) and noted of lesbians:

> What we do . . . considerably less frequently, takes on the average, considerably more than 8 minutes to do. Maybe about 30 minutes at the least. Sometimes maybe an hour. And it is not uncommon that among these relatively uncommon occurrences, an entire afternoon or evening is given over to activities organized around doing it. The suspicion arises that what 85% of heterosexual married couples are doing more than once a month, and what 47% of lesbian couples are doing less than once a month is not the same thing. (Frye, 1992, p. 110)

Thus, it is important that counselors raise questions with their lesbian and bisexual women clients about cultural and societal messages that contribute to their sexual self-definitions.

Nongenital sexual experiences such as flirting, hugging, stroking, massaging, kissing, and romantic behavior should be validated, as physical affection is an important aspect of lesbian romantic relationships (Johnson, 1990). In addition, the ebb and flow of sexual desire should be normalized (Hall, 2001). This is not to say that the absence of genital sex does not signify a problem. Absence of overt sexual activity in a relationship that has previously been sexual may be a consequence of tiredness, illness, overwork, hormonal imbalances, substance use, or relationship problems. Working through problems and resentments in the relationship will free the couple to more easily address their sexual desires, hopes, and expectations. The domestication of a relationship may contribute to the routinization of activities to the point that even sex becomes ordinary, just one more thing to do (Loulan, 1987). The couple may have established patterns of sexual activity at one time that are no longer fulfilling and could benefit from fantasizing about what might make sex more exciting (Loulan, 1987). Although some couples explore an open sexual relationship, this is rarely a cure for sexual or other problems in a relationship, and its success depends on the health of the primary relationship.

Open relationships engender strong feelings in many people, including counselors. Depending on one's values, personal experiences, and politics, nonmonogamy may be perceived positively or negatively. Lesbian and bisexual women, though affected by sex-phobic attitudes of the dominant heterosexual culture, may also tend to be sexually explorative and sex-positive. Kassoff (1989) characterized lesbians as "sexual explorers" (p. 181). Sex-positive attitudes extend to polyamory, or responsible nonmonogamy (Fassinger & Morrow, 1995). Unlike stereotypes of heterosexual partners "cheating" on each other or gay men's acceptance of non-monogamy as long as the "affair" is strictly sexual, polyamorous relationships tend to be characterized by honesty, caring, respect, and an attempt to process the feelings of those involved. Among feminist lesbian and bisexual women, polyamory may be seen as a challenge to possessive, patriarchal relationship forms (Nichols, 1987). Sex-positive practices also include the exploration of fantasy, power, and sexual aids or "toys." The lack of information and education in these areas has led counselors to confuse dominance-submission in sexual expression with partner violence (Fassinger & Morrow, 1995). Counselors working with lesbian and bisexual women should become aware of these possibilities as well as exploring their own values and feelings about alternative forms of sexual expression.

## Violence in Women's Relationships With One Another

Because of an early feminist analysis of patriarchal power and male dominance as the source of the abuse of women and children, battering in same-sex, especially women's, relationships remained in the closet for many years (Lobel, 1986). It is difficult for women, particularly feminists, to acknowledge that women do, in fact, batter other women. Although lesbian communities have in many ways moved beyond the secretiveness that once characterized this issue since the publication of the first book on the subject, *Naming the Violence: Speaking Out About Lesbian Battering* (Lobel, 1986), we are still grappling with continued impacts of lesbian and bisexual women's invisibility. Lesbian communities are still reluctant to "air dirty laundry" by making this issue public, and feminists experience a "loss of innocence" as they grapple with losing the ideal that women's relationships with women are more egalitarian, more ideal, and more kind than those with men (Ristock, 2002).

Counselors need to examine the relationship between power and battering (McLaughlin & Rozee, 2001; Morrow & Hawxhurst, 1989). This relationship may not be as obvious in a same-sex relationship where physical power may be relatively equal. A feminist perspective on power recognizes that gender is one of many axes of power in relationships (Morrow & Hawxhurst, 1989). Others include race/ethnicity/skin color, culture, sexual orientation, socioeconomic class, physical appearance, and disability. Class differences, communication skill level, and other power imbalances have been correlated with violence in lesbian relationships (Goode, 1971). Often violence is triggered over struggles for independence and autonomy in relationships (Lockhart, White, Causby, & Isaac, 1994). It is important to note that women in "triple jeopardy" (e.g., women of color, women with disabilities) are even more vulnerable to abuse because of their marginalized status (Poorman, 2001). The interaction of battering, heterosexism, and minority stress (Balsam, 2001) creates additional factors that contribute to lesbian battering. Balsam (2001) described internalized homophobia as a contributor to battering, as negative feelings about self and the partner make violence a possibility.

It is important for counselors to understand both personal dynamics as well as social forces that contribute to woman-to-woman partner abuse (Poorman,

2001). In addition, counselors must explore their own views about lesbian violence. Therapists tend to view lesbian partner violence as "mutual" or a result of codependency and to view heterosexual violence as more physically harmful than that in same-sex relationships between women (Poorman, 2001). This could result in failure to address safety issues for the victim and to recognize the dangers in proceeding with couples' counseling for the lesbian couple.

Partner abuse is a personal as well as a community, social, and political issue (Kaschak, 2001): "The offense is an offense against one woman at a time, but also against the entire community and particularly the lesbian community. It is an individual act of violence, but it is not only that" (p. 4). Thus, it is crucial that the therapist understand the community ramifications of domestic violence in woman-to-woman relationships. Counselors can be advocates for the development of services for women who are battered in lesbian relationships. The paucity of services, combined with homophobia in battered women's shelters, underscores the importance of the community developing resources and for lesbian therapists to be involved in this process. Additionally, Kaschak (2001) noted that, "In part, batterers abuse because they can" (p. 5). Just as silence about abuse in heterosexual relationships perpetuates violence, silence in the lesbian community allows battering to continue unchecked. What can counselors do? We can speak out, educate, and create an environment in which victims can come forward. Poorman (2001) recommended forging community links that would develop effective prevention and intervention strategies.

## CONCLUSION

This chapter has just scratched the surface of the many issues affecting lesbian and bisexual women. Noticeably absent are parenting and family issues, women with disabilities, substance use and abuse, and religion and spirituality. It is safe to say that, on the one hand, issues that concern lesbian and bisexual women are the same issues that concern everyone. On the other hand, lesbian and bisexual women are impacted uniquely by personal, interpersonal, and social forces that make their experiences of common problems uncommon.

Imbedded within a feminist counseling approach is the value that counselors are advocates for their clients. Particularly in working with populations where invisibility and silence characterize many aspects of their lives, it is imperative that counselors become knowledgeable about resources in the community. Possible sources of information include college and university gender or women's studies programs, counseling centers, women's or LGB centers; feminist and LGB community and political organizations; the local American Civil Liberties Union; community mental-health centers; religious organizations such as Dignity (for LGB Catholics) and Affirmation (for LGB Mormons); Metropolitan Community Church; and many Unitarian churches.

In addition to the role of advocate and resource, a feminist counselor is also an activist, taking a stand on social issues that affect lesbian and bisexual women; taking the lead in establishing shelters or in educating staff of existing shelters, mental health providers, and counseling centers; and working to impact legal and legislative systems. Activism is incorporated into the counseling process as the counselor and client together explore ways in which the client can positively effect change in systems that oppress her. Thus, empowerment is more than simply helping a woman to find her personal sense of power, though that is important; it is also working together as collaborators to change the systems and structures that contribute to personal pain and powerlessness. In this process, both counselor and her lesbian or bisexual woman client find that "yes" within themselves and within each other that goes beyond the impact each counselor can make on an individual life, and we are transformed in the process.

# Cases and Questions

1. You are a counselor at a community mental health agency. Ana, a Mexican American woman, and June, who is European American, have come to see you about a relationship conflict. Both are in their early 30s and have been in a relationship for 10 months. June is an activist in the lesbian community and is "out" to her friends and family, whereas Ana is a high school teacher and is not "out" at work or with her family, who live in another state. As they consider living together, Ana fears that June's activism will lead to people identifying Ana as a lesbian. As they anticipate making a commitment, June wishes that Ana would come out to her family and friends so that they could be seen as a real couple.

   (a) What are the cultural considerations that would be important to help June and Ana be aware of?

   (b) What risks could you anticipate if Ana were to decide to come out in the various circumstances in her life? If June agreed not to be so open about her lesbianism?

   (c) What are some possible resolutions to this conflict?

2. Melissa is a 19-year-old community college student who has come to see you at the college counseling center. She tearfully relates that her first romantic relationship with another woman has just ended and that she does not know if she is a "real lesbian." She has not been in any serious romantic relationships before this, and she really does not know if she is attracted to men or even any other women besides her first love. She asks you to help her figure out if she is a lesbian.

   (a) What questions might you want to consider exploring with Melissa to help her gain insight into her concerns?

   (b) Given what you know about young lesbian and bisexual women, how might you help alleviate Melissa's urgency about arriving at a clear identity?

(c) How would you go about identifying resources and support networks that would be affirming and helpful to her exploration? Identify some specific types of resources that you might look for.

## REFERENCES

Abelove, H. (1993). Freud, male homosexuality, and the Americans. In H. Abelove, M. A. Barale, & D. M. Halperin (Eds.), *The lesbian and gay studies reader* (pp. 381–393). New York: Routledge.

Abousleman, T. M., Morrow, S. L., & University of Utah Women's Resource Center. (2002, August). *Feminist therapy outcomes model.* Poster session presented at the 110th Annual Convention of the American Psychological Association, Chicago, IL.

Balsam, K. F. (2001). Nowhere to hide: Lesbian battering, homophobia, and minority stress. *Women and Therapy, 23*(3), 25–37.

Barrett, S. E. (1998). Contextual identity: A model for therapy and social change. *Women and Therapy, 21*(2), 51–64.

Blumstein, P., & Schwartz, P. (1983). *American couples.* New York: William Morrow.

Brown, L. S. (1994). *Subversive dialogues: Theory in feminist therapy.* New York: Basic Books.

Browning, C., Reynolds, A. L., & Dworkin, S. H. (1991). Affirmative psychotherapy for lesbian women. *The Counseling Psychologist, 19,* 177–247. Also in D. R. Atkinson & G. Hackett. (1998). *Counseling diverse populations* (2nd ed., pp. 317–334). Boston: McGraw-Hill.

Burch, B. (1986). Psychotherapy and the dynamics of merger in lesbian couples. In T. S. Stein & C. J. Cohen (Eds.), *Contemporary perspectives on psychotherapy with lesbians and gay men* (pp. 57–71). New York: Plenum Press.

Constantine, M. G. (2002). The intersection of race, ethnicity, gender, and social class in counseling: Examining selves in cultural contexts. *Journal of Multicultural Counseling and Development, 30,* 210–215.

Davies, D. (1996). Towards a model of gay affirmative therapy. In D. Davies & C. Neal (Eds.), *Pink therapy: A guide for counsellors and therapists working with lesbian, gay and bisexual clients.* (pp. 24–40). Buckingham, England: Open University Press.

Dunker, B. (1987). Aging lesbians: Observations and speculations. In the Boston Lesbian Psychologies Collective (Eds.), *Lesbian psychologies: Explorations and challenges* (pp. 72–82). Urbana: University of Illinois Press.

Downing, C. (1996). *Myths and mysteries of same-sex love.* New York: Continuum.

Enns, C. Z. (1997). *Feminist theories and feminist psychotherapies: Origins, themes, and variations.* Binghamton, NY: Haworth.

Espín, O. (1994). Feminist approaches. In L. Comas-Díaz & B. Greene (Eds.), *Women of color: Integrating ethnic and gender identities in psychotherapy* (pp. 265–286). New York: Guilford Press.

Esterberg, K. G. (1997). *Lesbian and bisexual identities.* Philadelphia: Temple University Press.

Faderman, L. (1984). The "new gay" lesbians. *Journal of Homosexuality, 10,* 85–95.

Falco, K. L. (1991). *Psychotherapy with lesbian clients: Theory into practice.* New York: Brunner/Mazel.

Fassinger, R. E. (2000). Applying counseling theories to lesbian, gay, and bisexual clients: Pitfalls and possibilities. In R. M. Perez, K. A. DeBord, & K. J. Bieschke (Eds.), *Handbook of counseling and psychotherapy with lesbian, gay, and bisexual clients* (pp. 107–131). Washington, DC: American Psychological Association.

Fassinger, R. E., & Morrow, S. L. (1995). Overcome: Repositioning lesbian sexualities. In L. Diamant & R. D. McAnulty (Eds.), *The psychology of sexual orientation, behavior, and identity: A handbook* (pp. 197–219). Westport, CT: Greenwood.

Frye, M. (1992). *Willful virgin.* Freedom, CA: Crossing Press.

Fukuyama, M. A., & Ferguson, A. D. (2000). Lesbian, gay, and bisexual people of color: Understanding cultural complexity and managing multiple oppressions. In R. M. Perez, K. A. DeBord, & K. J. Bieschke (Eds.), *Handbook of counseling and psychotherapy with lesbian, gay, and bisexual clients* (pp. 81–105). Washington, DC: American Psychological Association.

Gainor, K. A. (2000). Including transgender issues in lesbian, gay, and bisexual psychology. In B. Greene & G. L. Croom (Eds.), *Education, research, and practice in lesbian, gay, bisexual, and transgendered psychology: A resource manual* (pp. 131–160). Thousand Oaks, CA: Sage.

Goode, W. J. (1971). Force and violence in the family. *Journal of Marriage and the Family, 33*(4), 624–635.

Greene, B. (1997). Ethnic minority lesbians and gay men: Mental health and treatment issues. In B. Greene (Ed.), *Ethnic and cultural diversity among lesbians and gay men* (pp. 216–239). Thousand Oaks, CA: Sage.

Hall, M. (2001). Not tonight, dear, I'm deconstructing a headache: Confessions of a lesbian sex therapist. *Women and Therapy, 24*(1/2), 161–172.

Hill, M., & Ballou, M. (1998). Making therapy feminist: A practice survey. *Women and Therapy, 21*(2), 1–16.

Horrocks, R. (1998). Historical issues: Paradigms of homosexuality. In C. Shelley (Ed.), *Contemporary perspectives on psychotherapy and homosexualities* (pp. 14–43). London: Free Association Books.

Irigaray, L. (1985). *The sex which is not one.* Trans. C. Porter. Ithaca: Cornell University Press. (Original work published 1977)

Johnson, S. E. (1990). *Staying power: Long term lesbian couples.* Tallahassee, FL: Naiad.

Kaschak, E. (2001). Intimate betrayal: Domestic violence in lesbian relationships. *Women and Therapy, 23*(3), 1–5.

Kassoff, E. (1989). Nonmonogamy in the lesbian community. In E. D. Rothblum & E. Cole (Eds.), *Loving boldly: Issues facing lesbians* (pp. 167–182). New York: Harrington Park Press.

Kinnish, K. K., & Strassberg, D. S. (June, 2002). *Gender differences in the flexibility of sexual orientation: A multidimensional retrospective assessment.* Paper presented at the annual meeting of the International Academy of Sex Research, Hamburg, Germany.

Kitzinger, C. (1988). *Social construction of lesbianism.* London: Sage.

Kitzinger, C., & Perkins, R. (1993). *Changing our minds: Lesbian feminism and psychology.* New York: New York University Press.

Kulkarni, C. (1998). Radicalizing Jungian therapy. In C. Shelley (Ed.), *Contemporary perspectives on psychotherapy and homosexualities* (pp. 87–116). London: Free Association Books.

Lobel, K. (1986). *Naming the violence: Speaking out about lesbian battering.* Seattle: Seal Press.

Lockhart, L. L., White, B. W., Causby, V., & Isaac, A. (1994). Letting out the secret: Violence in lesbian relationships. *Journal of Interpersonal Violence, 9*(4), 469–492.

Lorde, A. (1978). *Uses of the erotic: The erotic as power.* Brooklyn: Out & Out Books.

Loulan, J. (1984). *Lesbian sex.* San Francisco: Spinsters Ink.

Loulan, J. (1987). *Lesbian passion: Loving ourselves and each other.* San Francisco: Spinsters/Aunt Lute.

Loulan, J. (1991). "Now when I was your age": One perspective on how lesbian culture has influenced our sexuality. In B. Sang, J. Warshow, & A. J. Smith (Eds.), *Lesbians at midlife: The creative transition* (pp. 10–18). San Francisco: Spinsters Book Company.

Masters, W. H., & Johnson, V. E. (1966). *Human sexual response.* Boston: Little, Brown.

McDougall, J. (1985). Homosexuality in women. In J. Chasseguet-Smirgel, *Female sexuality: New psychoanalytic views* (pp. 171–212). London: Maresfield.

McLaughlin, E. M., & Rozee, P. D. (2001). Knowledge about heterosexual versus lesbian battering among lesbians. *Women and Therapy, 23*(3), 39–58.

Milton, M., Coyle, A., & Legg, C. (2002). Lesbian and gay affirmative psychotherapy: Defining the domain. In A. Coyle & C. Kitzinger (Eds.), *Lesbian and gay psychology: New perspectives* (pp. 175–197). Oxford, England: BPS Blackwell.

Morrow, S. L., & Hawxhurst, D. M. (1989). Lesbian partner abuse: Implications for therapists. *Journal of Counseling and Development, 68,* 58–62.

Morrow, S. L., & Hawxhurst, D. M. (1998). Feminist therapy: Integrating political analysis in counseling and psychotherapy. *Women and Therapy, 21*(2), 37–50.

Mowbray, C. T. (1995). Nonsexist therapy: Is it? *Women and Therapy, 16*(4), 9–30.

Nichols, M. (1987). Lesbian sexuality: Issues and developing theory. In Boston Lesbian Psychologies Collective (Ed.), *Lesbian psychologies: Explorations and challenges* (pp. 97–125). Urbana: University of Illinois Press.

Nicolosi, J. (1991). *Reparative therapy of male homosexuality.* Northvale, NJ: Jason Aronson.

Oppenheimer, J. (1998). Politicizing survivors of incest and sexual abuse. *Women and Therapy, 21*(2), 79–87.

Pearlman, S. F. (1987). The saga of continuing clash in lesbian community, or will an army of ex-lovers fail? In the Boston Lesbian Psychologies Collective (Eds.), *Lesbian psychologies: Explorations and challenges* (pp. 313–326). Urbana: University of Illinois Press.

Poorman, P. B. (2001). Forging community links to address abuse in lesbian relationships. *Women and Therapy, 23*(3), 7–24.

Ristock, J. L. (2002). *No more secrets: Violence in lesbian relationships.* New York: Routledge.

Rust, P. (1996). Managing multiple identities: Diversity among bisexual women and men. In B. A. Firestein (Ed.), *Bisexuality: The psychology and politics of an invisible minority* (pp. 53–83). Thousand Oaks, CA: Sage.

Ryan, J. (1998). Lesbianism and the therapist's subjectivity: A psychoanalytic view. In C. Shelley (Ed.), *Contemporary perspectives on psychotherapy and homosexualities* (pp. 44–57). London: Free Association Books.

Sang, B. E. (1993). Existential issues of midlife lesbians. In L. D. Garnets & D. C. Kimmel (Eds.), *Psychological perspectives on lesbian and gay male experiences* (pp. 500–516). New York: Columbia University Press.

Schneider, M. S. (1986). The relationships of cohabiting lesbian and heterosexual couples: A comparison. *Psychology of Women Quarterly, 10,* 234–239.

Schoonmaker, C. V. (1993). Aging lesbians: Bearing the burden of triple shame. *Women and Therapy, 14*(1/2), 21–31.

Shuster, R. (1987). Sexuality as a continuum: The bisexual identity. In the Boston Lesbian Psychologies Collective (Eds.), *Lesbian psychologies: Explorations and challenges* (pp. 56–71). Urbana: University of Illinois Press.

Socarides, C. (1978). *Homosexuality.* New York: Jason Aronson.

Smith, B., & Smith, B. (1981). Across the kitchen table: A sister-to-sister dialogue. In C. Moraga & G. Anzaldúa (Eds.), *This bridge called my back: Writings by radical women of color* (pp. 113–127). Watertown, MA: Persephone.

Tafoya, T. (1997). Native gay and lesbian issues: The two-spirited. In B. Greene (Ed.), *Ethnic and cultural diversity among lesbians and gay men* (pp. 1–10). Thousand Oaks, CA: Sage.

Velten, E. (1998). Acceptance and construction: Rational emotive behaviour therapy and homosexuality. In C. Shelley (Ed.), *Contemporary perspectives on psychotherapy and homosexualities* (pp. 190–221). London: Free Association Books.

Walker, L. E. A. (1990). Feminist ethics with victims of violence. In H. Lerman & N. Porter (Eds.), *Feminist ethics in psychotherapy* (pp. 214–226). New York: Springer.

Weasel, L. H. (1996). Seeing between the lines: Bisexual women and therapy. *Women and Therapy, 19*(2), 5–16.

Weiner, K. M. (1998). Tools for change: Methods of incorporating political/social action into the therapy session. *Women and Therapy, 21*(2), 113–123.

Worell, J., & Remer, P. (2003). *Feminist perspectives in therapy: Empowering diverse women* (2nd ed.). New York: Wiley.

Wyche, K. F., & Rice, J. K. (1997). Feminist therapy: From dialogue to tenets. In N. G. Johnson (Ed.), *Shaping the future of feminist psychology* (pp. 57–71). Washington, DC: American Psychological Association.

# CHAPTER 17

# Affirmative Counseling With Gay Men

Eric C. Chen, Thomas I. Stracuzzi,
and Daniel E. Ruckdeschel,
Fordham University

The past decade has witnessed considerable advances in our understanding of diversity issues in counseling with clients across social-cultural divides (Fassinger, 2000a; Ponterotto, Fuertes, & Chen, 2000). The pressing need for mental health professionals to develop competence in working with a diverse clientele has similarly been embraced in many counseling and psychology training programs (e.g., Ponterotto, 1997; Quintana & Bernal, 1995), due, in part, to the accreditation and ethical standards of professional organizations such as the American Counseling Association (ACA, 1995), the American Psychological Association (APA, 2002a, 2002b), and the Council for Accreditation of Counseling and Related Educational Programs (CACREP, 2001). With respect to counseling lesbian, gay, and bisexual (LGB) individuals, furthermore, the need for counselors to increase their competence in working with this population has been driven by social, political, and demographic changes. The increasing visibility of LGB characters in the face of the mass media, the AIDS epidemic over the past two decades, the "Don't Ask, Don't Tell" policy in the U.S. military, a great number of horrendous hate crime cases in recent years, the lost and shattered lives of LGB individuals and their loved ones following the September 11 events, and the abuse of youth by priests, have, in ways both positive and negative, heightened the public's awareness of the experiences of LGB individuals in contemporary U.S. society.

Mental health professional organizations have long been at the vanguard of the effort to urge counselors and psychologists to recognize and address the unique needs of diverse clients (e.g., ACA, 1995; APA, 1993, 2002c). Relative to LGB clients, APA (1991a, 2000) has specifically issued guidelines and policy statements to guide its members in the delivery of services to this population. The addition of books (Perez, DeBord, & Bieschke, 2000; Ritter & Terndrup, 2001) on counseling LGB clients, and the special issues in the *Career Development Quarterly* (1993, 1995) on career counseling with this population, have further provided specific guidance. Added to this expanding body of literature are conceptual and empirical works that address a broad range of concerns and issues within the contexts of individual counseling (e.g., Dworkin, 2000; Shannon &

Woods, 1991), career counseling (e.g., Croteau, Anderson, Distefano, & Kampa-Kokesch, 2000), and group counseling (e.g., DeBord & Perez, 2000). It is important, therefore, to note the distinctions between this chapter and the existing approaches and frameworks.

Differing in race, sexual orientation, religion, professional experience, and theoretical orientation, we firmly believe that any counselor has the potential to provide affirmative counseling with LGB individuals, and that one's competence, or lack thereof, in working with LGB clients is not directly linked to one's sexual orientation. By using the term *affirmative counseling,* we underscore the need for the counselor to shift from more passive, nonjudgmental modes, which may be tolerant of the potentially harmful "conversion therapy" (see Shidlo & Schroeder, 2002, for a review), toward one that is active in the celebration of human dignity and diversity. In essence, affirmative counseling calls for "political analysis and action, personal empowerment, cultural awareness and sensitivity, and intervention logistics that move beyond the 50-minute office visit" (Fassinger, 2000b, p. 122).

Maps vary in kind (e.g., political, terrain) for different purposes; we conceptualize this chapter as a "tourist map" that highlights the main points of interest, as opposed to a "road map" that provides detailed instructions on navigating an unknown area in order to reach a specific landmark. Accordingly, we identify the target reader of this tourist map as a *novice* counselor who is interested in affirmative counseling with gay men. We further assume that the clientele with whom the target reader will most likely work at this stage of professional development are gay men in late adolescence and early to mid adulthood. Although the experiences and concerns of bisexual men differ in many respects from those of gay men, space constraints preclude coverage of their unique issues in this chapter; interested readers are referred to more specific works for in-depth discussion (e.g., Matteson, 1996; Weinberg, Williams, & Pryor, 1994).

The guiding question of this chapter is: What awareness, knowledge, and skills would the novice counselor need to develop prior to the provision of effective, affirmative counseling practice with gay men? In response to this question, the space constraint, and the potential redundancy with other chapters in this volume, the focus of our chapter is thus on connecting various strands of literature to offer implications for counseling gay men. We assume the reader has acquired basic knowledge about individual, group, and career counseling theories and approaches, as well as some familiarity with gay identity development models (e.g., Cass, 1979; Troiden, 1988; see chapter 15, this volume).

The remainder of this chapter is composed of four sections. In the first section we highlight issues that often affect the gay male client's well-being in the realms of relationships and intimacy, work, and health. The choice of emphasis here does not diminish the importance of associated topics and issues, such as religion and spirituality, dual career concerns, or gay parenting, many of which are covered elsewhere in the literature. The two sections that follow concern counseling gay men, with emphases on counseling challenges and principles, as well as on interventions in individual and group counseling. In the final section, two case vignettes are developed within the contexts of individual and group counseling, each with questions for reflection, followed by some closing comments.

## COMMON PRESENTING CONCERNS

Although gay men can present for counseling with a wide array of issues, this section covers their common concerns, with primary focus on the links between gay identity and presenting concerns in the domains of family, friendship, and romantic relationships; work; and health. Obviously, the series of issues described next are far from exhaustive; they are selected and presented as an introduction to some of the typical issues confronting gay male clients, and issues that can help the novice counselor gain a general understanding of gay men's experiences.

### Interpersonal Relationships

Gay male clients' concerns are often related to the management of their gay identity, both psychologically and interpersonally (see chapter 15, this volume). Unlike their heterosexual counterparts, LGB individuals constantly have to make decisions based on their sexual identity and confront the implications of these decisions. As a result, LGB individuals wind up expending more of their resources being gay or lesbian than heterosexuals expend being heterosexual (Trujillo, 1997).

At the core of this concern are the uncertainty and anxiety surrounding the disclosure, or lack thereof, in interpersonal relationships. When a gay man interacts with people in various contexts, lurking in the back of his mind often is the question of how his sexual orientation, and his disclosure or nondisclosure of his sexual orientation, may affect the dynamics of these relationships. Confronting the question of whether or not to "pass" as heterosexual in a new environment becomes almost a daily exercise. Although disclosing one's sexual orientation has been associated with feelings of relief and satisfaction, it also may be accompanied by emotional distress (Caitlin & Futterman, 1997; Gonsiorek, 1995; Trujillo, 1997), perceived or real rejection (Shannon & Woods, 1991), abandonment, loss of support, decreased feelings of respect or closeness, discrimination, and violence (Smith, 1997). This task of negotiating his gay identity within interpersonal relationships occurs at various developmental stages throughout the gay man's life and holds direct links, in ways large and small, to his psychological health, well-being, and resilience.

During adolescence, LGB individuals are likely to experience and internalize homophobia, often as a result of their experience of societal, institutional, and individual negative attitudes, beliefs, and behaviors toward their sexual orientation (Fassinger, 2000a). When they enter counseling, they often present concerns over monitoring, understanding, and making decisions based on their sexual orientation, both in their family and school lives. Anxiety about others' perceptions, and fear or experience of isolation and prejudice, when augmented by others' intentional and unintentional disparaging remarks, can cause considerable distress for LGB teenagers, often resulting in depression, behavioral problems, or even suicidal thoughts or actions (Caitlin & Futterman, 1997).

Throughout adulthood, the task of managing sexual identity is no less daunting. Gay men may lack the means for developing romantic relationships, particularly in environments or locales that are perceived as homophobic or isolated. Even if a romantic relationship is established, in addition to the common issues that most intimate relationships hold, gay men may have to deal with the additional stressors of isolation or exclusion from important events and rituals (i.e., recognized marriage in a Catholic church), harassment or prejudice, and limited legal protection based on their sexual orientation (Fassinger, 2000a; Gonsiorek, 1995).

When the gay male client enters counseling with issues of managing his gay identity in interpersonal relationships, it is critical to not view gay identity as a fixed or necessarily integrated identity across all situations (Dworkin, 2000). Similarly, one's gay identity should not be assessed on the basis of the dichotomy of "out" or "not out," or in terms of degree of "outness," because there are many paths to the development of a gay identity, as evidenced in Fassinger and Miller's (1996) research. Familiarity with the existing gay identity development models can assist the client in wrestling with the task of developing his gay identity in the interpersonal domain, a task that is oriented toward a cost-benefit analysis of his varying needs in different contexts across the life span.

## Work

For gay men, a host of work and career-related issues may be linked to their sexual orientation and gay identity development. Major career development theorists (e.g., Holland, 1985; Super, Savickas, & Super, 1996) emphasize the importance of understanding and integrating one's personal identity, values, and multiple life roles when making career choices. The development and integration of a personal identity, which takes place in adolescence, is often an even more challenging process for young gay men than for heterosexual men. For gay men, the tasks and process of integrating personal and vocational identities are further complicated by a possible lack of role models and social supports (Prince, 1995). When these tasks are not satisfactorily negotiated, gay men may be more uncertain and less fulfilled with their career choices compared with their heterosexual counterparts (Etringer, Hillerbrand, & Hetherington, 1990). Next we briefly describe career-related concerns gay men may bring to counseling, including those involving career choice, implementation of career plans, and work adjustment and discrimination.

**Issues of Career Choice**    Gay men in earlier stages of gay identity development may face the difficulty of having to conceal not only their sexual orientation but also their career interests if they are found to be incongruent with prevailing social norms around masculinity. This may constrict their career options, whereby gay men might feel pushed or pulled toward certain career paths. They might, for instance, feel drawn toward the "safe occupational environments" of stereotypically gay career choices (e.g., fashion, interior design), or careers where they might easily find support from other gay men, even when their actual career interests may lie elsewhere. The opposite pattern may also occur, where gay men shy away from these career choices even if they have a real interest, due, in part, to their desire to maintain a more "straight" identity or appearance, or to avoid real or perceived discrimination against gay men within those fields.

When gay men present issues concerning career choices, they may attempt to assess what careers they are interested in as well as what careers and work environments will be most conducive to their gay identity. Thus, aside from exploring areas of interest and possible career options, they may need assistance in exploring the reciprocal influences between their career choices and their gay identity, as well as the nature and types of supports for and barriers against their gay identity development in future work environments. Any occupational stereotypes or misconceptions about work environments may be challenged through talking to other gay men in the workforce.

**Issues of Implementing Career Plans**    In light of Campbell and Cellini's (1981) taxonomy of adult career problems, the difficulties gay men face during the process of implementing their career plans can be characterized as either external or internal in nature. The "Don't Ask, Don't Tell" policy of the U.S. military certainly imposes an external barrier for LGB individuals, whereas a failure to undertake the steps necessary to implement a career plan due to one's excessive, unfounded fears is an example of internal barriers. Helping clients tap into community resources and gather information such as institutional policies often ameliorates their stress during the job search process.

**Issues of Work Adjustment and Discrimination**    Once a job position has been acquired, gay men's adjustment to a new work environment may be influenced by their sexual orientation and gay identity. As with the development of a gay identity, the degree of openness concerning one's sexual orientation in the workplace also exists on a continuum. Griffin (1992) has identified four distinct levels of disclosure within the workplace: "passing," "covering," "implicitly out," and "explicitly out." Greater degrees of "outness" in the workplace have been found to be associated with the existence of nondiscrimination policies and lower levels of internalized homophobia (Rostosky & Riggle, 2002). Although being "explicitly out" in the workplace allows a greater degree of integration between various aspects of the self, it may also stimulate discrimination or harassment in more homophobic work environments. When employers or coworkers treat gay employees unfairly based on their sexual orientation, it can be considered workplace discrimination.

Although laws have been passed in some cities and states that protect sexual minorities from workplace discrimination, they are far from prevalent and sometimes vague in nature. Workplace discrimination is usually not the result of formal policies; a more "informal" discrimination can be found in work environments where LGB employees are routinely passed over for promotion or subjected to harassment by coworkers and supervisors (Levine & Leonard, 1984). Informal workplace discrimination can also take subtler forms, such as the use of antigay jokes or exclusion from social events by coworkers or supervisors (Croteau, 1996; Waldo, 1999). Regardless of the nature and type of informal discrimination, each produces psychological distress, to varying degrees, for the LGB people in the workplace. Although LGB individuals who are open about their sexual orientation in their work environments risk experiencing more direct, explicit discrimination, they may be more satisfied with their work lives than their less open counterparts (Croteau & Lark, 1995; Croteau & von Destinon, 1994).

When the gay male client brings work adjustment issues to counseling, counselors should be prepared to work with him at whatever level of workplace disclosure he is comfortable with at the moment. Although counselors can assist him in assessing the risks and benefits of workplace disclosure, they should respect the client's current position on the continuum while supporting him in mobilizing and strengthening his social network in his work environment, particularly in the absence of nondiscrimination policies (Rostosky & Riggle, 2002).

## Health

Although not unique to gay men, HIV/AIDS and substance abuse are health-related concerns that affect gay men differently than heterosexual men. The growing visibility and acceptance of LGB individuals within the larger society, coupled by the growing body of research specific to the health needs of gay men, offer ample implications for counselors and their gay male clients alike.

One health issue that has been of great concern for the gay male community in the past two decades is HIV/AIDS. Although HIV/AIDS is a concern for all sexually active people, the gay male population was one of the first and one of the hardest hit by the epidemic as it emerged in the 1980s (Shilts, 1987). With medical advances, AIDS has become generally viewed as a chronic disease rather than a terminal one (Beaudin & Chambre, 1996). Young gay men, however, may underestimate the seriousness and prevalence of the epidemic, because they may not have been exposed to the immense devastation that AIDS once inflicted on the gay male community (Kalichman, Nachimson, Cherry, & Williams, 1998).

Almost two decades after the onset of the AIDS epidemic, individuals, and gay men in particular, have become increasingly aware of the risks involved in unprotected sex and the measures necessary to decrease these risks. Counseling emphasis, therefore, will unlikely be placed on HIV/AIDS education. Nevertheless, counselors working with gay men should make a routine of asking them about safer-sex behaviors in a nonjudgmental fashion, particularly during intake assessment. When clients continue to practice risky sexual behaviors, the psychological basis for these behaviors would need to be explored.

Differences also exist among gay men with respect to how they deal with certain lifestyle choices such as dieting and body image, as well as alcohol and substance use. Young gay men in particular have been found, on average, to have a greater dissatisfaction with their bodies than lesbians and heterosexual men (Siever, 1994). The desire to maintain a certain body image (usually toned and muscular) should be of particular concern to counselors when accompanied by the use of hormones, steroids, and unhealthy eating or exercise patterns.

Alcohol abuse rates were once found to be higher in gay men than in the general population (Kauth, Hartwig, & Kalichman, 2000). More recently, it has been found that although few gay men abstain from alcohol entirely, rates of abuse are comparable with those of men in the larger population. A change in these findings over time may be related to generational differences. Bars were once the primary social gathering place for gay men. Now that the gay male community establishes its own community centers, churches, and sports teams in many metropolitan areas, gay men may have a wider range of opportunities to develop relationships with others in alcohol-free environments.

Changes in alcohol abuse rates may correlate to a larger trend toward positive health and wellness behaviors in the gay male community (Kauth et al., 2000). Just as concealment of sexual orientation may be related to a greater likelihood of somatic complaints, research shows that individuals who are accepting of their gay identity are less likely to suffer from substance abuse problems and depression, and they are less likely to engage in risky sexual behaviors (Cole, Kemeny, Taylor, & Visscher, 1996; Sadava & Thompson, 1986; Siever, 1994).

In conclusion, although gay male clients may present a host of different health concerns, these concerns may best be viewed as resulting from the interaction of individual attributes and environmental factors (Fassinger, 2000a). Sensitive to the unique health concerns of gay men, particularly alcoholism and substance abuse, sexual compulsiveness, and eating disorders (Shannon & Woods, 1991), the competent counselor reinforces behaviors conducive to their health and well-being, while exploring "risk" behaviors in a nonjudgmental fashion. Furthermore, it behooves the counselor to explore the function and contexts within which these risk behaviors occur, thereby building a bridge between gay men and the larger health care community.

## COUNSELING GAY MEN: CHALLENGES AND PRINCIPLES

As has been pointed out in the multicultural counseling literature, the counselor's general knowledge about a specific cultural group should not be used to stereotype the client (Pope & Vasquez, 1998). Moreover, the link between cultural knowledge or multicultural competence and effective counseling has not been established either conceptually (Ponterotto et al., 2000; Sue & Zane, 1987) or empirically (Constantine & Ladany, 2000). For these reasons, instead of offering a cookbook approach to counseling gay men, which may be viewed as prescriptive, we present our perspective on counseling gay men in two ways, with the intention of stimulating counselor creativity in developing effective counseling interventions. We first outline two main challenges confronting the counselor in the delivery of affirmative counseling with this population. Three overarching counseling principles and their implications are then described.

### Challenges

One main challenge for counselors is to become aware of and manage their own personal reactions to the client, and homosexuality in general, in the counseling relationship. Not uncommonly, counselors are presented with issues involving themes of race, class, politics, religion, and morality. Ignoring or denying their own values and beliefs in these areas can create an unnecessary roadblock to effective counseling, because these reactions, or, loosely defined, manifestations of countertransference, will sooner or later resurface in the counseling context and influence counselors' assessments and interventions. One main difference between competent and incompetent counselors, therefore, resides *not* in the elimination of personal values or beliefs, but in *what they do with them* in the counseling relationship and process.

If effective counseling with gay men requires a solid knowledge base about addictive disorders, including alcoholism and substance abuse, sexual compulsiveness, and eating disorders, as noted by Shannon and Woods (1991), then counselors should be equipped to address these issues in counseling. Exploring their values and beliefs concerning homosexuality in general, and gay men's sexual behavior (e.g., monogamy and promiscuity) and health-related concerns in particular, would help counselors identify these "pressure points," enabling them to prepare for the possible discomfort or anxiety they may experience in the counseling session. Moreover, for gay men with concerns involving the differences between their religious beliefs and personal experiences, counselors' awareness also facilitates the exploration of this conflict.

Addressing this counseling challenge is not an easy process but may start by counselors examining and establishing comfort with their own sexual identity (Hancock, 1995). Models of heterosexual identity development (e.g., Mohr, 2002; Worthington, Savoy, Dillon, & Vernaglia, 2002) and gay identity development (e.g., Cass, 1979; Troiden, 1988) can aid heterosexual and LGB counselors, respectively, in understanding their own sexual identity development as well as in identifying potential barriers to effective counseling practice with gay men. Such awareness and reflection also helps counselors to engage their supervisor in monitoring the influence of their sexual identity on the development of the working alliance (Gelso & Mohr, 2001).

Another challenge is to avoid the trap of framing the gay male client's presenting concerns solely through the lens of sexual orientation. Counselors may unintentionally shift in focus from the client's pressing concerns to issues of sexual orientation (APA, 1991a; Davison, 1991; Hancock, 1995), due, in part, to their heightened awareness of LGB concerns, or to their fear of being perceived as homophobic. Thus, counselors can actually become trapped in two different ways, through either inadequate attention to other factors beyond sexual orientation or through ignorance of within-group differences.

To ensure that adequate attention is paid to the influence of variables other than sexual orientation on the gay male client's urgent concerns (e.g., the client's being laid off due to poor work performance), a thorough assessment of the nature of presenting concerns is needed to locate the appropriate role sexual orientation plays in the LGB client's concerns (Dworkin, 2000). A developmental-contextual perspective (e.g., Vondracek, Lerner, & Schulenberg, 1986) (see the subsection in the following "Principles" section) is also of help in acquiring an understanding of the gay male client's sexual orientation against the backdrop of his life context.

Additionally, the counselor's ignorance of the within-group differences present within the gay male clientele (e.g., racial and ethnic factors, religious affiliations, socioeconomic status) may create a roadblock to effective counseling. Not only does one's identity occur and change at human, group, and personal levels (Kluck-hohn & Murray, 1953; Leong, 1996), but the relative importance of one's identity may shift in differing contexts. Counselors, hence, need to examine characteristics the gay male client shares with all human beings (e.g., the need for belonging) (human level); those that are specific to gay men (e.g., experiencing homophobia), as well as any other sociocultural groups to which the client may belong, such as racial or religious groups (group level); and those that are unique to him as an individual (e.g., a unique outlook on life) (personal level). Engaging the client in this assessment of his identity at these three levels and across contexts can assist the counselor in gaining a better understanding of a gay male client's intrapersonal and interpersonal identities and relationships.

## Principles

In this section we argue that effective counseling interventions are typically guided by: (a) a developmental-contextual perspective, (b) an integration of personal and career counseling, and (c) a synthesis of intentionality and reflection. We briefly describe each of the three principles, and the implications for affirmative counseling with gay men: The first two pertain to the counseling process, and the third, to the counselor.

**A Developmental-Contextual Perspective**    Characteristic of this developmental-contextual perspective (e.g., Vondracek et al., 1986) is the contention that human behavior changes over time and the meaning of behavior is embedded in and inseparable from context. As such, one's roles, values, needs, goals, and tasks change across the life span and in various contexts (e.g., family, school, work, community, society). The client's psychological health and well-being should be examined within and across domains, as should the changing nature of presenting concerns and the manifestations of these concerns across time and contexts. Behaviors that may be viewed as maladaptive may actually be developmentally appropriate or contextually adaptive.

Incorporating a developmental-contextual perspective in counseling helps the counselor understand gay men's well-being and presenting concerns through an identification of their developmental needs and tasks, on one hand, and of the ways in which they respond to supports and barriers within the context, on the other. In essence, we emphasize that counselors consider the vast influence of the interpersonal and contextual environments that envelop gay male clients and that, over time, shape and influence their behavior and their perceptions of themselves and others.

In collectivist cultures, for example, privacy is regulated psychologically rather than through the use of physical space, as in individualist cultures (Gudykunst & Ting-Toomey, 1988). An Asian gay man's reluctance to disclose his sexual orientation to others may not be due to shame or a negative gay identity, but, rather, to his cultural norm of privacy regulation. Furthermore, given the emphasis on marriage and carrying the family name in the Asian culture, a counselor in this developmental-contextual perspective may view this client's nondisclosure as actually adaptive, so that his alliances with the family and the community would not be disrupted. With the goal of striking a balance between attending to intrapersonal and interpersonal needs, both currently and in the future, the counselor assists the client in taking a proactive approach in anticipating and addressing issues and tasks that may occur later in life, consistent with the principle of preventive intervention (Jordaan, Myers, Layton, & Morgan, 1968).

**Integrating Personal Counseling and Career Counseling**  In an effort to focus on the needs of "the whole person" (Gysbers, 1997), the counselor should reduce artificial boundaries between career and noncareer interventions. As Richardson (1993) argued, the traditional view of career in vocational psychology, with its focus almost exclusively on activities and behaviors in the occupational sphere, is a narrow, if not biased, one. Work, as a basic human function, offers multiple meanings and should be integrated with other aspects of human life experiences. Underlying this view is a caution against unduly making distinctions between career and personal developments, because many life roles (e.g., student, worker, consumer, family member) operate within multiple contexts, as suggested by the developmental-contextual perspective. Reflecting this shift in perspective is the body of empirical literature that has focused on the interface of work and nonwork, as evidenced by research on sexual harassment, dual-career couples, and work-family conflicts (Hackett, 1993). Relative to counseling practice, clients' quality of life may be enhanced when attention is paid to their psychological well-being across domains (Robbins & Kliewer, 2000). The effectiveness of counseling interventions, conversely, is likely diminished by the creation of a flawed dichotomy of personal and career counseling (Croetau & Thiel, 1993; Hackett, 1993; Richardson, 1996).

The salience of the work and nonwork interface, and, in particular, of the reciprocal influence between identity development and career development, is further underscored for gay men (Croetau & Thiel, 1993; Fassinger, 2000a). If gay men, for example, may intentionally enter incongruent occupations as a result of either real or perceived prejudice or discrimination in society, interventions that focus exclusively on either enhancing their gay identity or exploring various occupational options are not likely to have a sustained impact.

The importance of integrating personal and career issues, and, by extension, personal and career counseling, cannot be overemphasized because it has the potential of affecting counselors' assessment of the nature of the gay male client's presenting concerns, and their choice of counseling goals and strategies (Croetau & Thiel, 1993). Although we emphasize the integration of work and nonwork issues, we do not suggest that in order for counseling to be effective that both personal and career counseling need to occur or receive equal attention. We recommend, instead, that counselors function like primary-care physicians who are generalists on the front line for clients with any complaints of illness and who provide referrals, if necessary, to see specialists for consultation or treatment.

**A Synthesis of Intentionality and Reflection**  *Intentionality,* or mindfulness, generally involves a sense of purposefulness in the counselor's deliberate selection of a behavior response from a range of alternatives to achieve a specific goal, and it includes two dimensions (Chen, 2001a). The *reason* aspect, or *why* the counselor does something, deals with both the understanding of the antecedent conditions of the behavior as well as the rationale for choosing a particular behavior, response mode, skill, or intervention to use over the other alternatives. The *plan* aspect, or *what* the counselor intends to accomplish, focuses on the anticipated effect of the behavioral response on the client. This understanding forms the basis on which the counselor chooses an intervention among the existing alternatives.

Although developed with a clinically sound rationale, the counselor's counseling goals and strategies may not yield the anticipated outcomes. *Reflection,* therefore, requires the counselor to subject the counseling encounter to the predetermined intentionality, that is, to undergo "an active, persistent, and deliberate consideration of any covert beliefs or tacit assumptions in light of the evidence that supports it and the immediate consequences it evokes" (Chen, 2001a, p. 811).

Given the diversity among the gay male clientele, intentional-reflective counselors are careful in the exploration of the client's presenting concerns, respectful of his experience and reactions, while examining the basis of their own assumptions about the client in the counseling process. The intentional-reflective stance, therefore, mitigates the negative effects of personal biases and the heterosexist language on the counseling relationship. Because counseling is most likely experienced differently by the client than by the counselor, this reflective inquiry allows counselors to uncover and identify their errors. In the subsequent session they can explore client reactions to these errors, and, when verified, they can be acknowledged openly and corrected. Through this cyclical process of remaining mindful and reflective, counselors are challenged to move beyond simply becoming technical experts to embracing the advocate role of bringing about social justice, consistent with Atkinson, Thompson, and Grant's (1993) call that when working with diverse clientele, counselors may need to assume other roles such as consultant or change agent.

## COUNSELING GAY MEN: MODALITIES AND STRATEGIES

Individual and group counseling are two modalities for which novice counselors are likely to receive the majority of training, as well as the most common counseling choices for gay men. In the remainder of this section, we outline possible intervention strategies within the contexts of individual and group counseling.

### Individual Counseling

Individual counseling can be one effective way in which gay men can learn how to develop a satisfying relationship with another individual. In this trusting, affirmative environment, they are encouraged to explore and experience their resilience in the negotiation of a myriad of contextual barriers to their personal and career development. More specifically, emotion-laden or anxiety-provoking concerns may be explored more fully as well. We believe individual counseling practice with gay men may be enhanced by (a) the use of nonheterosexist and gay-affirming language, (b) a thorough assessment of client concerns, and (c) modifications of theory-driven interventions.

**Building a Therapeutic Alliance Through the Use of Nonheterosexist and Gay-Affirming Language**   As opposed to the use of heterosexist language that often stifles communication (Dorland & Fischer, 2001), the utilization of non-heterosexist and gay-affirming language (APA, 1991b) from the outset of counseling facilitates the development of an optimal therapeutic relationship, one that is "secure, developmentally flexible, [and] fundamentally caring" (Mahoney & Patterson, 1992, p. 680). Gay-affirming language and attitude provides the building block from which other therapeutic interventions become possible. It can open the door to effective interpersonal communication with the gay man rather than providing ammunition for him to dismiss a counselor's attempts to help.

There are additional benefits to be reaped with the use of gay-affirming language. Such language increases the counselor's capacity to be empathic as a result of a shift toward the vantage point of the LGB person (Morrow, 2000), one that is client-centered and reflects a heightened awareness of the continued prevalence of prejudice, oppression, and discrimination experienced by LGB individuals in U.S. society. This empathic understanding provides insight into the psychological and contextual basis of behaviors that appear to pose threats to their psychological health, well-being, and resilience. The use of gay-affirming language has relevance for the practice of all counselors but concerns particularly male counselors who might be suspected by the gay man to be homophobic. The likelihood for misunderstanding, impasses, conflicts, or premature termination decreases when the counselor establishes a policy, either individually or institutionally, to monitor and reflect on the use of language through supervision and consultation, as well as by checking out client reactions to that language.

**Conceptualization of Presenting Concerns Through a Thorough Assessment**
As in any counseling relationship, an appropriate assessment of client concerns is a precursor to the identification of appropriate counseling goals and interventions. To view the gay male client's concerns as directly related to his sexual orientation or gay identity can lead to an incomplete, if not biased, picture, because adequate attention also needs to be given to biological, developmental, and contextual factors. Although initially developed in the context of career counseling, the use of Crites's (1979) career assessment model offers the counselor a systematic method to address the work and nonwork interface in gay men's lives. With equal emphasis on the interactions of internal and external factors, it is also consistent with the interactive view of LGB clients' concerns (Fassinger, 2000a). A modification of Crites's (1979) interactive approach suggests that counselors engage the gay male client in collecting, organizing, and interpreting relevant data, in three areas: *person, problem,* and *prognostic.*

Central to the *person* appraisal is an exploration of the gay male client's status on psychological, sociological, and physical dimensions; present life roles, health, well-being, and functioning; and developmental history. Questions in assessing the client's present life roles, for instance, may include: "Among your various life roles, which ones seem to be most important to you currently? How are your own needs fulfilled, neglected, or compromised in assuming these roles? How satisfied are you in relation to these roles? How do you see your sexual orientation affecting, if at all, your capacity in the fulfillment of these roles?" Specific attention should be paid to internalized homophobia, the coming-out process, and erotic fantasies, attractions, and behaviors (Dworkin, 2000). We also suggest that counselors matter-of-factly check with the client's health-related behavior, including alcohol and substance use, dieting and exercise, and safer sex practices.

In contrast to person appraisal, which is much broader in scope, *problem* appraisal examines the nature of the client's presenting concerns, his strengths and weaknesses in addressing these concerns, and internal and external factors associated with the development and resolution of concerns. Specific questions that may be raised, for example, include: "In what way, if any, might your concerns be related to your sexual orientation? What barriers or supports have you experienced in addressing these concerns? What strengths or limitations do you have that may affect your capacity to address these concerns?"

Finally, the focus of *prognostic* appraisal is on predictions about the client's future behavior in counseling, and adjustment in the school, career, or personal domains. Examples of questions pertaining to future adjustment include: "How likely do you see these concerns resurfacing in the future, say, 5 years from now? What barriers and resources might you experience at that point in time in addressing these concerns? How might your sexual orientation enhance or interfere with your capacity to overcome barriers or utilize resources?"

The assessment process is not an interview that consists of a series of questions and answers, but a collaborative inquiry that allows meanings to emerge more fully. In contrast to objective assessment through tests or inventories, qualitative assessment methods, such as card sorts, guided imagery, or genogram, have less rigid parameters and are particularly helpful for use in counseling gay men. In the person appraisal, the Personal Career Development Chart (Worell & Remer, 1992) or variation of the lifeline approach (Goldman, 1990), for instance, may be utilized to identify critical developmental and career-related events, experiences, and daydreams at different points in the gay man's life. The possible linkage of these events and his perceptions of life roles and contextual barriers may then be explored.

In short, as a result of such an assessment, both counseling participants can achieve a better understanding of the client's presenting concerns relative to his current life roles and needs within various contexts. This assessment also shapes the design and implementation of interventions that are more grounded in the gay male client's experience.

**Modifications of Theory-Driven Interventions**  Specific intervention strategies derived from traditional counseling theories, when modified appropriately, are useful in counseling gay men. Relative to psychotherapy, Fassinger (2000b) offered an excellent analysis of the prospects and limitations of each theoretical approach to counseling LGB clients. Echoing Fassinger's view, we believe that the major career counseling and psychotherapy approaches each offer unique possibilities as well as pitfalls in their application to counseling gay men. The task confronting the counselor, however, is to make necessary modifications so that these interventions may yield maximum effectiveness with the minimum risk of inflicting harm.

Theory-driven strategies can be modified in several ways. First, as discussed previously, the counseling principles of developmental-contextualism and the integration of personal and career counseling function as a yardstick against which the applicability of strategies, techniques, and skills from a given theoretical approach to working with gay men may be measured.

Second, modifications of theory-driven interventions may be made through a consideration of the appropriate counselor roles to be assumed. Initially developed in the context of counseling ethnic minority clients, Atkinson et al.'s (1993) three-dimensional cube model delineates eight counselor roles, depending on three factors: (1) acculturation level (low to high), (2) goal of helping (preventive or remedial), and (3) source of problem (internal or external). Aside from the roles of counselor and psychotherapist, the others are facilitator of indigenous support system, facilitator of indigenous healing methods, adviser, advocate, consultant, and change agent. Although the factor of acculturation level needs to be reexamined in the application of the Atkinson et al. model to the context of counseling LGB clients, counselor familiarity with this model, nevertheless, facilitates a consideration of roles beyond traditionally assumed ones. The counselor, for instance, may assume the role of facilitator of support system by providing the isolated gay male client bibliotherapy, as well as resources available within the community or through the Internet (e.g., see the appendix in Ritter & Terndrup, 2001). For a gay male client with coming-out issues, the appropriate roles and intervention strategies may be notably different from those the counselor uses when working with a gay man who has generally resolved these issues, even though both clients present distress resulting from an oppressive work environment.

In the third way of modifying theory-driven interventions, counselors consider the common factors perspective as described by Fischer, Jome, and Atkinson (1998), an alternative to the culture-specific view (i.e., that unique counseling strategies need to be developed for effective counseling with diverse clientele). According to Fischer et al., four factors transcend theoretical approaches to counseling diverse clientele, and, as a result, it is not necessary to develop unique counseling strategies for clients in each cultural group. The application of the Fischer et al. perspective serves as a framework for guiding the counselor working with gay men in raising questions relative to the four common factors:

1. *Therapeutic relationship:* What knowledge or skills do I need to acquire in order for me to develop a therapeutic alliance with *this* gay male client? What aspects of myself, personally and professionally, may threaten the development of that alliance?

2. *Shared worldview between client and counselor:* How do I know what worldview *this* gay male client holds? In what way do I share or not share his worldview? How do *we* work together as a result of these similarities and differences in worldview?

3. *Meeting client expectations:* How do I know his expectations for counseling in general, and for working with *me* in particular? How do I know that I have met his expectations?

4. *Culturally relevant and appropriate interventions:* How do I know that he shares the same confidence as I in the use of interventions that are relevant and appropriate to his experience as a member of the group(s) central to his identity?

Through a consideration of these questions and the acquisition of requisite knowledge of the gay male client's cultural contexts, counselors can then modify their general counseling skills accordingly. Shannon and Woods (1991) emphasized incorporating a cost-benefit analysis in the design and implementation of counseling interventions. Conducting this type of cost-benefit analysis of values and needs with the client allows both for exploration of potential reactions and outcomes to the interpersonal situation and for processing of internal reactions in counseling. In assisting the client in weighing the risks and benefits within the range of possible outcomes, counselors also aim at enhancing his coping skills and support network in the event of an adverse outcome.

## Group Counseling

In contrast to individual counseling, a counseling group is a complex entity composed of multiple, interactive parts (Furhiman & Burlingame, 1994; Kivlighan, Coleman, & Anderson, 2000). Much more than the sum of its members, leaders, subgroups, and whole group identities, each group contains interactions at numerous levels, including the intrapersonal, interpersonal, and group-as-a-whole levels. Whereas individual counseling provides gay men a secure base within which to enhance their capacity to deepen their connections to another individual, the opportunity for learning to develop intimate relationships with other gay men, or with people from all walks of life, is multiplied in a counseling group.

In light of Yalom's (1995) therapeutic factors, group counseling as a modality is effective for gay male clients because many therapeutic factors may be in full operation (see DeBord & Perez, 2000, for details). In a gay men's counseling group, the therapeutic value of universality and instillation of hope is maximized. Not only does the group function as a great source of support, but it also provides members the opportunity to recognize the universality of their concerns, and to share their experience of vulnerability and resilience as members of underrepresented, stigmatized groups in a predominately heterosexual society. Within this safe environment, anxiety-laden concerns such as alcoholism, HIV/AIDS, and sexual compulsiveness can be explored more fully, as can value systems that may be unhealthy or self-defeating.

Counseling group as a social microcosm suggests that the group is "a miniaturized presentation of each [member's] social universe" (Yalom, 1995, p. 42). In a group that is heterogeneous with respect to sex, race, ethnicity, and sexual orientation, the social microcosm of the counseling group enhances the therapeutic value of interpersonal learning, because members bring unique social and cultural values, beliefs, and expectations to each interpersonal encounter (Rutan & Stone, 2001). Group counseling, consequently, challenges members across sociocultural divides to identify and reflect on interpersonal perceptions, relationships, and conflicts that arise from these differences (Chen, 2001b). Self-disclosure, or the act of revealing oneself fully to another individual, when followed by acceptance and affirmation by others, affords gay men an opportunity to liberate their voice by exploring with greater depth issues or feelings they may otherwise find difficult to examine outside the group. Growth occurs when they use interpersonal learning to develop adaptive ways of relating to others, first with fellow group members, and subsequently with significant others outside the group.

Invariably, the growth process hinges on, to a large extent, the level of the group counselor's competence in assisting gay male clients in their negotiation and management of their interpersonal risks and emotional vulnerability. In the presence of the compassionate, skilled group counselor, clients would in the end be rewarded with a more meaningful way of relating to others. The competence of the group counselor is delineated next in relation to four leadership roles, drawn primarily from Chen, Thombs, and Costa (in press): historian, norm-shaper, participant-observer, and technical expert.

**Group Counselor as Historian**   The counselor in the role of historian keeps in mind the original goals of each group member, as well as the events that unfold in the group. The main goal is to develop an understanding of each individual's personal history, because a knowledge of the member's personal history vastly enhances the counselor's ability to look out the client's window (Yalom, 2002). Each member's personal history is then utilized to facilitate the self-disclosure necessary for the mutual understanding of experiences, both convergent and divergent, as gay men. The establishment of the gay man's ability to respond to the often painful experiences of other members allows cohesion to develop in a group composed of members with diverse histories and life experiences.

**Group Counselor as Norm-Shaper**   Because of the pervasive experience of homophobia in society, the counselor as a norm-shaper ensures that the social microcosm of the group does not simply replicate societal norms of oppression, prejudice, and discrimination. Furthermore, the effort to facilitate the development of mutual understanding among group members is linked to the points of tension that exist in relation to norms on three different levels: those of the group, those of the society, and those of gay culture. To this end, the counselor takes an active role in eliciting reactions from all group members about their perceptions and expectations about one another. Through modeling intercultural curiosity, sensitivity to diversity, and self-disclosure, the counselor helps the members develop norms under which differences across sociocultural boundaries are viewed as opportunities to confront stereotypical beliefs and unwarranted assumptions about LGB individuals. Throughout the group process, and particularly in the early stages most crucial for the development of group culture, members are encouraged to reflect on their own assumptions and stereotypes about others as manifested in their interpersonal encounters in the group.

**Group Counselor as Participant-Observer**   In the role of participant-observer, the counselor faces the task of understanding an interaction from the perspective of an insider, while maintaining the objectivity to describe what is happening in the group. The counselor strives to strike a delicate balance between data collected as an objective outsider versus that gleaned as a subjective insider, relative to the incidents both unfolding within *and* absent from the group. In a heterogeneous counseling group, for example, the focus of observation may be placed on how the quality of interaction is influenced by group members' sexual orientation. Would gay members constantly interrupt or cut off other heterosexual members, and vice versa? In a gay men's counseling group, questions for observation may concern the extent to which an exchange of information, ideas, views, or feedback occurs between members of different cultural backgrounds. Does there seem to be a special bond between two members because of their similarities or differences in their gay identity? With data collected in relation to these questions, the counselor will be better equipped to formulate hypotheses and plan possible interventions.

**Group Counselor as Technical Expert**   The role of the counselor as a technical expert refers to the application of specific techniques utilized to influence the direction of the group (Yalom, 1995). In a gay men's group, for instance, the role of technical expert is emphasized in the pregroup screening and preparatory process, in which prospective members are informed that, despite their individual differences, members all share the common experience as gay men in society.

With the goal of facilitating members' self-disclosure and feedback exchange, the counselor utilizes two main categories of counseling skills: caring and meaning attribution. In the "caring" category are skills that focus on affect and facilitate members' experience of warmth, support, empathy, and compassion from others in the group. With an emphasis on cognitive understanding, "meaning attribution" skills (e.g., cognitive reframing, interpretation) aim at uncovering meanings embedded in interpersonal experiences and interactions. The selection of appropriate skills from each category depends, in large part, on the counselor's intention. If the counselor intends to increase the curative value of universality, he or she may use the skill of empathy to increase perceived similarity among the members. If the intention is to address tension related to racial or ethnic differences, making process comments (Yalom, 1995) may heighten members' awareness that racism may certainly exist within the gay community as well.

In conclusion, although differing in focus and specificity, the four leadership roles are employed to promote personal growth, which is rooted in trusting interpersonal connections. To be an effective group counselor, one must shift among these roles by keeping in mind, among other factors, the goals of the group and individual members, the group composition, and the stages of group development. At the beginning stage of group development, to increase the motivation and involvement of a gay male member in a men's group with predominately heterosexual men, for instance, the counselor may intentionally focus on the therapeutic value of cohesion and universality. After inviting members to share an experience of rejection by others, the counselor may use skills in the caring and cognitive understanding categories, and shift the leadership roles back and forth in the process, to produce the intended impact. The counselor's reflection of the impact of interventions would then offer guidance for future counseling sessions.

## CONCLUSION

In this chapter we have presented an overview of presenting concerns, counseling challenges and principles, as well as intervention strategies central to affirmative counseling with gay men. We do not join Yalom's (2002) call for a new therapy for each client. Nor, on the other hand, do we intend to encourage a greater reliance on or adherence to a counseling protocol, one that includes a prescribed sequence, a schedule of topics and exercises to be followed with each gay male client. Instead, we urge counselors to create an assortment of innovative interventions tailored toward the gay man's needs to enhance his well-being and quality of life. At its very core, affirmative counseling cannot be provided in isolation from an ethical responsibility for effecting systemic and social changes, one that focuses on the elimination of problems, rather than on simply treating clients whose experience of stigmatization, religious prejudice, harassment, discrimination, or violence is often a manifestation of social injustice. It is our hope that the perspectives and ideas presented throughout this chapter may enhance counselors' effective, affirmative counseling practice with the gay male client by offering them a new vision of their work, and an inquiry that may lead to the fertile territory of professional competence.

# Cases and Questions

1. You are a practicum student in an urban university counseling center, working with your new client, Brian, a White, 20-year-old business major from a small town in the Midwest. He has reported to you that lately he has been feeling increasingly anxious in completing his schoolwork. His grades have been gradually decreasing over the past two semesters, and he is contemplating switching his major. Living in the dorm by himself, Brian has expressed feelings of isolation as well as apprehension about going home at the end of the semester. His parents have suggested that, if he likes, he could bring home a girlfriend for the holiday. Brian states that he has been aware of his attraction to men since the sixth grade and has only disclosed his sexual orientation to a few childhood friends. He seems ill at ease when asked about his relationship with his boyfriend of 3 months.

(a) How would you describe Brian's current level of functioning and the nature of his presenting concerns from a developmental-contextual perspective? In what ways might his sexual orientation and gay identity be related to his well-being and presenting concerns?

(b) On the basis of Crites's (1979) model, what specific questions in each of the three assessment areas (i.e., person, problem, and prognosis) might you consider important to explore further? Why?

(c) Describe the practical utility of existing theories of career development and psychotherapy in relation to this case. What modifications of your personal and career counseling approaches would you make in order for *you* to provide affirmative counseling with him?

2. You started facilitating a gay men's counseling group a few weeks ago at a mental health center affiliated with a university. The group, predominately White, is composed of eight men in their early to late 20s. At the beginning of a recent session, one ethnic minority member described a breakup with his boyfriend of 6 months after finding out his boyfriend was dating another man. After expressing mixed feelings of sadness, guilt, and anger, he questioned the norm of promiscuity in the gay men's culture. His remarks led to a heated exchange among several members, with notable silence from several others throughout the remainder of the session. You are aware that two of the silent members had a history of promiscuous behavior.

(a) Which of the therapeutic factors would you want to emphasize for this group in the next session? How so?

(b) At what level (e.g., individual member, subgroup, group-as-a-whole), in what role(s) (e.g., historian, participant-observer), and with what skills (e.g., caring, meaning attribution) would you intervene intentionally? How would you assess the impact of your interventions?

(c) How might your group members, individually and collectively, relate to you, if you are different from them with respect to sex, sexual orientation, or race-ethnicity?

## REFERENCES

American Counseling Association. (1995). *Code of ethics and standards of practice.* Alexandria, VA: Author.

American Psychological Association. (1991a). *Bias in psychotherapy with lesbians and gay men: Final report of the Task Force on Psychotherapy with Lesbians and Gay Men.* Washington, DC: Author.

American Psychological Association, Committee on Lesbian and Gay Concerns. (1991b). Avoiding heterosexual bias in language. *American Psychologist, 46,* 973–974.

American Psychological Association. (1993). Guidelines for providers of psychological services to ethnic, linguistic, and culturally diverse populations. *American Psychologist, 48,* 45–48.

American Psychological Association. (2000). *Guidelines for psychotherapy with lesbian, gay, and bisexual clients.* Washington, DC: Author.

American Psychological Association. (2002a). *Ethical principles of psychologists and code of conduct. American Psychologist, 57,* 1060–1073.

American Psychological Association. (2002b). *Guidelines and principles for accreditation of programs in professional psychology.* Washington, DC: Author.

American Psychological Association. (2002c). *Guidelines on multicultural education, training, research, practice, and organizational change for psychologists.* Washington, DC: Author.

Atkinson, D. R., Thompson, C. E., & Grant, S. K. (1993). A three-dimensional model for counseling racial/ethnic minorities. *The Counseling Psychologist, 21,* 257–277.

Beaudin, C. L., & Chambre, S. M. (1996). HIV/AIDS as a chronic disease: Emergence from the plague model. *American Behavioral Scientist, 39,* 684–706.

Brook, D. W., Gordon, C., & Meadow, H. (1998). Ethnicity, culture and group counseling. *Group, 22,* 53–80.

Caitlin, R., & Futterman, D. (1997). *Lesbian and gay youth: Care and counseling.* Philadelphia: Hanley & Belfus.

Cass, V. C. (1979). Homosexual identity formation: A theoretical model. *Journal of Homosexuality, 4,* 219–235.

Campbell, R. E., & Cellini, J. V. (1981). A diagnostic taxonomy of adult career problems. *Journal of Vocational Behavior, 19,* 175–190.

Chen, E. C. (2001a). Multicultural counseling supervision: An interactional approach. In J. G. Ponterotto, J. M. Casas, L. A. Suzuki, & C. M. Alexander (Eds.), *Handbook of multicultural counseling* (2nd ed., pp. 801–824). Thousand Oaks, CA: Sage.

Chen, E. C. (2001b, August). Integrating multicultural competencies into training for group therapists. In R. Trammel & E. C. Chen (Co-Chairs), *Working with diverse populations in groups: Competencies, issues and challenges.* Paper presented at the annual meeting of the American Psychological Association, San Francisco.

Chen, E. C., Thombs, B., & Costa, C. (in press). Building connection through diversity in group counseling: A dialogical perspective. In D. B. Pope-Davis, H. L. K. Coleman, W. M. Liu, and R. L. Toporek. (Eds.) *Handbook on multicultural competencies* (2nd ed.). Thousand Oaks, CA: Sage.

Cole, S. W., Kemeny, M. E., Taylor, S. E., & Visscher, B. R. (1996). Elevated physical health risk among gay men (age 18–24). *Journal of Acquired Immune Deficiency Syndromes and Human Retrovirology, 8,* 208–211.

Constantine, M. G., & Ladany, N. (2000). Self-report multicultural counseling competence scales: Their relation to social desirability attitudes and multicultural case conceptualization ability. *Journal of Counseling Psychology, 47,* 102–115.

Council for Accreditation of Counseling and Related Educational Programs. (2001). *Accreditation standards and procedures manual.* Alexandria, VA: Author.

Crites, J. O. (1979). Career counseling: A review of major approaches. *The Counseling Psychologist, 4*(3), 3–23.

Croteau, J. M. (1996). Research on the work experience of lesbian, gay and bisexual people: An integrative view of methodology and findings. *Journal of Vocational Behavior, 48,* 195–209.

Croteau, J. M., Anderson, M. Z., Distefano, T. M., & Kampa-Kokesch, S. (2000). Lesbian, gay, and bisexual vocational psychology: Reviewing foundations and planning construction. In R. M. Perez, K. A. DeBord, & K. J. Bieschke (Eds.), *Handbook of counseling and psychotherapy with lesbian, gay, and bisexual clients* (pp. 383–408). Washington, DC: American Psychological Association.

Croteau, J. M., & Lark, J. S. (1995). On being lesbian, gay or bisexual in student affairs: A national survey of experiences on the job. *NASPA Journal, 32,* 189–197.

Croteau, J. M., & Thiel, M. J. (1993). Integrating sexual orientation in career counseling: Acting to end a form of the personal-career dichotomy. *Career Development Quarterly, 42,* 174–179.

Croteau, J. M., & von Destinon, M. (1994). A national survey of job search experiences of lesbian, gay and bisexual student affairs professionals. *Journal of College Student Development, 35,* 40–45.

Davison, G. C. (1991). Constructionism and morality in therapy for homosexuality. In J. C. Gonsiorek & J. D. Weinrich (Eds.), *Homosexuality: Research implications for public policy* (pp. 137–148). Newbury Park, CA: Sage.

DeBord, K. A., & Perez, R. M. (2000) Group counseling theory and practice with lesbian, gay, and bisexual clients. In R. M. Perez, K. A. DeBord, & K. J. Bieschke (Eds.), *Handbook of counseling and psychotherapy with lesbian, gay, and bisexual clients* (pp. 183–206). Washington, DC: American Psychological Association.

Dorland, J. M., & Fischer, A. R. (2001). Gay, lesbian, and bisexual individuals' perceptions: An analogue study. *The Counseling Psychologist, 29,* 532–547.

Dworkin, S. H. (2000). Individual therapy with lesbian, gay, and bisexual clients. In R. M. Perez, K. A. DeBord, & K. J. Bieschke (Eds.), *Handbook of counseling and psychotherapy with lesbian, gay, and bisexual clients* (pp. 157–181). Washington, DC: American Psychological Association.

Etringer, B. D., Hillerbrand, E., & Hetherington, C. (1990). The influence of sexual orientation on career decision making: A research note. *Journal of Homosexuality, 19,* 103–111.

Fassinger, R. E. (2000a). Gender and sexuality in human development: Implications for prevention and advocacy in counseling psychology. In S. D. Brown & R. W. Lent (Eds.), *Handbook of counseling psychology* (3rd ed., pp. 346–378). New York: Wiley.

Fassinger, R. E. (2000b). Applying counseling theories to lesbian, gay, and bisexual clients: Pitfalls and possibilities. In R. M. Perez, K. A. DeBord, & K. J. Bieschke (Eds.), *Handbook of counseling and psychotherapy with lesbian, gay, and bisexual clients* (pp. 107–131). Washington, DC: American Psychological Association.

Fassinger, R. E., & Miller, B. A. (1996). Validation of an inclusive model of sexual minority identity formation on a sample of gay men. *Journal of Homosexuality, 32,* 53–78.

Fischer, A. R., Jome, L. M., & Atkinson, D. R. (1998). Reconceptualizing multicultural counseling: Universal healing conditions in a culturally specific context. *The Counseling Psychologist, 26,* 525–588.

Fuhriman, A., & Burlingame, G. M. (1994). Group psychotherapy: Research and practice. In A. Fuhriman & G. M. Burlingame (Eds.). *Handbook of group psychotherapy: An empirical and clinical synthesis* (pp. 3–40). New York: Wiley.

Gelso, C. J., & Mohr, J. J. (2001). The working alliance and the transference/countertransference relationship: Their manifestation with racial/ethnic and sexual orientation minority clients and therapists. *Applied and Preventive Psychology, 10,* 51–68.

Goldman, L. (1990). Qualitative assessment. *The counseling psychologist, 18,* 205–213.

Gonsiorek, J. C. (1995). Gay male identities: Concepts and issues. In A. R. D'Augelli & C. J. Patterson (Eds.), *Lesbian, gay, and bisexual identities over the lifespan* (pp. 24–47). New York: Oxford University Press.

Griffin, P. (1992). From hiding out to coming out: Empowering lesbian and gay educators. In K. M. Harbeck (Ed.), *Coming out of the classroom closet* (pp. 167–196). Binghamton, NY: Harrington Park Press.

Gudykunst, W. B., & Ting-Toomey, S. (1988). *Culture and interpersonal communication.* Newbury, Park, CA: Sage.

Gysbers, N. C. (1997). Involving counseling psychology in the school-to-work movement: An idea whose time has come. *The Counseling Psychologist, 25,* 413–427.

Hackett, G. (1993). Career counseling and psychotherapy: false dichotomies and recommended remedies. *Journal of Career Assessment, 1,* 105–117.

Hancock, K. A. (1995). Psychotherapy with lesbians and gay men. In A. R. D'Augelli & C. J. Patterson (Eds.), *Lesbian, gay, and bisexual identities over the lifespan* (pp. 323–336). New York: Oxford University Press.

Holland, J. L. (1985). *Making vocational choices: A theory of vocational personalities and work environments.* Englewood Cliffs, NJ: Prentice-Hall.

Jordaan, J. E., Myers, R. A., Layton, W. C., & Morgan, H. H. (1968). *The counseling psychologist.* Washington, DC: American Psychological Association.

Kalichman, S. C., Nachimson, D., Cherry, C., & Williams, E. (1998). AIDS treatment advances and behavioral prevention setbacks: Preliminary assessment of reduced perceived threat of AIDS-HIV. *Health Psychology, 17,* 546–550.

Kauth, M. R., Hartwig, M. J., & Kalichman, S. C., (2000). Health behavior relevant to psychotherapy with lesbian, gay, and bisexual clients. In R. M. Perez, K. A. Debord, & K. J. Bieschke (Eds.), *Handbook of counseling and psychotherapy with lesbian, gay, and bisexual clients* (pp. 435–456). Washington, DC: American Psychological Association.

Kivlighan, D. M., Jr., Coleman, M. N., & Anderson, D. C. (2000). Process, outcome, and methodology in group counseling research. In S. D. Brown & R. W. Lent (Eds.), *Handbook of counseling psychology* (3rd ed., pp. 767–796). New York: Wiley.

Kluckhohn, C., & Murray, H. A. (1953). Personality formation: The determinants. In C. Kluckhohn & H. A. Murray (Eds.), *Personality in nature, society, and culture* (pp. 35–48). New York: Knopf.

Leong, F. T. L. (1996). Toward an integrative model for cross-cultural counseling and psychotherapy. *Applied and Preventive Psychology, 5,* 189–209.

Levine, M. P., & Leonard, R. (1984). Discrimination against lesbians in the workforce. *Signs: Journal of Women in Culture and Society, 9,* 700–710.

Mahoney, M. J., & Patterson, K. M. (1992). Changing theories of change: Recent developments in counseling. In S. D. Brown & R. W. Lent (Eds.), *Handbook of counseling psychology* (2nd ed., pp. 665–689). New York: Wiley.

Matteson, D. R. (1996). Counseling and psychotherapy with bisexual and exploring clients. In B. A. Firestein (Ed.), *Bisexuality: The psychology and politics of an invisible minority* (pp. 185–213). Newbury Park, CA: Sage.

Mohr, J. J. (2002). Heterosexual identity and the heterosexual therapist: An identity perspective on sexual orientation dynamics in psychotherapy. *The Counseling Psychologist, 30,* 532–566.

Morrow, S. B. (2000). First do no harm: Therapist issues in psychotherapy with lesbian, gay, and bisexual clients. In R. M. Perez, K. A. DeBord, & K. J. Bieschke (Eds.), *Handbook of counseling and psychotherapy with lesbian, gay, and bisexual clients* (pp. 137–156). Washington, DC: American Psychological Association.

Perez, R. M., DeBord, K. A., & Bieschke K. J., (Eds.). (2000). *Handbook of counseling and psychotherapy with lesbian, gay, and bisexual clients.* Washington, DC: American Psychological Association.

Ponterotto, J. G. (1997). Multicultural counseling training: A competency model and national survey. In D. B. Pope-Davis & H. L. K. Coleman (Eds.), *Multicultural counseling competencies: Assessment, education and training, and supervision* (pp. 111–130). Thousand Oaks, CA: Sage.

Ponterotto, J. G., Fuertes, J. N., & Chen, E. C. (2000). Models of multicultural counseling. In S. D. Brown & R. W. Lent (Eds.), *Handbook of counseling psychology* (3rd ed., pp. 639–669). New York: Wiley.

Pope, K. S., & Vasquez, M. J. T. (1998). *Ethics in psychotherapy and counseling* (2nd ed.). San Francisco: Jossey-Bass.

Prince, J. P. (1995). Influences upon the career development of gay men. *Career Development Quarterly, 44,* 168–177.

Quintana, S. M., & Bernal, M. E. (1995). Ethnic minority training in counseling psychology: Comparisons with clinical psychology and proposed standards. *The Counseling Psychologist, 23,* 102–121.

Richardson, M. S. (1993). Work in people's lives: A location for counseling psychologists. *Journal of Counseling Psychology, 40,* 425–433.

Richardson, M. S. (1996). From career counseling to counseling/psychotherapy and work, job, and career. In M. L. Savickas & W. B. Walsh (Eds.), *Handbook of career counseling theory and practice* (pp. 347–360). Palo Alto, CA: Davies-Black.

Ritter, K. Y., & Terndrup, A. I. (2001). *Handbook of affirmative psychotherapy with lesbians and gay men.* New York: Guilford Press.

Robbins, S. B., & Kliewer, W. L. (2000). Advances in theory and research on subjective well-being. In S. D. Brown & R. W. Lent (Eds.), *Handbook of counseling psychology* (3rd ed., pp. 310–345). New York: Wiley.

Rostosky, S. S., & Riggle, E. D. B. (2002). "Out" at work: The relation of partner workplace policy and internalized homophobia to disclosure status. *Journal of Counseling Psychology, 49,* 411–419.

Rutan, J. S., & Stone, W. N. (2001). *Psychodynamic group psychotherapy* (3rd ed.). New York: Guilford Press.

Sadava, S. W., & Thompson, M. M. (1986). Loneliness, social drinking, and vulnerability to alcohol problems. *Canadian Journal of Behavioral Science, 18,* 133–139.

Shannon, J. W., & Woods, W. J. (1991). Affirmative psychotherapy for gay men. *The Counseling Psychologist, 19,* 197–215.

Shidlo, A., & Schroeder, M. (2002). Changing sexual orientation: A consumers' report. *Professional Psychology: Research and Practice, 33,* 249–259.

Shilts, R. (1987). *And the band played on.* New York: St. Martin's Press.

Siever, M. D. (1994). Sexual orientation and gender as factors in socioculturally acquired vulnerability to body dissatisfaction and eating disorders. *Journal of Consulting and Clinical Psychology, 62,* 252–260.

Smith, A. (1997). Cultural diversity and the coming out process: Implications for therapy practice. In B. Greene (Ed.), *Ethnic and cultural diversity among lesbians and gay men* (pp. 279–300). Newbury Park, CA: Sage.

Sue, S., & Zane, N. (1987). The role of culture and cultural techniques in psychotherapy. *American Psychologist, 42,* 37–45.

Super, D. E., Savickas, M. L., & Super, C. M. (1996). The life-span, life-space approach to careers. In D. Brown, L. Brooks, & Associates (Eds.), *Career choice and development* (3rd ed., pp. 121–178). San Francisco: Jossey-Bass.

Troiden, R. R. (1988). Homosexual identity development. *Journal of Adolescent Health Care, 9,* 105–113.

Trujillo, C. M. (1997). Sexual identity and the discontents of difference. In B. Greene (Ed.), *Ethnic and cultural diversity among lesbians and gay men* (pp. 266–278). Newbury Park, CA: Sage.

Vondracek, F. W., Lerner, R. M., & Schulenberg, J. E. (1986). *Career development: A life-span developmental approach.* Hillsdale, NJ: Erlbaum.

Waldo, C. R. (1999). Working in a majority context: A structural model of heterosexism as minority stress in the workplace. *Journal of Counseling Psychology, 46,* 218–232.

Weinberg, M. S., Williams, C. J., & Pryor, D. W. (1994). *Dual attraction: Understanding bisexuality.* New York: Oxford University Press.

Worell, J., & Remer, P. (1992). *Feminist perspectives in therapy.* Chichester, England: Wiley.

Worthington, R. L., Savoy, H. B., Dillon, F. R., & Vernaglia, E. R. (2002). Heterosexual identity development: A multidimensional model of individual and social identity. *The Counseling Psychologist, 30,* 496–531.

Yalom, I. D. (1995). *The theory and practice of group counseling* (4th ed.). New York: Basic Books.

Yalom, I. D. (2002). *The gift of therapy.* New York: HarperCollins.

# Part VI    IMPLICATIONS

# CHAPTER 18

Diversity Imperatives for Counseling Practice, Training, and Research

In this chapter we highlight several aspects of counseling practice that we feel need special attention. We also discuss changes that are needed in counselor training programs to adequately prepare counselors to work with diverse populations. Finally, we propose necessary changes in counseling research to reduce research bias against people with disabilities, older people, women, and LGB people.

## COUNSELING PRACTICE

In addition to the counseling practices specifically directed toward the four minority groups discussed in chapters 6 through 17, we feel it is important to draw attention to three practice topics that are relevant to all four groups. These topics are language, ethics, and advocacy.

### Language

Counselors and other mental health practitioners often unintentionally use imprecise and demeaning language that serves to reinforce stereotypes of people with disabilities, older people, women, and LGB people. Practicing counselors can help reduce discrimination against these groups and take a major step toward increasing their credibility and effectiveness with diverse clients by eliminating imprecise and demeaning language from their vocabulary, and by sensitively and knowledgeably using the terminology employed by their clients. In general, it is best to respect the client's preference for self-reference, and to recognize that this language changes over time.

Sometimes the counselor is in a situation where it is not possible to determine the client's preference for language of self-reference, as when the client is not present. When it is not possible to determine the client's preference for language of self-reference, it is helpful to have a general knowledge of appropriate terminology to use with diverse populations. In the following sections we examine some general guidelines for the appropriate and inappropriate use of language with each of the four diverse populations groups discussed in this book.

**People With Disabilities**   Perhaps no group has had more demeaning terms directed toward them both intentionally and unintentionally than people with disabilities. Concern over the widespread use of inappropriate language in reference to persons with disabilities has been a theme in the rehabilitation counseling literature since about 1980.

Hadley and Brodwin (1988) reviewed the rehabilitation literature and developed four simple principles that they recommended rehabilitation counselors follow when discussing people with disabilities:

1. *Precision:* Language should convey a speaker's or writer's intended meanings exactly and unambiguously.
2. *Objectivity:* One should avoid language that (a) implicitly expresses biases or unwanted surplus meanings or (b) treats opinions, interpretations, or impressions as facts.
3. *Perspective:* When one communicates about a person, the language chosen should emphasize the person and represent any disability in its proper perspective among his or her many other characteristics. This perspective is governed by the issues at hand; if disability is totally irrelevant to these issues, it may be omitted entirely.
4. *Portrayal:* People with disabilities should be portrayed as actively going about the business of living as other people do, *not* as passive victims, tragic figures, or superheroes. (p. 147)

Hadley and Brodwin (1988) pointed out that all professional counselors, not just rehabilitation counselors, should be concerned about the use of language since people with disabilities often seek out counselors in other specialties to discuss problems with living that are unrelated to their impairment. They made several concrete suggestions about the use of language, although they qualified their suggestions by pointing out that the most appropriate use of language is often situation specific:

1. A form of the verb *to have* is usually the most effective way to express the link between a person and a disability.
   a. A person "has arthritis," *not* "is an arthritic"; "has diabetes" is preferable to "is a diabetic."
   b. One should scrupulously avoid words such as "victim" or "afflicted" to express this link. These words carry surplus emotional meaning.
   c. The word *patient* correctly expresses a relationship with a medical service provider such as a physician or a hospital; it is a poor word choice for other uses. "Is a lupus patient" is an *imprecise* substitute for "has lupus."
   d. To have a disability is not necessarily to "suffer from" it. Such gratuitous use of "suffer" conveys a stereotypical attitude. . . . If one wants to say a particular person is suffering, this point should be developed explicitly.
2. A disability should never be represented as causing (a) an individual's emotional or behavioral reactions to it or (b) sequelae to these reactions. We prefer to represent people as the causes of their own feelings and behavior, although disability often serves as a cue. For example:
   a. It is neither precise nor objective to say that a disability or any other circumstance "makes" a person feel any particular way. "She feels depressed about her hearing loss" is better than "her hearing loss is making her depressed."

    b. Neither blindness nor paraplegia has ever caused alcoholism. People have reacted to these conditions, however, with patterns of drinking that caused alcoholism.

3. A disability should not be represented, either explicitly or implicitly, as the sole cause of circumstances resulting from social reactions to it. For example, a person should not be described as unemployed because he or she has impaired vision, if the reason is employers' discriminatory hiring.

4. Wheelchairs, prostheses, and other assistive devices are tools that people use in their various activities; word choices should represent this fact. For example:

    a. A client with paralyzed legs *uses* a wheelchair. The common expression, "confined to a wheelchair," is obviously imprecise and carries many of the same surplus meanings as "wheelchair-bound." Although "is in a wheelchair" is somewhat less offensive, . . . this expression . . . portrays the person as "passive."

    b. It is preferable to say a person "walks with" crutches rather than "has to use" or "is on" crutches. (Hadley & Brodwin, 1988, pp. 148–149)

Similarly, Byrd, Crews, and Ebener (1991) identified the following points that should be considered when making written or verbal reference to persons with disabilities:

1. Only make reference to a person's disability when it is important to the context;
2. Avoid using adjectives as nouns;
3. Place persons or individuals before the disability;
4. Avoid value laden descriptions;
5. Do not sensationalize the effects of disability;
6. Avoid statements that qualify the person with a disability (e.g., he uses a wheelchair, but is very bright);
7. Avoid implying sickness when discussing disability conditions. (p. 40)

Researchers and academicians, as well as practitioners, need to be concerned about the terms they use in reference to people with disabilities. The American Psychological Association's *Publication Manual* (APA, 2001) offers the following advice to authors of manuscripts submitted to APA journals for publication:

> The guiding principle for "nonhandicapping" language is to maintain the integrity of individuals as human beings. Avoid language that equates persons with their condition (e.g., *neurotics, the disabled*); that has superfluous, negative overtones (e.g., stroke *victim*); or that is regarded as a slur (e.g., *cripple*).
>
>     Use *disability* to refer to an attribute of a person and *handicap* to refer to the source of limitations, which may include attitudinal, legal, and architectural barriers as well as the disability itself (e.g., steps and curbs handicap people who require the use of a ramp). *Challenged* and *special* are often considered euphemistic and should be used only if the people in your study prefer those terms. As a general rule, 'person with ____," "person living with ___," and "person who has ___" are neutral and preferred forms of description. (p. 69)

Putting the person ahead of the disability is sometimes referred to as "people-first language." People-first language is clearly intended to avoid the inherent objectification and negative stereotyping associated with terms used in the past to identify people with disabilities. However, people-first language has been criticized recently for reinforcing medical interpretations of normalcy and for associating abnormality with individuals rather than conceptualizing disability as a function of handicapping environments and failed social policy (Titchkosky, 2001). Titchkosky has suggested that

> an openness to a diversity of terms and expressions of disability would be beneficial to all. Diverse expressions make possible transgressions of the singular conception of disability. Thus, the point is not "say it this way. . . ." The point is, instead, to examine what our current articulations of disability are saying in the here and now. An openness to alternative linguistic formulations of disability might lead to, and grow from, the understanding that disability, its social meaning, exceeds and even defies strictly medicalized articulations of "people-first." (p. 138)

Titchkosky made an important point that we think readers should keep in mind: People-first language has not separated people from a medical view of the problem residing with the individual; it has only put some distance between the individual and the "disability." Until a better lexicon comes along, however, we believe that people-first language does provide a more acceptable way of referring to people with disabilities than terms that have been used in the past.

**Older People**   The acceptability of terms applied to older people is also evolving. Cohen (1990) reviewed 60 issues of the *Gerontologist,* 30 issues of *Generations,* and a number of miscellaneous articles and monographs published by the federal government and reported having turned up

> an array of negative terms applied to or describing the elderly. . . . The following is a partial list of words and phrases that reinforce the elderly mystique from a variety of literatures, learned, policy, and legal. Elderly-at-risk, frail elderly, impaired elderly, institutionalized elderly, homebound elderly, chairbound elderly, bedridden elderly, wheelchairbound elderly, vulnerable elderly, dependent elderly, patient (rather than consumer), and "the Alzheimer" (referring to the person who has the disease). (p. 14)

Schaie (1993) pointed out that ageist attitudes and language permeate both empirical research and psychological practice. With regard to research, he identified a number of language problems related to the description of the research topic, the study design, the methodology and choice of participants, and the analysis and interpretation of research findings. Schaie's recommendations for avoiding these problems in research with older people are as follows:

I.  Recommendations related to description of research topic
    a.  Recognize that older persons constitute a diverse population. Heterogeneity should be stressed and gender should always be considered.
    b.  Recognize that ageism can apply to individuals at any age, not only to those who are old.
    c.  Consider a life span context in formulating the research topic.
    d.  Carefully reference existing literature on older persons, and in reviewing previous studies evaluate their possible age bias.
    e.  Consider the impact of possible findings on public policy.
II.  Recommendations related to the design of the study
    a.  Examine the choice and definition of hypotheses. Is there a causal inference that involves age or aging? Is it influenced by age bias?

    b. Consider whether chronological age is the most relevant variable. Would classification by other variables, such as educational level, income, duration of marriage, retirement, duration of retirement, or generational membership, be more appropriate?

    c. Document that the constructs used in a study retain the same meaning at different ages. . . . Acknowledge that use of measures of such constructs developed for younger adults may introduce bias into a study of elders.

III. Recommendations related to research methods

    a. Instruments should be evaluated to ensure that they do not contain explicitly or implicitly age bias.

    b. Avoid uncalled-for assumptions.

    c. Beware of experimenter bias about how questions are asked of various age groups.

    d. Check measures for inappropriate questions.

    e. Consider use of alternative definitions for chronological age, such as subjective age or functional age.

IV. Recommendations related to data analysis and interpretation

    a. Age-group differences should be characterized as such and not be labeled as *decline*. Often the term *age/cohort differences* is to be preferred.

    b. Age differences often can be explained by other variables and interactive effects; these should be discussed and ruled out before age is assumed to be the cause of differences in the dependent variable.

    c. In some instances it would be more desirable to use age as the dependent variable.

    d. Consider the practical significance of an age difference, especially when the data are relevant to public policy or might result in recommendations leading to important changes in an individual's life situation.

    e. Consider the impact of ageist assumptions and models applied to data analysis and interpretation. Formulate competing models that test for alternate interpretations.

    f. Use caution in generalizing results.

    g. Beware of interpreting trends or marginally significant findings, especially when they either fit or contradict social stereotypes about aging and older persons.

    h. Avoid value-laden language that implies negative characteristics for all study participants. (pp. 49–51)

    Recently, Polizzi and Millikin (2002) provided support for Schaie's recommendations for research methodology. These researchers found that using ageist terminology in research instructions does affect research outcome. Specifically, they determined that substituting "old" and "elderly" for "70–85 years of age" contributed to endorsement of more negative attitudes toward older people.

    Likewise, the APA *Publication Manual* (APA, 2001) suggests that in scientific writing, it is best to give a specific age range for participants rather than referring to them with a label. The *Publication Manual* also indicates that *"elderly* is not acceptable as a noun and is considered pejorative by some as an adjective" (p. 53). In place of *elderly,* the *Publication Manual* recommends use of *older person.* We have adopted the terms *older people, older persons,* and *older adults* for use in this text, recognizing that the terms *elder* and *elderly* may be offensive to some older people.

**Women**   "Gender rules embedded in written and spoken language inform children (and adults) about the place and value of women and the relationship between men and women" (Worell & Remer, 2003, p. 51). Psychologists have also been guilty of reinforcing sexism through the use of imprecise and derogatory language. The *Publication Manual of the American Psychological Association* first addressed this issue in 1974 in its second edition by suggesting that journal authors "be aware of the current move to avoid generic use of male nouns and pronouns when content refers to both sexes." This position was strengthened and elaborated upon in 1977 when the APA published the "Guidelines for Nonsexist Language in APA Journals" in the *American Psychologist*. In 1982, the APA Publications and Communications Board adopted a formal policy that requires authors who are submitting manuscripts to APA journals to use nonsexist language.

The current edition of the APA *Publication Manual* (APA, 2001) points out that by choosing the appropriate nouns, pronouns, and adjectives to describe the participants, an author can avoid ambiguity in sex identity and sex role and avoid sex bias:

> For example, using *man* to refer to all human beings is simply not as accurate as the phrase *men and women.* . . . (pp. 62–63)

> Sexist bias can occur when pronouns are used carelessly: when the masculine pronoun *he* is used to refer to both sexes, or when the masculine or feminine pronoun is used exclusively to define roles by sex (e.g., "the nurse . . . *she*"). The use of *man* as a generic noun or an ending for an occupational title (e.g., *policeman*) can be ambiguous and may imply incorrectly that all persons in the group are male. Be clear about whether you mean one sex or both sexes. . . . There are many alternatives to the generic *he,* including rephrasing, using plural nouns or plural pronouns, . . . replacing the pronoun with an article, . . . and dropping the pronoun. (p. 66)

Eichler (1988) suggested five questions to ask to ensure nonsexist language; a *yes* to any indicates the need for modifications:

1. Are any male (or female) terms used for generic purposes? [e.g., referring to all clients as "she"]
2. Are any generic terms employed when, in fact, the author(s) is (are) speaking about only one sex?
3. Are females and males in parallel situations described by nonparallel terms? [e.g., man and wife]
4. When both sexes are mentioned together in particular phrases, does one sex consistently precede the other? [e.g., "men and women"]
5. Are the two sexes consistently discussed in different grammatical modes? [e.g., using the passive voice when referring to women, but the active voice when referring to men] (p. 137)

However, being aware of nonsexist guidelines for written communication is not sufficient; psychologists and counselors must be aware of sexism in language in all of its forms (written, spoken, intentional, unintentional, etc.). Differential labeling of women often reflects biased ideology, for example, use of the phrase "man and wife"; deprecating or belittling labels for women and girls is likewise problematic (Worell & Remer, 2003).

**Lesbian, Gay, and Bisexual People**   Issues of appropriate language usage are also complicated when referring to gay men, lesbians, and bisexuals. Obviously, attention to the language issues raised in chapter 1 is a starting point. The terms *gay men, lesbians,* and *bisexual men* or *women* are preferable to *homosexual* to distinguish gay identity from sexual behavior (APA, 2001). Mental health practitioners must remain sensitive to the fact that individuals may self-identify differently given the same behavior. For example, many individuals who engage in sexual activities with the same sex may not self-identify as gay, lesbian, or bisexual (Reynolds & Hanjorgiris, 2000). Further, "the terms *heterosexual* and *bisexual* currently are used to describe both identity and behavior; adjectives are preferred to nouns" (APA, 2001, p. 67).

The term *sexual orientation* rather than *sexual preference* reminds us that LGB people do not choose their sexual orientation any more than non-LGB people choose to be heterosexual. It is also extremely important that counselors not confuse sexual orientation with other descriptors such as gender role, gender identity, transvestism, or transsexuality. And, of course, counselors should not only refrain from using any of the vast array of derogatory labels for gay people in their professional roles but must also extend this behavior to their personal lives, as such usage only serves to perpetuate the homophobia that is the primary source of oppression for gays. Beyond these basics, however, the issues become muddier.

When counseling LGB people, it is incumbent upon the counselor to understand the client's preferences for self-labels. There is often a considerable time gap (sometimes years) between a gay individual's first awareness of feelings for the same sex and his or her full acceptance of a gay identity (Dworkin, 2000; Dworkin & Gutierrez, 1992). In the earliest stages of the coming-out process, clients may not accept that they are LGB, and the counselor must consequently be careful in attaching labels to clients; however, neither should the counselor assume that homoerotic feelings are "just a phase." Understanding the coming-out process is vital to affirmative counseling with LGB people (Dworkin, 2000; Garnets, Hancock, Cochran, Goodchilds, & Peplau, 1991). Even clients who are fairly comfortable with being gay, lesbian, or bisexual may prefer one self-descriptor over others; for example, a woman who prefers to call herself gay rather than lesbian or a man in a relationship with another man who self-identifies as bisexual rather than gay. Counselors must always recall that LGB clients are no more immune from the effects of homophobia than non-LGB clients are. Finally, some gay men, lesbians, and bisexual men and women have reclaimed some of society's derogatory labels (e.g., queer or dyke), using them in an LGB-affirmative manner. It is usually wise for the non-LGB counselor to refrain from such usage because of possible misinterpretations.

In all aspects of practice, counselors must scrupulously avoid heterosexist assumptions and language reflecting those assumptions. As we previously discussed, *heterosexist bias* is defined as "conceptualizing human experience in strictly heterosexual terms and consequently ignoring, invalidating, or derogating homosexual behaviors and sexual orientation, and lesbian, gay, and bisexual relationships and lifestyles" (Herek, Kimmel, Amaro, & Melton, 1991, p. 958). Even with non-LGB clients (or clients who are presumed to be non-LGB) counselors must take care to examine the ways in which the assumption that everyone is heterosexual can influence practice. A common example is assuming the gender of a client's significant other or partner (e.g., with a male client, assuming that the partner is female).

APA's Committee on Gay and Lesbian Concerns (1991) summarized the goals for reducing heterosexual bias in language:

1. *Reducing heterosexual bias and increasing visibility of lesbians, gay men, and bisexual persons.* Unless an author is referring specifically to heterosexual people, writing should be free of heterosexual bias. Ways to increase the visibility of lesbians, gay men, and bisexual persons include the following:
   a. Using examples of lesbians, gay men, and bisexual persons when referring to activities (e.g., parenting, athletic ability) that are erroneously associated only with heterosexual people by many readers.
   b. Referring to lesbians, gay men, and bisexual persons in situations other than sexual relationships. . . .
   c. Omitting discussion of marital status unless legal marital relationships are the subject of the writing. . . .
   d. Referring to sexual and intimate emotional partners with both male and female terms (e.g., "the adolescent males were asked about the age at which they first had a male or female sexual partner").
   e. Using sexual terminology that is relevant to lesbians and gay men as well as bisexual and heterosexual people (e.g., "when did you first engage in sexual activity?" rather than "when did you first have sexual intercourse"?).
   f. Avoiding the assumption that pregnancy may result from sexual activity. . . .
2. *Clarity of expression and avoidance of inaccurate stereotypes about lesbians, gay men, and bisexual persons.* . . . An example such as "Psychologists need training in working with special populations such as lesbians, drug abusers, and alcoholics" is stigmatizing in that it lists a status designation (lesbians) with designations of people being treated.
3. *Comparisons of lesbians and gay men with parallel groups.* . . . For example, contrasting lesbians with the "general public" or "normal women" portrays lesbians as marginal to society. More appropriate comparison groups might be "heterosexual women," "heterosexual men and women," or "gay men and heterosexual women and men." (p. 974)

## Ethics and Ethical Issues

Most professional mental health associations have made it clear in their ethical codes that it is unethical to discriminate against clients with disabilities, older clients, women clients, and LGB clients. For example, the APA *Ethical Principles of Psychologists and Code of Conduct* (2002a; hereafter referred to as the APA *Ethics Code*) contains specific directives to psychologists regarding their treatment of diverse populations. Principle E (Respect for People's Rights and Dignity) states:

> Psychologists are aware of and respect cultural, individual, and role differences, including those based on age, gender, gender identity, race, ethnicity, culture, national origin, religion, sexual orientation, disability, language, and socioeconomic status and consider these factors when working with members of such

groups. Psychologists try to eliminate the effect on their work of biases based on those factors, and they do not knowingly participate in or condone activities of others based upon such prejudices. (APA, 2002a, p. 4)

Several of the standards that make up the APA *Ethics Code* (APA, 2002a) make specific reference to psychologist behavior regarding diverse populations.

Standard 2.01 (b) (Boundaries of Competence): Where scientific or professional knowledge in the discipline of psychology establishes that an understanding of factors associated with age, gender, gender identity, race, ethnicity, culture, national origin, religion, sexual orientation, disability, language, or socioeconomic status is essential for effective implementation of their services or research, psychologists have or obtain the training, experience, consultation, or supervision necessary to ensure the competence of their services, or they make appropriate referrals. (p. 5)

Standard 3.01 (Unfair Discrimination): In their work-related activities, psychologists do not engage in unfair discrimination based on age, gender, gender identity, race, ethnicity, culture, national origin, religion, sexual orientation, disability, socioeconomic status, or any basis proscribed by law. (p. 5)

Standard 3.03 (Other Harassment): Psychologists do not knowingly engage in behavior that is harassing or demeaning to persons with whom they interact in their work based on factors such as those persons' age, gender, gender identity, race, ethnicity, culture, national origin, religion, sexual orientation, disability, language, or socioeconomic status. (p. 6)

Readers may want to consult the ethical codes for the American Counseling Association (www.counseling.org/resources/ethics.htm#ce), Commission on Rehabilitation Counselors (www.iit.edu/departments/csep/PublicWWW/codes/coe/crcc-a.htm), American Association for Marriage and Family Therapy (www.aamft.org/resources/LRMPlan/Ethics/ethicscode2001.htm), American Mental Health Counselors Association (www.amhca.org/ethics.html), National Association of Social Workers (www.socialworkers.org/pubs/code/default.asp), and/or other relevant professional organizations to examine the provisions made for ethical practice with diverse populations.

In addition to the professional/ethical mandates prohibiting discrimination against diverse populations by psychologists, counselors should be aware of the ethical dilemmas they are likely to confront when working with people with disabilities, older people, women, and LGB people. The ethical principles of autonomy, beneficence, nonmaleficence, justice, and fidelity identified by Kitchener (1984) as those "most critical for the evaluation of ethical concerns in psychology" (p. 46), along with the ethical principle of paternalism, will be used to highlight the nature of these dilemmas. Briefly, and in the context of a counseling relationship, *autonomy* refers to the client's freedom of action and freedom of choice. The principle of *beneficence* implies that the counselor should promote the client's welfare, while the principle of *nonmaleficence* mandates that the counselor should do no harm to the client. According to Kitchener (1984), *justice* in the broadest sense means "fairness" and "suggests that equal persons have the right to be treated equally and nonequal persons have a right to be treated differently if the inequality is relevant to the issue in question" (p. 49). *Fidelity* has to do with trustworthiness and in counseling requires the counselor to maintain confidentiality and obtain the client's informed consent to treatment. The principle of *paternalism* requires that counselors care for and safeguard the interests of their clients who cannot do so themselves (Steininger, Newell, & Garcia, 1984).

Ethical dilemmas result when the mandates of ethical principles, codes of ethics, statutory law, common law, and the counselor's own moral standards come into conflict. The thorniest of these potential conflicts may be when counselors hold religious beliefs that conflict with their professional role. For example, to act ethically, counselors must be accepting and affirming toward LGB people. Whether that is possible when a counselor holds strongly to the conviction that homosexuality is a sin is highly questionable (see Nelson, 1985, for discussion of religious perspectives on homosexuality). The counselor might confront an infinite number of specific ethical dilemmas when working with diverse populations; a thorough review of the dilemmas that can arise from conflicts between the ethical principles alone is beyond the scope of this text. Instead, we cite a few conflicts between ethical principles as examples of dilemmas that the counselor may face when working with people with disabilities, older people, women, and LGB people.

Patterson, Patrick, and Parker (2000) surveyed practicing rehabilitation counselors to determine the ethical issues they encountered in promoting choice for their clients with disabilities. The most frequently cited ethical dilemma the respondents encountered was balancing autonomy with beneficence or justice. According to Patterson et al.:

> If a counselor views the vocational choice of an individual as unrealistic, given the individual's intelligence, aptitudes, age, past work experience, or functional limitations, the counselor is faced with honoring a choice that (a) may not be in the individual's best interest (beneficence) or (b) would spend taxpayers' dollars on a decision the counselor cannot support (justice)" (p. 206).

Conversely, justice is not served if a client with a disability is restricted in his or her occupational choices because the counselor judges the accommodations that an employer must make to address the client's functional limitations to be excessive.

Conflicts between the principles of autonomy and paternalism or beneficence frequently create dilemmas for counselors working with older people. The principle of autonomy (and treatment issues related to empowerment) dictates that the older client should be allowed to exercise freedom of choice and action. However, the counselor may feel that due to the client's limited cognitive functioning (as in the case of people with developmental disabilities as well as some older people), the client is not in a position to exercise autonomy in a beneficial way. This situation frequently arises when an older person must make a major life decision that affects not only the person but also family members. Autonomy, beneficence, and paternalism also come into conflict when an older client is living at risk in the community. In this situation, respect for personal freedom is often sacrificed out of concern for the welfare of the client and significant others (Strang, Molloy, & Harrison, 1998).

Schwiebert, Myers, and Dice (2000) examined the current American Counseling Association (ACA) ethical standards and identified three situations in which they do not provide adequate guidelines for working with older people:

(a) older adults with cognitive impairments; (b) older adults who are victims of abuse; and (c) older adults with a terminal illness. The ACA standards simply do not address the issue of informed consent for cognitively impaired older adults. With respect to older adults who are victims of abuse, an ethical dilemma may arise out of conflict between mandated reporting requirements and the older client's fear of institutionalization if abuse by the care provider is reported. And an older adult's desire to end his or her suffering by committing suicide may come in conflict with the ACA ethical expectation that a counselor break confidentiality to prevent a client from harming himself or herself. Clearly, counselors working with older clients need to keep abreast of the current standards, issues, trends, and laws that relate to counseling older adults and constantly weigh the relative merits of the various ethical principles involved.

Cayleff (1986) suggested that the paternalism inherent in the counselor-client relationship reinforces societal values that deny women a full measure of autonomy. "To discern the true autonomy of women, it may be necessary to establish women's own beliefs, as opposed to their socialized, sex-specific propensity to accommodate and attempt to please others" (Cayleff, 1986, p. 346). Counselors who neglect to examine the effects of gender-role socialization on their clients' attitudes and choices often unwittingly serve to reinforce the status quo. Counseling that serves to support limited, sex-specific career and personal goals for women violates the ethical principles of beneficence and nonmaleficence as well as the ethical principle of autonomy.

Paternalism, beneficence, and autonomy also can create ethical dilemmas for the counselor working with gay or lesbian adolescents. Sobocinski (1990) pointed out that adolescence is a transitional period during which a young person moves from dependence to independence, a change that has special relevance for counseling clients around issues of emerging sexuality and acknowledging sexual orientation. After analyzing the competing ethical principles, Sobocinski (1990) concluded:

> There does not appear to be, a priori, reason to declare youth incompetent to consent to treatment dealing with issues of sexual orientation. Because of the inevitability of internalized negative stereotypes and stigma surrounding lesbians and gays in society, one cannot hope that the resolution of gay and lesbian adolescents' emerging sexuality will be facilitated in a manner in which their autonomy is respected until and unless these factors are addressed within therapy. Only when adolescents view their sexuality as acceptable and worthy can they be truly autonomous and free of the coercive, controlling influences of family, peers, and society. (p. 246)

The American Psychological Association's *Guidelines for Psychotherapy with Lesbian, Gay, and Bisexual Clients* (APA, 2000) strongly reinforce this conclusion; Guideline 11 specifically addresses the need for psychologists to understand the unique problems of LGB adolescents.

## Advocate and Change-Agent Roles

A theme throughout this book is that many of minority clients' problems are the result of the oppression they experience and that counselors may need to assist their diverse clients to overcome the effects of oppression. This suggests that counselors need to function as advocates and/or social change agents.

In the advocacy role, the counselor speaks on the client's behalf (Bradley & Lewis, 2000). This role is called for when the client is unable to speak for himself or herself and when the client's grievances are not being addressed by those in a position to effect some needed social or environmental change. This might be the case for older clients with limited English-speaking ability or clients with a disability that limits their ability to speak for themselves. In the change-agent role, the counselor attempts to change the oppressive environment, either by directly or indirectly promoting the empowerment of the oppressed group. Collectively, the advocacy and change-agent roles are sometimes referred to as advocacy, or social justice, counseling.

Kiselica and Robinson (2001) pointed out that counselors need to have certain attributes and skills to provide effective advocacy counseling. These include

> the capacity for commitment and an appreciation for human suffering; nonverbal and verbal communication skills; the ability to maintain a multisystems perspective and to use individual, group, and organizational change strategies; knowledge and use of the media, technology, and the Internet; and assessment and research skills. (pp. 391–392)

In particular, group counseling skills are needed because counselors may need to facilitate empowerment among groups of people who are affected by an oppressive social environment. Organizational change skills are needed to identify and influence organizational policies in need of change. And telecommunications skills are needed because the success of advocacy work often depends on the ability of activists to involve as many people as possible in their cause.

Ruth and Blotzer (1995) suggested that "psychotherapeutic work to empower people with disabilities is in its toddlerhood, a stage of hypothesis-generating and small-scale clinical experimentation" (p. 3). However, a number of authors have described how service providers can serve as advocates and change agents for people with disabilities. With respect to advocacy, the counselor's efforts may be as simple as calling attention to the language used in reference to a person with a disability. Bruce and Christiansen (1988) proposed that therapists "confront persons using pejorative language in their spoken and written communication by politely drawing attention to the negative effects of such language and suggesting preferred word alternatives" (p. 191). Advocacy also may involve extending rights to people with disabilities in the context of therapy. Brown (1995) developed a "Bill of Rights for People with Disabilities in Group Work" that helps to identify rights that people with disabilities should be accorded in various groups (e.g., task groups, psychoeducational groups, counseling groups, psychotherapy groups). Sharing and implementing this "Bill of Rights" is another way in which counselors can advocate for people with disabilities. Psychologists and counselors can also serve as advocates for people with disabilities through both political and research efforts; Kewman (2001) suggested that psychologists "advocate for federal and state research funding to substantiate the benefits of interventions that promote participation in social roles and that reduce environmental barriers" (p. 117).

Cunconan-Lahr and Brotherson (1996) surveyed individuals with disabilities and parents of individuals with disabilities who had taken part in an advocacy training program to identify supports for, and barriers to, subsequent advocacy activities in which they had engaged. Three major themes emerged as supports for successful advocacy: (1) empowering our voices; (2) networking with others; and (3) attitudes of courage and leadership. Empowering our voices consists of knowing the mechanics of communication (persuasion, negotiation, compromise), the persons to target for communication, what content to communicate, and when to time specific communication. Networking includes networking with partners and community to develop a common unity and networking with policymakers to share knowledge and resources. Attitudes of courage and leadership consist of recognizing personal skill such as courage, passion, self-confidence, and risk, and personal resources, such as family and friends needed in advocacy. Cunconan-Lahr and Brotherson also found that time, money, and emotions were barriers to advocacy.

Mitchell and Buchele-Ash (2000) suggested that the most effective way to address maltreatment of people with disabilities is through public policy. The motivation to change public policy often comes out of anger about current conditions, but these authors pointed out that effective communication with policymakers is "planned and organized, then delivered in an assertive but diplomatic manner" (p. 237). Providing honest, accurate information will help advocates build trust with policymakers. Advocates need to be persistent, willing to invest time and effort, and prepared to compromise. Strategies proven effective in influencing policymakers include (a) personal visits, (b) written communication (letters and e-mail messages), (c) telephone contacts, (d) public testimony, (e) media coverage, and (f) ongoing communication (Mitchell & Buchele-Ash, 2000, p. 239).

Counselors also can serve as change agents by empowering families to act on behalf of a family member who has a disability. Munro (1991) has described a step approach model to training families of persons with severe developmental, psychiatric, or neurological disabilities to be effective advocates. Eight common-sense rules define this model:

*Rule # 1: Never use a cannon where a pea-shooter will do!* (p. 2)
The advocate who is overly negative, aggressive, or obnoxious may alienate potential supporters and problem solvers and may do more harm than good.
*Rule # 2: "Get the big picture."* (p. 2)
By gathering facts about all the factors influencing the institutional decision-making process, the advocate is in a good position to establish realistic goals and to develop effective strategies.
*Rule # 3: Time your advocacy strategies carefully.* (p. 3)
To ensure proper timing, the advocate should (1) make sure his or her own motivation and energy level is at its highest before raising a concern; (2) present his or her case when the potential problem solver is most willing and able to listen to the concern; (3) identify needs as early as possible and before a crisis develops.

*Rule # 4: "Use the cards you've been dealt."* (p. 3)
Assess your skills as an advocate and attempt to maximize those skills in the advocacy process. If you are better as a speaker than a writer, present the case verbally and recruit someone else to present the case in writing.

*Rule # 5: Don't "go it alone."* (p. 3)
Recruit other advocates; there is power, strength, and support in group advocacy.

*Rule # 6: Be willing to compromise.* (p. 3)
Politics are inherent in all social institutions. Negotiating a workable compromise can lay the groundwork for future successes.

*Rule # 7: Humanize the concern.* (p. 3)
A personal testimony from the client or the client's family can often be much more effective than a mountain of statistics.

*Rule # 8: Express appreciation and show support to helpful problem solvers.* (p. 3)
Failing to express appreciation to helpful decision makers ultimately may be self-defeating. A pat on the back may help ensure future cooperation.

Similarly, counselors can be advocates and change agents for older people. At the local level, advocacy can simply involve putting older clients and/or their families in touch with existing resources. For example, most communities have an Area Agency on Aging, a private, nonprofit organization for coordinating health care, and advocacy for older adults. For the older adult client who is caring for a parent with disabilities, the Area Agency on Aging can usually put the client in touch with caregiver services, such as adult day care and respite care. For the older client in need of personal assistance, the Agency can usually refer the client to services related to finances, housing, house repair and maintenance, nutrition, and health insurance coverage. Counselors can also serve as advocates by helping educate older clients, their families, health care providers, third-party payers, nursing home administrators, and nursing home staff as to what constitutes quality services and then following up to ensure that these services are provided. They can make their older clients and their clients' families aware of state-administered ombudsman programs that are intended to advocate on behalf of older people (the Comprehensive Older Americans Act Amendment of 1978 mandated that each state designate an ombudsman for older adults at the state level). In cases where older clients have no immediate family and are incapable of initiating efforts on their own behalf, the counselor may need to advocate by making resource contacts for the client. The Agency can usually put older clients in need of social contact and/or meaningful activity in touch with social centers and volunteer programs for older adults. At the community level, the counselor might organize older adults into self-help groups to address a particular concern or bring about needed social change. At the public policy level, mental health workers can join various aging advocacy organizations and participate in collective efforts to influence legislation affecting older people (e.g., American Association of Retired People, 2002; National Council on Aging, 2001; National Senior Citizens Law Center, 2002). Some organizations, such as the National Senior Citizens Law Center, even offer training in advocacy. The key to all these forms of advocacy is knowing what resources are available at the local, state, and national levels for assisting older people.

In making the case for gender-aware or feminist approaches to counseling, we have already implicitly suggested a social advocacy approach to counseling women. Because so many of the concerns female clients present to counselors are heavily influenced by their gender, we argue that counselors perform a disservice to their female clients if the counselor is not sensitive to gender influences and gender inequities. However, a wide range of effective options exists to work with gender in counseling.

The earliest forms of feminist counseling were the grassroots consciousness raising (CR) groups of the early 1970s, which emerged out of the feminist movement. These were not originally conceptualized as "therapy" groups, but rather as a political force; participants came together to share their perceptions and discuss their experiences as women, with the common goal of social change (Enns, 1997). However, it soon became clear that CR participants often reported improvements akin to those we expect from counseling, such as enhanced self-esteem, increased autonomy, and other personal changes, as well as modifications in interpersonal relationships.

> As the therapeutic benefits of CR groups became apparent to women, they were sometimes recommended as an adjunct to therapy. . . . Women therapists, who became members of CR groups, were changed and radicalized through their interactions with other women and expressed interest in using their skills to combat oppression in their professional work. . . . [Therapy] groups that were modeled after CR experiences . . . became the preferred modality for a substantial number of feminist therapists. . . . Groups were seen as an effective antidote to negative gender socialization in that women could gain power by practicing skills in a safe environment. (Enns, 1993, pp. 6–7)

Gradually, as the limitations of CR groups as the only form of feminist assistance to women became apparent, other methods of feminist and gender-aware therapy emerged focusing more on the personal issues and concerns of women. Today there are a wide range of feminist approaches, some still intimately tied to political activism, others less overtly activist but retaining some of the basic principles of the earlier feminist CR groups.

Although feminism simply refers to the advocacy of equality between women and men, several feminist philosophies have been articulated. Each adopts a slightly different stance on the presumed reasons for gender inequality and the manner in which inequalities and gender influences ought to be addressed. Feminist therapy, therefore, is not a monolithic entity; feminist therap*ies* exist, corresponding to different feminist philosophies, each suggesting somewhat different strategies for effecting social change within and outside of counseling (Enns, 1997; Enns & Hackett, 1990; Hackett, Enns, & Zetzer, 1992). Some of the major traditions within feminist thought have been the liberal, radical, socialist, Marxist, cultural, and woman of color feminist philosophies. Of these, the liberal and radical feminist philosophies have been drawn from most heavily by feminist therapists:

Liberal feminist writers emphasize current inequalities in educational opportunities and civil rights, focusing on the elimination of these inequalities, especially through legal and educational reform, as the mechanism for achieving a sex-fair society. . . . Consequently, the liberal feminist counselor focuses on expanding clients' awareness of gender role socialization, social barriers, and discrimination, in the context of exploring personal goals and options. Radical feminist theorists . . . see sexism as the fundamental oppression. Radical feminist theorists all share the assumptions that historically women were the first oppressed group, that women's oppression is the most widespread and pervasive form of oppression, and that women's oppression is the hardest to eradicate and cannot be removed by other social changes such as legal or educational reform. (Enns & Hackett, 1990, p. 34)

One of the fundamental differences between the liberal and radical perspectives in counseling is that the radical feminist counselor will be much more active in assisting clients to identify social barriers and structural inequalities and will be more likely to encourage (though not coerce) the client to engage in external change efforts and political action. The liberal feminist counselor will be more likely to support, but not necessarily actively encourage, clients' social change efforts. Although these philosophical distinctions are helpful in understanding the varieties of feminist approaches to counseling, we must also caution the readers that, in real life, the distinctions are often blurred.

What these approaches all have in common is an emphasis on empowering women: The social construction of gender [and feminist therapy] relocates women's problems from individual and internal to societal and external. The feminist construction of gender redefines the nature of women's and men's relationships in terms of the expression and maintenance of power. Emergent client populations were "discovered" where problems were never thought to exist [e.g., sexual abuse, sexual harassment, eating disorders]. The challenge of these new client populations stimulated the development of theories, research, and procedures to address their concerns. The combined efforts of women's groups in both the lay and professional communities have resulted in a new agenda for women's mental health. (Worell & Remer, 1992, p. 4)

In essence, counselors who address and explore gender socialization, gender-related beliefs and constraints, and structural influences on and barriers to women, by default engage in a form of social advocacy for all women. The reader is referred to chapters 12–14 in this book and to Worell and Remer (2003) for coverage of a range of feminist approaches to empowering women.

Social advocacy for lesbians, gay men, and bisexual women and men is also necessary and encouraged by the major professional associations:

In 1975, the American Psychological Association (APA) took a strong stance regarding bias toward lesbians and gay men, resolving that "homosexuality per se implies no impairment in judgment, reliability, or general social and vocational abilities." . . . The APA urged psychologists "to take the lead in removing the stigma of mental illness long associated with homosexual orientations." (Garnets et al., 1991, p. 964)

Despite this exhortation, issued over 25 years ago, ongoing discrimination against gay people underscores the necessity of continuing efforts on the part of counselors and psychologists in educating ourselves, our clients, and the public at large. Our professional organizations have been involved in public policy debates on issues of concern to gay men and lesbians; for example, APA issued a review of the scientific research supporting lifting the ban on gays in the military and has also issued briefs on other civil rights issues of concern to gay people (Herek, 1993; Melton, 1989). More recently, APA (2000) published the *Guidelines for Psychotherapy with Lesbian, Gay, and Bisexual Clients,* an invaluable guide to LGB affirmative counseling and therapy. Yet therapists and counselors themselves have not universally surmounted the deeply ingrained negative attitudes toward gay people. For example, in the 1990s it was reported that although 99% of service providers reported having counseled at least one gay client (that they knew of), the majority (58%) were also personally aware of incidents of biased or inappropriate treatment of gay clients "including cases in which practitioners defined lesbians or gay men as 'sick' and in need of change, and instances where a client's sexual orientation distracted a therapist from treating a person's central problem" (Garnets et al., 1991, p. 970). Clients' LGB orientation is still too often either viewed as the cause of psychological difficulties or ignored totally, effectively blinding counselors/therapists to the complexities and social context of their clients' lives (APA, 2000). Clearly, social change advocacy for LGB clients must begin with each individual counselor. Our earlier review of language usage is a starting point, and the chapters on LGB affirmative counseling (chapters 15 and 17) contain many suggestions useful to the counselor attempting to grapple with anti-LGB bias.

However, social advocacy must eventually extend beyond one's own attitudes and can take many forms. For example, Garnets et al. (1991), in their discussion of exemplary practice with LGB clients, stated that "a therapist is familiar with the needs and treatment issues of gay male and lesbian clients, and uses relevant mental health, educational, and gay male and lesbian community resources" (p. 970). This type of behavior with individual clients alone constitutes a form of advocacy: "A gay man, a client of mine, age 20, told me he particularly appreciated my willingness to gather information about coming out, including meeting with campus representatives, which he was not yet ready to do, having just concluded in therapy he was gay" (Garnets et al., 1991, p. 970). At some point, however, counselors must begin to engage in more visible advocacy efforts. Recommendations for exemplary practice with gay clients also include public advocacy:

> A therapist recognizes the importance of educating professionals, students, supervisees, and others about gay male and lesbian issues and actively counters misinformation or bias about lesbians and gay men: [for example] A colleague told me of how they changed the intake forms at the agency to include gay/lesbian and space for "significant other" identification instead of spouse. [And] I observed a colleague, at a case conference, ask the presenter if he had asked his single male patient about homosexual experience. The presenter had assumed that because he had never had a girlfriend or been married, he was asexual. (Garnets et al., 1991, p. 970)

## COUNSELOR TRAINING

One justification for training counselors to work with diverse populations is their representation among users of counseling and psychological services. As suggested in chapter 1, women alone make up the majority of clients being seen by counselors and psychologists. Older people also represent a significant (and growing) proportion of the population, as do LGB people and people with disabilities. It is imperative that future counselors receive training that prepares them to work with these populations.

Justification for training counselors and psychologists to work with special populations is also provided by the professional and ethical standards of the major professional counseling and psychology associations. For example, Standard 2.01 of the APA *Ethics Code* (2002a) makes it clear that psychologists are to seek training in order to ensure that they can work with diverse populations. Furthermore, the APA *Guidelines and Principles for Accreditation of Programs in Psychology* (APA, 2002b; hereafter referred to as the *Accreditation Guidelines*) includes the following characteristics that programs require to be eligible for accreditation:

> The program engages in actions that indicate respect for and understanding of cultural and individual diversity. . . . The phrase "cultural and individual diversity" refers to diversity with regard to personal and demographic characteristics. These include, but are not limited to, age, color, disabilities, ethnicity, gender, language, national origin, race, religion, sexual orientation, and social economic status. (p. 7).

> The program has and implements a thoughtful and coherent plan to *provide students with relevant knowledge and experiences* [italics added] about the role of cultural and individual diversity in psychological phenomena as they relate to the science and practice of professional psychology. (p. 12)

Furthermore, the APA *Accreditation Guidelines* (APA, 2002b) also mandate that programs not discriminate against diverse populations in their student and faculty recruitment, retention, and development processes:

> Respect for and understanding of cultural and individual diversity is reflected in the program's policies for the recruitment, retention, and development of faculty and students, and in its curriculum and field placements. The program has nondiscriminatory policies and operating conditions, and it avoids any actions that would restrict program access or completion on grounds that are irrelevant to success in graduate training or the profession. (p. 7)

Similar statements can be found in the *Code of Ethics and Standards of Practice* of the American Counseling Association and the accreditation requirements of the Council for Accreditation of Counseling and Related Activities (CACREP, 2001). It is clear from these statements that training counselors to work with diverse populations is not only a desired function of counselor training programs, it is a mandated one.

We believe that to train counselors to work with diverse populations, three components are needed: (1) a faculty sensitive to diversity issues; (2) a curriculum that is designed to train counselors to work with special populations; and (3) students who are receptive to such training. All three are essential ingredients; the absence of any one of these components will seriously jeopardize the effectiveness of the training program.

## Faculty Sensitivity to Diversity Issues

Although the major professional organizations require that counselors and psychologists recognize differences among people and that accredited training programs provide training in client diversity, they have not addressed the issue of faculty development and renewal with respect to diversity. Unfortunately, many professors in counselor and psychologist training programs were themselves trained before current professional and accreditation standards were in place mandating training for counseling of diverse populations. This places the responsibility for designing curricula related to client diversity in the hands of individuals who often have no systematic training on the topic. It seems clear that faculty must actively seek out development and renewal activities to acquire both the attitudes and knowledge needed to train counselors and psychologists to work with diverse populations. Further, it is unreasonable to assume that graduate students will acquire the necessary sensitivity to and competency with client differences if the counselor training faculty cannot model these attributes.

> An alarming number of heterosexist and stereotypical comments made by instructors, seen in textbooks, and heard from supervisors in practicums and internship have been documented; some of these vividly illustrate that students continue to have interactions with psychologists who believe, teach, and practice on the basis of outdated and empirically unsupported notions that homosexuality and bisexuality are inherently pathological. (Phillips, 2000, p. 338)

Such findings do not promote confidence that minimal standards, for example, the absence of homophobia and heterosexism, are present in many of our training programs, let alone that they meet professional guidelines, such as that the climate in counseling programs should be supportive for LGB students and promote LGB affirmative attitudes and behaviors among novice practitioners.

Although it is important for counseling professors trained over the past 50 years to develop sensitivity to diversity issues through their own professional development and renewal, it is imperative that future faculty appointments include sensitivity to diversity issues such as a selection criterion. Because faculty serve as professional models for the students with whom they work, we believe that sensitivity to diversity issues should be one of the top priorities in selecting counselor educators. Faculty and administrators responsible for selecting new faculty should examine each candidate's background to determine familiarity with diversity issues and include questions related to sensitivity in this area in any interviewing that is done.

In addition to selecting faculty who are sensitive to diversity issues, every effort should be made to ensure that people with disabilities, women, and LGB people are represented among the faculty proportionate to their representation in the general population (most counselor training programs already include a diversity of ages). As indicated earlier, the APA (2002b) and CACREP (2001) accreditation guidelines require that accredited programs recruit, retain, and develop faculty as well as students from diverse populations. Research support for this requirement was provided by Bluestone, Stokes, and Kuba (1996), who found that female and ethnic minority faculty provided superior coverage of diversity issues in their courses compared with European American males. This suggests that faculty who are themselves minorities are more likely than nonminorities to address issues of diversity. Although data on faculty members with disabilities and sexual minority faculty are generally not available, data on female representation among counselor education faculties is not encouraging.

Anderson and Rawlins (1985) reported that in 1983, although slightly over 50% of the new Ph.D.s and Ed.D.s in counselor education were women, only 22.5% of the faculty in counselor education programs were women and most of these were in the lower ranks. They suggested a concentrated effort was needed to recruit, select, and advance women in counselor education. We believe, despite increases of women among faculty ranks in recent years, that this recommendation is still valid and applies to faculty members with disabilities and lesbian, gay, and bisexual faculty as well. In the area of recruitment for faculty positions, Anderson and Rawlins suggested networking to identify qualified women applicants and including women, and we would add women of color, on selection committees. In the area of selection they suggested that screening committees be made familiar with discriminatory questions that are prohibited by law and that faculty discuss the "invisible discrimination of perceptual bias." To support the professional development of female faculty of all ethnic backgrounds, these authors suggested research support groups, academic mentors, and selective committee involvement for female faculty. Each of these suggestions can be generalized to the recruitment, selection, and support of faculty with disabilities and LGB faculty as well.

Those university counseling centers, Veterans Administration centers, and mental health hospitals that participate in training counselors and psychologists through pre- and postdoctoral internships should also take steps to ensure that their training staff is sensitive to and knowledgeable about client diversity. Efforts should be made to expose all interns to the full range of client diversity seen at each agency.

## Counselor Training Curriculum

Before examining suggestions for course content that address diverse populations, we review the current status of counselor and psychologist training for work with people with disabilities, older people, women, and LGB people and the training models that have been proposed for providing this training.

**Training Currently Provided**    To ensure that counselors are trained to effectively counsel clients from diverse populations, counselor training programs need to focus attention on these groups as part of their curricula. Although most counselor education programs now integrate some training on gender and ethnic diversity into their curriculum, problems regarding inadequate attention to gender issues and feminist counseling in training programs remain (Worell & Remer, 2003). Furthermore, Bluestone et al. (1996) found that training for other types of diversity is much less likely to be integrated into required coursework; they found that sexual orientation and physical disability were the topics least likely to be covered. Olkin (1999) surveyed APA-accredited clinical psychology programs in 1989 and 1999 and found that there were actually fewer programs offering disability courses (11%) in 1999 than in 1989 (24%).

Some progress has been made with regard to coursework in gerontological counseling in ACA programs. Myers (1995) reviewed the 20-year history of the gerontological counseling specialty and cited the following five outcomes as evidence that "gerontological counseling is well established as a specialty within the counseling profession" (Myers, 1995, p. 146): (1) five national projects on aging sponsored by ACA, (2) an ACA division with a focus on the adult years (Association for Adult Development and Aging), (3) CACREP (ACA accrediting agency) accreditation of programs in community counseling that specialize in gerontological counseling, (4) NBCC (ACA certification agency) establishment of a national certification in gerontological counseling, and (5) identification of gerontological competencies for counselors (Myers & Sweeney, 1990). However, she also acknowledged that only about one third of all counselor training programs offered coursework to prepare counselors to work with older people and that strong leadership at the national level and active advocacy at all levels will be needed if the specialty is to be maintained and enhanced.

A similar lack of training is evident among clinical and counseling psychologists. Hinrichsen (2000) surveyed psychology externs and interns at a medical center and found that only 41% had any coursework in adult development or geriatric mental health. He also found disconcerting gaps in their knowledge about mental health and aging. Qualls, Segal, Norman, Niederehe, and Gallagher-Thompson (2002) surveyed a representative sample of practitioner members of the APA and found "very few of the practitioners providing services to older adults had formal training in geropsychology, with the vast majority relying on informally acquired clinical experience or on-the-job training" (p. 440).

Similarly, very few counselor or psychology training programs (other than rehabilitation counseling programs) offer coursework related to clients with disabilities. Leigh, Corbett, Gutman, and Morere (1996) pointed out that psychology programs appear to be ignoring deafness altogether, even though the ADA mandates that "anyone operating a business of any size or providing services, including psychological services in any setting (such as hospitals, clinics, and private or home offices) must anticipate providing accommodations for clients with disabilities, including those whose disability affects communication accessibility" (p. 364).

Graduate students with disabilities enrolled in regular counselor education and psychology programs may feel marginalized, given the little attention given during their training to people with disabilities. Furthermore, these students are often presented with accessibility barriers when they leave campus for external practica or internship sites. Olkin, Schwartz, and Bourg (2001, cited in Olkin, 2002) found that

70% of externship and internship sites had had no employees or students with physical or sensor disabilities in the past 3 years, 50% had at least one floor that was not accessible by elevator, 20% lacked handicapped parking, and 25% had no wheelchair ramps. Also, only 16% of external practica and internship sites had Braille signage, only 38% had emergency alarms with both visible and audible warnings, and 78% had no TTY (teletype phone device for deaf and hearing callers). Hauser, Maxwell-McCaw, Leigh, and Gutman (2000) described discriminatory experiences that two of the authors experienced as deaf students applying for psychology internships in 1998, many of which violated antidiscrimination policies of the ADA. Clearly, training programs are providing inadequate preparation for counselor trainees to work with clients with disabilities as well as fieldwork sites that are inaccessible to counselor trainees with disabilities.

Very little research or attention has been devoted to coverage of LGB issues in counselor preparation programs (Iasenza, 1989). Graham, Rawlings, Halpern, and Hermes (1984), in a study of practicing therapists' attitudes, knowledge, concerns, and counseling approaches with lesbians and gay men, reported a strong need for additional training in this area. Therapists were generally uninformed about the literature on gay lifestyles, many held inaccurate beliefs about gay people, and a significant minority (37%) stated that they would work with clients on the goal of changing sexual orientation (Graham et al., 1984). McDonald (1982) found misleading information and misrepresentation of data on gay people in a survey of introductory psychology textbooks, a finding that does not bode well for the undergraduate preparation of students entering graduate programs in mental health. Buhrke (1989a) found that almost one third of female counseling psychology students reported no exposure to gay or lesbian issues during their graduate experience; 70% were in programs where no faculty were engaged in research on gay issues; and almost one half of the respondents had not seen any gay or lesbian clients. More recent studies indicate that students and recent graduates from counseling and other mental health programs

> believe that their programs have not trained them adequately to work with LGB clients or perceive heterosexism in their education. Mental health practitioners, including psychologists and psychologists in training, have reported feeling less competent and less well prepared to work effectively with lesbian and gay clients, . . . and even less well prepared to work with bisexual clients. (Phillips, 2000, pp. 337–338)

Nor is the problem confined to courses and practicum experiences. "Students also perceive heterosexism in their experiences with research in their programs, including both lack of support and overt discouragement from faculty from pursuing LGB research interests" (Phillips, 2000, p. 338).

Although inclusion of training for competence with diverse populations is beginning to have an impact on counselor training programs, clearly actual training of counselors to work with diversity populations still lags behind professional and accreditation standards that mandate such training.

**Training Models**   Although there is general agreement that training must be provided, there is disagreement about the kind of training model that is most effective as a means of sensitizing counselors to work with special populations. Some authors have argued for specialized training related to specific groups, and others have argued for changes in the basic curriculum. Copeland (1982) identified four models for training counselors to work with special populations, the separate course model, area of concentration model, interdisciplinary model, and integrated model.

In the *separate course* approach, information about special populations is provided in one course. Usually this course would have as its goals the development of sensitivity to the experience of being a minority person, knowledge about each group discussed, and competency in adapting counseling strategies to the groups studied. The separate course can focus on only one population, in which case a number of separate courses must be offered. Or the course can focus on the effects of discrimination across all minority groups (a human rights approach). In response to the need to increase student awareness, knowledge, and skills for counseling special populations, many counselor education programs have started to offer separate courses for each group. Margolis and Rungta (1986), addressing the issue of separate courses for ethnic groups, offered the following criticisms of this approach:

1. "Adding more and more special courses to an existing program may be feasible because of budget constraints, the total number of courses that can be imposed on students, and availability of expert faculty." (p. 643)
2. A proliferation of separate courses for special groups may accent differences among them and lead to a separate set of standards and strategies for each group that in turn may lead to unequal treatment.
3. By focusing on one characteristic we may fail to recognize the total person. If we focus on a person's ethnicity, sex, age, socioeconomic class, sexual orientation, or disability, we may fail to recognize important other characteristics or the unique combination of characteristics.
4. Another consequence of providing separate courses for each group is that it may limit the ability of counselor trainees to transfer their learning from one population to another. Margolis and Rungta argued that the common experiences of discrimination among minority groups suggest that some course content should be generalized across groups.

In the *area of concentration* model, students are offered several courses and perhaps a practicum that focuses on special populations. These courses are either part of an elective concentration within a larger program or the entire program is identified as having a focus on a special population. In the former case it is only helpful for some of the students and in the latter case, only those students enrolled in programs that make the commitment to resources for this model benefit. Also, those programs that focus on one client population, say older clients, may fail to provide proper training in other types of diversity.

In the *interdisciplinary* model, the program makes use of courses that are taught in other departments in order to provide an area of concentration. The interdisciplinary model appears to be inherent in the criteria for certification as a national certified gerontological counselor. The National Board for Certified

Counselors requires three graduate courses in gerontology (along with an intern-ship in a gerontological setting and two years of professional gerontological counseling experience) for certification as a gerontological counselor (Myers, 1992). The interdisciplinary approach, assumes, of course, that such courses are available through other departments on the same campus. It also assumes the co-operation of other units on campus.

As applied to diverse populations, the *integrated* model incorporates infor-mation about people with disabilities, older people, women, and LGB people in all counselor training courses. For example, a human development course would address the sociopsychological development of people with disabilities, older people, women, and LGB people. Similarly, a vocational psychology course would address the special vocational and avocational needs of women and people with disabilities and the employment problems experienced by all four groups. Certainly all ethics courses should contain specific content about the legal and ethical dilemmas and issues encountered in counseling the four groups. The inte-grated model was selected by CACREP in developing recently adopted standards for training in gerontological counseling (Myers, 1992). This approach requires that all the faculty be familiar with diversity issues that are related to their courses and be willing to incorporate this content in their courses. Furthermore, the APA *Accreditation Guidelines* (APA, 2002b) appear to mandate that training related to diverse populations be integrated into all courses in accredited programs.

**Curriculum Content**    Earlier authors have identified curriculum content needed to train counselors who will work with one of the four diverse populations discussed in this book. Most of these authors have recommended either an inte-grated or separate course approach. Some identify specific content that should be included in the curriculum; others focus on process more than content.

Most multicultural training models suggest that the first step toward becoming a multiculturally sensitive counselor is for counselors (or counselor trainees) to ex-amine their own racial/ethnic biases (Atkinson, Morten, & Sue, in press). The same is true with regard to becoming more sensitive to the needs and experiences of all diverse populations. Hays (1996) created the acronym ADRESSING to emphasize the need for counselors and counselors-in-training to address their biases with re-spect to age, disability, religion, ethnicity, social status, sexual orientation, indige-nous heritage, national origin, and gender diversity. The ADRESSING model de-scribed by Hays can be used to facilitate this process. Multicultural advocates who are concerned that combining ethnicity and culture with other forms of diversity will take away from multicultural competence should be reassured by Bluestone et al.'s (1996) finding that courses receiving the highest rating for other types of di-versity also received high ratings for multicultural content, suggesting that focusing on other types of diversity did not detract from multicultural competence.

As we suggested earlier, another major step that counselors and psycholo-gists can take toward becoming more credible and effective helpers is to eliminate from their vocabularies imprecise and stereotypic language with respect to mi-norities. However, can a course designed to teach the use of appropriate termi-nology have an impact on actual language usage? To answer that question with respect to people with disabilities, Byrd et al. (1991) randomly assigned 107 students to hear either a lecture on appropriate language usage when referring to persons with disabilities or to a lecture on cultural divergence. Based on the results of a test administered 1 week after the examination, the authors concluded that "students do change their writing behavior, when making reference to persons with disabilities, if they receive a short training module on appropriate use of language" (Byrd et al., 1991, p. 41). Although it can be hypothesized that appropriate use of written language will generalize to oral language, the authors suggested that oral language may require consistent reinforcement to produce consistency in language usage.

Lofaro (1982) suggested that although counselor education curricula may need to be modified to prepare counselors to work with disability-related concerns, new coursework may not be the most desirable alternative. Rather, exercises and course content may be integrated into the existing curriculum. Lofaro went on to describe a number of activities that could be included in basic counseling courses to generate sensitivity to disability-related issues and to develop competence in working with clients who have disabilities. Filer (1982) also described a number of activities that could be integrated into existing counselor education courses to better prepare high school counselors for working with students with disabilities. These activities are designed to (1) motivate counselor trainees to work with children with disabilities, (2) teach counselor trainees the skills and resources needed to work with children with disabilities, (3) teach counselor trainees how to promote social interaction between students with disabilities and other students, and (4) teach counselor trainees how to help students with disabilities optimize their mainstreaming experience. Some evidence indicates that counseling trainees who receive training in disability issues develop a sensitivity to those issues: Kemp and Mallinckrodt (1996) found that counselors who received no training on disability issues were more likely than counselors who received such training to focus on extraneous issues and less likely to focus on appropriate themes for a sexual abuse survivor with a disability.

The outcomes of several court cases since the passage of the Americans with Disabilities Act suggest that counselors, psychologists, and other mental health workers may need to take courses in American Sign Language (ASL) in the future. Raifman and Vernon (1996) reviewed three state and federal court cases and concluded that "recent ADA court activity appears to have the consequence of requiring psychologists to become fluent in ASL before offering psychotherapy and psychodiagnostic services to deaf clients" (p. 377). They recommended that APA establish a subspecialty for service training and in-service training that will help psychologists learn ASL and recognize the special culture of deafness and its psychological implications.

Myers and Blake (1986) described how course content related to counseling older people can be integrated into all counselor training courses, employing a model that could be generalized to other special populations as well. They suggested that the nine core areas of study and supervised experience included in the *Accreditation Manual* of CACREP "provide an adequate and appropriate framework for the incorporation of specialized course work on counseling older persons into a counselor education curriculum" (Myers & Blake, 1986, p. 139). Myers and Blake provided a number of examples of aging-related content that could be included in the core areas of human growth and development, social and cultural foundations, the helping relationship, group dynamics, career development, appraisal of individuals, research and professional orientation. Table 18.1 summarizes the course content these authors suggested for these nine CACREP core areas. They proposed that an integrated model is the best means of ensuring that all students learn about aging and is most adaptable for a program training

**TABLE 18.1**   Course Content on Counseling Older People by Core Areas of Study from CACREP* *Accreditation Standards*[1]

| Core | Course Content |
| --- | --- |
| Human Growth and Development | Life-span development<br>Theories of aging |
| Social and Cultural Foundations | Older persons as a minority group<br>Older women<br>Changing population demography and increased numbers of older people<br>Leisure and lifestyle of older people |
| The Helping Relationship | Impact of counselor and client age on interactions<br>Ageist attitudes and beliefs<br>Theories of personality and aging<br>Techniques for use with older persons (such as life review therapy) |
| Group Dynamics, Processes, and Counseling | Pros and cons of groups for older people<br>Structural versus unstructured groups<br>Life review therapy groups<br>Educational and guidance groups<br>Support groups |
| Lifestyle and Career Development | Sources of occupational and educational information for older people<br>Retirement adjustments<br>Use of leisure time |
| Appraisal of Individuals | Validity of tests with older people<br>Special techniques for testing older people<br>Instruments for use with older people<br>Renorming instruments for use with older people |
| Research and Evaluation | Obtaining access to older subjects<br>Grant funding in aging<br>Accommodating needs of older persons as research subjects |
| Professional Orientation | Professional associations in gerontology<br>Gerontology certificate programs<br>Roles of gerontological counselors<br>Legal and ethical issues in gerontological counseling |
| Supervised Experiences | Aging network agencies<br>Geriatric mental health hospitals and agencies<br>Settings where older persons comprise a large segment of the clientele |

*CACREP = Council of Counseling and Related Activities
[1]Adapted from Myers & Blake (1986, pp. 139–140).

counselors for a variety of settings. Myers (1995) identified competencies that counselors who plan to specialize in working with older clients should have. Myers recommended specialized courses taught on an interdisciplinary basis as the best approach to training counselors to work with older clients as a specialty.

Thomas and Martin (1992) cited efficiency and effectiveness as reasons why counselors should be trained to run groups for their older clients. They pointed out that to train counselors to run reality orientation, remotivation, psychotherapy, reminiscing, and other types of groups for older clients, counselor educators need to "bridge the training gaps by combining and connecting . . . three separate professional standards" (p. 57). The three training standards to which they refer are the standards for specialists in group work (Association for Specialists in Group Work, 1991), the standards for gerontological counselors (Myers & Sweeney, 1990), and the standards for counselors in general (CACREP, 1990). Agresti (1992) provided a rationale for the inclusion of specialized training in ethics for gerontological counselors. He cited the variability among states concerning the reporting of abuse of older people, older adult ability to participate in decisions regarding his or her care, and the complex questions surrounding long-term care as examples of how counseling with older adults may present unique ethical issues. Some evidence has been found that a geropsychology fieldwork experience can positively affect students' attitudes about older people. Hinrichsen and McMeniman (2002) found that students who completed a geropsychology practicum or internship had more knowledge of geriatric mental health issues, fewer negative attitudes toward older adults, and more interest in geropsychology than did students without such a placement.

Similarly, several authors (Buhrke, 1989b; Burhrke & Douce, 1991; Phillips, 2000; Norton, 1982) have offered suggestions for integrating current information on gay people into the core counselor training curriculum. Beginning with the introductory course, counselor educators should ensure that if a course in the psychology of sexuality is offered it contain current, nonhomophobic information. Such a course should be not relied on as the sole training experience related to LGB issues, however, and current issues on LGB people should be worked into all courses in counseling education. According to Norton (1982):

> There is not a course in counselor education in which gay issues are not appropriate. It is better that the topic appear as but a minor part of all courses, so that students get a feel for the pervasiveness of the gay group, but also a feel for the fact that this special population is really an integral part of the entire population. (p. 211)

Graham et al. (1984) offered a useful overview of the content on gay people that ought to be included in counselor preparation programs. Therapists and counselors need information about (1) lesbian/gay lifestyles and social networks; (2) homophobia and heterosexism; (3) self-esteem in lesbian and gay male clients, especially low self-esteem as a function of internalized homophobia; and (4) appropriate and inappropriate therapeutic goals, that is, gay-affirmative approaches. There are now numerous books, journal articles, and special issues of journals that are rich sources of information to inform course development, including the *Handbook of Counseling and Psychotherapy with Lesbian, Gay, and Bisexual Clients* (Perez, DeBord, & Bieschke, 2000) and the *Guidelines for*

*Psychotherapy with Lesbian, Gay, and Bisexual Clients* (APA, 2000). Phillips (2000) presented more detailed information about coverage of LGB issues in courses across the curriculum but also argued that every program should have a stand-alone course on LGB issues as well.

In terms of specific courses, introductory courses often include an overview of client concerns and populations; this is a good place to begin to introduce discussions of lesbians, gay men, and bisexuals, for example, through case examples (Norton, 1982). Glenn and Russell (1986) suggested that training experiences that include ambiguous-sex clients can be used in existing courses to assess and confront subtle forms of heterosexual bias. Counseling theories must also be examined for heterosexist bias, for example, Freud's views on heterosexual development (Buhrke, 1989b); heterosexual bias in assessment and diagnosis should also be an important aspect of any testing or measurement course. In group counseling courses, gay issues may be introduced in discussions of screening for group participation (e.g., a struggling gay adolescent in high school would probably not be a good candidate for a general counseling group), and gay support groups should be addressed (Buhrke & Douce, 1991). LGB men and women experience unique career concerns that warrant coverage in career development courses, for example, occupational stereotypes, employment discrimination, dual career issues, and the work-nonwork interface (Buhrke, 1989b; Phillips, 2000).

LGB issues should be incorporated into multicultural courses in two ways: (1) counselors must be sensitive to the unique experiences and special needs of gay people of color, for example, the multiple and interactive sources of oppression experienced by lesbian African Americans; and (2) counselors need to develop an understanding of gay men, lesbians, and bisexuals as minorities in this society (Buhrke, 1989b; Phillips, 2000). And, of course, LGB issues should be well integrated into the practicum sequence. In prepracticum, students should be exposed via role plays to the range of issues experienced by gay and lesbian clients (Buhrke & Douce, 1991). In practicum, attention to the effects of heterosexism on the counseling process and building gay-affirmative counseling skills is vital (Buhrke & Douce, 1991). Buhrke and Douce (1991) also provided recommendations for incorporating gay issues into predoctoral internship training.

The promotion of gender equity in counselor training, and creating a program that will equip counselors with the skills to engage in gender-aware counseling, requires an in-depth knowledge of the literature on gender along with an examination of some fundamental beliefs about women (Fassinger, 2000; Good, Gilbert, & Scher, 1990). It may also require changes in almost all aspects of most training programs. The Division 17 guidelines for counseling/psychotherapy for women have provided the basis for the content that must be integrated into counselor education programs (Fitzgerald & Nutt, 1986). In addition, Worell and Remer (2003) offered a detailed overview of the literature on counseling women and provide recommendations for revamping training programs.

Introductory counseling courses might address attitude biases, including sexism and homophobia, and contain information about gender and gender-role issues in counseling; students can be introduced to the clinical concerns of special importance to women, for example, depression, eating disorders, sexual abuse, and sexual assault (Worell & Remer, 2003). Theory courses ought to include attention to feminist critiques of counseling theories, new developments in the psychology of women, and the current literature on counseling women (e.g., Enns, 2000; Fassinger, 2000). Assessment courses should include an analysis of the gender bias literature; standardized tests should be critically examined for gender bias; and gender bias in clinical assessment and diagnosis can be introduced. Feminist alternatives to traditional assessment, for example, gender-role analysis, might be included (Hackett & Lonborg, 1993). Courses in career development ought to encompass gender bias in career development theories, gender-role stereotyping, the changing roles of men and women, and the special career counseling needs of women (e.g., dual career and multiple role counseling) (Walsh & Osipow, 1993). Practicum supervisors themselves must be conversant with the literature to be able to assist counselor trainees in addressing gender issues in the counseling process, and to provide training in gender-aware and feminist approaches to counseling (Cook, 1993; Worell & Remer, 2003). At a more global level, Chin and Russo (1997) identified the key principles for a feminist curriculum, each of which has implications for curriculum content and skills: diversity, egalitarianism and empowerment, self-determination, complexity, connection, and social action.

**Our Views on Training Models and Course Content**   We believe that all counselors and other mental health providers should receive training to work with diverse populations, particularly the four populations discussed in this book. Furthermore, we believe a combination of the integrated and separate course models is the most effective way to train counselors to work with diverse populations. Ideally, issues related to people with disabilities, older people, women, and LGB people should be integrated into all counselor training courses. As suggested earlier, however, this requires that each faculty member is sensitive to and knowledgeable about these special populations. Because many professors in counselor training programs were educated before training in diversity was mandated, we feel that a separate course will be needed to supplement attempts to integrate diversity issues into all counselor training courses for at least the next decade.

We also recognize that the resources available to a particular program will probably dictate which model is followed. Some programs, due to a unique mix of faculty, may find their faculty resources best suit an area of concentration model. It is important that the faculty of each program assess their resources and adopt an appropriate model for training counselors to work with diverse populations.

We believe a counselor training program designed to prepare counselors to work with diverse clients will include three components: (1) experiences designed to confront students with their own biases and to sensitize them to the discrimination minority populations experience; (2) course content designed to familiarize students with the lifestyle and mental health needs of diverse populations; and (3) training in counseling strategies that are most effective with minority groups. As suggested earlier, we believe these components should be included in a separate class on diverse populations, as well as integrated into all the courses in the counselor training program.

We suggest that each counselor training program develop a master plan for ensuring that content relevant to each diverse population is included in all required courses. This plan could be based on accreditation requirements, or it could be based on the program's own unique curriculum. In developing a plan, it is important to have direct input from representatives of the four groups discussed in this book. To the extent they are not represented on the faculty, the programs should seek out a consultant from nonrepresented groups who can help identify needed appropriate curriculum content and experiences.

The first step in developing a plan is to identify the knowledge and experiences counselors need with respect to each minority group. The second step is to match knowledge and experiences with appropriate courses. We offer the following outline as an example of the kind of knowledge and experiences that should be integrated into the core counselor training program.

A. People with Disabilities
   1. Counselor Attitudes, Values, Biases
      a. Discussion of negative attitudes toward disability
      b. Methods of uncovering and addressing negative attitudes toward disabilities
      c. Promotion of positive attitudes toward people with disabilities
   2. Summary of Knowledge Competencies
      a. Medical information for counselors working with people with disabilities
      b. Knowledge of psychological aspects of physical disability
      c. Knowledge of abuse, abuse theories, and abuse reporting laws
      d. Knowledge of psychological aspects and adjustment to mental and emotional disabilities
         (1) Learning disabilities
         (2) Mental retardation
         (3) Knowledge of social conditions
         (4) Discrimination
         (5) Employment
         (6) Health care
         (7) Social services
         (8) Laws
   3. Counseling Techniques
      a. Couples and family counseling
      b. Vocational counseling/rehabilitation
      c. Social change advocacy
      d. Environmental change focus
B. Older People
   1. Counselor Attitudes, Values, Biases
      a. Negative attitudes toward aging
      b. Geriophobia
      c. Positive perspectives on aging
   2. Summary of Knowledge Competencies
      a. Definitions of aging

      b.  Life-span development and life transitions in old age

      c.  Counseling needs

      d.  Physical and cognitive limitations associated with aging

      e.  Social conditions

         (1)  Discrimination

         (2)  Economics

         (3)  Health care

         (4)  Social services

         (5)  Victimization

         (6)  Abuse, abuse theories, abuse-reporting laws

         (7)  Laws

  3.  Counseling Techniques

      a.  Consciousness-raising

      b.  Group work

      c.  Social change advocacy

C.  Women

  1.  Counselor Attitudes, Values, Biases

      a.  Sexism: Subtle and blatant

      b.  Gender-role stereotyping

      c.  Feminism

  2.  Summary of Knowledge Competencies

      a.  Gender-fair models of mental health

      b.  Biological sex differences

      c.  Gender bias in psychological theories

      d.  Gender-related concerns

      e.  Psychology of women

      f.  Psychology of women of color

      g.  Knowledge of social conditions

         (1)  Discrimination

         (2)  Sexual harassment

         (3)  Women and work

         (4)  Multiple-role conflicts and issues

         (5)  Health care

         (6)  Social services

         (7)  Laws

         (8)  Violence

  3.  Counseling Techniques

      a.  Gender-aware and feminist approaches to counseling

      b.  Use of nonsexist psychological tests and interest inventories

      c.  Feminist alternatives to traditional assessment (e.g., gender-role analysis)

      d.  Career counseling for women

      e.  Social change advocacy

D.  Gay Men, Lesbians, and Bisexuals

  1.  Counselor Attitudes, Values, and Biases

      a.  Homophobia

      b.  Heterosexist bias

      c. Appreciation vs. tolerance of gay men, lesbians, bisexuals

      d. Counselor's awareness of their own sexuality

  2. Summary of Knowledge Competencies

      a. Past and current research on homosexuality

      b. Awareness of differences between being LGB and non-LGB

      c. Awareness of differences between lesbians, gay men, and bisexuals

      d. Awareness of issues of gay men, lesbians, and bisexuals of color

      e. Awareness of issues of transgendered individuals

      f. Theories of gay identity development

      g. The stages of the "coming-out" process

      h. Internalized homophobia

      i. LGB relationships, lifestyles, and families

      j. Sources of societal oppression

         (1) Discrimination

         (2) Employment

         (3) Health care

         (4) Laws

         (5) Violence

  3. Counseling Techniques

      a. LGB-affirmative counseling

      b. LGB support groups

      c. LGB lifestyle resources/referrals

      d. HIV/AIDS counseling

      e. Addictions counseling

      f. Social change advocacy

Until such time as knowledge and experiences related to client diversity are integrated into all counseling classes, we feel there is a need to focus on diversity issues in a separate class. A separate class should examine the societal conditions that create oppression and discrimination as well as the mental health implications of oppression. It should also include a discussion of human rights counseling, with a focus on changing the environmental and social conditions that create client problems, rather than focusing exclusively on changing client attitudes and behaviors. A separate course of this type should teach skills that can be generalized to any minority group.

## Selection of Counselor Trainees

Assuming a faculty and curriculum are sensitive to client diversity, a key component of preparing counselors competent to work with diverse clients is the raw material the program starts with; that is, student receptiveness to diversity. Because diverse populations are discriminated against and because discriminatory attitudes are difficult to change, it is important for counselor training programs to include assessment of discriminatory attitudes in their student selection process. We believe a personal interview with questions that address issues related to the various forms of diversity is the best way to detect discriminatory attitudes. A background questionnaire also may be useful in the selection process; the purpose of the background questionnaire is to identify activities in which the applicant engaged that suggest discrimination against special populations, or conversely, that demonstrate interest and experience in working with diversity.

With respect to people with disabilities, women, and LGB people, efforts should be made to ensure proportional representation in the student cohort. Selection of underrepresented populations for counselor training involves three phases: recruitment, admission, and support. Although no comparable data are available regarding recruitment of students with disabilities and female students, Bidell, Turner, and Casas (2002) reviewed application packets from clinical and counseling psychology programs and found that few of them specifically stated a commitment to LGB training, mentioned LGB-focused coursework, or listed faculty engaged in research on LGB issues. By comparison, most training programs included such information to recruit ethnic minority students.

Because the possibility of admission bias against people with disabilities, women, and LGB people may be inherent in the selection process, every effort must be made to ensure they are recruited, admitted, and supported equitably by training programs. This should begin with a careful analysis of the selection process to determine if any built-in biases are operating. Another hedge against bias in the selection process is to have representatives of the minority group involved in all aspects of the selection process. A masked review of application materials, whenever appropriate, is another safeguard. Counselor training programs must cultivate an environment of support for and affirmation of diversity to enhance the success and satisfaction of all students.

*One Final Point*    Special provisions need to be made to accommodate people with disabilities in the selection process. As Hauser et al. (2000) pointed out, internship sites are required by the ADA to make reasonable accommodations for applicants with disabilities in the application and interview process, and to not discriminate against them when final selections are made. The same expectation applies to training programs; reasonable accommodations must be made to ensure that applicants with disabilities are not disadvantaged in applying for admission as a student. Department chairs may feel that making accommodations for applicants (e.g., an interpreter for Deaf applicants, application materials in Braille for blind applicants) will stretch their departmental budget. However,

> internship [and training] programs should be aware that if these cases go to court, the resources of the entire institution will be examined to see if there is an undue burden, not just the budget of the psychology training program, the department where it is housed, or even the individual campus if it is multicampus system. (p. 572)

## COUNSELING RESEARCH

It is evident from psychology's treatment of diverse populations as reviewed in chapters 2 through 5 that past research has often been biased, usually based on a deficit model of the group being studied. This biased research, and the theories on which it has been based, have had a tragic impact on individuals and society alike. For example, disengagement theory and research have led many older people and their care providers to believe that after age 65 an individual's interest in social interaction should be expected to decline. We now know that older people will remain engaged in meaningful, productive interactions as long as social structures exist for their involvement and as long as their health allows for their involvement. Also, assumptions that mentally limited people cannot benefit from treatment have impeded research on the effectiveness of psychotherapy with this population (Butz, Bowling, & Bliss, 2000).

Similarly, the variability hypothesis of sex differences was used as an argument in the early part of the 20th century against admitting women to institutions of higher learning. Sex bias has been apparent in almost every area of psychological research and is still with us today (Enns, 2000). Psychological research has often denied the very existence of LGB people; and when LGB people are studied, they are often stigmatized (Bieschke, McClanahan, Tozer, Grzegorek, & Park, 2000; Herek et al., 1991). Even in LGB affirmative research, generalizations are problematic because of problems with the representativeness of the sample (Bieschke et al., 2000). Morin (1977), in a discussion of heterosexual bias in psychological research, pointed out that

> there is no such thing as a representative sample of lesbians or gay men. Researchers are sampling what is essentially a hidden or invisible population. Therefore, when homosexual samples are used, expanded subject descriptions that permit adequate replication are needed. (p. 636)

McHugh, Koeske, and Frieze (1986) described three major types of barriers to sex-fair research that we believe can be expanded to research with any non-ethnic-minority group. The three barriers are (1) excessive confidence in traditional methods of research, (2) bias in explanatory systems, and (3) inappropriate conceptualization and operationalization.

Widely shared beliefs and biases may creep into the research process even though efforts are made to follow established research procedures (Denmark, Russo, Frieze, & Sechzer, 1988; McHugh et al., 1986). Excessive confidence in traditional methods of control is not warranted if these methods produce situations that are not reflective of "real-life" situations. "Context stripping" has been an ongoing problem in the study of gender issues (Enns, 2000; Gilbert, 1992). That is, many gender-related phenomena are manifest in specific social contexts; research that studies gender out of context may be seriously misleading. Further, excessive confidence in established (published) findings may cause them to be "cited repeatedly as evidence for a generalization when they are consistent with prevailing paradigms about human behavior, whereas important counter evidence may go unpublished or uncited" (McHugh et al., 1986, p. 881). In other words, studies may be (unintentionally) designed to confirm stereotypes of older people, people with disabilities, women, and LGB people; studies with results that support existing stereotypes are most likely to get published and, once published, most likely to get cited.

Bias in explanatory systems refers to a model that is used to explain behavior for all members of the group when in fact the model applies to only a few members, if any at all. Biases that can affect explanatory systems include multiple and imprecise use of terminology (as when the term *handicapped* is applied to persons of differing ability regardless of situational factors), imprecision of explanatory model (as when simple biological, psychological, or sociocultural models are proposed to explain homosexual behavior), and "difference models" based on stereotypic assumptions (as when sex differences are proposed to explain differing performance levels between the sexes).

Inappropriate conceptualization and operationalization can occur when cultural ideologies about differences between groups of people influence psychological research and theory. For example, religious values play a prominent role in the deviance view of homosexuality that still underlies the thinking of many psychology researchers and practitioners. Any research that examines human behavior from the standpoint that behavior displayed by one group is inferior to or less desired than behavior displayed by another group may be conceptualizing differences in culturally biased terms rather than descriptive terms.

Other problems with research on diverse populations that can be generalized from the McHugh et al. (1986) concerns with sexist research include the facts that research topics are usually selected by researchers outside the group, minority group samples are often selected without concern for how representative they are of the entire group, tasks employed in an experimental setting may be familiar or salient for one group but not another, and identification of the experimenter as an outsider may affect how minorities respond to the study.

Although more recent studies have begun to dispel some of the myths generated by past research, caution needs to be exercised to ensure that potential biases are reduced in future research. Eliminating all bias in psychological research is probably impossible, but we feel the most effective way to reduce research bias against any diverse population is to include members of the group in the research initiating and reviewing processes (Kewman, 2001). Following are suggested procedures for including diversity in the research initiating and reviewing processes:

1. All members of research teams conducting studies on diverse populations should be informed about the special issues of these groups and be committed to examining their own stereotypes and attitudes that might bias their research. Research questions should reflect the experiences and needs of the group, rather than be imposed from the outside.

2. Research that includes a diverse population (people with disabilities, older people, women, gay men, lesbians) as the subject population should include a member of that population on the research team. The representative from the diverse population should be involved in all phases of the research project, including the design, implementation, data collection, data analysis, and reported phases of the project. Publication credit should be assigned on the basis of the representative's contribution to the final product.

3. All research, whether funded by the federal government or not, should be reviewed by an independent human subjects' committee. Whenever a research project that includes a minority group as a subject population is under review, the human subjects' committee should ensure that a member of the group is

included in the reviewing process. In the case where the group to be studied is not represented by a standing member of the human subjects' committee, a representative should be added as a voting member for the purposes of reviewing the relevant proposal.

4. Similarly, research funding agencies should include a representative of each minority group that is included as a subject population as part of their review team.

5. Editorial boards of professional journals should include representatives of diverse populations at a parity with their representation in society. Every manuscript considered for publication should be reviewed by at least one board member who represents the minority group included as a subject population.

## SUMMARY

Until counselor training and counseling research practices are brought in line with professional ethical and accreditation standards, direct services to diverse clients are likely to fall short of ideal practice. The suggestions offered here for changes in counselor training and counseling research should be viewed as a beginning point; at this point in the development of counseling as a profession we have yet to determine the most effective ways of teaching and researching client diversity.

## REFERENCES

Agresti, A. A. (1992). Counselor training and ethical issues with older clients. *Counselor Education and Supervision, 32,* 43–50.

American Association of Retired People. (2002). Legislation and elections. Washington, DC: Author. Retrieved December 6, 2002, from http://www.aarp.org/legislative/.

American Psychological Association. (2000). *Guidelines for psychotherapy with lesbian, gay, and bisexual clients.* Washington, DC: Author.

American Psychological Association. (2001). *Publication manual of the American Psychological Association* (5th ed.). Washington, DC: Author.

American Psychological Association. (2002a). *Ethical principles of psychologists and code of conduct.* Washington, DC: Author. Retrieved November 29, 2002, from http://www.apa.org/ethics/.

American Psychological Association. (2002b). *Guidelines and principles for accreditation of programs in professional psychology.* Washington, DC: Author. Retrieved December 4, 2002, from http://www.apa.org/ed/G&P2.pdf.

American Psychological Association, Committee on Gay and Lesbian Concerns. (1991). Avoiding heterosexual bias in language. *American Psychologist, 46,* 973–974.

Anderson, J. A., & Rawlins, M. E. (1985). Availability and representation of women in counselor education with strategies for recruitment, selection, and advancement. *Counselor Education and Supervision, 25,* 56–65.

Association for Specialists in Group Work. (1991). Professional standards for the training of group workers. *Together, 20*(1), 9–24.

Atkinson, D. R., Morten, G., & Sue, D. W. (in press). *Counseling American minorities: A cross-cultural perspective* (6th ed.). New York: McGraw-Hill.

Bidell, M. P., Turner, J. A., & Casas, J. M. (2002). First impressions count: Ethnic/racial and lesbian/gay/bisexual content of professional psychology application materials. *Professional Psychology: Research and Practice, 33*, 97–103.

Bieschke, K. J., McClanahan, M., Tozer, E., Grzegorek, J. L., & Park, J. (2000). Programmatic research on the treatment of lesbian, gay, and bisexual clients: The past, the present, and the course for the future. In R. M. Perez, K. A. DeBord, & K. J. Bieschke (Eds.), *Handbook of counseling and psychotherapy with lesbian, gay, and bisexual clients* (pp. 309–335). Washington, DC: American Psychological Association.

Bluestone, H., Stokes, A., & Kuba, S. A. (1996). Toward an integrated program design: Evaluating the status of diversity training in a graduate school curriculum. *Professional Psychology: Research and Practice, 27*, 394–400.

Bradley, L., & Lewis, J. (2000). Introduction. In J. Lewis & L. Bradley (Eds.), *Advocacy in counseling: Counselors, clients, and community* (pp. 3–4). Greensboro, NC: ERIC Clearinghouse on Counseling and Student Services.

Brown, B. M. (1995). The process of inclusion and accommodation: A bill of rights for people with disabilities in group work. *Journal for Specialists in Group Work, 20*, 71–75.

Bruce, M. A., & Christiansen, C. H. (1988). Advocacy in word as well as deed. *American Journal of Occupational Therapy, 42*, 189–191.

Buhrke, R. A. (1989a). Female student perspectives on training in lesbian and gay issues. *The Counseling Psychologist, 17*, 629–636.

Buhrke, R. A. (1989b). Incorporating lesbian and gay issues into counselor training: A resource guide. *Journal of Counseling and Development, 68*, 77–80.

Buhrke, R. A., & Douce, L. A. (1991). Training issues for counseling psychologists in working with lesbian women and gay men. *The Counseling Psychologist, 19*, 216–234.

Butz, M. R., Bowling, J. B., & Bliss, C. A. (2000). Psychotherapy with the mentally retarded: A review of the literature and the implications. *Professional Psychology: Research and Practice, 31*, 42–47.

Byrd, K., Crews, B., & Ebener, D. (1991). A study of appropriate use of language when making reference to persons with disabilities. *Journal of Applied Rehabilitation Counseling, 22*, 40–41.

Cayleff, S. E. (1986). Ethical issues in counseling gender, race, and culturally distinct groups. *Journal of Counseling and Development, 64*, 345–347.

Chin, J. L., & Russo, N. F. (1997). Feminist curriculum development: Principles and resources. In J. Worell & N. G. Johnson (Eds.), *Shaping the future of feminist psychology* (pp. 93–120). Washington, DC: American Psychological Association.

Cohen, E. S. (1990). The elderly mystique: Impediment to advocacy and empowerment. Generations: *Journal of the Western Gerontological Society, 14*(Suppl.), 13–16.

Cook, E. P. (Ed.). (1993). *Women, relationships, and power: Implications for counseling.* Alexandria, VA: American Counseling Association.

Copeland, E. J. (1982). Minority populations and traditional counseling programs: Some alternatives. *Counselor Education and Supervision, 21,* 187–193.

Council for Accreditation of Counseling and Related Educational Programs. (2001). *Council for Accreditation of Counseling and Related Educational Programs: The 2001 Standards.* Alexandria, VA: American Association for Counseling and Development. Retrieved December 2, 2002, from www.counseling. org/cacrep/2001standards700.htm.

Cunconan-Lahr, R., & Brotherson, M. J. (1996). Advocacy in disability policy: Parents and consumers as advocates. *Mental Retardation, 34,* 352–358.

Denmark, F., Russo, N. F., Frieze, I. H., & Sechzer, J. A. (1988). Guidelines for avoiding sexism in psychological research. *American Psychologist, 43,* 582–585.

Dworkin, S. H. (2000). Individual therapy with lesbian, gay, and bisexual clients. In R. M. Perez, K. A. DeBord, & K. J. Bieschke (Eds.), *Handbook of counseling and psychotherapy with lesbian, gay, and bisexual clients* (pp. 157–181). Washington, DC: American Psychological Association.

Dworkin, S. H., & Gutierrez, F. J. (Eds.). (1992). *Counseling gay men and lesbians: Journey to the end of the rainbow.* Alexandria, VA: American Association for Counseling and Development.

Eichler, M. (1988). *Nonsexist research methods: A practical guide.* Winchester, MA: Allen & Unwin.

Enns, C. Z. (1993). Twenty years of feminist counseling and therapy: From naming biases to implementing multifaceted practice. *The Counseling Psychologist, 21,* 3–87.

Enns, C. Z. (1997). *Feminist theories and feminist psychotherapies: Origins, variations, and themes.* New York: Harrington Park Press.

Enns, C. Z. (2000). Gender issues in counseling. In S. D. Brown & R. W. Lent (Eds.), *Handbook of counseling psychology* (3rd ed., pp. 601–638). New York: Wiley.

Enns, C. Z., & Hackett, G. (1990). Comparisons of feminist and nonfeminist women's reactions to variants of nonsexist and feminist counseling. *Journal of Counseling Psychology, 37,* 33–40.

Fassinger, R. E. (2000). Gender and sexuality in human development: Implications for prevention and advocacy in counseling psychology. In S. D. Brown & R. W. Lent (Eds.), *Handbook of counseling psychology* (3rd ed., pp. 346–378). New York: Wiley.

Filer, P. S. (1982). Counselor trainees: Attitudes toward mainstreaming the handicapped. *Counselor Education and Supervision, 22,* 61–69.

Fitzgerald, L. F., & Nutt, R. (1986). The Division 17 principles concerning the counseling/psychotherapy of women: Rationale and implementation. *The Counseling Psychologist, 14,* 180–216.

Garnets, L., Hancock, K. A., Cochran, S. D., Goodchilds, J., & Peplau, L. A. (1991). Issues in psychotherapy with lesbians and gay men. *American Psychologist, 46,* 964–972.

Gilbert, L. A. (1992). Gender and counseling psychology: Current knowledge and directions for research and social action. In S. D. Brown & R. W. Lent

(Eds.), *Handbook of counseling psychology* (2nd ed., pp. 383–416). New York: Wiley.

Glenn, A. A., & Russell, R. K. (1986). Heterosexual bias among counselor trainees. *Counseling Education and Supervision, 25,* 222–229.

Good, G. E., Gilbert, L. A., & Scher, M. (1990). Gender aware therapy: A synthesis of feminist therapy and knowledge about gender. *Journal of Counseling and Development, 68,* 376–380.

Graham, D. L. R., Rawlings, E. I., Halpern, H. S., & Hermes, J. (1984). Therapists' needs for training in counseling lesbians and gay men. *Professional Psychology, 15,* 482–496.

Hackett, G., Enns, C. Z., & Zetzer, H. A. (1992). Reactions of women to nonsexist and feminist counseling: Effects of counselor orientation and mode of information delivery. *Journal of Counseling Psychology, 39,* 321–330.

Hackett, G., & Lonborg, S. D. (1993). Career assessment and counseling for women. In W. B. Walsh & S. H. Osipow (Eds.), *Career counseling for women* (pp. 43-85). Hillsdale, NJ: Erlbaum.

Hadley, R. G., & Brodwin, M. G. (1988). Language about people with disabilities. *Journal of Counseling and Development, 67,* 147–149.

Hauser, P. C., Maxwell-McCaw, D. L., Leigh, I. W., & Gutman, V. A. (2000). Internship accessiblity issues for Deaf and hard-of-hearing applicants: No cause for complacency. *Professional Psychology: Research and Practice, 31,* 569–574.

Hays, P. A. (1996). Addressing the complexities of culture and gender in counseling. *Journal of Counseling and Development, 74,* 332–338.

Herek, G. M. (1993). Sexual orientation and military service: A social science perspective. *American Psychologist, 48,* 538–549.

Herek, G. M., Kimmel, D. C., Amaro, H., & Melton, G. B. (1991). Avoiding heterosexual bias in psychological research. *American Psychologist, 46,* 957–963.

Hinrichsen, G. A. (2000). Knowledge of and interest in geropsychology among psychology trainees. *Professional Psychology: Research and Practice, 31,* 442–445.

Hinrichsen, G. A., & McMeniman, M. (2002). The impact of geropsychology training. *Professional Psychology: Research and Practice, 33,* 337–340.

Iasenza, S. (1989). Some challenges of integrating sexual orientations into counselor training and research. *Journal of Counseling and Development, 68,* 73–76.

Kemp, N. T., & Mallinckrodt, B. (1996). Impact of professional training on case conceptualization of clients with a disability. *Professional Psychology: Research and Practice, 27,* 378–385.

Kewman, D. G. (2001). Advancing disability policy: Opportunities and obstacles. *Rehabilitation Psychology, 46,* 115–124.

Kiselica, M. S., & Robinson, M. (2001). Bringing advocacy counseling to life: The history, issues, and human dramas of social justice work in counseling. *Journal of Counseling and Development, 79,* 386–397.

Kitchener, K. S. (1984). Intuition, critical evaluation and ethical principles: The foundation for ethical decisions in counseling psychology. *The Counseling Psychologist, 12*(3), 43–55.

Leigh, I. W., Corbett, C. A., Gutman, V., & Morere, D. A. (1996). Providing psychological services to deaf individuals: A response to new perceptions of diversity. *Professional Psychology: Research and Practice, 27,* 365–371.

Lofaro, G. A. (1982). Disability and counselor education. *Counselor Education and Supervision, 21,* 200–207.

Margolis, R. L., & Rungta, S. A. (1986). Training counselors for work with special populations. *Journal of Counseling and Development, 64,* 642–644.

McDonald, G. (1982). Misrepresentation, liberalism, and heterosexual bias in introductory psychology texts. *Journal of Homosexuality, 6,* 45–60.

McHugh, M. C., Koeske, R. D., & Frieze, I. H. (1986). Issues to consider in conducting nonsexist psychological research. *American Psychologist, 41,* 879–890.

Melton, G. B. (1989). Public policy and private prejudice: Psychology and the law on gay rights. *American Psychologist, 44,* 933–940.

Mitchell, L. M., & Buchele-Ash, A. (2000). Abuse and neglect of individuals with disabilities: Building protective supports through public policy. *Journal of Disability Policy Studies, 10,* 225–243.

Morin, S. F. (1977). Heterosexual bias in psychological research on lesbianism and male homosexuality. *American Psychologist, 32,* 629–637.

Munro, J. D. (1991). Training families in the "step approach model" for effective advocacy. *Canada's Mental Health, 39*(1), 1–6.

Myers, J. E. (1992). Competencies, credentialing, and standards for gerontological counselors: Implications for counselor education. *Counselor Education and Supervision, 32,* 34–42.

Myers, J. E. (1995). From "forgotten and ignored" to standards and certification: Gerontological counseling comes of age. *Journal of Counseling and Development, 74,* 143–149.

Myers, J. E., & Blake, R. H. (1986). Preparing counselors for work with older people. *Counselor Education and Supervision, 26,* 137–145.

Myers, J. E., & Sweeney, T. J. (1990). *Gerontological competencies for counselors and human development specialists.* Alexandria, VA: American Association for Counseling and Development.

National Council on Aging. (2001). *Advocacy.* Washington, DC: Author. Retrieved December 6, 2002, from www.ncoa.org/advocacy/advocacy.htm.

National Senior Citizens Law Center. (2002). NSCLC's Services for Advocates. Washington, DC: Author. Retrieved December 6, 2002, from www.nsclc.org/.

Nelson, J. B. (1985). Religious and moral issues in working with homosexual clients. In J. C. Gonsiorek (Ed.), *A guide to psychotherapy with gay and lesbian clients* (pp. 163–175). New York: Harrington Park Press.

Norton, L. (1982). Integrating gay issues into counselor education. *Counselor Education and Supervision, 21,* 208–212.

Olkin, R. (1999). *What psychotherapists should know about disability.* New York: Guilford Press.

Olkin, R. (2002). Could you hold the door for me? Including disability in diversity. *Cultural Diversity and Ethnic Minority Psychology, 8,* 130–137.

Patterson, J. B., Patrick, A., & Parker, R. M. (2000). Choice: Ethical and legal rehabilitation challenges. *Rehabilitation Counseling Bulletin, 43,* 203–204.

Perez, R. M., DeBord, K. A., & Bieschke, K. J. (Eds.). (2000). *Handbook of counseling and psychotherapy with lesbian, gay, and bisexual clients.* Washington, DC: American Psychological Association.

Phillips, J. C. (2000). Training issues and considerations. In R. M. Perez, K. A. DeBord, & K. J. Bieschke (Eds.), *Handbook of counseling and psychotherapy with lesbian, gay, and bisexual clients* (pp. 337–358). Washington, DC: American Psychological Association.

Polizzi, K. G., & Millikin, R. J. (2002). Attitudes toward the elderly: Identifying problematic usage of ageist and overextended terminology in research instructions. *Educational Gerontology, 28,* 367–377.

Qualls, S. H., Segal, D. L., Normans, S., Niederehe, G. W., & Gallagher-Thompson, D. (2002). Psychologists in practice with older adults: Current patterns, sources of training, and need for continuing education, *Professional Psychology, 33,* 435–442.

Raifman, L. J., & Vernon, M. (1996). Important implications for psychologists of the Americans with Disabilities Act: Case in point, the patient who is deaf. *Professional Psychology: Research and Practice, 27,* 372–377.

Reynolds, A. L., & Hanjorgiris, W. F. (2000). Coming out: Lesbian, gay, and bisexual identity development. In R. M. Perez, K. A. DeBord, & K. J. Bieschke (Eds.), *Handbook of counseling and psychotherapy with lesbian, gay, and bisexual clients* (pp. 35–55). Washington, DC: American Psychological Association.

Ruth, R., & Blotzer, M. A. (1995). Toward basic principles. In M. A. Blotzer & R. Ruth (Eds.), *Sometimes you just want to feel like a human being* (pp. 1–14). Baltimore: Paul H. Brookes.

Schaie, K. W. (1993). Ageist language in psychological research. *American Psychologist, 48,* 49–51.

Schwiebert, V. L., Myers, J. E., & Dice, C. (2000). Ethical guidelines for counselors working with older adults. *Journal of Counseling & Development, 78,* 123–129.

Sobocinski, M. R. (1990). Ethical principles in the counseling of gay and lesbian adolescents: Issues of autonomy, competence, and confidentiality. *Professional Psychology: Research and Practice, 21,* 240–247.

Steininger, M., Newell, J. D., & Garcia, L. T. (1984). *Ethical issues in psychology.* Homewood, IL: Dorsey Press.

Strang, D. G., Molloy, D. W., & Harrison, C. (1998). Capacity to choose place of residence: Autonomy vs beneficence? *Journal of Palliative Care, 14,* 25–29.

Titchkosky, T. (2001). Disability: A rose by any other name? "People-first" language in *Canadian Society. Canadian Review of Sociology and Anthropology, 38,* 125–140.

Thomas, M. C., & Martin, V. (1992). Training counselors to facilitate the transitions of aging through group work. *Counselor Education and Supervision, 32,* 51–60.

Walsh, W. B., & Osipow, S. H. (Eds). (1993). *Career counseling for women.* Hillsdale, NJ: Erlbaum.

Worell, J., & Remer, P. (1992). *Feminist perspectives in therapy: An empowerment model for women.* New York: Wiley.

Worell, J., & Remer, P. (2003). *Feminist perspectives in therapy: Empowering diverse women* (2nd ed.). New York: Wiley.

# Credits

# Author Index

I

# Subject Index